ADVENTIST CLASSIC LIBRARY

Reprints of Important Publications
in the Adventist Tradition

Edited by
George R. Knight

A SERIES BY ANDREWS UNIVERSITY PRESS

Current Volumes in the Adventist Classic Library

Questions on Doctrine, Annotated Edition
Life Incidents, by James White
Autobiography of Joseph Bates
Memoirs of William Miller, by Sylvester Bliss
Earliest Seventh-day Adventist Periodicals
Historical Sketches of Foreign Missions
Second Advent History, by Isaac Wellcome

Projected Volumes (Partial List)

The Sanctuary Service, by M. L. Andreasen
History of the Sabbath, by J. N. Andrews
Answers to Objections, by Francis D. Nichol
Life Sketches of James and Ellen White (1888 edition)
Early Sabbath Tracts, by Joseph Bates
Bible Adventism and other early works, by James White
Our Firm Foundation (the report of the 1952 Bible Conference, 2 volumes)
A History of the Origin and Progress of Seventh-day Adventists, by M. E. Olsen
The Midnight Cry, by Francis D. Nichol
Evidence from Scripture and History of the Second Coming of Christ about the Year 1843 and other works, by William Miller
The Cross and Its Shadow, by S. N. Haskell
Christ and His Righteousness and other writings, by E. J. Waggoner
Thoughts, Critical and Practical, on the Books of Daniel and the Revelation (1867, 1873 editions), by Uriah Smith
The Story of Our Health Message, by D. E. Robinson
Millerite Autobiographies, by Luther Boutelle, Hiram Munger, and Henry Bear

The term "Adventist" in this series is used broadly. While most of the selections in the Adventist Classic Library will be directly related to Seventh-day Adventist heritage, some will come from Millerism and other branches of the Millerite tradition.

SECOND ADVENT HISTORY

BY ISAAC WELLCOME

Introduction by Gary Land

ANDREWS UNIVERSITY PRESS

BERRIEN SPRINGS, MICHIGAN

Andrews University Press
Sutherland House
Berrien Springs, MI 49104-1700
Telephone: 269-471-6134
Fax: 269-471-6224
Email: aupo@andrews.edu
Website: http://universitypress.andrews.edu

Original Edition (1874): History of the Second Advent Message and Mission, Doctrine and People, by Isaac C. Wellcome. Yarmouth, ME. 1874.

Reprint Edition (2008): Second Advent History. By Isaac Wellcome. Introduction by Gary Land.

Note of appreciation: The Center for Adventist Research, a service of the James White Library at Andrews University, provided the original copy of Wellcome's volume that was used as the basis for this facsimile reproduction.

Printed in the United States of America
12 11 10 09 08 5 4 3 2 1

ISBN 978-1-883925-59-8
Library of Congress Control Number: 2007942407

Project Director	Ronald Alan Knott
Project Consultant	Deborah L. Everhart
Typesetter	Thomas Toews
Indexer	Eike A. Mueller
Cover Designer	Robert N. Mason

Adventist Classic Libary

General Editor	George R. Knight
Series Director	Ronald Alan Knott

For reading convenience and balanced layout on the page, the facsimile reprint of the type from the original edition is enlarged by about 30 percent.

Typeset: 10.5/12.6 Sabon MT

HISTORICAL INTRODUCTION

Thirty years after the Millerite "Great Disappointment" of October 22, 1844, Isaac C. Wellcome published the first general history of the movement that had promoted the belief that the Second Advent of Jesus would take place on that date. By 1874 the Adventists had developed into several separate groups, among them the Evangelical Adventists, the Advent Christians, the Church of God, and the Seventh-day Adventists. Each group claimed to be the legitimate heir of William Miller and his teachings. Wellcome belonged to the Advent Christian branch and wrote his work not only to maintain memory of the Millerite movement, but also to demonstrate that the Advent Christians continued the original Millerite faith while, among competing groups, the Seventh-day Adventists had their origins in fanaticism and existed outside the recognized boundaries of Adventism. Part history and part apologetics, Wellcome's *History of the Second Advent Message* nonetheless has become recognized as an important source of information about early Adventism that also gives insight into the movement's self-understanding as it sought to define and preserve itself in the wake of bitter disappointment.

Biographical Sketch

Isaac Wellcome was born in Minot, Maine, on May 8, 1818, to what was apparently a farming family, for he stated that while growing up he worked hard at farming and lumbering. Although Wellcome wrote that his father was "a thoroughly read and zealous believer in Universalism and possessed a large amount of that kind of literature," he also said that his parents were not Christians.[1] This latter comment suggests that his parents may actually have been Deists, which was popularized in Northern New England by Ethan Allen.[2] At this point in time, Universalism was a Christian movement that advocated the belief that God had elected all humankind to be saved,[3] whereas Deism denied such cardinal Christian doctrines as the inspiration of the Bible and the Incarnation. Of course, with Wellcome's conservative doctrinal views, it is possible that he regarded Universalism as non-Christian, despite the opinions of contemporary society. In any case, while he had little formal education, Isaac was a voracious reader and "having an opportunity to read infidel works...soon became 'a fool' by denying the existence of any God but nature."[4]

In the midst of the Second Great Awakening, which moved back and forth across New England to the western frontier throughout the first half of the nineteenth century,[5] Wellcome's elder brother, Michael, converted to Christianity when Isaac was about eighteen years old. This event prompted Isaac to begin reading the Bible and Universalist writings, leading him to become a "confirmed, praying Universalist."[6] Increasingly under the conviction that he was a sinner, Isaac accepted Jesus as his savior and joined the Methodist Episcopal Church in 1840.

Meanwhile, William Miller, a New York farmer, had come to the conclusion, based upon his study of the prophecies of Daniel, that the Second Coming of Christ would occur about the year 1843. Under the leadership of Joshua V. Himes, a Boston Christian Connection minister, Miller's ideas had produced a movement that published its first paper and held its first conferences in 1840 and soon was sending preachers and printed materials throughout the Northeast.[7] Wellcome, who seems to have already believed the premillennial doctrine of Christ's return, in 1842 first read Miller's *Evidence from Scripture and History of the Second Coming of Christ About the Year 1843*, a collection of Miller's lectures first published in 1836. After studying for two years and hearing a number of Millerite sermons, "he was constrained to acknowledge that the Bible fully sustained the general views taught by Adventists, excepting the time. This was a subject he considered too deep for him then. He had neither the books nor the ability to decide that the Lord would come on any given year."[8]

Wellcome's advocacy of Millerite views resulted in conflict with the Methodist church, which he left in September 1844 to join the Adventists, who in many cases were now separating from the established churches, which they frequently described as "Babylon." One writer states that Isaac's brothers, Michael and Solomon, also abandoned Methodism for the Millerites.[9] A few weeks later, largely on the basis that he respected those who were teaching it, Wellcome accepted the message of the 7th-month movement, which asserted that Jesus would return on October 22, 1844. After the Great Disappointment, when Jesus did not return as expected, Wellcome restudied the Millerite interpretations, concluding that the general understanding of prophecy was correct but that God had not revealed the time of Christ's coming. About this same time, he accepted the doctrine of conditional immortality, the belief that humans "sleep" in death until the Second Coming when the saved receive immortality. This doctrine was becoming influential in Adventist circles.

Despite the Disappointment, the Wellcome brothers maintained their faith in Adventism. In 1846 Michael Wellcome left Maine for Wisconsin to preach the Adventist message. Solomon joined him three years later, opening a drug store and in 1870 receiving ordination as a lay preacher for the Advent Christian Church. Jacob, a physician, joined these brothers in 1857, apparently also participating with them in preaching services.[10]

Isaac, however, remained in Maine. Although called to preach, he resisted until 1848 because of illness and financial problems. After preaching for about two years, he received ordination in Boston from the General Annual Conference of Adventists. Subsequently, he traveled extensively throughout Maine, as well as elsewhere in New England and what is now called the Midwest. According to his account, he preached 100 to 200 times and traveled between 2,000 and 4,000 miles annually, all at his own expense, and supported himself through publishing religious works and operating a small drug store.[11] Advent Christian minister and historian Albert Johnson stated that Wellcome "preached nearly every Sunday, attended over one hundred campmeetings and was blessed in winning many souls to Christ."[12]

As the Adventist movement gradually developed more formal organization, Wellcome actively participated in what eventually became the Advent Christian Church. He served as a minister in the State Conference of Maine for some twenty years after it was organized in 1854 and was elected Vice-president for the State of Maine when the American Advent Mission Society formed in 1865. He also served for four years on the Board of the Advent Christian Publication Society and one year on the editorial committee of *The World's Crisis,* the emerging denomination's paper.[13]

But it was as an independent writer and publisher that Wellcome achieved his greatest influence. He wrote a number of pamphlets, among them *A Treatise on Matthew 24th and 25th Chapters* (1854), *A Pamphlet on War* (1862), and *The Duty and Object of Christian Baptism* (1863), as well as two books, *The Plan of Redemption* with Clarkson Goud (1866) and *History of the Second Advent Message* (1874). He also compiled Bible readings in *The Berean's Casket and Repository* (1869).

With coworkers he organized The Scriptural Publication Society and the Home and Foreign Tract Mission in 1872. Johnson stated that he "took a very deep interest in foreign tract and mission work, and actively engaged in sending Adventual literature to several countries across the sea."[14] In 1882 Wellcome recalled:

> About 1870, a few Swedes, in Illinois, were converted to the faith of the Lord's coming, and beginning with scanty means, translated and published in the Swedish language several of my works, and those of others. In 1881 they opened correspondence with me, asking the privilege to translate more, and my aid to publish more extensively. I had no funds of my own, but the Lord had, and I promised them help. They then organized the "Swedish Biblical Tract Society," with its business head and printing office at Bishop Hill, Ill. Bro. John Chaiser, agent, Myself, treasurer, Yarmouth Me.…I then sent out several thousand circulars, with sample tracts to our brethren in the faith, asking for money to carry on this work among the Swedes, and other nations also.[15]

Subsequently, he reported, this literature went to Swedes in North America, Sweden, Egypt, France, and England.

In addition to this Advent Christian related literature, Wellcome published other authors whom Advent Christian historian Clyde Hewitt has described as "broadly Adventist and conditionalist and not confined to Advent Christian writers."[16] Among these works were J. H. Pettingell's *The Unspeakable Gift* (1884) and *Views and Reviews in Eschatology* (1887), Charles E. Copp's *Rod and Staff* (1889), A. C. Palmer's *The One Fold and the Only Door* (1885), and Daniel Buck's *Scripture Symbolism in Three Parts* (1887).[17] Regarding Pettingell, Johnson wrote that he "was again and again refused access to the columns of the papers of his own denomination, for friendly articles or reviews on the question [of conditional immortality] and turned to publishers of this faith for the issue of his later works and affiliated closely with Adventists in his last days."[18]

Wellcome suffered a stroke in 1894. At its 1895 midwinter meeting the Advent Christian convention described him as "a father among this people" and resolved to "remember with appreciation the loyalty and earnestness with which he stood by his convictions of faith and duty in the service of his Master and…express for him our prayerful sympathy in this crucial experience, for which we feel that he is by rich grace abundantly prepared."[19]

After Wellcome's death in 1895 the Advent Christian Publication Society stated: "In his decease we recognize a great loss to the cause of truth and its dissemination, and greatly miss his venerable presence from the numerous gatherings of our people…we regard his missionary work…as a most noble labor of great interest and value to our whole people and the general spread of adventual truth...we consider his work as a publisher to have been a great advantage to the cause of truth and worthy of a very special record in our history."[20] Four years later this organization absorbed Wellcome's Scriptural Publication Society.

Looking back in 1986 on Wellcome's life, Hewitt wistfully observed that had he, along with others, "triumphed" over Miles Grant, an influential Advent Christian editor and evangelist, "subsequent Advent Christian history would undoubtedly have been quite different than it was."[21] Whereas Grant was "cautious and conservative with a rather narrow view of the ways the Advent Christian people could serve their Lord," Hewitt continued, Wellcome was among those who had a "broader vision with liberal and aggressive views" that sought to make the Advent Christian Publication Society "a large-scale, forward-looking operation."[22] Certainly, Wellcome's own work testified to his energetic vision, for after his death it was estimated that between 1872 and 1895 he had published and distributed 10 million tracts, 150 thousand books and pamphlets, and 200 thousand copies of the *Berean Quarterly,* the organ of the Scriptural Publication Society.[23]

Early Millerite Historiography

Wellcome's *History of the Second Advent Message* made an important contribution to a developing Millerite historiography. The Millerites had never expected to write histories of their movement, for they believed that Jesus's Second Coming in 1843 or 1844 would end the present age and usher in the Millennium. The fact that Jesus did not return as predicted strongly influenced the histories that Miller's spiritual descendents produced,[24] as they continued to assert the fundamental validity of his teaching and at the same time sought to come to terms with the error that, at least in popular consciousness, lay at the heart of the movement he spawned.

Writing in the immediate aftermath of a series of disappointments in 1843 and early 1844 when "the time is expired,"[25] Josiah Litch, a former Methodist minister and prominent Millerite preacher, sought to sustain the Adventist faith with its first historical account, published in May 1844. He affirmed the movement's accomplishments as God-led and defended it against criticism. Dividing the movement's development into five somewhat vaguely defined periods or phases, Litch said that the first stage began with Miller's initial publications in the *Vermont Telegraph* in 1831 and was characterized by "individual effort."[26] Publication of *The*

Signs of the Times and the convening of the first General Conference in 1840 introduced a new more organized phase in which the movement spread throughout New England and New York. The development of camp meetings and the purchase of the "Great Tent" in 1842 "shook the nation," culminating with Philadelphia where in February 1843 "the city was convulsed throughout with the influence of the lectures."[27] In addition to its own publications and the efforts of its lecturers, the spread of the movement benefited, according to Litch, from debate over Miller's teachings in both the religious and secular press.[28] Meanwhile, Adventism moved west into places such as Cincinnati and Pittsburgh and made largely unsuccessful forays into the South. Finally, in 1843 and early 1844 the movement entered into a period of crisis as a series of expected dates for Christ's return passed without incident.

Despite the disappointments, Litch continued to believe in the validity of Miller's teaching. Miller himself had a "powerful native intellect," a "most undoubted probity in his moral and Christian character," and was used by God as "his chosen instrument."[29] Litch defended the movement against its critics, arguing that rather than profiting financially from their publications, both Miller and Joshua V. Himes, Adventism's principal publicist, had drawn on their own resources.[30] Furthermore, he stated that Miller had never changed his mind regarding the time of Christ's return and that stories of ascension robes and gatherings in grave yards were "idle and foolish."[31] Anticipating the interpretations of subsequent historians, he asserted that particular dates for Christ's appearing were not the central element of the movement's teaching.

> The doctrine does not consist in merely tracing prophetic periods, although that is an important part of the work. But the whole prophetic history of the world is given in the pages of inspiration, is recorded in history, and affords indubitable evidence of the fact, that we have approached a crisis. And no disappointment respecting a definite point of time can move them [the Adventists], or drive them from their position, relative to the speedy coming of the Lord. And it remains to be shown that our calculations of time are not correct, and are only in error relative to the event which marked its close. This is the most likely.[32]

Those who opposed Adventism did so, according to Litch, primarily because of "a want of readiness to meet the Lord *now*."[33] The diverse and conflicting arguments of his critics were sufficient proof of the truth of Miller's teaching, he believed, for they overthrew one another. In contrast, Adventist writings had turned people's attention to history and, more importantly, to Scripture, giving "the church and world a simple, plain, common-sense system of interpretation of the sacred canon."[34]

Writing primarily from his own memory, Litch also drew upon such sources as Miller's published lectures, *The Signs of the Times* and *The Midnight Cry*, and his own previously published work. But he did not approach his subject as a dispassionate historian with time for careful research and critical analysis of either sources or findings. Rather, he was writing a historical apologetic to both restore and build faith in a movement that in the late spring of 1844 needed to lay plans for pressing forward with the message of Christ's soon return.

A similar apologetic purpose lay behind the publication of *The Memoirs of William Miller* in 1853. A Millerite preacher named Apollos Hale wrote the first three chapters but an associate, Sylvester Bliss, completed the bulk of the work and appeared as the author. Joshua V. Himes, who published the *Memoirs,* wrote a preface that left no doubt regarding the book's objective. He wanted the impartial reader to "be able to form a just estimate of one who has occupied so conspicuous a position before the public." Further, "As the public learns to discriminate between the actual position of Mr. Miller and that which prejudice has conceived that he occupied, his conservativeness and disapprobation of every fanatical practice will be admitted, and a more just estimate will be had of him."[35]

The authors drew upon interviews and their own memories but for the most part let Miller speak for himself through large extracts from his correspondence, sermons, and other papers. And throughout they built a positive image, presenting him as a man of piety, patriotism, and considerable mental ability. Hale, for instance, wrote that Miller "possessed a strong physical constitution, an active and naturally well-developed intellect, and an irreproachable moral character."[36] A few chapters later, Bliss described him as "a good citizen, a kind neighbor, an affectionate husband and parent, and a devoted Christian."[37]

Bliss also argued that Miller's preaching had brought genuine religious revivals, stating that conversions from "sin to holiness" were "a common feature in all his labors" and prompted many who did not agree with his views to nonetheless invite him to speak in their churches.[38] Regarding Miller's biblical interpretations, he stated that the man's teachings were similar to those of his critics, different only in the fact that he brought into one systematic whole points that they held individually. Bliss argued: "Mr. Miller laid no claim to *originality* in his position respecting any of [his specific teachings]; but maintained that they were established opinions of the church.... While his opponents attacked the view he took of these points, no one of them assailed the whole; but each admitted his correctness on some of the points; and, among them, the whole were admitted."[39]

Finally, the volume portrayed Miller as a strong opponent of fanaticism. In 1842 John Starkweather, a Congregational minister, had come into the Millerite movement and soon began promoting his belief in the necessity of personal sanctification manifested by such bodily phenomena as loss of strength. In addition to including an 1843 letter in which Miller condemned these teachings, Bliss also commented that Miller and his associates "took a decided position against all fanatical extravagances. They never gave them any quarter."[40] Similarly, the book included correspondence that demonstrated Miller's opposition after the "Great Disappointment" of 1844 to such "fanatical views and practices" as the "shut door" teaching, foot washing, "religious kissing," and "bodily exercises and mesmeric ecstasies."[41]

In all of these points Hale and Bliss established lines of argument that later Adventist apologists would follow and in their volume preserved much primary material upon which subsequent historians could rely. Their book maintained some popularity into the early twentieth century, providing nearly all of the text of Seventh-day Adventist James White's 1875 biography of Miller[42] and appearing in an abridged edition with some added material published by the Advent Christians in 1895.[43]

Wellcome's *History of the Second Advent Message*

By the time that Isaac Wellcome published his history of Adventism in 1874, the Advent Christian strand had become an established and distinctive element of the Millerite legacy.[44] In addition to providing another historical apologetic for William Miller's movement, therefore, Wellcome also sought to justify the Advent Christians as its legitimate heir.

Explaining the purpose of his book, Wellcome clearly expressed his apologetic motivation. "Every religious, political, or moral movement...," he wrote, "is worthy of being set fairly before the inquiring multitudes in truthful history, that the uninformed may learn the merits or demerits of the principles which produce such revolution."[45] As he explained his purposes further, Wellcome stated that he intended to show the positive religious effects of Adventism, the theological and practical problems of those who opposed the movement, and the reproach brought on the cause by various bigots and fanatics.[46] "It must be acknowledged that this message is a 'DISPENSATIONAL TRUTH,'" he concluded, "which the Lord intended should be published at this time, and which he has accompanied with his special blessing that it may prepare a people for his coming and kingdom."[47]

To accomplish this purpose, Wellcome followed essentially the same method as had Hale and Bliss in their *Memoirs of William Miller*. In addition to drawing upon memories, both his own and those of others, Wellcome presented many quotations and long extracts from contemporary materials, largely tracts and newspapers, in what might be called a "scissors and paste" approach. For instance, pages 13 to 28 were taken from Bliss's book *Time of the End*. Pages 92 to 127 reproduced the introduction, table of contents, and one lecture from Miller's *Evidences from Scripture*, and pages 181 to 197 reprinted an 1839 English tract on the second coming of Christ. Readers, however, need to carefully read Wellcome's text to determine when he used such extracts, for he often did not identify them clearly. He stated in one place, for example, that "we give here the title-page, some testimonials, the table of contents, and a section of [Josiah Litch's] address."[48] Two pages later the reader finds "Section VI" (easily confused as Wellcome's own "Chapter 6"), which, although being the promised excerpt, is not otherwise identified as having been written by Litch.[49]

In addition to long inserts such as these, Wellcome also included shorter quotations from such sources as the *Signs of the Times*, the *Hartford Universalist*, the *Boston Post*, the *Advent Herald*, and *The World's Crisis*, among many others. In compiling these quotations, Wellcome performed a service for future historians, for in several cases the original source material no longer exists. Wellcome also included throughout his book more than thirty-five biographical sketches of various Millerite and Advent Christian leaders, although it is unclear whether he wrote them himself, collected them from others, or—as seems most likely—did some of both.

Although Wellcome entitled his book a "*History*," he framed his account with several essentially theological chapters. The volume opened with a chapter on the function of prophecy that argued that "God's time had come" for the proclamation that Christ's second coming was at hand.[50] Although Wellcome did not specifically mention the Millerite movement in this chapter, he clearly wanted his readers to recognize that he was writing about events that are divinely ordained. Chapter 5, which came in the midst of his discussion of the Millerite movement, both illustrated the method and content of Millerite biblical interpretation and sought to convince the reader of its validity.

Wellcome commented that his excerpt from Miller's lectures "contains much valuable instruction for all"[51] and similarly stated that the selection from Litch "contains such an amount of instruction we think it should be given to all our readers."[52] Following his discussion of the Great Disappointment and its immediate aftermath, Wellcome devoted much of Chapter 15 to evidence from a number of writers affirming the "year-day principle of interpretation" and the expectation that the mid-nineteenth century marked the end of the time prophecies of Daniel.[53] Clearly, Wellcome was attempting to establish that although the Millerite movement was obviously wrong in its expectation that Christ would return in 1843 or 1844, its general approach to prophetic interpretation fell within the accepted range of nineteenth-century biblical interpretation and remained valid. Finally, Wellcome closed his volume with two chapters that outlined "some of the chief points of doctrine which the main body of believers in the immediate personal advent of Christ teach as included in the true foundation of the Christian faith and hope."[54] Ultimately, Wellcome was writing a believer's history that affirmed God's hand in an effort that had "produced great results, yet the work is not finished, perhaps much more is to be accomplished. The Lord will have the Church and world thoroughly warned."[55]

In his narrative of the Millerite movement, Wellcome sought to establish its reasonable character and spiritual effectiveness. First, similar to Litch, he repeatedly stated that identification of a date for Christ's second coming was not the movement's most important element. "IT WAS NOT SO MUCH THE BELIEF THAT CHRIST MIGHT COME IN 1843 as it was the *certainty* of that event," he wrote, "with the conviction that they were not prepared to hail his coming with joy."[56] Nearly two hundred pages later, he entitled a chapter section, "DEFINITE TIME NOT THE BURDEN OF THE MESSAGE."[57] Probably reflecting his own reluctance in 1842 and 1843 to accept the time message, he described those who confidently predicted Christ's return in 1843 to be affirming more than "they were warranted in Scripture" and further argued that even among those who held this belief strongly, few "regarded the specific *time* (unless it should prove correct) as properly constituting a portion or burden of the midnight cry."[58] By the end of his book he was calling those who continued to set dates for Christ's coming "timists," stating that God had not revealed such information to the church.[59]

In contrast to downplaying the emphasis on time, Wellcome called attention to the premillennial character of Miller's teaching. The real illusion, he seemed to believe, was the postmillennialist concept that

God's spirit would rule the earth for a thousand years before Jesus came to receive His kingdom. The expectation of Christ's soon return was the "true gospel hope" which contrasted "with the modern fable of the world's conversion and a temporal millennium."[60] Elsewhere, he again referred to these postmillennial beliefs as "delusive" and "unscriptural."[61] Whereas such doctrines tended to remove any sense of urgency for preaching and conversion, the message of "Christ's immediate coming" awakened "a deep interest and a heart searching with many of the lovers of Christ while it brought many sinners to repentance, and to Christ for salvation."[62]

Unfortunately, in addition to conversion the Millerite message also brought extremism and fanaticism, which Wellcome sought to explain and, as with the time predictions, separate out from the essential nature of the movement. He noted that throughout the history of the Christian church evil spirits had conducted their work through either the "disordered brains" of sincere believers or "some unsanctified elements of the carnal mind."[63] Similar to Litch, Wellcome applied the label "FANATICISM" to John Starkweather's efforts to promote loss of strength "and other cataleptic and epileptic phenomena," which the latter believed were evidences of true sanctification.[64] He also condemned the "come out of Babylon" theme promoted by Charles Fitch and others in 1843 and 1844 as an "unjustifiable position," a "false cry" that was "shameful and destructive" and taught by "misguided ones."[65] Wellcome called attention to the fact that Miller and other leaders of his movement strongly condemned this teaching and sought to have its promoters "take a wiser course."[66]

Establishing that the "come out of Babylon" movement was among the "foreign elements, foisted upon the Advent cause"[67] lay the groundwork for Wellcome's argument that the emergence of the Sabbatarians was a further move away from true Adventism. He noted that James White and other Sabbatarians "claimed to be the true successors" of those who called for separation from the Protestant churches, stating that "this we shall not dispute."[68] The Sabbatarians, according to Wellcome, also picked up the shut door doctrine, which he stated had been originally put forward by Joseph Turner in 1845. This doctrine, as Wellcome described it, taught that on October 22, 1844, the door of mercy had closed, a belief he regarded as "a snare, a base fraud"[69] that diverted people from proclaiming the soon coming of Jesus. He claimed that Ellen G. Harmon, who later married James White and with him and Joseph Bates established the Seventh-day Adventist Church, confirmed the shut door teaching through vision. "She had seen Christ in heaven," Wellcome wrote, "that he had ceased mediating, left the mercy seat, come out from 'the holiest of all' and organized his kingdom, composed of his saints, including all who held fast to their experience in the 1844 movement. She also claimed to see that all those who gave up that experience, calling it an error, had their names blotted out of the book of life, they being 'foolish virgins.'"[70] In writing to others years later, Ellen (Harmon) White stated that she had indeed seen in vision that a door had been shut in 1844, but "it was only the class who had despised the light from heaven that the Spirit of God could not reach." The door had only been shut upon those who had heard but rejected the first and second angels' messages. It did not prevent those who had not yet received "the light" from later accepting it.[71] But in Wellcome's view, Ellen White's visions had just been "the product of the over-excited imagination of her mind."[72]

While Wellcome said little regarding the doctrine of the seventh-day Sabbath, he seems to have regarded it as the logical outworking of the "come out of Babylon" teaching.[73] He was most concerned, however, to demonstrate that the Sabbatarians were not true Adventists. He called James White's claim that Adventists were agreed on the shut door teaching "another specious statement. It can only be true by denying that the many who *did not* embrace the time calculation were Adventists; and it cannot be regarded as *true* of those who *did* fully believe in the time *only for a single day,* for as soon as that day passed without bringing the Lord the mass of believers concluded it an error which they had believed for truth."[74] Wellcome criticized as the product of "a disordered brain or a fanatical faith" White's subsequent efforts to establish that Jesus had entered into the Most Holy Place of the heavenly sanctuary on October 22, 1844,[75] a belief that Seventh-day Adventists now generally term the "sanctuary doctrine."[76] Although Wellcome acknowledged White's ability "as a financier," "theological manager," and institution builder, he regarded Seventh-day Adventism as a "system of dictatorial ecclesiastical government...established for a class of believers in the Advent near."[77]

Having labored extensively to establish that Seventh-day Adventism lay outside the pale of true Adventism, Wellcome then sought to demonstrate that conditional immortality or "soul sleep," a new concept within the movement but one with which he was in sympathy, was consistent with its mainstream. Although only a few Millerites, especially George Storrs and Charles Fitch, had advocated the doctrine of soul sleep prior to the 1844 "Great Disappointment," Wellcome pointed to the inherent contradiction between the Millerite advocacy that the dead would be resurrected at the time of Christ's Second Advent and their belief, along with most of the Christian world, in the immortality of the soul.

> But the mystery of "the immortal soul," considered the responsible agent, the real man, being separated by death from the body, to live on in "fulness of joy" or in "untold agonies" for a time, and then compelled to come back and enter a new, resurrected body, to be brought to judgment and then returned to its respective place of happiness or misery, was not solved. Nay, this theory seemed more illogical and produced a more complicated difficulty than before.[78]

Nonetheless, the leaders of the Millerite movement regarded conditional immortality as "an innovation, and sought to avert the discussion of it," a "pestilent error," and "an old battered heresy."[79] Wellcome, however, excused the leaders, for they had not taken the time to study and reflect on the degree to which "superstition and Papal corruptions" had moved from Catholicism into Protestantism. He then briefly traced the historical development of the belief in natural immortality within Christianity, beginning with Origen. Despite the influence of such reformers as Martin Luther and William Tyndale, he asserted, by the time of the Reformation this belief "controlled the masses and was taught in all the schools."[80] In nineteenth-century America, however, Henry Grew and George Storrs once again brought the doctrine of soul sleep to prominence. Within a short time after Fitch published a letter on the doctrine in May 1844, he argued, "a large number of the Advent ministry embraced" the new understanding, a "number [that] has continually increased, until perhaps seven-eighths of the body now believe them."[81]

Recognizing that conditional immortality was a controversial doctrine not generally accepted by the Millerites for several years, Wellcome nonetheless regarded it, in contrast to the "come out of Babylon" and "shut door" teachings, as consistent with the movement because of its inherent logical connection with the doctrine of the resurrection of the dead and its faithfulness to the biblical text. This viewpoint enabled him, therefore, to regard as true Adventists those who congregated around *The World's Crisis* and formed in 1860 the Advent Christian Association, even though he also recognized that these people were by this point "separated from the main body" of "Evangelical Adventists," as the non-conditionalist Millerites were called by the mid-1850s. "From that time onward," Wellcome wrote, "the World's Crisis has been a denominational paper, the organ of the great majority of the Second Adventists in New England, the Middle States and of many West and South, for the Materialists [advocates of conditional immortality] have greatly outgrown the

Evangelical class, as they now embrace about one thousand ministers and some thirty State and sectional annual Conferences."[82]

In the end, Wellcome recognized three principal groups of Adventists. The Advent Christians, with which he identified, had no central organization but had organized several state conferences which supported publication and mission societies. The Evangelical Adventists, who differed from the Advent Christians primarily over the issue of conditional immortality, had formed the American Millennial Association and held annual sectional conferences and camp meetings. Finally, he noted the Seventh-day Adventists, indicating that they held several state conferences, but suggested their questionable relationship to true Adventism by simply saying "we do not have the means at hand to give any representations of them."[83] Wellcome looked forward in hope to the "sublime, awful, yet glorious fact that the Lord is coming soon," despite the divisions within Adventism. "The work of awakening and preparation will go on amid the darkness, unbelief, scoffing, and ridicule," he wrote, "until the final hour when our Redeemer shall come with the suddenness of the flood upon the ante-diluvians, and of the fire upon the Sodomites, and the terrific word is pronounced, 'It is done.'"[84]

Later Advent Christian Historiography

The Advent Christian historians who followed Wellcome were somewhat less concerned than he with arguing that their denomination was the faithful descendent of the Millerite movement. Rather, they sought to establish the historical and theological legitimacy of Miller's prophetic interpretation and conditionalism within the Christian tradition and the nineteenth-century American church. They also attempted to explain the post-Millerite trajectory of the Advent Christian denomination, focusing on its difficulties in developing a viable organizational structure and the effect that this experience had on the church's growth.

About a half century after the appearance of Wellcome's *History*, Albert C. Johnson, an Advent Christian minister, published *Advent Christian History* under the sponsorship of the denomination's Publication Society. Although much of his account of the Millerite movement appears to have been dependent on Bliss and Wellcome, Johnson devoted approximately one-half of his book to the development of the Advent Christian Church from the 1850s to 1918. Restrained by time and requested to write a work that was "brief, concise, and yet comprehensive," Johnson stated that "we have been deeply interested in the different branches of the cause and have tried to give as impartial and comprehensive a history as possible within the limits assigned."[85]

Johnson began his work by placing the Millerite movement within the context of Christian history, arguing that it had revived a faith in the "glorious return and reign of Christ"[86] that had been held by the Church for the first three hundred years of its existence. But with the emergence of Catholicism this primitive faith had "slumbered" until it emerged again in the Protestant Reformation,[87] only to be overcome once again by the post-millennial doctrine of Daniel Whitby, which taught the "conversion of the whole world before the advent."[88] But in the nineteenth century, interest in the premillennial return of Jesus arose in England and, more importantly, in the United States where "it will thus be seen, by unprejudiced minds, that the Miller movement came at the right time and place, greatly served the cause of true millennial faith, and reveals the providence of God still working on behalf of his truth."[89] In the face of the apostasy of the dominant postmillennialism and the development of religious skepticism in America, Johnson argued, "the church was in a state of peril; at this time of need came the great Advent Awakening in this country, the call back to the apostolic faith and to the voice of prophecy."[90] For Johnson, the Millerite movement was fundamentally a restorationist or primitivist movement inspired by God to bring back the ancient Christian faith in the premillennial advent of Jesus.

Writing from the perspective of the early twentieth century, Johnson noted positive aspects of the Millerite movement. Nearly everywhere they preached, he stated, William Miller and the other Adventist speakers prompted reformation and revival, including the conversion of skeptics and infidels. "We have not learned of any other movement in this country," Johnson wrote, "so fruitful in this regard."[91] Although he appears to have been more willing than Wellcome to accept what he called "the definite time feature" as a major element of the movement, giving two pages to a detailed account of Miller's calculations, Johnson also pointed out that early in the movement men such as H. Dana Ward, Henry Jones, and N. N. Whiting had urged that "great caution should be exercised on the time question."[92] Further emphasizing that Miller and his associates were "men of sober mind, of deliberate judgment, and utterly opposed to fanaticism,"[93] Johnson called attention to their opposition to such ideas as emphasis on "power" and "gifts" and the "come out of Babylon" movement prior to the Great Disappointment, and the shut door theory, foot washing, and religious kissing afterwards.[94]

Despite these positive characteristics of a movement that he believed had been raised up by God, Johnson seemed to have had a greater sense than Wellcome of the distance, perhaps even isolation, of the Adventist movement from the rest of society. He sadly sought to explain why the Christian churches took a critical stance toward the Adventists.

> Thus the independent Advent movement was caused by the fact that the church at large had from various sources received doctrines that displaced the primitive faith of the personal Advent as the great hope of believers, and its kindred truths, and therefore they rejected this message and its advocates, and generally church and pulpit were closed. This state of things was somewhat accented by the time feature, and some unfortunate doings of untrained and ill-balanced persons, but had not these elements entered in the result could hardly have been different, as there was not then or later on, "room in the inn" for hearty, earnest Adventual teaching and faith.[95]

Like Wellcome, Johnson also defined whom he believed constituted the true descendents of the Millerite movement. Indeed, in making his case regarding Seventh-day Adventists he drew on "the testimony of Eld. I. C. Wellcome, a man of faithful, honorable record and of sterling character, who was himself an eye-witness of these movements."[96] He regarded Seventh-day Adventism as a "schism" that arose out of the fanatical shut door teaching and strongly criticized Sabbatarian attempts to deny that they had ever advocated this view, pointing to several documents "all bearing the date of 1850 and all advocating the shut-door claim."[97] Strongly separating Seventh-day Adventism from the Adventist movement, he stated "but it was from the start a faction and a schism, and not representative of the Advent cause in general, either Millennial or Christian, nor of those therein who adhered to the name Christian."[98] In addition to the shut door teaching, Johnson also criticized the seventh-day Sabbath doctrine, contrasting it with the Advent Christian advocacy of the "new covenant," including observance of the Lord's day on the first day of the week, "which is historically traceable to Apostolic example."[99] Despite this strongly worded criticism, he also stated: "Nevertheless many of them are excellent people and they have able ministers, have a most thorough system of organization and benevolence, and have in recent years become a numerous people with extensive missions. They have certainly shown a zeal worthy of a better cause."[100]

Perhaps the "better cause" that Johnson had in mind was his own Advent Christian denomination, which had its origins as a distinct branch of Adventism in the doctrine of conditional immortality. The belief in natural immortality, which was accepted by most Christians at the time, also provided the basis for the doctrine of eternal hell, which, according to Johnson, had produced in America a reaction known as Universalism, the belief that everyone would be saved. "At this opportune season," he wrote, the "pre-eminently Biblical doctrine" of conditional immortality emerged to provide a "middle ground."[101] As with belief in the premillennial advent of Jesus, the resurgence of conditional immortality was a revival of an "ancient faith" that had emerged with such individuals as Elias Smith and Henry Grew in the early nineteenth century and came into Adventism through the efforts of George Storrs.

Although Johnson said little about conditional immortality within the Millerite movement in the 1840s, he noted that by 1856 it was producing such controversy that a general convention was called. When this meeting voted to call for an end of preaching on the question of immortality, many of those associated with the paper *The World's Crisis* had such strong convictions that their "movement overcame all restraints and spread more and more among unprejudiced Bible students."[102] In contrast, the *Advent Herald,* which represented the American Millennial Association or Evangelical Adventists, "began to be quite pronounced as the advocate of eternal torment." Johnson referred to the estimate of D. T. Taylor, an Adventist minister, that twenty-five of the sixty Adventist ministers and about half of the laymen who read the *Advent Herald* took the conditionalist view. "If this estimate be correct there was a very strong leaning toward immortality only in Christ at that time," Johnson wrote, "and this movement soon developed into the organization and work of the Advent Christian body."[103]

In the second half of his book Johnson focused on the subsequent history of the Advent Christians, discussing first the organization of the various state conferences and other organizations and then examining the many Advent Christian publications and their editors. Because of the opposition that they had experienced from the established churches, Johnson argued, many Advent Christians opposed church organization. "But it should be recorded that early in the progress of the cause," he observed, "there were able leaders who saw the futility of this lawless policy and who advocated church order."[104] Although a number of conferences had organized in the Northeast by the mid-1860s, church members failed to give adequate financial support. Despite some improvements, "the work has always suffered from lack of systematic, proportionate and liberal giving, never being permitted to come to its full possibilities," Johnson wrote. "In several cases, and we fear in many, men have gone to untimely graves from hardship endured because the people failed to recognize that the 'laborer was worthy of his hire.'"[105]

Although they had established several organizations—the Advent Christian Association and Advent Christian Publication Society in 1860, the Western Advent Christian Publishing Association in 1864, and the American Advent Mission Society in 1865—denominational leaders continued to push for a stronger and more unified structure. Recounting such efforts in the late 1870s, Johnson commented "that it was indeed a time of remarkable opportunity, the full measure of which was not recognized."[106] In 1893 the Advent Christian Association revised its constitution to form "a kind of general conference" that served, according to Johnson, "as a bond of fellowship between these Publication Societies and a kind of central union and headship of the same, though exercising only advisory influence in this capacity."[107] Again in 1915 and 1916 efforts to strengthen the General Conference resulted in constitutional changes that Johnson hoped would "secure that larger inspiration, co-operation and efficiency that has been so much desired."[108]

Johnson concluded his book with an optimistic assessment of the state of his denomination. The central doctrines of the premillennial advent of Jesus and conditional immortality "have proven sound, salutary, and of practical efficient assistance in winning men of all classes to the Christ and the church."[109] And despite the continuing struggle over organizational issues, he noted several positive developments, including better organized local churches, increased educational efforts, and more active foreign mission work. While he recommended a stronger evangelistic and foreign mission effort, more ministers, and a "broad vision," he believed that the future carried the promise "for successful work and increase."[110]

Although later Advent Christians wrote two important Ph.D. dissertations[111] and a small book[112] on aspects of their history, the next major publication was a series of books written by Clyde E. Hewitt, published between 1983 and 1990. Fearful that the present generation knew little of the denomination's heritage, the president of the Advent Christian General Conference, Joe Tom Tate, had called on the organization in 1978 to authorize a new publication addressing its history. The following year the church's executive council voted to republish Johnson's volume together with a second volume that would carry the story up to the present. The committee appointed to accomplish this task subsequently decided that rather than republishing Johnson it would commission a seven-volume history of the church. It chose Clyde E. Hewitt, former chair of the history department at Aurora College and a graduate of the University of Chicago, to write the first volume of what ultimately became a three-volume series.[113]

Midnight and Morning,[114] the first volume of the series, covered the Millerite movement and briefly described the various groups that emerged from it. For this book, Hewitt relied primarily on Bliss, Wellcome, and William Miller's *Apology and Defense*, as well as several recent secondary works. The remaining two volumes—*Responsibility and Response,* which focused on publications and editors, and *Devotion and Development,*[115] which examined geographical expansion and organizational developments—drew on extensive research in primary sources such as Advent Christian papers and periodicals, minutes of the General Conference and other entities, and oral history interviews.

Reflecting his training as a professional historian, Hewitt examined the Millerite movement within the context of American society in the mid-nineteenth century, something neither Wellcome nor Johnson had done. Noting that it arose within an era and geographical region surging with reform efforts, Hewitt called Millerism the "ultimate reform movement," for it looked forward to the "complete eradication of evil from this world by the return of Christ and the establishment of His kingdom forever."[116] Calling attention to secular developments as well as other Bible expositors who understood the prophecies similarly to Miller, Hewitt interpreted the Millerite movement as part and parcel of its time rather than being "an isolated phenomenon."[117]

But the Millerite movement, according to Hewitt, had distinctive elements as well. Its challenge to postmillennialism and emphasis on the very soon return of Christ set it apart from most other Christians. The degree of publicity the movement generated from friend and foe alike put it in a class by itself. Although not as distinctive, the use of large prophetic charts in preaching and the role of women speakers, of which there were at least eight, also gave Millerite meetings a unique flavor. Finally, in contrast to the emotionalism and spiritual "exercises" that frequently characterized camp meetings of the period, the Millerite meetings were restrained. Hewitt wrote:

> Miller and his followers preached a closely argued, well-reasoned exposition of prophetic utterances from the Scriptures. They compared one with the other and sought to demonstrate their fulfillment by reference to historical events. Theirs was essentially a scholarly approach. Conviction that they were right, or might very well be right, and that the world would come to an end *very shortly* in fire and judgment was an awful and

solemn thought to them and to their hearers. Deep emotions, including weeping, at the realization of one's lack of preparation for that event, could be inspired by such preaching, but typically not ecstatic emotional outbursts.[118]

Drawing upon David T. Arthur's doctoral dissertation, Hewitt sympathetically but critically examined the thrust toward separatism, as Millerites experienced at the same time both criticism and exclusion by the established churches and increasingly large and sympathetic crowds. "It became easy for them [the Millerites] to believe and publicly proclaim," Hewitt stated, "that their opponents were guilty of the same suppression of divine truth which Protestants generally believed had turned the early church into the 'Whore of Babylon' of Revelation prophecy."[119] Rather than seeing the "come out of Babylon" movement as fanatical and outside of mainstream Millerism, as had Wellcome and Johnson, Hewitt regarded it as the logical development of the movement's thought and experience. Nonetheless, it had tragic results, for after the Great Disappointment the Millerite believers often found themselves unchurched and, at the same time, faced grave difficulties in establishing their own denominations because of their antiorganizational convictions.

Addressing the aftermath of the Great Disappointment, Hewitt gave a careful and balanced account of the emergence of the various Adventist groups. In addition to recounting the debate over whether the Adventists should organize at all, he also explored the emerging issue of conditional immortality. Unlike Wellcome he made no effort to establish its Millerite credentials, stating that it had made "little impression" on the movement by 1844 and describing the 1845 Albany conference as "adamant" in its opposition to the doctrine.[120] But by 1852, he stated, conditional immortality was attracting a significant hearing among the Adventists, leading within a few years to a division between the Evangelical Adventists, who rejected the doctrine, and the Advent Christians, who accepted it. Not content with simply recounting the development of conditional immortality among the Adventists, Hewitt spent considerable time explaining its biblical foundations and history within the Christian Church.[121] Referring to the individuals and movements he had identified as supporting conditionalism, Hewitt observed that the list "does not prove that the Conditionalist contention is correct. It does indicate that it is a doctrine that has intellectual and scriptural respectability."[122]

Publications, Hewitt noted, played a major role in the conditional immortality debate and ultimately became the focal points around which not only the Evangelical Adventists and Advent Christians formed, but also the other distinct groups that emerged out of the Adventist movement: the Life and Advent Union, the "Age to Come" Adventists who later formed the Church of God, the Seventh-day Adventists, and the Church of God (Seventh Day). Although Hewitt noted that contemporary Adventists regarded the Sabbatarians as "another form of the fanaticism which they had long fought,"[123] he observed that the very distinctiveness of some Seventh-day Adventist beliefs and practices had produced an individual and corporate sense of purpose that explained much of its success. Furthermore, he concluded, "today, as from the beginning, this denomination agrees in its overall theology with most of Protestantism," a decided contrast to the views of Wellcome and Johnson.[124]

The remaining two volumes of Hewitt's series surveyed the development of the Advent Christian Church but, surprisingly for a denominationally-sponsored work, took a chastened view of that history. Coming to grips with the fact that the church had experienced a decline in membership during the past hundred years, Hewitt sought to explain its lack of advance. Belief in the soon coming of Jesus, he stated, "was a poor doctrine on which to build a denomination,"[125] for such an institution requires organizational structure, the training of ministers, strategic planning, and financial support, none of which is encouraged by a belief that the world is shortly coming to its end. Throughout the nineteenth century and into the twentieth, publications, many of them independently produced, were "the life blood of the Advent Christian denomination."[126] By the 1980s, however, the scores of different publications had been reduced to two, both published by the organized church. Hewitt wondered if there might be a relationship between reduction in publications and reduction in membership.

This sense of missed opportunities became even clearer in the third volume where, after four chapters in which titles implied expansion—"Westward Ho!," "The Far West," "Into Apalachia," and "The Deep South"—the remaining titles all suggested decline: "Contraction," "Hesitantly Forward," "The Rise and Fall of the Forward Movement," and "Structure without Power." Discussing the closing of churches, Hewitt commented that the Advent Christians "as a people—as a generality—[are] flawed in their application of their distinctive doctrines to their life as a church....they are great on the future life, not so great on the present life."[127] Among the flaws, he identified a lack of appeal to young people, failure to provide financial support for pastors, an attitude of exclusiveness, and an "acceptance of and resignation to the group's smallness."[128]

Writing about the many failed attempts in the nineteenth century to develop a stronger Advent Christian organization, Hewitt identified several "missed opportunities" that "may have doomed the denomination to a smallness of outlook which would limit its service to the Lord and its growth in the future."[129] Similarly, after describing the effort in the 1920s to establish a unified denominational budget, Hewitt stated that the Advent Christian membership lacked sufficient vision to make the plan a success.[130] Explaining why these problems persisted, he pointed to regional tensions that led different areas to be "suspicious of the motives and program favored by those in another section"[131] and the relatively low socioeconomic level of the church membership.[132] In the last pages of his book, Hewitt called for strong action by a future General Conference session to require that churches financially support a unified budget. If the churches did not do so, he proposed, they should no longer be allowed to send delegates to the session. "Obviously, this is a drastic proposal not likely to appeal to the faint-hearted," he wrote. "But, I am faint-hearted enough not to want to face the specter of our continuing decline toward denominational extinction."[133] These were strong words with which to close an official history—words that differed greatly from the hopeful outlook of Isaac Wellcome in 1873 and the more muted optimism of Albert Johnson in 1918.

Wellcome and the Historians

In addition to being an important source for Advent Christian historians, Wellcome's *History* has also been valuable to other scholars as well. David Rowe, a historian from outside the Adventist tradition, described the *History* as "the best published account" of the Millerite movement, although he made little direct use of the volume in his *Thunder and Trumpets*.[134] Three historians from Seventh-day Adventist backgrounds but nonetheless engaged in reevaluating the denomination's history took a similar position. In his revisionist examination of Ellen G. White's relationship to American health reform, University of Wisconsin historian Ronald L. Numbers called Wellcome's work "generally reliable"[135] and in an edited collection of papers on the Millerite movement he and Jonathan M. Butler, a historian teaching at the La Sierra campus of Loma Linda University, described the book as "a relatively dispassionate account."[136] Stating much the same thing, Ingemar Lindén, a Swedish scholar writing about the early development of Seventh-day Adventism, commented that it was "a remarkable work for being written by a layman historian"[137] and "a comprehensive and valuable history of the Adventist revival."[138]

From a different angle, Francis D. Nichol, a Seventh-day Adventist editor who wrote an extensive defense of the Millerite movement, commented that Wellcome's volume was "particularly valuable because of biographical sketches of various men who participated in the movement."[139] And most recently, Merlin D. Burt, director of the Center for Adventist Research at Andrews University, in an introduction to a reprint of the *Memoirs of William Miller* stated that Wellcome's book "remains an essential resource for study of Millerite Adventism."[140]

Although they did not make general evaluations of Wellcome's *History,* the major Seventh-day Adventist writers on the Millerite movement used it as a significant source, which attests to the volume's value and accuracy. The first few histories were written by ministers and provided a Seventh-day Adventist alternative to Wellcome's interpretation. J. N. Loughborough's two general histories, published in 1892 and 1905,[141] made no specific reference to Wellcome, but M. Ellsworth Olsen's 1925 work drew upon Wellcome as a source of quotations from Millerite primary sources at least eight times.[142] Everett N. Dick wrote the first scholarly study of Millerite history as his Ph.D. dissertation at the University of Wisconsin, completing it in 1930. Although he revised the dissertation for book publication, it did not appear in print until 1994.[143] In this work Dick used Wellcome as a source eight times, in each case relying on the book for factual information.[144] While more an apologist than a historian, Leroy E. Froom nonetheless did extensive research for his four-volume *Prophetic Faith of Our Fathers*. In his section on the Millerite movement, published in 1954, Froom used Wellcome as a source for quotations from contemporary materials twice[145] and for information more than twenty-five times.[146] At one point he wrote, "Considerable draft is made in this section on Historian [sic] Wellcome, for he was a contemporary, with access to all contemporary facts and sources."[147] Marking the 150th anniversary of the "Great Disappointment," George R. Knight, then professor of church history at the Seventh-day Adventist Theological Seminary, synthesized much recent scholarship in *Millennial Fever*, a popular general history of the Millerite movement and its aftermath. Knight used Wellcome extensively, drawing upon him some ten times for quotations from other primary source materials,[148] more than twelve times for information on the movement,[149] and three times as a primary source witness.[150] For all of these writers, the numbers stated here should be taken as approximate rather than precise, for it is easy to miss a reference in a heavily footnoted work, but they give a good indication of Wellcome's value to Dick, Froom, and Knight and the continuing significance of the book to those interested in the Millerite movement.

Not surprisingly, one area in which Seventh-day Adventist scholars differed significantly from Wellcome was in their treatment of the shut door controversy. Two related issues were at stake in their discussion. First, in conflict with Wellcome and Johnson, among others, these writers sought to establish Seventh-day Adventism as the legitimate offspring of the Millerite movement. Second, they defended Ellen G. White against charges that she taught a clearly erroneous doctrine on the basis of her visions.

Among the several Adventist writers who have examined the shut door issue,[151] three specifically addressed Wellcome's views. While disagreeing among themselves regarding the proper interpretation of the shut door episode, each made a similar assessment of Wellcome's treatment of the subject. In contrast to Wellcome, Gerard Damsteegt, who taught at the Seventh-day Adventist Theological Seminary, provided evidence that rather than originating with Joseph Turner and Apollos Hale, the concept of the shut door could be traced back to comments made by William Miller as early as 1838.[152] Distinguishing between what he called extreme and moderate versions of the shut door doctrine, Damsteegt placed Wellcome in the camp of those who believed that Ellen White "advocated the extreme shut-door view for a number of years."[153] Rolf Pöhler, at the time a graduate student at the theological seminary, wrote a significant paper in which, while differing from Damsteegt regarding the use of sources, he described Wellcome and other critics of Seventh-day Adventism and the shut door as "being as polemical (or even more so) as their opponents were defensive."[154] Even Lindén, who departed from Damsteegt and Pöhler in his empathy with Wellcome and other critics of the shut door teaching, recognized that Wellcome was writing polemics in dealing with this issue: "It is true that Wellcome exposed himself as a kind of bitter critic of the competing and growing Sabbatarian Adventists. He even conceded that immediately after the October disappointment he had been baptized by James White, a ceremony he much regretted a few weeks later on. Such circumstances explain at least some of the polemical phrases quoted here. When it comes to the radical shut-door concept in the Whites, however, other documents show that in principle Wellcome was correct in his report."[155]

Generally agreeing with the work of Damsteegt and Pöhler, Knight argued that the shut door concept originated with William Miller as early as 1836[156] and that most Millerites accepted the doctrine in the immediate aftermath of October 22 "because the interpretation was built into their belief system." Beginning in early November, however, Himes had led "the Adventist majority (including Miller) away from the October date and the shut-door belief."[157] According to Knight, all of the Sabbatarian Adventist leaders accepted the shut door doctrine, a point on which he seemed to agree with Wellcome, although he did not address the role of Ellen White's visions in supporting this belief. Gradually, Knight further explained, the Sabbatarian Adventists reinterpreted the shut door within the context of their understanding that Jesus had entered the Most Holy Place of the heavenly sanctuary on October 22, 1844.[158] Reflecting a century of Seventh-day Adventist historiography, he concluded that "in the heated post-1844 battle over which group had the 'original advent faith,'...it appears that the Sabbatarians were correct in their claim to be the only genuine continuation of Millerism."[159] In this general interpretation, Knight challenged Wellcome and the historiographic tradition that he had established.

Despite differences among scholars and other writers, it is clear that Wellcome's history remains an important source of information regarding the Millerite movement and a significant example of the Advent Christian side in the struggle to claim the mantle of William Miller. The modern reader needs to approach the book with the understanding that Wellcome did not write it as a disinterested observer of the movement but rather as a partisan in the debates over Miller's legacy. One must, therefore, not only attempt to distinguish fact from opinion but also ask why Wellcome included particular facts rather than others and presented them in the manner that he chose. When David Rowe discussed Wellcome's work, he commented that the physical volume was "difficult to find."[160] That situation is now rectified with the publication of this reprint, which offers the opportunity for new readers to approach the work with the respect and critical understanding that it deserves.

1. Isaac C. Wellcome, *History of the Second Advent Message and Mission, Doctrine and People* (Yarmouth, ME: I. C. Wellcome, 1874), 567.

2. See Henry F. May, *The Enlightenment in America* (New York: Oxford University Press, 1976), 122–26.

3. See Ann Lee Bressler, *The Universalist Movement in America, 1770–1880* (New York: Oxford University Press, 2001), 9–42.

4. Wellcome, *History*, 567.

5. For a brief description of the Great Awakening, see Mark A. Noll, *A History of Christianity in the United States and Canada* (Grand Rapids, MI: William B. Eerdmans, 1992), 166–80.

6. Wellcome, *History*, 568.

7. For the history of the Millerite movement, see George R. Knight, *Millennial Fever and the End of the World: A Study of Millerite Adventism* (Boise, ID: Pacific Press, 1994).

8. Wellcome, *History*, 568.

9. William Hoffman, "The Long View from the Watonwan River: The Millenarian Odyssey of Pioneer Druggist Henry Wellcome." http://www.mbbnet.umn.edu/hoff/hsw_art.html (accessed 13 October 2005).

10. Ibid.

11. Regarding the drug store, see ibid.

12. Albert C. Johnson, *Advent Christian History: A Concise Narrative of the Origin and Progress, Doctrine and Work of This Body of Believers*, Introduction by O. R. Jenks (Mendota, IL: Western Advent Christian Publication Society, 1918), 397.

13. Clyde E. Hewitt, *Responsibility and Response*, Foreword by Freeman Barton (Charlotte, NC: Venture Books, 1986), 64; and Wellcome, *History*, 571.

14. Johnson, *Advent Christian History*, 333–34.

15. Quoted in ibid., 334.

16. Hewitt, *Responsibility and Response*, 64.

17. Johnson, *Advent Christian History*, 397.

18. Ibid., 180.

19. *World's Crisis* (20 February 1895), 1, quoted in Hewitt, *Responsibility and Response*, 65.

20. *World's Crisis* (13 November 1895), 7, quoted in ibid.

21. Ibid., 45.

22. Ibid., 44.

23. Johnson, *Advent Christian History*, 397.

24. For a survey of Millerite historiography through 1994, see Gary Land, "The Historians and the Millerites: An Historiographical Essay," in Everett N. Dick, *William Miller and the Advent Crisis, 1831–1844*, with historiographical introduction and editorial notes by Gary Land (Berrien Springs, MI: Andrews University Press, 1994), xiii–xxviii; also published in *Andrews University Seminary Studies* 32 (Autumn 1994): 227–46; and Merlin D. Burt, "Historical Introduction," in Sylvester Bliss, *Memoirs of William Miller with Appendices Containing Three Other Contemporary Biographical Sketches*, reprint, Adventist Classic Library (Berrien Springs, MI: Andrews University Press, 2005), xvii–xxii.

25. [Josiah Litch], "The Rise and Progress of Adventism," *The Advent Shield and Review* (May 1844), 93.

26. Ibid., 60.

27. Ibid., 71.

28. Ibid., 86–87.

29. Ibid., 51.

30. Ibid., 83–86.

31. Ibid., 73–74.

32. Ibid., 80.
33. Ibid., 82.
34. Ibid., 88–90.
35. Sylvester Bliss, *Memoirs of William Miller Generally Known as a Lecturer on the Prophecies, and the Second Coming of Christ*, Preface by Joshua V. Himes (Boston, MA: Joshua V. Himes, 1853), iii–iv.
36. Ibid., 13.
37. Ibid., 80.
38. Ibid., 158.
39. Ibid., 185.
40. Ibid., 239.
41. Ibid., 293–99.
42. James White, *Sketches of the Christian Life and Public Labors of William Miller, Gathered from His Memoir by the Late Sylvester Bliss, and from Other Sources by James White* (Battle Creek, MI: Steam Press of the Seventh-day Adventist Publishing Association, 1875). White added several notes commenting on aspects of Bliss's text from a Seventh-day Adventist perspective.
43. *A Brief History of William Miller the Great Pioneer in Advental Faith* (Boston, MA: Advent Christian Publishing Society, 1895). The same publisher produced subsequent editions of this volume in 1910 and 1915. The Review and Herald Publishing Association, a Seventh-day Adventist institution, also published an edition of this work in 1915.
44. As George Knight observes, "statistics among the Adventist groups were not easy to come by in their early years." In an 1860 census, D. T. Taylor estimated that there was a total of 54,000 Adventists, but he did not differentiate them by specific beliefs. Knight notes that various sources suggest that there were about 3,000 Sabbatarians at this same time, about five percent of the total number of Adventists. Taylor also determined that in 1860 the Advent Christian *World's Crisis*, with 2,900 subscribers, led all Adventist publications. The Sabbatarian *Review and Herald* was second, with 2,300 subscribers. By 1890, a United States government census revealed that the Seventh-day Adventists, with 28,991 members in the United States, had grown to be the largest Adventist group. The Advent Christians were the next largest, with 25,816. See Knight, *Millennial Fever*, 328–29. See also Johnson, *Advent Christian History*, 267, and Clyde E. Hewitt, *Midnight and Morning: An Account of the Adventist Awakening and the Founding of the Advent Christian Denomination, 1831–1860*, Foreword by Joe Tom Tate (Charlotte, NC: Venture Books, 1983), 254–55.
45. Wellcome, *History*, 9.
46. Ibid., 10–11.
47. Ibid., 12.
48. Ibid., 128–29.
49. Wellcome's incorporation of sources into his text without clear delineation appears to have sometimes confused historians. George Knight, for instance, stated that Wellcome, as well as Litch, "claimed that Miller had

personally told them in 1839 that Christ would come between the spring of 1843 and March 21, 1844." See Knight, *Millennial Fever*, 127. As indicated earlier, Wellcome stated that he became a Christian in 1840 and a Millerite in 1842; thus, such a conversation seems improbable although not impossible. More significantly, a careful examination of the passage on which Knight's statement is based and the footnote that comes about three pages later suggests that the style is quite different from that of Wellcome and the text actually came from a Millerite paper, the *Advent Shield*, rather than from Wellcome himself. See Wellcome, *History*, 282–85. Similarly, Clyde E. Hewitt said that in 1843 Wellcome and a few friends attempted to preach the Millerite message in Maryland. See *Devotion and Development* (Charlotte, NC: Venture Books, 1990), 70. The source for this statement appears to come from an article by Litch, also in the *Advent Shield*. See Wellcome, *History*, 290. In both cases the historians seem to have been thrown off by the phrase "the writer," which rather than referring to Wellcome came from the original author of the *Advent Shield* articles he excerpted but did not clearly identify as such. That such excellent scholars as Knight and Hewitt can misread Wellcome's text suggests that all readers must approach it with both caution and care in distinguishing Wellcome's own writing from that of the sources he quoted.

50. Ibid., 35.
51. Ibid, 92.
52. Ibid., 129.
53. Ibid., 460–82.
54. Ibid., 651.
55. Ibid., 13.
56. Ibid., 86.
57. Ibid., 251.
58. Ibid., 356, 451–52.
59. Ibid., 486–87.
60. Ibid., 250.
61. Ibid., 545.
62. Ibid., 63.
63. Ibid., 381.
64. Ibid., 386–94.
65. Ibid., 405, 442–43.
66. Ibid., 395.
67. Ibid., 397.
68. Ibid., 405.
69. Ibid., 401.
70. Ibid., 397. After the appearance of Wellcome's book, Ellen G. White stated that she "had no recollection of being in meetings with I. C. Wellcome. I might have been, but I have no acquaintance with him, and never knew him by sight." Ellen G. White to J. N. Loughborough, Battle Creek, MI, 24 August 1874. L-002 1874 J. N. Loughborough, Ellen G. White Estate, Silver Spring, MD.

71. See Ellen G. White, *Selected Messages from the Writings of Ellen G. White*, vol. 1 (Washington, DC: Review and Herald, 1958), 61–64, 74. See also Ellen G. White, *Early Writings of Ellen G. White* (Washington, DC: Review and Herald, 1945), 42–45; and Robert W. Olson, "The 'Shut Door' Documents: Statements Relating to the 'Shut Door,' the Door of Mercy, and the Salvation of Souls by Ellen G. White and Other Early Adventists," unpublished manuscript, Ellen G. White Estate, Silver Spring, MD, 1982.

72. Wellcome, *History*, 402.

73. Ibid., 405, 407.

74. Ibid., 403.

75. Ibid., 407.

76. For an overview of Seventh-day Adventist understanding of the sanctuary doctrine, see Gerhard F. Hasel, "Divine Judgment," in *Handbook of Seventh-day Adventist Theology*, Commentary Reference Series, vol. 12, ed. Raoul Dederen, et al. (Hagerstown, MD: Review and Herald, 2000), 833–46.

77. Wellcome, *History*, 406.

78. Ibid., 507.

79. Ibid., 509–10.

80. Ibid., 514.

81. Ibid., 517.

82. Ibid., 600.

83. Ibid., 607.

84. Ibid., 650.

85. Johnson, *History*, iii.

86. Ibid., 11.

87. Ibid., 13–17.

88. Ibid., 21.

89. Ibid., 26–27.

90. Ibid., 87.

91. Ibid., 89–93.

92. Ibid., 79–83. See also Johnson's assertion that it is a mistake to say that "it was the definite time movement that made us a people," ibid., 136–37.

93. Ibid., 78–79.

94. Ibid., 123–24.

95. Ibid., 130.

96. Ibid., 197.

97. Ibid., 196.

98. Ibid.

99. Ibid., 199.

100. Ibid.

101. Ibid., 135.

102. Ibid., 176.

103. Ibid., 177.

104. Ibid., 207.

105. Ibid., 223.

106. Ibid., 307.

107. Ibid., 447.
108. Ibid., 449–50.
109. Ibid., 583. To provide further support for these central doctrines, in a chapter entitled "European Witnesses and Kindred Movements" Johnson identified and discussed several nineteenth-century individuals outside of the American Adventist movement who advocated similar views. See ibid., 538–64.
110. Ibid., 586–91.
111. David Tallmadge Arthur, "'Come Out of Babylon': A Study of Millerite Separatism and Denominationalism, 1840–1865" (Ph.D. diss., University of Rochester, 1970) and David Arnold Dean, "Echoes of the Midnight Cry: The Millerite Heritage in the Apologetics of the Advent Christian Denomination, 1860–1960" (Th.D. diss., Westminster Theological Seminary, 1977). Dean described Wellcome as "astute" and called both Wellcome and Johnson "Christian historian-apologists." See Dean, *Echoes*, 131, 476.
112. Clarence J. Kearney, *The Advent Christian Story* (n.p.: by the author, 1968).
113. Joe Tom Tate, "Foreword," in Hewitt, *Midnight and Morning*, ix–x.
114. For further comments on *Midnight and Morning*, see Gary Land, "The Millerites: An Advent Christian View," *Adventist Heritage: A Journal of Adventist History* 11 (Fall 1986): 61–64.
115. Clyde E. Hewitt, *Devotion and Development* (Charlotte, NC: Venture Books, 1990).
116. Hewitt, *Midnight and Morning*, 46.
117. Ibid., 64.
118. Ibid., 127.
119. Ibid., 148.
120. Ibid., 193, 227.
121. Ibid., 221–27, 291–96.
122. Ibid., 222.
123. Ibid., 186.
124. Ibid., 277–78.
125. Hewitt, *Responsibility and Response*, 9. See also Hewitt, *Devotion and Development*, 211–12.
126. Hewitt, *Responsibility and Response*, 237.
127. Hewitt, *Devotion and Development*, 148.
128. Ibid., 146–62.
129. Ibid., 192.
130. Ibid., 236.
131. Ibid., 248.
132. Ibid., 252.
133. Ibid., 373.
134. David L. Rowe, *Thunder and Trumpets: Millerites and Dissenting Religion in Upstate New York, 1800–1850* (Chico, CA: Scholars Press, 1985), 164. By "direct use" I am referring to reference to Wellcome in footnotes. Two other major studies of Millerism that appeared around the same time as Rowe's

made no direct use of Wellcome. See Michael Barkun, *Crucible of the Millennium: The Burned-over District of New York in the 1840s* (Syracuse, NY: Syracuse University Press, 1986) and Ruth Alden Doan, *The Miller Heresy, Millennialism, and American Culture* (Philadelphia, PA: Temple University Press, 1987).

135. Ronald L. Numbers, *Prophetess of Health: Ellen G. White and the Origins of Seventh-day Adventist Health Reform*, revised and enlarged edition of *Prophetess of Health: A Study of Ellen G. White* with psychological profile by Janet S. Numbers and Ronald L. Numbers and introduction by Jonathan M. Butler (Knoxville, TN: University of Tennessee Press, 1992), 318.

136. Ronald L. Numbers and Jonathan M. Butler, "Introduction," in *The Disappointed: Millerism and Millenarianism in the Nineteenth Century*, eds. Ronald L. Numbers and Jonathan M. Butler, illustrations selected by James R. Nix (Bloomington, IN: Indiana University Press, 1987), xvi.

137. Ingemar Lindén, *The Last Trump: An Historico-Genetical Study of Some Important Chapter in the Making and Development of the Seventh-day Adventist Church* (Frankfurt am Main, Germany: Peter Lang, 1978), 76.

138. Ingemar Lindén, *1844 and the Shut Door Problem* (Stockholm, Sweden: by the author, 1982), 84.

139. Francis D. Nichol, *The Midnight Cry: A Defense of the Character and Conduct of William Miller and the Millerites, Who Mistakenly Believed that the Second Coming of Christ Would Take Place in the Year 1844* (Washington, DC: Review and Herald, 1944), 557.

140. Merlin D. Burt, "Historical Introduction," xviii.

141. J. N. Loughborough, *Rise and Progress of the Seventh-day Adventists with Tokens of God's Hand in the Movement and a Brief Sketch of the Advent Cause from 1831–1844* (Battle Creek, MI: General Conference Association, 1982); John N. Loughborough, *The Great Second Advent Movement* (Nashville, TN: Southern, 1905).

142. M. Ellsworth Olsen, *A History of the Origin and Progress of Seventh-day Adventists* (Washington, DC: Review and Herald, 1925), 103, 122–23, 162–64.

143. See Gary Land, "Foreword," in Dick, *William Miller*, vii–ix.

144. Dick, *William Miller*, 7, 11, 30, 35, 48, 67, 72, 144.

145. Leroy E. Froom, *The Prophetic Faith of Our Fathers*, vol. 4 *New World Recovery and Consummation of Prophetic Interpretation* (Washington, DC: Review and Herald, 1954), 507, 839.

146. Ibid., 508, 512, 609, 611, 631, 633, 640, 669, 677, 706, 715, 752–56, 772–82, 816, 838, 952.

147. Ibid., 752.

148. Knight, *Millennial Fever*, 8, 49, 50, 62, 100–01, 102, 129, 249–50, 260, 279.

149. Ibid., 67–68, 83, 98, 102, 115, 116, 119–20, 134, 149, 170, 212, 260, 291.

150. Ibid., 150, 290, 318.

151. Rolf J. Pöhler provides an excellent historiographical account of the shut door, covering works written through the mid-1970s, in "'...And the

Door was Shut:' Seventh-day Adventists and the Shut-door Doctrine in the Decade After the Great Disappointment," unpublished paper, Seventh-day Adventist Theological Seminary, 1978, James White Library, Andrews University, Berrien Springs, MI, 10–66. Although it does not address historiographical issues, the most recent study of early Seventh-day Adventist doctrinal development, including the shut door, is Merlin D. Burt, "The Historical Background, Interconnected Development, and Integration of the Doctrines of the Sanctuary, the Sabbath, and Ellen G. White's Role in Sabbatarian Adventism from 1844 to 1849" (PhD diss., Andrews University, 2002).

152. P. Gerard Damsteegt, *Foundations of the Seventh-day Adventist Message and Mission* (Grand Rapids, MI: William B. Eerdmans, 1977), 43, 107.

153. Ibid., 149; see also 176.

154. Pöhler, "'...And the Door Was Shut,'" 15, 34, 57–60.

155. Lindén, *1844*, 84–85.

156. Knight, *Millennial Fever*, 236–37.

157. Ibid., 238.

158. Ibid., 313.

159. Ibid., 318.

160. Rowe, *Thunder and Trumpets*, 164.

CONFERENCE OF THE ANCIENT PROPHETS.

HISTORY

OF THE

SECOND ADVENT MESSAGE

AND MISSION,

DOCTRINE AND PEOPLE.

BY ISAAC C. WELLCOME,

AUTHOR OF VARIOUS WORKS ON GOSPEL THEMES.

ILLUSTRATED.

"Behold, the Lord hath proclaimed unto the end of the world, Say ye to the daughter of Zion, Behold, thy salvation cometh; behold, his reward is with him, and his work before him. —Isa. lxii. 11.

"He which testifieth these things saith, Surely I come quickly, Amen. Even so, Come Lord Jesus."—Rev. xxii. 20.

YARMOUTH, ME:

PUBLISHED BY I. C. WELLCOME.

BOSTON:

ADVENT CHRISTIAN PUBLICATION SOCIETY, 160 HANOVER STREET.

NEW YORK:

A. A. PHELPS, 75 BARCLAY STREET.

LONDON:

KALLAWAY & CO., 78 NEWGATE STREET.

1874.

B. THURSTON & CO., PRINTERS, PORTLAND.

PREFACE.

When contemplating the preparation of this work, for the Press, we were well aware it was no enviable task. While the chief subjects to be presented, such as the proclamation of the immediate coming of our Lord, accounts of the awakening of many of his servants to engage in it, the manifestations of the "guiding hand," and attending power of God's grace in bringing vast multitudes to repentance and reformation through it, are pleasing themes, and of vast importance in cheering, instructing and strengthening the true disciples of Christ. But in connection with these there are many incidents that develop the depravity, malignity and unbelief of the human heart, which are very unpleasant to recall. We would never place such acts of unkindness, intolerance, meanness and unchristian conduct, conspiciously before the public, did not the cause of truth and righteousness sometimes demand it. It is indeed humiliating to poor human nature to reconsider its depravity, ignorance and weakness.

We felt incompetent to select, from the mass of facts connected with this theological and religious revolution, such portions as were most important for the public, and prepare such a work as the merits of the cause demand and as should be produced from the abundant material at hand: and we have long waited in hope that, as time lingered, some man of literary ability, with a living interest in this subject, would write a history. Several have proposed to do so, but did not; perhaps it presented too many complicated phases.

Without any claim to literary attainments, we have entered upon the work, believing duty led in that direction, and here present the results of our efforts, in the following pages. Not for the eye of the literary critic, but for the study, information, and contemplation of sober thinkers. It contains a large amount of valuable information for all Christian students, whether they accept all the views of Advent believers or not. We have aimed to collect the most important historical matters and many valuable criticisms bearing on the subject at issue, whether they favored our views or otherwise.

We have recorded many things which will be exceedingly gratifying to all believers; and also matters that will be bitterly complained of by some, and perhaps disputed. On points which affect personal views or conduct, or party views and interests, we have given what seemed to us duty, regardless of what may be said or thought by the parties.

We write for Christ and his cause, not for persons or parties.

We may have erred as to duty; we may have made mistakes. We do not claim infallibility. When errors are pointed out we shall gladly do what we can to make corrections.

In going through the vast amount and great varieties of matter we have examined, from which to make our selections, we have found it often difficult to decide what was best to cull and what to leave. We have been lured by the many excellent things we have gazed upon; and then nearly overwhelmed by the opposition, the hate, the unbelief and rude conduct of many who professed to be Christians; and thus we have occupied many pages we intended to reserve for theological arguments. Some will conclude it had been better to cull only the good, the pleasant matters, and passed the evil by. But our work was *history*. Justice and righteousness demand a recognition of facts, when we know them, of various classes. This is the Bible rule. Yet had we this work to write again, after going through the matter as we have, we should treat many of the opposers with greater leniency and charity.

Although we are, if possible, more confirmed that this is a dispensational truth—a God-given message, yet we recognize more fully than ever the results of ignorance, the strong influence of association, the power of prejudice; and also the great importance of "patience"—long patience with the erring.

The fact is very apparent too, that the believers have not all been "wise as serpents, and harmless as doves." Not all of such deportment as to "commend themselves to every man's conscience in the sight of God."

Poor human nature is weak indeed, but God is Almighty, and he has accomplished a mighty work through the "earthen vessels" he has called to this mission, and he has more work for them to do.

We have commended, not flattered, many of the pioneers and writers. "Esteem them highly for their work's sake," says Paul. But this will displease some. They will gladly have their favorite ministers commended, but others are to them of little account, and as for some we esteem highly they think unworthy of confidence. They have heard bad things, hard stories about them. Doubtless you have. The devil and mean men, unworthy aspirants, and bad men, are always defaming God's ministers, especially the most useful ones.

But if you speak of men's lives and labors, why not do as the Lord caused the Scripture writers to do—give the good and the bad? We are not the judge, nor are we divinely inspired to know the hearts of all men.

The Scripture says, "By their fruits ye shall know them." We therefore decide Christian character, not by reports of "Madam rumor," nor by the statements of sour-minded, or bitter-hearted men, nor of "party men," but by the general course of life, labors, sacrifices and constant toils of such as bring men to Christ, and build up the believers in Christ.

All are mortal. If men are to be turned over to destruction, for a fault, a rash act, a misstep, or a scar from the attack of the enemy, then all must go, for all have faults. But we have commended none we believe to be bad men, and we are not intending to help blacken the characters of the Lord's servants although they are faulty. "Be not puffed up for one against another."

We have, by the advice of many, added Portraits of Pioneers, Editors, and Authors. Some we could not obtain. Some who promised, afterwards declined. Some also declined giving us any facts of their history that we might give sketches of them. We have used no partiality in these matters.

We present it as it is with the prayer that the Lord will make it a blessing to many, and with the hope that our labor expended upon it has not been in vain, in the Lord.

I. C. W.

YARMOUTH, ME., July 1, 1874.

TABLE OF CONTENTS.

INDEX OF PORTRAITS.

CHAPTER I.

IMPORTANCE OF HISTORY—OUR OBJECT—THE MESSAGE OF CHRIST'S SECOND ADVENT—OBSTACLES—EXTREMES—DISPENSATIONAL TRUTHS—GOD REVEALS COMING EVENTS—PROPHECY NOT UNDERSTOOD TILL NEAR ITS FULFILLMENT—TIME OF THE END SUBJECT OF PROPHECY—PROPHECIES FORESHADOWING THE END—MISAPPREHENSIONS CORRECTED—THE APOCALYPSE THE UNSEALING OF PROPHECY—INDIFFERENCE TO PROPHECY DISPLEASING TO JEHOVAH—A SEARCHING OF THE BIBLE—DEVELOPMENT OF ERRORS—SAD CONFLICT—THREE POINTS OF CHOICE—A NEW ORGANIZATION.

EVERY religious, political, or moral movement which sufficiently agitates the public mind to produce a radical revolution in any considerable portion of society, whether for good or evil, is worthy of being set fairly before the inquiring multitudes in truthful history, that the uninformed may learn the merits or demerits of the principles which produce such revolution.

To furnish such a history requires a clear statement of the incipient stages of the movement, of the fundamental principles producing it, the theological structure reared thereon by those who have been the chief instruments in discovering and applying them, in distinction from the deductions of novices, the sayings of erratics, reports of the uninformed, and perversions and misrepresentations of opponents.

The moral working of those principles upon the lives and best interests of their adherents and those directly affected by their influence, should also be developed by well attested facts. Such is our object in writing A HISTORY OF THE MESSAGE OF THE IMMEDIATE COMING OF CHRIST, with brief sketches of pioneers and authors. We shall give a brief statement of the chief doctrines put forth by its messengers, a synopsis of discussions with opponents, and with each other, some examples of the treatment it has received from opposing parties; of the increasing interest it has awakened throughout all christendom; of the success God has given it in the conversion of infidels and sinners of all grades, in retarding the progress of gigantic errors, reclaiming of wanderers, reforming the theology, increasing the religious power, and improving the moral conduct of many thousands in the churches.

While it has now become well known that a body of Christians exists in America and Europe called "Second Adventists," who are said to hold and teach doctrinal views widely and essentially differing from those of other churches, yet but few, comparatively, know anything properly of them, as many vague, strange, and false representations have been constantly set afloat by opposers, concerning their doctrine, objects, influence, numbers, social standing, moral culture, principles, and conduct, causing many erroneous ideas to be entertained by honest persons concerning them and their views.

Without attempting to give a history of the doctrine of the church throughout the Christian dispensation on the subject of Christ's second coming, we shall enter upon that of the special interest which was awakened in the hearts of certain devoted Bible students and sincere Christians since A. D. 1820, and of its progress in constantly awakening and enlisting others until the present, on this subject, and of their distinct and earnest proclamation that the event is soon to transpire.

It will be expected that we give the principles, the arguments, and the evidences upon which this proclamation is based, together with a statement of the increase of knowledge of the Scriptures on this all-important subject, and several others adjacent to it, and dependent upon it, which has been attained by the accumulated numbers of faithful, studious, Christian scholars, who have become deeply interested in the study of the prophecies concerning these matters.

It will be in place to give fair specimens of the chief criticisms and best efforts of learned and able writers who have attempted the overthrow of these principles and conclusions.

We purpose to show from current records, the great awakenings, deep religious interest, increased study of the Scriptures, greatly advanced Christian experiences, genuine reformation of sinners, radical conversions of infidels and sceptics, through this prophetic mission, who had enjoyed all the advantages of other church institutions and teachings, without being reformed or awakened.

We shall also produce records of some of the dodges, evasions, perversions of Scripture, corruptions of history, and wanderings from old and demonstrated principles of interpretation; of abandonments of main articles of Christian doctrine held by the founders of all Protestant churches, by many teachers of high standing, who have risen up against this judgment message and its mission. We shall think it our duty, also, to note some of the disastrous results to the church, which have followed these efforts to rid themselves of the cross which must be borne, by accepting this message and doctrine as truth.

It will be our duty, also, to give proper attention to the reproach brought upon this cause by ambitious aspirants, religious bigots and egotists, who have associated themselves with, and made efforts to shape and control it.

While we may give some accounts of the work of novices and zealots, the careful reader will contrast between it and that of the more advanced, candid, stable, enlightened "laborers together with God," as true disciples in the school of Christ, our teacher and master.

We shall not shun to record and confess the mistakes and grave errors which some of the true hearted and faithful have fallen into, producing evil results, affording illustrations of human weakness, and also of God's special providence and mighty workings, in preserving this cause from destruction, and prosecuting his purpose of warning a slumbering church and guilty world, through these "earthen vessels," of impending judgment.

Over-heated zeal and bad measures, vague ideas, immatured thoughts and incongruous utterances, of good men of impetuous minds, have been associated with all good causes, and must of necessity have opportunity for development and correction. They are found associated with this message, and we confess they have had an open field in which to develop and learn wisdom.

The nature of the subject—the proclamation of the immediate coming of our Lord Jesus Christ to call the dead to life, to execute righteous judgment upon all, to reward every one of the race of man—is calculated to enlist all classes of human mind, to awaken the deepest emotions of the heart, and call into action every faculty of the soul. Added to this is another element of much force to produce uncommon excitement and extreme action. During the incipient stages of this judgment-message, those who became its advocates met with violent opposition and great contempt from all other classes of society. Under these circumstances it would be no strange thing for some to become restive and rash in their conclusions and movements. And, taking advantage of the excitement caused by severe opposition and bitter denunciation, the enemy of righteousness, who always seeks to pervert what he cannot destroy, acting by direct influences and through human agencies, succeeded in pushing some over the line of gospel faith, and some into a fanatical spirit and unscriptural practices, well calculated to injure the work they wished to promote. It has been the work of the arch enemy of truth from the days of Adam to mix falsehood with the most important truths; to produce false lights, false issues, false messages, false alarms, and counterfeit spirits, to cause strife and alienation thereby. These were his tactics in the days of the apostles; they are the same now.

Were there no false messages, false alarms, false spirits, strifes and divisions connected with the bearers of the Second Advent message, they might well distrust its genuineness.

But it is to be deplored that some have been so ignorant of Satan's devices as to allow him to divert their attention and divide their strength in so many instances, when all should have been united in the specific work of building up the church of Christ on her most holy faith, and warning and saving sinners, through the publishing of "this gospel of the kingdom of God," now nigh at hand, with the evidences of the fact; together with the stupendous events dependent upon the return of Christ, and involving the great principles of human redemption.

Yet we will give everlasting praise to God for the mighty work he has accomplished with these human agencies. Truly the Lord's hand has wrought mightily in the work to produce such grand results against such seeming obstacles.

When the circumstances under which this people commenced their career as a distinct class of Christians, are well considered, and the vast amount of Christian mission work which has been accomplished through their labors, with the great number of genuine Christian converts resulting therefrom, the immense amount of valuable scriptural publications they have issued, and the numerous reforms in theological teachings in other churches produced by their literature, it must be acknowledged that this message is a "DISPENSATIONAL TRUTH," which the Lord intended should be published at this time, and which he has accompanied with his special blessing that it may prepare a people for his coming and kingdom.

The instrumentalities have been confessedly feeble, as far as the people are concerned, but the word of God is mighty, and being accompanied by the Holy Spirit has produced great results, yet the work is not finished, perhaps much more is to be accomplished. The Lord will have the Church and world thoroughly warned.

DISPENSATIONAL TRUTHS.

God, in his providential dealings with his Church, has caused a revelation of his purposes of mercy and of judgment to be made and proclaimed to all generations. When he purposed special blessings or special judgments, he caused a proclamation of such purpose to be made to the people, and messengers were qualified and imbued with the spirit and importance of the message, and sent to declare it. Such was the case concerning the flood. Gen. vi. Also, concerning the covenant of mercy with believers in God. Gen. xii., xiii., and xv. Again, concerning the deliverance of Lot from Sodom; Gen. xix.; of Israel from Egypt; Exod. iii. and iv.; of judgments on Egypt; Exod. vii. to xi. In the case of Israel's bondage in Babylon, also their release. Jer. xxv. 8–11. Isa. xlv. In the case of the first advent of Christ. Isa. xi. Mal. iii. Matt. iii. The above instances are but samples of the divine principles of government.

We will here introduce an extract from a valuable work of Mr. Bliss on this point, which fully agrees with the remarks we have already made upon this subject.

GOD REVEALS COMING EVENTS.

No truth of inspiration can be more clearly enunciated than that "Surely the Lord God doeth nothing, but he revealeth his secret unto his servants, the prophets." Amos iii. 7. He does not necessarily do this by a special revelation, nor by visible manifestations; his communications with men being different in different ages of the world. "God, who at sundry times and in divers manners spake in time past unto the fathers by the prophets, hath in these last days spoken unto us by his Son." Heb. i. 1, 2. And the prophets by whom he now speaks are the faithful men who are called in his providence, and qualified by his grace, to become "ambassadors for Christ;" and he revealeth his secrets to them by moving them to the study, and enlightening them to comprehend the import of the

"Sure Word of Prophecy, whereunto," says an inspired apostle, "ye do well that ye take heed, as unto a light that shineth in a dark place, until the day dawn, and the day-star arise in your hearts."

It is not to be truthfully disputed that, during the last half-century, the attention of the church has been called to the study of the prophetic Scriptures, in a manner never before witnessed, and with an intensity and earnestness of investigation that is irreconcilable with any theory that denies that God is thus moving upon the people, and preparing his chosen ones for some manifestation of his dealings with them, the nature of which can only be known by a careful and prayerful study of his Word.

That he should thus give admonition of the future is in harmony with the record of all his past doings. Said the Rev. John Hooper: "As God is *one*, having one will and one purpose, so his dealing with mankind has ever been the same. What he was to man at the beginning, and what he was to him in after ages, that he is *now* and ever will be; 'Jesus Christ, the same yesterday, to-day, and forever.' He changeth not, neither can change. To this the Psalmist beareth witness, saying, 'Thy *memorial*, O, Lord, endureth throughout all ages.' Now, one great feature in God's dealing towards his people is, that he revealeth himself to them according to the age in which they live, and according to their need in their day and generation, that they, knowing his will and purpose concerning them, might worship him truly, and serve him acceptably, and so be prepared for greater manifestations of his glory, and dwell forever in his presence." Apoc. p. 12.

In accordance with this principle, when man had fallen from the created innocence in which God had placed him, one of God's first acts towards him was to reveal his purpose of redemption, by the triumph of the seed of the woman over the head of the serpent. When the wickedness of man had become great on the earth, and it was necessary to destroy all flesh by a flood of waters, God revealed his purpose to Noah, and instructed him to build an ark, so that as many as believed might enter in, and be saved from the coming judgment. During one hundred and twenty years the long-suffering of God then waited, and men doubtless were faithfully admonished and entreated; and though the unbelieving multitude knew not the nearness of the judgment till the flood came and swept them all away, yet those that believed were in the secret of God, entered into the ark at the appointed time, and were all saved. At a later period, when the nations had become sunk into idolatry, and Abraham, apparently, was alone faithful, God communicated his purpose to make his seed a blessing to all the nations of the earth, revealed the length of their sojournings, and made known the time of their restoration. When the destruction of wicked Sodom was determined on, the Lord said (Gen. xviii. 17), "Shall I hide from Abraham that thing which I do, seeing that Abraham shall surely become a great and mighty nation, and all the nations of the earth shall be blessed in him?" And due notice was given to righteous Lot, who, with his daughters, was preserved; and none, even in that guilty city, perished without due warning. When "the time of the promise drew nigh, which God had sworn unto Abraham" (Acts vii. 17), we find the children of Israel (Ex. i. 23) sighing by reason of their bondage, and crying unto God for deliverance. We also find that Moses was divinely moved to visit his brethren, supposing they "would have understood how that God by his hand would deliver them; but they understood not," till the period of their Egyptian servitude was more nearly fulfilled; when Moses spake unto them the words of Jehovah and performed wonders in their sight, and "the people believed." This was a prerequisite for their deliverance; and so (Ex. xii. 41) "it came to pass at the end of the four hundred and thirty years, even the self-same day it came to pass, that all the hosts of the Lord went out from the land of Egypt." As we come down through the periods of Jewish history, and it became necessary to punish them for their transgressions (2 Ch. xxxvi. 15), "the Lord God of their fathers sent to them by his messengers, rising up betimes, and sending; because he had compassion" on them. When "they mocked the messengers of God, and despised his words," so that his wrath "arose against his people, till there was no remedy," they were graciously informed of the duration of their punishment,—that it was to be in Babylon for seventy years. As what is once written needs no repetition by a special revelation, so the record of Jeremiah (xxv. 11) was amply sufficient to make known the end of the Babylonish servitude. And, accordingly, we read that Daniel (ix. 2) "understood by books the number of years, whereof the word of the Lord came to Jeremiah, the prophet, that he would accomplish seventy years in the desolations of Jerusalem;" and, therefore, he set his heart towards God to seek its accomplishment. To him, also, was made known (Dan. ix. 25–27) "that from the going forth of the commandment to restore and to build Jerusalem unto the Messiah the Prince, shall be seven weeks, and three-score and two weeks" of symbolic time, or four hundred and eighty-three years. And in just that period from the date of the decree which Artaxerxes the king gave to the priest Ezra (vii. 11), we hear "a voice from heaven (Matt. iii. 17) saying, This is my beloved Son in whom I am well pleased." And the Saviour affirms the accuracy of the prediction when he declares (Mark i. 15), "*The time is fulfilled*, and the kingdom of God is at hand: repent ye, and believe the Gospel." Previous to the appearing of our Lord, there were those among the Jews who understood from the Scriptures that the time of his advent drew near, and who were "waiting for the consolation of Israel." To one of these, the "just and devout" Simeon (Luke ii. 26), "it was revealed that he should not see death till he had seen the Lord's Christ." And there was a widow also (v. 36), "one Anna, a prophetess," "of about four-score and four years, which departed not from the temple, but served God with fastings and prayers night and day," who "spake of him to all them that looked for redemption in Jerusalem." Not only (Matt. xiii. 17) "many righteous men desired" to see his day, but the opinion was so general, that when the Baptist preceded him (Luke iii. 15), "the people were in expectation, and all men mused in their hearts of John, whether he were the Christ or no." Nor was the belief confined to Palestine, that some remarkable personage was about to appear in Judea. Says Suetonius, a Roman historian, "An ancient and settled persuasion prevailed throughout the East, that the Fates had decreed some one to proceed from Judea, who should attain universal empire." And Tacitus, another Roman historian, says, "Many were persuaded that it was contained in the ancient books of their priests, that at that very time the East should prevail, and that some one should proceed from Judea, and possess the dominion." When he came, the glad tidings of his birth were announced by angelic voices to shepherds who were keeping watch over their flocks by night; and wise men, recognizing his star in the East, came to worship him. A forerunner was sent to prepare the way before him; and those who received him not were rejected, "because," as he said to Jerusalem (Luke xix. 44), "thou knewest not the *time* of thy visitation." When he laid down his life, he first revealed, not only to his disciples, but to the entire nation, that in three days he should rise again; and when he ascended on high, he left the promise of the bestowal of the Holy Spirit, till the reception of which the disciples were commanded to tarry at Jerusalem. If these illustrations are not sufficient, we have on record the Saviour's prediction of the destruction of Jerusalem during the continuance of the generation that rejected him, which was fulfilled in less than forty years subsequent to his crucifixion. And, that the Christians living in Judea might escape its impending doom, they were told (Luke xxi. 20) that when they should "see Jerusalem encompassed with armies," or, in other language (as in Matt. xxiv. 15), "the abomination of desolation spoken of by Daniel the prophet stand in the holy place," they were to "flee to the mountains;" which admonition they heeded, and escaped safe to Pella.

Such is the testimony of inspiration respecting the uniform dealings of God with his people in past ages; in view of which is it to be supposed that an unchangeable Being should pursue an opposite policy respecting events of the future, particularly when that future is to witness the "crowning consummation of all prophetic declarations?" Under every dispensation, the near coming of every great event has been known to his people. In every important instance he has told them what he was about to do; so that none of them were ignorant of it, or unprepared for it, who regarded his revelations respecting it—those only being left in darkness who disregarded and wickedly closed their eyes and ears to the instruction which God gave them. Therefore it cannot be that God will withhold from his people, in any age, such knowledge of their own times as is needed for their serving him acceptably in the performance of the duties pertaining to their respective age. And that he would not do so respecting the time of the closing of the present, and the ushering in of the Millennial dispensation, may be clearly inferred from the considerations already presented.

PROPHECY NOT UNDERSTOOD TILL NEAR ITS FULFILLMENT.

It is not in accordance with God's providential dealings to suppose that the epoch of the occurrence of events should be *fully* known for a long period previous to their fulfillment; for such knowledge is not needed by those who live in earlier periods of the world's history. Forty years before the deliverence of Israel from Egypt (Acts vii. 25), "they understood not" that God would deliver them by the hand of Moses. When Daniel inquired respecting the end of wonders that extended to the resurrection, he was told (Dan. xii. 9) that "the words are closed up and sealed till the time of the end." And when (1 Pet. i. 10—12) "prophets have inquired and searched diligently, who prophesied of the grace that should come unto you: searching what, or *what manner of time*, the Spirit of Christ which was in them did signify, when it testified beforehand of the sufferings of Christ, and *the glory that should follow*," it was revealed unto them, "that not unto *themselves*, but unto *us* they did minister."

The declaration that the words were sealed up till "the time of the end," implies that, at the period referred to, the obscurity, in which they might be shrouded from the understanding of those living in previous ages, would be penetrated, so that their import should be no longer a sealed mystery. Not only so, but, in the context, it is expressly declared (Dan. xii. 4) that, at the time or period of the end, "many shall run to and fro, and knowledge shall be increased." And it is also added (v. 10), that "many shall be purified and made white, and tried; but the wicked shall do wickedly: and none of the wicked shall understand; but the wise shall understand." That which they were to understand was that which was to be closed up and sealed till that period of understanding should arrive, and which, by its being denominated a "*time*," may, perhaps, be understood as comprising a period of three hundred and sixty years, * commencing, not unlikely, with the Protestant reformation, during which knowledge was to be disseminated, and to be continually increased by the running to and fro of many,†—their running to and fro being

* If the date of the Reformation be 1517, a time, or three hundred and sixty years, carries us to 1877, the period within which the mystery of God should be finished.—*Rev. Edward Bickersteth's Practical Guide to the Prophecies.*

† Others reckon the time of the end to be 75 years—the difference between the 1335 days and the 1260 days of Dan. 12.—*Editor.*

not a movement in space, but put by substitution for the various and often contradictory interpretations which should be advanced, each serving to call attention and adding interest to the subject, until the true light should have gradually dawned on the minds of believers, who should earnestly give themselves to the study of unfulfilled prophecy. For (Prov. xviii. 15) "the ear of the wise seeketh knowledge;" and, said the prophet (Hos. xiv. 9), "Who is wise, and he shall understand these things; prudent, and he shall know them?" Such will delight in the study of "the things which shall be revealed."

THE TIME OF THE END A SUBJECT OF PROPHECY.

That the period of the advent will be known, may not only be inferred from the analogy of God's providence in past ages, but it is clearly demonstrable from the testimony of Holy Writ. When inquired of by his disciples (Matt. xxiv. 3), "What shall be the sign of thy coming and of the end of the world?" the Saviour told them the signs that should precede those events. And though (v. 36) "of that day and hour knoweth no man, no, not the angels in heaven, but my Father only," so that none may presumptuously dogmatize respecting particular dates, yet in reference to the signs he had given, he said (vs. 32, 33), "Now learn a parable of the fig-tree: When his branch is yet tender, and putteth forth leaves, ye know that summer is nigh; *so likewise* ye, when ye shall see all these things, know that it is near, even at the doors." Or, as Luke expresses it (xxi. 28), "When these things begin to come to pass, then look up and lift up your heads, for your redemption draweth nigh." They would know enough of its nearness to induce watchfulness and a preparation for the event; but their knowledge would not be sufficiently definite to make it safe to postpone the event, in their own minds, to a period beyond any present moment; and so the Saviour said (Matt. xxiv. 42, 44), "Watch therefore: for ye know not what hour your Lord doth come. . . . Therefore be ye also ready: for in such an hour as ye think not the Son of man cometh." But, while (1 Th. v. 24) "the day of the Lord so cometh as a thief in the night," "sudden destruction cometh" only on those who "shall say peace and safety;" which Christ's children will not do: for, addressing them, the apostle says, "Ye, brethren, are not in darkness, that that day should overtake you as a thief. Ye are all the children of the light and the children of the day; we are not of the night nor of the darkness. Therefore let us not sleep as do others, but let us watch and be sober."

Thus the nearness of the end was to be known for a period previous to its occurrence; and not only so, but ignorance or indifference respecting its approach may be attended with serious consequences; for, otherwise, there would be little significancy in the Saviour's admonition (Luke xxi. 34—36), "Take heed to yourselves, lest at any time your hearts be overcharged with surfeiting and drunkenness, and cares of this life, and so that day come upon you *unawares*. For as a snare shall it come," not on those who know that their redemption draweth nigh, but "on all them that dwell on the face of the whole earth. Watch ye, therefore, and pray always, that ye may be accounted worthy to escape all these things that shall come to pass, and to stand before the Son of Man,"—of whom Paul says (Heb. ix. 28), that, "Unto them that *look for him* shall he appear the second time without sin unto salvation." Thus Christians were expected to live (Titus ii, 13), "looking for that blessed hope, and the glorious appearing of the great God and our Saviour Jesus Christ."

THE TRUTH APPLICABLE TO EACH AGE IMPERATIVE ON THAT AGE.

While no truth is to be neglected in the dispensation of the Word, it is particularly the duty of Christ's ambassadors, and it is made imperative on them, to instruct the church and make known to the world, in a more emphatic manner, those truths which have a specific application to the times in which they live, whether they have respect to sins which prevail then more than at other times, duties whose performance is then more imperatively demanded, or predictions which are then near to be fulfilled. And this, in the beautiful imagery with which the Saviour illustrated his teachings, is called giving "meat in due season," by the faithful servant who is made ruler over the household; and, to neglect to do this, is to be unfaithful to the charge committed by Christ to his ministers. Said the Saviour (Matt. xxiv. 45—51), "Who then is a faithful and wise servant, whom his lord hath made ruler over his household, to give them meat in due season? Blessed is that servant, whom his lord when he cometh shall find so doing. Verily, I say unto you, that he shall make him ruler over all his goods. But and if that evil servant shall say in his heart, My lord delayeth his coming; and shall begin to smite his fellow-servants, and to eat and drink with the drunken, the lord of that servant shall come in a day when he looketh not for him, and in an hour that he is not aware of, and shall cut him asunder, and appoint him his portion with the hypocrites; there shall be weeping and gnashing of teeth;" and (in Mark xiii. 34) "The Son of man is as a man taking a far journey, who left his house, and gave authority to his servants, and to every man his work, and commanded the porter to watch." Can the porter be negligent of his duty without incurring the displeasure of the Master?

What, then, is implied in the duty of watching? The context shows that it has reference to the Master's return; which, being shrouded in a kind of definite indefiniteness, if the paradoxy may be allowed, makes the duty constant and unceasing. Said the Saviour (vs. 35, 36), "Watch ye, therefore; for ye know not when the Master cometh,—at even, or at midnight, or at the cock-crowing, or in the morning; lest, coming suddenly, he find you sleeping."

As a porter, watching for his master's return, would be mindful of all the tokens which the master had given as indications of his coming, so should the servant of him who has promised to return again, familiarize himself with all the predictions which are left on record respecting that return, the events that were to precede it, and the periods that measure his absence. And, if we are indeed living in the time of the end (which who dare deny?), then they are culpably indifferent and ignorant, who seek not to "understand by books," as did Daniel of old, the "number of years" which are to intervene between given epochs and the end, or to approximate as near to such knowledge as the means which God has furnished them will allow.

PROPHECIES FORESHADOWING THE END.

Among the prophecies which were given for instruction respecting the end, there stands prominent the great Image (Dan. ii. 28), by which the "God in heaven" made "known to the king Nebuchadnezzar what shall be in the latter days." (Vs. 32, 33.)—"This image's head was of fine gold, his breast and his arms of silver, his belly and his thighs of brass, his legs of iron, and his feet part of iron and part of clay." The king saw (vs. 34, 35) "Till that a stone was cut out of the mountain without hands, which smote the image upon his feet that were of iron and clay, and brake them to pieces: then was the iron, the clay, the brass, the silver and the gold, broken to pieces together, and became like the chaff of the summer threshing-floors; and the wind carried them away, that no place was found for them; and the stone that smote the image became a great mountain, and filled the whole earth." Such was the king's dream, which Daniel proceeded to interpret as symbolic of a succession of empires, beginning with that of Nebuchadnezzar, which was represented by the head of gold. An inferior one, that was to arise after him, corresponded to the breast and arms of silver; and succeeding ones corresponded to the brass and the iron of the image. When the last should have existed for a period in a divided state, then, said the prophet (v. 44), "shall the God of heaven set up a kingdom, which shall never be destroyed; and the kingdom shall not be left to other people, but it shall break in pieces and consume all these kingdoms, and it shall stand for ever."

Parallel with this prophecy is that other in the 7th of Daniel, in which the prophet saw in vision by night (v. 3), "four great beasts come up from the sea, diverse one from another,"—the last of which had ten horns; and among them (v. 8) came up another "little horn," with "eyes like the eyes of a man, and a mouth speaking great things." Then followed a symbolic representation of the session of the Ancient of Days, the slaughter of the beasts, and the investure of one like the Son of Man with the kingdom. In harmony with the former vision, the interpreter, of whom Daniel inquired the meaning of this said (vs. 17, 18), "These great beasts, which are four, are four kings which shall arise out of the earth. But," he added, "the saints of the Most High shall take the kingdom, and possess the kingdom for ever, even for ever and ever." As Daniel would know more particularly of the beast with many horns, and of that horn which "prevailed until the Ancient of Days came, . . . and the time came that the saints possessed the kingdom," the angel replied (v. 23—27) "The fourth beast shall be the fourth kingdom upon earth, which shall be diverse from all kingdoms, and shall devour the whole earth, and shall tread it down, and break it in pieces. And the ten horns out of this kingdom are ten kings that shall arise; and another shall rise after them, and he shall be diverse from the first, and he shall subdue three kings. And he shall speak great words against the

Most High, and shall wear out the saints of the Most High, and think to change times and laws; and they shall be given into his hand until a time and times and the dividing of time. But the judgment shall sit, and they shall take away his dominion, to consume and to destroy it unto the end. And the kingdom and dominion, and the greatness of the kingdom under the whole heaven, shall be given to the people of the saints of the Most High, whose kingdom is an everlasting kingdom, and all dominions shall serve and obey him."

In the chapter following, when the first-named kingdom was about to pass away, Daniel had a corresponding vision, in which (v. 3) a ram that "stood before the river" symbolized (v. 20) "the kings of Media and Persia;" and (v. 21) a "rough goat the king of Grecia." It was shown (v. 22) that in the place of the first king of the last kingdom, "four kingdoms should stand up out of the nation," — corresponding to Alexander's successors, — which were to be followed (v. 23), "in the latter times of their kingdom," by "a king of fierce countenance, and understanding dark sentences," who should "stand up against the Prince of princes," and "destroy the mighty and the holy people," till the sanctuary and the host should be trodden down (v. 14) for "two thousand three hundred" prophetic days; at the end of which "shall the sanctuary be cleansed."

A prophecy commencing with the 11th of Daniel, notices more particularly the same events, and closes with the deliverance (xii. 1–3) of "every one that shall be found written in the book," the awaking of "many of them that sleep in the dust of the earth," and their shining "as the brightness of the firmament," and "as the stars, for ever and ever." It is in connection with these predictions that the angel (v. 7) lifts "his right hand and his left hand to heaven, and sware by him that liveth for ever, that it shall be for a time, times and an half;" and that "when he shall have accomplished to scatter the power of the holy people, all these things shall be finished." He also reveals (v. 11) that "from the time that the daily shall be taken away, and the abomination that maketh desolate set up, there shall be a thousand two hundred and ninety days;" and adds a blessing (v. 12) to him "that waiteth and cometh to the thousand three hundred and five and thirty days." This is the prophecy before referred to, the words of which (v. 9) were "closed up and sealed till the time of the end," and respecting which, then, knowledge was to be increased by the running to and fro of many.

We come then to the New Testament, and, in answer to questions of the disciples respecting the time of the destruction of Jerusalem, and the sign of his coming and end of the world, we have in the 24th chapter of Matthew's gospel a prophecy given by the Saviour which answers both of those questions by a glance at the occurrences which should transpire before the end; and he emphatically announced (v. 14) that "This gospel of the kingdom shall be preached in all the world as a witness unto all nations; and," said the Saviour, "then shall the end come."

MISAPPREHENSIONS CORRECTED.

The Saviour was ever ready to correct any misapprehension on the part of his children respecting the time of the event. On one occasion (Luke xxi. 11–13) "He added and spake a parable . . . because they thought that the kingdom of God should immediately appear. He said, therefore, A certain nobleman went into a far country to receive for himself a kingdom, and to return. And he called his ten servants, and delivered unto them ten pounds, and said unto them, occupy till I come." And, after a long time, when he was returned, he called his servants, and reckoned with them, rewarded those found faithful, and destroyed those who disregarded his authority. When the Saviour was about to leave his disciples to go into that far country, they asked of him (Acts i. 6, 7), "saying, Lord, wilt thou at this time restore the kingdom to Israel? And he said unto them, It is not for you to know the times or the seasons which the Father hath put in his own power." The "time" had not come,—the period in which was to be gradually removed the seal which was set on them till "the *time* of the end." Their specific mission was to make known the resurrection of Jesus, and the *fact* of his second coming; and therefore the Saviour said (v. 8) "But ye shall receive power after that the Holy Ghost is come upon you; and ye shall be witnesses unto me, both in Jerusalem and in all Judea, and in Samaria, and unto the uttermost parts of the earth,"—to which the gospel must be preached before the end could come. Accordingly we find that the sum of their preaching was (Acts xvii. 18) "Jesus and the resurrection." They taught men (1 Th. i. 9, 10) to turn "to God from idols, to serve the living and true God, and to wait for his Son from heaven, whom he raised from the dead, even Jesus, which delivered us from the wrath to come."

When, under such preaching, the Thessalonian brethren were led to regard the day of the Lord as more imminent than the sacred oracles warranted them in believing, the apostle Paul promptly called their attention to the desolating power prophesied of in Daniel, and reminded them (2 Th. ii. 3) that "that day shall not come except there come a falling away," or an apostasy, "first, and that Man of Sin be revealed, the Son of Perdition," "whom the Lord shall consume by the spirit of his mouth, and shall destroy with the brightness of his coming."

THE APOCALYPSE AN UNVEILING OR UNSEALING OF PROPHECY.

That the drooping spirits of his children might not be left to faint under the long absence of the nobleman who had gone to the far country till his enemies be made his footstool, before the beloved disciple was laid asleep in Jesus there was given (Rev. i. 1, 2) "The Revelation of Jesus Christ, which God gave unto him, to show unto his servants things which must shortly come to pass; and he sent and signified it by his angel unto his servant John, who bare record of the word of God, and of the testimony of Jesus Christ, and of all things that he saw." When the Saviour was on earth he told his servants many things; but he had also (John xvi. 12) "yet many things to say" to them which they could not then bear; but in this Revelation to John they are shown a long series of events which were shortly to come to pass, or, literally, which were shortly to begin to come to pass, and extended down to the binding of the dragon, the resurrection, and the new creation. It will be seen, also, that this Revelation comprised "times and seasons," which, at the time of the ascension (Acts i. 7), were reserved in the Father's own power, but which have here been given to Jesus Christ, shown unto his servants, signified by an angel to John, and written by John to the churches.

The words of this Revelation are not sealed like those given to Daniel; for John was commanded (Rev. xxii. 10) to "*seal not* the sayings of the prophecy of *this* book." It was given, also, through the medium of "the appointed heir of all things" (Heb. i. 2), by whom God was to speak in these last days, and who alone (Rev. v. 2) "is worthy to open the book, and to loose the seals thereof." Not only (v. 5) hath "the Lion of the tribe of Judah" prevailed to open the book and to loose the seals, but it is declared (i. 3) that "Blessed is he that readeth, and they that hear, the words of this prophecy, and keep those things which are written therein."

Thus prepared, there follows a succession of visions, which John wrote, and whose significance was communicated to him. First, we have (chap. v.) the successive loosening of the seals of a book; and, as each symbolic seal is broken, successive portions of the writing in the book become accessible, showing the gradual manner in which the church would be enabled to understand the full import of the revelations which God has given for its instruction, and closing with the appearance of "a great multitude, which no man could number, of all nations, and kindreds, and peoples, and tongues," which (vii. 9) "stood before the throne and before the Lamb, clothed in white robes, and palms in their hands,"—the result of the preaching of the Gospel as a witness to all nations.

Then follows (chap. viii.) a vision of the sounding of a succession of trumpets, marking periods which are covered by those of the seals, symbolizing events which were to transpire during those respective periods, and closing with the seventh trumpet, at the sounding of which (xi. 15–18) are heard "great voices in heaven, saying, The kingdoms of this world are become [that] of our Lord and of his Christ; and he shall reign for ever and ever." And then also is come (v. 18) "the time of the dead that they should be judged," those who serve the Lord being rewarded, and those who destroy the earth being destroyed.

In harmony with these visions, others follow, in which is more minutely symbolized,—under the imagery of a great red, seven-headed and ten-horned dragon (chap. xii.), of a seven-headed, ten-horned leopard beast (chap. xiii.), and of a seven-headed, ten-horned, scarlet-colored beast, with a woman seated on it (chap. xvii.), and corresponding to Daniel's (vii. 7) ten-horned nondescript fourth beast,—"the fourth kingdom on the earth," or Rome, under its five forms of united rule, its division into decem-regal governments, and the period of its papal supremacy. In the connection are (xi. 2) the treading down of the holy city "forty and two" prophetic months (v. 3), the prophesying of the witnesses in sackcloth "a thousand two hundred and three-score" prophetic days, the fleeing of the woman into the wilderness (xii. 6), where she was to be fed for the same period, or

(v. 14) nourished for a time and times, and half a time, from the face of the serpent, the "forty and two months" (xiii. 5) that it was to be given to the blasphemous mouth of the beast to speak blasphemy, the "five months" (ix. 5) that the locusts were to torment men, and (v. 15) the "hour and a day, and a month, and a year," in which they were to have power to kill. And the whole series closes with the symbol of the destruction of Babylon, the battle of Armageddon, the new heavens and new earth, the descent of the New Jerusalem, and the establishment of "the tabernacle of God with men."

INDIFFERENCE TO PROPHECY DISPLEASING TO JEHOVAH.

Such prophecies being committed to the church, for its instruction and profit, to denominate them a sealed book, to declare their study unprofitable, or to affirm that they are incapable of being understood, is to deny that they were given for the church's edification, or that there is a blessing pronounced on those who read and keep them; and it dishonors God, by imputing to him communications unintelligible by those to whom they are addressed. Said the apostle, Heb. xii. 25, "See that ye refuse not him that speaketh; for if they escaped not who refused him that spake on earth, much more shall not we escape if we turn away from him that speaketh from heaven."

THE PROPHETIC PERIODS NECESSARILY OBSCURE TO THE EARLY CHRISTIANS.

The canon of Scripture being closed with the book of Revelation, and important portions of the Old Testament predictions being a sealed book till a "time" then in the distant future, the views which then prevailed, respecting the meaning of the symbolic prophecies and the nearness of the end, were necessarily somewhat indistinct and imperfect.

The symbolic nature of the prophetic periods was not preceived by the early Christians,—with the exception of the seventy weeks of the 9th ch. of Daniel, which were regarded as weeks of years, both by Jews and Christians.* The prophetic "days" and "times" were

---

* Prof. Bush, in speaking of the year-day calculations of prophecy, says: "It is the solution naturally arising from the construction put in *all ages* upon the oracle of Daniel, respecting the SEVENTY WEEKS, which by Jews and Christians have been interpreted weeks of years; on the principle of a day standing for a year. This fact is obvious from the Rabbinical writers *en masse,* where they touch upon the subject; and Eusebius tells us (Dem. Evang., b. viii., p. 258—Ed. Steph.) that this interpretation in his day was generally, if not universally, admitted."—*Hierophant,* v. 1, p. 243. They are not, however, in the prophecy called weeks of days; and might naturally be understood as weeks of years, independent of the year-day calculation.

not supposed to be other than literal denominations of time. The prophecies of Daniel that had been fulfilled prior to the time of Josephus, are interpreted by him (in his Antiquities, B. x., ch. xi., § 7) in harmony with the views of modern expositors. But, in attempting to give the significance of the 2300 days,—a designation of time then sealed up from the vulgar gaze,—he applies them to the times of Antiochus Epiphanus; and, to make them fit, he unjustifiably changes them to "one thousand two hundred and ninety-six." And previous to the Protestant Reformation, when the seal from the prophecies began gradually to be removed, no one interpreted the prophetic "days" or "times" as symbolic periods;* for the time had not come when their significancy was to be appreciated. Josephus doubtless expressed the opinion then prevalent among the Jews; and, strange as it may seem, the apostate Papal church still holds the same views, and some Protestant writers, who have labored to prove the end in the distant future, have followed Josephus in applying that prophecy to Antiochus—though some of them have considered the 2300 days as so many whole, and some as so many half-days;† but in so doing, have acknowledged that they departed from the common Protestant interpretation.—*Time of the End, pp. 17–24, by S. Bliss.*

Therefore the Christian church had the right to expect the Lord would continue to work by the same principles with them to the end; and that in the prophetic scriptures concerning this greatest of all events, there would be clear and distinct statements of the closing up of the dispensation of mercy, of the ushering in of the eternal rest, of the removal of all mortal things, and of the great change which would precede and introduce the everlasting kingdom of our Lord; that the events would be so clearly recognized by the watchmen that they would be assured by the unfolding of prophecy and signs of the times, that the day of the Lord was indeed at hand, and sound the note of warning to the people, of what was about to occur in the divine administration. The prophecies of Daniel, Christ, and his apostles, fully warrant such expectation and more. They not

---

* "It does not appear that any man ever interpreted days as meaning years, during the first *fifteen* centuries of the Christian era."—*An Elucidation of the Prophecies,* by JOSEPH TYSO London ed., 1838, p. 68.

† The Rev. Doctors Dowling and Chase interpreted them as half-days, or 1150 days, while Prof. Stuart regarded them as 2300 literal days.

only announce the events to take place, but show, also, that prior to the close of the gospel dispensation, there would be a class of messengers sent forth to proclaim the immediate coming of the Lord to judgment. Thus we read:

"Go through, go through the gates; prepare ye the way of the people; cast up, cast up the highway; gather out the stones; lift up a standard for the people. Behold, the Lord hath proclaimed unto the end of the world, say ye to the daughter of Zion, Behold, thy salvation cometh; behold, his reward is with him, and his work before him." Isa. lxii. 10, 11.

"But thou, O Daniel, shut up the words, and seal the book, even to the time of the end; many shall run to and fro, and knowledge shall be increased." Dan. xii. 4.

"So likewise ye, when ye shall see all these things, know that it is near, even at the doors. . . . Who, then, is a faithful and wise servant, whom his lord hath made ruler over his household, to give them meat in due season? Blessed is that servant, whom his lord when he cometh shall find so doing. Matt. xxiv. 33, 45, 46.

"And at midnight there was a cry made, Behold, the bridegroom cometh, go ye out to meet him." Matt. xxv. 6.

The above and other Scriptures as clearly show that there was to be a message of the second advent of Christ proclaimed to the people just prior to his coming, as can be shown from any other Scriptures that any message of an event of the past was ever given, prior to the event.

It should be well considered that in the early stages of this proclamation, its messengers and adherents were then members of all the various branches of the Christian church, and entertained no thought that it would cost them the sacrifice of their church relations, or that they would be drawn together to form a distinct society, made up of men of all shades of religious tenets and church customs, to occupy an indefinite space of time in the future, to perform gospel labor, and meet the reproaches and trials that have since followed.

They had no system of theology matured and pledged to, embodying in form the specific truths which suddenly shone into their minds, as they heard the stirring cry, "Behold, the bridegroom cometh, go ye out to meet him." Neither had they any concerted plan for a theological course of study for their rapidly increasing young and inexperienced ministers, who seemed suddenly called from the farm, the mechanics' shop, the mill, the merchandise, the ship, and from all other departments of business, to preach the good news of Jesus soon coming.

Neither had they any system of church polity to regulate their then unexpected societies and future missions.

A SEARCHING OF THE BIBLE.

While a few watchmen were deeply stirred by the evidences they saw of the judgment being near, and began to preach and publish it as a scriptural fact, each man, woman, and youth, who entertained the thought, turned eagerly to the Bible, and "searched as for hid treasure," to learn what was there revealed concerning it.

Many determined to learn for themselves what the Scriptures taught. They knew their church creeds and confessions of faith, and their ministers stated that Christ was to come some time in the future, and raise the dead and judge the world, consign the wicked to hell and take the righteous to heaven, where they were supposed to have gone already without judgment.

A DEVELOPMENT OF ERRORS.

A careful investigation of the Scriptures soon revealed to them that in some important points the ministry generally had embraced and led them into theories and traditions in direct conflict with the Bible.

It was being generally taught that all mankind were to be converted to Christianity, that the Jews were to return to Judea, and a millennium, or thousand years of universal peace would be enjoyed before the resurrection and judgment. This was soon found to have no foundation in Scripture to sustain it.

It was generally supposed the dead were in heaven or hell, enjoying or suffering their rewards. This idea was soon seen to be unfounded.

It was taught almost universally that heaven was the final abode of the saints; while the Bible, from Genesis to Revelation, declared that "the meek shall inherit the earth," "and dwell therein forever;" that it shall be renewed for them, and they shall possess it. Gen. xvii. 8. Psa. xxxvii. Matt. v. 5. Rev. xxi. 1–7.

It was being very generally taught that Christ was now a reigning king in heaven, and on earth also, while a mediator. But the

Scriptures revealed that his reign begins when the seventh angel sounds. Matt. xxv. 31. Rev. xi. 15–18.

A SAD CONFLICT.

An investigation of these and several other points led to an examination of the "Old Paths," when it was soon found the church had drifted far from the course laid down in the chart, and from the views of the expounders of it in all former times.

This soon brought the ministry in conflict with each other, and the laymen in conflict with most of their teachers, who generally refused to study the subjects presented to them, or to attempt to reconcile the glaring discrepancies between their teaching and the Bible, but often accused their brethren of studying their Bibles too much, of racking their brains to find out God's mysteries, and of listening to dangerous teachers.

It also became evident that many of the guardians of the churches in America, wherever the advent message was proclaimed, were too deeply imbued with German Neology, *rationalism*,—or with the theories of the Mystics and Spiritualists, to give a critical and careful investigation of this subject, or to tolerate their brethren who strictly adhered to and advocated it as a scriptural doctrine. We are not entering any complaint; they seemed to think it their duty.

While it is true that the probable time for Christ's return was fixed upon and earnestly advocated by a few, yet the consecutive fulfillment of prophecy, the signs foretold by our Lord and his apostles were urged as more positive evidence that the end was near, if the point of time fixed upon was incorrect.

To this the great mass of teachers responded, that we could not know anything about it, whether near or far off, and that it was none of their business to study it. Yet they had time; they had set the time a thousand years ahead of the conversion of the entire world.

But time was not the only, nor the most obnoxious point, or objectionable feature of the message, as our future pages will show. They objected to it as a whole. They were infatuated with another system of doctrine which eclipsed their vision, and they cared not to refer to this only to oppose it and stigmatise it under the name of "Millerism." There were honorable exceptions, as we shall show,—those who did examine, embrace and publish the message,—and others who neither embraced nor opposed it, while many others secretly believed, but "loved the praise of men more than the praise of God;" so it appears to those who know them.

Under these and other crushing influences which constantly increased, with but little lenity and great efforts to induce the believers, by proscriptions, threats and flatteries, to "give up the whole thing," as it was often expressed, there remained

THREE POINTS OF CHOICE.

1st. Be silent upon this all-important, God-begotten, soul-quickening, blessed gospel hope, and hear it constantly stigmatized, perverted, defamed, and classed with the most corrupt apostasies and false religions, or,

2d. Stand firm to their convictions of truth, and declare faithfully what the Bible teaches, as the only true hope, and labor earnestly to reform the views of the church on these important subjects, and warn sinners to prepare to meet their God; against the remonstrances of friends, opposition of brethren, and the reproofs of church officials, as heretical in doctrine and dangerous in influence, with the prospect of being dismissed from the church, or,

3d. Obtain a discharge from what had been the church of their choice and their religious home, to maintain the right to think and decide for themselves what is truth, and go out among the masses single-handed to combat the evils of the times, bearing the brand of "heresy" upon them, to cause a feeling of distrust and disfellowship in the hearts of "Orthodox Christians," while they wait the unfolding of God's providence, and Christ's return.

Each of the above choices have been made, and the Lord has clearly indicated, by his divine blessing, which has been the most pleasing to him; we doubt not the sincerity of each class mentioned.

But in struggling with these difficulties, the faithful, self-sacrificing, God-fearing soldiers of the cross have sometimes given away to human passion, and indulged in the censorious, bitter, retaliating spirit, and self-will, to their own hurt, to the injury of the cause they loved, and the exposure of much of the sin and shame existing amongst their opposers.

Being harrassed by violent opposition, and greatly reproached by their brethren for their disappointment in the event of time, and for continuing to feel assured that the Lord would come soon; also realizing that many of the churches were in a cold and faithless condition, and were fast uniting with the world in vanity and folly; originating plays and gambling to pay church expenses; some of the advent preachers, who were but novices in the faith, and others with more zeal than wisdom, and more rashness than patience, now began to preach that the Protestant churches constitute the Apocalyptic Babylon, and to proclaim "come out of her, my people," to the disgust and humiliation of the better informed and more charitable portion of their brethren, and the disgrace of the advent cause and believers.*

This false message and unrighteous denunciation of the churches was followed by immediate legitimate results. It embittered and chilled the feelings of the good and charitable, who were in the churches, and were themselves in great trials because of the little love, humility, and genuine piety existing, and the pride and worldly spirit which was rapidly increasing. It also furnished an apparently good pretext to the opposers of the Advent Message to close the doors of the few houses of worship which were yet accessible, against not only rash zealots, but against all faithful, judicious, and devoted Christian ministers who persisted in proclaiming that the Lord was coming soon.

The breach widened; and in the blindness of their zeal to defend the churches and cleanse them from all heresy, the managers made but little distinction between the rash fanatic and the stable, sober Christian minister or member. Many seemed pleased with an excuse to banish the very sound of the coming of the Lord from their communities, and many were turned out of the churches, which they were afterward very anxious to receive in again, and who were heartily welcomed if they returned.

This only increased the anxiety of the devoted lovers of Christ and his appearing, to be separated from such unpleasant and unlovely church companions; and in the short space of one year, probably

---

* We do not mention this to cast reproach upon these brethren; many of them were devout and godly men, who had sacrificed all for Christ and his cause, and when we consider the facts in our possession concerning the condition and practices of many churches, ministers and members, in those days, we do not wonder that those not well instructed in the prophecies on the harlot power (Rev. 17) and the history of its career, should be inclined to make the application they did. But such indications do not justify their blunder, nor such want of information atone for the mischief it produced.

over thirty thousand ministers and members were excommunicated, or left by their own request.* Some whole churches were excommunicated from conferences. This course of procedure caused an absolute necessity, with the Advent believers, of

FORMING A NEW ORGANIZATION TO CONTINUE CHRIST'S WORK.

Many church officials and other members have usually expressed the intensity of their opposition to the Advent Message by the statement: "It deludes and takes from our churches the very best, the most useful and pious, of our ministers and members."

If this testimony is true, then it would follow that the Lord allows the devil to steal away his best shepherds and sheep, or that he himself has made a wise selection in calling them to such an important trust, and noble, yet trying work, as that of giving the judgment message to a slumbering church and sinking world.

When the vastness of the subject which has attracted and absorbed the attention of this class of Christians is carefully considered, and the great importance of the doctrine involved in the prophetic and symbolic Scriptures which map out the Christian and gentile age, and terminate with the judgment of the world and the establishment of the everlasting kingdom of God, is taken into the account, together with the very limited knowledge possessed at that time, by the church and ministry generally, upon the laws governing symbols, metaphors, tropes and parables, and the general doctrine of the Scriptures, and then trace the opening and development of this subject as it awakened in the church the intense desire to learn the truth and obey it; with imaginations and thoughts wholly unbridled from creed or church etiquette, and gathering strength from advancement in wisdom, sincerity of purpose, deepened piety, and greatly increasing numbers, of all classes and grades, with all types and shades of religious views and trainings, yet drawn together by the mighty magnet of truth—the gospel of the kingdom of God, and of the immediate coming of our Lord Jesus Christ; it must be admitted that no human wisdom could have formed a creed or framed a compact to

---

* The same course, with less rigor, has continued among the churches until now, making it a necessity that these believers in such cases, should unite in a separate body, or church, in order to maintain the ordinances of the Lord's house, and labor successfully in the work of the gospel.

occupy such a position and maintain such ground against such human odds and evil influences of wealth and worldly policy combined. It must be the work of God through his truth and Spirit, by the instrumentality of a people, who consecrated their reputation, talents, honor, wealth, ease, influence, time, and whatever they possessed or had hoped to be, to the work of promulgating an unpopular and unwelcome message to the world and world-loving church members; but a message due the church and world. God's time had come to have it proclaimed, and he prepared a people through whom he could perform this work, as in times past he has prepared men to give other unwelcome messages to their respective generations.

Were it a mere change of religious views or of church policy or a differing on church rites and ceremonies, we would not attempt to write a history of it. But there is something to record in this history of the work of God, which is deeper and more broad than anything known to the church since the days of the apostles. The movement is of God for the preparation of the church to enter the everlasting rest prepared for her.

Already it has reformed thousands of its members, deepened the piety and enlarged the experience and increased the usefulness of many thousands more, while it has been the means of the conversion of tens of thousands of sinners of all grades; and the work is not yet completed. Others are to be warned, the cry "Behold the bridegroom cometh, go ye out to meet him," is to continue until all the virgins have heard. If any of those now engaged falter, the Lord will prepare others to "cast up the highway, and gather out the stones," and "raise up a standard for the people."

In its aggressive work it has gained accessions from all quarters and from all churches, Protestant, Catholic, and Greek. It has won the hearts and faith of many ministers and members who had strongly opposed it; it has reached the citadel of infidels, scattered their weapons, and brought many of them to Christ.

CHAPTER II.

Opening of the 19th century—Progress of human freedom—Bible societies—Prosperity in worldly equipage—False hope of the future—Pre-millennial views revived—First religious newspaper —Mr. Wm. Miller's conversion—Experience—Call to preach—Begins to preach and write.

The chief events in christendom during the closing years of the eighteenth and the opening years of the nineteenth centuries, were such as produced great enthusiasm in the hearts of the friends of Christianity, and were well calculated to inspire much confidence in the minds of those Christians who had not carefully studied the prophetic Scriptures, that the *new theory* of Mr. Daniel Whitby, D. D., which had already been endorsed by several eminent clergymen, and obtained considerable favor in some churches, was true, and consequently that all the inhabitants of the earth would become Christians, and that the church would soon enter upon the enjoyment of a *millennium*—a thousand years of universal peace on earth, prior to the second coming of Christ, and the final judgment. This was Mr. Whitby's new view; a very pleasing one.

Though there were some eminent students of prophecy and faithful gospel ministers, who saw in these events the true omens of a preparation for the harvest, and the return of the Son of Man to judge the world, and in their writings we find them telling how the prophecies were to be fulfilled in the remaining portion of time, just as they have since been accomplished, which shows their views of the prophetic word to be in all the main features correct.

The "Great Reformation," which began in Germany under Luther in the sixteenth century, had, through the mighty power of the gospel, accompanied by the Holy Spirit, worked wonderful revolutions through Europe, crushing the power of papal superstitions, checking the progress of priest-craft, and of papish dogmas in other nations also; and producing reforms in civil government, in educational systems and in religious teachings; thus improving arts and sciences, religious toleration, and opening the way for the general diffusion of knowledge. The Scriptures now began to be translated into many languages, and sent abroad among the masses, which enabled many to learn the real nature of Christianity, the character of papal corruption and usurpation, and the duty to oppose its farther aggressions upon the civil and religious rights of the people.

The great importance of Christian missions began to be realized, as in apostolic times, and was acted upon with commendable zeal. Germany, England, and some of the smaller States of Europe had been reformed by Protestantism; but France had been driven mad by papal tyranny and priestly avarice, and to clear herself from it staggered to the most revolting extreme of infidelity. The re-action of it caused the French Assembly in A. D. 1797, to grant the free right to circulate the Bible throughout that country. The triumph of Napoleon I, over Rome and papal arrogance, in A. D. 1801; the action of the Holy Alliance in A. D. 1815, which restricted the civil power of the papacy to the ten States of Italy, all conspired to "set an open door" before the church, inviting her to leave the wilderness, whither she had "fled from the face of the serpent," Rev. xii. 14, and re-enter upon her extensive mission work. She improved it, "and no man can shut it," since God has opened it.

A few persons in London assembled and established what has since been called the "Bible Society." In A. D. 1804, the "British and Foreign Bible Society" was incorporated, and between then and A. D. 1830, FIFTY-THREE other Bible Societies were instituted in various parts of the world, which have published the Bible in nearly all the languages of the nations of the earth.

The missionary spirit accompanied the work, and Christian Mission Societies were also instituted, to carry and "preach this gospel of the kingdom in all the world, for a witness unto all nations" before "the end should come." The Lord turned the hearts of many, who were not Christians, to aid in this work, for it was his work, which he had declared should be done; see Matt. xxiv. 14, Rev. xi. 11. Great success attended these movements of the church, and millions were converted to Christ, and prepared for the marriage supper of the Lamb; such mighty results dazzled the eyes of some and caused them to feel as did those disciples who came to Christ, saying, "master, even the devils are subject to us through thy name." They had overlooked those Scriptures which showed the real province of the gospel, in the grand purpose of God, to announce the kingdom, to prepare a people for it, to visit the gentiles, "to take out of them a people for his name," Acts xv. 14, and "for a witness to all nations."

Great prosperity often causes poor mortals to lose sight of the source of their success, and the real object of life, and become prodigal of the means put in their hands, laying out work for themselves and undertaking to do what was never designed by their master to be done. Such was the condition of the great mass of the christian churches in A. D. 1820; they had become strong in numbers, were organized for work, had a large supply of means, and abundance of equipage for entensive business, and had decided that the Jews were a people especially favored of God, to whom he had made great promises, which must be fulfilled, and they be restored to Palestine and converted, and that all the gentiles must be converted also. Their plans were large, and they began to lavish their means upon home institutions, building immense church edifices, extensive theological schools, and making extravagant outlays, while they dreamed of "the good time coming," and sang of "the golden age;" forgetting that Christ had warned them to "watch" for his return to gather out "the tares," to "divide the sheep from the goats," and "to execute judgment upon all."

Although Luther, Crannaer, Rutherford, Calvin, Tyndale, Dr. Goodwin, Dr. Gill, Wesley, Fletcher, and others, had left their dying testimony concerning the evils which would accumulate, and afflict the faithful in the last days, citing the Scriptures of the Old and New Testaments, which declare the "time of trouble," the "departure from the faith," the "abounding of iniquity", the "perilous times" likened to "the days of Noah," and "the days of Lot," and that signs would show the church when Jesus was about to come, and the faithful watchmen would declare it, while the "evil servant" would "say in his heart, my lord delayeth his coming;" yet the teachers who professed to follow their footsteps had gradually changed their views; and instead of singing with anxious expectancy, with the pious Watts;

"The God of Glory down to men,
Removes his blest abode,"

or with the longing fervency of the Wesley's;

"The church in her militant state
Is weary and cannot forbear,
The saints in an agony wait,
To see him again in the air."

They were training the church to sing;

"Death is the gate to endless joys,
Why should we dread to enter there?"

But the Lord was preparing the way for awakening the virgins from their slumbers by the distinct proclamation of his immediate coming.

It is true that Luther, Melancthon, Latimer, and others of their time, had studied the prophecies and the prophetic numbers, in good earnest, to ascertain when Christ would return, and they at first concluded, from their manner of applying them, that he would come in the sixteenth century. After getting better light Luther said, "I persuade myself verily, that the day of judgment will not be absent full three hundred years longer." Since then Messrs. Goodwin, Mede, Bishop Newton, Sir Isaac Newton, Messrs. Faber, Keith, and Cunningham, of Scotland, and others, had given to the church and world their views that the periods of Daniel would end in the nineteenth century, and bring the advent of Christ and his millennial reign. These were European writers; comparatively few of the ministry in America possessed their works.

The first pre-millennial work known to have been written and printed in America, was by Samuel Hutchinson, of Boston, in 1667. From that time to the close of the eighteenth century, about fifty more of the same character were issued by the American press.

In A. D. 1796, Eld. Joshua Spaulding, an eminent minister of the gospel at the Tabernacle, Salem, Mass., published a series of nine sermons "concerning the COMING AND KINGDOM OF OUR LORD JESUS CHRIST, and the restitution of all things." This was a very important work but was not widely circulated, being violently opposed by the ministry generally, their ears were closed to a proclamation of the personal pre-millennial advent and reign of Christ on earth. Mr. Spaulding was an educated, able and godly minister, highly esteemed for his piety, learning and usefulness. In A. D. 1800, Benjamin Farnham, published a work of one hundred and fifty-five pages, at East Windsor, Ct., on the pre-millennial advent of Christ. A little later,

Eld. Titcomb; Baptist minister, in Brunswick, Me., published a small work, advocating that the periods of Daniel would end about 1866, and that epoch would bring the Lord to judge the world; several others who had studied the prophecies, and the conclusions of former writers on this subject, held and preached that Christ would soon come in judgment and in glory.

A. D. 1808, THE FIRST RELIGIOUS NEWSPAPER.

In A. D. 1808, Eld. Elias Smith, a Christian Baptist minister, produced the first religious newspaper ever published in the world, at Portsmouth, N. H.; viz, "The Herald of Gospel Liberty," advocating the pre-millennial personal, and soon coming of Christ, and nearly every other feature of doctrine now called "adventism." He was an able gospel minister, obtained an extensive influence as a Christian reformer; very many sinners were brought to Christ, many ministers and other members of the churches were brought to see new beauties and excellences in the character and work of Christ through his labors, that they had not seen under other instructions, and which greatly reformed their theological views. Meeting and long enduring a storm of bitter opposition, hatred, vituperation and slander, he finally became weary and vacillated for awhile and ceased his public efforts, but the fruits of his labors yet live.

A little after this several students of prophecy, in different parts of the world, and wholly unknown to each other, had their attention awakened by observing that the seventy weeks of Daniel's prophecy, were a part of the 2300 days (or years), and that they commenced together, and that of course the 2300 days would end eighteen hundred and ten years after the end of the seventy weeks; some of them concluded that the seventy weeks ended with the death of Christ, and consequently the 2300 wonld end in A. D. 1843; others concluded the seventy weeks ended four years after the death of Christ and the balance would end in 1847, and bring the judgment. Thus reasoned Mr. A. J. Krupp, of Philadelphia, M. Davis, of South Carolina, Mr. David McGregor, of Falmouth, Me., Mr. Wm. Miller, of New York State, Mr. Edward Irving, and Mr. Way, of England, and Mr. Joseph Wolff, the Jewish-missionary in Asia. Each writing and teaching the second personal advent of Christ, to take place about 1843 to 1847, while others, whom we shall hereafter notice, calculated on later dates.

I remain yours affectionately
Wm Miller

Page 41.

A. D. 1816, AN IMPORTANT ACCESSION.

In A. D. 1816, a Deist, by the name of Wm. Miller, was converted to Christ in Low Hampton, N. Y. He was a man of much moral worth, as a citizen, of very respectable parentage; brought up a farmer among the mountains of Vermont, of industrious habits, had served his country under a captain's commission in the war of 1812, and was held in high esteem by his associates and acquaintances generally.

With Mr. Miller's conversion, his subsequent studies and labors, we trace the first real tangible awakening of the church in America on the subject of Christ's speedy return. It may be truthfully said that with his labors commenced effectively the proclamation of the Second Advent Message in this country, although others had taught it.

We shall therefore feel at liberty to give a brief extract from his biographer, Mr. Sylvester Bliss, a congregationalist, concerning him, and his labors, and afterward give some extracts of his letters and sermons.

"The name of William Miller, of Low Hampton, N. Y., is too well known to require an extended introduction; but while well known, few men have been more diversely regarded than he. Those who have only heard his name associated with all that is hateful in fanaticism, have necessarily formed opinions respecting him, anything but complimentary to his intelligence and sanity; but those who knew him better esteemed him as a man of more than ordinary mental power,—a cool, sagacious, and honest reasoner, an humble and devout Christian, a kind and affectionate friend, and a man of great moral and social worth, . . . However his public labors may be regarded by a majority of the community, it will be seen by a perusal of his life, that these were by no means unproductive of great good. The revivals of religion which attended his labors are testified to by those who participated in them; and hundreds of souls will ever refer to him as a means, under God, of their awakening and conversion. His erroneous calculations of the prophetic periods he frankly confessed; and those who regarded his views of prophecy as dependent on that, may be surprised to learn that he distinguished between the *manner* and the era of their fulfillment."

"The attention which was given to his arguments caused many minds to entirely change their preconceived opinions respecting the millennial state, who have since remained devoted Christians, ardently looking for the Nobleman who has gone into a far country to receive for himself a kingdom, and to return, Luke xix. 12.

"As the public learn to discriminate between the actual position of Mr. Miller, and that which prejudice has conceived that he occupied, his conservativeness and disapprobation of every fanatical practice will be admitted, and a more just estimate will be had of him,"[1] Mr. Miller, in speaking of his experience after his conversion, says:

"The Bible now became my chief study, and I can truly say, I searched it with great delight, I found the half was never told me, I wondered why I had not seen its beauty and glory before, and marvelled that I could have ever rejected it, I found everything revealed that my heart could desire, and a remedy for every disease of the soul; I lost all taste for other reading and applied my heart to get wisdom from God."[2]

The above will show that the Lord had set his mind in the right direction to receive the truth which would better qualify him for a teacher of the Christian religion than all other schools could do. We will now quote another passage from his biographer, and then allow him to tell a little more of his own history, and how the Lord fitted him to bring out those mighty truths which have since stirred all Christendom.

"Mr. Miller immediately erected the family altar; publicly professed his faith in that religion which had been food for his mirth, by connecting himself with the little church that he had despised; opened his house for meetings of prayer; and became an ornament and pillar in the church, and an aid to both pastor and people. The die was cast, and he had taken his stand for life as a soldier of the cross, as all who knew him felt assured; and henceforth the badge of discipleship, in the church, or world, in his family or closet, indicated whose he was and whom he served.

"His pious relations had witnessed with pain his former irreligious opinions: how great was their rejoicing now. The church favored with his liberality, and edified by his reading,[3] but pained by his at-

[1] Life of Miller, pp. 3, 4.

[2] Life of Miller, p. 67.

[3] Mr. M. had been accustomed to read printed sermons to the church in the absence of their pastor, by their request, before his conversion.

tacks on their faith, could now rejoice with the rejoicing. His infidel friends regarded his departure from them as the loss of a standard-bearer. And the new convert felt that henceforth, wherever he was, he must deport himself as a Christian, and perform his whole duty. His subsequent history must show how well this was done.

"To the church, the devotion of himself to his Master's service was as welcome as his labors were efficient. The opposite party, especially the more gifted of them, regarded him as a powerful, and therefore, a desirable antagonist. He knew the strength of both parties. That of the former he had often tested, when, in his attacks, though they might have been silenced, he had felt that he had a bad cause; and the weakness of the latter had been forcibly impressed on him in his fruitless efforts to assure himself that they were right. He knew all their weak points, and where their weapons could be turned against them. They were not disposed to yield the ground without a struggle, and began their attack on him by using the weapons and assailing the points which characterized his own former attacks on Christianity; and to this fact, under God, is probably owing his subsequent world-wide notoriety.

"He had taunted his friends with entertaining 'a blind faith' in the Bible, containing, as it did, many things which they confessed their inability to explain. He had enjoyed putting preplexing questions to clergymen and others,—triumphing in their unsatisfactory replies. These questions had not been forgotten; and his Christian friends, also, turned his former taunts upon himself.

"Soon after his renunciation of Deism, in conversing with a friend respecting the hope of a glorious eternity though the merits and intercession of Christ, he was asked how he knew there was such a Saviour. He replied, 'It is revealed in the Bible.'—'How do you know the Bible is true?' was the response, with a reiteration of his former arguments on the contradictions and mysticisms in which he had claimed it was shrouded.

Mr. Miller felt such taunts in their full force. He was at first preplexed; but, on reflection, he considered that if the Bible is a revelation of God, it must be consistent with itself; all its parts must harmonize, must have been given for man's instruction, and, consequently, must be adapted to his understanding. He, therefore, said, 'Give me time, and I will harmonize all these apparent contradictions to my own satisfaction, or I will be a Deist still.'

He than devoted himself to the prayerful reading of the Word. He laid aside all commentaries, and used the marginal references and his Concordance as his only helps. He saw that he must distinguish between the Bible and all the peculiar and partisan interpretations of it. The Bible was older than them all, must be above them all; and he placed it there. He saw that it must correct all interpretations; and, in correcting them, its own pure light would shine without the mists which traditionary belief had involved it in. He resolved to lay aside all preconceived opinions, and to receive, with child-like simplicity, the natural and obvious meaning of Scripture. He pursued the study of the Bible with the most intense interest,—whole nights, as well as days, being devoted to that object. At times delighted with truth, which shone forth from the sacred volume, making clear to his understanding the great plan of God for the redemption of fallen man; and at times puzzled and almost distracted by seemingly inexplicable or contradictory passages, he persevered, until the application of his great principle of interpretation was triumphant. He became puzzled only to be delighted, and delighted only to persevere the more in penetrating its beauties and mysteries.

His manner of studying the Bible is thus described by himself:

"I determined to lay aside all my prepossessions, to throughly compare Scripture with Scripture, and to pursue its study in a regular and methodical manner. I commenced with Genesis, and read verse by verse, proceeding no faster than the meaning of the several passages should be so unfolded as to leave me free from embarrassment respecting any mysticisms or contradictions. Whenever I found anything obscure, my practice was to compare it with all collateral passages; and, by the help of Cruden, I examined all the texts of Scripture in which were found any of the prominent words contained in any obscure portion. Then, by letting every word have its proper bearing on the subject of the text, if my view of it harmonized with every collateral passage in the Bible, it ceased to be a difficulty. In this way I pursued the study of the Bible, in my first perusal of it, for about two years, and was fully satisfied that it is its own interpreter. I found that, by a comparison of Scripture with history, all the prophecies, as far as they have been fulfilled, had been fulfilled literally; that all the various figures, metaphors, parables, similitudes, etc., of the Bible, were either explained in their immediate connection, or the terms in which they were expressed were defined in other portions of the Word; and, when thus explained, are to be literally understood in accordance with such explanation. I was thus satisfied that the Bible is a system of revealed truths."

In thus continuing the study, he adopted the following

RULES OF INTERPRETATION.

I. Every word must have its proper bearing on the subject presented in the Bible. *Proof*, Matt. v. 18.

II. All Scripture is necessary, and may be understood by a diligent application and study. *Proof*, 2 Tim. iii. 15—17.

III. Nothing revealed in Scripture can or will be hid from those who ask in faith, not wavering. *Proof*, Deut. xxix. 29. Matt. x. 26, 27. 1 Cor. ii. 10. Phil. iii. 15. Isa. xlv. 11. Matt. xxi. 22. John xiv. 13, 14; xv. 7. James i. 5, 6. 1 John v. 13—15.

IV. To understand doctrine, bring all the Scriptures together on the subject you wish to know; then let every word have its proper influence; and if you can form your theory without a contradiction, you cannot be in error. *Proof*, Isa. xxviii. 7—29; xxxv. 8. Prov. xix. 27. Luke xxiv. 27, 44, 45. Rom. xvi. 26. James v. 19. 2 Pet. i. 19, 20.

V. Scripture must be its own expositor, since it is a rule of itself. If I depend on a teacher to expound to me, and he should guess at its meaning, or desire to have it so on account of his sectarian creed, or to be thought wise, then his guessing, desire, creed or wisdom, is my rule, and not the Bible. *Proof*, Ps. xix. 7—11; cxix. 97—105. Mat. xxiii. 8—10. 1 Cor. ii. 12—16. Ezk. xxxiv. 18, 19. Luke xi. 52. Matt. ii. 7, 8.

VI. God has revealed things to come, by visions, in figures and parables; and in this way the same things are oftentime revealed again and again, by different visions, or in different figures and parables. If you wish to understand them, you must combine them all in one. *Proof*, Ps. lxxxix. 19. Hos. xii. 10. Hab. ii. 2. Acts ii. 17. 1 Cor. x. 6. Heb. ix. 9, 24. Ps. lxxviii. 2. Matt. xiii. 13, 34 Gen. xli. 1—32. Dan. ii, vii and viii. Acts x. 9—16.

VII. Visions are always mentioned as such. 2 Cor. xii. 1.

VIII. Figures always have a figurative meaning, and are used much in prophecy to represent future things, times and events,—such as mountains, meaning governments, Dan. ii. 35, 44; beasts, meaning kingdoms, Dan. vii. 8, 17; waters, meaning people, Rev. xvii. 1, 15; day, meaning year, etc., Ezk. iv. 6.

IX. Parables are used as comparisons to illustrate subjects, and must be explained in the same way as figures, by the subject and Bible. Mark iv. 13.

X. Figures sometimes have two or more different significations, as day is used in a figurative sense to represent three different periods of time, namely, first, indefinite, Eccles. vii. 14; second, definite, a day for a year, Ezk. iv. 6, and third a day for a thousand years, 2 Pet. iii. 8.

The right construction will harmonize with the Bible, and make good sense; other constructions will not.

XI. If a word makes good sense as it stands, and does no violence to the simple laws of nature, it is to be understood literally; if not, figuratively. Rev. xii. 1, 2; xvii. 3—7.

XII. To learn the meaning of a figure, trace the word through your Bible, and when you find it explained, substitute the explanation for the word used; and, if it make good sense, you need not look further; if not, look again.

XIII. To know whether we have the true historical event for the fulfillment of a prophecy; If you find every word of the prophecy (after the figures are understood) is literally fulfilled, then you may know that your history is the true event; but if one word lacks a fulfillment, then you must look for another event, or wait its future development; for God takes care that history and prophecy shall agree, so that the true believing children of God may never be ashamed. Ps. xxii. 5. Isa. xlv. 17—19. 1 Pet. ii. 6. Rev. xvii. 17. Acts iii. 18.

XIV. The most important rule of all is, that you must have *faith.* It must be a faith that requires a sacrifice, and if tried, would give up the dearest object on earth, the world and all its desires,—character, living, occupation, friends, home, comforts and worldly honors. If any of these should hinder our believing any part of God's word, it would show our faith to be vain. Nor can we ever believe so long as one of these motives lies lurking in our hearts. We must believe that

God will never forfeit his word; and we can have confidence that he who takes notice of the sparrow's fall, and numbers the hairs of our head, will guard the translation of his own word, and throw a barrier around it, and prevent those who sincerely trust in God, and put implicit confidence in his word, from erring far from the truth.

"While thus studying the Scriptures,"—continuing the words of his own narrative,—"I became satisfied, if the prophecies which have been fulfilled in the past are any criterion by which to judge of the manner of the fulfillment of those which are future, that the popular views of the spiritual reign of Christ—a temporal millennium before the end of the world, and the Jews' return—are not sustained by the word of God; for I found that all the Scriptures on which those favorite theories are based are as clearly expressed as are those that were *literally* fulfilled at the first advent, or at any other period in the past. I found it plainly taught in the Scriptures that Jesus Christ will again descend to this earth, coming in the clouds of heaven, in all the glory of his father: [1] that, at his coming, the kingdom and dominion under the whole heaven will be given to him and the saints of the most high, who will possess it forever, even for ever and ever: [2] that, as the old world perished by the deluge, so the earth, that now is, is reserved unto fire, to be melted with fervent heat at Christ's coming; after which, according to the promise, it is to become the new earth, wherein the righteous will forever dwell: [3] that, at his coming, the bodies of all the righteous dead will be raised, and all the righteous living be changed from a corruptible to an incorruptible, from a mortal to an immortal state; that they will all be caught up together to meet the Lord in the air, and will reign with him forever in the regenerated earth: [4] that the controversy with Zion will then be finished, her children be delivered from bondage, and from the power of the tempter, and the saints be all presented

---

[1] See John xiv. 3; Acts i. 11; 1 Thess. iv. 16; Rev. i. 7; Matt. xvi. 27; xxiv. 30; Mark viii. 38; xiii. 26; Dan. vii. 13.

[2] Dan. vii. 14, 18, 22, 27; Matt. xxv. 34; Luke xii. 32; xix. 12, 15; xxii. 29; 1 Cor. ix. 25; 2 Tim. iv. 1, 8; James i. 12; 1 Pet. v. 4.

[3] 2 Pet. iii. 7—10; Isa. lxv. 17—19; Rev. xxi. 22.

[4] 1 Cor. xv. 20, 23, 49, 51—53; Phil. iii. 20, 21; 1 Thess. iv. 14—17; 1 John iii. 2.

to God blameless, without spot or wrinkle in love; [1] that the bodies of the wicked will then all be destroyed, and their spirits be reserved in prison until their resurrection and damnation; [2] and that, when the earth is thus regenerated, the righteous raised, and the wicked destroyed, the kingdom of God will have come, when his will will be done on earth as it is done in heaven; that the meek will inherit it, and the kingdom become the saints.[3] I found that the only millennium taught in the word of God is the thousand years which are to intervene between the first resurrection and that of the rest of the dead, as inculcated in the twentieth of Revelation; and that it must necessarily follow the personal coming of Christ and the regeneration of the earth: [4] that, till Christ's coming, and the end of the world, the righteous and wicked are to continue together on the earth, and that the horn of the Papacy is to war against the saints until his appearing and kingdom, when it will be destroyed by the brightness of Christ's coming; so that there can be no conversion of the world before the advent; [5] and that as the new earth, wherein dwelleth righteousness, is located by Peter after the conflagration, and is declared by him to be the same for which we look, according to the promise of Isa. lxv. 17, and is the same that John saw in vision after the passing away of the former heavens and earth; it must necessarily follow that the various portions of Scripture that refer to the millennial state must have their fulfillment after the resurrection of all the saints that sleep in Jesus.[6] I also found that the promises respecting Israel's restoration are applied by the apostle to all who are Christ's,—the putting on of Christ constituting them Abraham's seed, and heirs according to the promise.[7]

"I was then satisfied, as I saw conclusive evidence to prove the advent personal and pre-millennial, that all the events for which the

---

[1] Isa. xxxiv. 8; xl. 2, 5; xli. 10—12; Rom. viii. 21—23; 1 Cor. i. 7, 8; iv. 14; xv. 54, 56; Eph v. 27; Col. i. 22; 1 Thess. iii. 13; Heb. ii. 13—15; Jude 24; Rev. xx. 1—6.

[2] Psa. i. 2; xcvii. 3; Isa. lx. 15, 16; xxiv. 21, 22; Dan. vii. 13; Mal. iv. 1; Matt. iii. 12; John xxv. 29; Acts xxiv. 15; 1 Cor. iii. 13; 1 Thess. v. 2, 3; 2 Thess. i. 7—9; 1 Pet. i. 7; 2 Pet. iii. 7, 10; Jude 6, 7, 14, 15; Rev. xx. 3, 13—15.

[3] Psa. xxxvii. 9—11, 22, 28, 29, 34; Prov. ii. 21, 22; x. 30; Isa. xl. 21; Matt. v. 5; vi. 10.

[4] Rev. xx. 2—7.

[5] Matt. xiii. 37—43; xxiv. 14; Dan. vii. 21, 22; 2 Thess. ii. 8.

[6] 2 Pet. 3; Isa. lxv. 17; Rev. xxi.; xxii.

[7] Rom. ii. 14, 15; iv. 13; ix. 6; x. 12; xi. 17; Gal. iii. 29; Eph. ii. 14, 15.

church look to be fulfilled [in the millennium] before the advent, must be subsequent to it; and that, unless there were other unfulfilled prophecies, the advent of the Lord, instead of being looked for only in the distant future, might be a continually-expected event. In examining the prophecies on that point, I found that only four universal monarchies are anywhere predicted, in the Bible, to precede the setting up of God's everlasting kingdom; that three of those had passed away,—Babylon, Medo-Persia, and Grecia,—and that the fourth—Rome—had already passed into its last state, the state in which it is to be when the stone cut out of the mountain without hands shall smite the image on the feet, and break in pieces all the kingdoms of this world. I was unable to find any prediction of events which presented any clear evidence of their fulfillment before the scenes that usher in the advent. And finding all the signs of the times, and the present condition of the world, to compare harmoniously with the prophetic descriptions of the last days, I was compelled to believe that this world had about reached the limits of the period allotted for its continuance. As I regarded the evidence, I could arrive at no other conclusion.

"Another kind of evidence that v ially affected my mind was the chronology of the Scriptures. I found, on pursuing the study of the Bible, various chronological periods extending, according to my understanding of them, to the coming of the Saviour. I found that predicted events, which had been fulfilled in the past, often occurred within a *given time.* The one hundred and twenty years to the flood, Gen. vi. 3; the seven days that were to precede it, with forty days of predicted rain, Gen. vii. 4; the four hundred years of the sojourn of Abraham's seed, Gen. xv. 13; the three days of the butler's and baker's dreams, Gen. xl. 12—20; the seven years of Pharaoh's, Gen. xli. 28—54; the forty years in the wilderness, Num. xiv. 34; the three and a half years of famine, 1 Kings xvii. 1; the sixty-five years to the breaking of Ephraim, Isa. vii. 8; the seventy years captivity, Jer. xxv. 11; Nebuchadnezzar's seven times, Dan. iv. 13—16; and the seven weeks, three score and two weeks, and the one week, making seventy weeks, determined upon the Jews, Dan. ix. 24—27; the events limited by these times were all once only a matter of prophecy, and were fulfilled in accordance with the predictions.

"When, therefore, I found the 2300 prophetic days, which were to mark the length of the vision from the Persian to the end of the fourth kingdom, the seven times' continuance of the dispersion of God's people, and the 1335 prophetic days to the standing of Daniel in his lot, all evidently extending to the advent, with other prophetical periods, I could but regard them as 'the times before appointed,' which God had revealed 'unto his servants the prophets.' As I was fully convinced that 'all Scripture given by inspiration of God is profitable,'—that it came not at any time by the will of man, but was written as holy men were moved by the Holy Ghost, and was written for our learning, that we, through patience and comfort of the Scriptures, might have hope,—I could but regard the chronological portions of the Bible as being as much a portion of the word of God, and as much entitled to our serious consideration, as any other portion of the Scriptures.

"I, therefore, felt that, in endeavoring to comprehend what God had in his mercy seen fit to reveal to us, I had no right to pass over the prophetic periods. I saw that, as the events predicted to be fulfilled in prophetic days had been extended over about as many literal years; as God, in Num. xiv. 34, and Ezek. iv. 4—6, had appointed each day for a year; as the seventy weeks to the Messiah were fulfilled in 490 years, and the 1260 prophetic days of the Papal supremacy in 1260 years; and as these prophetical days extending to the advent were given in connection with symbolic prophecy, I could only regard the time as symbolical, and as standing each day for a year, in accordance with the opinions of all the standard Protestant commentators. If, then, we could obtain any clue to the time of their commencement, I conceived we should be guided to the probable time of their termination; and, as God would not bestow upon us an useless revelation, I regarded them as conducting us to the time when we might confidently look for the coming of the chiefest among ten thousand, the one altogether lovely.

"From a further study of the Scriptures, I concluded that the seven times of Gentile supremacy must commence when the Jews ceased to be an independent nation, at the captivity of Manasseh, which the best chronologers assigned to B. C. 677; that the 2300 days commenced with the seventy weeks, which the best chronologers dated from B. C. 457;[1] and that the 1335 days, commencing with the

[1] Others place their commencement at later points, which have also proved incorrect.

taking away of the daily, and the setting up of the abomination that maketh desolate, Dan. xii. 11, were to be dated from the setting up of the Papal supremacy, after the taking away of Pagan abominations, and which, according to the best historians I could consult, should be dated from about A. D. 508.[1] Reckoning all these prophetic periods from the several dates assigned by the best chronologers for the events from which they should evidently be reckoned, they would all terminate together, about A. D. 1843. I was thus brought, in 1818, at the close of my two years' study of the Scriptures, to the solemn conclusion, that in about twenty-five years from that time all the affairs of our present state would be wound up; that all its pride and power, pomp and vanity, wickedness and oppression, would come to an end; and that, in the place of the kingdoms of this world, the peaceful and long-desired kingdom of the Messiah would be established under the whole heaven; that, in about twenty-five years, the glory of the Lord would be revealed, and all flesh see it together,—the desert bud and blossom as the rose, the fir-tree come up instead of the thorn, and instead of the briar the myrtle-tree,—the curse be removed from off the earth, death be destroyed, reward be given to the servants of God, the prophets and saints, and them who fear his name, and those be destroyed that destroy the earth.

"I need not speak of the joy that filled my heart in view of the delightful prospect, nor of the ardent longings of my soul for a participation in the joys of the redeemed. The Bible was now to me a new book. It was indeed a feast of reason; all that was dark, mystical or obscure to me in its teachings, had been dissipated from my mind before the clear light that now dawned from its sacred pages: And O how bright and glorious the truth appeared! All the contradictions and inconsistencies I had before found in the Word were gone; and, although there were many portions of which I was not satisfied I had a full understanding, yet so much light had emanated from it to the illumination of my before darkened mind, that I felt a delight in studying the Scriptures which I had not before supposed could be derived from its teachings. I commenced their study with no expectation of finding the time of the Saviour's coming, and I could at first hardly believe the result to which I had arrived; but the evi-

---

[1] Several able writers have placed commencement of the 1335 days, at A. D. 533—538, which time has proved to be incorrect, others are beginning them at 540—553, and are as liable to err.

dence struck me with such force that I could not resist my convictions. I became nearly settled in my conclusions, and began to wait, and watch, and pray for my Saviour's coming."

Such were the conclusions to which he arrived, and such the course of study which lead him to them, and which prepared his heart to adore the author of salvation, and to labor for the salvation of others yet in darkness.

Mr. Miller writes "With the solemn conviction that such momentous events were predicted in the Scriptures, to be fulfilled in so short a space of time, the question came home to me with mighty power regarding my duty to the world, in view of the evidence that had affected my own mind. If the end was so near, it was important that the world should know it. I supposed that it would call forth the opposition of the ungodly; but it never came into my mind that any Christian would oppose it. I supposed that all such would be so rejoiced, in view of the glorious prospect, that it would only be necessary to present it, for them to receive it. My great fear was, that, in their joy at the hope of a glorious inheritance so soon to be revealed, they would receive the doctrine without sufficiently examining the Scriptures in demonstration of its truth. I therefore feared to present it, lest, by some possibility, I should be in error, and be the means of misleading any.

"Various difficulties and objections would arise in my mind, from time to time; certain texts would occur to me, which seemed to weigh against my conclusions; and I would not present a view to others, while any difficulty appeared to militate against it. I therefore continued the study of the Bible, to see if I could sustain any of these objections. My object was not merely to remove them, but I wished to see if they were valid.

"Sometimes, when at work, a text would arise like this: 'Of that day and hour knoweth no man,' etc.; and how, then, could the Bible reveal the time of the advent? I would then immediately examine the context in which it was found, and I saw at once that, in the same connection, we are informed how we may know when it is nigh, even at the doors; consequently, that text could not teach that we could know nothing of the time of that event. Other texts, which are advanced in support of the doctrine of a temporal millennium, would arise; but, on examining their context, I invariably found that they were applicable only to the eternal state, or were so illustrative of the spread of the gospel here, as to be entirely irrelevant to the position they were adduced to support.

"Thus all those passages that speak of the will of God being done on earth as in heaven, of the earth being full of the knowledge of the glory of God, etc., could not be applicable to a time when the Man of Sin was prevailing against the saints, or when the righteous and wicked were dwelling together, which is to be the case until the end of the world. Those which speak of the gospel being preached in all the world, teach that, as soon as it should be thus preached, the end was to come; so that it could not be delayed a thousand years from that time, nor long enough for the world's conversion after the preaching of the gospel as a witness.

"The question of the resurrection and judgment was, for a time, an obstacle in the way. Being instructed that all the dead would be raised at the same time, I supposed it must be so taught in the Bible; but I soon saw it was one of the traditions of the elders.

"So, also, with the return of the Jews. That question I saw could only be sustained by denying the positive declarations of the New Testament, which assert: 'there is no difference between the Jew and the Greek;' that 'the promise that he shall be the heir of the world was not to Abraham and his seed through the law, but through the righteousness of faith;' that 'there is neither Jew nor Greek, bond nor free, male nor female;' but that 'if ye are Christ's, then are ye Abraham's seed, and heirs according to the promise.' I was, therefore, obliged to discard an objection which asserts there *is* a difference between the Jew and Greek; that the children of the flesh *are* accounted for the seed, etc.

"In this way I was occupied for five years,—from 1818 to 1823,—in weighing the various objections which were being presented to my mind. During that time, more objections arose in my mind than have been advanced by my opponents since; and I know of no objection that has been since advanced which did not then occur to me. But, however strong they at first appeared, after examining them in the light of the divine Word, I could only compare them to straws, laid down singly as obstacles, on a well-beaten road,—the car of truth rolled over them, unimpeded in its progress.

"I was then fully settled in the conclusions which seven years previously had begun to bear with such impressive force upon my mind; and the duty of presenting the evidence of the nearness of the advent to others,—which I had managed to evade while I could find the shadow of an objection remaining against its truth,—again came home to me with great force. I had previously only thrown out occasional hints of my views. I then began to speak more clearly my opinions to my neighbors, to ministers, and others. To my astonishment, I found very few who listened with any interest. Occasionally, one would see the force of the evidence; but the great majority passed it by as an idle tale. I was, therefore, disappointed in finding any who would declare this doctrine, as I felt it should be, for the comfort of saints, and as a warning to sinners."

His correspondence during this period shows ardent longings for the salvation of his relatives and friends.

EXTRACT FROM A LETTER TO A FRIEND IN 1826, ON THE SECOND ADVENT.

Come, blessed Saviour! nor let time delay
The sacred morn of that expected day,
When all the happy throng, the heavenly band,
Descending from above, "the spirit land;"
When the seventh trump its solemn blast shall sound,
And Gabriel's voice shall shake the solid ground.
Then sleeping myriads from their graves shall rise,
And meet their Saviour in those nether skies;
While those who yet remain, by men oppressed,
Will feel a sudden change and join the bless'd;
Where, in one chorus joined, the song be raised,
To God, the Father, Son,—"Ancient of days."

I sometimes almost flatter myself I shall live to see this glorious day. "Fanatical," say you. Very well; I should not be surprised if you and I should both be on this earth, alive,—

When from the east we see a cloud arise,
And bring to view a Saviour long despised;
When we shall hear that trumpet's dreadful roll,
That shakes the earth from center to the pole;
When, from the great white throne, indignant ire
Shoots forth its blaze, and sets the world on fire:—
Then all the wicked, all that pride can boast,
Shall be as stubble, saith the Lord of hosts;
When kings, and captains, tyrants, mighty men,

Are the great supper for the fowls of heaven;
And kingdoms, thrones, and powers, dominions riven,
Like chaff before the angry whirlwind driven.
The dragon, papal beast, and great arch foe,
Shall sink in endless night, eternal woe;
The orb of day, his face be hid in gloom,
And the old reeling earth in Nature's tomb.

"Then you believe in annihilation?" methinks I hear you say. No, sir; I believe

That this dark orb shall from its ashes rise,
And the new heavens, descending from the skies,
The happy bride, adorned in righteousness,
Shall with the Bridegroom enter to his rest.
Then, O my soul, will you, permitted, view
This word fulfilled, "created all things new;"
And all be banished—trials, sins, and fears,
To live and reign with Christ a thousand years.
The beloved city, filled with boys and men,
Will constitute the New Jerusalem,
And there, as priests to God, with Christ to dwell,
While Satan and his hosts are chained in hell.
But, lo! a thousand years are past and gone,
Since the new world was from the old one born;
When death gives up the particles of dust,
And hell lets loose the spirits of the cursed.
Then on the surface of the earth they stand,
A company unnumbered as the sand;
For in their flesh they sinned in time that's passed,
So in the flesh must they be judged at last;
Driven and gathered, round the city roam,
To hear their sentence and receive their doom.
But can they scale those walls, so great and high?
No; nothing enters that doth make a lie.
Lo! on the golden walls, from tower to tower,
See saints stand judging them in this dread hour!
There justice, from above, in fiery breath,
Destroys the rebels—"this the second death!"

I am almost persuaded to believe that we shall never meet again until that day when the Sun of righteousness shall rise

With healing wings, and grace on grace distill,
And cleanse the church on Zion's holy hill;
Where sin no more controls, nor death by sin,

But justified and glorified with him:
No need of sun or moon, for he's our light;
No changing seasons there, nor gloomy night;
No parting there of friends, nor farewells given,
But gathered all in one from earth and heaven.
On this my faith is fixed, my hope is raised—
To him the glory, and his name the praise.
Then, while I stay in this unfriendly state,
Lord, give me grace, and patiently I'll wait.

The above is written to you, my brother, hoping that you may catch some of the feelings and exercises of the author's heart, while he has often read and pondered over the blessed passages to which you are referred in the conclusion, under head of "Proof-texts." I can only claim your indulgence; merit I claim not.

For poets say, and surely they can tell,
To read a poet right, "drink from his well;"
To feel the spirit, catch the spirit's flame,
And kindred spirits kindle back again.
Then read the proof, my brother, and believe,
If I'm not right, I'm happy being deceived;
For hope's an anchor,—all in this agree,—
And faith a helmsman—so at least with me;
The word of God my compass, love the pole,
Experience are my sails, and Christ the whole.
Grace is my ballast, for it keeps me low;
The Spirit is the wind, that bears me through;
Perfection is the haven for which I run,
Consigned to him who gave for me his Son;
Life is the voyage, and I am "homeward bound,"
Time is my log-book, death my anchor-ground;
The resurrection is my ship o'erhauled,
Eternity unites us all in all.

WILLIAM MILLER.

August 17, 1826.

MR. MILLER'S CALL TO PREACH.

It will be in place here to give, in his own language, the experience of Mr. Miller on his call to proclaim the advent message.

He continued to make the Bible his daily study, and became more and more convinced that he had a personal duty to perform respecting what he conceived the Bible to teach of the nearness of the advent. These impressions he thus describes:

"When I was about my business, it was continually ringing in my ears, 'go and tell the world of their danger.' This text was constantly occurring to me: 'when I say unto the wicked, O wicked man, thou shalt surely die; if thou dost not speak to warn the wicked from his way, that wicked man shall die in his iniquity; but his blood will I require at thy hand. Nevertheless, if thou warn the wicked of his way to turn from it; if he do not turn from his way, he shall die in his iniquity; but thou hast delivered thy soul.'—Ezek. xxxiii. 8, 9. I felt that, if the wicked could be effectually warned, multitudes of them would repent; and that, if they were not warned, their blood might be required at my hand. I did all I could to avoid the conviction that anything was required of me; and I thought that by freely speaking of it to all, I should perform my duty, and that God would raise up the necessary instrumentality for the accomplishment of the work. I prayed that some minister might see the truth, and devote himself to its promulgation; but still it was impressed upon me, 'go and tell it to the world; their blood will I require at thy hand.' The more I presented it in conversation, the more dissatisfied I felt with myself for withholding it from the public. I tried to excuse myself to the Lord for not going out and proclaiming it to the world. I told the Lord that I was not used to public speaking; that I had not the necessary qualifications to gain the attention of an audience; that I was very diffident, and feared to go before the world; that they would 'not believe me nor hearken to my voice;' that I was 'slow of speech, and of a slow tongue.' But I could get no relief."

In this way he struggled on for nine years longer, pursuing the study of the Bible, doing all he could to present the nearness of Christ's coming to those whom circumstances threw in his way; but resisting his impressions of duty to go out as a public teacher. He was then fifty years old, and it seemed impossible for him to surmount the obstacles which lay in his path, to successfully present it in a public manner.

MR. MILLER BEGINS TO PREACH.

The public labors of Mr. Miller, according to the best evidence to be obtained, date from the autumn of 1831. He had continued to be much distressed respecting his duty to "go and tell it to the world," which was constantly impressed on his mind. One Saturday, after breakfast, he sat down at his desk to examine some point, and, as he arose to go out to work, it came home to him with more force than ever, "go and tell it to the world." He thus writes:—

"The impression was so sudden, and came with such force, that I settled down into my chair, saying, 'I can't go, Lord.' 'Why not?' seemed to be the response; and then all my excuses came up—my want of ability, etc.; but my distress became so great, I entered into a solemn covenant with God, that if he would open the way, I would go and perform my duty to the world. 'What do you mean by opening the way?' seemed to come to me. 'Why,' said I, 'if I should have an invitation to speak publicly in any place, I will go and tell them what I find in the Bible about the Lord's coming.' Instantly all my burden was gone, and I rejoiced that I should not probably be thus called upon; for I had never had such an invitation. My trials were not known, and I had but little expectation of being invited to any field of labor.

"In about half an hour from this time, before I had left the room, a son of Mr. Guilford, of Dresden, about sixteen miles from my residence, came in, and said that his father had sent for me, and wished me to go home with him. Supposing that he wished to see me on some business, I asked him what he wanted. He replied, that there was to be no preaching in their church the next day, and his father wished to have me come and talk to the people on the subject of the Lord's coming. I was immediately angry with myself for having made the covenant I had; I rebelled at once against the Lord, and determined not to go. I left the boy, without giving him any answer, and retired in great distress to a grove near by. There I struggled with the Lord for about an hour, endeavoring to release myself from the covenant I had made with him; but I could get no relief. It was impressed upon my conscience, 'will you make a covenant with God, and break it so soon?' and the exceeding sinfulness of thus doing overwhelmed me. I finally submitted, and promised the Lord that, if he would sustain me, I would go, trusting in him to give me grace and ability to perform all he should require of me. I returned to the house, and found the boy still waiting. He remained till after dinner, and I returned with him to Dresden.

"The next day, which, as nearly as I can remember, was about the first Sabbath in August, 1831, I delivered my first public lecture on the second advent. The house was well filled with an attentive audience. As soon as I commenced speaking, all my diffidence and embarrassment were gone, and I felt impressed only with the greatness of the subject, which, by the providence of God, I was enabled to present. At the close of the services on the Sabbath, I was requested to remain and lecture during the week, with which I complied. They flocked in from the neighboring towns; a revival commenced, and it was said that in thirteen families all but two persons were hopefully converted.

"On the Monday following I returned home, and found a letter from Elder Fuller, of Poultney, Vt., requesting me to go and lecture there on the same subject. They had not heard of my going to Dresden. I went to Poultney, and lectured there with similar effect.

"From thence I went, by invitation, to Pawlet, and other towns in that vicinity. The churches of Congregationalists, Baptists, and Methodists, were thrown open. In almost every place I visited, my labors resulted in the reclaiming of backsliders, and the conversion of sinners. I was usually invited to fields of labor by the ministers of the several congregations whom I visited, who gave me their countenance; and I have never labored in any place to which I was not previously invited. The most pressing invitations from the ministry, and the leading members of the churches, poured in continually from that time, during the whole period of my public labors, and with more than one-half of which I was unable to comply. Churches, were thrown open everywhere, and I lectured to crowded houses through the western part of Vermont, the northern part of New York, and in Canada East; and powerful reformations were the results of my labors."

Soon after he began to lecture on the subject, Mr. Miller began to be importuned to write out and publish his views. In a letter to Elder Hendryx, dated January 25, 1832, he says:

"I have written a few numbers on the coming of Christ and the final destruction of the Beast, when his body shall be given to the burning flame. They may appear in the Vermont Telegraph; if not, in pamphlet form. They are written in letters to Elder Smith, of Poultney, and he has liberty to publish."

On the same occasion, he adds: "I am more and more astonished at the harmony and strength of the word of God; and the more I read, the more I see the folly of the infidel in rejecting this word."

The articles referred to were sent as anonymous to the editor of the Telegraph, who declined their publication unless informed of the name of the writer. This being communicated to him, they appeared, in a series of sixteen articles, over the initials of W. M. The first article was published in the paper of May 15, 1832, and they caused much conversation and discussion.[1]

These articles awakened such interest among the ministers and other Bible students that they soon opened correspondence with Mr. Miller, and nearly flooded him with letters filled with inquiries respecting the advent of Christ and the evidences of its nearness, or stating objections they wished removed.

MR. MILLER'S FIRST BOOK.

Mr. Miller was finally induced to prepare a small work on the subject—a pamphlet of 64 pages, entitled,

"Evidences from Scripture and History of the Second Coming of Christ, about the year 1843, and of His Personal Reign of One Thousand Years." Brandon, Vt., Telegraph Office, 1833.

This pamphlet was scattered gratuitously mostly, in response to letters of inquiry, or in places he could not visit, when requested.

In a letter to Elder Hendryx, dated Feb. 8, 1833, Mr. Miller writes: "The Lord is scattering the seed. I can now reckon eight ministers who preach this doctrine, more or less, besides yourself.

THE BIBLE IS THE SURE WORD.

"And where your hearers are not well indoctrinated, you must preach *Bible;* you must prove all things by *Bible;* you must talk *Bible;* you must exhort *Bible;* you must pray *Bible*, and love *Bible;* and do all in your power to make others love *Bible*, too. One great means to do good is to make your parishioners sensible that you are in earnest, and fully and solemnly believe what you preach. If you wish your people to feel, feel yourself. You can do them more good by the fire-sides, and in your conference circles, than in the pulpit."

---

[1] Life of Miller, pp. 73, 100.

Then, speaking of the prospect of the harvest of the world being near, Mr. M. continues:

"See! see! the angel with his sharp sickle is about to take the field! See yonder trembling victim fall before his pestilential breath! High and low, rich and poor, trembling and falling before the appalling grave, the dreadful cholera. Hark!—hear those dreadful bellowings of the angry nations! It is the presage of horrid and terrific war. Look!—look again! See crowns, and kings, and kingdoms tumbling to the dust! See lords and nobles, captains and mighty men, all arming for the bloody, demon fight! See the carnivorous fowls fly screaming through the air! See,—see these signs! Behold, the heavens grow black with clouds; the sun has veiled himself; the moon, pale and forsaken, hangs in middle air; the hail descends; the seven thunders utter loud their voices; the lightnings send their vivid gleams of sulphurous flame abroad; and the great city of the nation falls to rise no more forever and forever! At this dread moment, look! look!—O, look and see! What means that ray of light? The clouds have burst asunder; the heavens appear; the great white throne is in sight! Amazement fills the universe with awe! He comes!—he comes! Behold, the Saviour comes! Lift up your heads, ye saints,—he comes! he comes!—he comes!

WM. MILLER.

We give the closing item of the above letter to show the vividness of mind and earnestness of manner, with which this faithful servant of God pressed home to the hearts of those to whom he wrote or spoke, this all absorbing theme; after presenting his argument from the Scriptures that these events were soon to be realized.

There is a power in these points of doctrine which gives force and edge to the communications of those who really believe and teach them, such as is not found with those who ignore or neglect them, however much other good doctrine they may present.

CHAPTER III.

HERALD OF THE COMING KINGDOM—DR. J. THOMAS—A WORD OF WARNING —WM. W. PYM—MILLER AGAIN IN THE FIELD—THREATS OF ENEMIES— HARDENED REBELS CONVERTED—1836—MILLER WRITES THE SIXTEEN LECTURES—1837—A BAPTIST MINISTER CONFOUNDED—1838—ONE HUNDRED INFIDELS CONVERTED—ELD. CHARLES FITCH A BELIEVER—ELD. J. LITCH EMBRACES AND PUBLISHES THE CRY—ELD. T. COLE BECOMES A BELIEVER —MILLER IN MASSACHUSETTS—GREAT REFORMATIONS—MILLER AND THE PROPHETS—ELD. HIMES' RECORD.

In 1834, Mr. John Thomas, M. D., published a journal devoted to the advocacy of the pre-millennial, personal, and immeditate coming and kingdom of Christ. Its title and place of issue at that time we are not able to give; it was subsequently published in Richmond, Va., entitled "THE HERALD OF THE COMING KINGDOM."

"A WORD OF WARNING IN THE LAST DAYS."

The above is the title of a pamphlet by Rev. Wm. W. Pym, A. M., vicar of William Hurts, England, published in England in 1835, and in Philadelphia, in 1837.

Mr. Pym takes the ground that the second advent of the *Lord Messiah* will take place about the year 1847. He says: "It may be well here to remind you of 'this present truth,' 2 Pet. i. 12, for which I am contending that the coming of our Lord draws nigh."

In his preface he says: "the principal motive which actuates me, is the daily increasing conviction of this truth, that the Lord is at hand. Impressed with a most firm belief in *the very near approach of Christ*, and alike impressed with the prevailing unbelief of this present truth,[1] my spirit is stirred within me to warn every man, with whom I have to do, that the Lord must shortly be revealed." 2 Thes. i. 7—10.

---

[1] Besides every age hath its peculiar truth. The apostle Peter, when he mentions his departure, tells them he would have them 'established in the present truth.' WM. W. PYM.

Thus the message of the gospel of Christ's immediate coming began to spread around the churches in America, and to awaken a deep interest and a heart searching with many of the lovers of Christ while it brought many sinners to repentance, and to Christ for salvation. It was not the special point of time, *i. e.*, the year for the end, that produced these great and glorious results; but the facts concerning the certainty of Christ's personal advent to judge the world, to renew the earth, and establish his glorious reign, preached as a reality, and as SURE TO COME SOON, with the prophetic Scriptures presented in a living, vivid manner by those who believed what they preached.

THREATS OF THE ENEMIES.

Under date of Oct. 23, 1834, Mr. Miller writes thus to Elder Hendryx: "the evidence is so clear, the testimony is so strong, that we live on the eve of the present dispensation, toward the dawn of the *glorious day*, that I wonder why ministers and people do not wake up and trim their lamps. Yes, my brother, almost two years since you heard the news, '*behold, the bridegroom cometh!*'—and yet you cry, 'a little more sleep, a little more slumber.' Blame not your people if they go to sleep under your preaching. You have done the same. . . . Awake! awake! O sluggard! Defend your own castle, or take sides with the word of God, *destroy*, or *build*.

"In every church where I have lectured on this important subject, many, very many, seem to awake, rub open their eyes, and then fall back to sleep again. But the enemy is waking up. In one town (North Beekmantown) I received a letter the day after my first lecture, from some bullies and blackguards, 'that if I did not clear out of the state they would put me where the dogs could never find me.' The letter was signed by ten of them. I staid, and, blessed be God! he poured out his Spirit and began a work which gainsayers could not resist.

"Some ministers try to persuade their people not to hear me; but the people will go, and every additional lecture will bring an additional multitude, until their meeting-houses cannot hold them. Depend upon it, my brother, God is in this thing; and he will be glorified; and blessed be his holy name! Do pray for me, my brother, that I may have grace equal to my need, and that I may always see my need, feel my weakness, and be kept humble, and that I may always declare the truth. *Do pray!*

"I remain yours in Christ,

Rev. T. HENDRYX. "WILLIAM MILLER."

Two days subsequent to the date of the above, Mr. M. was again in the field; and, according to his memorandum-book, gave lectures as follows: Oct. 25 and 26, at Paulet, Vt.; Nov. 6, 8, and 9, at Orwell, Vt.; 10 and 12, in Cornwall, Vt.; and Nov. 16, in Hampton, N. Y. His success in the above places is indicated in the following extract from a letter which he wrote Elder Hendryx from Low Hampton, on the 28th of Nov., 1834.

"I have had good success since I wrote you before. The Lord has been with me. I have been into a number of towns in Vermont. Some old, hardened rebels have been brought to plead for mercy, even before my course of lectures was finished. Blessed be the holy name of God! He has given me more than I should have dared to ask. How good, my brother, it is to preach, having God for paymaster! He pays down. He pays in souls. He paid the Shepherd thus, and he was satisfied: will he not pay his servants too? Yes, yes. Bless his name, O my soul, for all his benefits!

"I find that studious Christians are the best hearers; and the reason is obvious. The more we know of mankind, the less room there is for bigotry, superstition, and prejudice. Those are evils, always attending ignorance."[1]

A. D. EIGHTEEN HUNDRED AND THIRTY-FIVE.

During all the year 1835, the work of reformation continued under the sounding of the midnight cry, sinners were awakened and converted, wanderers returned to Christ, and Christians greatly quickened. Mr. Miller found more work than he could do all through the year.

He visited Stillwater, N. Y., according to invitation, and continued there one week, lecturing each day. On the 13th he was at Bristol. On the 1st of November he visited Middletown, N. Y., and gave a course of eight lectures. He then lectured again, five days, at Bristol, commencing on the 15th of November; and, beginning on the 29th, he labored five days longer at Middletown, usually giving two

---

[1] Life of Miller, p. 119.

lectures each day. On the 6th of December he was at Whitehall, N. Y.; on the 20th, at Poultney, Vt.; and on the 27th, at Westhaven. This terminated his labors for the year 1835.

MR. MILLER WRITES HIS COURSE OF LECTURES.

He says: "In 1836 I wrote my series of sixteen lectures, which were published by Elder Wescott, in Troy, New York, the profits of which I gave to him.—All the copies I received of that edition, I purchased at his regular prices.

The first assistance I received from any source to defray my expenses, were two half dollars which I received in Canada, in 1835. The next assistance I received was the payment of my stage fare to Lansingburg, in 1837. Since then I have never received enough to pay my traveling expenses; so that my labors have been of no pecuniary advantage to me. I should not have alluded to this, were it not for the extravagant stories which have been circulated to my injury."[1]

After writing the above work Mr. Miller again lectured in Dresden, N. Y., on the 7th of August; in Orwell, Vt., on the 11th of September; and in Keesville, N. Y., on the 18th. He then gave courses of lectures, beginning at Lawrence, N. Y., on the 22d; Stockholm, on the 29th; Parishville, on the 7th of October; Massena, N. Y., on the on the 14th. He gave ten lectures at Fort Covington, N. Y., beginning on the 20th, and was at Chatauguay, N. Y., on the 27th. This terminated his labors for the year 1836. In allusion to these last visits, he wrote on the 23d of December:

"I have not visited a place where the Lord has not given me one or two souls for my hire. I have spent eight weeks in St. Lawrence county, and delivered eighty-two lectures this fall. Next week I am going to Shaftsbury and vicinity."

A. D. EIGHTEEN HUNDRED AND THIRTY-SEVEN.

He visited Shaftsbury, Vt., on the 23d of January, 1837, and gave his full course of sixteen lectures. At the close of one lecture, a Baptist clergyman arose, and stated that he had come there for the purpose of exposing the folly of Mr. M., but had to confess that he

---

[1] Miller's apology and defense.

was confounded, convicted, and converted. He acknowledged that he had applied various unhandsome appellations to Mr. Miller, calling him "the end of the world man," "the old visionary," "dreamer," "fanatic," and for which he felt covered with shame and confusion. That confession, evidently so honest, was like a thunderbolt on the audience.

Very few particulars of interest have been gathered respecting his labors during the year 1837. According to his memorandum-book, he lectured in Wells, Vt., on the 3d of February; in Shrewsbury, Vt., on the 3d of March; in Andover, Vt., from the 5th to the 12th of March; in Weston, Vt., four days, beginning with the 13th; in Mt. Holly, Vt., on the 17th; in Orwell, Vt., on the 23d of April and 7th of May; in Danby, Vt., on the 14th of May; in Poultney, Vt., eight days, beginning with the 21st of May; in Orwell, again, on the 4th of June; in North Springfield, Vt., from the 11th to the 17th; in Ludlow, Vt., from the 19th to the 21st; in Mt. Holly, Vt., from the 25th of June to the 2d of July; in Orwell, Vt., on the 9th of July; at Fairhaven, Vt., from the 11th to the 20th; in Whiting, Vt., on the 23d; in Fairhaven, Vt., on the 13th of August; in Moriah, Vt., from the 14th to the 22d of October; in Ludlow, Vt., from the 29th to the 6th of November, and at Stillwater, N. Y., on the 31st of December.

A. D. EIGHTEEN HUNDRED AND THIRTY-EIGHT.

With the 1st of January, 1838, he commenced a second course of lectures at Lansingburgh, N. Y., in compliance with the urgent request of the Baptist church in that place, and of E. B. Crandall, their pastor. The lectures continued nine days, and were listened to by crowded and attentive audiences. The result was also most heart-cheering. Infidelity had several strongholds in that neighborhood, and many of that class attended his lectures, and were greatly affected by them. In a letter dated on the 25th of that month, two weeks after the close of the lectures, a gentleman of that place writes to Mr. Miller:

"I have never witnessed so powerful an effect in any place, as in this, on all who heard. I am of the opinion that not less than one hundred persons, who held infidel sentiments, are brought to believe the Bible. Infidelity is dumb in this place, as if frightened, and converts are many."

ONE HUNDRED INFIDELS CONVERTED.

The following testimony of one who was converted from infidelity during these lectures, is copied from the Boston Investigator (an infidel paper) of January, 1845:

"MR. EDITOR:—I was a warm supporter of the views of Abner Kneeland, attended his lectures and *protracted dances*, disbelieved in Divine Revelation and a future existence, and fully accorded with Mr. Kneeland's views of religion. Having read every work of note that I could obtain, and having heard many lectures opposed to God and the Bible, I considered myself prepared to overthrow the Christian faith, and feared no argument that could be brought from the Bible. With these feelings, I attended a full course of Mr. Miller's lectures. He gave his rules of interpretation, and pledged himself to prove his position. I approved of his rules,—to which I refer you,—and the result was, he established the fact that the Bible is what it purports to be—the word of God—to my mind, beyond a doubt; and I have taken it as the man of my counsel. I notice your doubts of the truth of the statement in relation to hundreds of infidels being converted under the preaching of Mr. Miller. This may possibly be owing to your never having given Mr. Miller a candid and thorough hearing. He is a man mighty in the Scriptures, and has done terrible execution in the ranks of the 'King's enemies,' with the sword of the Spirit, which is the word of God. I am personally acquainted with nearly one hundred, who held to similar views with Abner Kneeland, who were converted under the preaching of Mr. Miller; and we did not yield the point without a struggle, nor without due consideration. Each and every prop and refuge of infidelity and unbelief were taken away from us, and our sandy foundation was swept by the truth of the Almighty as chaff is driven by the wind. Yet we parted with them much as a man parts with a *diseased tooth.* We tried to cure and keep it there, and when made to know that the *root* and foundation was rotten, it was painful to part with; but we rejoiced and felt better after the separation; for there is balm in Gilead—there is a Physician there.

"LANSINGBURGH, N. Y., January, 1845."

On the 14th of January, Mr. Miller lectured at Westhaven, N. Y., and two weeks from that day at Low Hampton, N. Y. On the 4th of February he commenced a course of lectures at Panton, Vt., which he continued eight days. He then returned to Westhaven, N. Y., and lectured seven days, beginning February 18th.

On returning to Low Hampton, he found the following letter from Rev. Charles Fitch, pastor at the Marlboro' Chapel, Boston. It was the beginning of an acquaintance between those dear brethren in Christ, and as such will be read with interest by all.

"Boston, March 5, 1838.

"My dear Brother:—I am a stranger to you, but I trust that, through the free sovereign grace of God, I am not altogether a stranger to Jesus Christ, whom you serve. I am the pastor of an Orthodox Congregational church in this city. A few weeks since your lectures on the Second Coming of Christ were put into my hands. I sat down to read the work, knowing nothing of the views which it contained. I have *studied* it with an overwhelming interest, such as I never felt in any other book except the Bible. I have compared it with Scripture and history, and I find nothing on which to rest a single doubt respecting the correctness of your views. Though a miserable, guilty sinner, I trust that, through the Lord's abounding grace, I shall be among those that 'love his appearing.' I preached to my people two discourses yesterday on the coming of our Lord, and I believe a deep and permanent interest will be awakened thereby in God's testimonies. My object in writing you, my dear sir, is twofold.

"1st. Will you have the kindness to inform me, by letter, in what history you find the fact stated that the last of the ten kings was baptized A. D. 508, and also that the decree of Justinian, giving the Bishop of Rome power to suppress the reading of the Scriptures, was issued in 538? All the other data which you have given I have found correct, and I know of no reason to doubt your correctness in these. But, as I have not yet been able to find a statement of those facts, you will do me a great favor by just informing me where I may find them; and I shall then feel prepared to defend the truth, and to point others to the right source of information.

"There is a meeting of our Ministerial Association tomorrow, and, as I am appointed to read an essay, I design to bring up this whole subject for discussion, and trust that I may thereby do something to spread the truth.

JOSIAH LITCH.— Page 69.

"2d. My second object in writing was to ask if you would put me in the way to obtain a dozen copies of your lectures. I know of none to be obtained here. I know of several individuals who are very desirous to obtain the work, and if you can tell me of any place where it can be obtained in this city, or in New York, you will greatly oblige me. If you can give me any information of importance on the subject, not contained in your book, I should greatly rejoice, because, as I stand a watchman on the walls, I wish to '*give the trumpet a certain sound*,' and to make that sound as full, and explicit, and convincing as possible.

"Yours in the faith of Jesus Christ,

"CHARLES FITCH."

ANOTHER WATCHMAN GIVING THE CRY.

Eld. Josiah Litch, member of New England Methodist Episcopal Conference.

This devoted servant of Christ was highly esteemed by his associates, as a man of thought, of much study, and of great promise for future labors.

"Early in A. D. 1838, a copy of Mr. Miller's lectures was put in Eld. Litch's hand, with the request that he should read it, and give his opinion of its merits. No doubt came into his mind but what he could entirely overthrow the whole system in five minutes. . . . However, to gratify a friend, and from a curiosity to know what arguments could be adduced in support of so novel a doctrine, the book was read. The first chapter was concerning the restitution, and reign of Christ. "Prejudice began to give way, and the idea of the glorious reign of Christ *on the earth renewed*, was most delightful." The reign of Papacy—the 1260 years came up, evidence appeared to be full that they commenced A. D. 538, and terminated 1798. The great argument against the coming of the Lord which appeared so strong and invulnerable, soon vanished, and a new face shone forth from Paul's argument, 2 Thes. ii. The substance of it was, the predicted period having gone by, and the Papacy having been consumed away by the spirit of the Lord's mouth, he is next to be destroyed by the brightness of Christ's coming. Then there can be no Millennium until Christ comes; for the reign of the Man of sin, and a glorious Millennium cannot co-exist. Thus the old fabled Millennium was lost.

"Before concluding the book, I became fully satisfied that the arguments were so clear, so simple, and withal so Scriptural, that it was impossible to disprove the position which Mr. Miller had endeavored to establish.

"The question of duty then presented itself thus:—'If this doctrine is true, ought not you, as a minister of the gospel, to understand and proclaim it?' Yes, certainly I had. 'Then why not do so?' Why, if it should, after all, prove false, where will my reputation be? And besides, if it is not true, it will bring the Bible into disrepute, after the time has gone by. But there is another view to be taken of this subject. How shall we know whether it is true or false? Can it be known except by the testimony of the Scriptures? What do they teach? This is the true question. If it is true that the Lord is coming soon, the world should know it; if it is not true, it should be discussed, and the error exposed. I believe the Bible teaches the doctrine; and while I believe thus, it is my duty to make it known to the extent of my power. It is a Scriptural subject, and one full of interest; and the discussion of it cannot do harm. These prophecies and periods are in the Bible, and mean something; if they do not mean this, what do they mean? Thus I reasoned, until the Lord showed me my own vileness, and made me willing to bear reproach for Christ, when I resolved, at any cost, to present the truth on this subject."

As soon as this decision was formed, Eld. L. wrote a synopsis of Mr. Miller's views, which was published in Lowell, Mass., in a pamphlet of 48 pages, entitled,

The Midnight Cry, or a Review of Mr. Miller's Lectures on the Second Coming of Christ, about A. D. 1843.

This pamphlet was circulated to some considerable extent through New England, and awakened a permanent interest in many minds, many of whom are yet alive and in the faith. This pamphlet was made, by the blessing of God, instrumental in saving souls.

Bro. L. began immediately to preach it wherever he went. He was the first minister in New England, except Eld. Charles Fitch, of Boston, who preached the Second Advent Message, in any specific form.[1]

---

[1] *Advent Shield,* Vol. 1, pp. 54, 56.

In June, 1838, Bro. L. prepared and published a second volume, of 204 pages, entitled,

"The Probability of the Second Coming of Christ, about A. D. 1843."

"It was in this work the calculation on the fall of the Ottoman supremacy on the 11th day of August, 1840, was first given to the world. The calculation was based on the dates in connection with the symbols which illustrate that power, as follows: The star in Rev. ix. 1, he, with most other writers, considered a symbol of Mahomet. Mr. L. commenced the "five months"—(symbolic time—making 150 years), with the supremacy of the Ottoman government, or empire, by Othman, July 27, A. D. 1299, which ended in 1449, when a change came, and the "first woe" closed. The "hour," "day," "month," and "year" of verse 15, he reckoned as symbolic, and made 391 years and 15 days, which, commencing in 1449, would end Aug. 11, 1840, when he calculated the Ottoman Power would lose its independence. So, also, the argument on the 1260 days, showing how all the events which were to precede the time, times and a half, centered in 538, while the decree of Justinian was given in 533."

This book was widely circulated through New England, and awakened more interest than the former work.

As the spring of 1840 opened and summer came, the awakened communities were on the tiptoe of expectation in reference to the anticipated events of Aug. 11th, the fall of the Ottoman empire. Many predicted the day would pass without the event being realized, and that then the spell would be broken, and Adventism would die. Others said, if this calculation proves correct, we will believe the Lord is soon coming. The day came and passed; great anxiety was felt, by believers and unbelievers, about the arrival of news from the east. When it came it informed the people that on the 11th day of August, 1840, the supremacy of the Mahomedan empire was transferred from the Sultan to the Christian powers. This fact discomforted the unbelieving hosts, while it strengthened the believers.

In another part of our book will be found the above calculation and the history of its fulfillment, with full evidence of the fact.

But this calculation and fulfillment of the periods involved are entirely independent of the periods of Daniel, which were expected to end in 1843; and, therefore, the fulfillment of the one is no proof of the correctness of the calculation on the others.

A GREAT INTEREST IN TROY, N. Y.

In compliance with urgent requests, Mr. Miller commenced a course of lectures at West Troy, N. Y., on the 8th of March, and continued till the 15th, when he began in East Troy, where he continued till the 25th. These were attended with happy results. In March of the next year, the Rev. Mr. Parke wrote Mr. Miller as follows:

"It is my privilege to say that God in mercy is doing a great work in West Troy. Old and young and middle-aged are alike made the happy recipients of grace. The Dutch Reformed church are enjoying an interesting state of things. The Methodists are full of the Spirit, and the Baptists are pressing on in the good cause. Praise the Lord! A number date their awakening to your lectures on the Second Coming of Christ. . . . You have great reason to rejoice that God is pleased to make you the honored instrument of awakening poor sinners."

In June following, he again visited his friends in Canada East, and lectured at Outlet on the 10th and 11th, and at Bolton from the 12th to the 14th,—returning home before the end of the month. After this he gave courses of lectures, commencing on the 26th of August, at Braintree, Vt.; on the 16th of September, at White Creek, Vt.; on the 3d of October, at Pittsfield, Vt.; on the 7th, at Randolph, Vt.; and on the 16th at Brookfield, Vt.

This last course was given at the urgent request of Rev. Jehiel Claflin and the Baptist church in that place. As early as the 26th of June, Mr. C. wrote him: "There are a great many people in this and the adjoining towns who are very anxious to hear you lecture on the subject of the Millennium." And, on the 16th of July, he wrote: "I received your favor of the 30th ult., and read the same with much delight, to find that you could gratify the wish of so many friends in this and the adjacent towns. I read your letter in meeting, yesterday, to my congregation; and, some being present from abroad, I consulted them according to your request, and found an increasing anxiety in their minds that you should come and lecture in this vicinity, or near by."

On the 7th of November, he commenced a course of lectures at Montpelier, Vt., which he continued there and in the neighborhood till the 23d. On the 17th, he writes from that place to his son:

"There is a great excitement on the subject in this place. Last night we had a solemn and interesting meeting. There was a great breaking down, and much weeping. Some souls have been born again. I can hardly get away from this people. They want me to stay another week; but I shall go to the next village on Monday. Mr. Kellogg, the Congregational minister here, is a good man, and his church are living Christians. Montpelier is quite a considerable village, and contains some very intelligent people, who appear to listen with much interest. This afternoon I meet the citizens, and am to give them an opportunity to ask questions and state objections. . . . May God help me to give his truth! I know my own weakness, and I know that I have neither power of body nor of mind to do what the Lord is doing by me. It is the Lord's doings and marvelous in our eyes."

A gentleman in this place, on the 20th of February following, wrote to Mr. M. as follows: "I am happy to inform you that your labors with us have been blessed, and twenty have united with our church [the Baptist] since you left Montpelier, and twenty or thirty more will soon join, all of whom date their awakening at the time you lectured here. Brother Kellogg (the Congregationalist minister) is strong in the faith, and his views are with Brother Miller on the second coming of Christ."

On the 24th of November, he commenced a series of lectures in Jericho, Vt., which continued till the 2d of December. On the 28th of this month, he went to Stockbridge, Vt., and on the 30th, to Rochester, where he continued till the 6th of January, 1839.[1]

THE MESSAGE IN MASSACHUSETTS CHURCHES.

In compliance with an invitation from Mr. Seth Mann, of Randolph, Mass., dated Jan. 15, 1839, Mr. Miller reached Randolph, and commenced his first course of lectures in Massachusetts on the 21st of April of that year. He closed his lectures there on the 28th; commenced in Stoughton, Mass., on the 29th, and continued to the 6th of May; lectured at Braintree, Mass., on the 7th and 8th, and from the 9th to the 13th in East Randolph, Mass. His lectures in these places were attended by powerful revivals. On the 27th of May, Mr. Mann wrote to him from Randolph, saying:

---

[1] Life of Miller, pp. 125 to 133.

"The Lord, we trust, is doing a gracious work in this place. There have been twelve or fourteen already converted, and at the close of the last meeting about twenty arose for prayers. Our last conference meeting was so crowded that we had to adjourn to the meeting-house. . . . There appears to be a great solemnity on the minds of nearly all in Mr. M'Leish's society. A powerful work is going on in East Randolph."[1]

Mr. M. writes: This was my first visit to that State. I lectured there, and in Stoughton, East Randolph, Lowell, Groton, and Lynn. I closed my lectures at Lynn on the 10th of June following, making 800 lectures which I had given since June 9, 1834. At Lowell, May 14th, I became acquainted with Elder T. Cole, who had written to me to visit him before I left home. He was among the first ministers in that State who embraced these views, and was the means of introducing me into many of the churches of the Christian connection.[2]

Previous to Mr. Miller's visit to Massachusetts, Elder T. Cole, of Lowell, had heard of the results attending his labors in Vermont, and had written for him to visit that city.

Mr. M. arrived in Lowell and lectured there from the 14th to the 22d of May, and again from the 29th to the 4th of June. A glorious revival followed, and Elder C. embraced his views in full, continuing a devoted advocate of them. On the 25th of July, Elder C. wrote Mr. M. that, since the lectures, he "had baptized about forty, sixty in all having joined the church; and there are yet some who are seeking the Lord." Mr. Miller says of his visit: "At Lowell I also became acquainted with my Bro. J. Litch, who had previously embraced my views, and who has since so aided their extension by his faithful lectures and writings, and energetic and consistent course."

Oct. 13th, Mr. M. commenced his lectures in Groton, Mass., and continued ten days. In reference to these lectures and others in neighboring towns, Eld. Silas Hawley, Congregational minister, wrote from Groton, on the 10th of April, 1840, as follows:

"Mr. Miller has lectured in this and adjoining towns with marked success. His lectures have been succeeded by precious revivals of religion in all those places. A class of minds are reached by him not

---

1 Life of Miller, p. 136.

2 Apology and defense, p. 20.

within the influence of other men. His lectures are well adapted, so far as I have learned, for shaking the supremacy of the various forms of error that are rife in the community."

The editor of the "Lynn Record" gave the following notice of Mr. Miller, and his visit to that place:—

"MILLER AND THE PROPHECIES.

"We took a prejudice against this good man, when he first came among us, on account of what we supposed a glaring error in interpreting the Scripture prophecies so that the world would come to an end in 1843. We are still inclined to believe this an error or miscalculation. At the same time we have overcome our prejudices against him by attending his lectures, and learning more of the excellent character of the man, and of the great good he has done and is doing. Mr. Miller is a plain farmer, and pretends to nothing except that he has made the Scripture prophecies an intense study for many years, understands some of them differently from most other people, and wishes, for the good of others, to spread his views before the public. No one can hear him five minutes without being convinced of his sincerity, and instructed by his reasoning and information. All acknowledge his lectures to be replete with useful and interesting matter. His knowledge of Scripture is very extensive and minute; that of the prophecies, especially, surprisingly familiar. His application of the prophecies to the great events which have taken place in the natural and moral world is such, generally, as to produce conviction of their truth, and gain the ready assent of his hearers. We have reason to believe that the preaching or lecturing of Mr. Miller has been productive of great and extensive good. Revivals have followed in his train. He has been heard with attention wherever he has been. . . .

"There is nothing very peculiar in the manner or appearance of Mr. Miller. Both are at least equal to the style and appearance of ministers in general. His gestures are easy and expressive, and his personal appearance every way decorous. His Scripture explanations and illustrations are strikingly simple, natural, and forcible; and the great eagerness of the people to hear him has been manifested wherever he has preached."

AN EFFORT TO RETARD THE WORK.

As Bro. Miller was the chief proclaimer of the glorious message at this time, reports were put in circulation that he was dead; and as soon as that was successfully contradicted, another was sent afloat that, on re-examining his calculations, he had discovered a mistake of one hundred years. Both of these rumors were several times subsequently revived, and had to be as often contradicted. These were but the beginnings of falsehood and slander which followed.

THE SAME EFFORT MADE IN MARTIN LUTHER'S DAY.

"In the beginning of A. D. 1545, a pamphlet was published by a Romanist, at Naples, to inform the world that Luther was dead, and it professed to give the particulars of his departure. In this veritable publication it was stated that Luther spent his time in gluttony and drunkenness and blasphemy. That perceiving his end to be near he commanded his attendants to place him upon an altar and worship him as a God; that he received the sacrament and immediately died, but the consecrated wafer leaped out of his stomach and remained suspended in the air, to the astonishment of all beholders; that he was buried in a frightful storm of thunder and lightning: the people thought the day of judgment had come. Next morning the tomb was empty, a smell of burning brimstone was intolerable to those who attempted to approach the tomb, and made every one sick, whereupon many repented and joined the Catholics." The landgrave of Hesse sent a copy of this pamphlet to Luther, who published a large edition of it in Italian and German, adding nothing but the following:

"Now, I, Martin Luther, Dr., acknowledge and testify by this present writing, that I received the foregoing angry tale respecting my death, on the 21st of March, and that I have read it with great mirth and jollity, excepting that such blasphemy and lies should be attributed to the high, Divine Majesty. For the rest, it tickles me to the right knee-pan, and my left heel, that the devil and his crew—the Pope and his priests—hate me so heartily. May God convert them from the devil. But if it be decreed that my prayer for a sin which is unto death cannot be answered, then God grant that they may speedily fill up the measure of their iniquity, and do nothing else for their own comfort and joy than to write such books as these.

"BIBLICAL REPOSITORY."

Thus it appears that the devil leads some Protestants into trouble to do the same tricks which bad Catholics did.

The cause of truth is generally rather strengthened than weakened by such efforts. Mr. Miller was living and his work was not finished in the vineyard of the Lord, as we shall learn. From the 2d to the 10th of November, he lectured in Haverhill, Mass., where he made the acquaintance of Eld. Henry Plummer, pastor of the Christian church, who embraced his views, and was a steadfast friend to him, and a faithful minister in the Advent cause, until his death.

On the 11th of November, Mr. Miller commenced a course of lectures in Exeter, N. H., which continued until the 19th. On the 12th, a conference of the Christian connection was in session there, and they called on Mr. Miller in a body. He was a stranger to nearly all of them; and few of them regarded his views with anything more than mere curiosity. Several of them questioned him respecting his faith; but they were speedily silenced by the quotation of appropriate texts of Scripture.

It was on this occasion that he became acquainted with Eld. Joshua V. Himes, then pastor of Chardon-street church, Boston. Eld. H. had written to Mr. Miller, on the 19th of October, inviting him to give a course of lectures in his chapel. He now renewed his invitation, and got promise of a course of lectures in December.

THE ADVENT MESSAGE HEARD IN BOSTON.

Mr. Miller arrived in Boston on the 7th of December, and from the 8th to the 16th lectured in the Chardon-street chapel,—his first course of lectures in that city.

On the 12th of December, Mr. Miller writes from Boston to his son:—"I am now in this place lecturing, twice a day, to large audiences. Many, very many, go away unable to gain admittance. Many, I am informed, are under serious convictions. I hope God will work in this city."

At this time he stopped at the house of Elder Himes, who had much conversation with him respecting his views, his plans for the future, and his responsibilities. Elder H. became impressed with the correctness of Mr. M.'s views respecting the nearness and nature of Christ's coming; but was not fully satisfied respecting the time. He was, however, sufficiently convinced that Mr. Miller was communicating important truths, to feel a great interest in their promulgation.

"When Mr. Miller had closed his lectures," says Elder H., "I found myself in a new position. I could not believe or preach as I had done. Light on this subject was blazing on my conscience day and night. A long conversation with Mr. Miller then took place, on our duties and responsibilities. I said to Bro. Miller, 'Do you really believe this doctrine?'

"He replied, 'Certainly I do, or I would not preach it.'

"'What are you doing to spread or diffuse it through the world?'

"'I have done, and am still doing, all I can.'

"'Well, the whole thing is kept in a corner yet. There is but little knowledge on the subject, after all you have done. If Christ is to come in a few years, as you believe, no time should be lost in giving the church and world warning, in thunder-tones, to arouse them to prepare.'

"'I know it, I know it, Bro. Himes,' said he; 'but what can an old farmer do? I was never used to public speaking: I stand quite alone; and, though I have labored much, and seen many converted to God and the truth, yet *no one*, as yet, seems to enter into the *object* and *spirit of my mission*, so as to render me much aid. They like to have me preach, and build up their churches; and there it ends, with most of the ministers, as yet. I have been looking for help,—I want help.'

"It was at this time that I laid myself, family, society, reputation, all, upon the altar of God, to help him, to the extent of my power, to the end. I then inquired of him what parts of the country he had visited, and whether he had visited any of our principal cities.

"He informed me of his labors,—as given in the foregoing pages.

"'But why,' I said, 'have you not been into the large cities?'

"He replied that his rule was to visit those places where invited, and that he had not been invited into any of the large cities.

"'Well,' said I, 'will you go with me where doors are opened?'

"'Yes, I am ready to go anywhere, and labor to the extent of my ability to the end.'

"I then told him he might prepare for the campaign, for doors should be opened in every city in the Union, and the warning should go to the ends of the earth!"

CHAPTER IV.

FIVE THOUSAND OF MILLER'S LECTURES PUBLISHED IN BOSTON—GREAT REFORMATION IN PORTSMOUTH—ELD. D. I. ROBINSON A CONVERT—MILLER'S TESTIMONY OF HIMES—GREAT REFORMATION IN WATERTOWN—MILLER IN PORTLAND—GREAT REFORMATION—ELD. L. D. FLEMING A CONVERT—THE MAINE WESLEYAN JOURNAL—A SINGULAR RESOLUTION—THE MESSAGE IN NEW YORK CITY.

A NEW ERA IN THE PROCLAMATION OF THE ADVENT MESSAGE.

With this epoch commenced an entire new era in the spread of the doctrine of the Advent. B. B. Mussey, Esq., a distinguished Boston publisher, undertook the publication of a revised edition, of five thousand copies, of Mr. Miller's Lectures, on condition that Mr. Miller would secure the copyright. Mr. M. did so, which subjected himself to some blame, where the reason for the act was not known. Mr. M. gave to Mr. Mussey the entire profits of the edition for two hundred copies of the work, which Mr. Mussey gave him.

On the 17th of December, Mr. M. lectured in Westford, where he was refused the use of the Congregational church,—the first place of worship that was ever closed against him. From the 19th to the 26th of December, he lectured in Littleton, Mass. The result of these lectures is indicated by a letter of Rev. Oliver Ayer (Baptist), who writes, in January:—"I baptized twelve at our last communion. I shall, probably, baptize from fifteen to twenty next time. There have been from thirty-five to forty hopeful conversions. There is also quite a work in Westford,—ten or twelve conversions, and twenty or thirty inquirers. The work is still going on."

On the 28th he retured to Boston, and repeated his course of lectures in Mr. Himes' chapel, closing on the 5th of January, 1840. The day following, by request of the Baptist church under the care of the Rev. Mr. Parker, he visited Cambridgeport, and lectured there each day till the 13th of January. From the 14th to the 20th, he gave a second course of lectures to Elder Plummer's society, in Haverhill, Mass.

A GREAT REFORMATION IN PORTSMOUTH.

On the 21st of January, 1840, he visited Portsmouth, N. H., and commenced his first course of lectures in that city. The following article, in reference to them, from the pen of Elder David Millard, pastor of the Christian Society there, appeared in the columns of the Christian Herald, a few weeks subsequently:

"On the 21st of January, Bro. William Miller came into town, and commenced, in our chapel, his course of lectures on the Second Coming of Christ. During the nine days that he remained crowds flocked to hear him. Before he concluded his lectures a large number of anxious souls came forward for prayers. Our meetings continued, every day and evening, for a length of time, after he left. Such an intense state of feeling as now pervaded our congregation we never witnessed before in any place. Not unfrequently from sixty to eighty would come forward for prayers on an evening. Such an awful spirit of solemnity seemed to settle down on the place that hard must be that sinner's heart that could withstand it. Yet, during the whole, not an appearance of confusion occurred; all was order and solemnity. Generally, as soon as souls found deliverance, they were ready to proclaim it, and exhort their friends, in the most moving language, to come to the fountain of life. Our meetings thus continued, on evenings, for six weeks; indeed, they have thus continued, with very little intermission, up to the present.

"Probably about one hundred and fifty souls have been converted in our meetings; but a part of these were from other congregations, and have returned to their former meetings. Among the converts are a considerable number from the Universalist congregation; these still remain with us. From our meetings this blessed work soon spread into every congregation in town favorable to revivals. In several of them it is at present spreading with power. For weeks together, the ringing of bells, for daily meetings, rendered our town like a continual Sabbath. Indeed, such a season of revival was never witnessed before in Portsmouth by the oldest inhabitant. It would be difficult, at present, to ascertain the exact number of conversions in town; it is variously estimated at from five hundred to seven hundred. We have received into fellowship eighty-one; nine of these were received on previous profession. We have baptized sixty-seven, and the others stand as candidates for baptism. Never, while we linger on the shores of mortality, do we expect to enjoy more of heaven than we have in some of our late meetings, and on baptizing occasions. At the water-side thousands would gather to witness this solemn institution in Zion, and many would return from the place weeping. Our brethren at the old chapel have had some additions, —we believe some over twenty."

The Rev. Mr. Peabody, of Portsmouth, in a sermon, published soon after, spoke of the revival which commenced there in connection with Mr. Miller's labors, as follows:

"If I am rightly informed, the present season of religious excitement has been, to a great degree, free from what, I confess, has always made me dread such times,—I mean those excesses and extravagances which wound religion in the house of its friends, and cause its enemies to blaspheme. I most cheerfully express my opinion that there will be, in the fruits of the present excitement, far less to regret, and much more for the friends of God to rejoice in,—much more to be recorded in the book of eternal life,—than in any similar series of religious exercises which I have ever had the opportunity of watching."

ELDER D. I. ROBINSON A CONVERT.

At the time of these lectures, Elder D. I. Robinson was stationed in Portsmouth, as the pastor of the Methodist church, and attended a part of the course. He writes:—

"I heard him all I could the first week, and thought I could stop his wheels and confound him; but, as the revival had commenced in the vast congregation assembled to hear, I would not do it publicly, lest evil should follow. I, therefore, visited him at his room, with a formidable list of objections. To my surprise, scarcely any of them were new to him, and he could answer them as fast as I could present them. And then he presented objections and questions which confounded *me*, and the commentaries on which I had relied. I went home used up, convicted, humbled, and resolved to examine the question."

The result was that Elder R. became convinced of the nearness of the Advent, and has since been a faithful preacher of the kingdom at hand. Elder Thomas F. Barry, also, at this time embraced Mr.

Miller's views, and continued an able and consistent advocate of the same till his death, at Oswego, N. Y., July 17, 1846.

On the 30th and 31st of January, Mr. M. again lectured in Exeter, N. H., and from the 2d to the 6th of February, in Deerfield, N. H., after which he returned to Boston.

PUBLICATION OF THE "SIGNS OF THE TIMES" COMMENCED.

From the 8th to the 29th of February, Mr. M. gave his third course of lectures in Boston, in the Marlboro' chapel and other places, as the doors opened. It was during this series of meetings that the publication of a journal, devoted to the doctrine of the Advent, was effected. Mr. Miller (in 1845) thus narrates its origin:—

"For a long time previous to this, the papers had been filled with abusive stories respecting my labors, and they had refused to publish anything from me in reply. I had greatly felt the need of some medium of communication to the public. Efforts had been frequently made to commence the publication of a paper which should be devoted to the advocacy of the doctrine, and the communication of information on the fulfillment of prophecy. We had, however, never been able to find a man who was willing to run the risk of his reputation and the pecuniary expense, in such a publication.

On my visit to Boston in the winter of 1840, I mentioned to Brother Himes my wishes respecting a paper, and the difficulties I had experienced in the establishment of one. He promptly offered to commence a paper which should be devoted to this question, if I thought the cause of truth would be thereby advanced. The next week, without a subscriber or any promise of assistance, he issued the first No. of the Signs of the Times, on the 20th of March [28th of February], 1840—a publication [now Advent Herald] which has been continued to the present time.

"With this commenced an entire new era in the spread of information on the peculiar points of my belief. Mr. Mussey gave up to him the publication of my lectures, and he published them in connection with other works on the prophecies, which, aided by devoted friends, he scattered broadcast everywhere to the extent of his means. I cannot here withhold my testimony to the efficiency and integrity of my Bro. Himes. He has stood by me at all times, perilled his reputation, and, by the position in which he has been placed, has been more instrumental in the spread of these views than any other ten men who have embarked in the cause. His course, both in laboring as a lecturer and in the manner that he has managed his publications, meets my full approval." [1]

ELDER JOSIAH LITCH'S SKETCH OF ELDER HIMES' WORK.

Mr. Miller's first course of lectures in Boston, constituted a new era in the history of the ADVENT MESSAGE. An excitement was produced in Boston which demanded light, and prepared the public mind to sustain the enterprise of hiring the Marlboro' chapel for a course of lectures. From that point an influence was extended through all the adjacent country; and such was the demand for light, that it was determined to issue a new and revised edition of the lectures. Bro. Himes cheerfully undertook the revision of the work and superintendence of publication (without fee or reward), which a Boston publisher agreed to do if he could have the profits arising from five thousand copies. This he had. After selling the five thousand copies, Mr. Mussey, the publisher, concluded that the demand was over. For the purpose of supplying the public, Mr. Himes then undertook, at the earnest solicitations and advice of friends, the publication of the work himself. At the same time he abandoned the copy-right, and thus, to save reproach on the cause, exposed himself to the competition of any and all who chose to compete with him. The same course has been pursued in reference to all his other publications.

"Notwithstanding all this, all that the tongue of slander could invent, has been heaped upon him for the stand he took and the self-denying course he pursued on this subject."

"At a juncture when the storm of opposition grew heavy, the providence of God raised up a man for this work also.

"That unwearied friend of the cause, J. V. Himes, who has so nobly stood in the front of the hosts and the hottest of the fire, came forward and threw himself into the enterprise, to make up the breach. On the 20th of March, 1840, without money, patrons, or scarcely friends, he issued the first number of the 'Signs of the Times.' The appearance of that sheet was hailed with joy by many a longing heart, waiting for the consolation of Israel. The paper was sustained for the first year at a considerable expense to the editor, besides his own unrequited toil. As might be expected, the enemies of the cause were greatly discommoded by the appearance of such a weapon, both offensive and defensive. . . . From the position he has occupied in the front of the battle, the most deadly shafts of the enemy have been aimed at him. The generous spirit of self-sacrifice, with which he came forward and exerted every nerve for the advancement of this great work, excited at once the envy, the wrath, the anger and calumny of the whole host of foes to the doctrine. And no means which could be devised to blast his influence has been wanting from

---

[1] Apology and defence, p. 21.

that to the present time. But through grace he has thus far triumphed. From the commencement of his course as an advocate of this cause, the writer has been on terms of intimacy with him, and has known his whole course, and feels it to be a great pleasure to say, that a more noble-hearted, generous, and self-denying man never engaged in any enterprise. That the Advent book establishment has yielded profits which might have enriched him is true; but that it has done this, is utterly false and groundless. The funds which have accrued from the sale of books, have been appropriated to the advancement of the work of God, the spreading of the glad tidings of his kingdom. The labors and fatigues he has endured in the work which has engrossed his attention, are too well known to require repetition here. No man can be found whose labors have been more abundant and arduous than his.

"This is a strain to which my pen is unused; and so it should remain, did not the vile and slanderous insinuations which have been made against him demand it at my hand. An attempt to give a history of the Second Advent cause would not be complete without such a testimony."[1]

After the issue of the first No., its printers, Messrs Dow & Jackson, proposed to Elder Himes to issue the paper semi-monthly for one year, he to furnish the editorial matter gratuitously, and they to have all the proceeds of it. These terms being accepted, they re-issued the first No. on the 20th of March, and continued it, as per agreement, for one year, when it reverted to Elder Himes, its projector, by whom it has been continued to 1858.

THE MESSAGE IN WATERTOWN, MASS.—GREAT REVIVAL.

On the 1st of March, 1840, Mr. M. visited Watertown, Mass., and commenced his first course of lectures in that place. These continued nine days, and were attended by a crowded audience. Mr. M. was much pleased with his reception there, and, after leaving, wrote to his son:—

"I have never seen so great an effect in any one place as there. I preached last from Gen. xix. 17. There were from a thousand to fifteen hundred present, and more than one hundred under conviction. One-half of the congregation wept like children when I parted from them. Mr. Medbury, the Baptist minister, a good man, wept as though his heart would break when he took me by the hand, and, for himself and people, bade me farewell. He and many others fell upon my neck, and wept and kissed me, and sorrowed most of all that they should see my face no more. We could not get away for

[1]Advent Shield, pp. 57, 58, 85, 86.

more than an hour, and finally we had to break away. About twenty were converted while I was there."

Rev. R. B. Medbury afterwards gave the following account of the result of Mr. Miller's lectures there, through the "Signs of the Times":—

"For several months past we have enjoyed, and are still enjoying, a pleasing work of grace among us. This revival, as stated in the account published in the Christian Watchman of the 8th instant, was in progress when Mr. Miller commenced lecturing here. In speaking of the results of his labors, however, it is but just to say that his influence here preceded him. It will be recollected that, some time in January, he lectured at Cambridgeport, about four miles from us. Many, both of our church and congregation, attended one or more of those lectures. The first two subjects of the present work among us, as well as some others, who have since been hopefully converted, regarded those lectures as instrumental of fastening permanent conviction upon their minds. Several Christians, too, were awakened to a new sense of their duty.

"There had, however, been rather more feeling than usual in several of our meetings previous to that time. And in the interval which elapsed between this time and the commencement of Mr. Miller's lectures here, the blessing of God had accompanied the means of grace at home to the hopeful conversion of about twenty. The work evidently received a new impulse while Mr. Miller was here. His lectures were attended by crowds, who listened with profound attention, and, we have reason to believe, in not a few cases with profit. Many persons from neighboring villages shared the benefit of his labors in common with us, and, in several cases, returned to their homes rejoicing. Other means of grace were, however, mingled with his labors, which were, no doubt, in a great degree owned and blessed of God.

"Among those who have since united with our church, many have mentioned Mr. Miller's lectures as the means, under God, of bringing them to repentance. They have generally stated that, for months or years, they had thought more or less on the subject; but that, on hearing him, they felt it was time to take a stand. The things of eternity assumed to them an unwonted reality. Heaven was brought near, and they felt themselves guilty before God.

IT WAS NOT SO MUCH THE BELIEF THAT CHRIST MIGHT COME IN 1843 as it was the *certainty* of that event, with the conviction that they were not prepared to hail his coming with joy. Many, however, who listened to his whole course of lectures with a heart unmoved, have since been melted into contrition, and become the hopeful subjects of renewing grace.

"Many Christians who attended Mr. Miller's lectures here have regarded them as the means of quickening them to new spiritual life. I know not that any one has embraced all his peculiar views; but many have been made to feel that time is short, that the coming of Christ is at hand, and that what they do for their fellow-men must be done quickly. They have felt that hitherto the doctrine of the second coming of Christ has had little or no practical effect upon them, and that, while they could suppose at least one thousand years between that event and the present time, its influence must be less than if it were a matter of constant expectation. They think that the contemplation of this subject has awakened feelings which the anticipation of death never kindled in their breasts. Earth has receded, and their attachment to all sublunary objects has been loosened. Eternity has seemed to open near before them, and its scenes have become more distinct objects of vision; while the soul, with all that pertains to its immortal weal or woe, has been felt to eclipse every other object of earth. In a word, they profess to have consecrated themselves unto the service of God, and to labor to be found watching whenever the Master of the house shall come, 'whether at even, or at midnight, or at the cock-crowing, or in the morning, lest, coming suddenly, he should find them sleeping.'

"WATERTOWN, May 21, 1840."

THE SECOND ADVENT MESSAGE IN PORTLAND, ME.—GREAT REVIVAL.

In compliance with the wishes of Elder L. D. Fleming, pastor of the Christian church in Portland, Me., Mr. Miller visited and gave his first course of lectures in that city, from the 11th to the 23d of March. The result of these was thus stated by Elder Fleming, in April following:

"There has probably never been so much religious interest among the inhabitants of this place, generally, as at present; and Mr. Miller must be regarded, directly or indirectly, as the instrument, although many, no doubt, will deny it, as some are very unwilling to admit that a good work of God can follow his labors; and yet we have the most indubitable evidence that this is the work of the Lord. It is worthy of note that in the present interest there has been, comparatively, nothing like mechanical effort. There has been nothing like passionate excitement. If there has been excitement, it has been out of doors, among such as did not attend Brother Miller's lectures.

"At some of our meetings, since Brother M. left, as many as two hundred and fifty, it has been estimated, have expressed a desire for religion, by coming forward for prayers; and probably between *one* and *two hundred* have professed conversion at our meetings; and now the fire is being kindled through this whole city and all the adjacent country. A number of rum-sellers have turned their shops into meeting-rooms, and those places that were once devoted to intemperance and revelry are now devoted to prayer and praise. Others have abandoned the traffic entirely, and are become converted to God. One or two gambling establishments, I am informed, are entirely broken up. Infidels, Deists, Universalists, and the most abandoned profligates, have been converted,—some who had not been to the house of worship for years. Prayer-meetings have been established in every part of the city, by the different denominations, or by individuals, and at almost every hour. Being down in the business part of our city, on the 4th inst., I was conducted into a room over one of the banks, where I found about thirty or forty men, of different denominations, engaged, with one accord, in prayer, at about eleven o'clock in the day-time! In short, it would be almost impossible to give an adequate idea of the interest now felt in the city. There is nothing like extravagant excitement, but an almost universal solemnity on the minds of all the people. One of the principal booksellers informed me that he had sold more Bibles in *one month*, since Mr. Miller came here, than he had in any four months previous."

AN ARTICLE IN THE MAINE "WESLEYAN JOURNAL"

gave the following account of his person, and style of preaching:

"Mr. Miller has been in Portland, lecturing to crowded congregations in Casco-street church, on his favorite theme, the end of the world, or literal reign of Christ for one thousand years. As faithful chroniclers of passing events, it will be expected of us that we should say something of the man and his peculiar views. Mr. Miller is about sixty years of age; a plain farmer, from Hampton, in the State of New York. He is a member of the Baptist church in that place, from which he brings satisfactory testimonials of good standing, and a license to improve publicly. He has, we understand, numerous testimonials, also, from clergymen of different denominations, favorable to his general character. We should think him a man but of common-school education; evidently possessing strong powers of mind, which, for about fourteen years, have been almost exclusively bent to the investigation of Scripture prophecies. The last eight years of his life have been devoted to lecturing on this favorite subject.

"In his public discourse, he is self-possessed and ready; distinct in his utterance, and frequently quaint in his expressions. He succeeds in chaining the attention of his auditory from an hour and a half to two hours; and in the management of his subject discovers much tact, holding frequent colloquies with the objector and inquirer, supplying the questions and answers himself in a very natural manner, and, although grave himself, sometimes producing a smile from a portion of his auditors.

. . . .

"Mr. Miller is a great stickler for literal interpretations; never admitting the figurative, unless absolutely required to make correct sense, or meet the event which is intended to be pointed out. He doubtless believes, most unwaveringly, all he teaches to others. His lectures are interspersed with powerful admonitions to the wicked, and he handles Universalism with gloves of steel."

In connection with the foregoing was appended a statement of Mr. M.'s opinions, which elicited from him the following comment:

"In all the cities which I have visited, the editors of religious newspapers have almost invariably misstated and ridiculed my views, doctrines, and motives; but in Portland I found, as I honestly believe, an honest editor. He gave a candid, honest, and impartial account."

A SINGULAR RESOLUTION.

The following resolution was passed by a conference of Baptist ministers, held in Boston on anniversary week, in 1840:

"Resolved, that this conference consider it an occasion of special

JOSHUA VAUGHAN HIMES.—Page 59.

gratitude to God that the revivals of religion, now so general through the land, have mainly commenced and proceeded under the ministrations of the regular pastors, aided by the members of the churches."

Who ever disputed this? Why such a resolution? Had they ever heard that many thousands were dating their convictions and conversion from hearing Mr. Miller's lectures?

THE SECOND ADVENT MESSAGE IN NEW YORK CITY.

Mr. Miller visited New York City, and delivered his first course of lectures there, from the 16th to the 29th of May, 1840, at the corner of Norfolk and Broome streets, to large assemblies of deeply anxious hearers; but we must not continue to detail so many particulars.

We have been led to detail many of these special points and labors of Mr. Miller thus far, because up to this period he was the chief laborer in giving this proclamation in this country; also, the accounts of the work of the Lord in the conversion of such vast numbers of souls, forms the most interesting and impressive feature of the history of this message.

The proclamation now begins to assume more important claims upon the people, as the instrumentalities increase for giving it an extensive circulation, and its votaries begin to multiply more rapidly. Books, tracts, and a paper devoted to this message, were soon issued to carry the "glad tidings" to all Christendom that "the King of kings" was coming soon, to establish a righteous government in all the earth. Surely, such news must be welcome to all lovers of righteousness and peace.

SKETCH OF ELD. J. V. HIMES, AND HIS LABORS.

Joshua Vaughn Himes was born in Wickford, R. I., May 19, 1805. He went to New Bedford in 1822; while there he was converted under the labors of Eld. Simon Clough, and united with the First Christian church Feb. 2, 1823. He became an earnest exhorter, and soon felt it his duty to preach the gospel; he commenced holding meetings in the neighboring school houses, and revivals followed his labors. In 1827 he left his secular calling and entered upon the work of the ministry, as the work of his life. He began in Plymouth, Mass., where a revival followed his labors, a church was soon organized and a chapel was built the first year. He was then appointed Evangelist by the Massachusetts Christian Conference to labor in the southern part of the State till the autumn of 1828, when he located at Fall River, Mass. Here there was an extensive revival, and a church of one hundred and twenty-five members was organized, most of whom he baptized in Founton River.

In the year 1830, Eld. Isaac C. Goff resigned the pastoral care of the First Christian church in Boston, Mass., and Elder Himes was invited to take the pastoral care of that people; he accepted and continued his labors with them till 1837, when he resigned. The church had been built up from about seven families, with which he began, and the house was filled during his ministry. In 1837 he organized the Second Christian church in Hanover street, who the next year built a chapel in Chardon street, and removed thither; the new church prospered and their new place of worship was filled.

In 1839 Eld. Himes, heard, examined, and embraced the views of Mr. Miller, relating to the prophecies, and the chronology of the age of the world, and the soon coming of Christ. From that until the present he has devoted his whole time, talent, energies, influence, and means to the proclamation of the great and glorious Second Advent Message, as will be readily seen in our history of it; for we find his name connected with almost every department of the work; his publications have been abundant. His zeal and devotion to this work placed him with Mr. Miller, in the front ranks as one of its most efficient agents and advocates. It should be expected that a man of his temperament—his zeal and success in the work—would provoke opposition, jealousy and ambition, which would subject him to the attacks, tricks, avarice and machinations of aspirants, and of foes, who might desire his position with its seeming advantages, or wish to destroy the good work they were not competent or disposed to equal. Eld. Himes has not escaped these head winds and rough seas, yet they have generally worked for the wider circulation of the message of the coming kingdom and for his greater usefulness.

He has published and superintended more papers, tracts, and books, and circulated more gratuitously, than any other man or society connected with the Second Advent Message. He has been supplied with liberal donations, and has used the earnings of his own exertions and labors, with which to do this vast amount of publishing. It was estimated by Mr. Bliss, his agent and editor, that he had issued over ten millions of publications from the Boston office alone, prior to 1854, beside the immense numbers from other offices. He has probably traveled more miles, preached more sermons, baptised more believers, discipled more to the faith, than any other one man on the American continent.

He has visited England, Scotland, and Ireland, as a missionary, he has traveled and labored in nearly all the States in the Union (California with the others), and the adjoining provinces. Open, frank, independent, courteous, liberal, sympathetic, and aggressive, he has a great faculty to enlist the attention and hearts of the people.

When thwarted or hindered by his enemies, through unguarded remarks or misplaced confidence in them, he has sometimes proved a severe antagonist, but exceedingly merciful, and too confiding, at the least approach of penitence on their part, and too ready to trust them before they *show fruits* of penitence.

In 1863, having several years previous transferred the "Advent Herald," and his entire interest in the Advent Herald Office, in Boston, to others, he established "The Voice of the West," in Buchanan, Mich.; now "Advent Christian Times," Chicago, Ill., a weekly paper wholly in the interest of the advent cause, and there published in connection with the paper, many valuable books and tracts on the advent doctrine and kindred subjects, which have been widely scattered over the western field with much success.

Having resigned his office as editor and manager of the office of the Western Advent Christian Publication Association, he still continues to travel and preach. At the age of about seventy years, his interest and ardor is unabated; though his bodily vigor and intellectual powers are somewhat diminished, he is yet full of faith and hope, expecting the glorious advent of Christ in this generation.

But in all this work the Lord has accomplished all that was good, and will have all the glory. Bro. H. is but a frail mortal, subject to the weaknesses and imperfections of us all; what has not been good is the work of fallen human nature. It is not to be expected that all the work, above alluded to, has been perfect; mistakes have been made, missteps have been taken, complaints have been heard, investigations had, inconsistencies and perhaps serious faults discovered, and confessed and corrected. Who of us could experience a life so eventful, with so much opposition, and such prosperity and success with less faults? Mercy and grace through Jesus' blood, is the only hope for any and all of us.

During his ministry of more than forty years, Eld. H. has organized over three hundred churches, assisted in organizing fourteen State and sectional conferences, and immersed over fifteen hundred souls. The greatest number he ever immersed at one time was *eighty-three,* in Mystic river, Charlestown, Mass., near Bunker Hill.

He has traveled some 20,000 miles a year a portion of the time, lecturing on an average of once each day much of the time, and during the forty years has held about 5,000 meetings.

He has been blessed in having the most of his family associated with him in the faith and work. His faithful wife has been in full sympathy with him in all his sacrifices and toils. His son, John L. G., was a faithful and active believer and worker, until he fell in death; his son, Edwin T., was a faithful, Christian, and earnest and judicious minister, greatly beloved by the friends of Christ. He sleeps in death. Wm. L. has been an earnest and faithful Christian, a great worker in the cause, an able editor, and is now a useful minister in preaching the gospel of the kingdom of God.

CHAPTER V.

THE INTRODUCTION TO MR. MILLER'S LECTURES.—RULES OF INTERPRETING PROPHECY, SYMBOLS, FIGURES, METAPHORS, PARABLES, AND TYPES.—INDEX TO HIS LECTURES.—LECTURE ON THE SEVEN CHURCHES OF ASIA.—LITCH'S LETTER.—J. D. BRIDGE IN ZION'S HERALD.—LITCH'S ADDRESS TO THE PUBLIC.—THE WOE TRUMPETS.

WE shall here give our readers Mr. Miller's "introduction" to his published lectures, because it contains much valuable instruction for all. Also, the "Index," containing the subjects treated upon. We also add one of his lectures, as it contains ideas of great importance, and gives a sample of the arguments which have done so much to bring the erring to Christ, and to awaken a slumbering church to look for the return of Christ to judge the world.

The errors of Mr. M. in his application of the prophetic numbers, we think, are not so wide from the truth, nor so injurious in their effects, as the errors and perversions of the learned doctors and professors who sought to stop his message.

INTRODUCTION.

IN presenting these Lectures to the public, the writer is only complying with the solicitations of some of his friends, who have requested that his views on the Prophecies of Daniel and John might be made public. The reader is therefore requested to give the subject a careful and candid perusal, and compare every part with the standard of Divine Truth; for if the explanation the writer has given to the Scriptures under consideration should prove correct, the reader will readily perceive that it concerns us all, and becomes doubly important to us, because we live on the eve of one of the most important events ever revealed to man by the wisdom of God,—the judgment of the great day.

In order that the reader may have an understanding of my manner of studying the Prophecies, by which I have come to the following result, I have thought proper to give some of the rules of interpretation which I have adopted to understand prophecy.

Prophetical scripture is very much of it communicated to us by figures and highly and richly adorned metaphors; by which I mean that figures, such as *beasts, birds, air or wind, water, fire, candlesticks, lamps, mountains, islands, &c.,*

are used to represent things prophesied of—such as kingdoms, warriors, principles, people, judgments, churches, word of God, large and smaller governments. It is metaphorical also, showing some peculiar quality of the thing prophesied of, by the most prominent feature or quality of the figure used, as *beasts*—if a *lion*, power and rule; if a *leopard*, celerity; if a *bear*, voracious; an *ox*, submissive; a *man*, proud and independent. *Fire* denotes justice and judgment in its figure; in the metaphor, denotes the purifying or consuming up the dross or wickedness; as *fire* has a cleansing quality, so will the justice or judgments of God. "For when thy judgments are in the earth, the inhabitants of the world will learn righteousness." Therefore almost all the figures used in prophecy have their literal and metaphorical meaning; as *beasts* denote, literally, a kingdom, so metaphorically good or bad, as the case may be, to be understood by the subject in connection.

To understand the literal meaning of figures used in prophecy, I have pursued the following method:—I find the word "*beast*" used in a figurative sense; I take my concordance, trace the word, and in Daniel vii. 17, it is explained to mean "kings or kingdoms." Again, I come across the words "*bird or fowl*," and in Isa. xlvi. 11, it is used, meaning a conqueror or warrior,—Cyrus. Also, in Ezekiel xxxix. 4–9, denotes armies or conquerors. Again, the words "*air or wind*," as used in Rev. ix. 2, and in 16, 17, to understand which I turn to Eph. ii. 2, and 4–14, and there learn that it is used as a fignre to denote the theories of worldly men or vain philosophy. Again, "*water or rivers*" are used as figures in Rev. xvii. 15, it is explained to mean "people or nations." "*Rivers*" of course mean the nation or people living on the river mentioned, as in Rev. xvi. 12. "*Fire*" is often used in a figurative sense; explained in Num. xxi. 27, 28, Deut. xxxii. 22, Psal. lxxviii. 21, Heb. xii. 29, to mean justice and judgment.

As prophecy is a language somewhat different from other parts of Scripture, owing to its having been revealed in vision, and that highly figurative, yet God in his wisdom has so interwoven the several prophecies, that the events foretold are not all told by one prophet, and although they lived and prophesied in different ages of the world, yet they tell us the same things; so you take away one, and a link will be wanting. There is a general connection through the whole; like a well regulated community they all move in unison, speaking the same things, observing the same rules, so that a Bible reader may almost with propriety suppose, let him read in what prophecy he may, that he is reading the same prophet, the same author. This will appear evident to any one who will compare scripture with scripture. There never was a book written that has a better connection and harmony than the Bible, and yet it has the appearance of a great store-house, full of all the precious commodities heart could desire, thrown in promiscuously; therefore, the biblical student must select and bring together every part of the subject he wishes to investigate, from every part of the Bible; then let every word have its own Scripture meaning, every sentence its proper bearing, and have no contradiction, and your theory will and must of necessity be correct. Truth is one undeviating path, that grows brighter and brighter the more it is trodden; it needs no plausible arguments nor pompous dress to make it more bright, for the more naked and simple the fact, the stronger the truth appears.

Let it be noticed that God has revealed to his prophets the same events in divers figures and at different times, as he has to Daniel in the second, seventh, and eighth chapters concerning the four kingdoms; or to Peter (see Acts x. 16); also, Isaiah and John. Then, to get the whole truth, all those visions or prophecies must be concentrated and brought together, that have reference to the subject which we wish to investigate; and when combined, let every word and sentence have its proper bearing and force in the grand whole, and the theory or system, as I have before shown, must be correct. I have likewise noticed that in those events, visions, and prophecies which have had their fulfillment, every word and every particular has had an exact and literal accomplishment, and that no two events have ever happened, that I can learn, which will exactly apply or fulfill the same prophecy. Take, for instance, the prophecies concerning the birth, life, and crucifixion of our Saviour, and in his history we find a literal fulfillment; yet in the birth, life, or death of any other individual it would be in vain to find a parallel. Again, take the prophecies which have been admitted, by Protestants at least, to apply to Cyrus, Alexander, Julius Cæsar, destruction of Jerusalem, and the church of Rome, and I have never been able to trace even a resemblance to the prophecies in question in any historical events except the true ones. If this is true, may we not suppose that the unfulfilled prophecies in their accomplishments will be equally as evident and literal?

There are two important points to which all prophecy seems to centre, like a cluster of grapes upon its stem—the first and second coming of Christ; the first coming to proclaim the gospel, suffer for sinners, and bring in an everlasting righteousness. His second coming, to which the ardent faith and pious hope of the tried and tempted child of God centres, is for complete redemption from sin, for the justification and glorification promised to all those who look for his appearing, the destruction of the wicked and mystical Babylon, the abomination of the whole earth.

His first coming was as a man, his human nature being only visible, his Godhead known only in his miracles. His second coming will be as God, his divine Godhead and power being most visible. He comes first, like the "first man of the earth, earthy;" his second coming is "the Lord from heaven." His first coming was literally according to the prophecies. And so we may safely infer will be his second appearance, according to the Scriptures. At his advent, his forerunner was spoken of—"one crying in the wilderness;" the manner of his birth—"a child born of a virgin;" the place where—"Bethlehem of Judea;" the time of his death—"when seventy weeks should be fulfilled;" for what he should suffer—"to make an end of sins, to make reconciliation for iniquity, and to bring in everlasting righteousness, to seal up the vision and prophecy, and to anoint the Most Holy." The *star* that appeared, the *stripes* he received, the *miracles* he performed, the *tauntings* of his foes—all were literally fulfilled. Then, why not suppose that all the prophecies concerning his second coming will be as literally accomplished as the former? Can any man show a single reason why it will not? If this be true, we can obtain much light by reading the Scriptures. We are there informed of the manner of his second coming—"suddenly, in the clouds, in like manner as he ascended;" the majesty of his coming—"on a great white throne, with power and great glory, and all his saints with him;" the object of his coming—"as the Ancient of Days, to send his angels into the four winds of heaven, gather his elect, raise the righteous dead, change the righteous living, chain Satan, destroy anti-Christ, the wicked, and all those who destroy the earth, judge, justify, and glorify his people, cleanse his church, present her to his Father, live and reign with her on the new heavens and new earth," the form of the old having passed away.

The time when these things shall take place is also specified, by some of the prophets, unto 2300 days (meaning years); then shall the sanctuary be cleansed, after the anti-Christian beast has reigned her "time, times, and a half;" after the two witnesses have prophesied "a thousand two hundred and threescore days, clothed in sack-cloth;" after the church captivity in the wilderness, "forty-two months;" after the "gospel should be preached in all the world for a witness, then shall the end come." The signs of the times are also given, when we may know he is near, even at the door. When there are many "lo heres and lo theres;" when the way of truth is evil-spoken of; when many seducers are abroad in the land; when scoffers disbelieve in his coming, and say, "Where is the promise of his coming;" when the wise and foolish virgins are called to trim their lamps, and the voice of the friend of the bridegroom is, "Behold, he cometh;" when the city of the nations is divided into three parts; when the power of the holy people is scattered, and the kings of the east come up to battle; and the church in her Laodicean state; when the seventh seal opens, the seventh vial is poured out, the last woe pronounced by the angel flying through the midst of heaven, and the seventh and last trumpet sounds;—then will the mystery of God be finished, and the door of mercy be closed forever; then shall we be brought to the last point, his second coming.

Again, prophecy is sometimes typical; that is, partly fulfilled in the type, but completely only in the antitype. Such was the prophecy concerning Isaac, partly fulfilled in him, wholly so in Christ; likewise concerning Israel, partly fulfilled in them as a nation, but never fully accomplished until the final redemption of spiritual Israel. Likewise the prophecies concerning the Jewish captivity in Babylon, and their return, are only partly accomplished in the history of past events. The description of those things in the prophets is so august and magnificent, that if only applicable to the literal captivity of the Jews and their return, the exposition would be weak and barren; therefore I humbly believe that the exact fulfillment can only be looked for in the captivity of the church in the wilderness, under the anti-Christian beast, destruction of mystical Babylon, and glorification of the saints in the New Jerusalem.

There are also in the 24th chapter of Matthew many things prophesied of, which were not fulfilled at the destruction of Jerusalem; such as the coming of the Son of Man in the clouds, the gathering his elect from the four winds of heaven, his taking one and leaving another. This shows a typical meaning in this prophecy, and that it will not all be fulfilled until the end of the world. Also, the transfiguration of Christ on the mount, prophesied of by himself eight days before, is noticed by Peter, 2d Epistle, i. 16—18, as being a type or figure of his second coming.

Who, that has read the prophecies with any degree of attention, will not acknowledge the great agreement between the Old Testament prophecies and the New? Almost every prophecy given by Christ and his apostles may be found, in the Old Testament prophets, represented by figures, which were familiar to the writers and readers of those times. The foregoing rules are some of the principal ones which I have observed in attempting to explain the prophecies of Daniel and John, and to give the time when the mystery of God will be finished, as I humbly believe it is revealed to the prophets.

If I have erred in my exposition of the prophecies,[1] the time, being so near at hand, will soon expose my folly; but if I have the truth on the subjects treated on in these pages, how important the era in which we live! What vast and important events must soon be realized! and how necessary that every individual be prepared, that that day may not come upon them unawares, while they are surfeited with the cares and riches of this life, and the day overtake them as a thief! "But ye, brethren, are not in darkness, that that day should overtake you as a thief," 1 Thess. v. 4. In studying these prophecies, I have endeavored to divest myself of all prepossessed opinions, not warranted by the word of God, and to weigh well all the objections that might be raised from the Scriptures; and after fourteen years' study of the prophecies and other parts of the Bible, I have come to the following conclusions, and do now commit myself into the hands of God as my Judge, in giving publicity to the sentiments herein contained, conscientiously desiring that this little book may be the means to incite others to study the Scriptures, and to see whether these things be so, and that some minds may be led to believe in the word of God, and find an interest in the offering and sacrifice of the Lamb of God, that their sins might be forgiven them through the blood of the atonement, "when the refreshing shall come from the presence of the Lord, and from the glory of his power," "when he comes to be admired in all them that believe in that day."

And now, my dear readers, I beg of you to lay aside prejudice; examine this subject candidly and carefully for yourselves. Your belief or unbelief will not

---

[1] In this remark Mr. Miller has reference to his adjustment of the prophetic periods, in which he felt conscious he might be in error. It proved an error, but that does uot at all affect his application of the other prophecies and promises.

affect the truth. If it is so, whatever you may think or do will not alter the revealed purposes of God. "Not one jot or tittle of his word will fail;" but you may, by your obedience in the faith, secure you an interest in the first resurrection, and a glorious admittance into the New Jerusalem, and an inheritance among the justified in glory, and you may sit down with Abraham, Isaac, and Jacob, in the kingdom of God. May this be your lot—is the prayer of your servant,

WM. MILLER.

HAMPTON, Washington County, N. Y.

INDEX.

LECTURE I.—The Second Appearing of Christ. Titus ii. 13.—Looking for that blessed hope, and glorious appearing of the great God, and our Savior Jesus Christ.

LECTURE II.—The First Resurrection. Rev. xx. 6.—Blessed and holy is he that hath part in the first resurrection; on such the second death hath no power—shall reign with him a thousand years.

LECTURE III.—The Two Thousand Three Hundred Days. Dan. viii. 13, 14.—And he said unto me, unto two thousand three hundred days; then shall the sanctuary be cleansed.

LECTURE IV.—Daniel ix. 24.—Seventy weeks are determined upon thy people and upon thy holy city, to finish the transgression, and to make an end of sins, and to make reconciliation for iniquity, and to bring in everlasting righteousness, and to seal up the vision and prophecy, and to anoint the Most Holy.

LECTURE V.—Pagan Rome numbered. Rev. xiii. 18.—And his number is six hundred threescore and six.

LECTURE VI.—Daniel's Vision of the Latter Days; or, an Exposition of the eleventh chapter of Daniel. Dan. x. 14.—Now I am come to make thee understand what shall befall thy people in the latter days.

LECTURE VII.—Daniel's 1260, 1290, and 1335 days explained. Daniel xii. 8.—And I heard, but I understood not; then said I, O my Lord, what shall be the end of these things?

LECTURE VIII.—The Three Woe Trumpets. Rev. viii. 13—Woe, Woe, Woe, to the inhabitants of the earth by reason of the other voices of the trumpet of the three angels which are yet to sound.

LECTURES IX AND X.—The Epistle to the Seven Churches of Asia, considered as applying to Seven Periods of the Gospel Church. Rev. i. 20.

LECTURE XI.—The New Song. Rev. v. 9.—And they sung a new song, saying, Thou art worthy to take the book, and to open the seals thereof; for thou wast slain, and hast redeemed us to God, etc.

LECTURE XII.—The Seven Seals, as representing Events to the End of Time. Rev. v. 5—Behold, the Lion of the tribe of Judah hath prevailed to open the book, and to loose the seven seals thereof.

LECTURE XIII.—The Two Witnesses, as having been slain in the French Revolution. Rev. xi. 3.—And I will give power unto my two witnesses, and they shall prophesy 1260 days, clothed in sack-cloth.

Lecture XIV.—The Woman in the Wilderness. Rev. xii. 6.—And the woman fled into the wilderness, where she hath a place prepared of God, that they should feed her there 1260 days.

Lecture XV.—The Seven Last Plagues, or Seven Vials. Rev. xvi. 17.—and the seventh angel poured out his vial into the air; and there came a great voice out of the temple of heaven, from the throne, saying, It is done.

Lecture XVI.—The Parable of the Ten Virgins. Matt. xxv. 1.—Then shall the kingdom of heaven be likened unto ten virgins, which took their lamps, and went forth to meet the bridegroom.

Lecture XVII.—On the Punishment of The People of God Seven Times for their Sins. Lev. xxvi. 23, 24.

Lecture XVIII.—Solomon's Songs, viii. 5.—Who is this that cometh up from the wilderness, leaning upon her beloved?

Lecture XIX.—Signs of the Present Times. Matt. xxvi. 3.—But can ye not discern the signs of the times?

LECTURE IX.—BY WM. MILLER.

Rev. i. 20.

The mystery of the seven stars which thou sawest in my right hand, and the seven golden candlesticks. The seven stars are the angels of the seven churches; and the seven candlesticks which thou sawest are the seven churches.

It has generally been believed that the seven churches to whom the angel instructed John to write, were seven different and distinct churches in Asia, and by almost all of our commentators at the present day are understood to mean seven literal churches. But your speaker is forced, from the reasons which will hereafter be produced, to believe that these seven churches of Asia are to be understood in a figurative sense, alluding to seven periods of the church militant, during the Christian dispensation, down to the first resurrection, and the commencing of the glorious reign of Christ on the earth, commonly called *The Millennium.* If this view of the subject should prove to be the correct exposition of the text, how important and interesting is the subject to us who live in the last stage of the church? Then we who live at this day, are particularly, and *solemnly* and *awfully*, admonished in what is said by Christ to *the church of the Laodiceans*, that church corresponding with our stage of the church immediately previous to the commencing of the millennial glory; and how necessary that we should know that these admonitions do most deeply concern us!

This view of the subject will then claim our first attention. Were the seven churches used as a figure of the whole Christian dispensation, or were they not? I answer, in my humble opinion, they were. Because, first, the book of Revelation does evidently contain a prophecy of things which did not concern those seven literal churches in Asia; for those churches have long since passed away and become extinct; yet the book of Revelation contains prophecies which are daily fulfilling, and have been for eighteen centuries. It is also said to be a revelation of things which must shortly come to pass. "The revelation of Jesus Christ which God gave unto him, to show unto his servants things which must shortly come to pass." Not things that have been. Yet if Christ is only giving admonitory advice to those seven literal churches, then he is only relating their characters as they then were, and so far as these churches were concerned it would cease to be a prophecy, and the very first verse in Revelation would be violated. Again, third verse, "Blessed is he that readeth and they that hear the words of this prophecy, and keep those things which are written therein; for the time is at hand." We see that it is called a prophecy in this verse, and must allude to the whole book; but who will pretend that the three chapters in the beginning of Revelation are a prophecy, if we understand them as relating the character of seven literal churches in Asia only? None, none.

Again: the word *seven* is often used in the word of God as a mystical number, meaning the whole, as seven spirits, seven stars, seven angels, seven candlesticks, seven seals, seven trumpets, seven vials, seven thunders, seven plagues, seven mountains, seven heads, seven eyes, seven horns, seven crowns, seven kings, and *seven churches.* All these are used in Revelation, and apply to or concerning the whole Gospel period. If, then, the number seven is used so often in this book in a figurative sense, may we not reasonably suppose that it is so used in the dedication of this book to the seven churches in Asia, and the history of those seven churches be prophetic? for no Scripture is given for any private interpretation, and surely the instruction in the introduction of the book carries us down to the coming of Christ in the clouds—"Behold, he cometh with clouds; and every eye shall see him, and they also which pierced him; and all kindreds of the earth shall wail because of him; even so, amen. I am Alpha and Omega, the beginning and the ending, which is, and which was, and which is to come, the Almighty." And why all this descriptive grandeur in the address to these seven churches, if they only were meant? Surely there were other churches of equal importance at that day. Where were the churches at Corinth, Cappadocia, Galatia, Thessalonica, Philippi, Collosse, Rome, Jerusalem, Bithynia, etc.? Our text shows that the seven churches were to be understood in a figurative sense. "The mystery of the seven stars which thou sawest in my right hand, and the seven golden candlesticks. The seven stars are the angels of the seven churches; and the seven candlesticks which thou sawest are the seven churches." These seven churches are represented by "seven lamps." See Zach. iv. 2, "And said unto me, What seest thou? And I said, I have looked, and behold a candlestick all of gold, with a bowl upon the top of it, and his seven lamps thereon, and seven pipes to the seven lamps which were upon the top thereof." These seven lamps are called "the eyes of the Lord which run to and fro through the whole earth." See Zach. iv. 10. If this is true, then it readily follows that the seven churches of Asia are only used as a figure representing the church "through the whole earth." Again: the seven lamps, which are the seven churches, are called the seven spirits of God. Rev. iv. 5, "And there were seven lamps of fire burning before the throne, which are the seven spirits of God." I have clearly proved, and I think it will be admitted by all, that the "seven eyes of the Lord," and "the seven spirits of God," are the seven churches to whom John was directed to write or dedicate his book, the Revelation of Jesus Christ.

And I will now show that these comprehended the whole church through the whole earth. See Rev. v. 6, "And I beheld, and lo! in the midst of the throne and of the four beasts, and in the midst of the elders, stood a lamb as it had been slain, having seven horns, and seven eyes, which are the 'seven spirits of God sent forth into all the earth.'" Again: when we compare the several characteristic marks or events, upon opening the seven seals, with those marks and instructions to the seven churches, we shall be led to admire the beauty, harmony, and consistency of the Revelation of Jesus Christ to his people. And I think the mind will rest satisfied that this view of the subject is the truth, because it so exactly agrees with Christ's manner of teaching by parables when he was with us in the flesh.

Some may inquire, "Why were those seven churches in Asia used as figures to represent the church militant in her several conditions to the end of her militant state?" I answer (if we may be allowed to answer the *whys* or *wherefores*), because the signification of the names of those seven churches describe the spirit and qualities of the several periods of the Christian church, which they are brought forward to represent, which we shall attempt to show in its proper place.

I shall now endeavor to take up the churches in the order in which they are laid down to us in Revelation. (Read Rev. ii. 1—7, inclusive.) 1st. The word EPHESUS, *desirable chief.* This is true concerning the first age of the church, in the apostles' days, when the Holy Ghost was given the power to work miracles, and the power to distinguish between good and evil spirits, and when all were of one heart and one mind, and the canon of the Holy Scriptures were filling up, and the inspired apostles were setting things in order, and establishing churches through the world. Yes, my brethren, these were desirable times surely. But to proceed: This church is addressed by the character "that holdeth the seven stars," the ministers and servants of him who holdeth them "in his right hand," under his immediate care and control, "who walketh in the midst of the seven golden candlesticks," and has said, where two or three are gathered together in his name, there will he be in the midst of them, and has promised that whatsoever they should ask in his name it should be granted unto them. He says, "I know thy works." In that day they brought forth fruits meet for repentance, and they went every where preaching that men should repent; and Paul said, when preaching at Athens, "But now commandeth all men every where to repent." Yes, all, saint or sinner, high or low, rich or poor; all, all must repent. And O! my brethren, how much we need these works at the present day! "Remember, therefore, from whence thou art fallen, and repent and do thy first works." Again he says, "I know thy labor." Did not the apostles labor night and day? 2 Thess. iii. 8, "Neither did we eat any man's bread for nought, but wrought with labor and travail night and day, that we might not be chargeable to any of you." See 1 Thess. ii. 8, 9, "So being affectionately desirous of you, we were willing to have imparted unto you, not the gospel of God only, but also our own souls, because ye were dear unto us. For ye remember, brethren, our labor and travail; for laboring night and day, because we would not be chargeable to any of you, we preached unto you the gospel of God." Again he says, "And thy patience." This, too, will apply to the apostles' days. For Paul says, 2 Cor. vi. 4, "But in all things approving ourselves as the ministers of God, in much patience, in afflictions, in necessities, in distresses." Also, xii. 12, "Truly the signs of an apostle were wrought among you in all patience, in signs, and wonders, and mighty deeds. And again the apostle says to Timothy, "But thou hast fully known my doctrine, manner of life, purpose, faith, long-suffering, charity, *patience*." And who can read the history of the first age of the church, but will admit that works, labor, and patience, were prominent features of that age, and virtues which adorned the Christian church in its infancy, more than any age since? "And how thou canst not bear them which are evil." Who can read Paul's instructions to his Corinthian brethren, in 1 Cor. v. 11, without seeing this text fulfilled? "But now I have written unto you not to keep company, if any man that is called a brother [as though such a one could not be a real brother, but only called so] be a fornicator, or covetous, or an idolater, or a railer, or a drunkard, or an extortioner; with such a one no not to eat." And had the servants of Christ at the present day the power of the apostles to discern the spirits by which we are governed, how many in this congregation would blush when "*fornicator*" is mentioned! How many "*covetous*" would hide their faces! How many "*idolaters*" would bow their heads, or "*railers*" would begin to murmur at the plainness of the speaker! How many "*drunkards*" would not have staggered into this house! And how many "*extortioners*" would have stayed at home! O God, thou knowest. Or who can read the 2d chapter of the 2d epistle of Peter, and John's first epistle, Jude, and others, and not be convinced that the apostles could not bear with them that were evil? Again: "Thou hast tried them which say they are apostles, and are not, and hast found them liars." This sentence was fulfilled in the apostles' days. Simon Magus, after he was professedly a disciple of Christ, was found out by Peter to be in the "gall of bitterness and bonds of iniquity." Hymeneus and Alexander, whom Paul delivered to Satan, that they may learn not to blaspheme. 1 Tim. i. 20. Also, Philetus, Demas, and Alexander the coppersmith, were all found to be liars, and many others who went out from them, as the apostle says, because they were not of them. And how many are there now, my brethren, among us, who, when tribulation cometh, will be offended, and go out from us! Lord, is it I? "And hast borne, and hast patience, and for my name's sake hast labored, and hast not fainted." Yes, my brethren, it was for the name of Jesus, that the primitive Christians bore the persecutions of their day. Acts xv. 25, 26, "It seemed good unto us to send chosen men unto you, with our beloved Barnabas and Paul, men that have hazarded their lives for the name of our Lord Jesus Christ." Acts ix. 16, "For I will show him what great things he must suffer for my name's sake." Verse 41, "And they departed from the presence of the council, rejoicing that they were counted worthy to suffer shame for his name." And, may I not inquire, how many of us are willing and would rejoice to suffer shame for the name of Christ? Perhaps none. We had rather be called Rabbi, Rev., Dr., etc. We are contending for our *names* at the present day; for Baptists, Congregationalists, Presbyterians, Methodists, Free-wills, Campbellites, etc. If we do not contend earnestly for our sect, they will decrease, and we shall come to nought. And I say, May God speed it; so that you all may fall on the word of God, and rally again under the name of Jesus. But we will proceed with our subject. 4th verse, "Nevertheless I have somewhat against thee, because thou hast left thy first love." Can this be true? Did the apostolic church, in its purity, so soon depart from the first principles of the gospel? Yes, in Acts xv. 24, "Forasmuch as we have heard that certain which went out from us have troubled you with words, subverting your souls, saying, ye must be circumcised, and keep the whole law, to whom we gave no such commandment." Gal. i. 6, "I marvel that ye are so soon removed from him that called you into the grace of Christ unto another gospel." 1 Timothy, i. 19, "Holding faith and a good conscience, which some having put away, concerning faith, have made shipwreck." 2 Tim. i. 15, "This thou knowest, that all they which are in Asia are turned away from me." And Paul further says, iv. 16, "At my first answer no man stood with me, but all men forsook me. I pray God lay not this sin to their charge."

Many more evidences might be brought, to prove that many, in that early state of the church, did fall away from the doctrine of grace, which Paul and the apostles taught. And now, my brethren, how is it with us? Are we built on the truth? Have we a "Thus saith the Lord," for all we believe and do? Are we built on "the prophets and apostles, Jesus Christ himself being the chief corner-stone?" Look well to your foundation—the day is coming that will try every man's works.

Verse 5, "Remember, therefore, from whence thou art fallen, and repent and do the first works, or else I will come unto thee quickly, and will remove the candlestick out of his place, except thou repent." In this verse the great Head of the church admonishes the Christians of their former sins in neglecting the doctrine of grace, and falling into the popular errors of the day, which I have before noticed, and warns them of their duty to repent, which is the first and great command under the gospel. He also gives them notice, that, except they repent, he will remove the "desirable" state of the church into the next, which would be a state of trial, persecution, and poverty.

6th verse, "But this thou hast, that thou hatest the deeds of the Nicolaitans, which I also hate." What the deeds of the Nicolaitans were, we are not able, from the word of God, to determine; but from some things hinted at by some ancient authors, we have good reason to believe that Nicholas, one of the seven deacons, departed from the doctrine which the apostles taught, and preached a doctrine which was repugnant to the gospel of Christ, viz., a community or plurality of wives, which led Paul in his instructions to say, "Let the deacons be the husband of one wife," 1 Tim. iii. 12. "He that hath an ear, let him hear what the Spirit saith to the churches." Here we have another evidence, that the branch of the church at Ephesus was not the only church addressed in this epistle and prophecy; for, if so, what propriety in using the word *churches*, in the plural, when only one church in Asia was spoken of? No, it could not be proper, neither would it have been, as it is so used in every epistle through the whole seven, had not Christ designed it for all the churches in a certain age. There is also an admonition contained in these last-quoted words, to read, hear, and observe the prophecy now given by the Spirit to John, the inspired servant of Christ; and for all the churches of the age spoken of, to be careful to apply to themselves the admonitions, designed by the Holy Spirit for their immediate benefit. "To him that overcometh will I give to eat of the tree of life, which is in the midst of the paradise of God." How precious is this promise to the faithful and tried soul, who places all his hope, and strength, and dependence, on one who is mighty to save, and on one who has promised to bring him off conquerer over all the enemies of grace, and the powers of hell! Yes, and, more than all, he has overcome and entered within the veil, as a forerunner for us who believe. May we all, by faith, have a right to this tree of life, this paradise of God.

I will now examine the prophecy to the second church, which I understand to commence about the close of the first century, and lasted about two hundred years, until the days of Constantine, A. D. 312.

8th verse, "And unto the angel of the church in Smyrna, write." The signification of the word *Smyrna*, is myrrh; denoting that the church in this age would be a sweet-smelling savor to God, while she was passing through the fiery ordeal of persecution and affliction, which always has served to weed out those obnoxious plants of pride, popularity, self-dependence—the bane and poison of true faith, piety, and devotion. And O, my brethren, could we learn wisdom, by what the church has already suffered in the days of our forefathers, we should be more humble, the more worldly peace and prosperity we enjoyed. For it is only in the midst of persecution and trial, that the church manifest great purity of doctrine or life. How well, then, might this age of the church be compared to *myrrh*, when she must have been separated from worldly honors, avarice, pride, popularity, and hypocrisy, when the hypocrite and worldling had no motives to unite with and destroy the union of the brotherhood, and when the hireling shepherd could expect no fleece, that would suit his cupidity, to filch from the lambs of Christ! "These things saith the first and the last, which was dead and is alive." In these words we learn the character speaking to the church. It is no less than the mighty God, the everlasting Father, the Prince of Peace. "I know thy works, and tribulation, and poverty." Now, their works were about to be tried; although God knew them that were his, yet he designed to manifest to a world who would be faithful even unto death, and to show that pure and undefiled religion would burn with a brighter flame in tribulation and poverty, and the richness of that faith, which would bring off the true Christian conqueror over the powers of the world, the temptations of Satan, and corruptions of the flesh. "But thou art rich." Yes, brethren, the true and genuine Christian is *rich*.

For charity can suffer long in tribulation, and the spirit of Christ will make us forsake all for his sake, and endure poverty for the name of Jesus. "And I know," says Christ, "the blasphemy of them which say they are Jews [1] (that is, people of God), and are not, but are the synagogue of Satan." Although Christ knew the hypocrites and false professors that had rushed into his visible church during a time of prosperity that the church had experienced in its Ephesian state, or apostolic age, yet now the time had come when that candlestick must be removed, and the next age of the church or candlestick be set up; and the same means used by God to purify the silver would purge out the dross, so that the church would again be cleansed of its worldly, hypocritical, and false professors.

10, "Fear none of those things which thou shalt suffer." The true child of God need not fear to suffer for Christ's sake, for the sufferings of this present evil world will work out for us a far more exceeding and eternal weight of glory. "Behold, the devil shall cast some of you into prison, that ye may be tried, and ye shall have tribulation ten days." The devil in this verse represents Pagan Rome. See Rev. xii. 9, 17, "And the great dragon was cast out, that old serpent, called the devil." "And the dragon was wroth with the woman, and went to make war with the remnant of her seed, which keep the commandments of God, and have the testimony of Jesus Christ." How exactly was this prophecy fulfilled in the days of Nero, Domitian, and other Roman emperors, and how faithful has history been to record the ten persecutions between the days of John's prophecy and the emperor Constantine! In these ten persecutions of the Roman Government, in the text called *ten days*, we learn by the history of those days the church suffered a great diminution in numbers by apostasy and fear; yet those that remained steadfast made up in graces what they lost in numbers; and it was truly a time of trial, for many were cast into prison, and many suffered torture and death, rather than to offer sacrifices to their Pagan gods.

---

[1] The name Jew was derived from the patriarch Judah, and given to the descendants of Abraham by his eldest son Isaac. It was considered, by those who bore it, to entitle them to all the blessings of God. Thus we read concerning it, "Salvation is of the Jews," John iv. 22. Yet, says Christ, "Think not to say within yourselves, we have Abraham to our father." Matt. iii. 9, "Behold, thou art called a Jew, and restest in the law, and makest thy boast of God." Rom. ii. 17. This shows why these hypocrites called themselves Jews.—*Editor*.

"Be thou faithful unto death, and I will give thee a crown of life."[1] Yes, my brethren, if we can believe the history of those days, many of the dear disciples of Christ were faithful unto death, and will soon receive the crown of life promised in this prophecy.

11, "He that hath an ear, let him hear what the Spirit saith to the churches. He that overcometh shall not be hurt of the second death." Here, then, we find some of those characters who will have part in the first resurrection, the blessed martyrs who were slain for the witness of Jesus. See Rev. xx. 4. And in this passage we are again commanded to hear what the Spirit saith to the churches—all, all who have ears; not the branch in Smyrna only, but all who have ears. We have long been in the habit of giving away Scripture to others when it belongs to us and our children; let us therefore apply it home.

12, "And to the angel of the church in Pergamos write." Very earthy elevated is the signification of the word *Pergamos;* and this church represents the age of Constantine, which lasted more than two hundred years, until the rise of anti-Christ, from A. D. 312 until A. D. 538. During this age the church became very earthy, having her worldly policy, and, like the church in the present day, attending more to the outward concerns, and the worldly part of religion, than to inward piety and graces of the spirit, looking more for *forms* and *ceremonies*, than for the *life*, *power*, and *spirit* of the religion of Jesus, spending much of their time in building elegant chapels, gorgeous temples, high places to educate their ministry, and adorning them with pictures and pleasant things, and filling the hearts of their worshippers with high, popular, and haughty notions. Yes, my brethren, the age of trial was gone; the holy and secret aspirations of piety fled away, and, now she had obtained an earthly emperor, her divine Master was forgotten. And here was the falling away mentioned by Paul, 2 Thess. ii. 3, "Let no man deceive you by any means; for

---

[1] The 1st persecution was under Nero, the tyrant. This 2d persecution was under Domitian, A. D. 95, when 4,000 were said to have been killed. The 3d under Trajan, A. D. 100. The 4th under Antonius. The 5th under Severus, A. D. 127. The 6th under Maximinus, A. D. 235. The 7th under Decius, A. D. 250. The 8th began A. D. 257, under Valerian. The 9th was under Aurelian, in 274. The 10th was under Dioclesian, A. D. 303. It is stated that 17,000 Christians were slain in one month, that in Egypt alone 144,000 Christians died by violence under the hands of their persecutors, besides 700,000 died through fatigues of banishment. Some histories state that 3,000,000 of Christians died by the persecutions of these Pagan Emperors. —*Ed.*

that day shall not come except there come a falling away first, and that man of sin be revealed, the son of perdition." This, then, was the age that prepared the church to receive that monster, the man of sin, the son of perdition, into her bosom, which stung the church with the poison of asps, and filled the temple of God with image worship, and the church with idolatry, selfishness, avarice, and pride.

"These things saith he which hath the sharp sword with two edges." By the sharp sword with two edges, we must understand the word of God, which denounces heavy judgments on the wicked, and cuts off the corruptions and errors from the church. The Psalmist says, cxlix. 5—7, "Let the saints be joyful in glory; let them sing aloud upon their beds. Let the high praises of God be in their mouth, and a two-edged sword in their hand, to execute vengeance upon the heathen, and punishments upon the people." Paul says, Heb. iv. 12, "For the word of God is quick and powerful, sharper than any two-edged sword, piercing even to the dividing asunder of soul and spirit, and of the joints and marrow, and is a discerner of the thoughts and intents of the heart." And John saw, Rev. i. 16, "And he had in his right hand seven stars; and out of his mouth went a sharp two-edged sword." Then this is the meaning of the passage under consideration, "These things saith he," which hath the word of God, and showing us the importance of attending to the subject following, by the importance of the speaker, "He that is Christ." And now, while we read or hear, let us keep in memory that it is no less a personage speaking, than him of whom the prophets did write; who holdeth the stars in his right hand, and created and preserves all things by the word of his power. Hear him.

"I know thy works, and where thou dwellest, even where Satan's seat is. Here, again, we have an evidence that this church is mystical, 'dwelling in Satan's seat,' the fourth kingdom, the great red dragon, imperial Rome, whereon the great mystical whore of Babylon sitteth. The church, in this age, became immediately connected with this power called Satan, which is the devil, *Pagan Rome*. 'And thou holdest fast my name, and hast not denied my faith.' In this time of popular religion, and when many, from political and worldly motives, united their names to the people of God, still there were some who held to the doctrine of Christ, and did not deny the faith.

"Even in those days, wherein Antipas was my faithful martyr, who was slain among you where Satan dwelleth." It is supposed that Antipas was not an individual, but a class of men who opposed the power of the bishops or Popes in that day, being a combination of two words, *Anti*, opposed, and *Papas*, father or Pope, and many of them suffered martyrdom at that time, in Constantinople and Rome, where the bishops and Popes began to exercise the power which soon after brought into subjection the kings of the earth, and trampled on the rights of the church of Christ. And, for myself, I see no reason to reject this explanation of the word *Antipas* in this text, as the history of those times are perfectly silent respecting such an individual as is here named. Yet many, who opposed the worship of saints and pictures, and the infallibility of the bishop of Rome, were excommunicated, persecuted, and finally driven out from among men, and in the next age of the church had to flee into the wilderness. All this happened in the kingdom of Rome, "where Satan dwelleth."

"But I have a few things against thee, because thou hast there them that hold the doctrine of Balaam, who taught Balak to cast a stumbling-block before the children of Israel, to eat things sacrificed unto idols, and to commit fornication." The world have always been endeavoring to draw the church of Christ into fellowship with them, and to a mixed communion of idolatry, as Balaam taught Balak to draw the children of Israel from their God and his commands, by mixing with the Jews in their worship, and, at the same time, by degrees, introduce their priests, their altars, and idol worship into their camp. In Constantine's day this mode of warfare was introduced with great success by Pagan worshippers, so that in little more than two centuries the greater part of the professed Christian church became the image of the beast of which we are now speaking, viz., Pagan Rome. Here, then, we see the rise of Papacy on the downfall of Pagan Rome. Whosoever will take the pains of comparing the Pagan manner of worship, forms, and ceremonies with Papacy, cannot help being forcibly struck with the similarity of the two. One deified their departed heroes and poets, the other her departed saints and votaries. The one consulted her oracles and priests for laws and instructions, the other her Popes and cardinals. The one had her altars, images, and statues, the other her chapels, pictures, and crosses. Both had them erected in every public place, for the multitude to fall before and worship. Both had their holy fire, holy water, and both claimed to perform miracles; the one by the response of her wooden oracles, and the other by her carnal priesthood. Here, then, we see how the church, in the fourth and fifth centuries, was led over the stumbling-block of Paganism, to eat things sacrificed to idols, and to commit fornication.

"So, also, hast thou them that hold the doctrine of the Nicolaitans, which thing I hate." This doctrine was promulgated in the fourth century. See the church history, and our former observations.

"Repent, or else I will come unto thee quickly, and will fight against them with the sword of my mouth." Again the Lord calls for repentance, and threatens the judgments of his word upon them that obey not. O! may we take warning, my brethren, and tempt not the heavy judgments of God upon us for our idolatry and fellowship of that which is not the religion of Jesus.

"He that hath an ear, let him hear what the Spirit saith unto the churches. To him that overcometh will I give to eat of the hidden manna, and will give him a white stone, and in the stone a new name written, which no man knoweth saving he that receiveth it." Again, all that have ears are commanded to hear, and those who remain faithful, that do not fall away, receive a promise of spiritual food, and a name and righteousness which none can know but they who receive it.

18, "And unto the angel of the church in Thyatira write." The signification of *Thyatira* is, a "sweet savor of labor or sacrifice and contrition," and is a description of the church, after she is driven into the wilderness by the anti-Christian beast. This church lasted until about the tenth century; and little of her history is known to the world; but some authors have pretended to trace her into the north-west part of Asia, and in the north-east part of Europe, where they lived until about the tenth century, unknown unto the rest of the world, or taking but little concern with the nations around them. Yet it is said they retained religion in its purity, and held to the doctrines of the word of God.* At any rate this church is repre-

*Whoever reads "The Israel of the Alps," a rare work of history of "the origin, manners, doctrine, and persecutions of the Waldensian church,—Vaudois, etc.," published in London, will not fail to see a clear illustration of this scriptural account of several stages of the church given by Christ to John, the Revelator.—EDITOR.

sented as being in a state of heavy trial, and subject to seduction by some power represented by *that woman Jezebel*, of which I shall speak in its place. "These things saith the Son of God, who hath his eyes like unto a flame of fire, and his feet are like fine brass;" representing, as in all the other declarations to the churches, that the character addressing them is no less than the mighty God, the omniscient, omnipotent, and omnipresent Jehovah, who says, "I know thy works, and charity, and service, and faith, and patience, and thy works; and the last to be more than the first." When this church existed, which was when anti-Christ began her reign, there was great need of the exercise of those graces of the Spirit which in this passage are enumerated. 1st. In works they had to, and without doubt did, combat the anti-Christian doctrines which began in the sixth century to overwhelm the Christian world, such as worshipping angels, departed saints, subjection to councils and bishops, infallibility of the Pope, etc. They, in charity, too, had many of their brethren to sustain while combatting these errors against the power of this beast. They did much service in holding up the hands of their pious teachers and pastors who were not led away by this wicked one. How much faith, too, must they have been in possession of to have withstood the power of their councils, the excommunications of the Pope, and a majority of their brethren who had fallen into Papal errors! how much "*patience*" to have remained unwavering amidst persecution when driven from their homes, their country and friends, into the wilderness, where God prepared a place for her! and how much more necessary were their last works to support each other in exile, poverty, and distress, the natural consequence of being driven from among men! But these things were so, according to the best account we can obtain of those times.

20, "Notwithstanding, I have a few things against thee, because thou sufferest that woman Jezebel, which calleth herself a prophetess, to teach and to seduce my servants to commit fornication, and to eat things sacrificed to idols." In this verse we have strong testimony that the exposition we have given of the seven churches is correct; for no character given the woman Jezebel will apply so exactly, as the woman sitting on the scarlet-colored beast, full of names of blasphemy, "having a golden cup in her hand full of abominations and filthiness of her fornication."

Jezebel is a figurative name, alluding to Ahab's wife, who slew the prophets of the Lord, led her husband into idolatry, and fed the prophets of Baal at her own table. A more striking figure could not have been used to describe the Papal abomination. See 1 Kings xviii. xix. xxi. chapters. It is very evident from history, as well as from this verse in Revelation, that the church of Christ did suffer some of the Papal monks to preach and teach among them. See the history of the Waldenses.

21, "And I gave her space to repent of her fornication, and she repented not." 22, "Behold I will cast her into a bed, and them that commit adultery with her into great tribulation, except they repent of their deeds." 23, "And I will kill her children with death; and all the churches shall know that I am he which searcheth the reins and hearts, and I will give unto every one of you according to your works." We cannot be mistaken in the character given to this mystical Jezebel, when we compare the descriptions here used, and the judgments threatened, with other passages of like import in Revelation, where mystical Babylon is described and threatened. See Rev. ix. 20, 21, "And the rest of the men which were not killed by these plagues, yet repented not of the works of their hands, that they should not worship devils and idols of gold, and silver, and brass, and stone, and of wood, which neither can see, nor hear, nor walk: neither repented they of their murders, nor of their sorceries, nor of their fornications, nor of their thefts."

If these last texts mean anti-Christ, of which I believe none have any doubt, that is, no commentator that I have been able to consult, then it is equally evident that this woman, called Jezebel, in this prophecy of the church in Thyatira, means the same; and the conclusion is strong that the Thyatira church represents the churches in some age of anti-Christ, and the prophecy contained in the verses we have already quoted are the judgments God has and will pour out on that great city that rules over the kings of the earth, and has for ages past trodden the church under foot, and contaminated the people of God by her seductions, sorceries, and fornications.

24, "But unto you I say, and unto the rest in Thyatira, As many as have not this doctrine, and which have not known the depths of Satan as they speak, I will put upon you none other burden." 25, "But that which ye have already, hold fast till I come." In these verses the church which have not fellowshipped the anti-Christian doctrine, and have not followed the practices of the satanic blasphemies of their abominations, are here promised to experience no other persecution except what they may experience from this beast or woman Jezebel, which is another proof of this being anti-Christ; for the church in Thyatira has long been extinct, and was when the man of sin was revealed; and yet they are promised to have none other burden until he come, as it is more than implied; and this power is to stand until he comes. For Paul says, "Whom he shall consume with the spirit of his mouth and destroy with the brightness of his coming." This is Daniel's fourth kingdom, which was to be broken without hand, and to be carried away like the chaff of the summer threshing-floor before the wind, that no place be found for it.

26, "And he that overcometh and keepeth my works unto the end, to him will I give power over the nations." 27, ("And he shall rule them with a rod of iron; as the vessels of a potter shall they be broken to shivers), even as I received of my Father. And I will give him the morning star." 29, "He that hath an ear let him hear what the Spirit saith to the churches."

In closing the prophecies to the churches, our divine Instructor carries them down to that day when he shall come to be admired in all them that believe, or to glorify his saints, to crown them in his kingdom of glory, to break in pieces all the kingdoms of the earth as a potter's vessel is broken to shivers, as the last text says, which proves that when Christ comes, he will bring all the saints (angels, see Matt. xxv. 31) with him, and this too when the kingdoms of this world and anti-Christ will be destroyed. And this proves another important point in which many good and pious people are greatly mistaken, viz., that there will not be a thousand years' happy reign previous to Christ's coming the second time without sin unto salvation. What happy reign can there be while the kingdoms of the earth stand as they now do; while the anti-Christian beast has power to seduce and draw the servants of God into idolatry, and lull to her serpentine folds thousands and tens of thousands human beings yearly, and deceive the nations by her siren song of *mother church;* while by means of her poison, subtle, secret, and deep plots, she is undermining and sapping the foundation of every religious sect but her own; of every civil government but such as will resign their power unto her control? And now, while I am speaking, she is exerting an influence in this once favored land, by means of her Jesuits, that will set father against son, and son against father, and drench our country in blood. Can this monster of murder, iniquity, and blood, retain her life, her standing in society, and we have a happy reign? No. She must and will sink like a millstone in the mighty deep, and God will avenge the blood of his servants. Her flesh must be eaten by dogs; yes, the kings of the earth shall eat her flesh, and God shall consume her with fire before the happy reign comes. "*Come, Lord Jesus, come quickly.*"

I have given my views of four of the churches spoken of in the text. Three more remain, which will complete the prophetic history of the church through all the ages of the New Testament times until the state of trial shall be fulfilled, and the church shall enter her glorified kingdom in triumph. You have undoubtedly been led, by the comparison of the churches with the history thus far, to admire the agreement of the prophecy of the four churches with the history of the times; and truly this is one of the greatest evidences we have of the truth of the divine inspiration of revelation, and this evidence fixes the authenticity of the Scriptures beyond a reasonable doubt. I shall now claim a few moments' indulgence while I attempt to show where and when the other three churches have been or will be fulfilled. See Rev. iii.

1, "And unto the angel of the church in Sardis write." Song of joy, or that which remains, is the signification of *Sardis.* The last signification is the one which the heavenly Instructor has affixed himself to this church in the second verse, "Be watchful, and strengthen the things which remain." The church preceding this had passed a long, dark, and benighted age of the world, and every writer of these times calls them the dark ages; and truly it was an age of superstition, bigotry, and ignorance; therefore we must reasonably suppose that but few were the true worshippers of God, and those few enjoying but a faint knowledge of divine things. But we will pursue our course. "These things saith he that hath the seven spirits of God, and the seven stars, I know thy works, that thou hast a name, that thou livest, and art dead." The same character that has addressed the other churches, still gives himself a quality by which we may know that it is he who is called God man, having the spirit of God, and as man governing his church as the star of Bethlehem. This church began about the tenth century, and lasted until the Reformation under Luther, Calvin, and others. "Thou hast a name, and art dead;" that is, she was or would be of little use to the rest of the world, hiding her influence within her own sphere, and of course did not manifest her light to the world, was inactive, idle, not performing the work which God had commanded them to perform, to set their light on the candlestand, that it might give light to all. This was the case with the church in the valleys of Piedmont during the time of the crusades to the Holy Land; and while the Pope had the command of all the armies of Europe, the church lived in these valleys of the Pyrenees, nearly in the centre of Europe, unknowing and unknown.

2d verse, "Be watchful, and strengthen the things which remain, that are ready to die; for I have not found thy works perfect before God." Although the church in this age retained some of the leading principles of the gospel, the ordinances were in part retained among them, yet towards the close of this Sardis age, the Papal monks and priests were sent in among them, and many of the Waldenses became corrupted by the Papal beast and her doctrine. Therefore the admonition, "Be watchful, and strengthen the things which remain."

3d verse, "Remember how thou hast received and heard, and hold fast and repent. If, therefore, thou shalt not watch, I will come on thee as a thief, and thou shalt not know what hour I will come upon thee." The judgment threatened in this verse, "I will come upon thee," is undoubtedly a prophecy of the persecution of the Waldenses and Lollards, by the Papal authority, and through the inquisition, as an instrument, about the close of the fourteenth century, when, for their departure from the true doctrine of the gospel, and the commands of God, they were persecuted and scattered among all nations, so that by the judgments of God, for their transgressions, they were made instruments in the hands of God of spreading the knowledge of the gospel among the nations, which they ought to have done in obedience to his word, and for the love of souls. And these judgments served the double purpose of punishment for sin, and opening a door for a more general display of salvation.

4th verse, "Thou hast a few names even in Sardis which have not defiled their garments, and they shall walk with me in white, for they are worthy." There were a few even in this age of moral darkness who followed Christ in his laws and ordinances, and they receive the promise of justification before God, "walk with me in white."

5th verse, "He that overcometh, the same shall be clothed in white raiment, and I will not blot out his name out of the book of life; but I will confess his name before my Father and before his angels." Whenever the phrase, "he that overcometh," is used, it always implies, I think, in the Scriptures, that the persons addressed are, or will pass through a time of persecution; and in this text the church in this age is shown that those only who can endure tribulation and persecution will be acknowledged at the bar of God as the children of faith. And then this church is again warned to hear and believe what the Spirit saith to the churches.

6th verse, "He that hath an ear, let him hear what the Spirit saith to the churches."

I shall now attempt to show to what age we may calculate the Philadelphia church should answer, and when this prophecy was fulfilled.

7th verse, "And to the angel of the church in Philadelphia write, These things saith he that is holy, he that is true, he that hath the key of David, he that openeth and no man shutteth, and shutteth and no man openeth." This verse is a description of the character addressing the church and gives an account of his holiness, his veracity, authority, and power, and leaves us without a doubt that it is Jesus the son of David, the Holy One of Israel, the faithful and true witness, he that hath all power in heaven and in earth. And he thus addresses them, 8th verse, "I know thy works: behold, I have set before thee an open door, and no man can shut it, for thou hast a little strength, and hast kept my word, and hast not denied my name." The signification of the name of this church, *Philadelphia*, is *brotherly love*, and this age began about the time of the Reformation; for then God opened an effectual door for the gospel to be spread which no man or set of men has been able to shut. And the early reformers displayed a zeal and fearlessness in their cause which astonished their friends and confounded their enemies. At this time, too, Christian love and fellowship was evidently one of the strongest marks of the day and manifested that the work was of God.

9th verse, "Behold, I will make them of the synagogue of Satan which say they are Jews and are not, but do lie." The characters here spoken of are the same as those who sit in Satan's seat, who profess to be Christians, but are anti-Christians; they are worshippers of the Papal beast, professing to be the *mother church*, but are only that part which are fallen away, as Paul has told us, "there should come a falling away first, and then the man of sin should be revealed, who opposeth (or is anti), and exalteth himself (calling themselves Jews, a figurative expression, or name for Christian) above all that is called God." "Behold, I will make them to come and worship before thy feet, and to know that I have loved thee." This sentence shows that anti-Christ would be humbled in this age of the church and brought to take the back ground, or in some measure lose her civil power over the Protestant church and be humbled at her feet. Has not this prophecy been accomplished strictly according to the letter? Witness Great Britain, Germany, and other nations. And to this day she has not been able to bring into subjection any of the Protestant states, and is only permitted to dwell among them by toleration. And although within a few years past she seems to be making an effort to regain her lost power and authority, yet it is but a last struggle, a dying gasp; for soon she must and will fall, to rise in civil power no more forever.

10th verse, "Because thou hast kept the word of my patience, I also will keep thee from the hour of temptation which shall come upon all the world to try them that dwell upon the earth." This part of the prophecy was fulfilled on or before the French revolution, when Atheism and Deism made such rapid progress through Europe or the Roman government, which in prophecy is called the earth. See Rev. xii. 9. And it is a fact, that through this age of profligacy and corruption, the church retained her principles as pure and with as little defection as any age in modern times; although men of the world were led away by the plausible writings of Voltaire, Hume, Tom Paine, and others, yet it had no effect on the Christian church: and the promise, "I will keep thee from the hour of temptation," was fully and faithfully accomplished; and the very means that Satan used to destroy the religion of Jesus Christ, or "the twelve fishermen," was the means of bringing the church out of the wilderness. And those governments of the world which had for more than twelve centuries persecuted the children of God, now granted free toleration for all men to worship God according to the dictates of their own conscience. And from this period we may see the "angel flying through the midst of heaven having the everlasting gospel to preach to them that dwell on the earth." Now the church began to awake to the subject of missions; and while the world was tempted and tried, the kingdoms of the earth shaken to their centre (yet not destroyed); while the civil power of the mother of harlots, the inquisition of Spain, and the horrible means of torture, persecution, slavery, and cruelty, were all swept away in one revolution,—the church, by the power of him who had promised to "keep them," passed through the fiery ordeal without the smell of fire on her garments.

11th verse, "Behold, I come quickly; hold that fast which thou hast, that no man take thy crown." In this verse we have notice of his second coming, and that it would be quickly; by which I understand that the age of the seventh church, which was yet to come, would be short, and the second coming of him, who will overcome and subdue all things, would be quickly. He likewise admonishes us to hold fast that which we have, giving us, as I understand, warning that the next age of the church would be an age of invention; of lo heres, of departure from the true faith, of denying the crown of the church, the twelve stars, the apostles' doctrine. And amidst the confusion of the doctrines and revelations of the present day, if any one should inquire of me what sentiment it would be best for them to embrace, I would first point them to the Bible, and second, back to the fathers and teachers of the last century, and say, Hold fast that they held; let no man take thy crown. Let us then, my brethren, be watchful, and remember "him that overcometh will I make a pillar in the temple of my God, and he shall go no more out; and I will write upon him the name of my God, and the name of the city of my God, which is New Jerusalem, which cometh down out of heaven from my God; and I will write upon him my new name." The blessings promised in this text are to be realized when the New Jerusalem comes down from God out of heaven; then shall the spiritual born child of heaven be a pillar in the temple of God, in that building made without hands; then, too, will he receive that rich inheritance that is laid up in heaven for those that love God, and there obtain that eternal crown, that immortal life which is now hid with Christ in God, and then and there realize that "blessed hope at the glorious appearing of the great God and our Saviour Jesus Christ." "And he shall go no more out" of that glorious temple; no tempting devil there, for he will be chained; no persecuting kingdom, for they will "all be destroyed and carried away like the chaff of the summer threshing-floor." Then will he receive the new name. "The Lord our righteousness," for the Lord is there. Then, too, a citizen of the glorified kingdom, the New Jerusalem, married to the Lamb, and shall live and reign with him forever and forever. "He that hath an ear, let him hear what the Spirit saith unto the churches." This closes the prophecy to the sixth church; and now let us see to it that we do not lose the blessings promised by refusing to hear what the Spirit saith to the churches. Hear, and your souls shall live; disobey, turn a deaf ear, refuse the offered grace, and you will die; for the soul that sinneth shall die.

It now remains for me to show the age of the seventh or Laodicean church, and the characteristic marks of that church or age. And if I am right in considering these churches in a typical sense, as our text more than implies, and our arguments and references strongly prove, in my humble opinion, then, this part of our subject becomes doubly interesting to us, who live in the very age of the fulfillment of this prophecy. Yes, my brethren, we live at the very time when the great head of the church says,

14th verse, "And unto the angel of the church in Laodicea write, These things saith the Amen, the faithful and true witness, the beginning of the creation of God." *Laodicea* signifies the judging of the people, and may have reference to the church in its last stage, when God would pour out his justice and judgment upon a guilty world, and upon a haughty, proud, and self-exalted church, and spue them out of his mouth. This idea may be warranted from the subject in connection. The address to this church begins by showing that it is the closing up of this dispensation, by saying, "These things saith the Amen." It also teaches us that it commences the judgment, or prepares for a judgment, by bringing forward "the faithful and true witness." It also shows the universality of this judgment by the knowledge of the witness being "the beginning of the creation of God."

15th verse, "I know thy works, that thou art neither cold nor hot: I would thou wert cold or hot." To be neither cold nor hot in religious things implies a profession of religion without a spiritual life, or the middle way between the world and Christ; taking much pains after worldly things, to the neglect of spiritual things; endeavoring to move between the doctrine of Christ and the doctrine of men; taking the middle ground, as I have often heard it expressed.

16th verse, "So then, because thou art lukewarm, and neither cold nor hot, I will spue thee out of my mouth." For this cause, that is, because they are engaged more for show, honors, or profits of this world than for God, he would spue them out of his mouth. The word *spue* is used in three places in Scripture, besides the one under consideration; in Levit. xviii. 28, xx. 22, Jer. xxv. 27; and in all these places stands connected with the judgments of God upon Israel, or the nations spoken of, and implies a shaking out or driving from their present standing, either among nations or in the church of Christ, as the case may be. And this passage, I suppose, alludes to the time when God hath promised, saying, "Yet once more I shake not the earth only, but also heaven," Heb. xii. 26. So we may expect a shaking of the church of Christ, if this is the age spoken of, that those things which cannot be shaken may remain. This, too, is the age when the wise and foolish virgins are sleeping and slumbering together.

17th verse, "Because thou sayest, I am rich, and increased with goods, and have need of nothing, and knowest not that thou art wretched, and miserable, and poor, and blind, and naked." Our heavenly Instructor has given us in this verse the reason why they are lukewarm; "because thou sayest, I am rich." The church in this Laodicean state, like the rich man, will be laying up goods, or making great calculations for the outward or worldly concerns of the church for many years to come, building places for worship, establishing colleges, high schools, academies, theological institutions, to raise up a popular ministry, that the world may be pleased, the ministry well supported, and they become the most popular sect of the day, "increased with goods." This, too, is the church. What shall be called the goods of the church? It is those contributions which are deposited for charitable and pious uses, such as Paul informed his brethren to lay by them in store on the first day of the week.

These will be increased to a great and astonishing degree in this age of the church. Theological writings and publications, too, are the goods of the church: there will be a great increase of these. "Come, see what great things we are doing," will be the general language of the church, and the names of donors and the sums they contribute will be published through the world. "And knowest not that thou art wretched." The corruptions of the church will be kept out of sight; and pride, popularity, self-righteousness, depravity, will be the besetting sins of the members and great body of public professors, and few, very few of the ministers of the churches will be valiant or bold enough to tell them the truth. "And miserable." Real piety will be very little enjoyed; the hopes of a large body of professors will be but the hope of a hypocrite. "And poor." Without a tried faith, suffering but little or no persecution, the church will lack those riches which are more precious than fine gold, the trial of their faith. "And blind," without faith, living by things seen more than on the promises of God. "And naked," having on their own righteousness. "I counsel thee to buy of me gold tried in the fire." That is, the Amen, the faithful and true witness, counsels the Laodicean church to buy the gold tried in the fire, which may mean either that faith which will stand the fiery trial of temptation and persecution, or that truth which is like "apples of gold in pictures of silver;" "*that thou mayest be rich;*" rich in faith or in the knowledge of the truth; "*and white raiment that thou mayest be clothed,*" that raiment which John saw the saints in heaven clothed with, which is the righteousness of the saints, the imputed righteousness of Christ, "*the Lord our righteousness.*" If it is not so, why counsel the church to buy of him?[1] Yes, my brethren, we are counseled to buy a raiment without spot or wrinkle, "and that the shame of thy nakedness do not appear." Truly, when Christ comes, and we find we have been trusting in self, although we have called ourselves by his name, we have worn our own clothing, and ate our own bread, and instead of being clothed upon, we shall find ourselves naked. Shall we not be ashamed before him at his coming, if we are in this situation when he comes? O, what an awful thought! Therefore let us now receive the further admonition, "And anoint thine eyes with eye-salve, that

---

[1] "Buy the truth and sell it not." "Thy word is truth."

thou mayest see." To anoint the eyes, in a figurative sense, is to examine the truth and evidences of Scripture, that we may see clearly our state and standing as it respects our character towards God and our hope in his future aid, promises, and blessings. It is to see our sins, and feel the need of help, to know our weakness, and trust in his strength—in one word, it is to repent and believe in the gospel of Jesus Christ. For he says, "As many as I love I rebuke and chasten: be zealous therefore and repent." Here, then, is one comfortable promise to this lukewarm church. If there is any tried, chastened, penitent soul in this church, this Laodicean state or age of the church, they have the promise of his love, his everlasting love, his unchangeable love; his loving kindness he will not take from him, although he should "visit their transgressions with a rod, and their iniquity with stripes." Be zealous, therefore, brethren, and repent.

20th verse, "Behold, I stand at the door and knock." He that is the "*Amen*" is now at the door. In this Laodicean age of the church he comes; he knocks by his judgments, by the fulfillment of the signs, by his word, by all the means of grace that God has ever used to alarm the sleepy, slumbering virgins of his approach. He gives the cautionary word, "Behold, I stand at the door and knock; if any man hear my voice and open the door, I will come in to him, and will sup with him, and he with me." In this passage of prophecy we are brought down to the marriage supper of the Lamb, another and a strong testimony that the churches are to be considered in a typical sense, and the language or subject prophetical. For this is certainly the saying of Jesus, the faithful and true witness; "for the testimony of Jesus is the spirit of prophecy." Rev. xix. 7–9, "Let us rejoice and be glad, and give honor to him; for the marriage of the Lamb is come, and his wife hath made herself ready. And to her was granted that she should be arrayed in fine linen, clean and white; for the fine linen is the righteousness of saints. And he saith unto me, Write, Blessed are they which are called to the marriage supper of the Lamb. And he saith unto me, These are the true sayings of God." We see, my friends, by the similarity of the sentiments given in the marriage supper, and those admonitions and prophecies to the Laodicean church, that they must mean one and the same event. To hear the voice of the bridegroom, and to open the door, and go out to meet him, is the way which the bride makes herself ready; and his supping with them and they with him, shows that it is when Christ shall come, and live, and reign with them.

"To him that overcometh will I grant to sit with me in my throne, even as I also overcame, and am set down with my Father in his throne." Here is another expression which proves we are brought down to the end of time, "*to him that overcometh.*" What can the faithful and true witness mean by this expression? He explains himself, "*even as I also overcame.*" How did Christ overcome when he sat down with his Father? I answer, By bursting the bands of death, by conquering the grave, he arose a glorious conqueror, and was seated at the right hand of God. Then this is the true meaning of the text, to him that hath part in the first resurrection, will I grant to sit with me in my throne. "Blessed and holy is he that hath part in the first resurrection; on such the second death hath no power; but they shall be kings and priests of God, and of Christ, and shall reign with him." What light may we not receive from the word of God, when taken together, when explained by its own language, when kept unbroken! "He that hath an ear, let him hear what the Spirit saith unto the churches." This closes what I call, and what Christ, I think, calls, a prophecy. "Blessed is he that readeth, and they that hear the words of this prophecy, and keep those things which are written therein; for the time is at hand."

The Laodicean church began about A. D. 1798. When this dispensation closes, the judgment will set, and the books will be opened; the hypocrites will be spued out of the church, and the sanctuary cleansed.

Will the situation of the church, the character of Christians, the doctrines taught, and the signs of the times warrant us to believe that we live in the Laodicean age of the church? Let us for a moment examine the evidence and see.

1st. The situation of the church, enjoying peace in and among the kingdoms of the earth, enjoying all the privileges of citizens without persecution, making great and many improvements in her worldly concerns, rich in this world's goods, having at her command many millions of funds, and almost swaying the destinies of the world; great, learned, and rich men enlisting under her banners, controlling the fashions, customs, and laws of the day, swaying a mighty influence over the education of our youth, and giving a general tone to the literature of the world, increasing her demands for power, establishing bishoprics, presbyteries, national and state conventions, conferences, councils, associations, consociations, societies innumerable; and all these controlled almost exclusively by her clergy. May we not say truly, "She is rich and increased in goods?" But is this all? No. Look at her colleges, theological schools, academies, depositories, public edifices, presses, theological writings and publications, in almost every nation, kingdom, state, and territory, and in this country in almost every county and town; and all this by contributions. Well may it be said, she has need of nothing. These things, too, among all sects and denominations, one cannot outdo another apparently, yet each is striving for the mastery.

2d. *The characters of Christians generally.* In speaking of the character of our brethren, it becomes the speaker to be very careful and unassuming, for God has not made him a judge over his brethren. Therefore, to judge this one is right, and that one wrong, we shall leave for the judgment seat of Christ. But on a general scale surely we may be allowed to examine and compare ourselves with the prophecies. In all ages back, Christians, when living godly, have been a poor, despised, persecuted people, pilgrims and strangers in the world, plainly showing that this is not their continuing city, but that they are seeking one to come. But is it so now? Have not professors generally, for more than thirty years, been seeking for the riches of this life, for the honors of the world, and following the fashions of the times as greedily as men of the world? Yes. And can we distinguish a professor of religion in our public assemblies from a man of the world, except we are informed? No. Where, then, do Christians plainly show they seek a better country? Nowhere. May we not live in the same neighborhood with professors for years, and not hear them recommend the religion they profess? Yes. But do we not hear the same persons talk freely, flippantly and zealously about the world, the politics, and the fashions of the day? Yes. Is it not a general complaint with all of our churches, of coldness, of a want of spiritual life, and a great failure in active spiritual duties? Yes. Has not a spirit of sloth and supineness seized upon professors generally? Do not many think, if they have a hired servant to talk religion, and visit the widow and fatherless, and keep themselves unspotted from the world, for them it is enough? Yes. And does not all this, and much more which might with truth be said on this point, declare loudly that the professors of Christianity, generally, are in a lukewarm state? Yes. We must respond, Yes.

The doctrine taught. Here again your speaker feels a diffidence in speaking on this subject, knowing that many great, learned, and good men differ on this point; but we must all stand or fall to our own Master, and I must answer how I speak or shun to declare the whole counsel of God. Your speaker believes that the depravity of the human heart, our dependence on God, and indebtedness to grace, are abundantly taught in the Scriptures. See Eph. ii. 4–13. But how stands this doctrine with our public proclaimers at the present day? Some few may preach it, but there are more than ten to one who do not preach it, or, if they do, they so cover it up by their plausible and specious reasoning, that the force of the doctrine and the object of the inspired writers are wholly lost. We are now taught that man can make himself a Christian as easily as he can turn about in the highway; that obedience or baptism is regeneration; that works are the medium of acceptance with God, and that the righteousness of Christ is not imputed. How can such doctrine be more clearly pointed out than it is by the "faithful and true witness" to the Laodicean church? "And knowest not that thou art wretched, and miserable, and poor, and blind, and naked." That is, they know not their depravity. "I counsel thee to buy of me (see here their dependence on God) gold tried in the fire, that thou mayest be rich; and white raiment, that thou mayest be clothed, that the shame of thy nakedness do not appear; and anoint thine eyes with eye-salve, that thou mayest see." Grace, grace, from the foundation to the top stone. Surely, my dear friends, no candid observer of the doctrine taught at the present day, but what must in his heart acknowledge that the doctrine taught by many, among the different sects, is the same described by our divine Master, in the prophecy to the Laodicean church.

The signs of the times. In the close of Christ's instructions to the church under consideration, he says, "Behold, I stand at the door and knock; if any man hear my voice," etc. Daniel says, "At that time shall Michael stand up, the great Prince that standeth up for the children of thy people." And Christ says, "For many shall come in my name, saying, I am Christ, and shall deceive many." These were particular signs given by Christ and the prophets. And how have these come to pass? Witness the great and many reformations which for thirty years have progressed in our land, in Europe, and the islands of the seas. See also the word of God published, in whole or in part, among all nations. See the missionaries of the gospel running to and fro through the whole earth. Do not these indicate that Christ stands at the door, and that his voice has gone out even unto the ends of the world. Yes. Again: how many new sects have arisen, how many false Christs have come in this blaze of gospel light, and are drawing away their hundreds and thousands after them! It is almost incredible, when we take into view the light and knowledge under which we live; but all go to prove that Christ is nigh, even at the door.

In reviewing our subject, we learn by the events of the Sardis church, and by the admonitions given, our duty to guard against the introduction of errors into the church, and to strengthen ourselves in the truth; and likewise of being active in all the duties of religion, that we may not only have a name to live, but have the life and power of the gospel, that we may resist all the temptations and fiery darts of the enemies of the church.

By the church of Philadelphia, we learn that if we keep the word of God and the testimony of Jesus Christ, he will keep us from those trials and judgments which he sends on an ungodly and rebellious people, and that God has opened a door for the spread of the gospel, which no power on earth will be able to shut, until the angel standing on the sea and on the land, shall swear that time shall be no longer. We also learn the importance of having brotherly love and perseverance in holy things, that no man take from us the crown which is laid up for those that love God, and which will be given to them who remain steadfast in Christ Jesus at his coming, which is promised quickly to this church.

By the Laodicean church, we learn the important lesson that we cannot serve two masters; we cannot love the present evil world, and at the same time be the servants of God; that to be lukewarm in religion is to be cast out of his presence, and call down the vengeance of God's final judgment upon our heads, and, while we may flatter ourselves that we are righteous, find to our everlasting shame, that we are wretched, miserable, poor, blind, and naked.

Think, O think, my dear friends, you that are trusting in your own goodness, when that day of justice shall come, and the faithful and true witness shall stand against you, when your goodness shall pass away like the morning cloud, and the righteous Judge shall pronounce the dreadful sentence, *Depart*—what must be your feelings! The world, which you here worshipped, is burning up; the friends with whom you here associated are gone to meet the Lord in the air, or are sinking with you into endless and hopeless misery.[1] The Saviour, whose name you are now ashamed to own, or whose righteousness you think you need not, is now your Judge, seated on a great white throne, from whose face the heavens and the earth shall flee away. Think, O sinner! where wilt thou be found!

ELD. LITCH'S FIRST LETTER IN SIGNS OF THE TIMES.

"ELD. J. V. HIMES:—I have just received your prospectus for the 'Signs of the Times.' I believe the time has come when such a publication is demanded; the subject it designs to discuss is fairly before the public, and before the excitement can subside, it must be thoroughly investigated. But this cannot be done in existing periodicals;—they are all, so far as I am acquainted, with the exception of Zion's Watchman, of New York, closed against the discussion of anything more than one side of the question, and that the old and popular side.

Your brother in Christ,

"EASTHAM, MASS., March 28, 1840. JOSIAH LITCH."

Elder Litch soon developed in his preaching and writings a studious and strong mind, with a disposition to investigate, and courage to advocate and defend what appeared to him as truth. He gave up his pastoral charge and traveled extensively in preaching the advent message, and soon became an associate editor of the "Signs of the Times." He has written much that is valuable, has published several excellent books on the prophecies (though not all in harmony with the general views of Adventists), and has performed a vast amount of missionary labor.

One of Bro. Litch's works, which was of unusual merit for those times, and had a wide circulation, greatly stirred the waters of the M. E. church, especially awakening opposition among the ministry of his association, calling forth many letters and objections.

---

[1] It will be seen by this expression that Mr. Miller believed the wicked would live in eternal conscious misery, while the larger portion of the Advent believers of the present time believe in their final destruction by "the second death."

As with the priesthood in the days of the ministry of Christ, so with the clergy now who are befogged by tradition, it seems exceedingly difficult for them to see or hear anything correctly which does not chime with their own views. If they attempt to refute an opponent's views, or to relate it to the public, or state it to their friends, they always give it incorrectly, setting it in a false light, for effect. We here quote a specimen.

An extract from an article of Elder J. D. Bridge, in Zion's Herald, March 25, 1840.

"It appears to me that the theory that Christ will come the second time in 1843, that the resurrection of the saints and the judgment will then take place, tends ultimately to the darkest and most destructive infidelity. . . . Bro. Litch does not seem so much as to entertain a *doubt* respecting the truth of his doctrine, or hardly to suppose it possible that the events of 1843 may annihilate the fair fabric of prophetic exposition, which with so much research and labor, he has been rearing. Supposing they live till 1843, and see that year pass away without any resurrection of the saints, or any appearance of the "great white throne" in the clouds of heaven. *What* will be the *effect* produced on *their own minds?* Certainly they must be very humble, teachable, implicit believers in the Bible still to claim that it contains a true revelation of the will of God. They will be likely to reason, 'Mine was the *true sense* and exposition of the prophetic part of the Bible;' but these predictions have not been fulfilled, therefore they have no foundation in truth! They will be likely to go farther than this and say—The prophecies are as true as any part of the Bible, but time and matter-of-fact have proved them false; therefore, the Bible does not contain the truth of God."

Extracts from Elder J. Litch's reply.

"Has my beloved Brother B. read the following from the preface of "Christ's Second Coming?" "All pretention to a spirit of prophecy, or to infallibility in the interpretation of prophecy, is utterly disclaimed. It has often been asked,—If the evidence does not come out as you believe, what will you then think? Will it not destroy your confidence in the Bible? To this it is replied—Not at all; for the writer has, in the course of his research on this subject, seen so much that has been literally fulfilled as predicted, that, although all he has written on this subject should be proved to have been founded in ignorance, he cannot doubt but the prophecies have a meaning, and that they will in due time be fulfilled."

J. LITCH."

Mr. Litch soon published an enlarged and improved edition of much importance, which had an extensive circulation, and produced deep impressions on many minds that the Lord would soon come. We give here the title-page, some testimonials, the table of contents, and a section of the address—which contains such an amount of instruction we think it should be given to all our readers.

An Address to the Public, and especially the Clergy, on the near approach of the glorious, everlasting kingdom of God on earth, as indicated by the word of God, the history of the world, and signs of the present times. By Rev. J. Litch.

We give the following testimonials of the former edition:

Extract of a Letter of the Rev. S. W. Coggeshall.

LITCH'S ADDRESS TO THE CLERGY.

Dear Brethren:—Permit me to call your attention to this work. It is well worthy of a most careful and attentive perusal. It exhibits much vigor of thought, depth of research, and logical acuteness. The work bears most evident marks of not having been hastily gotten up, or of having been sent hastily into the world without due reflection. The author, in general, seems to be well satisfied with the correctness of his own conclusions; and if there is any man who is able to overthrow them, I hope he will read the book and then do it.

The doctrine of a temporal millennium, I think, may be considered as utterly exploded. As for the restoration of the Jews, for which some are looking, without doubt, it is a notion equally untenable, and as fully exploded. Remember, brethren, the words of inspiration, "he that judgeth a cause before he heareth it, is a fool;" and how much more true is this of those who proceed still further, even to *sneer* at those things which they understand not. Therefore, brethren, read brother Litch's book before you presume to pass judgment upon its contents, and especially to esteem it lightly. When I sat down, I did not intend to argue the case, even so far as I have, but merely to call your attention to the book. Read it, brethren, and then judge for yourselves.

S. W. COGGESHALL.

Note from Rev. Daniel Wise.

Rev. J. Litch,—Dear Brother:—I have read your Address to the Clergy with much pleasure. When I took it up, my mind was deeply prejudiced against the theory it advocates, but when I laid it down those prejudices were greatly softened. Still I am not *convinced,* but merely set on a train of inquiry into the subject, that I intend shall result in a perfect settlement of my opinion on the questions involved. Very respectfully yours,

DANIEL WISE.

Extract of a Letter from Rev. John A. Sillick.

To Rev. J. Litch:—"Since last year I have been a subscriber to the Literalist, which I have read with great interest, and from which I have received much interesting light and information. The idea of the personal appearing and reign of Christ with all his saints upon *this earth* was new and enrapturing. I was convinced, from a fair investigation of the subject, that my former views had been traditional rather than scriptural. Though I was much pleased with the general views set forth in the Literalist, yet there were many things which I could not subscribe to.

"Your little work gave me a more clear, and, I think, scriptural view of the subject. I think it must strike the mind of every candid reader with the force of the truth. Whether you are correct in fixing the dates of the prophetic time, will soon be determined. At any rate, if the general theory is correct, the time is near, even at the door; and it becomes us to sound the midnight cry, Behold, the bridegroom cometh. The more I examine the prophecies and compare these prophetic periods with history, the more I am convinced that you are not far out of the way."

CONTENTS.

SECTION VI.

THE THREE WOES AND THE TWO WITNESSES.

ENCOURAGEMENT FOR STUDYING THE BOOK OF REVELATION.

As the limits I have prescribed for myself in this work will not admit of my entering so fully into an examination of the book of Revelation as I could wish, I shall content myself with remarking upon some of the *most important* (if it is proper to use the term) points presented in that most deeply interesting book.

I am not unaware of the prejudice existing in the Christian world, against the study of this book, with the idea of understanding its meaning; but so long as I believe it to be, what it professes in its introduction to be, "THE REVELATION OF JESUS CHRIST, *which God gave unto him, to show unto his servants things which must shortly come to pass;* and he sent and signified it by his angel unto his servant John; who bare record of the word of God;" so long shall I feel justified in studying this sacred book. And again, while it is recorded, "*Blessed* is he that *readeth*, and *they that hear the words of this prophecy, and keep those things which are written therein*," I shall be encouraged, whatever my fellow-creatures may think of it, to endeavor, according to my ability, to *read and understand* these words; for God has pronounced his blessing on such a work. Can we ask, then, for stronger encouragement for reading and endeavoring to understand the book? It is Heaven's own book, and as such, it is every way worthy of our perusal. We will, therefore, enter on the examination of one of the subjects presented in this interesting prophetic book, viz., the sounding of the three woe trumpets spoken of in the 9th, 10th and 11th chapters. I have selected this particular subject, because it affords some striking and tangible evidence of the near approach of the *everlasting kingdom* of the Lord Jesus Christ. For, when the sixth angel has done sounding, the second woe will be passed, and the third woe and the seventh trumpet will come quickly. And when the seventh trumpet does sound, and third woe come, then, "the kingdoms of this world shall become the kingdoms of our Lord and his Christ; and he shall reign forever and ever."

THE ANGEL OF THE BOTTOMLESS PIT, REV. IX.

"And the fifth angel sounded, and I saw a star fall from heaven unto the earth: and to him was given the key of the bottomless pit. And he opened the bottomless pit; and there arose a smoke out of the pit, as the smoke of a great furnace; and the sun and the air were darkened by reason of the smoke of the pit. And there came locusts out of the smoke on the earth; and unto them was given power, as the scorpions of the earth have power. And it was commanded that they should not hurt the grass of the earth, neither any green thing, neither any tree; but only those men which have not the seal of God in their foreheads. And to them it was given that they should not kill them, but that they should be tormented FIVE MONTHS."

There is a very general agreement at the present day, among prophetic expositors, that the subject of this prophecy is Mohammedism. I shall not, therefore, enter into a particular explanation of the various figures used in the prophecy, but take it for granted that those who thus apply it are correct, and confine myself principally to the examination of the prophetic periods mentioned in the chapter, and endeavor to show their fulfillment. If this can be done, it is in itself the stongest evidence that a right application is made of the prophecy, when it is applied to Mohammedism.

The first prophetic period which occurs in the chapter, is in the 5th verse; "*that they should be tormented five months.*" A prophetic month consists of 30 days, as in Rev. xiii., and each day represents a year. Five months will amount to 150 years. During 150 years the locusts (or warlike armies of horsemen) which came out of the smoke (the Mohammedan errors), for the propagation of his religion, were to torment a certain nation of men. But what nation? And when were they to begin the work? These are questions to be settled.

I shall endeavor to determine the first question by settling the second. *When, then, were the Mohammedan armies to commence their torment on a certain people for 150 years?*

Verse 10, the period is again referred to. "And their power was to hurt men five months." The 11th verse pointed out the time when those months were to commence. "And they had a king over them, which is the angel of the bottomless pit, whose name in the Hebrew tongue is Abaddon (that is, a destroyer), but in the Greek tongue he hath his name Apollyon" (destroyer).

The beginning of the five months, then, is when these armies *have* ONE *king* over them, of the character above described.

After the death of Mohamet, his followers were divided into various factions, under several leaders. In this state they continued, until the close of the 13th century. They were then united under one government, under Othman, the founder of the Ottoman or Turkish empire. The founder of the government, as well as the government itself, was truly described when called Abaddon, or Apollyon, a destroyer.

But this king was to be the *angel*, or *chief minister*, of the bottomless pit, or of the religion which arose from thence under Mohamet. Such was Othman; and such have been his successors. Like the Pope of Rome, the Turkish Sultan has exercised supreme power, both civil and ecclesiastical, throughout his dominions. This empire was established A. D. 1299. "And on the 27th day of July, 1299, Othman first invaded the territory of Nicomedia," to commence his attack on the Greek empire. (See Gibbon's History of the Decline and Fall of the Roman Empire.)

Beginning in 1299, the 150 years would end A. D. 1449. In that year, John Palealogus, the Greek emperor, died, and left no children to succeed him in the throne; and his brother, Constantine Deacozes, was to succeed him. But, from some cause or other, although it was a time of peace, before he dared to ascend his brother's throne, he sent ambassadors to Amurath, the Turkish Sultan, to ask his permission; and having obtained it, he assumed the government of the empire. Thus, for 150 years, from 1299 to 1449, although the two powers were almost continually engaged in broils and contentions, yet the Turks could not prevail against the Greeks. "Their power was to torment," by sudden excursions. Thus far they might go, but no farther. The 150 years ended, and with it virtually ended the Greek empire; because from that time the Greek emperor only reigned by permission of his deadly foe. Thus closed the sounding of the fifth angel, and thus ended the first woe. The men then which they were to torment were the Greeks.

SOUNDING OF THE SIXTH ANGEL.

Verses 12—15. "One woe is past, *and* behold there come two woes more hereafter. And the sixth angel sounded, and I heard a voice from the four horns of the golden altar which is before God, saying to the sixth angel which had the trumpet, Loose the four angels which are bound in the great river Euphrates. And the four angels were loosed, which were prepared for an hour, and a day, and a month, and a year, to slay the third part of men."

One woe ended with the 5 months or 150 years, and two more were to succeed it. The second woe began when the sixth angel began to sound. The same power which had restrained the Ottomans to the work of tormenting men five months, on the sounding of the sixth angel commanded that restraint to be taken off. "*Loose the four angels which are bound in the great river Euphrates. And the four angels were loosed.*"

"The four angels" are the four principal nations of which the Ottoman empire is composed, located in the neighborhood of the Euphrates. They had hitherto been confined to the work of tormenting the Greeks, without politically putting them to death. But from this time they were to slay, politically kill, that nation.

Accordingly, when the 150 years ended, the Turks were loosed, and the independence of the Greeks ceased, by their voluntarily acknowledging that they only existed politically by the permission of the Turkish Sultan.

But the duration of their dominion over the Greek empire is limited to "*an hour*," 15 days; "*and a day*," one year; "*and a month*," 30 years; "*and a year*," 360 years; the whole amounting to 391 years and 15 days. Both periods, *the 150 years, and 391 years and 15 days*, are 541 years and 15 days. The first period was fulfilled, and the four angels were loosed. Hence, we may expect that when the second period closes, with it will close the reign of the Ottomans in Constantinople. If the time for commencing the periods was at the time of the first onset of the Ottomans upon the Greeks, July 27, 1299, THEN THE WHOLE PERIOD WILL END IN AUGUST, 1840.

All observers of the signs of the times must acknowledge that from present appearances in the eastern world, there is nothing improbable in the idea that the Turkish power will fall in the course of the present year. If it does, we shall be furnished with another demonstration of the fulfillment of prophetic periods, and shall be able to decide with certainty that the ninth chapter of Revelation predicts the Mohammedan government. The conclusion, also, that the sounding of the last trump is at the door, will be inevitable and irresistible to all who believe the word of God.

I wish to invite the reader's particular attention to this point. It is, on some accounts, the most important event of time predicted, and to take place in futurity. After the fall of Constantinople, or the Turkish power located there, we may not look for any very signal event to take place as an index of the coming of the Lord, until the mystery of God is finished.

ACCOMPLISHMENT OF THE FOREGOING CALCULATIONS.

When the above was written, the result was in futurity, and was purely a matter of calculation; but *now*, however, the time is passed, and it is proper that we should inquire whether the event has answered the calculations.[1]

1. HAS, THEN, THE OTTOMAN SUPREMACY IN CONSTANTINOPLE BEEN BROKEN, OR HAS IT BEEN LOST?

1st Testimony. The *London Morning Herald*, after the capture of St. Jean d'Acre, speaking of the state of things in the Ottoman empire, says: "We (the allies) have conquered St. Jean d'Acre. We have dissipated into thin air the *prestige* that till lately invested as with a *halo* the name of Mehemet Ali. We have, in all probability, destroyed forever the power of that hitherto successful ruler. *But have we done aught to restore strength to the Ottoman empire?* WE FEAR NOT. WE FEAR THAT THE SULTAN HAS BEEN REDUCED TO THE RANK OF A PUPPET; AND THAT THE SOURCES OF THE TURKISH EMPIRE'S STRENGTH are ENTIRELY DESTROYED."

"If the supremacy of the Sultan is hereafter to be maintained in Egypt, it must be maintained, we fear, by the *unceasing intervention* of England and Russia."

What the *London Morning Herald* last November feared has since been realized. The Sultan has been entirely, in all the great ques-

[1] This calculation and this part of this discourse was made and published first in 1838, as we have before recorded.

tions which have come up, under the dictation of the Christian kingdoms of Europe; and on them he has been dependent for support against Mehemet.

2d Testimony. The following is from Rev. Mr. Goodell, missionary of the American Board at Constantinople, addressed to the Board, and by them published in the Missionary Herald, for April, 1841, page 160:

"The power of Islamism is broken forever; and there is no concealing the fact, even from themselves. They exist now by mere sufferance. And though there is a mighty effort made by the Christian governments to sustain them, yet at every step they sink lower and lower with fearful velocity. And though there is a great endeavor made to graft the institutions of civilized and Christian countries upon the decayed trunk, yet the very root itself is fast wasting away by the venom of its own poison. How wonderful it is, that, when all Christendom combined together to check the progress of Mohammedan power, it waxed exceedingly great in spite of every opposition; and now, when all the mighty potentates of Christian Europe, who feel fully competent to settle all the quarrels, and arrange all the affairs of the whole world, are leagued together for its protection and defense, down it comes, in spite of all their fostering care."

This, let it be remembered, is the clear, positive testimony of an eye-witness, a man who is on the spot, and who knows whereof he affirms. For truth and veracity, he has the confidence of the American Board of Commissioners for Foreign Missions, and they, in their official organ, have given publicity to the testimony. Reader, please review this witness's testimony, and mark its point and strength.

3d Testimony. The following is an extract from a London paper: the article is headed, "The Waning of the Ottoman Empire." It has been copied into most of the leading journals of this country, without one word of dissent on the part of any. Thus the whole editorial corps in this country have given it their official sanction.

The object of the writer is to show the relative condition of the Turkish and Christian powers of Europe. In former times the Turkish empire exceeded in power every kingdom in Europe. But the scene is changed; the Turks are weakened and the Christian nations strengthened. The article concludes thus: "*The day they* (the nations of Europe) *counted their numbers, was to be the last of Constantinople;* AND THAT DAY HAS EVERYWHERE COME."

So, according to all our leading periodicals, the last of Constantinople has come.

4th Testimony. Dr. Bond, editor of the *Christian Advocate and Journal*, New York, in one of the May numbers of that paper, concludes his account of Eastern affairs thus: "*The Mohammedan nations are effectually in the hands and at the mercy of the Christian governments.*"

This is granting all we ask. Turkish supremacy is gone, and is in the hands of Christian powers. With these I shall close the testimony on this point; and proceed to inquire—

2. WHEN DID THE OTTOMAN INDEPENDENCE DEPART?

Perhaps it may be said in reply, "It has been decaying for years." True, it has. But if its power is broken forever, as Mr. Goodell declares, there must have been a point when it was broken. If it is dead, there was a moment when it ceased to be alive, and became dead. When was that crisis? To answer this question understandingly and clearly, it will be necessary to take a view of the Eastern difficulty, and the means adopted for its settlement.

For some years, Mehemet Ali, Pacha of Egypt, had manifested a disposition to throw off the Turkish yoke and maintain an independent government. He gradually increased in power, and extended his conquests, wresting one province after another from the Sultan, adding it to his own dominions. In 1839, a war broke out between Mehemet and the Sultan, in which the Sultan's army were cut up, and his fleet taken by Mehemet and carried to Egypt, which he refused to surrender and return to the Sultan; threatening to burn it, if an attempt should be made to take it.

The following extracts from the translation of an official document which appeared in the "*Moniteur Ottoman*," *of Aug. 22, 1840*, will show the turn of the affair at this juncture:

"Subsequent to the occurrence of the disputes alluded to, and after the reverses experienced, as known to all the world, the ambassadors of the great powers at Constantinople, in a collective official note, declared, that their governments were unanimously agreed upon taking measures to arrange said differences, and the sublime Porte, with a view of putting a stop to the effusion of Mussulman blood, and to the various evils which would arise from a renewal of hostilities, accepted the intervention of the great powers. His excellency *Shekiah Effendi*, the Bey likgis, was therefore dispatched a *plenipotentiary*, to represent the sublime Porte, at the conference which took place in London (July 15, 1840), for the purpose in question.

The conference was composed of England, Russia, Austria, and Prussia, together with the Sultan's ambassador. The following extract from the same official document above quoted, shows the decision of that conference:

"It having been felt that all the zealous labors of the conferences of London in the settlement of the Pacha's pretensions were useless, and that the only public way was to have recourse to coercive measures to reduce him to obedience in case he persisted in not listening to pacific overtures, the powers have, together with the OTTOMAN PLENIPOTENTIARY, drawn up and signed a treaty whereby the Sultan offers the Pacha the hereditary government of Egypt, and of all that part of Syria extending from the Gulf of Suez to the Lake of Tiberias, together with the province of Acre, for life; the Pacha, on his part, evacuating all other parts of the Sultan's dominions now occupied by him, and returning the Ottoman fleet. A certain space of time has been granted him to accede to these terms, as the proposals of the Sultan and his allies, the four powers, *do not admit of any change or qualification, if the Pacha refuse to accede to them, it is evident that the evil consequences to fall upon him will be attributable solely to his own fault.* His EXCELLENCY RIFAT BEY, Musteshar for foreign affairs, has been dispatched to Alexandria in a government steamer, to communicate their ultimatum to the Pacha."

The reason why the Sultan thus submitted the decision of the question to the Christian powers is intimated in a manifesto which he issued about the 20th of August, and caused to be read in the mosques, day after day. It was because he felt his weakness and the danger of his throne.

"The Porte in order to counteract this (the pretensions of Mehemet), has deemed it necessary to publish a manifesto, laying before its subjects a statement of affairs from the commencement of the quarrel up to the present time, and proving to them, by the clearest arguments, that the Pacha himself is the enemy of their religion, AND THAT THE OBJECT HE IS AIMING AT IS TO DETHRONE THE SULTAN."—*Corres. Lond. Morn. Chronicle.*

If we can place any confidence in the declaration of the Sultan, he did feel his throne to be in danger; and this was his reason for throwing himself on his allies for support.

The ultimatum of the London conference, it seems, was put into the hands of the Sultan, to treat with Mehemet, and if possible settle the difficulty without the further intervention of his allies. But if Mehemet refused to accede to the terms, which admitted of no change or qualification, the great powers were pledged to use coercive measures. While, therefore, the Sultan held the ultimatum in his own hands, his independence was maintained; but the question once submitted to Mehemet, and it was beyond his control. True, if Mehemet accepted the ultimatum, the Ottoman independence would remain; but if he rejected it, there was no alternative but for the Christian powers to interpose and put him down.

Rifat Bey left Constantinople for Egypt, with the ultimatum, August 5th, 1840.

"He arrived at Alexandria on the 11th of August, and was by Mehemet's orders placed in quarantine until the 16th." Thus on the 11th of August the question of war or peace was taken from the Sultan's hands and placed in Mehemet's, so that the Sultan could no longer control the affair.

The 541 years 15 days, commencing July 27th, 1299, would end on the 11th of August; just the day Rifat Bey arrived at Alexandria.

On the 15th of August, Mehemet gave his answer to the Sultan in the following note:

"Wallah, hillah, tillah," (an oath, by God.) "I will not yield a span of the land I possess, and if war is made against me, I will turn the empire upside down and be buried in its ruins.

MEHEMET ALI."

This was the decisive stroke, and under it the Ottoman power was thrown into the hands of the Christian nations of Europe. And the very next day, the 16th, the consuls of the four powers took up the affair and remonstrated with him for his course, and threatened him if he did not submit. Since then, the Sultan has been under the necessity of submitting to the dictation of the European powers in all the affairs of his empire.

I am now entirely satisfied that *on the 11th day of August*, ACCORDING TO PREVIOUS CALCULATION, THE END OF 541 YEARS 15 DAYS, THE OTTOMAN SUPREMACY DEPARTED; and that on the 15th of August, the control of the empire was thrown into Christian hands, from which it had departed 391 years 15 days before. Thus the Ottomans were loosed and prepared for an hour, a day, a month, and a year, to slay the third part of men. That time ended, and their power was broken, and Christian power restored to Constantinople.

After the prediction of the Turkish power, the Revelator continues, chap. 10th, and relates what he saw farther. He saw an angel stand upon the sea and upon the earth, who "lifted up his hand to heaven, and sware by him that liveth forever and ever, who created heaven and the things that therein are, and the earth, and the things that are therein, and the sea, and the things that are therein, that there should be time no longer. But in the days of the voice of the seventh angel, when he shall begin to sound, the mystery of God should be finished; as he hath declared to his servants the prophets."

The Revelator was here permitted to anticipate the sounding of the seventh angel, and the event of his sounding, but the way was not yet prepared for presenting in due form the sounding of the seventh trumpet.

The history of the Greek church and their oppression by the Mohammedans was given in the 9th chapter, which brought us down to the ending of the second woe; but before the event of the third woe could be fully presented, another line of prophecy must be brought up to the same period. That line was to give the suffering and depressed condition of true religion in the west, and its triumph before the end.

THE LITTLE BOOK AND ITS CONTENTS. REV. TENTH AND ELEVENTH CHAPTERS.

The Revelator was directed to go and take a little book out of the angel's hand and eat it up. This he did: and was then told that he must prophesy again, before many peoples, and nations, and tongues, and kings.

The events of the little book are the events predicted in the 11th chapter. And it was those events he was to predict before peoples, nations, tongues, and kings, before he could fully present the third woe.

THE TWO WITNESSES PROPHESY IN SACKCLOTH.

Chapter xi. 1, 2. "And there was given me a reed like unto a rod; and the angel stood, saying, Rise and measure the temple of God, and the altar, and them that worship therein. But the court which is without the temple leave out, and measure it not; for it is given unto the Gentiles; and the holy city shall they tread under foot forty *and* two months."

The temple here spoken of, and which the Revelator was commanded to measure, is the church of Christ, composed of his living members, whether Jews or Gentiles. See Eph. ii. 19–22. This is emphatically the temple of God; and it was the church he was to measure.

"But the court . . . leave out . . . it is given unto the Gentiles, and the holy city shall they tread under foot 42 months."

In the ancient temple at Jerusalem the outer court was devoted to the Gentiles; into that they were permitted to enter and present their sacrifice to the priest.

So also in the Christian temple, there are those who, although professed members of Christ's body, are no more than Gentile or outer court worshippers, after all. Such is, and has been, the character of the church of Rome. She, while God has had a seed to serve him, has been treading that holy city under foot, and for 42 months, or 1260 years, the saints were given into her hand to oppress, persecute, and put to death. This church was not, in measuring the true church, to be taken into the account as forming any part of the temple of God.

Verse 3d. "And I will give power unto my two witnesses, and they shall prophesy a thousand two hundred and threescore days, clothed in sackcloth." Verse 4. "These are the two olive trees, and the two candlesticks standing before the God of the earth."

The 4th verse seems to be a reference to Zach. 4th chapter. The prophet was presented in vision with a view of two olive trees. He asked, What are these? and was told, "This is the WORD OF THE LORD unto Zerubbabel."

The two olive trees, then, represent the word of the Lord. Had we no farther evidence as to the character and person of the two witnesses, this ought to be sufficient. But we have other evidence. John v. 39. Jesus said to the Jews, "Search the Scriptures, for in them ye think ye have eternal life; and they are they which testify of me." Here the Saviour explicitly asserted that the Old-Testament Scriptures bore witness of him. And hence they are his witness.

Again; Matt. xxiv. 14. He said, "This gospel of the kingdom must be preached in all the world, for a witness unto all nations." What is this but calling the gospel his witness? The Old and New Testaments are, therefore, Christ's two witnesses. They were to "*prophesy*," testify the truth of God, during all that long dark night of papal rule.

"*Clothed in sackcloth.*" Sackcloth is the emblem of sorrow or mourning. So the word of God is represented as mourning over the desolation of the church during that reign of wickedness. But still it bore a faithful testimony, and many by its heavenly light were led to the Saviour.

"If any man will hurt them, fire proceedeth out of their mouth and devoureth their enemies."

If any man add to the words of this book, it testifies that God will add to him the plagues written therein. And if any take away from the words of this book, his part shall be taken from the book of life, and from the holy city. Again, John xii. 48. "He that rejecteth me, and receiveth not my words, hath one that *judgeth him; the word that I have spoken*, the same shall judge him in the last day." Thus fire proceedeth out of the mouth of these witnesses and devoureth all who would hurt them.

"*These have power to shut heaven that it rain not.*" When the word of God was obscured, the rain of grace, the genial influences of the gospel, were withheld; revivals of religion, during the greatest part of papal rule, were almost unknown. "*And have power over waters to turn them to blood.*" While the restraints of the word of God were withdrawn, the nations of the earth were continually involved in war and bloodshed.

"*And when they have finished their testimony,*" or, according to Faber, when they are about to finish their testimony, "*the beast that ascendeth out of the bottomless pit shall make war against them, and shall overcome them, and kill them.*"

The beast from the bottomless pit is the same as the willful king, Dan. xi. 36, *revolutionary France.* That infidel government, so far as it could be done, made war on, and put to death, both the Bible and the God of the Bible. The one they declared, by a formal enactment, a lie, and prohibited its use; and the other they declared a nonentity, a being which did not exist.

They not only declared the Bible a lie and prohibited its use, but gathered it in heaps and burned it. At other times it was dragged through the streets with every circumstance of contempt.

"*And their dead bodies shall lie in the streets of the great city, which spiritually is called Sodom, and Egypt, where also our Lord was crucified.*"

"Streets of the great city." *Paris.* "Spiritually is called *Sodom.*" The crying sin of *Sodom* was its licentiousness. But probably in no part of the world, since the ruin of Sodom, has this sin ever been carried so far as in France during the reign of terror. On the 6th of June, 1794, a formal enactment was passed in the city of Paris, to establish fornication by law. A parallel cannot be found.

It is also spiritually called "*Egypt.*" The crying sin of Egypt was her atheism. "Who is the Lord, that I should let the people go? I know not the Lord, neither will I let the people go," was the language of Pharaoh. So also was it in France. One infidel, after the existence of God had been denied, declared that he and his fellows "*detested God.*"

"*Where also our Lord was crucified.*" The motto and watchword of the infidel crew was "*Crush the wretch,*" meaning Christ. Nor was it an empty cry. All who bore the name of Christ were either banished from France or seized and put to death. It might be also in reference to the murder of the 30,000 Christians, members of Christ's body, on St. Bartholomew's eve, that it is said to be the great city "where our Lord was crucified."

"And they of the people, and kindreds, and tongues, and nations, shall see their dead bodies three days and a half, and shall not suffer their dead bodies to be put in graves." The nations of the earth saw and heard of the dangers of the French revolutionists in regard to the Bible, but did not suffer it to be buried out of sight. It still stood out prominently in Great Britain. "*Three days and a half.*" The decree condemning the Bible and establishing atheism was passed Aug. 26, 1792. And that decree continued in force until March, 1796, a period of about three and a half years. During those three and a half years they lay dead in Paris in sight of the nations.

"And after three days (years) and a half, the spirit of life from God entered into them." The decree by which they were condemned was repealed, and the Bible was again permitted to be read.

"And they heard a great voice from heaven, saying unto them, Come up hither. And they ascended up to heaven in a cloud; and their enemies beheld them."

The great voice from heaven is the great demand which the world has made for the Bible since that time. The 1260 years of the prophesying in sackcloth of the two witnesses ended with the fall of Popery, 1798. In 1801 the British and Foreign Bible Society was formed, which, by the aid of the American Bible Society, has translated and printed the Bible, either in whole or in part, into more than 150 different languages. And missionary societies have been multiplying beyond even the most sanguine expectations of the warmest friend of the heathen world forty years ago, and the work is still going forward with unparalleled rapidity. The gospel will continue thus to spread until it has reached the last heathen nation as Christ's witness; "then," according to his declaration, "shall the end come." And the same fact is presented in Rev. xi. 14, 15. "The second woe is past, and behold the third woe cometh quickly. And the seventh angel sounded; and there were great voices in heaven, saying, The kingdoms of this world have become the kingdoms of our Lord and his Christ; and he shall reign forever and ever."

If the calculation on the periods of the 9th chapter are correct, we are upon the very verge of the time when this text will begin to be accomplished. For as soon as the second woe passes, the third will come QUICKLY. How soon, it is impossible to tell. The only safety any one can have, will be in securing an interest in the Lord Jesus Christ. The third woe will come as a thief in the night. It will come when the world are crying peace and safety. Of the day and the hour, no man knoweth. But rest assured, reader, when you see the Turkish empire fall (it has now fallen), that it is nigh, even at the door. And by the close of 1843,[1] we may expect that all these things will be finished, and the righteous glorified.

Now, I ask those who contend for a *temporal millennium*, to show me where it is to find a place between the sounding of the seventh angel, when the kingdoms of this world shall become the kingdoms of our Lord and his Christ, and he begins his everlasting reign, "and the time of the dead (verse 18), that they should be judged, and that God should give reward unto his servants, the prophets, and to the saints, and them that fear his name, small and great; and destroys them that destroy the earth?"

Where, again I ask, is the place for the millennium to be found?

Then "let Zion's watchmen all awake." Let them cry aloud and spare not, until a slumbering world is awake to its danger, and flies to Christ for refuge. For now it is especially true, that "He which testifieth these things, saith, Surely I come quickly. Amen. Even so, come, Lord Jesus." "The grace of our Lord Jesus Christ be with you all. Amen." Revelation xxii. 20, 21.—*Second Advent Library, Vol. 5.*

"But, above all, in her own light arrayed,
See Mercy's grand apocalypse displayed;
The sacred book no longer suffers wrong,
Bound in the fetters of an unknown tongue;
But speaks with plainness, art could never mend,
What simplest minds can soonest comprehend."

Cowper.

[1] This expectation was, of course, not realized, yet this does not at all affect the argument on these trumpets. The term quickly measures more time than was expected.—*Editor.*

CHAPTER VI.

A. D. EIGHTEEN HUNDRED AND TWENTY-ONE TO EIGHTEEN HUNDRED AND THIRTY-FOUR.

THE MESSAGE IN ASIA—DR. JOSEPH WOLFF—WAY'S DESCRIPTION OF WOLFF—HIS JOURNAL, CORRESPONDENCE, PREACHING, CONVERSATIONS—DR. RAMSEY—DR. POOR—CHARLOTTE ELIZABETH—HER CONVERSION TO THE FAITH—HER POEM.

While the Lord was awakening and preparing servants on the American continent to "proclaim to the daughters of Zion, Behold, thy salvation cometh; his reward is with him, and his work before him." He was also preparing others on the Eastern continent and sending them forth to do the same work in those parts of the world.

We will therefore examine some of the results of his wondrous grace as manifested in the proclamation of the immediate coming of Christ, by one of the missionaries of the cross.

Here we find among those who are preaching the crucified and risen Christ and Saviour, one by the name of Joseph Wolff, a man of very remarkable qualifications for missionary work, proclaiming, from A. D. 1821 to 1834, to the churches in the East, and to Kings, Rulers, Princes, Priests, and peasants of all grades and religions, and in many tongues, that Jesus Christ is about to come in person and in glory, to reign on David's throne, over the earth made new, with all his saints raised from the dead to immortality.

Mr. Wolff's "Researches and Missionary Labors" were published in "four separate volumes," while "his labors in England, Scotland, Ireland, Holland, and again in the Mediterranean, were published in the 'Jewish Expositor.'" We have but one volume; from that we gather interesting facts not generally known to the public; we shall therefore give copious extracts.

The book containing the Journals of Dr. Wolff, from which I make extracts, was published in Philadelphia, by Oren Rogers, entitled

Researches and Missionary Labors among the Jews, Mohammedans, and other sects, by the Rev. Joseph Wolff, during his travels between the years 1831 and 1834.

The preface of this book is dated, Malta, Jan. 29, 1835, in which he says, "The object of my journey was solely to proclaim the gospel of the kingdom of Christ among the Jews, and the tribes whom I have visited." According to his Journals, between the years 1821 and 1845, he "proclaimed the Lord's speedy advent in Palestine, Egypt, on the shores of the Red Sea, Mesopotamia, the Crimea, Persia, Georgia, throughout the Ottoman Empire, in Greece, Arabia, Turkistan, Bokhara, Affghanistan, Cashmere, Hindostan, Thibet, in Holland, Scotland, and Ireland, at Constantinople, Jerusalem, St. Helena, also on ship-board in the Mediterranean, and in New York city, to all denominations." He declares he has preached among Jews, Turks, Mohammedans, Parsees, Hindoos, Chaldeans, Yeseedees, Syrians, Sabeans, to Pachas, Sheiks, the kings of Organtsh and Bokhara, the Queen of Greece, etc., and of his extraordinary labors the *Investigator* says:—"No individual has, perhaps, given greater publicity to the doctrine of the second coming of the Lord Jesus Christ than this well-known missionary to the world. Wherever he goes, he proclaims the approaching advent of the Messiah in glory."

Mr. Wolff preached at nearly all the Christian missionary stations in the whole East, and held conversations with most of the missionaries in those fields of labor.

Thus it will be seen that the message of Christ's speedy coming began to be proclaimed extensively in those Eastern countries at the same time it was being heard among the Christian churches in America. And we find that there among those barbarous and semi-barbarous nations, God's special blessing attended the proclamation, and many were turned to the Lord through it.

We will give below some sketches concerning this man of God, which will show something of the kind of instrumentalities the Lord chooses to perform important work where great obstacles are to be overcome.

JOSEPH WOLFF.

Dr. Brownlee says, "the following amusing portait of this most remarkable man was, some years ago, given by his attached friend and fellow-traveler, the Rev. Lewis Way:—

"'A man who, at Rome, calls the Pope 'the dust of the earth,' and tells the Jews at Jerusalem that 'the Gemara is a lie;' who passes his days in disputation, and his nights in digging the Talmud; to whom a floor of brick is a feather bed, and a box a bolster; who finds or makes a friend alike in the persecutor of his former or present faith; who can conciliate a Pasha, or confute a patriarch; who travels without a guide, speaks without an interpreter, can live without food, and pay without money;—forgiving all the insults he meets with and forgetting all the flattery he receives; who knows little of worldly conduct, and yet accommodates himself to all men, without giving offence to any; such a man (and such and more is Wolff) must excite no ordinary degree of attention in a country, and among a people, whose monotony of manners has remained undisturbed for centuries. . . . By such an instrument, whom no school hath taught, whom no college could hold, is the way of the Judean wilderness preparing.'

"Such is a striking (though somewhat hyperbolical) delineation of a man, who, for laboriousness, may be classed with Wesley and Whitefield, and for eccentricity, may be ranked with Berridge, Everton, and Rowland Hill."—*History of the Jews, p.* 303.

"This oddity among men in the missionary field was born in the little village of Weilersbach, near Bamberg, in Bavaria, in the year 1796. His father was a Jewish rabbi. In early life he became interested in religious matters, and in his search for the truth entered the Roman Catholic church. In Rome he studied theology, but while there he "heard many sentiments and saw many practices in the church against which his conscience revolted," and being "openly obliged to protest against them," Pius VII. and Cardinal Litta decreed his banishment from the city. In course of time his peregrinations brought him to England, where a gentleman with whom he had become acquainted in Rome "recommended him to the London Society for promoting Christianity amongst the Jews, as a person likely to prove a valuable missionary for Jerusalem and the East;" and on examination he was received, and entered upon a course of study which prepared him for his work. He left England in the summer of 1821, on his first missionary tour in the Orient.

At what time Dr. Wolff embraced the doctrine of the pre-millennial advent we know not, but find him on his first tour, in conversation with his countrymen, advocating the coming of our Lord Jesus Christ before his reign of righteousness and peace.

The year 1847 was the one to which he looked forward with much interest, as the time when some of the prophetic periods would terminate and the Lord's last advent be likely to take place. But in this he was disappointed. In his latter years, he settled down as an Episcopal clergyman in England, but still clung to the idea of the Lord's coming as an event to take place at no distant day. On May 5th, 1862, he died in the faith of Christ, and in hope of a "part in the first resurrection.'"—*Advent Herald.*

Dr. Wolff, was one of those bold, direct conversational men, who make their business and message known at once, and proceed to tell what they have to say, and to ask information on any point they wish to know. He preached Christ, and his soon coming, to thousands, in tents, in palaces, in private rooms and public halls, in large assemblies, and in private dwellings, on ship board and in caravans. He conversed and corresponded with kings, queens, prime ministers, politicians, priests and laymen, doctors and lawyers, teachers and school men; always interchanging thoughts and doctrinal views on religion, and openly controverting the false views of the eastern nations and sects, yet in so kind a manner that they could but highly respect him.

But he several times found those who threatened his life. Persistently, but patiently, he would inquire of all, what they thought of Jesus Christ, and of his second advent; thereby he obtained many important facts of their various beliefs and traditions. He was a man of deep and rich Christian experience and heart religion, and fearing God always, he often astonished those different tribes, who declared they had "never seen a European before who was really interested in God and religion."

From his travels in the east we gather the following traditions, current among the Asiatic nations:

In ARABIA the Jews of *Yemen*, the *Rechabites*, and the children of Israel, of the tribe of *Dan*, expect the speedy arrival of the Messiah in the clouds of heaven. The children of Rechab say: "We shall one day fight the battles of the Messiah and march towards Jerusalem." *Rabbi Alkaree*, one of the Jews of Yemen, said: "We do expect the coming of the Messiah. . . There is war in the wilderness unprecedented in our memory."

In THIBET, one of their chiefs said: "When you shall see corn growing upon my grave, then the day of resurrection is nigh at hand." The people of *Cashmere* assured me that corn had begun to grow upon his grave, and therefore they considered my words to be true, that Jesus will come.

THE JEWS IN PERSIA say the world is to exist six thousand years, and that the Messiah will appear, and the sabbatical year shall have its commencement. One of their Rabbis read to Mr. Wolff, from

Maimonides, that "The King Messiah shall rise to make the kingdom of David return to its former condition and power," that "whosoever does not hope in his coming denies the words of the prophets and the law of Moses," that "in his days the Messiah shall rule alone, and only he," that "on his arrival the battle of Gog and Magog shall be fought," that "we must wait for his coming," and that, "at that time there shall be hunger and war no more, and envy and anger shall cease among us."

THE GUEBERS of India and Persia who worship fire are acquainted with the history of the fallen angels, and believe in the deluge, and that a time is coming when this world will pass away and another will be created. The Musselmans, the worshippers of Ali and Mohammedan Jews and Mullahs, many of them believe in the coming of a deliverer called "Mohde" (translated from Shiloh), who shall restore all things before the day of judgment, and be proclaimed sovereign: a messenger going on before him. They told Wolff that they were glad to find he expected the speedy arrival of the Messiah Jesus; for the signs of the times prove that Mohde must soon come, one stating to him that she had discovered by the book called "Khorooj Namah," that Christ will come again in the year 1861. "They derive," says Wolff, "most of this from their *Hadees* or traditional prophecies."

The HINDOOS have a tradition that VISHNOO is to come to destroy the world for a season, a belief analogous to the advent of Christ to judgment. They have also a record of the submersion of the world by a deluge.

The following dialogue occurred between Mr. Wolff and a Persian Dervish:

Wolff.—What will become of this world?

Dervish.—The world will become so good that the lamb and the wolf shall feed together, and there shall be general peace and fear of God upon the earth; there shall be no more controversy about religion, all shall know God truly; there shall be no more hatred, etc.

Wolff.—Who then shall govern the earth?

Dervish.—JESUS.

Dr. Wolff says they got this from their *Hadees;* and he adds, that in his opinion more light is to be found among them than among the most learned neologists and infidels in Europe.

In Yemen (Teman of Scripture) a Rabbi told Mr. Wolff that his tribe did not return to Jerusalem after the Babylonish captivity. When Ezra by letters invited their princes in Tanaan to return, they replied, "Daniel predicts the murder of the Messiah, and another destruction of Jerusalem and the temple; therefore we will not go up until He shall have scattered the power of the holy people—till the 1290 days (meaning years) are over. . . . But we do expect the coming of the Messiah," etc.

"Rabbi Pinehas Ben Simha told me, that according to the opinion of his late father-in-law, Rabbi Joseph Mooghrebee, three events were to happen before the arrival of the Messiah:

First, Russia shall force her Jewish subjects to become soldiers.
Second, The Ottoman Power shall subdue Russia.
Third, The Ottoman Power shall again be subdued by Russia."

"Rabbi Pinehas Ben Simha told me, that 146 days before the arrival of the Messiah the son of David, the Messiah the son of Joseph must appear. I desired him to solve the difficulty in Psalm cx. 1. 'The Lord said unto my Lord, sit thou at my right hand.' 'Who was,' I asked him, 'the Lord of David?' Rabbi Pinehas replied, 'The prophet said to David, 'the Lord saith to my (the prophet's) Lord, *i. e.* David, remain for a while with the Yeminite, *i. e.* Saul, until I have made thine enemies thy footstool.'" In the first instance I showed him that David did not remain with Saul until his enemies were subdued, for he had to subdue them after Saul's death: beside this I showed him the grammatical incorrectness of it.

March 14, 1832.—A Jew from Bashgala called on me, by whom I got an exact statement of the Jews in Curdistan belonging to Persia, which I have already inserted in the first part of my late journal about Tabreez.

Rabbi Matathia called on me. I showed to him Isaiah vii. 14, and desired him to translate *virgin*, and he translated it *virgin*.[1]

I. Who was the son of that virgin?

Matathia. The Messiah.

I. Why is the birth of a son of a virgin such a stupendous miracle, as described in Isaiah vii. 11?

M. She must have had a son without a husband.

I. When did such an event take place?

M. I do not know.

I. It took place at the birth of Jesus, son of the virgin Mary.

---

[1] A great proof, that the Christians have translated correctly those passages is, that Jews, who do not know of the controversy which is going on between Christians and Jews, give to those words the same interpretation as Christians do.

A long conversation then followed about Jesus and him crucified, which lasted a whole night; for it is not the case, as some assert, that since I believe the personal reign of Christ, I have ceased to preach Jesus Christ crucified: I preached the personal reign of Christ at Jerusalem, because it is a consolation to Jew and Gentile, and a holding out of a beautiful prospect to the Jews; Christ crucified is the medicine, the remedy, and the only consolation to the afflicted sinner. The cross of Christ is the banner to be lifted up against the enemy, when he surrounds us.

March 16.—I proclaimed the cross of Christ to Rabbi Gaday and to many other Jews.

My Turkomaun Awaz, who had brought me from Sarakhs to Bokhara, called on me; he advised me to go back with him to Sarakhs, saying, that he had heard that three Englishmen had been killed some years ago on their way to Bokhara. Awaz added, that if ever Hakham Eliahu from Bagdad, who wanted to make me suspected in the eyes of Goosh-Bekee, should come to Sarakhs, the Turkomauns would put him to death. I told him not to do such things.

March 19, 1832.—This day was a joyful day to me: Rabbi Pinehas Ben Simha professed his belief in the Lord Jesus Christ; he was fully convinced by the prophecies I pointed out to him. He told me that Rabbi Pinehas the elder had been convinced of the same truth; he advised me however not to speak with every Jew at Bokhara about religion, as many Jews are ignorant and obstinate. I have addressed the following

LETTER TO RABBI PINEHAS THE ELDER, GREAT RABBI OF THE JEWS OF BOKHARA.

"The Lord gives his covenant of peace, unto Rabbi Pinehas.

Know ye, that I, Joseph Wolff, believe, that Jesus of Nazareth is the Messiah, who was cut off, but not for himself; and that Jesus of Nazareth is the Messiah, who has given himself up unto death, and interceded for his enemies; and that Jesus of Nazareth is that Messiah, who shall come like the son of man in the clouds of heaven, and shall redeem Israel, saith Joseph Wolff, the Englishman."

THE TWO CLASSES OF PROFESSORS OF RELIGION.

Dr. Wolff says: In every denomination of religion, there are among its professors two kinds of people: first, those who content themselves with a cold orthodox creed, whilst they do not seek after internal religion, and close communion with God. This is the case among the professors of the Christian religion, and this I found to be the case with the Mohammedans. To the first class, the Mullahs of Bokhara belong; to the second class, the Dervishes of Bokhara, who are generally Sooffees, but of a different character from those of Persia. The Sooffees of Bokhara, are people who really try, as they express themselves, "to come nearer to God," by a moral life, separation from the world, meditation, prayer, and reading the books of other religious sects. Many of them are like Cornelius of Cesarea, whose prayers and alms went up as a memorial before God. These are termed hypocrites by the Mullahs; and as there are some hypocrites among the Bokhara Sooffees, they believe it right to reject the whole sect.

ARRIVED AT BALKH.

April 7.—I arrived at Balkh, the mother of cities, and lodged with Mullah Yehoodah Cashi, the Jew, my fellow-traveler, in the Jewish quarter, which is closed in by a gate, and shut up on a Sabbath day. Both chief Rabbis Mullah Benjamin Cashi, for whom I had a letter from the Jews of Meshed, and Mullah Simha called on me. I entered with them into an argument about Jesus Christ the very first hour of my arrival: they desired the Gospel in Hebrew, but alas, I had it not to give them. I promised to send it to them after my arrival in India. Mullah Yehoodah Cashi behaved very badly to me, for which he was reproved by the Rabbis: he first put me into a most filthy apartment; but when he saw that I wanted to go to the caravan-seray, he gave me a very nice room up stairs; he actually gave me nothing to eat, except some Indian corn, and cheated me as much as he could. My servant told me after this, that Yehoodah Cashi had told him, that he would try to get rid of me as soon as possible, in order that I may not infect the Jews with my doctrine; and that he believed he should be doing an acceptable thing before God, to cheat me as much as he could; for I was a heretic, and not a real Jew.

April 8.—I proclaimed the gospel to Mullah Benjamin, and proved to him, that Joseph's history was a type of Jesus of Nazareth. I scarcely ever saw a Rabbi so teachable as Mullah Benjamin.

April 9.—I was again visited by Mullah Benjamin, to whom I preached that Jesus was the Son of God. The more I see of this country, the more I am convinced that there is not a more hopeful field for a Missionary than Toorkestaun. The Persian likes to read the Bible, and to converse about religion for the sake of curiosity; but the Turkomauns in the desert, with all their barbarity, and the people of Bokhara, with all their corruption, and the inhabitants of Balkh, like to converse about religion, and to hear of it, from a genuine feeling for religion. The Jews of Balkh, and even the bigoted Yehoodah permitted me to read in the Law of Moses in their synagogue, and to preach to them Christ.

Mr. Wolff circulated a great number of Bibles and Testaments in various languages in all parts of the East where he traveled. He also found many who possessed it already, and were not ignorant of its contents.

We feel constrained to give the following extract from his journal, to show his deep interest in the welfare of humanity, and also the true spirit of Christian sympathy and gospel charity which animated the heart of this arduous and faithful servant of Jesus Christ:

CONVERSATION WITH TWO FAKEERS.

"Two Fakeers came to beg charity: one was naked, and the other had dust on his face.

Myself. (To the first.) What is your occupation?

Fakeer. The service of God.

M. How do you serve God?

F. By walking and dancing about like a fool, the whole day and the whole night; (and saying this, he began to dance about, exclaiming continually, 'O God! nothing but thou; O God, nothing but thou.')

M. (To the second.) Why have you dust on your face?

F. I am a Moored of Imam Jaapar Sadek, buried at Medinah. Man is dust, and therefore he must have dust on his face.

I proclaimed to them Jesus Christ, the Man of sorrows, the man who died upon Calvary; and showed them the unreasonableness of their present pursuits. The one washed the dust off his face with spittle, and the other ceased to dance, and exclaimed, "We have been convinced." It is striking, that as well in Persia, as in Hindostan, the Fakeers and Dervishes look with contempt upon every written word of God, and every outward ceremony of religion, and believe themselves to have obtained such a degree of perfection, that all these things, necessary for the generality of people, are not necessary for them. I think this is a great proof that all men descended from one common father, Adam; and that the human mind, and human thoughts, are the same in England, as among the Fakeers and learned men in Persia; though in different forms and shapes; in the one they are more refined and more clear than in the other. The system of Jacob Boehme, of Swedenborg, of Liebnitz, Emanuel Kant, Schelling, and Fichte, may be traced, and surely discovered in Persia, and among the Fakeers in the Himmalayah mountains; the law of celibacy, and in a great degree, the spirit of Roman Catholics, are both to be found among the Lamas at Ladak; and many a Catharine of Siena, and many a nun like Theresa of Cordova, may be found in the female convents of the Tshomo or Ane (Nuns) of Ladak and Lassa.

Thus it is with the relationship of human errors, and thus it is with the light of truth. The Spirit of God, I am convinced, now guides a Mohammed Shah Nakhshbande in the city of Cashmeer, and a Joseph of Talkhtoon in the desert of Mowr, in the same way as it did Cornelius and Job of old; for though the truth is incontrovertible, that there is only one name given by which men can be saved, the name of Jesus Christ, God blessed forever, I am convinced, that he brings many to himself, in a way that we know not; concerning which St. Augustin says beautifully: "Multæ oves foris, multi lupi intus." "Many sheep without, many wolves within." And Thomas Aquinas boldly says, that God sends to many a man in the wilderness an angel from heaven to enlighten him. Thou silent sufferer, Job, though not a son of Abraham, thou knewest that thy Redeemer lived, and that thou wast to see him in the flesh; and I hope to see thee, oh Pius VII. in heaven. Venerable old man! how often was I edified and inflamed by thy unaffected and heart-penetrating devotion! What a beautiful day shall this be, when Pius VII. and Luther, Count Stolberg and Huss, Ganganelli and Melancthon, Francis Xavier and Henry Martin, leading each the flock which they have fed with the bread of life, and shining like the brightness of the firmament, shall embrace each other before Jesus, the Lord and Saviour of all, sit down at his table, and enter into his eternal rest. Thou, O Lord Jesus, alone readest the heart. Thou only softenest it with the dew of holiness. Thou, Shepherd of the Israelite and the Gentile, alone knowest thy own sheep; shed light upon the paths of all those who wander in darkness, and gather them all quickly into thy fold."—"*Wolff's Missionary Labors*," pp. 237, 238.

The question naturally arises here, why have not the missionary records a more full account of the labors of this faithful and unwearied laborer in so important a field? Why not more frequent allusions to the fruits of his toils? Not because there was no good to record, nor because of evil resulting from these labors. But the man proclaimed with the authority of a preacher of Jesus Christ, that his Master was about to return to judge the world, and he received the same opposition from his religious friends in America, which others shared who were proclaiming the same message here.

In a note on a fly-leaf of his journal we find the following, which Mr. Wolff purposely had placed there to show others how he was estimated by some religious teachers.

AMERICAN FRIENDS.

"In editing this new edition, I subjoin the following recommendation I got from the Quarterly Review; beside, you will be aware that Dr. Seabury, the editor of the New York Churchman, has declared me to be insane. JOSEPH WOLFF, Missionary."

Recommendation.—The Reverend Joseph Wolff,—a religious fanatic.—*Quarterly Review, 1834.*

Wm. Ramsey, D. D., Missionary in India, and Dr. Poor, Missionary in Asia, were also believers in the soon coming of our Lord Jesus Christ to raise the dead and change the living saints to reign with him on the redeemed and renewed earth. They preached it to the people, and declared it to be the true hope of the church.

CHARLOTTE ELIZABETH.

Charlotte Elizabeth is a name well known to all missionaries in the East, and to most of those whose interest in Christian missions has led them to read mission records. She was an English lady, the only daughter of Rev. Michael Browne, Norwich, born A. D. 1792, and died 1846. Her life was given to the work of Christian missions in India. She was a lady of high rank, deep piety, and superior talent, combined with great fortitude and perseverance. "She was the author of a large number of religious books and tracts. A collection of twelve volumes have been preserved." While engaged in teaching "Jesus and the resurrection," the Lord opened her heart to see the truth concerning his coming and kingdom.

From that time to the end of her mortal life her voice and pen proclaimed extensively, and in the true earnestness of Christian love and hope, the glorious fact that Jesus Christ is soon coming in person to reign in righteousness on David's throne. But we shall let her tell her experience in her own words. At what point of time she embraced and commenced teaching these views we are not informed, but it must have been between A. D. 1820 and 1840.

ADVENT EXPERIENCE.

"I have noticed in previous letters that I did not go with Mr. Howels on the subject of the Second Advent: I could not. In fact, I was a Millennarian against my will. The three particulars on which

I did not believe myself to be convinced were, the vengeful dispensation against the Lord's enemies preparatory to the thousand years of blessedness; the literal nature of the first, Pre-millennial resurrection, and the personal reign. With regard to the first, I wished to believe that the gospel would be universally victorious, subduing every heart, and bringing the whole world in peaceful submission to acknowledge the Lord as King. I had once, as before stated, been startled by a reference to the sixty-third of Isaiah, and lulled to sleep again by the far-fetched comments of good Matthew Henry: and I confessed I had taken up the missionary cause on the gratuitous assumption that we were to convert everybody, and could not agree to a less extensive triumph. Well, I did not choose to bring this to the test of Scripture, because I did not wish to be undeceived; but just after the Irish meeting, one was held in reference to the Jews, at which I was present; and forth stepped my valued friend M'Neil, whom I had not seen for a year, and with his little Bible in his hand, preached the doctrine, to my infinite annoyance and conviction! He took up my precise objection without knowing it; he spoke of those who could not see that a part of God's *mercy* was his *judgment;* and with that glowing ardor, tempered with deep solemnity, that always gives him so much of the prophetic characteristic, if I may so speak, he read from the 136th Psalm: 'To Him that smote Egypt in their first-born; *for his* MERCY *endureth forever:* and slew famous kings, *for his* MERCY *endureth forever.*' This was the key-note of a strain that I deeply felt resounded through the whole Scripture, though I had refused to heed it; and then he turned to the 61st of Isaiah, and read the first and part of the second verse, as quoted by our blessed Lord in the 4th of St. John, to where he shut the book, saying, 'This day is *this* Scripture fulfilled in your ears.' But did the Scripture end here? No: the first advent fulfilled so much of it; and He who then proclaimed 'the acceptable year of the Lord,' should at his second coming proceed with that unfinished Scripture, 'The day of vengeance of our God.' And go on thence 'To comfort all that mourn: to appoint unto them that mourn in Zion,'—and so the whole beautiful picture of Millennial gladness and glory on which Isaiah expatiates rose before me, as consequent upon that 'day of vengeance,' which Christ has not yet in person proclaimed. How angry I felt with that dauntless champion of God's whole truth, for trampling upon my darling prejudices! nevertheless he had done it; and thenceforth I opened my mind to drink in the pure, simple meaning of the literal promise.

"The first resurrection I considered to be a resurrection of the souls of the martyrs, whose spirits were to animate the happy race of believers during a thousand years. I confess some things puzzled me sorely in this interpretation: for instance, how could a soul be buried; and if not buried, how did it rise? Again, those souls were under an altar in heaven, waiting for the completion of their company by means of a new persecution on earth, and it seemed rather a heathenish doctrine to transmigrate them into other bodies; more especially as their own bodies would need them again. Besides, they were with Christ personally in heaven; and to be without Christ personally on earth, was by no means an additional privilege. I found the thing untenable, and resolved to consider it as wholly figurative; but if so, then the final judgment, described also in that chapter, might be figurative too. I would not look my own inferences in the face; so I wished to let the subject alone; but then a blessing was distinctly pronounced on such as should read or hear the words of that prophecy; and I did not like to lose a blessing.

"Thus the matter stood; I had rigidly forborne to read any book, pro or con, or to be talked to about it. One day when the subject forced itself upon me, I resolved to strengthen myself against the modern view (as I wisely supposed it), by prayerfully reading again what I already so well knew—the 15th chapter of 1st Corinthians. I did so: and was suddenly struck by a recollection of the passage where the 'saying' is written, 'Death is swallowed up in victory.' I turned to Isa. 25, read it, and found it unequivocally a description of the church's blessedness on earth—the Millennium—at the outset of which the saying is written which 'shall come to pass,' when Christ's people rise from the dead. But will not all rise then? I went over the apostle's description once more, and found no word of the resurrection unto condemnation. The corruptible then raised would all put on incorruption; the weakness, power; the mortal, immortality; having borne the image of the earthly, they were to bear the image of the heavenly. I was quite overpowered: could I reply against God? The passage that I thought so formidable on my side failed me—'Afterwards they that are Christ's at his coming. *Then* cometh the end.' . . . From this starting-point I explored the Scriptures in reference to a literal resurrection of Christ's people, at a literal coming previous to the thousand years of Satan's binding, and the peace of the church. I saw it clearly: I received it fully: and I hold it firmly at this day. . . .

"It has often struck me what efforts the enemy has made to stifle this doctrine. . . . But shall the abuse of a sublime truth by the great enemy lead us to reject it? As well may we blot out the ninety-first Psalm, because the devil quoted it, and for a truly devilish purpose. No; he knows that the shedding forth of greater light on this important branch of Christian knowledge is one of the signs of Christ's actual coming; a token that his own time is short; therefore he endeavors to stifle it; and ere long he will bring us false Christs, to deceive, if it were possible, the very elect. We have need to be found watching!"—*Charlotte Elizabeth.*

We subjoin a poem which has been published extensively by the lovers of Christ's return, and doubtless read by millions for the grandeur and sublimity of the composition. It shows that the subject of coming glory, and restitution, and righteousness, had taken deep hold of her heart.

SIGNS OF THE TIMES—BY CHARLOTTE ELIZABETH.

When from scattered lands afar,	Matt. xxiv. 6, 8.
Spreads the voice of rumored war,	Luke xxi. 25.
Nations in tumultuous pride,	Haggai ii. 7.
Heave like ocean's roaring tide,	Heb. xii. 26, 29.
When the solar splendors fail,	Matt. xxiv. 29.
When the crescent waxeth pale,	Rev. xvi. 12.
And the powers that starlike reign,	Matt. xxiv. 39.
Sink dishonored to the plain,	Joel ii. 10, 31.
World! do thou the signal dread,	Luke xxi. 26, 36.
We exalt the drooping head;	Luke xxi. 37, 38.
We uplift the expectant eye,	Eph. i. 14.
Our redemption draweth nigh.	Rom. viii. 19, 23.
When the fig-tree shoots appear,	Matt. xxiv. 32, 33.
Men behold their summer near;	Luke xxi. 29, 31.
When the hearts of rebels fail,	Isa. lix. 18, 19.
We the coming Conqueror hail.	Rev. xix. 11, 16.
Bridegroom of the weeping spouse,	Rev. xix. 7, 9.

Listen to her longing vows;	Rev. vi. 10.
Listen to her widowed moan,	Luke xviii. 3, 7, 8.
Listen to Creation's groan.	Rom. viii. 22, 23.
Bid, O bid Thy trumpet sound,	1 Thess. iv. 16.
Gather thine elect around,	Matt. xxiv. 31.
Gird with saints Thy flaming car,	Jude 14.
Summon them from climes afar,	Isa. xxiv. 13, 15.
Call them from life's cheerless gloom,	Matt. xxiv. 40, 41.
Call them from the marble tomb,	Rev. xx. 4, 6.
From the grass-grown village grave,	Luke xiv. 14.
From the deep dissolving wave,	Psalm xlix. 14, 15.
From the whirlwind and the flame,	1 Thess. iv. 17.
Mighty Head, Thy members claim.	Col. i. 15.
Where are they whose proud disdain,	Luke xix. 12, 27.
Scorned to brook Messiah's reign?	Matt. xiii. 41, 42.
Lo, in waves of sulphurous fire,	Luke xvi. 29, 30.
Now they taste His tardy ire;	Rev. xix. 20, 21.
Fettered till the appointed day,	Rev. xx. 3, 5, 9.
When the world shall pass away.	2 Peter iii. 9.
Quelled are all Thy foes, O Lord,	Rev. xix. 15, 21.
Sheathe again the dreadful sword.	Psalm cx. 5, 7.
Where the Cross of anguish stood,	Isa. liii. 3, 5, 12.
Where Thy life distilled in blood,	Mark xv. 27.
Where they mocked Thy dying groan,	Mark xv. 29.
King of Nations, plant Thy throne.	Isa. xxiv. 23.
Send Thy law from Zion forth,	Zach. viii. 3.
Speeding o'er the willing earth,	Dan. ii. 35, 44.
Earth, whose Sabbath glories rise,	Isa. xl. 1, 9.
Crowned with more than Paradise;	Psalm lxvii. 6.
Sacred be the impending vail!	1 Cor. xiii. 12.
Mortal sense and thought must fail,	1 John iii. 2.
Yet the awful hour is nigh,	Luke xxi. 31.
We shall see Thee, eye to eye.	Rev. i. 7.
Be our souls in peace possessed,	2 Thess. iii. 5.
While we seek our promised rest,	Heb. iv. 9.
And from every heart and home,	2 Tim. iv. 8.
Breathe the prayer, "O Jesus come!"	Rev. xxii. 20.
Haste to set the captive free.	Isa. xlix. 9.
All Creation groans for Thee.	Rom. viii. 19.

CHAPTER VII.

ELD. HENRY JONES—THE JEW QUESTION—PROSPECTS OF THE JEWS—A DISCOURSE BY MR. MILLER—THE TWO THEORIES BY ADVENT BELIEVERS—ELD. L. D. FLEMING—ELD. H. D. WARD—MILLER IN THE VINEYARD—A GREAT REVIVAL FOR TWO YEARS—LETTER FROM SCOTLAND—REV. JOHN HOOPER, ENGLAND.

The publishing of a paper devoted to discussion and instruction on the fulfillment of prophecy, the promises to, and prospects of, the church, the signs of the coming of the Lord to judge the world, the nature of the millennium, and kingdom of God, awakened the attention, and called into action the thoughts and the talents of the devout, sincere, and studious Christians in the churches as no other work could do. It also called forth the energies and talent of those who had "graduated"—had obtained, as they seemed to think, all the light that could be had from the Bible—to oppose the "new light" as they reproachfully stigmatized it. But all helped to make the truth shine more conspicuously.

"THE SECOND ADVENT."

In June, 1840, a new publication with the above title was commenced, in connection with the "Signs of the Times." The first issue contained a valuable discourse on the signs of the times, from Eld. John Hooper, of England. It was first published in England in A. D. 1830. He agrees with Mr. Miller in the main features of his views.

ELD. HENRY JONES, CONGREGATIONALIST,

in New York city, listens to the message of the immediate coming of Christ, and after much prayerful study, embraces it with a whole heart. He was a man of brilliant talents, and an active worker in the vineyard of the Lord. He wrote many valuable communications on the coming of Christ. Also a tract entitled, "Scripture Searcher," and finally published a paper. He also published a pamphlet entitled, "Modern Phenomena in the Heavens," which had an extensive circulation. While he preached and proved by many evidences that the end was near at hand, yet he rejected definite time conclusions for the event, as being uncertain, and therefore unsafe to teach. He was a very successful laborer in the Advent faith, and did much to extend the message and establish the cause.

"THE LITERALIST."

Mr. Oren Rogers, of Philadelphia, Pa., commenced a semi-monthly publication with the above title, in 1840. This was a Pre-Millennial Advent production, devoted mostly to the return of the Jews and the immediate coming of Messiah.

THE JEW QUESTION.

The subject of the return of the Jews to Palestine, occupied the attention of most writers on the prophecies at this time. It had been one of the leading topics of discussion among the English and Scotch commentators and writers for a long period, since the relapse of the Lutheran Reformation. Some felt assured that the Jews would return and all be converted to Christ, with all the Gentiles, then would come the millennium, then the judgment. Others, called "Millennarians," looked for the Advent of Christ in connection with the return of the Jews, some of them advocating that they return before, as a sign of his Advent; others that they will return immediately after his Advent. Others took the view that the only return yet to be expected is the return of the true Israel—Christians of all ages, from the dead, to the land promised Abraham and his seed. See Gen. xv. 7; xvii. 8; Rom. iv. 13, 16; Gal. iii. 16, 29. Thus with the great awakening caused by the Advent Message, one of the questions which stood in the foreground was the Jew question. Those who looked for their universal conversion before the Lord's return, could not receive any light or evidence from the Bible, or any quarter, that the judgment was near, because of their idea about the Jews. Others who looked for Christ in connection with their return, measured the evidence of the immediate Advent of Christ by the prospects of a general movement among the Jews of all countries to return to Jerusalem. Every omen was closely watched, and every word from Jews, relative to going to Jerusalem, whether on pilgrimage or to abide, was interpreted as favoring a universal move. But this subject was met by those who were the pioneers in giving the proclamation in America, of the Advent near, with arguments and applications of Scripture which they considered unanswerable; showing that no return of the Jews, as such was taught in the Bible, neither did the prospects, the action, or the desire of the Jews favor such an idea. They were on a level with all other sinners, "the middle wall of partition was broken down," they were invited, and required to believe in Christ, and as many as would, became the children of Abraham, and heirs of his inheritance. And they who would not accept of Christ as their Messiah, had, as a class, become too sceptical in regard to the promises of God, which their fathers interpreted as embracing their literal restoration, to be interested in them, or to expect any blessings through them.

David Levi, a learned Jew, who, in A. D. 1796, published "Dissertations on the Prophecies of the Old Testament," observes in that work, "that deism and infidelity have made such large strides in the world, that they have at length reached even the Jewish nation; many of whom are at this time so greatly infected with scepticism, by reading Bolingbroke, Hume, Voltaire, etc., that they scarcely believe in a revelation; *much less have they any hope in their future restoration.*"

"PROSPECT OF THE JEWS' RETURN."

We find an article with the above caption in the "Signs of the Times," by one who had just returned from the East. He says:

MR. EDITOR:—Having lately returned from the East, I would be glad of the privilege of corroborating the sentiments contained in an article in your paper Sept. 22, on 'the prospects of the Jews.' Much more than ordinary interest is manifested in this country, in reference to the Jews return to Palestine, and every item bearing on the subject, is seized upon with avidity. Many believe that within a year or two the Jews have commenced moving to that land by thousands from all parts of the world. The exact truth on this subject ought to be known, and I venture to say that I am not aware, nor is it the opinion of the missionaries there, that the number of the Jews in Palestine is increasing. In all Palestine there are not 10,000 (about the same as in New York city), who are found in the four cities, Jerusalem, Hebron, Tiberias, and Safed.

"H. A. H."

The above letter was probably called out by an article written by

Bro. Miller, on the return of the Jews, and published in the "Signs of the Times."

The article was written to meet an objection urged by Elders Ethen Smith, D. Campbell, Phelps, and others, against the idea that the Lord was about to return.

It is so pertinent to the subject, and full of instruction, we give it space in our book, as an item of "the controversy of Zion."

MR. MILLER ON THE RETURN OF THE JEWS.

Mr. M. keenly felt the danger of religious teachers teaching what would tend to put off immediate repentance. He begins this subject thus:

"Those souls whom I have addressed in my six months tour are continually before me, sleeping or waking; I can see them perishing by thousands, and when I reflect on the accountability of their teachers, who say, 'peace and safety,' I am in pain for them. How many souls will Bros. Phelps, Campbell,[1] and others, who are sticklers for the Jews return and for a temporal millennium, be the means of lulling to sleep, and while they are flattering themselves that their teachers are right, find to their eternal cost, that their preparation for the eternal world was delayed a few days too long, on the vain supposition that the Jews must return and a millennium intervene? Why will they not listen to reason and Scripture? Peter was converted from such a selfish and bigoted mind, when he said, 'I perceive that God is no respecter of persons,' Acts x. 34, 35. And yet, truly, if the Jews ever return, they must be respected of God, for will not all acknowledge that they are to be gathered by God out of all nations, etc.

See Isa. lxvi. 20, 'And they shall bring all your brethren for an offering unto the Lord out of all nations upon horses, and in chariots, and in litters, and upon mules, and upon swift beasts, to my holy mountain Jerusalem, saith the Lord, as the children of Israel bring an offering in a clean vessel into the house of the Lord.'

They are not gathered because they work righteousness, or by being children of faith; but because they are *God's ancient covenant people.* For if they believe, they are graffed in among the Gentile believers, and are no more Jews in that sense.

Rom. x. 12, 'For there is no difference between the Jew and the Greek: for the same Lord over all is rich unto all that call upon him.'

Now if the Jew be restored because he is a Jew, then Peter needed another conversion: for he said he perceived God was no respecter of persons. What

---

[1] These are two Orthodox clergymen who had written books to refute Mr. Miller's views. They claimed that the Jews must return to Palestine and the world be converted before Christ could come.

a pity that Peter had not had Bro. Phelps and his deacon to teach him better.

Again,—how foolish Paul must have been to have wished himself accursed. Rom. ix. 3, 'For I could wish that myself were accursed from Christ for my brethren, my kinsmen according to the flesh.'

When Bros. Phelps, Skinner, and the notorious T. Whitmore,[1] if they had lived in his day, could have told him in five words: Father Paul, God will not cast away his ancient covenant people; for all Israel shall be saved. Once more, If James had lived in the days of the Boston trio, he might have written a very different epistle, when he wrote to the 'twelve tribes scattered abroad.' Instead of pointing to the law of liberty and faith in Christ Jesus as their justification and respect of persons, he might have told them to remain steadfast as Jews, and in the end they would all be gathered and saved. Yes, how different would James have written, if he had believed in the return of the Jews. If then, the Jew, as a Jew, in the flesh, must have another day, God must have respect of persons without any reference to the work of righteousness. Or God must give the Gentile another day, after the Jew.

Rom. i. 16, 'For I am not ashamed of the Gospel of Christ; for it is the power of God unto salvation to every one that believeth; to the Jew first, and also to the Gentile.'

Here we are plainly taught that the Jew has had his day, and now the Gentile.

Rom. ii. 7, 'To them, who, by patient continuance in well doing, seek for glory and honor and immortality, eternal life.'

11, 'For their is no respect of persons with God.'

28, 'For he is not a Jew, which is one outwardly; neither is that circumcision which is outward in the flesh.'

29, 'But he is a Jew, which is one inwardly; and circumcision is that of the heart, in the spirit, and not in the letter; whose praise is not of men, but of God.'

These passages show plainly that the Jews have had their day, and have been visited with the indignation and wrath of God, of which they are a sample unto us who afterwards should live ungodly. Now, if they, as unbelievers, after suffering the vengeance of God as a nation, are to be gathered again, and restored to their privileges, land, and laws, then the Gentiles, after suffering the vengeance of eternal life, are to be restored again to their present privileges, country, and laws.

Will the trio agree to this?

I think not, yet the type must agree with the anti-type.

But the gospel promise which was before the law, made to Abraham, was promised in Christ unto all them which believe, both Jew and Gentile.

This is certainly the apostle's reasoning in the 3d and 4th chapters of Ro-

---

[1] O. A. Skinner and Thomas Whitmore, two Universalist clergymen who were much gratified with and united to sustain the views of Phelps, who opposed Miller, and who had behaved very ungentlemanly when Mr. Miller lectured in Boston.

mans, and he says not one word about the Jews' return, when he sums up the advantage the Jew has over the Gentile.

Rom. iii. 1, 'What advantage hath the Jew? or what profit is there of circumcision?'

2, 'Much every way: chiefly, because that unto them were committed the oracles of God.'

3, 'For what, if some did not believe? Shall their unbelief make the faith of God without effect?

4, 'God forbid: yea, let God be true, but every man a liar; as it is written, That thou mightest be justified in thy sayings, and mightest overcome when thou art judged.

5, 'But if our unrighteousness commend the righteousness of God, what shall we say? Is God unrighteous, who taketh vengeance?' (I speak as a man.)

6, 'God forbid: for then how shall God judge the world?'

7, 'For if the truth of God hath more abounded through my lie unto his glory, why yet am I also judged as a sinner?'

8, 'And not rather (as we be slanderously reported, and as some affirm that we say) Let us do evil, that good may come? whose damnation is just.'

9, 'What then? are we better than they? No, in no wise: for we have before proved both Jews and Gentiles, that they are all under sin.'

Not a word about this return and inheriting Judea again; yet, if so, their restoration would be a great advantage over the Gentile, Deut. xxx. 7.

Isa. xxiv. 14, 'They shall lift up their voice, they shall sing for the majesty of the Lord, they shall cry aloud from the sea.'

15, 'Wherefore glorify ye the Lord in the fires, even the name of the Lord God of Israel in the isles of the sea.'

Isa. liv. 7, 'For a small moment have I forsaken thee; but with great mercies will I gather thee.'

8, 'In a little wrath I hid my face from thee for a moment; but with everlasting kindness will I have mercy on thee, saith the Lord thy Redeemer.

Hos. i. 11, 'Then shall the children of Judah and the children of Israel be gathered together, and appoint themselves one head, and they shall come up out of the land: for great shall be the day of Jezreel.'

If these passages mean the Jews, then certainly they will rule over the Gentiles, and this would be an unpardonable neglect in the apostle to the Gentiles, not to give us warning of it.

But he doth tell us that the chief advantage of the Jew was, that God had called them first.

So it is the Jew first, and also the Gentile.

Again, if the Jew is to be gathered to his own land and never pulled up again, Amos ix. 15, 'And I will plant them upon their land, and they shall no more be pulled up out of their land which I have given them, saith the Lord thy God.' How can Paul reconcile Gal. vi. 15, 'For in Christ Jesus neither circumcision availeth anything, nor uncircumcision, but a new creature.'

Eph. i. 10, 'That in the dispensation of the fullness of times, he might gather together in one all things in Christ, both which are in heaven and which are on earth: even in him.'

Eph. ii. 12, 'That at that time ye were without Christ, being aliens from the commonwealth of Israel, and strangers from the covenants of promise, having no hope, and without God in the world.'

13, 'But now, in Christ Jesus, ye who sometimes were far off, are made nigh by the blood of Christ.'

14, 'For he is our peace, who hath made both one, and hath broken down the middle wall of partition between us.'

15, 'Having abolished in his flesh the enmity, even the law of commandments contained in ordinances; for to make in himself of twain one new man, so making peace.'

16, 'And that he might reconcile both unto God in one body by the cross, having slain the enmity thereby.'

And how would our dear Saviour explain John x. 16, 'And other sheep I have, which are not of this fold: them also I must bring, and they shall hear my voice; and there shall be one fold, and one shepherd.'

If the Jew is to be a separate people again, and never pulled up, when will Christ break down the partition wall? When will he unite Jew and Gentile in one body? And if the church be the fullness of him, see Eph. i. 22, 'And hath put all things under his feet, and gave him to be the head over all things to the church.' 23, 'Which is his body, the fullness of him that filleth all in all.' How can the Jew, as a Jew, be a part of his body, inheriting old Jerusalem, while the church is the fullness of him who inherits all things, and possess the new Jerusalem? Can Bro. Phelps, or Campbell, his prompter, answer these questions?

Let us have plain, distinct answers: keep to the point.

But, say these teachers, what shall we do with all those passages in the prophets, that speak of the Jews' return to their own land? I answer, Sirs, will you be so good as to notice that all the passages which you dare quote to prove your doctrine were written or prophesied before the Jews were restored from Babylon, and had their literal fulfillment in that event. But you say some of them were not all fulfilled, such as they should 'never be pulled up,' 'David shall be their king forever,' etc., etc.

Very well, gentlemen, if you will examine your Bibles you will find every prophecy which could not be fulfilled literally, have a direct allusion to the new covenant, and cannot be fulfilled under the old. There, *Israel*, *Judah*, and *my people*, are to be understood spiritual Israel, as in Isa. xi. 10, 'And in that day there shall be a root of Jesse, which shall stand for an ensign of the people; to it shall the Gentiles seek: and his rest shall be glorious.'

11, 'And it shall come to pass in that day, that the Lord shall set his hand again the second time to recover the remnant of his people, which shall be left, from Assyria, and from Egypt, and from Pathros, and from Cush, and from Elam, and from Shinar, and from Hamath, and from the islands of the sea.'

12, 'And he shall set up an ensign for the nations, and shall assemble the outcasts of Israel, and gather together the dispersed of Judah from the four corners of the earth.'

The 11th verse speaks of the gathering of the remnant of his people. The 10th and 12th verses show that it is under the new covenant. Also, Jer. xxxii. 37, 'Behold, I will gather them out of all countries, whither I have driven them in mine anger, and in my fury, and in great wrath; and I will bring them again unto this place, and I will cause them to dwell safely.'

38, 'And they shall be my people, and I will be their God.'

39, 'And I will give them one heart, and one way, that they may fear me forever, for the good of them, and of their children after them.'

40, 'And I will make an everlasting covenant with them, that I will not turn away from them, to do them good; but I will put my fear in their hearts, that they shall not depart from me.'

Verses 36 and 37 speak of their gathering out of Babylon. 38th and 40th show plainly that it is under the new covenant.

Again, Ezek. xxxvii. 21, 'And say unto them, Thus saith the Lord God; Behold, I will take the children of Israel from among the heathen, whither they be gone, and will gather them on every side, and bring them into their own land.'

22, 'And I will make them one nation in the land upon the mountains of Israel; and one king shall be king to them all: and they shall be no more two nations, neither shall they be divided into two kingdoms any more at all.'

23, 'Neither shall they defile themselves any more with their idols, nor with their detestable things, nor with any of their transgressions; but I will save them out of all their dwelling-places, wherein they have sinned, and will cleanse them: so shall they be my people, and I will be their God.'

24, 'And David my servant shall be king over them; and they all shall have one shepherd: they shall also walk in my judgments, and observe my statutes, and do them.'

25, 'And they shall dwell in the land that I have given unto Jacob my servant, wherein your fathers have dwelt; and they shall dwell therein, even they, and their children, and their children's children forever: and my servant David shall be their prince forever.'

26, 'Moreover I will make a covenant of peace with them; it shall be an everlasting covenant with them: and I will place them, and multiply them, and will set my sanctuary in the midst of them for evermore.'

27, 'My tabernacle also shall be with them: yea, I will be their God, and they shall be my people.'

28, 'And the heathen shall know that I the Lord do sanctify Israel, when my sanctuary shall be in the midst of them for evermore.'

The 21st and 22d verses speak of the children of Israel being gathered; the 23d and 24th show the new covenant; 25th speaks of their dwelling in the land forever; 26th and 28th, of the new covenant.

These specimens show how the prophecies may be understood, and have the

Scriptures harmonize. But if we take into consideration the names and phrases used by the prophets under the Old Testament, we must see, unless we are willingly ignorant, that no other name would or could be used with propriety, but such as have been used. And every Bible student must have discovered this, which, if it is not so, in vain might we look for any prophecy in the Old Testament concerning the church in the New.

By thus having the veil over their faces and thus construing Scripture, Skinner and Whitmore can throw all judgment on the poor Jew; and Phelps and Campbell give them all the promises. But Father Paul gives to each a portion in due season.

'Tribulation and anguish, upon every soul of man that doeth evil, of the Jew first, and also of the Gentile. But glory, honor, and peace to every man that worketh good, to the Jew first, and also to the Gentile.'

"LOW HAMPTON, N. Y., March 31, 1840. WM. MILLER."

The above argument was not directed against the "Millennarians" who hold to the return of the Jews after the Advent of Christ, but those who expect that event and a thousand years of universal righteousness before the Advent, yet if his position is correct, it greatly damages the other view also.

It will be of service to some of our readers to state here

THE TWO GENERAL THEORIES ADVOCATED BY THOSE WHO BELIEVE THE ADVENT NEAR.

It is well known to many that there are two prominent theories advocated by the believers in the pre-millennial advent. The *first* teaches that the consummation will not take place till the close of the millennium. The *second* teaches that the consummation will take place at the commencement of the millennium. There is considerable difference between these theories; both agree, however, in the personal reign and speedy coming of Christ.

I. *The theory teaching that the consummation will not take place till the close of the millennium.*

This is given in the works of James A. Begg, of Glasgow, Scotland, and other works of the millennarians, and may be stated in substance as follows:

"The Jews shall return to their own land, and Jerusalem shall be rebuilt. The Lord will descend from heaven and dwell in Jerusalem. 'Then the moon shall be confounded and the sun ashamed, when the Lord of hosts shall reign in mount Zion and in Jerusalem, and before his ancients gloriously.' He will continue his personal presence on earth certainly 1,000, and probably 365,000 years. The nations will go to see him, and to worship in Jerusalem, and keep the annual feasts. The man of sin shall be destroyed by the Lord in person or by the brightness of his coming, and the race of evil-doers shall generally be cut off. A resurrection of the saints and martyred witnesses of Christ precedes the millennial reign. This is the first resurrection, and shall precede the second from 1,000 to 365,000 years. The earth and the atmosphere will be changed. A more genial climate and a more fruitful soil will reward the labors of the husbandmen. Still the earth's identity and its present localities shall continue; and 'although it will be a period of unprecedented holiness and happiness, neither sin nor death will be wholly excluded.' 'The child shall die a hundred years old, and the sinner being a hundred years old shall be accursed.' And therefore, during the millennial dispensation, this world will be the abode of men in the flesh, who will have intercourse with the immortal men who are reigning with Christ. But of the nature of the employment of the reigning saints, and of their intercourse with mortal men, he has no knowledge.

A short apostasy will succeed the millennium. Satan will be set free from his captivity, but will ultimately be destroyed. Then comes the general resurrection of all that died during the millennium, and those who were not raised at its commencement, which will be followed with the general judgment and eternal rewards and punishments."[1]

II. *The theory teaching that the consummation takes place at the appearing of Christ, in the beginning of the millennium.*

This may be stated in substance as follows:

"When Christ makes his Second Advent, all the righteous dead with all infants, will be raised immortal, and all the righteous and infants then living, 'shall be changed in a moment,' and together caught up to meet the Lord in the air. Matt. xxiv. 30, 31; 1 Thess. iv. 15, 18; Isa. xxvi. 19, 20; 1 Cor. xv. 51, 52; Rev. xv. 2. 'This is the first resurrection,' see Isa. xxvi. 19; Luke xiv. 14; xx. 35; 1 Cor. xv. 23; Phil. iii. 11; Rev. xx. 4, 6. 'Then will be celebrated the marriage of the lamb,' Rev. xix. 7. The nations of the wicked who are alive on the earth will then 'be angry,' and engage in 'the battle of the great day of God Almighty,' Rev. xi. 15, 18; Jer. xxv, 31, 33; Rev. xvi. 14, 18; Isa. xxiv. 17, 18, 21, 22; Rev. xix. 13—18. Thus the wicked will all suffer the Adamic death when cut off by sword, pestilence, famine, and fire. The angels of God will be associated with Christ in this exterminating war. The devil will be bound a thousand years, see Psa. cxlix. 6, 7; Matt. xxv. 31; Jude 14; Rev. xix. 14; xx. 3. Then the firmament (heaven) and the earth will be cleansed by fire, Gen. i. 8; Psa. xlvi. 6; cii. 26; Isa. li. 6; Dan. viii. 14; 2 Pet. iii. 10; Rev. xxi. 1. Christ and his church will then occupy the new earth and reign for a thousand years (the New Jerusalem being the capitol of the king-

---

[1] This class of believers are called "Millennarians," and form a distinct class from the class called "Second Adventists," though in some instances they unite in their labors and in churches.

dom of God), which constitutes the millennium, see Psa. ii. 8, 9; lxxii. 8, 9; lxxxix. 27—37; cxxxii. 11; Luke i. 33; Rev. ii. 21; v. 10; xi. 15; xx. 4, 6; xxi. 1, 5. When the thousand years have expired, Satan shall be loosed out of his prison, the rest of the dead, *i. e.* all the wicked raised from death, come up upon the breadth of the earth, led by the deceiver, determined to retain the earth and dislodge the saints, when fire from God comes down and devours them—submerges them 'in the lake which burneth with fire and brimstone,' where they experience 'the second death,' see Job. xxi. 30; Isa. xxiv. 22, 23; John v. 29; Acts xxiv. 15; 1 Cor. xv. 24, 25; Rev. xx. 5, 7; xxi. 8. Then Christ will reign with his church, eternally, on the earth redeemed from all usurpers and the curse, Dan. ii. 44; vii. 14, 27; Psa. lxxxix. 34, 37; Luke i. 33."

There are various shades of view with each class as to certain points above stated. There is also a class who hold that the first resurrection is a moral one, and is past, that the millennium is also past, and that all the dead will be raised at, or near, the same time; who co-operate with and constitute a part of the body of believers in the Advent near. This view they claim is taught in such statements as couple the resurrection and reward of both classes together, as Matt. iii. 12; xiii. 41, 42; xxv. 32, 33; John v. 38, 39; Rev. xx. 12, 13. But these are held as minor points by the body of believers.

ELD. L. D. FLEMING, MINISTER OF THE CASCO STREET CHURCH, PORTLAND, ME.,

after hearing and examining the evidences, with much prayer, on which the Second Advent Message was based, heartily embraced and preached it. He was one of the ablest of the ministry of the "Christian church," of deep piety, and fine qualifications for teaching.

He wrote several works on the immediate coming of Christ, which were published at the "Signs of the Times" office, in 1840, one entitled, "Synopsis of Evidences of Christ's Second Coming." Another, "The Midnight Cry."

Eld. F. was a faithful, energetic, and useful minister of Christ, and devoted himself to the work of saving men, by preaching the gospel of the kingdom and Christ's immediate coming, until his voice failed, when he was obliged to leave the work of the ministry. But he did not leave the truth nor the work of Christ until death. He entered upon the practice of medicine, and used his means and his pen to sustain the proclamation which had so greatly cheered his heart, and had given him such success in his ministry. He now sleeps, but sleeps in Jesus, soon to "have part in the first resurrection."

ELD. HENRY DANA WARD, AN EPISCOPAL MINISTER,

of New York city, now entered into the work and gave his extensive influence in sounding "THE CRY." He was a graduate of Harvard College, of brilliant talent, large experience, and deep piety. We find much of his writings in "the Signs of the Times," and "the Midnight Cry." He wrote one of the most accurate and interesting accounts of the shower of stars of Nov. 13, 1833, of which he was an eye-witness. In that event he recognized the fulfillment of Christ's words, Matt. xxiv. 29, and a sign of his immediate coming. We find him associated in, and a President of the first conference of Second Advent believers, held in Boston, and one of the chief speakers. In A. D. 1840, he wrote a work entitled

"GLAD TIDINGS,"

which was published at the office of the "Signs of the Times."

This was soon followed by several others; one was entitled the "Telescope of Faith." He has traveled and lectured on the subject of Christ's coming, the "Promises to Abraham," "The kingdom of God," and "Restitution of the earth," in America and in Europe. He has recently written several valuable books on the same.

During the summer of 1840, the number of believers and laborers in the cause was greatly increased. Books and tracts were now circulating, thousands were reading, praying, and inquiring on the subject. Bro. Miller was constantly traveling, and lecturing nearly every day in the week, to large and anxious audiences. Accounts of conversions of sinners in all parts of the country are found in the records of his labors and in others' reports also. He is unable to comply with but few of the calls for his services.

We here give an extract from the record of his labors, to show that the Lord wrought graciously with the Message. After giving several series of lectures in Canada, he returned to Low Hampton, and lectured on the 12th of July.

He remained at home about four weeks, when he visited Dresden, N. Y., and lectured from the 9th to the 12th of August. Of that place he writes, under date of August 13: "We had a good time; the Lord was there." He then adds: "I do not know what to say about coming to Massachusetts again. Day after to-morrow I begin a course of lectures at Fort Ann. The next week I go north, where I have three places, which will take three weeks at least. I have more business on hand than any two men like me should perform. I must lecture twice every day. I must converse with many—answer a host of questions—write answers to letters from all points of the compass, from Canada to Florida, from Maine to Missouri. I must read all the candid arguments (which I confess are not many) which are urged against me. I must read all the slang of the drunken and sober. . . . The polar star must be kept in view; the chart consulted, the compass watched; the reckoning kept; the sails set; the rudder managed; the ship cleared; the sailors fed; the voyage prosecuted; the port of rest, to which we are destined, understood; and to the watchman call, 'Watchman, what of the night?'"

On the 15th of August, 1840, he commenced his anticipated lectures at South Bay, in the town of Fort Ann, N. Y., and continued to the 20th.

On the 22d, in compliance with a previous invitation, he commenced a second course of lectures in Colchester, Vt., which terminated on the 29th. Of these meetings, Elder Columbus Green thus writes:

"The audiences were very large, notwithstanding it was a time of great excitement, and our place of worship was as still as death. His lectures were delivered in the most kind and affectionate manner, convincing every mind that he believed the sentiments he uttered. He made the most powerful exhortations that I ever heard fall from the lips of any one. A deep solemnity pervaded the minds of the community. Young men and maidens, amid the pleasures of early years; men in the meridian of life, hurrying on with locomotive speed in pursuit of the treasures of earth; gray-haired sires, and matrons whose hoary locks gave evidence that many winters had passed over them, all paused and pondered on the things they heard, inquiring, 'Am I ready?' Many came to the conclusion that they were unprepared to meet their Saviour, repented of their sins, and, through the merits of Jesus, obtained pardon full and free. For two years after this, there was a constant state of revival in that place; and many were the souls that dated their convictions of sin at that time, when the faithful old man warned them of the world's approaching doom. No man was more highly esteemed than he was; and it was not uncommon for impenitent men to vindicate his character when his motives were impeached.

"Many there regarded him as 'a chosen vessel of the Lord,' who had been instrumental in building them up 'in the most holy faith;' who had taken them, as it were, to Pisgah's top, and shown them the promised land, that better country for which patriarchs and prophets sighed. Among the public servants of the Most High, to them most dear, our departed brother held a conspicuous place. Years have passed since I enjoyed those happy seasons with them, and swift-rolling rivers and snow-capped hill-tops now lie between us. But, in whatever light they may now regard the efforts of him who sleeps in death, they then appreciated them. For one, I have never since seen the time when I was not thankful to God that I was counted worthy to see the light, and rejoice in it. And my prayer is that the torch of truth may illume our path through time, and that we may at last have an abundant entrance into the everlasting kingdom of our Lord Jesus Christ.[1]

"MONTGOMERY, VT., March 14, 1850."

ENGLAND AND SCOTLAND.

Extract from a letter from J. A. Begg, of Scotland, to "Signs of the Times:"

"Sept. 16, 1840.

"Many thanks for the 'Signs of the Times.' I regard the very existence of such a periodical as itself one of *the signs of the times.* The cry, 'Behold, the bridegroom cometh,' has now been raised in many lands, but in no other country, besides our own, do I know of any periodical specially devoted to proclaim the Saviour's advent near.

"We have had, in Great Britain and Ireland, the 'Morning Watch,' the 'Christian Herald,' 'The Watchman,' 'The Investigator,' and 'The Inquirer,' all either exclusively or chiefly occupied with the illustrations or enforcement of the truths of the sacred prophecies, and hundreds of the heralds of the cross are also heralds of the crown."

The following extract is from the "Present Crisis," by Rev. John Hooper, England, 1840:

EXTRACT.

It was a prominent characteristic of the primitive Christians "that they *loved* (*Christ's*) *appearing,*" and looked forward to it as the period that would consummate their happiness. Surely, if our affections were placed on the Saviour—if he was to us the chief among ten thousand, and altogether lovely

---

[1] Life of Miller, p. 152.

—if we had none in heaven but him, or on earth that we desired in comparison of him—we should desire his *return*—we should long to "*see him as he is*"—should pray, "*thy kingdom come*"—"*Come, Lord Jesus, come quickly.*" "*Why is his chariot so long in coming? Why tarry the wheels of his chariot?*" The observations of Mr. Drummond on this subject, in a speech which that gentleman delivered at the Eleventh Anniversary of the Continental Society, are so much to the point, that I cannot refrain from quoting them. "Let us suppose," says he, "for instance, a woman whose husband is a long way absent from her, perhaps in the East Indies. She is possibly very diligent in the management of his affairs, and conducts herself with perfect outward propriety, but always breaks out into a passion whenever any one speaks to her of her husband's return: 'Oh no,' she says, 'he cannot be coming yet; I expect to be much better off before he comes; I expect his estate under my management to be much more extensive; if he were to come now, he would disarrange all my plans; besides, what is the use of thinking about his coming—I may die first, and that will be exactly the same as his coming to me.' Let her asseverations of love and affection be what they may, you cannot believe otherwise than that her heart is alienated from her lord, and probably fixed upon another. Now let us suppose another woman in the same situation: see her constantly reading his letters, and especially those parts of them which describe the time and the circumstances attendant upon his return; hear her talking of it to her children, and teaching them to look forward to it as the consummation of her and their fondest wishes. Mark the silent scorn with which she treats a judicious friend who would try to persuade her that there was no use in looking out for his return, for that he had never mentioned the month, far less the day or the hour, when it was to take place. Though she may make no noisy protestations of love; though she may speak but little about him, except to her children, and to those whose hearts are tuned in unison with her own, we cannot for a moment entertain a doubt of the real state of her affections. Let us apply this figure to ourselves: and of this I am certain, and I wish I could make the warning ring through every corner of our professing land, that a dislike to hear of the coming of the Lord is a more decided proof of the affections of the religious world at large, being alienated from Christ, and, therefore, in an unholy, unsanctified, and unconverted state, than all the noisy protestations at annual meetings, all the Bibles and tracts circulated, and missionaries sent out, are proofs of the REVERSE."

CHAPTER VIII.

First general conference—The report—Circular address—Spirit of the conference—The kingdom of God, by Eld. J. Litch.

THE FIRST GENERAL CONFERENCE OF ADVENT BELIEVERS.

Several friends of this cause united in a call for a general conference to be held in Boston, Oct. 14, 1840.

This proved to be an important measure. Many ministers and laymen who had heard and read upon the subject of the soon coming of the Lord, and held correspondence with each other, with hearts full of interest, and open to accept truth from any source, and also full of love for all who loved Christ, had never seen each other, nor met with the faithful servants of the Lord, whose writings had been to them like cool water to a thirsty soul.

This was the first conference of the kind ever called. It was not a call for Methodists, Congregationalists, Baptists, Presbyterians, Episcopalians, Lutherans, or any other single class of organized churchmen, but for all who love our Lord Jesus Christ and his appearing, of every name and class, to come together and confer with each other; to examine the Scriptures, compare views, exchange thoughts, and worship the Lord together, regardless of church relations or sectional bonds. The doctors and professors had seen the omens of union of Christian hearts on this broad basis of love for the return of Christ, and they had covered the moral heavens with thick clouds of misstatements, and commenced their clerical *thunder*. They had free access to the secular and religious press, and had told the masses that "these Millerites" were fanatics, madmen, ignoramuses, crack-brained, deluded, low, illiterate, speculators, humbugs, etc., etc.

The day arrived, and with it came large delegations of believers, of awakened and convicted ones, of inquirers, of doubters, and of the curious. But they did not meet in vain. The Lord graciously smiled upon the scene, and the Holy Spirit was performing its blessed work of witnessing to the words of Holy writ, which were spoken, and accepting and sealing the sacrifices of position, reputation, of church livings, of worldly ambition and gain, of self and selfish interests, which were being there offered upon the altar of truth, which revealed the glorious prospects to the believer of soon obtaining, through Christ, an eternal home in an immortal state, in the new earth, with all the family of the redeemed.

This conference convened in Chardon street Chapel, Oct. 14, at 10 o'clock A. M. Eld. J. V. Himes, the pastor, read the call of the conference, as follows:

"The undersigned, believers in the Second Coming and Kingdom of the Messiah '*at hand*,' cordially unite in the call of a general Conference of our brethren of the United States and elsewhere, who are also looking for the advent near, to meet at BOSTON, MASS., OCT. 14, 1840, AT 10 O'CLOCK A. M., to continue two days, or as long as may then be found best. The object of the Conference will not be to form a new organization in the faith of Christ; nor to assail others of our brethren who differ from us in regard to the period and manner of the advent; but to discuss the whole subject faithfully and fairly, in the exercise of that spirit of Christ in which it will be safe immediately to meet him at the judgment seat. By so doing we may accomplish much in the rapid, general, and powerful spread of 'the everlasting gospel of the kingdom' at hand, that the way of the Lord may be speedily prepared, whatever may be the precise period of his coming."

Prayer was offered by Eld. David Millard, Baptist. Eld. Henry Dana Ward, Episcopal, was chosen president of conference, who then delivered a solemn and instructive address, on the "near coming of our Lord in his kingdom."

Eld. Josiah Litch, Methodist, followed with another address.

The board of officers of conference was then chosen as follows:

Henry Dana Ward, President; David Millard, Josiah Sevey, J. Lord, R. W. Reed, Assistants; Henry Jones, P. R. Russell, Secretaries; J. V. Himes, Joseph Bates, J. Litch, Charles F. Stevens, Stephen Goodhue, Committee of Arrangements; Daniel Merrill, Wm. Clark, Calvin French, Nathaniel Billings, Committee of Finance.

A letter was then read from Bro. Miller's son, Low Hampton, N. Y., stating the illness of his father, which deprived the conference of much anticipated satisfaction in his presence.

Two days were occupied in the above conference, several very able and important addresses were given, and some read from those not present.

The table of contents of the full report shows the following subjects:

This report was published in full, with an address to the public, and widely scattered. It contains a great many important truths which were gathered and presented by those brethren at a time especially needed to silence the *false charge* of "new doctrine," and to enlighten the ignorant on the old truths, and guide them into "the old paths." The most of these truths on the history of the faith and hope of the church have since been published in various works among us, and are yet performing their mission.

From that gathering of the saints went out a "report" which confirmed many in the faith of Christ's immediate coming, and awakened many more to study and learn it to be a Bible truth.

CIRCULAR ADDRESS FROM THE GENERAL CONFERENCE of Advent believers, assembled in Boston, Oct. 14 and 15, 1840, to the brethren abroad.

AN EXTRACT.

"When the apostasy had corrupted the body of the church, and the glory had departed from Israel, the calamity of the holy people was manifest in their indifference toward the deferred hope of the Lord's coming, and in their lively worship of departed spirits, relics of saints, and graven images.

"The darkness which overcast the horizon of Christendom after this has procured, for a long period, the name of 'the dark ages.' The eye of faith was feebly directed to the Lord's near coming, and the church was given 'over to believe the lie' that the blessed God had given the dominion of this world to the administration of one bishop. And in that same day in which the intrepid reformers encountered the Latin heirarchy, and threw off the papal yoke, they revived the fainting hope of the Lord's appearing for the overthrow of anti-Christ, and the dispensation of the final judgment.

"Whether the reformers were right or not, in this view of the Lord's doctrine, they girded their loins, they fought the battle, and they won the victory of the reformation; and, right or not, in this view of the Lord's doctrine, they accorded exactly with the faith of the ancient church; and in this view they laid the foundations of the creeds and standards, and confessions of faith, of every Protestant denomination; so that on them no man can build the hope of a kingdom for Christ, or his people, in this world; and as they were right in this view of the Lord's doctrine, and the ancient church was right in the same view, the great majority of their nominal followers are wrong; for now the church of the reformation, also, has forsaken her *first* love, and holds the doctrine of the kingdom in *this* world,—a doctrine never admitted at all in the ancient church, nor in the churches of the reformation until within the last century.[1]

"*Our object* in assembling at this time, our object in addressing you, and our object in other efforts, separate and combined, on the subject of 'the kingdom of heaven at hand,' is to revive and restore this ancient faith, to renew the ancient landmarks, to 'stand in the ways, and see and ask for the old paths, where is the good way' in which our fathers walked and the martyrs 'found rest for their souls.' We have no purpose to distract the churches with any new inventions, or to get to ourselves a name by starting another sect among the followers of the Lamb. We neither condemn, nor rudely assail, others of a faith different from our own, nor dictate in matters of conscience for our brethren, nor seek to demolish their organizations, nor build new ones of our own;[2] but simply to express our convictions like Christians, with the reasons for entertaining them which have persuaded us to understand the word and promises, the prophecies and the gospel, of our Lord, as the first Christians, the primitive ages of the church, and the profoundly learned and intelligent reformers, have unanimously done, in the faith and hope that the Lord will 'come quickly,' 'in his glory,' to fulfill all his promises in the resurrection of the dead.

"As believers in this glorious and yet 'terrible day of the Lord' 'at hand,' it does not become us to judge, censure, or condemn others who see not as we do in regard to this subject, nor to show our zeal for the faith by personally denouncing scoffers and gainsayers. We desire to be humble before the Lord, to defer all judgment to that tribunal, before which we ourselves must shortly stand; and mindful of his goodness who rescued us from the snare of delusion, in which we were taken once in common with the rest of our brethren, we would be charitable toward all, and especially patient with opposers and revilers, who substitute abuse for argument, and pervert our opinions before they venture to try them by the law and the testimony. We seek not the honor of this world, nor do we fear its frown; but in the meek and quiet spirit

---

[1] For full proof of the correctness of this statement, see "Voice of the Church," an elaborate work on the faith of the church from Christ's ascension to the present century, by D. T. Taylor.

[2] It was never attempted until thousands were ex-communicated and pressed out of the churches for their faith; then necessity required them to organize.—*Editor*.

of the gospel, we would walk in all the ordinances of our respective churches blameless, and exhibit in the purity of our lives the holiness and power of the doctrine we profess, in the hope of the appearing of our Lord in his heavenly kingdom.

"Though in some of the less important views of this momentous subject we are not ourselves agreed, particularly in regard to fixing the year of Christ's second advent, yet we are unanimously agreed and established in this all-absorbing point, that the coming of the Lord to judge the world is now specially 'nigh at hand.'

"We are also agreed and firmly persuaded, that the popular theory of a thousand years, or more, of the spiritual and invisible reign of Christ '*in this present evil world*,' where death reigns unto the coming of the Lord in his glory, is altogether unscriptural, and naturally tending to comfort sinners in their evil ways, and to dishearten the faithful; inasmuch as it takes away heavenly and eternal promises from the latter, only to convert them to the temporal use of the former, should they live, as they hope, to witness and enjoy millennial bliss in the conversion of themselves, and of this world."

THE SPIRIT OF THIS FIRST CONFERENCE.

We give below an account of this conference written by one who was present. It speaks for itself, and shows an example worthy of imitation by all who gather to worship, and examine the Scriptures in search of the truth.

"It is well known, though with grief to many of the saints, that of late it has been common in conventions of reform, so called, to witness much debate and perhaps severe clashing or sharp contention.

"And some, no doubt, have concluded, of course, that such would be the case also at our conference, on the Second Advent, inasmuch as it was publicly known that there were differences of opinion among the speakers and members, on points, thought by some, of great importance, particularly on the times and seasons of prophecy. But the friends of Christ may rejoice, even should others regret, that during the two days and evenings of this conference, among the brethren never before met, of the various formerly conflicting orders; with views immatured and uncompared, on the general subject, there was not, from first to last, a single contradiction, nor argument arrayed against argument, nor the least appearance of controversy or contention on any point discussed; there was the greatest harmony, apparent Christian union and good feelings, with deep and solemn interest manifested throughout the meetings, both for worship and business, so that in case of every vote or resolution moved and seconded, it passed unanimously, and yet no time was spent in discussing the subject of union or sectarianism." J.

A MANIFESTATION OF "THE GUIDING HAND."

In A. D. 1839, Capt. A. Landers, Liverpool, Eng., published a valuable pamphlet on the Second Coming of Christ at hand, entitled,

"THY KINGDOM COME."

1200 copies of them were sent to America in A. D. 1840, addressed to "Christians in America." They arrived in Boston, and remained in the custom-house for some time, as no one claimed them, and then were sold at auction to pay duties. Some one bid them off at a nominal price for paper stock. One fell from the package and was picked up by a Christian gentleman who was present; he took it home and read it. Finding it an important work on the soon coming of the Lord, he returned to the custom-house, traced out the name and place of the purchaser, found him, bought the package, carried them to the Signs of the Times office, where they were scattered to be read.

THE KINGDOM OF GOD RESTORED TO THE TRUE ISRAEL.

Acts i. 6, 7—"When they, therefore, were come together, they asked of him, saying, Lord, wilt thou at this time restore again the kingdom to Israel? And he said unto them, It is not for you to know the times and seasons which the Father hath put in his own power."

The question of the disciples in this text implies three things: 1. That Israel once had a kingdom. 2. That it was then subverted, and had been taken from them. 3. That they understood that it was some time or other to be restored *again.*

The answer of Christ, so far from correcting their views, or intimating that they were mistaken in their expectations, tended directly to confirm them in the opinion they already entertained. "It is not for YOU to know," &c. As much as to say, although there are appropriate times and seasons for the occurrence of what you anticipate, and they are yet future, it is not for *you* to know them.

If it be affirmed that the disciples of Christ expected a *temporal* kingdom under the Messiah, it is denied, and the proof is demanded. That they expected a visible kingdom is true; but they expected also that it would be eternal in its duration, and not temporal. Their opinion was based on the Scriptures, which everywhere represented the kingdom of Messiah to be everlasting, without end. That they erred in respect to the subjects of that kingdom, is freely admitted—*they* supposing the Jews were the favorites of heaven.

In pursuing the subject, we shall consider,—

I. The Kingdom of Israel—what it was.

II. Its subversion—when and for what cause.

III. The Restoration of the Kingdom—its heirs and subjects.

I. THE KINGDOM OF ISRAEL—WHAT IT WAS.

The God of glory appeared unto our father Abraham, when he was in Mesopotamia, before he dwelt in Haran, when he was probably an idolator, and called him into Canaan, with the promise that he would give it to Abraham and his seed for an *everlasting* possession; and yet according to Stephen, Acts 7th chapter, he did not give Abraham enough, when alive, to set his foot on; yet he promised he would give it *him* for a possession, when as yet he had no child. God assured him that his seed should sojourn in a strange land, and be entreated evil 400 years, and afterward come forth and serve him in that land of promise. When the time drew near that the people should be returned to the land of promise, Moses was raised up to deliver them from Egypt. He brought them through the Red Sea into the wilderness, where a civil and political government was organized, derived immediately from *Jehovah*, their Great King. The system of civil and political jurisprudence, as well as their religious institutions, were of heaven's own legislation. The administrators of this government were of Divine appointment. Under this government, the people, with Joshua, by divine appointment the successor of Moses, at their head, entered the "land of promise," as God had spoken to Abraham. After casting out and destroying their enemies, the land was divided among them by lot, and the political institutions given to Moses were carried into effect. For 450 years, until Samuel, God governed them by Judges, and was himself their King. So it was in fact a kingdom, even under the Judges. But the people became dissatisfied with this system, and requested a king, like the nations around them. Samuel complained to God that he was rejected; "And the Lord said unto Samuel,—Hearken unto the people in all that they say unto thee, for they have not REJECTED THEE, but they have REJECTED ME, that I should not REIGN OVER THEM." 1 Sam. viii. 7. He then raised up Saul, of the tribe of Benjamin, to reign over Israel; and God again legislated for them, and adapted their laws to a kingly government. He gave them the manner of the kingdom. Saul sinned, and was put away, and David, the son of Jesse, of the tribe Judah, filled his place.

We find the identity of this kingdom to lie in—*The royal house—The territory—The heirs and subjects—The capital and government.*

I. *In the house of David, God promised to perpetuate the royalty of the Kingdom forever.* 1 Chron. xvii. 9—14.

"9. Also I will ordain a place for my people Israel, and will plant them, and they shall dwell in their place, and shall be moved no more; neither shall the children of wickedness waste them any more, as at the beginning.

"10. And since the time that I commanded judges to be over my people Israel. Moreover, I will subdue all thine enemies. Furthermore, I tell thee that the Lord will build thee a house.

"11. And it shall come to pass, when thy days be expired, that thou must go to be with thy fathers, that I will raise up thy seed after thee, which shall be of thy sons; and I will establish his kingdom.

"12. He shall build me a house, and I will establish his throne forever.

"13. I will be his father, and he shall be my son, and I will not take my mercy away from him, as I took it from him that was before thee.

"14. But I will settle him in my house and in my kingdom FOREVER; and his throne shall be established for EVERMORE."

From this text we learn, 1. That David's throne and kingdom was to be ETERNAL. 2. That the son of David, who should fill that throne, will be THE SON OF GOD. So Paul applies it, in Heb. i.: "To which of the angels said he at any time, thou art my son?" And again, "I will be to him a father and he shall be my son." 3. That the kingdom in which he should reign, is "the kingdom of God." "I will settle him in 'my house' and in MY KINGDOM forever: and his throne shall be established for evermore." 4. That this promise is unconditional and immutable. "I will not take my mercy away from him as I took it away from him that was before thee." Saul sinned and was REJECTED ENTIRELY; David was elected to the office FOREVER. But, said God, "If his children forsake my law, and walk not in my judgments; if they break my statutes, and keep not my commandments; then will I visit their transgression with a rod, and, their iniquity with stripes. Nevertheless, my loving-kindness will I not utterly take from him, nor suffer my faithfulness to fail. My covenant will I not break, nor alter the thing that is gone out of my lips. Once have I sworn by my holiness, that I will not lie unto David. His seed shall endure FOREVER, and his throne as the sun before me. It shall be established FOREVER as the moon, and as a faithful witness in heaven." Ps. lxxxix. 30—37.

The heir of David's throne is thus described by Isaiah, ix. 6, 7,—"For unto us a child is born, unto us a son is given: and the government shall be upon his shoulder: and his name shall be called Wonderful, Counsellor, the Mighty God, the Everlasting Father, the Prince of Peace. Of the increase of 'his' government and peace 'there shall be' no end, upon the throne of David, and upon his kingdom, to order it, and to establish it with judgment and with justice from henceforth even forever. The zeal of the Lord of Hosts will perform this.

This king is "THE MIGHTY GOD—THE EVERLASTING FATHER." The government is on "*the throne of David and his kingdom.*" Is not the kingdom of God on earth and the kingdom of David one and the same thing? But who is this child? Luke, first chapter, answers—"And shalt call his name Jesus; and he shall be great, and shall be called the Son of the Highest; and the Lord God shall give unto him the throne of his father David, and he shall reign over the HOUSE OF JACOB FOREVER." There can be no doubt but that Christ is the true and promised heir to David's throne, and under him it is to endure FOREVER.

Solomon was a type of Christ, and built an house of cedar—but Christ is to build a church or temple of living stones—a habitation of God through the Spirit.

2. *The territory over which David bare rule, was the land of promise,* described by God to Abraham thus—"Unto thy seed have I given this land, from

the river of Egypt to the great river, the river Euphrates." Gen. xv. 18. Over this territory, the kingdom of Israel was extended in the days of Solomon. 1 Kings iv. 21, 24, "And Solomon reigned over all kingdoms from the river unto the land of the Philistines, and unto the border of Egypt: they brought presents, and served Solomon all the days of his life. For he had dominion over all the region on this side the river, from Tiphsah even to Azzah, over all the kings on this side the river: and he had peace on all sides round about him."

3. *The heirs and subjects of the kingdom were an elect people.* 2 Chron. vi. 5, 6. "Since the day that I brought forth my people out of the land of Egypt, I chose no city among all the tribes of Israel to build an house in, that my name might be there: neither chose I any man to be over my people Israel. But I have chosen Jerusalem, that my name should be there; and I have chosen David to be over my people Israel." Israel is an elect people. Abraham was elected from all the families of the earth to be the father of the whole church of God—the father of the faithful—the father of many nations—the family in whom all the families of the earth should be blessed. And this promise was when he had no child. His first-born, and the natural heir, Ishmael, was rejected, and the second, Isaac, was elected. In Isaac shall thy seed be called. Of Isaac's seed, to whom the promise was confirmed, Esau was rejected and Jacob chosen, and his name was called Israel. Of his seed, God raised up a church, and gave it an independent and divine system of civil and political government, under his own supervision—the twelve tribes of Jacob were its heirs. Others were conditionally elected to the same privileges. A provision was established in the law of Moses, by which Gentiles might be admitted to a participation in the privileges and immunities of the kingdom. But they came in by identifying themselves with the elect family.

4. *The metropolis, or capital of the kingdom, was Jerusalem.* 2 Samuel v. 3—9. "So all the elders of Israel came to the king, to Hebron; and king David made a league with them in Hebron, before the Lord; and they anointed David king over Israel. David was thirty years old when he began to reign, and he reigned forty years. In Hebron he reigned over Judah seven years and six months; and in Jerusalem he reigned thirty and three years over all Israel and Judah. And the king and his men went to Jerusalem, unto the Jebusites, the inhabitants of the land; which spake unto David, saying, Except thou take away the blind and the lame, thou shalt not come in hither; thinking, David cannot come in hither. Nevertheless, David took the stronghold of Zion: and the same is the city of David. And David said on that day, Whosoever getteth up to the gutter, and smiteth the Jebusites, and the lame and the blind, that are hated of David's soul, he shall be chief and captain. Wherefore they said, The blind and the lame shall not come into the house. So David dwelt in the fort, and called it the city of David. And David built round about from Milo and inward." Also, 2 Chron. vi. 6. "I have chosen Jerusalem, that my name might be there, and have chosen David to be over my people Israel." The reader can find abundant testimony on this point by a little pains.

From the foregoing particulars, we learn that the identity of the kingdom consists, 1. In the royalty of David's house. 2. The territory, the land promised Abraham and his seed. 3. Subjects and heirs, an elect people of Abraham's seed or family. 4. The capital at Jerusalem, and the government of divine origin.

II. THE SUBVERSION OF THE KINGDOM—WHEN, AND FOR WHAT CAUSE.

Although God promised unconditionally, and by an oath, to perpetuate David's throne, kingdom, and seed *eternally;* yet the temporal succession was conditional. "Yet, so that *thy children* take heed to their way to walk before me as thou hast walked before me." Again, "If thy children transgress my law," etc., "then will I visit their transgressions with a rod, and their iniquities with stripes; nevertheless, my loving-kindness will I not utterly take from him, nor suffer my faithfulness to fail." The Lord also made the same covenant with Solomon, 1 Kings ix. 2—7: "The Lord appeared to Solomon the second time, as he had appeared unto him at Gibeon. And the Lord said unto him, I have heard thy prayer and thy supplication that thou hast made before me. I have hallowed this house, which thou hast built, to put my name there forever; and mine eyes and my heart shall be there perpetually. And if thou wilt walk before me, as David thy father walked, in integrity of heart, and in uprightness, to do according to all that I have commanded thee, and wilt keep my statutes and my judgments; then will I establish the throne of thy kingdom upon Israel forever, as I promised to David, thy father, saying, There shall not fail thee a man upon the throne of Israel. *But* if ye shall at all turn from following me, ye or your children, and will not keep my commandments and my statutes which I have set before you, but go and serve other gods, and worship them; then will I cut off Israel out of the land which I have given them; and this house, which I have hallowed for my name, will I cast out of my sight; and Israel shall be a proverb and a by-word among all people." The conditions of this covenant are plain. If Solomon and his children were obedient, his throne should continue, and the promise to David, "There shall never fail thee a man upon the throne of Israel." But if either he, or his children, turned from God's commandment, "*Then will I cut off Israel out of the land which I have given, and Israel shall be a proverb and a by-word among all people.*" Solomon violated that covenant, and the kingdom was rent from his son. 1 Kings xi. 6, 9, 13: "And Solomon did evil in the sight of the Lord, and went not fully after the Lord, as did David his father. And the Lord was angry with Solomon, because his heart was turned from the Lord God of Israel, which had appeared to him twice; and had commanded him concerning this thing, that he should not go after other gods; but he kept not that which the Lord commanded. Wherefore the Lord said unto Solomon, Forasmuch as this is done of thee, and thou hast not kept my covenant and my statutes which I have commanded thee, I will surely rend the kingdom from thee, and will give it to thy servant. Notwithstanding, in thy days I will not do it, for David thy father's sake; but I will rend it out of the hand of thy son. Howbeit, I will not rend away all the kingdom, but will give one tribe to thy son, for David my servant's sake, and for Jerusalem's sake, which I have chosen." When the ten tribes were rent from the house of David and given to Jeroboam, it was with this declaration on the part of Jehovah: "And I will afflict the seed of David, but not forever." 1 Kings xi. 39.

After Solomon's death, Rehoboam his son reigned in his stead in Jerusalem. He oppressed the house of Israel, and the ten tribes revolted from him, and left only Judah and part of Benjamin to the house of David. Rehoboam reigned over them in Jerusalem on the throne of David, and Jeroboam reigned over Israel in Samaria. Hoshea was the last king of the ten tribes, and was carried captive by the king of Assyria, B. C. 742. 2 Kings xvii. 1—6, 13—23. "In the twelfth year of Ahaz, king of Judah, began Hoshea the son of Elah, to reign in Samaria over Israel nine years. And he did that which was evil in the sight of the Lord, but not as the kings of Israel that were before him. Against him came up Shalmaneser, king of Assyria, and Hoshea became his servant, and gave him presents. And the king of Assyria found conspiracy in Hoshea, for he had sent messengers to So, king of Egypt, and brought no present to the king of Assyria, as he had done year by year; therefore the king of Assyria shut him up, and bound him in prison. Then the king of Assyria came up throughout all the land, and went up to Samaria, and besieged it three years. In the ninth year of Hoshea, the king of Assyria took Samaria, and carried Israel away into Assyria, and placed them in Halah and in Habor by the river of Gozen, and in the cities of the Medes. Yet the Lord testified against Israel, and against Judah, by all the prophets, and by all the seers, saying, Turn ye from your evil ways, and keep my commandments, and my statutes, according to all the law which I commanded your fathers, and which I sent to you by my servants the prophets. Notwithstanding, they would not hear, but hardened their necks, like to the necks of their fathers, that did not believe in the Lord their God. And they rejected his statutes, and his covenant that he made with their fathers, and his testimonies which he testified against them; and they followed vanity, and became vain, and went after the heathen that were round about them, concerning whom the Lord had charged them, that they should not do like them. And they left all the commandments of the Lord their God, and made them molten images, even to calves, and made a grove, and worshipped all the host of heaven, and served Baal. And they caused their sons and their daughters to pass through the fire, and used divination and enchantments, and sold themselves to do evil in the sight of the Lord, to provoke him to anger. Therefore, the Lord was very angry with Israel, and removed them out of his sight; there was none left but the tribe of Judah only. Also, Judah kept not the commandments of the Lord their God, but walked in the statutes of Israel which they made. And the Lord rejected all the seed of Israel, and afflicted them, and delivered them into the hands of spoilers, until he had cast them out of his sight. For he rent Israel from the house of David; and they made Jeroboam the son of Nebat king: and Jeroboam drove Israel from following the Lord, and made them sin a great sin. For the children of Israel walked in all the sins of Jeroboam which he did; they departed not from them. Until the Lord removed Israel out of his sight, as he had said by all his servants the prophets. So was Israel carried away out of their own land to Assyria unto this day."

The supremacy of Judah was broken, B. C. 677, in the days of Manasseh, king of Judah. 2 Chron. xxxiii. 9—11. "So Manasseh made Judah and the inhabitants of Jerusalem to err, and to do worse than the heathen, whom the Lord had destroyed before the children of Israel. And the Lord spake to Manasseh, and to his people; but they would not hearken. Wherefore the Lord brought upon them the captains of the host of the king of Assyria, which took Manasseh among the thorns, and bound him with fetters, and carried him to Babylon." This was the first time the whole house of Israel was entirely broken. Judah had previously been afflicted, and Israel remained independent—Israel had been in bondage, and Judah remained independent. But at the time of Manasseh's captivity, Israel had also been broken, that it was no more a people; and Judah also went into captivity. Mannasseh repented, and was reprieved and restored as a tributary to his kingdom. From that time, the house of David never regained its independence. Kings, however, of the house of David, continued to reign on David's throne in Jerusalem, as tributaries to Assyria and Babylon, until the captivity of Zedekiah, king of Judah. 2 Kings xxiv. 18—20; and xxv. 1—10. "Zedekiah was twenty and one years old when he began to reign; and he reigned eleven years in Jerusalem. And his mother's name was Hamutal, the daughter of Jeremiah of Libnah. And he did that which was evil in the sight of the Lord, according to all that Jehoiakim had done. For through the anger of the Lord it came to pass in Jerusalem and Judah, until he had cast them out from his presence, that Zedekiah rebelled against the king of Babylon. And it came to pass, in the ninth year of his reign, in the tenth month, in the tenth day of the month, that Nebuchadnezzar, king of Babylon, came, he and all his host, against Jerusalem, and pitched against it; and they built forts against it round about. And the city was besieged unto the eleventh year of king Zedekiah. And on the ninth day of the fourth month the famine prevailed in the city, and there was no bread for the people of the land. And the city was broken up, and all the men of war fled by night, by the way of the gate between two walls, which is by the king's garden: (now the Chaldees were against the city round about:) and the king went the way toward the plain. And the army of the Chaldees pursued after the king, and overtook him in the plains of Jericho: and all his army were scattered from him. So they took the king, and brought him up to the king of Babylon, to Riblah; and they gave judgment upon him. And they slew the sons of Zedekiah before his eyes, and put out the eyes of Zedekiah, and bound him with fetters of brass, and carried him to Babylon. And in the fifth month, on the seventh day of the month (which is the nineteenth year of king Nebuchadnezzar, king of Babylon), came Nebuzaradan, captain of the guard, a servant of the king of Babylon, unto Jerusalem: and he burnt the house of the Lord, and the king's house, and all the houses of Jerusalem, and every great man's house burnt he with fire. And all the army of the Chaldees, that were with the captain of the guard, brake down the walls of Jerusalem round about."

This ended the temporal dynasty of David's house. When Nebuchadnezzar came up and besieged Jerusalem, and took it, God, by the mouth of Ezekiel, pronounced its doom. Ezek. xxi. 25—27. "And thou, *profane, wicked prince of Israel,* whose day is come, when iniquity shall have an end; thus saith the Lord God, REMOVE THE DIADEM, AND TAKE OFF THE CROWN; this shall not be the same: exalt him that is low, abase him that is high. I WILL OVERTURN, OVERTURN, OVERTURN IT; AND IT SHALL BE NO MORE UNTIL HE COME WHOSE RIGHT IT IS; AND I WILL GIVE IT HIM."

It was under this doom Zedekiah was carried away to Babylon: and since then, no king of David's house has reigned in Jerusalem. *The kingdom was subverted under Hezekiah, by the hand of Nebuchadnezzar,* B. C. 588. *The cause of it was God's indignation at their sins.* It was on this account that God gave his people into the hand of the Assyrians, and is thus declared by Jehovah, Isa. x. 5—7: "*O Assyrian, the rod of mine anger;* AND THE STAFF IN THEIR HAND IS MINE INDIGNATION. I will send him against an hypocritical nation, and against the people of my wrath will I give him a charge, to take the spoil, and to take the prey, and to tread them down as the mire of the strees. Howbeit, *he* meaneth not so. But it is in his heart to destroy and cut off nations not a few." Had it not been for God's INDIGNATION, the Assyrian and Chaldean could not have prevailed against Israel.

Under the Medo-Persians, the government of Israel was restored, but as a tributary government. See Neh. ix. 32—37.

We learn from this passage, that from the times of the kings of Assyria to that day, Israel had been in a state of suffering; and that they were then servants to the kings who were over them. Those kings had dominion over their bodies, and over their cattle, and they were distressed at the pleasure of those kings.

This sentiment was uttered when the kings of Persia had, at their own expense, ordered the temple at Jerusalem to be rebuilt, the worship of God restored and maintained, and had granted an order of protection to the Jews in the enjoyment of all their privileges. Yet they were servants in their own land. And they ever after remained tributary to, or dependent on some one of the great Gentile nations, except when in a state of actual rebellion against their enemies to throw off the yoke.

When Christ was born, even David's royal house went up to Bethlehem to be taxed. When he was crucified, the Jews acknowledged no king but Cæsar. That they have never regained their liberty since then, is too notorious to need remark.

THE CHURCH, WHETHER JEWISH OR CHRISTIAN, STILL IN BONDAGE.

The Christian church is equally in bondage with the Jews. True, Christians have equal privileges with others in the various governments where they live;

but they have no political and civil government of their own. Daniel and his companions in Babylon, were exalted to political power next the king; still they were in bondage. When the king made an image, and called on all his subjects to worship it, they could refuse to do so, to be sure, but only on condition that they should go into the burning fiery furnace. They did refuse, and went into the fire. Thus, the Christian is at liberty to obey the law of God in preference to human laws. But life, limb, liberty or property, must pay for his temerity. As long as we, as Christians, can go along with those laws, they are not felt; but let them but come in collision with our conscience and the laws of God, and the iron enters the soul. All Christians are, as Nehemiah was (under the kings and governments where they reside), servants; —they have dominion over our bodies and property. If it be said, in our own government, Christians have a controlling influence in consequence of the elective franchise, and can model the government as they please through the ballot-box; it is answered—true, if they could out-vote the world, and were united among themselves—neither of which is true. They are but a moiety of the people. If all Christians could be gathered in one body, they might become independent of the world; but this is not the case; they are scattered all over the earth—"The power of the holy people" is "*scattered.*" Dan. xii. 7. And until Michael begins his reign, they will never be delivered from their dispersion. They must be in political bondage until then. But *the Son will then make them free*, and they "*shall be free indeed.*" The Jews, when this sentiment was uttered by the Saviour, resented it, saying, "*We be Abraham's seed, and were never in bondage to any man! And how sayest thou, the Son shall make you free?*" So, in all probability, will many American Christians scorn the thought in the same way. But it is true nevertheless. It was on this principle that Christ directed Peter to take a fish, find a piece of money in his mouth, and give it to Cæsar's tax-gatherer—"*Lest we should offend them.*" So should all Christians be good and peaceable subjects of the governements under which they live, so far as they can with a good conscience. When they cannot do that, then do as did the worthies in Babylon, obey God, and suffer the human penalty.

Our Sovereign is the rightful heir of all the kingdoms of the world, but is now an exile, and his dominion is in the hand of the usurper. But he will come, and in due time bind the strong man, and cast him out, and then he will spoil his goods, and take possession of his house.

III. THE RESTORATION OF THE KINGDOM—ITS HEIRS AND SUBJECTS.

The identity of the kingdom is found, as under our first head, in—*1. The territorial dominion being the land of promise. 2. The heirs and subjects being an elect people, of Abraham's family. 3. The royalty of the kingdom is in the house of David—and the government of Divine origin. 4. The capital, Jerusalem.*

When it is restored, therefore, we must find all these marks in the kingdom.

1. The territory will be the land of promise—the land God promised to "Abra-

ham and his seed." The territory of David's dominion was from the river of Egypt to the great river, the river Euphrates. But there is another promise—Abraham is the father of many nations—and in him and his seed all the families of the earth are to be blessed. "The promise that he should be the HEIR *of the* WORLD was not to Abraham or his seed, through the law, but through the righteousness of faith." Rom. iv. 13. Thus, "THE WORLD" is the land of promise *to Abraham and his seed.* But not in its present ruinous condition. For he sought "a better country, that is, an heavenly:"—*The new heavens and new earth.* Heb. xi. 16.

The promise of *the heirship* of the *world* is given to Christ, the seed and heir of Abraham. "Yet have I set my king upon my holy hill of Zion. I will declare the decree; the Lord hath said unto me, THOU ART MY SON, this day have I begotten thee. Ask of me, and I shall give thee the heathen for thine inheritance, and the uttermost parts of the earth for thy possession." Ps. ii. 6—8.

But what will he do with the heathen, and the uttermost parts of the earth, when they are given to him? Just what God directed his people to do to the inhabitants of the land when he brought them out of Egypt to put them in possession of the land of promise—utterly destroy them—their iniquity is full. "*Thou shalt break them with a rod of iron, and shalt dash them in pieces like a potter's vessel.*" "Those mine enemies that would not that I should reign over them, bring them hither and slay them before me." Luke xix. The land of promise is the new earth, "*the world to come.*" The dominion of it is promised to Christ, Ps. viii.; applied by Paul, Heb. ii. 5—8. *A paradisical earth, with all its creatures, animate and inanimate.* The stone which will dash in pieces the great image (Dan. ii.) will then fill the earth.

2. *The heirs and subjects will be an elect people of Abraham's family.*

God exercised his sovereignty, his elective franchise, in the selection of Abraham from all other families, to be the holy family, and progenitor of the Messiah, in whom all the families of the earth were to be blessed. This *election* was made when as yet Abraham "had no child," and *before circumcision*, "that the promise might be sure to all the seed." Of the two sons of Abraham, *Ishmael* was *rejected* and *Isaac elected;* and the promise renewed to him and his seed, before he had any child. Of his two sons, *Jacob* was *elected* and *Esau rejected.* Thus God reserved to himself the right of *election*, even in the holy family. Did he lose that right when the twelve sons of Jacob were born? Not at all. He had the same right to make another *election* in the family of Jacob, that he had in Abraham and Isaac. He has made *another* and *final election;* and that "*elect*" "*in* whom [his] soul is well pleased," is Christ. He is the seed promised to Abraham, in whom all the families of the earth are blessed. And he is the heir of all the promises. The election is still in the original family, the house of Abraham.

Who, then, is heir to the land of promise? THE JEW? *In no wise.* Let us listen to the apostle Paul while he argues the case. *First,* he lays down a principle of law:—that a covenant once made and confirmed, cannot be changed, "though it be but a man's covenant." How much less God's covenant! To whom, then, does the original deed or covenant convey the land of promise? He answers, "Now to *Abraham and his* SEED were the promises made;—he saith not, and to SEEDS, as of many, but as of one; and to THY SEED, which is Christ."

But the Jew comes up again, and claims it on the ground of the law—that under the law of Moses, God gave it to his fathers. Paul answers, "This I say that the law which was four hundred and thirty years after, cannot disannul, that it should make the promise of none effect. For if the inheritance be of the law, it is no more of promise: but God gave it to Abraham by promise." That is, a law 430 years later than the promise to Christ, cannot take the inheritance from Christ and give it to the Jews. Who then owns the land? Christ.

But says the Jew, "*Wherefore serveth the law?*" If it does not entitle us to the inheritance, why did God make it, and under it bring in our fathers and put them in possession of the inheritance? Paul replies, "It was added because of transgression, *until the seed should come to whom the promise was made.*" "Wherefore, the law was our schoolmaster that it might bring us to Christ, that we might be justified by faith. But after faith is come, we are no longer under a schoolmaster. For ye are all the children of God by faith in Jesus Christ. For as many of you as have been baptized into Christ have put on Christ. There is neither Jew nor Greek, bond nor free, male nor female, but ye are all one in Christ Jesus. And if YE be *Christ's*, then are YE *Abraham's seed*, and *heirs according to promise.*"—Gal. iii. 15—22.

"Baptized into Christ" (under the influence of the Holy Ghost), the *body* of the Christian is as literally a temple of the Holy Ghost, the seed and principle of *eternal life*, as our natural bodies are temples of the blood of Adam—the principle of our mortal life. We shall be filled with, and quickened by that spirit in the resurrection, as we are now filled with and quickened by the blood of Adam. God has made of *one blood* all nations of men that now dwell on the face of the earth. He will then make of *one spirit* all who dwell on the new earth. "The *first Adam* was made *a living soul*, the last Adam, *a quickening spirit.*" "As we *have borne* the image of the earthly, we *shall bear* the image of the heavenly." "Flesh and blood cannot inherit the kingdom of God." It must be our mortal BODY QUICKENED *by the spirit which raised up Christ from the dead. A spiritual* but not *ethereal* body. *Spiritual*, because quickened by spirit; and because *spiritual*, incorruptible, immortal and glorious. Thus all who have that spirit by which Christ was quickened from the dead, have put on Christ, are members of his body—are Abraham's seed, and heirs to the inheritance, "*according to promise.*"

Then not the *Jews*, all Abraham's seed through Jacob—but *Christians*—all Abraham's seed through faith in Christ, the seed of Jacob, are heirs.

THE FALL AND RECOVERY OF THE JEWS.

What is the FALL *of the Jews? From what and how did they fall?*

This subject is fully discussed by Paul in the 11th of Romans, verse 12.

"Now if THE FALL of them be the riches of the world, and the DIMINISHING of them the riches of the Gentiles, how much more their fullness."

The figure Paul has chosen to illustrate the subject, is an olive tree. We may as well follow it. The Jews are its *natural* branches; the believing Gentiles its *engrafted* branches; Christ is the good olive tree. He is so because he is the promised seed of Abraham, in whom the world was to be blessed. That blessing *is salvation—eternal life.* The Jews were the legal heirs and representatives of Abraham, through Isaac and Jacob, to Christ, when the *final election* from Abraham's family took effect. They were of the same blood of Abraham with Christ, and were by that tie one common body; the same as the church is by the spirit of Christ. That was the *only* relation the Jews sustained to him by their natural birth—*a blood relation.* Now let us suppose a case. Suppose Christ to be of the blood or life of Abraham, and to have no other principle of life than that blood. He lives forever by it, and is the source of *life eternal* to all who are saved. He gives them life. Can they inherit more than he possesses? that is the blood or life of Abraham. Then in the resurrection he must quicken into life those who are saved, by that blood; and none but those who are its partakers could live by it. He would call forth the *natural* branches and quicken them,—but he could not impart the blood of Abraham to the Gentile, and quicken him by it, and thus engraft him into the good olive tree, the Abrahamic family.

But Christ shed his blood and *dissolved* his *natural* relation to the Jews. The SHEDDING OF CHRIST'S BLOOD—*his death*—WAS THE FALL OF THE JEWS. Christ was no more their brother in his death, than he was of the Hottentot. He was brother by natural ties to neither the one nor the other. He was dead, and if he ever lived again it must be by some other principle of vitality than blood. That principle was the quickening Spirit of God. Abraham is dead, and if he ever lives again, it will be by the same Spirit, and in Christ. He can never benefit the natural seed by his natural life. Abraham, the father of the faithful, and Christ the promised seed, are both dependent on the Spirit of God for eternal life. The death of Christ being the fall of the Jews, they can never be restored to that from which they fell until Christ lives again by the blood of Abraham.

The DEATH OF CHRIST was both *the riches of the world,* and *the fall of the Jews.* Let the reader pause here, and settle this question. If THIS was not "*the fall of them,*" what was? What else but the shedding of Christ's blood enriched the world? If nothing else did enrich the world, that *death* must be the *Jewish fall!!*

"*The* DIMINISHING OF THEM *the riches of the Gentiles.*" The Jews all fell from their *natural* relation to Christ, but all did not fall from their *spiritual* relation, and cease to be branches:—for some Jews were in Christ when he died, and remained in him in his resurrection. Thus the natural branches of Christ were diminished, and the diminishing was the riches of the Gentiles;—that is, the Gentiles were brought on the same ground with the Jews:—they could be branches of the good olive tree on the condition of faith.

If, by the diminishing of the Jews, or if the Gentiles are enriched when only a few Jews are brought in, how much more rich the church and the world would be if they had all remained as spiritual branches! It was necessary to the salvation of the world, Jews as well as Gentiles, that the Jews should fall from their natural relation, by the death of Christ: but not that they should fall from their spiritual relation. The Gentiles would be just as rich had they remained.

Again: "*If the casting away of them be the reconciling of the world, what shall the receiving of them be but* [*except*] *life from the dead.*"

"The casting away of them," is the same as "the fall of them." They were cast away from the election, as natural branches, by the death of the Saviour. "What," then, "shall the receiving of them be *but* [except] life from the dead;" or a participation of the spirit of Christ, the seed of eternal life, and the principle by which they are to be raised from the dead? They can only be restored, as the Gentile is, by the new birth.

They must be like Christ—*spiritual.* He is the "first fruit,"—"the root,"—and is *spiritual* not *natural;*—then "the lump—the branches"—must be like him.

If God took some branches of the wild olive-tree, the Gentiles, and grafted them in among the branches which remained of the good olive-tree, and made them living, fruitful branches, he can and will take the natural branches, which were broken off by their unbelief, and if they continue not in unbelief, graft them in again, and make them flourishing branches. But their restoration is wholly conditional—"if they continue not in unbelief."

"For I would not, brethren, that ye should be ignorant of this mystery, lest ye should be wise in your own conceits: that blindness in part is happened to Israel until the fullness of the Gentiles be come in."

"*What is the fullness of the Gentiles?*" Either the full number of Gentiles who will ever be saved, will be gathered in, and the door of mercy be closed to them; or the times of the Gentiles, spoken of by the Saviour, Luke xxi. 25, will be accomplished, and the church delivered from her bondage to the Gentiles. In either case it will not end until Christ comes. For as long as he sits on the mercy-seat, "there is no difference between the Jew and the Greek." But "*whosoever* shall call on the name of the Lord shall be saved." And when the dispensation of mercy closes, unless God raises up again the middle wall between the Jew and Greek, and has respect of persons, it will cease with the Jew as well as Greek.

It is not true that the Jews have not had an equal privilege with the Gentiles—for they have had the same chance. God never cast them away from that privilege. They had their privilege before Christ—they have had it equally with the Gentiles. Will they have another exclusive privilege after the Gentiles are shut out? It is objected, if blindness is happened to them, how have they had an equal chance with the Gentiles? I answer, it is only in part; and it is the same with the Gentiles. They do not all see. Or, if it means "*the times of the Gentiles,*" then the Lord's determination is, "to gather the nations, to assemble the kingdoms, to pour upon them his indignation, even all his fierce anger."

Isaiah has settled the question of the national conversion of the Jews,—vi. 8—13.

"Also I heard the voice of the Lord, saying, Whom shall I send, and who will go for us? Then said I, Here *am* I: send me. And he said, Go, and tell this people, hear ye indeed, but understand not; and see ye indeed, but perceive not. Make the heart of this people fat, and make their ears heavy, and shut their eyes; lest they see with their eyes, and hear with their ears, and understand with their hearts, and convert and be healed. Then said I, Lord, how long? And he answered, Until the cities be wasted without inhabitant, and the houses without man, and the land be utterly desolate: and the Lord have removed men far away, and *there be* a great forsaking in the midst of the land. But yet in it *shall be* a tenth, and it shall return, and shall be eaten; as a teil-tree, and as an oak, whose substance is in them, when they cast their leaves: so the holy seed shall be the substance thereof."

From this quotation we learn, 1. That blindness and hardness is happened to the Jewish people, "*lest they* CONVERT *and be* HEALED!" 2. That this blindness is to continue on the nation until *the cities be* WASTED WITHOUT INHABITANTS, the houses *without man*, and the *land be* UTTERLY DESOLATE, or as in the margin, "DESOLATE WITH DESOLATION." Will such a desolation ever occur until the scene described, Isa. 24th chapter, and 2d Pet. 3d chapter? Until then, the blindness is on them as a nation. Will it be said, that the "*land*," "*cities*," "*houses*," etc., are only the land of Palestine; and was fulfilled in the destruction of Jerusalem by the Romans? If so, then the blindness was then ended. *But is it so?* If not, it cannot be terminated until the end of the present state of things.

But there is to be a *tithe* who will return, after this desolation ends. That *tithe* is the "HOLY SEED."

"*All Israel shall be saved.*" But "they are not all Israel," *do not constitute* "ALL ISRAEL, who are of Israel; neither, because they are the seed of Abraham, are they all children: but in Isaac shall thy seed be called." The *elect* of Abraham's family, not all his descendants, are the *Israel of God.* "We, brethren," says Paul, "as Isaac was, are the children of promise." The salvation of Israel, here spoken of, is not the conversion of the Jews, but the gathering of the holy seed into the heavenly inheritance, by the resurrection of the just. ETERNAL SALVATION. "As it is written," in Isa. lix. 20:—"And *the Redeemer shall come to Zion*, and unto them that turn from transgression in Jacob." Let the reader keep in mind, that the *elect* seed of Abraham's family, according to the *last election*, is CHRIST *and his* CHILDREN. "Behold I, and the children which thou hast given me," is his language. The Jew has *now* no more right to the promise, than *Ishmael*, after Isaac's birth; or *Esau*, after *Jacob* was chosen of God. The subject of the *latest election* being come, it is in his family alone. *Ishmael* and *Esau* have the same right in him, as *Isaac* and *Jacob*, provided they come in at the door. "Henceforth," then, "know we no man after the flesh, yea, though we have known Christ after the flesh, yet now (since his death) know we him so no more." He *was* a Jew, but is not so *now*. He is henceforth the Son of God, because he lives by the quickening Spirit of God. He laid down his blood or life, *an* ETERNAL SACRIFICE, and is now a new creature. Therefore, if any man be in him, he is a new creature, a *spiritual heir* of Abraham.

That when the kingdom is restored, it will not be restored to the Jews, is clear from Christ's parable, Matt. xxi. 33—45; where, by the parable of the householder, he taught the Jews, that for their rejection and murder, *first* of God's prophets, *and then* of his Son, the heir of the inheritance, *that when he shall come*, he will *take* THE KINGDOM OF GOD *from them*, and give it unto a "nation bringing forth the fruit thereof." That nation, Dan. vii. 18, 27, is "THE SAINTS OF THE MOST HIGH." *The elect people, the heirs and subjects of the future "kingdom of Israel," are "the house of Jacob," through Christ—the saints of the Most High.*

3. The royalty of the kingdom is in David's house, and the government of divine origin.

The heir of David's throne has already been shown to be Christ. Acts ii. 30, further illustrates the same point. "Being a prophet, and knowing that God had sworn with an oath unto him, that of the fruit of his loins according to the flesh, HE WOULD RAISE UP CHRIST TO SIT ON HIS THRONE; he seeing this before, spake of the *resurrection* of Christ." David well knew that a mortal man could not fill his throne forever; hence he predicted the resurrection of Christ from the dead, to endure forever.

Solomon, also, in his dedicatory prayer, understood Christ to be the promised heir of David's throne. Rehearsing the promise to his father David, that there should not fail him a man to sit on his throne, he prays that God might remember, and fulfill his promise. "But," he exclaims, "*will God in very deed dwell with men on the earth?*" Thus he evidently believed the kingdom of God and the kingdom of David or Israel to be one; and that Christ, the son of David, would reign personally on the earth. Christ, likewise, claims to have the key of the house of David, and to be able to shut, and no man open, and open, and no man shut. See Revelation iii. 7.

When God subverted the kingdom of Israel by Nebuchadnezzar, as shown under our second head, he declared, Ezekiel xxi. that "IT SHALL BE NO MORE UNTIL HE COMES WHOSE RIGHT IT IS, AND I WILL GIVE IT HIM." Christ has come once, but that he did not at that time restore the kingdom is clear from our text, which was utterred just as he was about to leave the world. "Wilt thou at this time restore," etc. "It is not for you to know," etc. Had the kingdom been then restored, it would have been perfectly easy to have corrected the impression of the disciples, that it had not been restored. Had he only told them, "My disciples, you are mistaken on this point, the kingdom is restored, only it is a spiritual kingdom; the reign of David's spiritual seed on David's spiritual throne;" it would have settled the question forever. But he could not have taken a course more directly calculated to establish them and the church, forever, in the opinion that the restoration is yet future, and will be at his second appearing. Indeed, all our opponents admit that the times referred to, are the times of Christ's second advent, by quoting this very text to prove that we can know nothing of that time. But when he comes again whose right it is, God will give the kingdom to him, and he will restore it to his people. "Come, ye blessed of my father," he will say, "and inherit the kingdom prepared for you from the foundation of the world." Matthew xxv. *Its royalty will then be in David's house forever.*

The Government will be of divine origin. Thus, the prophet Isaiah—xxxiii. 22. "*The Lord is our Lawgiver, the Lord is our Judge, the Lord is our King, and he will save us.*" Ezekiel xxxvii. 14—24, God has promised to put his Spirit in them, and cause them to walk in his statutes, etc.

4. The capital of the kingdom is Jerusalem. The election of *Jerusalem* was made when David was chosen king. "I HAVE CHOSEN JERUSALEM, THAT MY NAME MIGHT BE THERE." 2 Chron. vi. 6. "The Lord hath chosen Zion, he hath desired it for his habitation. This is my rest forever, here will I dwell, for I have desired it." Ps. cxxxii. 13, 14. "The time to favor Zion, yea, the set time is come, for thy servants take pleasure in her stones, and favor the dust thereof." "When the Lord shall build up Zion, he shall appear in his glory." Ps. cii. Also, Isa. xxiv. 23. "Then the moon shall be confounded and the sun ashamed, when *the Lord of hosts* SHALL REIGN *in* MOUNT ZION, *and in* JERUSALEM *and before his ancients* GLORIOUSLY." "Nor by Jerusalem, for it is the city of the great king," said the Saviour.

Again, Matthew, 23d chapter: addressing Jerusalem as distinguished from her children, the inhabitants, he says, "Ye shall not see me henceforth, until ye shall say, Blessed is he that cometh in the name of the Lord." Then he will return to Jerusalem, and find a race of children who shall say, "BLESSED;" not the children of the old "Jerusalem, which is in bondage, with her children;" but the children of the "Jerusalem which is above and is free:" the children of promise—the *glorified saints.* Ezekiel, 37th chapter, where, under the symbol of the valley of dry bones, the resurrection of the just is predicted, God promises to set his sanctuary among them forevermore. "My tabernacle also shall be with them; yea, I will be their God, and they shall be my people." John, in vision, witnessed the fulfillment of the scene, when he said, BEHOLD THE TABERNACLE OF GOD IS WITH MEN, and HE WILL DWELL WITH THEM, and they shall be his people, and GOD HIMSELF shall be with them, and be their God." This TABERNACLE is the NEW JERUSALEM. There Jesus Christ will dwell in the midst of them forevermore. There "THE LORD OF HOSTS will reign in Mount Zion and in Jerusalem, and before his ancients gloriously." Then Jerusalem shall enlarge the place of her tent, and stretch forth the curtains of her habitation. She shall break forth on every side, as foretold in Isaiah, 54th chapter. The city, according to Rev. 21st chapter, will be 12,000 furlongs, i. e., 1500 miles square.

"*It is not for you to know the times and seasons, which the Father hath put in his own power.*" Thus said the Saviour, when about to leave the disciples and ascend into heaven. It is a clear intimation that there were appointed times for the event, but they were then future, and not to be understood by the apostles. Those times are referred to by the Saviour, Luke, xxi. 25, "Jerusalem shall be trodden down of the Gentiles, until THE TIMES OF THE GENTILES BE FULFILLED." Until then it cannot become the capital or kingdom of Israel. Until then, also, the people of God are to be carried captive into all nations. The Psalmist also speaks of the times, in Ps. cii. 13. "The *time* to favor her (Zion), yea, the *set time*, is come." "This shall be written for the generation to come." "When the Lord shall build up Zion he shall appear in his glory."

"It is not for you to know the times and seasons which the Father hath put in his own power." So SAID the Saviour, and he SAID it because it was true. It was not for those disciples to know. But he did not mean to contradict himself where he had said to his disciples who should live to see the signs of his coming, "THEN KNOW that it is near, even at the door." But had he meant that it would never be known, he would have contradicted both himself and Daniel, who declares that at the time of the end, "the wise shall understand." And Paul to the church, "Ye, brethren, are not in darkness, that that day should overtake you as a thief." Christ, then, cannot come till his humble, watchful people know it. Reader, prepare and watch. Amen.

"O how I long to see that day
When the redeemed shall come
To Zion, clad in white array,
Their blissful, happy home.

To hear the alleluiahs roll
From the unnumbered throng;
The kingdom spread from pole to pole,
And join redemption's song.

To see all Israel safe at home,
Singing on Zion's height;
And Jesus crowned upon his throne;
Creation own his right.

Jerusalem I long to see,
Blest city of my King!
And eat the fruit of life's fair tree,
And hear the blood-washed sing!

All hail! the morn of glory's nigh,
The pilgrim longs to see;
That dries the tear from every eye—
Creation's jubilee!

My longing heart cries out, O, come!
Creation groans for thee!
The weary pilgrim sighs: O, come!
Bring immortality."

CHAPTER IX.

Echoes of the seven thunders—Smoke of doctors and editors—The monthly miscellany—F. Parkman, D. D.—A roman catholic—O. A. Skinner—John Dowling, A. M.—Christian Witness—D. Campbell—Weekly Messenger—Popish proscription—J. E. Hood—Editor Brown—Professor Stuart—Catholics supported—Universalists—Strengthened—The trumpet astonished—Christ already come—The witness—Dr. Bushnell—Christ not to come personally—Hartford Universalist gladdened—Lutheran confession—Dr. Eck and the duke of Batavia.

It is a mark of courage and persistence, if not of dignity and piety, for men to oppose and seek to destroy whatever doctrine or system may arise which is contrary to their position, and is calculated to supersede what they have publicly taught.

When victory can be won by sound logic, thorough argument backed up with a proper application of truth, it is honorable and christian to oppose an opposite view and to "contend earnestly for the faith once delivered to the saints." But in recognizing efforts which have been made to oppose and destroy the influence and results of the Second Advent Message, we must introduce a class of men, of high position in society, whose courage and persistency appear to eclipse their piety, dignity, honor, and wisdom.

As the facts we have already recorded show, the proclamation that Christ was coming soon, was taking deep root in the hearts of many of the devout ministers and members of all the churches, and gaining a strong hold upon the masses who were privileged with hearing. This was disturbing those who were "at ease in Zion," damaging to the prevailing teaching concerning "the good time coming," and striking a deadly blow at the worldly, ambitious schemes of many who were getting above the position appointed them by their Divine Master.

What must be done? Christian candor, Divine direction, and

Berean example, would reply, "Let us consider the whole matter," "Search the scriptures daily, whether these things are so." But was this done? Oh, yes, it was by many, and it made converts to the faith, until it was considered a true mark of an Advent believer to be seen studying his Bible *much,* or to be known as carrying his Bible with him. Many were told that they studied the Bible too much. The writer of this history has been often told so. Those who were "*established* in their own views," those who had "not *changed* an item" of their "views for forty years," and those who seemed to forget that the Bible is the standard of truth, must try some other means to stop this message. Did they stop it? They tried. Strong men tried. Giant-minded men tried. Highly educated men tried. Men in high, social, educational, and religious position tried. This encouraged weak men, men of less brains, men without education, men of no culture, men without religion, drunkards, scoffers of low grade; they all tried. These classes so different in quality, in position, in general pursuits, became fellow-helpers in one common cause. Whether they met in council in "the plains of Ono," or mutually consulted "the gods of the nations," does not concern us. But for once, ah, not for the first time, they are found in sympathy in a general effort. And what was that effort? To close the ears of the people against the gospel of the kingdom of God. And what did they use as weapons? The sword of the spirit? Let us inspect their armor. We shall find no fault with any proper effort, any Scriptural, historical, or chronological argument, to show that the calculation on 1843 was unsound.

THE MONTHLY MISCELLANY FOR MAY, 1840, contained an article headed "*Predictions of the End of the World,*" signed F. P., supposed to be from the pen of Francis Parkman, D. D., of Boston, intended to associate Mr. Miller with the false prophets, instead of meeting his views with Scriptural arguments. In his closing paragraph he says:

"That much remains to be done before ancient prophecy is completed, whoever reads may understand.[1] That the world will continue, and generations succeed after we have left it we may be assured. How long, or how many, this shall be, is with the secret things that belong to God, 'whose glory it is

---

[1] But why did he not tell us what we were to look for, if he knew? To correct error we should give instruction.

to conceal a matter,' and whose wisdom and kindness are displayed alike in what he has revealed and in what he has hidden."

If this D. D. has given us the true principle on which God's book is to be read, how then can we know that future generations are to come? On what does *he* base *his prophecy*, that the world will continue. Had Mr. Miller prophesied on the subject we cannot see why he had not as good authority for it as has Dr. P. Do titles give authority to predict? There are many who appear to think thus.

ROMAN CATHOLICS, PROTESTANTS, AND JEWS AGREE.

In A. D. 1840 two books were issued in Boston with these titles. First. "*Miller Overthrown*, or the false prophet confounded," by one who signed himself "*A Cosmopolite*—a Roman Catholic." He tells us "the prophecies of Daniel were fulfilled in Antiochus Epphanes." This became a text book for many Protestant teachers, who repeated it in all their efforts to show that the prophecies of Daniel could not give us any clue to the time we occupy. The second—"Miller's theory utterly exploded," by O. A. Skinner, Universalist. He puts all these prophecies on the destruction of Jerusalem. Not agreed as to events, but all agree to interpret so as that the events are in the past, or the prophecies which give a chain extending to the coming judgment, must be so interpreted as to break the connecting links.

But just now another and greater enters upon the work of teaching on the prophecies, and we are glad to see every man do what he can, yet of some, "their strength is to sit still." It should not be so with doctors of divinity. However, we have now what claims to be "An exposition of the prophecies supposed by Wm. Miller to predict the second coming of Christ in 1843, with a supplementary chapter upon the True Scriptural Doctrine of a Millennium prior to the Judgment, by John Dowling, A. M." Mr. D. says on page 24:

"It is necessary to use argument and fact to knock down the foundation upon which his (Mr. Miller's) theory is based, and *nothing else will satisfy* a candid and inquisitive mind."

This is well said, and sounds like one who has decided to pursue this course. But after bringing certain objections to Mr. Miller's interpretation and application of the predictions of Daniel and John, and pointing out what he calls inconsistencies and errors in his reasonings, and after departing from all Protestant use of the periods of

Daniel, he leaves his readers in possession of the following statements, for "argument and facts" (The learned doctor says on page 111):

"I am asked the question—As you reject the interpretation Mr. Miller gives of these three prophetic times, can you furnish a better? I reply, I DO NOT FEEL MYSELF BOUND TO GIVE ANY."

Is this a "knock-down argument?" Are these the "facts with which to satisfy a candid and inquisitive mind?" We then have his arguments and facts on "A Millennium before the Judgment," on page 167, thus:

"The doctrine I hold in relation to the millennium, and for which I think I am indebted to the Bible, is, That the reign of Christ on earth will not be a personal, but a spiritual reign, that it will be preceded by the overthrow of Popery, Mahommedanism, Paganism, and all false systems: that it will consist in the universal prevalence of righteousness and true holiness, throughout the whole world; that during its continuance, war, rapine, robbery, and oppression, shall be unknown; there shall be nothing to hurt or destroy, and universal love shall govern the actions of all mankind; that this glorious age shall pass away, and be succeeded by a brief but dreadful period of wickedness, after which the Lord Jesus shall be revealed."

If the doctor is indebted to the Bible for all this we think he ought to have passed over a little of the Bible which teaches such as he "holds to." True, he quotes some texts and refers to some passages of history in his knock-down effort with Mr. Miller's theory, but these may be in place in another part of our work.

But we should not fail to acknowledge that Dr. Dowling's book, "Reply to Miller," received a splendid puff by the "Christian Witness." Its editor thinks Dowling has "thoroughly upset Miller's theory," and adds:

"It contains a brief treatise upon the Scripture doctrine of the millennium, showing reasons for believing that we are *not to expect a personal* reign of Christ on earth for a thousand years, but a spiritual reign, denoting the universal prevalence of Christianity."

We will here present the testimony of an impartial witness as to the general character of Dr. Dowling's book, which will, perhaps, be important as to notice his many palpable misstatements and shallow efforts.

Dr. Breckenridge speaks of it as follows:

"As for this disquisition of Mr. Dowling, we may confidently say that it is hardly to be conceived that anything could be printed by Mr. Miller, or Mr.

Any-body-else, more shallow, absurd and worthless. There is hardly a point he touches, on which he has not managed to adopt the very idlest conjectures of past writers on the prophecies; and this so entirely without any coherent system, that the only clear conviction a man of sense or reflection could draw from his pamphlet, if such a man could be supposed capable of believing it, would be that the prophecies themselves are a jumble of nonsense."—*Spirit of the XIX Century.*

But Dr. D.'s predicted millennium seems not likely to come, his much admired book died "the death," with its grandeur, while the doctrine of Christ's speedy return lives and progresses, and the abounding of iniquity shows the harvest near.

Eld. David Campbell writes a book to meet the demand for light. It is a strange medley.

"ILLUSTRATIONS OF PROPHECY."

He attempts to expound "the seals," "the trumpets," and "the vials" of Revelation, the "beasts" and "horns" of Daniel, with an effort to set aside Miller's application. He claimed the Papacy fell in A. D. 1672: that the little horn of Dan. VIII. symbolized a person—Mahomed; that the millennium was to be before the advent of Christ; that the Jews were to return to Palestine, etc. This book finds admirers, and receives such praise as the following. The New York Weekly Messenger says of it:

"In these days of fanaticism and false doctrine, when the world is full of speculations concerning the near approach of the millennium and the day of judgment, a clear understanding must be of the utmost importance. Miller and his coadjutors are now doing more harm to the cause of religion than they can ever hope to repair, and all efforts to avert the mischief they are producing should be encouraged by the Christian world. Mr. Campbell's work is the very thing that is needed to bring about such a result. By illustrating in a clear and understanding manner, the meaning of those prophecies which enthusiastic teachers have misapprehended, he shows that all who are willing to inquire, may so far acquaint themselves with the truth, as at least, to see the absurdity of the thousand erroneous interpretations of prophecy which are now before the public."

The above notice was inserted in a hand bill with an advertisement of Mr. Campbell's book, and then circulated among the audiences at the door where Mr. Miller was lecturing in New York City; yet it increased the interest.

But Mr. Campbell's book did not meet the demand. It was found to be entirely wanting in proper rules of interpretation. It was an anomaly, and died "the death." No stone marks its grave.

The anxious, disturbed public demanded instruction on the prophecies which should ease their minds on the subject of the judgment. It might be near. The views of "these fanatics" rest on the literal reading of the Bible, and appear to chime with all the events of past and present history. But what do they know of the Scriptures? Our doctors ought to know. They must know. Why do they not give us some clear, plain Bible argument on these things? This was the prevailing thought, and this the oft-repeated question. We here meet another form of argument, that the world cannot end at present. It is as old as the Papacy.

POPISH PROSCRIPTION.

The following appears in the "Signs of the Times," and is afterwards confirmed by the admission of Mr. Cogswell: "We are informed by a letter from J. E. Hood, a student of Dartmouth College, addressed to the Rev. Wm. Cogswell, D. D., Secretary of the American Education Society, that '*beneficiaries* of that institution are to be withheld from any *who embrace the doctrines of Miller* in reference to the end of the world,' that 'any young man embracing them would be denied further aid.'"

Mr. J. E. Hood writes a letter to the Rev. Wm. Coggswell, D. D., Secretary of the American Education Society, Hanover, N. H.:

"HANOVER, July 8, 1840.

"DEAR SIR:—At a private interview with myself on the 1st inst., you said to me: 'The Educational Society will not hereafter aid any man who adopts the doctrines of Miller in reference to the end of the world. . . . I was puzzled and pained to hear from your lips such a declaration. I could with difficulty credit my own senses, until you had explicitly and emphatically repeated the statement. . . . Finally, I am not a Millerite, yet I believe it wrong to proscribe my brethren for their religious opinions. I believe that the Education Society has turned out of its primitive path for the purpose of crushing a 'small and despised sect' who are guilty of no crime but that of holding 'new and strange doctrines.' I therefore feel it my duty respectfully to decline any further aid from its funds, and return the last appropriation.

"J. E. HOOD."

MR. BROWN, EDITOR OF ZION'S HERALD,

Comes out with a false statement, and makes a cloud of dust for the eyes of his readers, stating that:

"Mr. Miller has long maintained that after the eleventh day of August, 1840, there would be no conversions, that Christians would lose their desire and their spirit of prayer for the conversion of sinners—in fine, that that day would close up the day of grace."

Mr. Miller had said no such thing. The above was a manufactured story, based on Miller's opinion that the 7th trumpet would close probation; on this he said in the "Signs of the Times," Sept. 1, 1840:

"To say positively when the door will be shut I cannot, for I do not know how much time may be included in the words 'when the seventh trumpet begins to sound.'"

Some other writers have argued that the "beginning to sound" in this instance embraces a space of perhaps several years.

ROMAN CATHOLIC INTERPRETATION SUPPORTED.

Prof. Moses Stuart, of Andover College, who some twenty years before wrote a valuable work against "German Neology," in which he cautions the churches in America against its encroachments upon their theology, now comes out with a work entitled

"HINTS ON THE INTERPRETATION OF PROPHECY."

At this time of special awakening among the ministers and studious members of all churches, either to learn the true voice of prophecy, or to find some construction of it that would ward off the current of mind which was setting in, favoring the message of the advent near, very much help was expected from so ripe a Biblical scholar as Mr. Stuart was supposed to be. The announcement of his work on this subject gratified the minds of many, supposing they would now have a satisfactory solution of these prophetic Scriptures which were brought forward by an old farmer, and other "ignorant and unlearned men" as proof that the judgment was soon to come. The book was obtained. In the preface Mr. Stuart says:

"It is time for the churches, in reference to matters now before us, to seek some refuge from the tumultuous ocean, on which they have of late been tossed."

Here again, at the onset, in the beginning of the book of this learned author, the expectations of the readers were raised yet higher, that "a refuge from" the deep interest existing and increasing on the Lord's speedy return, was at last found and pointed out. But O, the surprise, dismay, mortification of these anxious fellow-scholars and fellow-teachers. Why, "Moses Stuart himself become a Neologist!" and he a leading teacher in one of our most important theological schools in America; exerting an influence over the minds, and directing the thoughts and studies of our young ministers, and young scholars in our churches; such as few, if any other teacher can do! But what position did Mr. Stuart take? He handled the prophecies of Daniel and John, as no other scholar had done in the Protestant Christian churches; he unhinged the arguments of all sound scholars of the former, and present generations, and endorsed those of papists. We will here give a few extracts from others, which show the character and influence of the work, and in another place we shall give some extracts from the book, with reviews.

Mr. Hinton, in his work on prophecy, page 231, says (of Mr. Stuart's work):

"We regret that in the midst of the great moral conflict, with anti-Christ, which is now carrying on, those into whose hands 'the saints' were so long 'given' should find so able a conductor. Without, of course, for one moment intimating any such ambitious design, we are clearly of opinion that the worthy doctor of Andover, has already earned a Cardinal's hat; and if his forthcoming work should be equally ingenious in behalf of Romanism, the pontificate itself would be only an adequate reward!

We have, however, no fears that Christians of sound common sense, and capable of independent thought, will, after a candid consideration of the scheme which excludes papacy from the page of prophecy, and that which traces in the prophetic symbols a faithful portraiture of its abominations, make a wrong decision."

THE UNIVERSALISTS STRENGTHENED.

The following is from the "Hartford (Ct.) Universalist." Its editor says:

"When we see such men as Professor Stuart, forced by the power of truth, to abandon the old, antiquated, erroneous notions concerning the Apocalypse, we are inspired with hope. In his zeal to overthrow Millerism, the Professor has involved himself in a dilemma from which *he will find it no easy matter to retreat.*"

"In his 'hints on the interpretation of prophecy,' he refutes Miller's views of the second coming of Christ, by taking Universalist's ground, and limiting the fulfillment of the predictions of the Revelator to a time not far distant from that in which they were made.

"The utterance of such doctrine by Moses Stuart is a new thing under the sun. 'It tends,' as we are told by a Presbyterian paper of repute, 'as the opinions of Professor Bush do, *fearfully* to Universalism.' Professors Stuart and Bush are liberalizing the minds and enlightening the understandings of the Calvinistic party, by administering small doses of *Universalism*, as the remedies for the popular tumults and excitements."

In the above samples may be seen the influence which men of giant minds, or high position, exert over the people who look to them for instruction, and how important that such "be taught of God," and "teach as the oracles of God."

It is not a matter of surprise that Universalists should sneer and jest when the subjects of Christ's coming and the judgment are faithfully taught, for they claim to be unbelievers in such doctrine. But when Christian ministers and doctors of divinity are bold to deny or pervert what their predecessors have taught as the most sacred and important truths, we must expect unbelievers to become more confirmed.

THE EDITOR OF THE TRUMPET, A UNIVERSALIST PAPER, published in Boston, makes a great flourish about the Miller excitement, in his paper. We extract an item.

He informs his readers that "Wm. Miller is a weak-minded, vain, and self-confident old man, who has learned some passages of Scripture by heart; but who in our judgment, either dishonestly perverts the sacred writings, or is almost totally ignorant of their true sense. He has been in the vicinity of Boston some two or three months. He is constantly giving lectures on his theory, which are attended by immense crowds. The meeting-houses are generally closed against him, except the two occupied by a sect calling themselves 'Christians.'

"But the most astonishing fact is yet to be disclosed. The Baptist Society in Cambridgeport, had their house open every day last week, for Miller, and their clergyman was in the pulpit with him, taking part in the services. We are surprised beyond measure, at this movement. . . . That such men as J. V. Himes, and P. R. Russell (the Christian ministers), should abet Miller's imposition, might have been expected. They are fit for such things. We agree with the Rev. Dr. Sharp, in a remark he is said to have made, 'that Miller's theory is *all moonshine;*' and we are astonished that a truly respectable society should give the least countenance to such deception."

THE ABOVE EDITOR AND A PHRENOLOGIST MATCHED.

Solomon's fools are found in all generations. We have often heard men talk of that they knew nothing.

The following will be interesting to some of our readers:

From the 6th to the 9th of March, Mr. Miller lectured in Medford, Mass. While here a friend took him to a phrenologist in Boston, with whom he was himself acquainted, but who had no suspicion whose head he was about to examine. The phrenologist commenced by saying that the person under examination had a large, well-developed, and well-balanced head. While examining the moral and intellectual organs, he said to Mr. Miller's friend:

"I tell you what it is, Mr. Miller could not easily make a convert of *this man* to his hair-brained theory. He has too much good sense."

Thus he proceeded, making comparisons between the head he was examining and the head of Mr. Miller, as he fancied it would be.

"O, how I should like to examine Mr. Miller's head!" said he; "I would give it one squeezing."

The phrenologist, knowing that the gentleman was a particular friend of Mr. Miller, spared no pains in going out of the way to make remarks upon him. Putting his hand on the organ of marvelousness, he said: "There! I'll bet you anything that old Miller has got a bump on his head there as big as my fist;" at the same time doubling up his fist as an illustration.

The others present laughed at the perfection of the joke, and he heartily joined them, supposing they were laughing at his witticisms on Mr. Miller.

"He laughed; 'twas well. The tale applied
Soon made him laugh on t' other side."

He pronounced the head of the gentleman under examination the reverse, in every particular, of what he declared Mr. Miller's must be. When through, he made out his chart, and politely asked Mr. Miller his name.

Mr. Miller said it was of no consequence about putting his name upon the chart; but the phrenologist insisted.

"Very well," said Mr. M.; "you may call it Miller, if you choose."

"*Miller, Miller*," said he; "what is your first name?"

"They call me William Miller."

"What! the gentleman who is lecturing on the prophecies?"

"Yes, sir, the same."

At this the phrenologist settled back in his chair, the personation of astonishment and dismay, and spoke not a word while the company remained. His feelings may be more easily imagined than described.

The following description of Mr. Miller's phrenological developments were furnished by a phrenological friend in 1842, and may be of some interest to those acquainted with that science:

ORGANS VERY LARGE.—Amativeness, Adhesiveness, Combativeness, Firmness, Conscientiousness, Benevolence, Constructiveness, Ideality, Calculation, Comparison.

LARGE.—Philoprogenitiveness, Alimentiveness, Acquisitiveness, Self-esteem, Imitation, Mirthfulness, Form, Size, Order, Locality, Eventuality, Time, Language, Casuality.

FULL.—Inhabitiveness, Concentrativeness, Caution, Approbation, Wonder, Veneration, Weight, Color, Tune.

MODERATE.—Marvelousness, Secretiveness, Hope, Individuality.

"CHRIST ALREADY COME."

Messrs. Noyes, editors of "The Witness," who advocate the doctrine of "Perfect Holiness," say as follows, in 1840:

"MILLER'S IMPOSTURE.

"Our readers are doubtless aware that Miller's famous doctrine of the speedy coming of Christ 'in the clouds of heaven,' is based on that old desperate delusion of Christendom,—the denial that *he has already come.*

"Miller thus adds to the long list of foolish, not to say blasphemous devices, by which ungodly men have sought these thousand years to turn aside and stultify the plainest and most solemn declaration of the Son of God. . . . On the other hand, we have reason to rejoice that this delusion makes occasion for many to examine honestly the subject of the Second Coming.

"All sober men must soon find themselves shut up to the acknowledgment that Christ came the second time according to his promise, within the lifetime of some of his followers."

NO PERSONAL ADVENT OF CHRIST TO BE LOOKED FOR.

Mr. Bushnell, D. D., Congregationalist minister in Hartford, Conn., comes to the help of Neology and Spiritism. He writes a book, in which he says many good things, gives much good practical instruction. This serves to gloss and cover the scepticism which the doctor has fallen into in regard to the doctrine of the Second Coming of Christ, the resurrection of the dead, the glorious restitution and the reign of the Lord Messiah. One of the objects prompting this eminent divine to publish this book seems to have been to attempt to show the church that their Lord and Master would never return in person to fulfill his gracious promises. Let us hear him on the Second Advent; for he writes upon the subject, and writes strangely.

The doctor quotes the following text and gives his comments:

"'Ye have heard how I said unto you, I go away, and come again unto you.' 'In what sense then is he going, and in what sense will he come again—what change of relationship he will inaugurate between himself and his followers, and as to what kind of a personal relation he undertakes to hold with them now, is the subject to which the author invites the attention of his auditors.'

"Christ says, 'It is expedient for you that I go away,' adding the promise, 'I will come to you.' He means by this that the time has now arrived when there must be a change of administration, when he must needs be taken away from their eyes, and begin to be set in a new spiritual relation which permits a universal access of men to him, and a universal presence of him with them.

"What is wanted now is an *unlocalized, invisible, spiritual presence, everywhere present Saviour*, such as all may know and receive, being consciously known and received by him, AND THIS WILL BE HIS COMING AGAIN, OR HIS SECOND COMING, such a kind of coming as shows him bearing rule in Providence, and riding in the clouds of heaven—rolling on the changes, unfolding the destinies of time, and preparing his universal kingdom. . . . In all of which Christ, you will perceive, is proposing to do exactly nothing which many of his disciples, taken by faith of his second coming, so fervently preach, and so earnestly magnify. They believe that he is to come in a body, and be visible as in a body. . . . Every ship that sails will be crowded with eager multitudes pressing on to see the visible Christ. Thronging in thus, month by month, a vast seething crowd of pilgrims, curious and devout, poor and rich, houseless and hungry, trampling each other down—many of them sick, not one of them truly in the enjoyment of God's peace, not one of a thousand getting near enough to see him—still fewer to hear him speak, how long will it take, under such kind of experience, to learn what Christ intended, and the solid truth of it when he said, 'It is expedient for you that I go away.'

"Nothing could be more INEXPEDIENT, OR A PROFOUNDER AFFLICTION THAN A LOCALLY DESCENDED, PERMANENTLY VISIBLE SAVIOUR. . . . We have no want then of a locally related, that is, of a bodily resident Saviour."

This, and much more of the same kind, writes Doctor Bushnell. Will such gospel cause any modern Felix to "tremble?" I do not wonder that doctors are being rapidly multiplied in the schools of the church at this time of sickly divinity. But such are some of the grave errors which have crept into the church, little by little, by imbibing heathen philosophers' deductions of the nature of the soul of man, and of the phenomena of death, which is poisoning much of the theology of the church, and charging God with a lie, and perverting the gospel of Christ, and strengthening rank infidelity.

"THE HARTFORD UNIVERSALIST" ENCOURAGED AGAIN.

This paper contains nearly four columns of rejoicing over "the positions taken by Dr. Bushnell of the North Congregational Church" of that city, relative to the future, and congratulating him for rejecting the personal advent of Christ. Such developments show what is the real influence of this class of instruction, and it should lead all candid thinkers to examine the foundation of such specious reasoning and religious infidelity.

We have thought it proper to insert a few of these strange and painful developments of scepticism; of wide departure from the primitive faith of the church; to awaken the minds of some who may read them, who have not known that such teachings exist. We are almost constantly meeting with remarks from sincere christians, who suppose they speak correctly, that "all christian ministers teach the second coming of Christ and the resurrection of the dead, and all members of christian churches believe in those doctrines."

We know of very many who do not, and could fill a book larger than this with their writings and sayings, involving even much deeper unbelief on these points than the above. And these infidel principles are nursed and strengthened in high places. And they are sapping the very foundation of the christian institutions of all christendom. We refer to and record them, not in the spirit of antagonism and exultation; but in sorrow and deep solicitude for the welfare of the flock of Christ, and of the perishing multitudes who are "without God and without hope" knowing not to whom to listen, among men, as guides to the true source of help and salvation. But in all these evils we see the fulfillment of prophecy and the sure tokens of the speedy redemption of the church of Christ.

When the reformers had gained a hearing before Charles V. and the Roman legates, and had read that "*Confession of faith*" which afterwards revolutionized all Europe, and at that time gained the secret approval of all its opposers who heard it, the bishop of Augsburg exclaimed: "All that the Lutherans have said is true, we cannot deny it." Dr. Eck was one of the most inveterate haters and opposers of the reformation. The Duke of Batavia said to him, in a reproachful tone: "Well, doctor, you had given me a very different idea of this doctrine and this affair." This was the general cry, accordingly the sophists were embarrassed. "But after all," said the Duke to them, "can you refute, by sound reasons, the Confession made by the Elector and his allies?" "With the writings of the Prophets and Apostles—no!" replied Doctor Eck; "but with those of the Fathers and of the councils—yes." "I understand," quickly replied the Duke, "I understand. The Lutherans, according to you, are in Scripture, and we are outside." Hist. of Ref., p. 499.

CHAPTER X.

Some account of the work of A. D. 1841—Religious revivals—Conference in Lowell—Eld. Litch visiting methodist conferences—Eld. G. F. Cox—Prof. Wheeden—P. E. Demmick—Definition of millerism—Conference in Portland—Conference in New York—Conference in Low Hampton—Protest against a set time—South Carolina—Eld. L. Boutelle—Eld. C. French—Eld. D. Churchill—Eld. T. M. Preble.

During the entire year of 1840, we find in the religious papers records of revivals of religious interest, and cheering accounts of the conversion of many sinners, while the evidences of Christ's immediate coming are being accepted, by a goodly number of Christians in all denominations, and many were added to the little company of faithful watchmen who were proclaiming the judgment at hand, notwithstanding the dust and smoke which had been raised by opponents to cover this shining light in the moral heavens. But much fervent prayer was constantly ascending to God by faithful Christians. Those who became fully convinced that the dogma of a temporal millennium was one of the "last-day fables" and had carefully examined the prophetic Scriptures to learn what part of them were already fulfilled, awoke as from a delusive dream and entered heartily into the work of the Lord, freely using their means and gifts to spread the good news of a speedily coming Saviour. Beside the names we have already mentioned, as preaching this message, we find those of Elders David Millard, P. R. Russell, Joseph Bates, Nathaniel Billings, Calvin French, A. Bridges, Edwin Burnham, Wm. Clark, V. Cushman, Richard Reed, Richard Walker, and others, who were now numbered among the "deluded world-burners," as they were often called by the last-day scoffers.

SECOND ADVENT WITNESS.

The above is the title of a new periodical published in New York, Eld. Henry Jones, editor. The first number contains a dissertation on the "Restoration of Israel to their own land." It is an able and thoroughly Scriptural production; it was the same that had been previously read by Eld. Jones before the first general conference in Boston.

GENERAL CONFERENCE IN LOWELL, MASS.

There were several general conferences held this season, the first of which was convened in Lowell, June 15th to 17th. There was a very large attendance, the word of the Lord was attended by the Spirit, and produced deep and abiding impressions for good upon the hearts of many, and the fruits of that meeting have been abundant since.

A few items will be of interest. The following officers were chosen, viz.:

For President, Eld. D. I. Robinson; Vice Presidents, Elds H. Plumer, A. Bridges, Joseph Bates, Richard Reed; Secretaries, J. V. Himes, Henry Jones; Business Committee, J. Litch, J. V. Himes, S. Goodhue, Timothy Cole, Edwin Burnham; Committee of Finance, Wm. Clark, Calvin French, Valentine Cushman, Richard Walker.

It was voted to raise $1,000; they took up in collections $649.04. The F. W. Baptist church of So. Boston sent to them Christian greeting with an address and four delegates claiming to be in "the faith" as a church.

RESOLUTIONS PASSED.

"*Resolved,* That we solicit the co-operation of all who heartily love the appearing of Christ in the clouds of heaven, as being near at hand, whatever may be their views of the prophetic numbers, on which some of us found our argument that the advent will take place about the year A. D. 1843.

"*Resolved,* That we will, as ministers and individuals, by the help of God, exert what influence we can, by the consecration of our all to the work of spreading far and wide the great Scriptural doctrine of Christ's coming and kingdom now in all respects especially nigh at hand."

During the summer, Eld. Josiah Litch visited several annual conferences of the M. E. church in various States, lecturing and distributing publications on the subject of Christ's immediate coming. The first was the R. I. conference, of which he was a member. It convened in Providence. Eld. L. was asked very impertinent questions, and in slang phrases, by the presiding Bishop, concerning his belief, but finding a man who knew his business and practiced good manners, he was allowed to go on without further abuse, at that time, while he spread some truth among them.

He next visited the N. H. conference, held in Dover, June 23d, and presented his message to the ministry there.

He next visited the New England conference, held at Worcester, June 30. Here he found the ministers of Christ shy, and having no interest in hearing about the return of their Master.

Eld. L. says, "I found less ministers interested than in any other State in New England."

He next visits the Maine conference, held at Skowhegan in July.

Here he was refused the privilege of preaching in the Methodist house, although a member of the R. I. conference of the same church.

But it being known that a man was in the place who was preaching about Christ's soon coming, a great interest was manifested to hear him, the Baptists came forward and opened their house for the message. Large audiences attended. Many ministers of the "Maine Conference" attended, and eagerly listened, and gladly received the publications which Bro. Litch presented them. He writes, "The prospects appear better for the truth concerning the Lord's soon coming to take effect in Maine, than in any other State in New England."

This visit of Bro. L., his lectures before so many ministers, and the scattering of publications which were carried to all parts of the State, marks the period of the introduction, into Maine, of this precious, glorious, God-given message. The seed then sown and introduced to be sown, spread for a time very rapidly, and many ministers and members of the Methodist, and other churches, became advocates of the cause until the higher officials forbade them. Eld. G. F. Cox, formerly editor of the "Maine Wesleyan Journal," when published in Portland, became convinced that the Lord would come soon, and was thoroughly converted out of his former traditions, and immediately wrote a series of valuable articles on the nature of the millennium, and the second coming of Christ, which were published in the "Christian Advocate and Journal." This series of articles calls out Prof. Wheeden, of the "Wesleyan University," and he devotes an entire chapter in a book in 1842, in reviewing Eld. Litch's writings on the judgment and the resurrection, but is evidently intended as a refutation of Cox, on the Millennium. Both the "Christian Advocate," and "Zion's Herald" were closed to a reply.

A Rev. P. E. Demmick, of the M. E. church, Newburyport, Mass., was also moved to preach a sermon, which was afterward published in a pamphlet, under the imposing and soothing title,—"THE END OF THE WORLD NOT YET," in which a strenuous effort is made to "overthrow Mr. Miller's theory." But what is meant by "Mr. Miller's theory?" What is involved in the term "Millerism?" Both embrace the same idea.

Why, they mean that delusive theory which so applies the prophetic periods as to teach that the Lord will come in 1843, say its opponents.

If this be the true interpretation of the terms, then why do all the writers and preachers who use them opprobriously, make constant efforts, in their attacks, to show that the millennium is of a temporal nature and in mortality, instead of being in the immortal state? Also that the kingdom of God is in this mortal state, that the earth under the curse, is the theater of Christ's reign and the inheritance of the saints; in opposition to the theory that it is to be in the "new earth and an immortal state?" Why such mighty efforts to prove that Christ is never to return personally to earth—that heaven is the final abode of the saints—that the resurrection is not to be literal—the dead not to be bodily raised—that the judgment day is not a fixed period, for rewards to be rendered to the race of man, but is constantly going on? Why all those efforts on these and several other vital points affecting the entire hope of the Christian church? Why is the term "Millerism" opprobriously applied until to-day—1874, to the doctrine of a millennium in the immortal state, the glorious restitution of the earth, the establishment of the kingdom of God, under Christ, eternally on the new earth, of the saints eternally inheriting it as their promised possession? Why the system of literal interpretation of the prophecies, and the application of them to the great events of our time, and a showing that these events are precursors of the immediate coming of our glorious Lord, stigmatized as "Millerism?" Ah, my friends, you are "deceiving or being deceived," if you claim that it was only the time, which has been supposed would bring the Second Advent, that has been, or is being, opposed by men of high standing. Time was but a small item of the system which has called out such efforts and enlisted so much talent to lull the church to sleep. The term "Millerism" is used as a bug-bear to terrify the people, while sceptics are tearing away the main pillars of the doctrine which has been the Christian hope in all the ages of the past. They have determined to build a new structure in place of the old, and thus the old faith and hope of the church is stigmatized with false names to bring it into disrepute, and the moral heavens filled with smoke and dust to hide the true "faith which was once delivered to the saints."

Such was the course pursued by the Roman Catholic church. Her doctors and priests branded the gospel, which the Reformers preached constantly, "Luther's new doctrine," "Lutheranism," "Heresy," "Don't go to hear them, you will be surely deceived. Don't hear a word from them," said the priests.

SECOND ADVENT CONFERENCE IN PORTLAND, ME.

Oct. 12th to the 14th, 1841, a general conference was convened in Casco street chapel, in Portland. This was the first conference of Second Advent believers ever held in Maine. According to the report in the Signs of the Times, it was a precious and joyous season to those who attended, and the attendance was very full. We notice the names of Elders T. F. Barry and Joel Spaulding, committee of arrangements, and of Elders J. Litch, E. B. Rollins, and J. V. Himes, and Dea. John Pearson, as officers of the conference. Many were in attendance from various parts of the State. Several important and elaborate addresses were made, and several important letters and addresses from Eld. H. Jones, of N. Y. City, Eld. J. N. T. Tucker, and Mr. Miller, N. Y., to the conference, were also read, on the prophecies, chronology, the duty of immediate repentance of all sin, the signs of Christ's immediate coming, the character of the kingdom of God, the restitution of the earth, the nature of the inheritance of the saints, and of the millennium; together with the duty of living wholly in the service of the Lord.

The gospel of the kingdom of God was accompanied by the Holy Spirit, and acted as "a refiner's fire" upon the hearts of many, who never heard the word of the Lord on this wise before. Glorious results followed this gathering and "sowing of the word." Many returned to their homes rejoicing in "the blessed hope of the glorious appearing of the great God and our Saviour Jesus Christ," and they carried the story home with them and told it to their brethren.

The effects were not wholly lost by the people of Portland. There are those yet living and enjoying the blessed hope of soon "seeing the king in his beauty," who were associated in this conference. Since that time many have been gathered to hear the message of the "coming and kingdom," in the meetings of the believers, and many sinners have been brought to Christ and converted from the error of their ways, through it, and many saints have been brought to see and embrace "this blessed" hope, and to rejoice in it. Though trials, divisions, afflictions, and tumults have been their lot, there is a faithful class who yet work and watch and wait, in Portland, for the Lord.

GENERAL CONFERENCE HELD IN NEW YORK CITY.

Oct. 25 and 26, 1841, a general conference convened in Broadway tabernacle, New York. Rev. John Lindsey, of the M. E. church, was president of the meeting. He announced the topic for their consideration, thus, "*The kingdom of heaven, as preached in the gospel, is a future dispensation near at hand.*" After making some very pertinent remarks upon the subject, Eld. Josiah Litch followed with an able address, Eld. Henry Dana Ward followed with another address, Eld. J. V. Himes followed with a third address, after which several others addressed the audiences. We give the following notice of the conference, as stated in the "New York Tribune:"

"The meeting was profoundly attentive, and the remarks of the speakers were received with unequivocal approbation, save only *the fixing a time*, which failed to convince and satisfy the audience.

"But, as far as awakening of public attention goes, the convention has been attended with the happiest results. The pastors of churches direct their studies toward the interesting theme, in many cases, with new emotions; and many Christians read the Bible with an inquiring mind to learn whether these things are so, and some are becoming daily more and more convinced of the truth and importance of the sentiments expressed by the chairman and made the theme of the discourses of the speakers."

We will now give the statement of the "Christian Intelligencer," copied by six other papers. It gives a strong contrast and discovers a large amount of popish bigotry in a small item:

"The dangerous and infidel tendency of the wretched attempts of Messrs. Miller, Jones, and Ward, to darken counsel by words without knowledge, by which persons are cheated out of their money by the purchase of such trash as the heresies of Miller, Jones, and Ward, 'false prophets,' 'deceiving many,' 'deceitful workers.'"

A GENERAL CONFERENCE WAS CONVENED IN LOW HAMPTON, N. Y., Nov. 2d to the 6th, 1841. This conference was very largely attended by those who had become believers through the labors of Mr. Miller, and others in former years. It was a meeting of great interest, the power of the word and spirit deeply affecting the mass, and making the hearts of the saints glad in the Lord. Among the business done by these joyful brethren, we find the following:

"*Resolved*, That, in our opinion, the time has fully come for announcing the midnight cry,—'Behold, the bridegroom cometh,' and that all who would have part in the first resurrection, should, without a moment's delay, arise, and trim their lamps, to be ready to meet the bridegroom."

A PROTEST AGAINST BELIEVING AND TEACHING A SET TIME, written by Eld. Henry Dana Ward, one of the active ministers of the Second Advent Message. The following is the position which he and very many other Second Advent ministers and members have always occupied. This was published in "The Signs of the Times," December, 1841:

"It is not for you to know the times or the seasons which the Father hath put in his own power." Acts i. 7.

"It is known to you, Messrs. Editors, that some of us, who heartily accord with you in respect to the duty of waiting for the coming of the Lord, have a different view of the set time, from that usually advocated in your columns; and it is my purpose, in this communication, to give some of our reasons in support of our views, that neither you, nor your readers, may be in doubt of the ground we occupy among the supporters of the 'Signs of the Times.' I do not write or send it in the spirit of *opposition*, but only of simple *declaration*, that all your readers may know the truth, as it seems to us, who refuse to receive the *date* of the Lord's coming, whether it be 1843, or 1866, or 2000, or a thousand years to come, at the hand of any man. The first reason I give, is this: The gospel dispensation is that under which we live, and the founder of this dispensation declared of his own coming to end it.

"Mark xiii. 32, 'But of that day and that hour knoweth no man, no, not the angels which are in heaven, neither the Son, but the Father.'

"33, 'Take ye heed, watch and pray: for ye know not when the time is.'

"Certainly the founder of this dispensation must be supposed to know the time of its end, better than any man; but he declares it was not revealed to him; and no new revelation for our guidance has been given since the sacred canon was closed up.

"Any distinction between 'that day and that hour,' and that year, seems to conflict with the general tenor of the Scriptures, and especially with the practical use which our Lord makes of the fact of our ignorance of the time, viz.,

'Take ye heed, watch and pray: for ye know not when the time is.' Mark xiii. 33. The second reason is, the text at the head of this article, 'It is not for you to know the times or the seasons which the Father hath put in his own power.' Acts i. 7.

"This is as true as when it was first spoken, and does not mean 'the times' of the natural day, or hour of the Lord's coming; but it means the times of the kingdom generally.

"The Father did not intend we should *know* then; and for this cause he 'has put them *in his own power*,' that men may be constantly on the watch, and never at liberty to say, 'The Lord will not come this day, this year, these thousand years, but he *will* come at *such* a time.' If the time were revealed, it would be put out of the Father's power: it must come according to the word, 'for the Scripture cannot be broken.' . . .

"Therefore, we learn to put no great confidence in the predictions of prophetic times made by our contemporaries. We rather 'hold fast the form of sound words.' . . .

"Before dismissing this topic, we observe, that the people, above all others, vexed at certain men for fixing dates to future events, are the same who have favorite *dates of their own* to watch for, and therefore their true vexation arises not so much against *the foretelling of times*, which they themselves practice, as against the *particular time foretold*, which conflicts with some favorite view of their own. Where is the sin, or shame, of *fixing a date* for the end of all things, more than for *fixing a date* within which that end cannot come?

"Both classes alike attempt to fix times, and the smaller class are not the greater sinners. Those who limit the times to two years, are no more transgressors for this, than those who extend them to a thousand or more. They are alike dealers in prophetic times, but the larger class on much the larger scale. Men think it *good* to calculate that this world will continue yet a thousand years at least, but to calculate that it will continue only two years, is the height of presumption, and it even excites the ridicule and contempt of the larger prophets. We have nothing to do with either of these but to moderate the assurance with which one calculates this, and another that *fixed* time; besides, we like to see fair play, and to defend a small minority for taking the liberty which the great majority freely use, to discuss and pre-determine the times.

"'But Mr. Miller and others undertake to say the world will end in 1843.' On the contrary, Dr. Scott and others undertake to say, 'The world will stand above a thousand years.' Neither party attempts this by any light, except through the Bible; and the American captain is as free to that for the foreseeing of *two* years, as the English doctor of divinity, for the foreseeing of *one thousand*. We blame neither, we thank both; they speak according to the wisdom given them. We thank them without following either, and we cheerfully maintain the right of the minority, however small, when the great majority are ready to trample and to scoff them down, at the same time they themselves are foretelling on a broader scale, five hundred to one. This is the length and breadth of our opinion relative to fixed times.

"HENRY DANA WARD."

THE MIDNIGHT CRY IN SOUTH CAROLINA.

We find in the "Signs of the Times" of 1841, that Eld. J. M. Thomas, a minister in the South, is said to be traveling in S. C., and giving the "midnight cry," and meeting with success. He makes an earnest appeal for Northern ministers to come to that field of labor and help him.

Second Advent Conferences were held in Corinna, and in Newport, Me., in the autumn of 1841, which produced excellent results, awakening a deep revival interest in those parts of the State, and spreading the news of Christ's soon coming among many of the churches, and producing thorough reforms in many hearts.

A SKETCH OF THE EXPERIENCE OF ELD. L. BOUTELL.

"In A. D. 1841, this faithful Christian minister resided in Groton, Mass. He was then a member of the Congregational church in that town. Hearing that Mr. Miller was to be in Lowell, to preach the 'new doctrine,' and being desirous to hear it, he and several other members conferred together, and decided to invite him to Groton, to preach on the subject of Christ's coming. The Congregational meeting-house was obtained for it, for one evening only. Mr. M. came and lectured one week, as we have elsewhere noticed, occupying the town hall, after the first evening. The interest became intense; all commenced studying the Bible in earnest, and praying for divine light. Bro. B. soon became convinced that there was important truth in this subject, as it seemed to show a harmony and fitness of adaptation as to the application of the sacred word. He soon *assented* to its truthfulness, and set himself to 'searching the Scriptures' to learn more concerning it; and after a few months, became *fully convinced* of its truth. He believed so strongly that duty required him to preach it, that he immediately went out with the cry, 'Behold, the bridegroom cometh: go ye out to meet him.' 'And, as by an unseen hand or power, the message went as on the wings of the wind, before I knew it;' he writes, 'I had left all to preach "this gospel of the kingdom of heaven" at hand. The calls became so great and numerous, and the movements so rapid, that I had no time to look back. Calls came from every direction for advent meetings. The believing ones,' he says, 'did not even doubt the propriety of leaving all to blow the trump of alarm, and like an electric shock, by a vitalizing power, were drawn from town to town; we could not stop if we would, and would not if we could.' . . . So strong was our faith that the Lord would come (in 1844), that corn and potatoes were left in the field without any regret, as never to be wanted, and this became general without conference, or consultation. Thus in harmony, with one soul, the believers so acted that 'the things they possessed they called not their own.'"

After the disappointment on the time, he did not become an infidel, as it was predicted these believers would, but held fast to the faith of the gospel of the kingdom.

"He says, 'It was hard to rally from the sad disappointment, but through trial, suffering, and affliction, the pillar of fire could be seen, with a word of comfort, "If it tarry, wait for it." Thus it is blessed to "call to remembrance the former days." I am still with those that have been going through the wilderness, loyal to the government, not ashamed of the leader, knowing that victory will be achieved when our hope is consummated, and that must be soon.'"

This brother has been an arduous and successful worker in the vineyard of the Lord. With a buoyant, cheerful spirit, he finds access to the hearts and sympathies of many where others could not approach.

He has traveled and labored as an evangelist in many parts of the New England and Middle States, in camp-meetings, conferences, tent, protracted, and other meetings, with good success, and is held in high esteem by those who become acquainted with him, as a beloved and faithful servant of the Lord.

Though his head is as white as the driven snow, he is vigorous and active in gathering souls to Christ, and in still crying, "Behold, he cometh," comforting the saints, and in recommending "good religion" to all. Eld. Boutell now resides in Chelsea, Mass.

A SECOND ADVENT GENERAL CONFERENCE IN DOVER, N. H.

A conference was convened in Dover, Dec. 14, 1841, which was fully attended, and a deep interest awakened upon the subject of Christ's immediate coming. According to the report in the "Signs of the Times," it was a meeting of much importance and great service in turning the attention of the people to the subject of a coming judgment. There is yet a company of faithful believers in that city, who are rejoicing in hope, and laboring for the salvation of men.

Eld. Calvin French, F. W. Baptist minister, became a believer in the message of the immediate coming of Christ, and entered upon the work in 1841, of proclaiming it. While holding a protracted meeting in Nashua, N. H., in December, where souls were being converted and a deep interest pervading the congregation, a mob entered and broke up the meeting. But the Lord mercifully protected him from injury. From various items of history we judge he was an active, devout, and useful minister of Christ. He traveled and preached much, the Lord worked by him in power, and great revivals of religious interest are reported as results of his preaching. He also wrote and published several instructive and useful books on the signs of the times, and on the state of man in death, and the wages of sin.

At one time he was brought into the snare of "Cochrainism," by following false impressions, which he considered the Holy Spirit, and which brought disgrace upon the truth. Faithful ministers visited him, condemned his course and views, and at once reported him to the public through the "Signs of the Times," withdrawing fellowship from him, according to the direction of Paul, 1st Cor. v.

This opened his eyes to see the snare and learn his danger and the mischief that would follow. He made a deep, humiliating, and thorough public confession of this wrong and wound, asking the forgiveness of the brethren, and was restored to continue in the ministry of the word.

This is the Bible mode of discipline, and is safe for the church to practice. A vast amount of sin might have been prevented, and fallen men and women recovered and saved by this course, which has been allowed to ripen to destruction, for fear of reproach, and of the ill will of the offenders.

A SKETCH OF ELD. DANIEL CHURCHILL'S LABORS.

This zealous and conscientious brother was converted to Christ in A. D. 1831, and had associated with the F. W. Baptist and Christian churches in Lowell, Mass. In 1840, he heard the message of Christ's soon coming, studied the Scriptures until he became convinced that it was the doctrine of the Bible, and heartily embraced it as such. Being deeply impressed that it was his duty to preach the gospel, and especially this message of it, he commenced in 1841, and labored as the way opened before him. In 1844, in company with Bro. Joseph Harvey, he visited the eastern part of Maine, and the province of New Brunswick, carrying some $80 worth of Advent publications furnished by Bro. J. V. Himes, which were scattered chiefly gratuitously. There he preached in several places, the Lord blessed the effort and good was accomplished. The seed has since sprung up and produced good fruit in the salvation of souls.

Bro. C. also traveled and labored in company with Eld. I. E. Jones. The Lord accompanied their labors with the power of his Spirit, and many souls were converted. His constitution broke down and he was obliged to refrain from constant preaching, yet has labored at home, in Lowell, and traveled to some extent, in various States and Provinces, and been associated with conferences, camp and other large meetings; many will never forget his earnest appeals to their consciences. He has been, and yet is, a conscientious, zealous, whole-hearted supporter of the message of the soon coming and kingdom of our Lord, and a judicious manager of what he undertakes to do in the

Lord's cause. Although now unable to preach, he enjoys the precious hope of soon seeing Jesus, and of being changed to immortality and brought into the land whose inhabitants will never be sick.

BOOKS ON THE SECOND ADVENT OF CHRIST.

In addition to a long list of American works which had accumulated and were being circulated, we find the following list of English works advertised for sale at the "Signs of the Times" office in 1841: "*Essays on the Millennium*, by Rev. Henry Woodward;" "*Apology for the Millennial Doctrine*, by Wm. Anderson;" "*Pre-Millennial Advent of the Messiah*, by Wm. Cunningham;" "*Thoughts on the Scriptural Expectation of the Church*, by Basilicus;" "*Political Destiny of the Earth*, by Wm. Cunningham;" "*Sermons on the Second Advent*, by Rev. Hugh McNelie;" "*The time to favor Zion*, by Rev. E. Bickersteth;" "*A brief inquiry into the prospects of the Church of Christ*, by Hon. Garrard T. Nole, A. M.;" "*Essays on the Advent and Kingdom of Christ*, by Rev. J. W. Brooks."

It was the purpose of those engaged at that time in the work of proclaiming the immediate coming of Christ, to circulate all works which bore directly on this subject, even though they might contain other matter they considered erroneous, thinking the end too near to allow time for the errors to take root, and divide the flock of believers. And at that time there was more respect paid to united action on the main question, and more importance attached to union in Christ, and less egotism, less persistent determination to maintain and propagate pet theories and individual deductions, to the sacrifice of Christian courtesy and healthful associated Christian influence.

One of the perilous features of the last days was to be that of self-will, high-mindedness, and recklessness. Christians have not wholly escaped these traits of character; hence, much of the division and strife arises from the determination of some to sustain their point, if it ruins the union and influence of Christian efforts.

SKETCH OF ELD. T. M. PREBLE'S EXPERIENCE AND LABORS.

Eld. Preble was formerly a minister in the Free Will Baptist church some five years. While on his second year, as pastor of a church in Nashua, N. H., in 1841, at the age of thirty-one years, he heard and embraced the message of Christ's soon coming. Bro. P. immediately started out to proclaim it, which resulted in his expulsion from the church in about six weeks; but this did not retard his progress, being of an ardent temperament, of a decided and positive disposition and exceedingly zealous, he was ready to meet opposition, and sufficiently acquainted with the Scriptures to silence any of the clergy, who stood opposed to the great truths embraced in the Advent Message.

Although sometimes blown off from the direct theological course by contrary winds, and drifted by agitated seas, Bro. P. has been a conscientious, devoted and earnest minister. Many sinners have been awakened and converted through his labors, and many Christians taught the gospel hope more perfectly.

At the time the spirit of fanaticism made an onset upon the believers in the Advent near, leading some astray into strange notions, and a party concluded it duty to keep the seventh-day Sabbath, instituted under Moses, Bro. P. accepted that message for a while, but on a careful examination he found it a *false message* for the gospel age, and gave it up, confessing the error, and keeping others out of this "yoke of bondage." He has since written a book to refute it, which contains much valuable matter, though it differs in position considerably from that of the Advent believers generally, who keep "the Lord's day."

He has extensively proclaimed the good news of the immediate advent of the Messiah, to give eternal life to his waiting people.

Early in his experience in examining the doctrine of Christ's Personal Advent he became a believer in the view of immortality through Christ only, and of the final destruction of the wicked, and has consequently published the gospel since on this principle.

He has traveled and preached in all the New England States, New York, Michigan, Illinois, Iowa, Wisconsin, and the Canadas. He has held written and oral discussions with Universalists, Mormons, Seventh-day Sabbath keepers, Non-resurrectionists, Age-to-come teachers, Immortal soul believers, and Temporal millennium believers. Besides his public preaching and discussions, Bro. P. has written various books. "The Two Hundred Stories for Children," pp. 234; "The Voice of God," pp. 84; "The Three Kingdoms," pp. 58; "The Two Adams," pp. 24; "The Ten Virgins," pp. 12, and the "First-Day Sabbath," pp. 471. May the Lord guide him the balance of his time and aid him in all his truth to the end.

CHAPTER XI.

THE YEAR 1842—MORALS—RESULTS OF THE MESSAGE—M. CHANDLER—POMFRET CONFERENCE—SANDY HILL CONFERENCE—GOLD CHAIN OFFERINGS—S. BLISS—GREAT WRATH—WEEKLY PAPER—HYMN BOOKS—SINGULAR MOVEMENT—MILLER AND HIMES IN NEW YORK—ASSOCIATION—R. E. LADD—LITCH IN CANADA—GREAT REVIVAL—FIRST CAMP-MEETING—MILLER IN NEWARK, SARATOGA, NEWBURYPORT—A MOB—THREE RIVERS—A GREAT REFORMATION—PORTLAND CONFERENCE—APOLLO HALE—CAMP-MEETINGS—S. S. BREWER—POEM—BANGOR CONFERENCE—SHIMEAL'S CHRONOLOGY—M. BATCHELOR—THE BIG TENT—THREE METHODIST MINISTERS—HIRAM MUNGER—CHICOPEE CAMP-MEETING—MILLER AT CASTINE AND NEW HAVEN—GREAT REVIVAL—JOHN COUCH—CAMP-MEETINGS AT CASTINE, ATKINSON, AND CONCORD—DEFINITE TIME—EDITOR'S ADDRESS—PETER HOUGH—UNCERTAIN SOUNDS—REVIEW OF STUART—CHARLES FITCH—LUTHER AND MELANCTHON.

The state of the Second Advent cause at the opening of the year 1842, was such as to give promise of much success in giving the proclamation a wide circulation, and of greatly promoting the cause of Christ, through the message of his immediate return, and the necessary preparation for a part in his kingdom.

A great amount of good had been already accomplished through this gospel of the kingdom which eternity alone will unfold, while much fruit was immediately seen. A large number of ministers were now so awakened, during the labors of the past year, to a sense of duty to investigate this subject, and to preach it, that many of them were induced to preach it more or less in their public ministrations. Several were now devoting themselves wholly to it, and had become efficient ministers of this cause. The current events of the times and the moral condition of Christendom were ominous of an approaching crisis. Morals were everywhere in a rapid decline, and infidelity developing itself, which led careful observers to see that sin in all its deceitful forms was increasing, notwithstanding the extensive revivals of religious interest in certain quarters, and great moral improvements in some points. There were numerous evils working disease and moral weakness in the Christian churches, arising from scepticism of various shades. The nations were in a state of ferment and jealousy, and were constantly reporting their forebodings of gigantic wars. The political and secular papers were continually showing that an alarming state of diplomacy existed among the nations, a rapidly increasing uneasiness and animosity which threatened universal war involving the destruction of Turkey and the Papacy.

The prophetic Scriptures which describe the moral and religious features "of the last days" were seen, by the awakened ones, to be fast fulfilling, giving convincing evidence that they were right in their general views of the end being near, if the time calculations should prove incorrect; but some were quite sure they would prove correct. Many of the ministry of the various churches in America had become deeply imbued with the conviction that the Lord was to come soon. The news from Europe showed that many were of the same opinion there. The preaching of the advent near, was marked by special results in constant revivals of religious interest, a deeper type of conversion of sinners, and a radical improvement in the lives of Christians. These points were so prominent that it was very commonly remarked concerning a living, faithful, conscientious, scrupulous Christian, or a specially active, earnest, zealous witness for Christ, "I guess he," or she (as the case might be), "is a Millerite." Such were the acknowledged results of the doctrine, while at the next moment, perhaps, they would claim that this message was doing great harm.

ELD. MOSES CHANDLER, A STANDARD BEARER.

The name of Bro. Chandler stands connected with many of the early conferences, camp and other meetings in the early history of the Advent cause. He was one of the many who were brought into the faith by hearing Mr. Miller on the subject. In 1842 he commenced preaching it, and amidst all the trials, persecutions, changes and apostacies, he has continued in the work and been associated with the body of believers. The Lord has given him souls as seals of his ministry, and the "blessed hope of eternal life, when the chief Shepherd shall appear."

His labors have been mostly in the western States. He is now residing in

Maquoketa, Jackson Co., Iowa, and travels as an evangelist over those western prairies to tell the people of Christ as a Saviour of sinners, and of his soon coming in regal power to establish a kingdom in righteousness, with all his saints on the NEW EARTH.

With this bright prospect before us, we can well afford to forego the ease, pleasures, salaries and social enjoyments of those who are at ease in Zion, that we may hear it said "well done" when the master comes to reckon with us.

A SECOND ADVENT GENERAL CONFERENCE IN POMFRET, CT.

A conference was convened in Pomfret, Jan. 18, 1842, being the eighth of a series of general conferences. This, as all the former ones had proved, was a decided success, leaving deep and abiding impressions on the minds of many for their benefit, and also enlisting the hearts of many Christians to examine and accept the neglected but glorious and sanctifying truths of the gospel. The gospel seed then sown has produced many grand results since, in that vicinity, and there are societies which are yet bearing the light to the masses around them, as the result of this conference.

A SECOND ADVENT GENERAL CONFERENCE AT SANDY HILL, N. Y.

A conference convened at Sandy Hill, Feb. 1, 1842, being the ninth of the series. Here also, a large company of believers and inquirers assembled to listen to the proclamation of the message of the coming judgment, and coming kingdom of our Lord Jesus Christ. The Holy Spirit attended the word with power, and produced precious results. Sinners were brought to Christ, Christians were awakened and quickened to renewed activity, were led out of former superstitious notions and false traditions into the great and glorious truths of the restitution, and the establishment of the kingdom of God in the new earth. A church of faithful believers was planted there, which has been a light, through the constant blessing of God and the labors of faithful pastors, to that place and the surrounding country, until now. After this period, conferences were held frequently, and, more or less, in all the New England and Middle States, and in the adjacent Provinces. Christian hearts were instructed, corrected, and gladdened, and sinners converted, as a common result of these gatherings, everywhere. Worldly ambition, pride, vanity, extravagance in dress and show, met with a decided and marked check, wherever this gospel of the coming kingdom was preached.

SYLVESTER BLISS.—Page 227.

GOLD CHAINS.

"We have received several gold chains of late to be sold and the proceeds used to aid the spread of the *Midnight Cry*."—*Signs of the Times*.

SYLVESTER BLISS, EDITOR OF THE "SIGNS OF THE TIMES."

During the year 1842, while the ministers who had embraced the doctrine of the Advent near, were preaching it with much success, others were writing books and tracts, reviews, criticisms and correspondence and instruction in the papers. Among these writers, Bro. Sylvester Bliss, of Hartford, Ct., a lay member of the Congregational church, soon became known as a young man of more than ordinary ability. He had become awakened to the subject of Christ's immediate advent, and investigated it until fully convinced of the great truths underlying the message which was being preached. He was liberally educated, of fine abilities to critically examine and analyze theological questions: becoming a believer and reading the books, sermons and papers which contained the efforts of the chief opposers he was more confirmed in its truths, his zeal for the Lord was throughly awakened to review the works of some of these champions who had entered the field of theological combat.

He wrote a few articles for the columns of the "Signs of the Times," in which his gifts and qualifications were so manifest to the manager of the paper, that his services were secured as an assistant editor, and he entered upon that relation in Nov., 1842. He sustained that relation for several years and then became the responsible editor of the paper, changed to "Advent Herald," and business agent of the publisher; which relation he sustained until his death in 1863.

The paper was conducted with much ability, and was the medium through which very much important biblical, historical, theological and critical information and Christian experience has been communicated to its readers, while under his charge, and since. He was a devout, conscientious Christian, and endowed with a discriminating mind which enabled him to select, generally, the best intellectual, moral and spiritual food for the readers of the paper, which is one of the chief qualities of a good editor. He was an able theologian, a good logician, and generally very reliable in his references to authors, history, or the events of the day. He was studious to avoid sensational, unreliable, fabulous floating articles and speculative, groundless opinions of political and religious novices and erratics; perhaps too much so to accept of some truths which had been long buried beneath papal dogmas and but just exhumed, for this has been the danger of all able men of great caution. But he was an excellent writer and editor.

The very reverse of his qualifications have been those of some who have attempted to edit papers for the Adventists, and have led parties into strange and speculative vagaries, as idle and as eager as the Athenians of Acts xvii. 21, to whom Paul once preached.

Bro. Bliss reviewed with much ability and great candor, the "lectures of Dr. N. Colver," against the views of Miller. The sermon of Rev. O. E. Daggett, preached to overthrow the faith of those who were looking for the Lord; the work of Dr. Weeks, which seemed to be prepared to weaken the faith of the people. The work of Dr. Jarvis, who had a better motive, but seemed out of the track of truth. The work of Prof. Geo. Bush, who denied the personal advent and the literal resurrection of the dead. The work of Prof. Sanborn, who denied the personal advent, the visible reign of Christ, the doctrine of the restitution, and nearly everything else which the Scriptures promise the Christian church. Bro. Bliss also prepared a "brief commentary on the Revelation," "Time of the End," an "Analysis of Sacred Chronology," and several smaller works. "The Analysis," and the "Time of the End," should be reprinted and in the market.

Although Bro. B. never embraced the views concerning the nature of man, his state in death, and the final reward of the wicked, which the great majority of his co-laborers have, and which we think his writings and reasonings helped some of them to find in the Sacred Word (though he opposed them and wrote against them), yet we remember him with much affection for his sincere Christian integrity, faithful labors and fellowship in the work of the gospel. And we cherish the blessed hope which animated his heart, causing him to toil and endure opposition, scoffs and derision for the truth's sake, expecting to see him redeemed from death, and to enjoy his society with Christ and the blood-washed church in a little while, on the new earth filled with the glory of God.

GREAT WRATH ABOUT "THE HOUSE OF PRAYER" IN ALBANY, N. Y.

A conference of believers was held in Albany, of several days' continuance. Eld. C. French was the chief minister. No house could be obtained for it except Grand street church, called "*The house of Prayer*." This was obtained and occupied.

While the meetings were in progress, and a deep and solemn interest pervading the masses in attendance, the following note was left at the door of one of the principal trustees:

"C. HEEPINSTALL,—Sir.—I am informed that you are the sole cause of letting French into Grand street church; unless you turn him from your house and shut the church from him, and his followers, you may expect damage done to your person and property for years to come, at such times as can be done in secret.

"If fair means will not do, foul will." BLANK.

The above writer seems to have taken lessons at Rome, or of some of her institutions.

"THE SIGNS OF THE TIMES" BECOMES A WEEKLY.

April 6, 1842, "The Signs of the Times" commenced its weekly issues, having previously been issued once in two weeks.

The number of the above date contains a letter from B. Clark, of the seventh day Baptist church, who desired to introduce their *views* of the obligation of the Christian church to observe the Seventh-day Sabbath of the Mosaic institution. But the managers declined to introduce such a topic into their paper. They believed the church to be under Christ and out from under the Sinaiac covenant, and had no wish to progress backward.

THE MILLENNIAL HARP.

The first hymn-book published by the Second Advent believers, bore the above title. Sheet music and a small collection of select hymns called "Millennial musings," had been published.

There are many valuable hymns in the standard hymn-books of the other churches. Some of the best ever written, on the subjects of the signs preceding, and on the Second Advent of Christ, the judgment, the kingdom of God, the personal reign of Christ, the resurrection of the dead, the crown of glory, and the holy city, but a portion of them were strangely mixed with erroneous views, opposite in their teachings, and one part nullifying the other. As "the path of the just—shineth more and more until the perfect day," and a great reform in theology was going on, it was important that there should be a corresponding reform in hymnology, for it is more obnoxious to truth to sing error than to preach it, because singing charms more, generally, than preaching.

Again, there were also some excellent poetical gifts among these believers, who, being illuminated with the divine light of the precious gospel hope, and pressed beyond measure by the opposing influences, were prepared to give some of the richest and most sublime poetic effusions ever produced. This is the testimony of those not belonging to the sect, concerning them. It was therefore considered best to produce a book of selected, corrected, and original hymns and tunes. But this has been a work of progression, as it is with the study of "the word." Several revisions have been made, and there is not a perfect hymn-book yet, though some very excellent ones, from which we shall extract a few hymns in another place.

"The Advent Harp," "The Harp," "The Christian Lyre," "Jubilee Hymns," "Spiritual Melodies," "Second Advent Minstrel," "Social Hymns," "Hymns of the Morning," and "Jubilee Harp," are the chief books; the last is the best, but this needs revision.

A NEW AND SINGULAR MOVEMENT.

The New York Observer issues a call for a convention to meet in New York City, May 10, 1842, to consider a subject of great importance—"the evangelizing the present generation of the heathen." "The convention is called for the express and only purpose of discussing the question of evangelizing the world, while the various topics which agitate and divide the friends of Christ, shall not be introduced." This call is signed by about sixty ministers, mostly Doctors of Divinity. It will be seen that the doctrine of Christ's coming to judge the world could not be referred to as a motive for energetic and faithful self-sacrificing action in prosecuting whatever could be done in such a glorious work.

NEW YORK CITY VISITED AGAIN.

The false reports and slanders which constantly issued from the press and the pulpits concerning this message, and the standard-bearers, had nearly obliterated the effects of former visits in proclaiming these truths in New York. Bro. Himes determined on sounding the cry more fully in that great city. In the month of May, himself and Bro. Miller went there and entered upon the work. They hired the Apollo Hall, on Broadway, at a heavy expense, and commenced meetings. None were found ready to bestow upon them hospitality, not even to invite them to their houses for a meal or a night's lodging. Accordingly, they used an ante-room adjoining the hall as a sitting and lodging room, until friends were awakened and brought in, who furnished them with a cot-bed, which they found easier than the hard floor. Two weeks, under these circumstances, they labored night and day, paying nearly all their own expenses, before an impression was made. The multitudes had been made to believe that Adventists were monsters, or anything else except civilized beings. Such were the prevailing impressions of the people that several days had passed and scarcely a lady dared to make her appearance in the meetings. As one after another ventured to attend and informed friends of the character of the meetings, others came and listened, prejudice gave way, and before the effort closed, the hall was filled with attentive hearers, and an interest secured.

The undertaking was great, and a glorious result followed for a series of years in that city. They meant business for the Lord, and did not wait for some missionary society to hire a hall, or pledge the money to pay them wages and hall rents. This series of meetings held through and closed on anniversary week.

SECOND ADVENT ASSOCIATION OF NEW YORK AND VICINITY.

Such is the title of an association formed May 18, 1842.

The members were to pay a sum monthly, to defray expenses of forwarding the message of Christ's immediate coming. The following brethren constituted the executive committee:

Dr. A. Doolittle, chairman; Elders Henry Jones, S. S. Brewer, H. V. Teal, G. M. Wendell, John G. McMurry, T. Hyatt, Wm. Tracy, Dr. Stevens, J. Williams, S. S. Joclyn, E. Jacobs, John Burditt, T. R. Henry; E. H. Wilcox, secretary.

These associations, conferences, camp-meetings, and rapidly increasing numbers of papers and books, show a deep and active conviction in the hearts of very many, that the Lord was indeed coming, and they had decided to do all they could do to awaken men upon the subject, and lead as many as possible to repentance, that they might be ready for the coming and kingdom of God.

The same season, the believers in Boston made a rally on anniversary week in that city. The Melodeon was hired for the occasion, and a grand gathering secured. The attendance was large throughout the week, and much truth was sent abroad. Immediately after the anniversary meetings were over, Eld. J. Litch visited Canada East, and commenced meetings in Stanstead.

"Before two weeks had passed, the people, for thirty or forty miles around were awakened to the subject of the Lord's coming. Immense concourses assembled, both in Canada and in Derby, Vermont, where a course of lectures was given. Such was the interest to hear, and the awakening among the people, that it was determined at once to hold a camp-meeting in Canada. A place was selected, the ground prepared, and the meeting held in the township of Hadley, Canada East. Such was the good effect of this first meeting, that the people of Bolton wished one to be held in their town. This was begun the next week after the Hadley meeting closed, and ended on the third of July. During that month's labor, as near as could be estimated, five or six hundred souls were converted to God." [1]

---

[1] Advent Shield, p. 68.

SKETCH OF ELD. R. E. LADD, AND HIS EXPERIENCE.

Bro. Ladd was a man of business, of high moral principles, and sterling worth; also, an official member of the Methodist E. church. In the winter of 1838-9, a copy of Mr. "Miller's Lectures" was placed in his hand, with the representation that it was "a very remarkable prophecy." He began to read, "became absorbed in its *unfoldings of the prophecies* of Daniel and John," and when he "had finished, the Bible became a new treasure" to him. The prophecies, which had always been dark mysteries to him, now became a source of constant study and thought. He talked with Christian friends, and sought light from every quarter, but found none who sympathized with him; many ridiculed the idea that the world would come to an end so soon. They said, "the world is to be converted," and the "glorious millennium come before Christ's coming." But he reasoned, "if the Lord is soon coming, *some* of his people will *know it* and proclaim it, and my faith will be confirmed;" but he then knew of no person except the writer of that book who *then* believed it. In 1840, Bro. Ladd moved from Connecticut, to Springfield, Mass., locating in Cabotville, one of its villages, and engaged in the baking business, in which he drove a "bread team" to all the neighboring villages. While on one of his visits to the city of Springfield, the Methodist minister introduced Eld. J. Litch to him, saying, "Bro. Litch is preaching the coming of Christ and the end of the world in 1843; I think you will be glad to see him." With a thrill of delight, he responded, "Glory to God; yes, this is the man I have been *expecting* to see, *if this* is God's truth," and cordially greeted him. He soon found that Bro. Litch was seeking a place among his Methodist brethren to preach the coming One, he invited him to ride to Cabotville, as they were having meetings there every evening, and where Bro. Ladd was an official member, with an "exhorter's license." He went; but the pastor of the church was fearful of having Bro. Litch preach on the coming of the Lord, lest it should interfere with a revival which was then in progress. This most wonderful objection has been urged in many places, to the great astonishment of faithful Christians. Consent was finally obtained, "and when he opened the Scriptures at the prophecy of Daniel, and unfolded that wonderful second chapter, and showed the progress and downfall of the *four* great kingdoms of earth's history and the time of the introduction of God's everlasting kingdom, it was overwhelming to the people," who were before entirely ignorant of these great Bible facts. "There was not a tongue in that great congregation that spoke against his preaching; all the people said, tell us more about this." "He tarried a few days lecturing every evening: the revival broke out with new interest and power, and souls were converted every night; more than one hundred were added to the church that winter." Before these lectures were concluded, Bro. Ladd was thoroughly converted to the doctrine, and gave his whole soul to the work, peddling bread and the Lord's coming, from house to house. In the spring of 1842, Eld. Charles Fitch went to Springfield, with the great chart which illustrated the symbols of Daniel and Revelation, and gave a course of lectures; the whole city was moved and a great revival followed.

R. E. LADD.—Page 232.

During the summer, Eld. Himes called on Bro. Ladd, and introduced himself and his business, which was, to secure a place for a camp-meeting. Bro. Ladd took him to Bro. Munger, where they negotiated for the camp-ground which the Methodists had just occupied, of which we have spoken in the " Sketch of H. Munger," and where an Advent camp-meeting was soon held, which resulted in the conversion of several hundreds of sinners. From that point, Bro. Ladd was thrust out to more public duties in proclaiming the soon coming and kingdom of Christ, and to do all he could for this cause, and seemed to be impelled by an unseen power. He, with about forty others, were expelled from the church without any charge of misconduct. "These formed the nucleus of a large and prosperous Advent society, which maintained its organization for many years, and where scores were brought to Christ and the knowledge of the truth."

Since Bro. L. took a public stand to proclaim and sustain the Advent Message, he has found the Lord to be his helper, in accomplishing much in his cause, and has always gloried in being identified as one of the bearers of this message. Though highly respected in all his business relations, and esteemed by his acquaintances as a sincere, stable, devout, and peaceful Christian man, yet he has been hung in effigy, lampooned in public prints, hissed in the public streets; his house once entered by a mob in pursuit of an Advent preacher supposed to be entertained there (which, by the way, has been the experience of many Advent preachers), yet the Lord has enabled him to endure it all for truth and righteousness' sake. Bro. L. wishes to add the following: "The passing of the time calculated by Wm. Miller as the probable period for the Advent, viz., 1843-4, produced very great changes among those who had been fully committed to the time question; factious parties sprang up among us; very many abandoned the subject altogether.

"But amid all these revolutions in sentiment I never lost faith in the general correctness of the interpretations of prophecy; I lost all confidence in *dates* and have steadily looked at *events* which have more than confirmed my faith in prophecy. I never *can* doubt that the great movement originating with Bro. Miller in this country, was *of God;* I would sooner doubt my identity. We have had to examine and re-adjust many things that were supposed to be settled; when we discovered error have cheerfully exchanged for truth, and still do not know it all. I am a learner still; but the sweetness of that first experience can never be erased from memory." But his public labor is done; his health has utterly failed, and he is waiting patiently, with earnest expectancy, for the coming Messiah, hoping soon to welcome him with all the blood-washed throng, to dwell with him in eternal life and glory.

On the 24th of April, Mr. Miller commenced a course of lectures in the large hall of the Apollo, 410 Broadway, in the city of New York, as usual to large audiences, closing on the 10th of May.

On the 7th of May, he visited Newark, N. J., and gave two discourses in the Universalist chapel in that city. In compliance with three very urgent requests from Rev. Joshua Fletcher, pastor, and the unanimous vote of the Baptist church, in Saratoga, N. Y., Mr. M. again visited that place, and lectured from the 14th to the 22d of May. From the 24th to the 28th of May, he gave his seventh course of lectures in Boston; and from the 29th of May to the 3d of June, 1842, he lectured in Newburyport, Mass. At the commencement of his lecture, in the evening of the first day, an egg was thrown into the hall, at him, but fell upon the side of the desk. At the close, stones were thrown through the windows, by a mob outside, who indulged in some characteristic hootings and kindred noises. The congregation dispersed without damage, save the glass of lamps and windows. Under those circumstances, the town authorities closed the hall, and the lectures were adjourned to the chapel in Hale's Court. They continued till Friday, June 3d—a goodly number having received Christ to the joy of their souls.

From the 4th to the 12th of June, he gave a second course of lectures in the Casco-street church, Portland, Me. They were attended by crowds of anxious hearers, and many Christians were refreshed, while some sinners were converted to God. From the 16th to the 26th of June, he lectured at Three Rivers (in Palmer, Mass.). A member of the Baptist church there, afterwards wrote, through the "Christian Reflector," the organ of that denomination, as follows:

"Dear Brother Graves:—It is with gratitude to God that I am able to turn aside from the joyful scenes around me, to inform the friends in Zion what God hath wrought for us. Rev. William Miller, on the 16th of June last, commenced a course of lectures on the Second Advent of Christ to this world in 1843. The lectures were delivered in our meeting-house, which, however, would hold but a small part of the audience, it being estimated at five thousand; and, notwithstanding prepossessions, prejudices, and the slanderous reports circulated about this man of God, the people gave heed to the word spoken, and seemed determined to examine the Scriptures, to see if these things were so; and deep solemnity pervaded the vast assembly. The children of God were soon aroused to a sense of their duty; sinners were seen weeping, and heard to say, 'Pray for me!' The number increased, until one hundred, in an evening prayer-meeting, were seen to arise to be remembered in the prayers of the saints. Soon, converts began to tell us what the Lord had done for them. Some Deists, some Universalists, and many of the thoughtless, of both the middle-aged and the youthful part of the community, have been brought to submit their hearts to God, and are now waiting for and hasting to the coming of the day of God. As to the character of the work, let me say, I have never seen a more thorough conviction of the total depravity of the heart, and the utter helplessness of the sinner, and that, if saved, it must be by the sovereign grace of God, than has been manifest in all that have given a relation of their experience."

A SECOND CONFERENCE OF BELIEVERS IN PORTLAND, ME.

A second conference was held in Casco-street church, Portland, commencing June 4th, which continued to the 12th. Elders G. F. Cox, J. V. Himes, M. Palmer, S. E. Brown, Wm. Miller, Andrew Rollins, Herman Stinson, and other ministers were in attendance. Bro. Miller gave a course of lectures in this conference, which awakened much interest; many, strangers to the faith, were greatly enlightened on the Scriptures, and returned home to instruct others in this glorious theme. The church was much strengthened and some sinners were converted. Had Casco-street church walked in the light and maintained the faith which enlightened, comforted, strengthened, and added such numbers to her communion from 1840 to 1843, she would have continued a shining light in that city, and been spared the many dissensions and apostasies which she has experienced Deacon John Pearson, Baptist, and his whole family were among the chief supporters of the Second Advent cause in Portland from the first.

SKETCH OF ELD. APOLAS HALE, AND HIS LABORS.

Bro. Hale was formerly a minister in the Methodist E. church. The first information we have of him is a statement in Zion's Herald, that he had "located in 1842, in order that he might extensively promote his views of the millennium," which meant that he had become deeply interested in the doctrine of Christ's immediate coming to *introduce* the millennium, and had determined to *preach* the Advent Message. We find him connected in an official capacity, with nearly all the early Second Advent conferences, camp meetings and public efforts to proclaim this great truth.

Bro. H. is a scholar, a deep thinker, a careful and critical writer, with an argumentative gift, and of deep piety; as a writer but few are his equals for logic and pointedness.

During several years he was associate editor of the "Signs of the Times" and "Advent Herald," in which are found many able, critical and valuable articles and reviews, on some of the most vital subjects connected with the Advent doctrine. We shall give his "Review of Prof. Chace" in another part of the book. He has also written several pamphlets.

As a minister he was able, clear, and full of logical argument, making him an effective worker, where formidable influences of opposition needed attention; as a counselor and friend he was cautious, considerate and safe. His constitution was frail and gave way under too constant application to study and labor, which obliged him, after a time, to abandon constant preaching and devote himself to secular business. Yet the glorious hope of an eternal inheritance, in a little while, has sustained him in his trials and loneliness (having buried his faithful wife), while he constantly waits in earnest expectation of Jesus' immediate advent. We believe Bro. H. designed several of the symbolic charts which have been published and used in the public ministrations of our lecturers.

The last work we have seen from his pen is a "Review of Thurman's Chronology," as connected with his "Sealed book of Daniel opened." This he wrote at the special request of some of its friends who thought Thurman unanswerable. The review is severe, and the more so because the work to be reviewed was so pompous, contained such decided errors, put forth in such egotistical language of dogmatism, that it needed, in his estimation, a through rebuke. The candid, critical reader, who had been an admirer of Thurman's "great work," could no longer admire it after reading the review. He could believe him sincere, pious and dogmatically egotistical, while reaching after things too high for him, and "patching" with an unskillful hand to make the garment whole. Those who are captivated by Thurman's assurances that he has found the "Philosopher's Stone," and "the key of Sacred Chronology," with which he has unlocked, or broken the seal, will think the "Review" is an abuse of Thurman, a persecution of his work, unless they have the ability and the disposition to critically analyze the subject for themselves. There are many not competent to do this, as it is a task which the most learned have not yet finished. We will therefore wait and watch.

ANOTHER NEW ERA—SECOND ADVENT CAMP-MEETINGS.

At the Second Advent conference held in Boston, May 24, 1842, a committee was appointed to prepare a place and appoint a time for holding a camp-meeting, "for Christians to worship God, to awaken sinners, and purify Christians by giving the midnight cry—viz., to hold up the immediate coming of Christ to judge the world." That committee was—E. Hale, jr., Elders Henry Plummer, T. Cole.

The first camp-meeting held was in Hadley, Lower Canada, commencing June 21, 1842, which we have already mentioned.

The first camp-meeting in the States was held in East Kingston,

N. H., commencing June 29th. There were twenty-six tents, from all parts of New England. The attendance was from seven to ten thousand people. The contributions to advance the cause amounted to $1,000. The report of it shows that it was one of the most interesting and important meetings ever held in this cause.

Eld. A. Hale was secretary, and in his report says, "it is a new era in the Second Advent cause."

We here insert a notice of it by a writer in the Boston Post, as follows:

"The Second Advent camp-meeting, which commenced at East Kingston, N. H., on Tuesday, June 29th, and continued from day to day until Tuesday noon, July 5th, was attended by an immense concourse of people, variously estimated at from seven to ten thousand. . . .

"The meeting was conducted with great regularity and good order from beginning to end. The ladies were seated on one side, and the gentlemen on the other, of the speaker; meals were served uniformly and punctually at the times appointed, and the same punctuality was observed as to the hours appointed for the services.

"The preachers were twelve or fifteen. Mr. Miller gave the only regular course of lectures—the others speaking occasionally. Many of the people, without doubt, assembled from motives of curiosity merely; but the great body of them, from their solemn looks and close attention to the subject, were evidently actuated by higher and more important motives. Each tent was under the supervision of a tent-master, who was responsible for the good order within the same, where religious exercises were kept up at the intermissions between the public exercises and meals, and where lights were kept burning through the night. . . .

"Some fault was found, or dissatisfaction felt, with that part of the regulations which precluded all controversy—*i. e.*, which prevented people of opposite theological sentiments from occupying the time or distracting the attention of the audience, which would otherwise have introduced confusion and defeated the object of the meeting. Nothing could be more reasonable than this regulation, and no peace-loving person would make any objection. . . . The meeting broke up with harmony and good feeling."

A few years later, a distinguished American writer and poet, J. G. Whittier, who was present at this meeting, made the following reference to it:

"Three or four years ago, on my way eastward, I spent an hour or two at a camp-ground of the Second Advent in East Kingston. The spot was well chosen. A tall growth of pine and hemlock threw its melancholy shadow over the multitude, who were arranged upon rough seats of boards and logs. Several hundred—perhaps a thousand—people were present, and more were rapidly coming. Drawn about in a circle, forming a background of snowy whiteness to the dark masses of men and foliage, were the white tents, and back of them the provision stalls and cook shops. When I reached the ground, a hymn, the words of which I could not distinguish, was pealing through the dim aisles of the forest. I know nothing of music, having neither ear nor taste for it—but I could readily see that it had its effect upon the multitude before me, kindling to higher intensity their already excited enthusiasm. The preachers were placed in a rude pulpit of rough boards, carpeted only by the dead forest leaves and flowers, and tasselled, not with silk and velvet, but with the green boughs of the sombre hemlocks around it. One of them followed the music in an earnest exhortation on the duty of preparing for the great event. Occasionally he was really eloquent, and his description of the last day had all the terrible distinctness of Anelli's painting of the 'End of the World.'

"Suspended from the front of the rude pulpit were two broad sheets of canvas, upon one of which was the figure of a man,—the head of gold, the breast and arms of silver, the belly of brass, the legs of iron, and feet of clay,—the dream of Nebuchadnezzar! On the other were depicted the wonders of the Apocalyptic vision—the beasts—the dragons—the scarlet woman seen by the seer of Patmos—oriental types and figures and mystic symbols translated into staring Yankee realities, and exhibited like the beasts of a traveling menagerie. One horrible image, with its hideous heads and scaly caudal extremity, reminded me of the tremendous line of Milton, who, in speaking of the same evil dragon, describes him as

'Swingeing the scaly horrors of his folded tail.'

"To an imaginative mind the scene was full of novel interest. The white circle of tents—the dim wood arches—the upturned, earnest faces—the loud voices of the speakers, burdened with the awful symbolic language of the Bible—the smoke from the fires rising like incense from forest altars—carrying one back to the days of primitive worship, when

'The groves were God's first temples, ere men learned
To hew the shaft, and lay the architrave,
And stretch the roof above it.'"

There were near thirty tents on the ground, and the interest of the meeting continued to the last.

SKETCH OF ELD. S. S. BREWER, A STANDARD BEARER AND POET.

Eld. Brewer commenced preaching the gospel A. D. 1834; being at that time a member of the Methodist E. church. The falling stars on the eve of Nov. 13, 1833, made a deep and lasting impression upon his mind. He then, and ever since, considered it a fulfillment of Rev. vi. 13, and a sign of the last days. The question of human rights had awaked a deep sympathy in his heart for the poor slaves, when it was considered a disgrace to plead for the helpless victims under bondage. The decided position he had taken upon this highly exciting subject, caused him great sorrow of heart, while witnessing the bitter feeling existing between the South and the North; this prevented him from making an effort to become a member of the itenerancy.

S. S. BREWER.—Page 238.

While laboring as a local preacher, he had the opportunity of hearing Wm. Miller and J. V. Himes, when they visited New York City the first time. What he then heard, and had previously read, convinced him of the truthfulness of the message. He at once became an advocate of the doctrines, which have distinguished us as a people, and has continued to proclaim them until the present, with unabated interest. Bro. B. soon became identified with the Advent believers, and faithfully labored in preaching, writing and publishing the glad tidings of the soon coming of Christ, to establish his kingdom and manifest his glory. He has traveled extensively and preached constantly, being active, zealous, earnest, courteous, a sympathetic, modest and ready speaker, argumentative, expository and conversational in his discourses. He is given to prophetical and historical study, and generally looks beyond the surface and beyond the dogmatic assertions of men; he does not dogmatise. Bro. B. is also a poet, and has added many contributions to the hymnology of Advent believers. In our hymn-books and poetic columns of our papers and sheet hymns, may be found some of the most sublime and logical hymns we have. We shall quote a few elsewhere. Himself and faithful wife being singers of the first class, have done much to interest and produce conviction in congregations, and to soothe and comfort the afflicted sons and daughters of sorrow and care, by their melodious songs of Scriptual musings.

Bro. B. has contributed much to the papers, and is author of several pamphlets and tracts, which have had a wide circulation, and are yet in much demand, among which are 1. The Wine of God's Wrath; 2. The Laodicean Church; 3. Last Day Tokens, Nos. 1, 2, 3; 4. Treatise on Rev. xiii; 5. Kingdom of God; 6. History of an Immortal Soul; 7. The Slaying of the Witnesses; 8. The days in which we live; 9. The Seventh Plague; 10. The Seven Seals; 11. The Seven Messages; 12. Evangels of the Coming One; 13. The Mystery of Iniquity; 14. Papal Rome, its Glory, its Gloom and Destiny.

Though now in old age, and worn with constant labors, this loving and devoted brother is constantly traveling as an evangelist, and preaching "Behold the bridegroom cometh, go ye out to meet him," and persuading sinners to repent and believe the gospel; while he urges the believers to a deeper heart work and thorough consecration of all to the Lord and his service, believing surely that Christ will come in "this generation," and is now, emphatically, soon to appear.

Below will be seen one of his poems which has been greatly admired by many, and is thought worthy of insertion here.

JERUSALEM.

Jerusalem, Jerusalem,
Foretold by prophets long,
The new creation's diadem,
The bride of sacred song;
Jehovah is thine architect,
The mighty God above;
There with our great Melchisedec,
The saints ere long will rove.

The temple of King David's Son,
That prophets long have told,
Built by the wise King Solomon,
With "manna pot" of gold; [rod,
Where budded Aaron's wondrous
With all those sacred things, [road,
And cherubs spread their wings ab-
The pride of Hebrew kings.

That was a type of what ere long
The pure in heart shall see,
And what th' Apocalyptic song
Reveals fair Salem is to be;
Thou citadel of earth and sky,
Of vast sublimity,
Where dwells the Lamb and the Most High,
To all eternity.

The son of Amos sang of thee,
Whose lips were touched with fire;
The stones all set with colors rare,
Foundations of sapphire;
He saw the windows of Agates,
Thy glory bright, sublime,
Thy massive carbuncle gates—
Oh! how those gems did shine.

O when, thou great Zerrubbabel (Zec. iv. 6, 7),
Wilt thou the headstone place,
When shouting millions loud shall tell
The wonders of free grace?
Shall I, O God, be with them there,
And join the choral song,
With all the sacramental host,
The Jubal strain prolong?

No cherubim nor seraphim
Behind the Holy Place,
Nor blue nor purple veil between,
But face shall answer face.
No Urim then nor Thummin there (Ex. xxviii. 30),
On Aaron's sacred breast,
But clad in vestments rich and rare,
God's ancient priest is drest.

No longer Moses now appears
From Sinai's awful brow,
With veil upon his shining face,
That gleams with glory now;
Nor when with Peter, James, and John,
Upon Mount Tabor's height,
That vision could not shed upon
His face such glory bright.

But, hark! that sweet, the loud acclaim
Through Salem's portals swells;
Behold He comes! it doth proclaim
The great Immanuel.
From pinnacle and parapet
Admiring myriads gaze,
And angels crowd her battlements
To see the Lamb's dear face.

O how the blood-besprinkled ones
Will wonder and admire,
When standing on thy streets of gold,
Aglow with sacred fire;
When he beholds his Lord and King,
Oh how his harp will trill,—
King David then will sweeter sing,
Than when on Zion's Hill.

Then how the martyrs from the stake,
Who praised God in the fires,
When they again to life shall wake,
Will sing 'mid angel choirs.
They suffered death their Lord to greet,
Beneath fair Salem's dome;
Oh! what a change, to tread thy streets,
From fagots to a throne!

No longer weeps Hilkiah's son
O'er Israel's fallen lot,
And Rachel's tears have ceased to run,
Because her loved were not.
Macpelah's cave, on Mamre's plain,
Hath yielded up its trust;
Good Abraham and Sarah too
Now shine amid the host.

O! there the robes of all God's saints
Transcendently do shine,
With crowns of gold in princely dress,
Prepared by hands divine.
Afar from the Ægean sea
The Seer of Patmos comes,
To join creation's jubilee,
And shout the harvest home.

No man the ransomed host can count,
Nor tell the number o'er,
So vast the multitude's amount,
Like sands on ocean's shore;
There 'neath thy dome, Jerusalem,
Their King in beauty see,
And bend in homage at his throne,
With pure felicity.

From out thy dazzling throne, O God,
For evermore is seen
A swelling river, deep and broad,
Life's ever-gushing stream;
Beside its vernal banks,
Beneath its blooming bowers,
Perpetually is seen
Sweet Eden's blooming flowers.

Ah! Lord, my heart is big with wo,
And weary with life's cares;
To Salem I would quickly go,
If thou wouldst hear my prayers.
Since I have read its wondrous fame,
I'd see without delay
Jerusalem—O, dear, sweet name!
Thou'st taken my heart away.

The marriage supper of the Lamb,
To celebrate I'd go,
'Mid the bright glories of "I AM,"
The rapturous height to know.
O Salem, dear, supremely grand,
Thy golden streets I'd tread;
Hard by the throne, Lord, let me stand,
And see my Living Head.

The nuptial hour, Lord, let it come;
The guests, dear Lamb, invite;
Fast speed the angels, bring them home,
Haste! end the weeper's night.
Our hearts pulsate with patience, Lord,
Though exiles here we roam,
And pray with the beloved John,
O come! Lord Jesus, quickly come.

SECOND ADVENT CONFERENCE IN BANGOR, ME.

July 12, 1842, a conference of Second Advent believers was held in Bangor, by Elders G. F. Cox, John W. Atkins, Methodists, and Elder J. V. Himes and others from Massachusetts; Eld. A. Hale, secretary.

A large number attended and many became believers. Several ministers date their experience in Second Advent views from this conference. The change of views from the *mystical* notions about the future, to the hope of real, tangible, immortal, eternal things, works such a change, and awakens such interest, produces such activity, devotion, and self-denying, cross-bearing results in believers, as to lead them to feel as though they had experienced a new conversion. This has often been expressed by them as a new conversion, and has been noticed by others who have been much perplexed on account of it. It has often caused opposers to say of them, "They throw away their conversion," or, "They don't believe any one is converted unless they believe the Advent doctrine." But this is not so. They find an addition, a deeper, greater joy in it, than they ever experienced before.

REV. R. C. SHIMEALL'S CHRONOLOGY.

Mr. Shimeall, a millennarian, member of the Presbytery of New York, published a book in 1842, entitled "Our Bible Chronology," in which he advocated the second personal advent of Christ in 1847. It is a work exhibiting much study, research, and ability in the millennarian line, and was well patronized by the ministry of his denomination. But much of his theory is foreign to the views of Adventists, and his exposition of some of the prophecies of Daniel very far from logical deductions.

SKETCH OF ELD. M. BATCHELOR, AND HIS LABORS.

This faithful gospel minister and devoted Christian brother was a Baptist preacher and pastor of a Baptist church in Wallingford, Ct., where he read and heard that the advent of our Lord was soon to be realized. This was in 1842; he studied, prayed, believed, rejoiced and began to preach it to his church; a revival followed, and continued for many months. He then preached it in the surrounding towns and cities; the word had free course and sinners were converted. In the spring of 1844 he visited Pownal, Vt., with no intention of staying but a day or two. The people flocked to hear, he continued preaching every day, for three weeks, the people flocking in from other towns. He then left for home, worn and weary, but within a few days received a letter urging him to return to Pownal, and become pastor of the Baptist church there; he decided to do so, and moved and settled his family among them, and "continued," as he says, "fifteen years, witnessing to small and great, 'saying none other things than those which Moses and the prophets did say should come to pass.'" By consent of the church he went on mission tours into other parts, and preached this glorious message from Canada to the Atlantic coast. When the discussion came up in relation to the mortality of man, and the penalty for sin, he took the literal side of the case, and has published the gospel on the principle of immortality and eternal life only through Christ, and total destruction as the end of the wicked.

During his faithful ministrations in the towns around him the ministry became chafed and jealous of encroachments upon their territory. They commenced labor with Bro. B. and the Baptist church, of which he was pastor, bringing them under the charge of heresy; he called a church meeting and proposed to leave, as he decided that the ministry were not aiming at the church but at him; but they declined to give him up, and then voted as a church to withdraw from the Shaftonbury Association; but refused to drop their name: Baptists. The association voted to withdraw from them the hand of fellowship for heresy, and advertised it in the Baptist paper "The Reflector," Boston. That church has been enabled to live out of doors ever since, and Bro. B. says: "We have all out of doors to think in." In 1859 he moved to Rutland, Vt., and labored there and in other places; preached in Low Hampton, N. Y., half the time for several years. In 1866 he moved to New Bedford, where he yet resides; but travels and preaches as an evangelist. He loves to preach the precious word, feeling more than ever assured that soon "we shall reap if we faint not." The Lord has wrought graciously with this dear brother and many sinners have been converted through his preaching. His work is not done, sinners are yet brought to Christ where he preaches, and the saints strengthened and built up. We trust he will come to the end of the days as a shock of corn fully ripe, and stand with Daniel in his lot, and that very soon.

THE TENT–MEETING ENTERPRISE.

It was thought by some to be a hazardous attempt for the few Advent believers to enter upon holding camp-meetings, but was soon seen that the Lord was greatly blessing the effort. That enterprise was in successful operation. The idea was now started for constructing a large tent sufficient to accommodate four thousand persons, to use in cities and towns where no houses were open for lectures. The people at once favored the plan and accepted the proposition. Eld. Himes, with the help of other friends, undertook the work. The tent was constructed, and pitched first in Concord, N. H., in July. The excitement and interest awakened by this movement was greater than that occasioned by Second Advent camp-meetings. The gatherings were immense, and the Lord worked graciously in the spread of truth and the salvation of sinners. The tent was next pitched in Albany, N. Y., then at Chicopee Falls, and at Salem, Mass., at Benson, Vt., and lastly, for that summer, in Newark, N. J. In each place the word of God took effect and produced great and glorious results among the people.

This tent was an immense Tabernacle. Its center pole was fifty-five feet high; the tent covered a circle of twenty-five rods in circumference, and, properly seated, would accommodate near four thousand persons. This "Tabernacle" was of heavy canvas, and was conveyed by cars, steamers, or teams, from place to place, and was literally worn out in the service of the gospel. Many hearts were instructed in the great truths of the gospel of the kingdom, and comforted by its blessed hope, while many hundreds of sinners were led to the Saviour at the meetings held under this canvas. This was another instrumentality brought into successful use, and since that, many other tents have been made and used for the same purpose, in the Eastern, Middle, and Western States, and thousands have been brought under the sound of the gospel of Christ by such means, who would never go to meeting-houses, and large numbers of such and of other classes have been thus brought to a saving knowledge of Christ.

THREE METHODIST MINISTERS SOUND THE MIDNIGHT CRY.

The editor of "Zion's Herald" informs its readers that

"Three of their ministers, Elders Apolos Hale, P. T. Kenney, and L. C. Collins, located in 1842, in order that they might extensively promote their views of the millennium; they accord, we understand, with those of Mr. Miller."

This was a correct statement of facts; but would it not have been still more to the point, when alluding to their views of the millennium, to have said: they accord, we understand, with those of the Christian church in all time since Christ until the days of Dr. Whitby. This would have left them without reproach.

Eld. L. C. Collins writes to "The Signs of the Times" Jan. 1, 1842, stating that he is deeply interested in the great subject of Christ's second coming and is trying to do something to spread the good news. Again Bro. C. writes from Oxford, N. Y., where he had been preaching the message: "The work of reformation is going on, new laborers are being raised up to give the midnight cry. The Methodist meeting house and vestry are closed against me, though the vestry is open for a debating club of unconverted young men."

The trustees passed a resolution which shut out one of their own ministers—Bro. Collins—for preaching that Jesus is soon coming. Here is a copy of the document; it speaks like Rome:

"*Resolved*, That we cannot, as trustees of the Methodist E. church of Oxford (Ct.), encourage, by opening the doors of our church, or in any other way, directly or indirectly, to Millerism." [1]

The ministers resorted to the school houses where they preached to the people; a glorious reformation followed in several districts in the town, and a society of believers was raised there to reflect the light they had received from the Lord, on that community.

SKETCH OF ELD. HIRAM MUNGER, AND HIS LABORS.

Bro. Munger is a singular man, unlike any other you ever saw. We shall not attempt to compare him with Rowland Hill, Lorenzo Dow, or Peter Cartwright; he has some of the rough, blunt, ready, shrewd gifts of each of them. He measures a plat of ground, a tree, a man, a situation or a congregation at a glance; he is sympathetic, kind, tender in spirit, careless in appearance, coarse in expression and very useful in his place. There are none like him, and it is well that the Lord brought him into the faith; he is in great demand at *camp-meetings*, and also in many other places; he is not perfect, for he makes some great blunders. Bro. Munger was converted among the Methodists, "when they stood in the liberty of the gospel" (as he remarks), and became a workman in the cause of God. His qualifica-

---

[1] Published in the Oxford Times.

HIRAM MUNGER.—Page 244.

tions for camp-meeting work were soon perceived, and he began to serve on camp-meeting committees. In this capacity, in 1842, serving at a Methodist encampment at Chicopee Falls, Mass., Eld. J. V. Himes found him and engaged the encampment of him, after some reluctance on his part, for a Second Advent camp-meeting, to follow directly after that of the Methodists. Eld. Himes engaged Bro. Munger also to oversee the encampment, as chief of the committee. Thus the way was opened for the

GREAT CAMP-MEETING AT CHICOPEE FALLS AUG. 25, 1842.

The committee of this meeting consisted of Hiram Munger, N. Branch, W. Billings, R. E. Ladd, Peter Dearborn, and M. Pendleton. We will allow Bro. Munger to give the report of it, while we give some account of him. It would cause all our Christian readers to *laugh* and *cry* to read his account of the meeting in full, as it is stated in the "Life of Hiram Munger," pp. 47–50. We shall give an item only, to open the way to his advanced experience. He says:

"The Methodists had just closed the best meeting they had ever held in New England. Over one hundred were reported to have been converted at the meeting." The Advent believers came on with their canvas tabernacle, and pitched it, its size and height was such that "I was more astonished than ever," says Bro. Munger; "I helped raise the tent; the novelty of the scene drove off my blues, for the tent covered all our seats and a rod all around besides; it was twenty-five rods around it; I never saw half so large a tent before. I and others *thought* and *said*, "Where are all the people coming from to fill it," for it was estimated to hold from three thousand to four thousand." The meeting commenced with a few, and all strangers, except a *very* few. The meeting was so different from the other that I took but little interest in it; excepting the $25 (promised him for his services), and I hoped they would not make out much;" but the people came more and more; finally, he says: "a great multitude came and many of my Methodist brethren came back and took possession of their tents, which they had left in my care." Again he says: "Sunday they began to come very early and continued to come until the whole tent was filled, and they came till the whole circle of the tents was full, and the whole grove literally filled with people, while the preaching was listened to with great attention; I could not hear much of it, for as the congregation was large, and some rowdyism began to appear, it took my attention mostly." . . . "But very good order prevailed and the meeting increased in interest, together with its vast numbers. The first time Bro. Himes attempted to call on sinners to come forward to the altar for prayers, I truly thought him beside himself, for our meeting had been crowned with such success that I did not think any would come forward, and I kept watch while the first three verses were being sung, when there was such a rush to the altar for prayers as I had never seen. This gave *me* the 'lock-jaw' for a while, for I was so astonished to see those forward who had stood through *our* meeting, that I did not speak for some time; truly I thought 'God was in the place and I knew it not;' and when prayer was offered such a work ensued as had not been seen on that ground before. Some of my friends were forward, and some church members: all pleading for mercy, I recollect asking Bro. Hawks (a Methodist minister), what he thought of it? He answered, 'It is the work of God in good earnest.' By this time a number had come out happy, and were rejoicing, which carried the evidence to us, that if *ours* was the work of God this must be. This meeting went through with power, and was instrumental in more conversions than the other, saying nothing of the truth that was received by thousands at this meeting. *I* did not receive the doctrine, for I had not time to examine it, nor did I want to. . . . The next week after this meeting closed, Bro. L. C. Collins offered me $25 to go to Plainville and take charge of another Advent camp-meeting, which I accepted. At this meeting a great many attended who were at the other meeting, although it was over fifty miles. Bro. Geo. Storrs was there, and other Advent preachers. I had more time here to examine their doctrine, and I was astonished when I read the Bible for myself, without a Papal comment upon it; I was convinced they had got the truth on the *nature of the* events, saying nothing of the *time*, and many things I learned that I never knew were in the Bible before; it was a new book indeed, and had some promises that I never had thought belonged to us; in fact I had never read expecting to understand for myself, and thousands are in the same situation, not able even to give the reason for the hope that is within them."

This commenced a new era in his Christian life, and set all the energies of his giant frame and eccentric mind to work to publish and aid in public efforts in publishing this glorious, God-given message to all around. Being fully convinced of the Bible facts of the events and their nearness, he further remarks: "I do not care if we never get a correct clue to the *time*, the *doctrines* will *stand the test* and the *practice of them* will give us a 'part in the first resurrection, on such the second death will not have power.'" To this principle Bro. M. has since adhered. A short time after, in 1843, Mr. Ransom, the Methodist Presiding Elder, with the advice of a lawyer, turned Bro. M. and eighty-four other members out of the church, at Chicopee, for heresy, without a trial. Eld. M. has traveled East and West and preached with good results in many places. He has attended one hundred and seventy-five camp-meetings since A. D. 1829. He has served on camp-meeting committees now forty-one years. Therefore the people have formed an acquaintance with him, and we need not add more than to say he is yet in the work of the Lord, and anxiously waiting the return of the nobleman, believing and teaching that all the dead will be raised, the righteous to receive the gift of immortality and eternal life through Christ, and the unrighteous to utterly perish in the second death.

"Mr. Miller remained at home till past the middle of August. On the 20th of that month he commenced a course of lectures at Brandon, Vt., which continued till the 28th. On the 25th, a large tent had been pitched at Chicopee, Mass., where Mr. Miller was anxiously expected; but he did not arrive so as to commence his lectures till the 1st of September. He then lectured each day till the 4th, when the meeting closed. That was a very large gathering, and, as was estimated, some four hundred or more found peace in believing.

From the 7th to the 11th of September, he lectured at Castine, Maine. On returning to Boston, on the 12th, at the request of the passengers, he gave a lecture on the boat. He went to Albany on the 13th, lectured there in the evening, and on the next day took the canal-boat, on which he also lectured, on his way to Granville, N. Y., where he lectured from the 18th to the 23d of September. From the 8th to the 16th of October, he lectured in Whitehall, N. Y., and from the 20th to the 30th, at Benson, Vt., where Mr. Himes held a tent-meeting in connection with his lectures.

On the 3d of November, Mr. Himes erected the Big Tent in Newark, N. J. Mr. Miller was not able to be present till the 7th, from which time to the 14th he gave fifteen discourses. Five days before the close of that meeting the weather became so inclement that the meetings could not be continued in the tent, and they were adjourned to the Presbyterian church in Clinton street, which was kindly opened during the week. On Sunday, the 13th, the meeting was held in the morning in Mechanics' Hall, which was crowded to suffocation, and found to be altogether too strait for them. At 2 P. M., Mr. Miller spoke from the steps of the court-house to near five thousand people. Notwithstanding the inclemency of the weather, and their being thus driven from pillar to post, the meetings were very interesting, and were productive of much good.

At the close of the meeting in Newark, he commenced a course of lectures in New York city, which continued till the 18th of November. On the 19th of November, he commenced a course of lectures in New Haven, Ct., in the M. E. Church, Rev. Mr. Law, pastor. On Sunday, the 20th, although the house was large, it was crowded; and in the evening many were unable to gain admittance. He continued there till the 26th, the interest continuing during the entire course. "The Fountain," a temperance paper published in that city, gave the following account of the meeting:

"Mr. William Miller, the celebrated writer and lecturer on the Second Advent of our Saviour, and the speedy destruction of the world, has recently visited our city, and delivered a course of lectures to an immense concourse of eager listeners in the First Methodist church. It is estimated that not less than three thousand persons were in attendance at the church, on each evening, for a week; and if the almost breathless silence which reigned throughout the immense throng for two or three hours at a time is any evidence of interest in the subject of the lectures, it cannot be said that our community are devoid of feeling on this momentous question.

"Mr. Miller was accompanied and assisted by Rev. J. V. Himes, who is by no means an inefficient coadjutor in this great and important work. We did not attend the whole course, the last three lectures being all we had an opportunity of hearing. We were utterly disappointed. So many extravagant things had been said of the 'fanatics' in the public prints, and such distorted statements published in reference to their articles of faith, that we were prepared to witness disgusting and perhaps blasphemous exhibitions of 'Millerism,' as the doctrine of the Second Advent is called.

"In justice to Mr. Miller we are constrained to say, that he is one of the most interesting lecturers we have any recollection of ever having heard. We have not the least doubt that he is fully convinced of the truth of the doctrine he labors so diligently to inculcate, and he certainly evinces great candor and fairness in his manner of proving his points. And he proves them, too, to the satisfaction of every hearer;—that is, allowing his premises to be correct, there is no getting away from his conclusions.

"There was quite a number of believers in attendance from other places, and a happier company we have never seen.

"We have no means of ascertaining the precise effect of these meetings on this community, but we know that many minds have been induced to contemplate the Scripture prophecies in a new light, and not a few are studying the Bible with unwonted interest. For our own part, this new view of the world's destiny is so completely at variance with previous habits of thought and anticipation, that we are not prepared to give it entire credence, though we should not dare hazard an attempt to disprove it.

"The best part of the story is, that a powerful revival has followed the labors of Messrs. Miller and company. We learn that over fifty persons presented themselves for prayers at the altar of the Methodist church on Sunday evening. On Monday evening the number was about eighty."

In the month of May following, Rev. A. A. Stevens (Orthodox Cong.), then a member of Yale College, in a letter to the "Midnight Cry," stated that "the powerful and glorious revival which then commenced continued for some two months, with almost unabated interest."—*Bliss' Life of Miller*, p. 168.

SKETCH OF ELD. JOHN COUCH'S EXPERIENCE AND LABORS.

Eld. John Couch has been a standard-bearer since 1842. He is a native of New Hampshire, was formerly a member of the Christian church. Hearing the message of the soon coming of Christ, he examined the Scriptures and became convinced that they taught it, and embraced it as a great Bible truth, in 1838. He soon felt impressed with the duty of preaching the gospel, and, in 1842, entered upon the important work. Since that point he has been zealously and actively "lifting up a standard for the people." Many thousands have listened to his faithful, earnest, and Scriptural arguments in presenting the facts concerning the coming and kingdom of our Lord, and the evidences graphically presented to show that the event is near at hand, and that all ought to seek an immediate preparation for it. We think none who are acquainted with him will accuse him of not dealing faithfully with the gospel, or with the people in regard to their relation to the future, or duty for the present. Bro. C. is an attractive preacher, enlisting and retaining the attention of the people by close reasoning and frequent illustrations, accompanied by thrilling exhortations. He has traveled much in many of the Eastern, and some in the Western States, and in the Provinces, and many have been brought to Christ and into the gospel hope through his labors. He is author of several valuable pamphlets and tracts, viz.: "Historic Echoes"—"Christian Union"—"The Two-Horned Beast"—"It is Heresy"—"The End at Hand"

—"Bible Sanctification"—"The Eastern Question"—and the prophetical part of "Good Tidings." During several years past he has been president of the New Hampshire Advent Christian Conference. He now resides in Chelsea, Mass. He has also served on the editorial committee of the World's Crisis. At the annual session of the A. C. P. Society in 1873, he was chosen editor-in-chief of that paper. We trust he will act a faithful part for the Lord and his truth to the end.

A SECOND ADVENT CAMP-MEETING IN CASTINE, ME.

A camp-meeting was held in Castine, commencing Sept. 6, 1842, which gathered large numbers of listeners to the word; Mr. Miller, Eld. Himes, Eld. A. Hale, and others attended to give the message, which awakened a deep interest in the hearts of many and brought several ministers into the work.

A CAMP-MEETING IN ATKINSON, ME., SEPT. 21, 1842.

The committee of arrangements was composed of Elders A. Hale, Yates Higgins, J. W. Atkins, J. Hamilton, A. Bridges, Israel Daman, S. H. Horn. The report shows it to have been an interesting and important meeting; there are good fruits of it yet in existence.

A CAMP-MEETING IN CONCORD, N. H.

The camp-meeting held in Concord was a success in sowing the good seed of the kingdom. The true gospel hope was shown in contrast with the modern fable of the world's conversion and a temporal millennium; and a goodly number of faithful Christian fathers and mothers in Israel joyfully accepted the true hope. They examined the prophetic Scriptures and the signs of the times, and became standard bearers of the message of Christ's soon coming. Concord has since had much faithful labor bestowed and received great blessings from the Lord; many faithful Christians have embraced and enjoyed this gospel message of Christ's soon coming, while many sinners have been turned to righteousness through it. But the enemy has torn and divided them and sown seeds of mischief, which is doing its destructive work; yet there are many living epistles—joyful Christians—who are working and waiting, while others sleep in Jesus, waiting the coming of the King of kings.

DEFINITE TIME NOT THE BURDEN OF THE MESSAGE.

The following is an editorial in the "Signs of the Times" of Aug. 3, 1842:

"The crisis has now come; the world is alarmed; the church is waked up from her dreamy slumbers. The ministry are aroused; some of them are embracing the truth, and others are defending the traditions of the past, saying, 'My Lord delayeth his coming.' The opposition have begun to put forth their energies to crush the advocates of the 'Midnight cry,' and to hush the voice of alarm to the slumbering virgins. The opposition now comes from high places. The schools of Orthodoxy in New England. Accordingly the attacks are now made upon us in almost every pulpit and newspaper under their control. Other sects follow, for though they are divided among themselves, they are united in opposing us.

"In this work of opposition we find a strange medley of Orthodox and Universalists—Apostates, Deists, Atheists, and professed Christians, of different denominations, all uniting in the cry of 'peace and safety' when sudden destruction is coming upon them." . . .

WHAT IS OUR WORK?

"It may be asked, what our work consists in? We reply:

"1. To expose the fallacious and soul-destroying doctrine of what is termed the *temporal millennium.* The promise of 'peace and safety,' a thousand years yet to come, before the Lord shall personally appear, a second time without sin unto salvation.

"We brand this doctrine a fable—a deception—a thing which is of recent origin, and therefore has no foundation in the word of God.

"2. To expose the doctrine of the literal political return and establishment of the Jews in Palestine as a nation. It has no foundation in the New Testament. In that covenant all are one in Christ, and if we are Christ's then are we Abraham's seed, and heirs according to the promise. The idea of the reëstablishment of the Jewish nation as an event to precede the coming of Christ, we can but regard as a stratagem of the devil, to blind both Jew and Gentile to the doctrine of Christ's speedy coming. As such we feel bound to treat it.

"3. The notion of the *world's conversion*, is another false notion which blinds the minds of the church and the world to the speedy coming of Christ. 'Christ cannot come as yet for a long time.' Why not? 'The world is to be converted.' Thus all are lulled to sleep." . . .

WHAT IS OUR DUTY?

"The only answer we can give, is, to sound the 'Midnight Cry;' to show that nothing remains to be fulfilled in historical prophecy but the coming of the Son of man in the clouds of heaven; to raise the righteous dead and set up his everlasting kingdom; and to warn the church and the world to prepare for this as the next great event before us. The prophetic periods have nearly run out. The vials, the seals, the trumpets, the signs of the times, all indicate the near approach of the coming of the Son of man, 'even at the doors.' We shall, therefore, in connection with our respected colleagues, continue to preach on the subject. We shall 'sound the alarm in God's holy mountain.' We shall publish more extensively, and scatter our publications more profusely than ever. We shall hold public meetings, and by every effort in our power endeavor to arouse the world to prepare for the coming of the Bridegroom. More than this we cannot do; less, we dare not." . . .

BUT WHAT AFTER ALL IF YOU SHOULD BE MISTAKEN?

"Well, if it will be of service to you, we will reason a little on this point. 1. If we are mistaken in the *time*, and the world still goes on after 1843, we shall have the satisfaction of having done our duty. Our publications are evangelical; they have, and now are producing the most salutary effect upon the church and the world. Our lectures and public meetings produce the same glorious results. Can we ever regret that souls were converted,—that the virgins were awakened and prepared to meet their Lord? If then we are mistaken about the *time*, what harm can result to the church or world?"

TO THIS OUR OPPONENTS REPLY:

"'*It will make infidels.* If your calculations fail, the faith of the people will be shaken in the Bible.' Let us look at this objection. Who will be made infidels? Not our opponents, for they don't believe us. It is all moonshine with them! Who, then, will be made infidels? Surely, none but Second Advent believers. Well, we will suppose a case to illustrate this matter. Believers in the Second Advent are students of prophecy. We have fifty positive predictions in the Bible which have been literally fulfilled. In all we will suppose there are fifty-one to be fulfilled. Fifty are already fulfilled, and have become matters of history. By these we know the Bible is the word of God. *This is settled forever.* Well, in the course of time, certain members of the church, by reading the Bible, and comparing Scripture with Scripture, come to the conclusion that the fifty-first event will take place in a given year, say 1843. No one in the meantime is able to disprove it, or show a better calculation. Well, we continue to look for the event until the time expires, and the last event does not take place as they had calculated. What will these believers do? They have fifty demonstrations of the truth of the Bible, and they have ONE mistake of their own in a mere calculation. Let common sense decide whether we should reject our Bibles? Make infidels!! It is a sceptical church that is making infidels."

We give below the resolutions passed at a conference in Albany, N. Y., in the summer of 1842, by a large delegation of ministers and laymen, who looked with interest for the return of their Lord. They will contrast strangely with some other resolutions of religious men, which we shall give a little later in the book.

ALBANY CONFERENCE RESOLUTIONS.

"*Resolved,* That we feel under deep obligations to our heavenly father for putting it into the hearts of his servants to come among us with the *midnight cry.*

"*Resolved,* That we rejoice in the hope of our Lord's speedy appearing to set up his kingdom, and our prayer is, 'Even so, come Lord Jesus, come quickly,' and our conviction is that that glorious event will transpire in 1843.

"The last clause in the above resolutions was passed with the understanding, that we did not express a fixed opinion with regard to the *time*; but from the light we at present have, we incline to think 1843 is the time rather than any other period."

"FROM THE CHRISTIAN PUBLIC."

"Mr. Miller continues to excite considerable interest by his new theory (?) of the millennium throughout New England. He meets with violent opposition and has to suffer many hard sayings and bitter reproaches from the clergy. Whether his theory is true or false, it can never be put down by such indiscriminate denunciation as the haughty kingdom of the clergy continually pours out upon him. We lack confidence in the correctness of his views; but we admire his independence of mind and the integrity of character which he evinces. The Signs of the Times, published by Joshua V. Himes, abounds in articles from the pens of Mr. Miller and other correspondents, among whom we recognize James A. Begg, of Glasgow, Scotland. Should the signs fail to point infallibly to 1843, it will at least elicit much light, which will be turned to a useful account by the thinking and practical."

SKETCH OF ELD. PETER W. HOUGH'S EXPERIENCE AND LABORS.

Elder Hough's father was a native of Connecticut, was deeply impressed by the darkening of the sun in 1780, which he witnessed and believed a sign of the coming of the Lord. He was a Christian man and talked of the subject of the Lord's coming with his friends, and found that it was their general impression that the event was very near, some were hoping they should live to see it. He afterward settled in Canada West, where he brought up a family of children and instructed them in the ways of the Lord, frequently impressing upon their minds the near approach of the day of judgment which produced in them an inclination to search the Bible to learn about it.

Peter became, early in life, deeply interested in the prophecies of Daniel and John; his father's old family Bible had the symbolic diagrams of those beasts in it, he longed to understand them, and talked with older persons about them. At the age of sixteen years he was converted and united with the Methodist church. He sought books to enlighten him on these prophecies. "The first help" he found "was Wesley's notes on the New Testament; this," he says, "gave me some precious light on the truth of the new earth, as the home of the saints, which gave me a greater relish to read the prophecies. This to me seemed so reasonable and proper and clothed the prophecies with majestic grandeur and importance, as connecting history with the incoming of that grand event. "In A. D. 1833, he witnessed that grand scene—the shower of stars—" It confirmed" he says, "my former convictions of the end being near and revived the history of the darkening of the sun, which gave shape and consistency to the whole."

About this time a book was published by the Methodist E. Book Concern, N. Y., entitled "*Introduction to Christianity*," with Nathan Bangs, D. D., commendation of it to the Christian public, Oct., 1832, viz., "by the printing of it in its present size and with these improvements, we hope it may have an extensive circulation, as it contains the most comprehensive arguments in favor of genuine Christianity of any book we are acquainted with, of the same dimensions, as well as a historical sketch of its early establishment and subsequent propagation."

Bro. H. obtained this book. In it he found the 2300 days of Dan. viii. 13, 14, called years, and explained to end with the setting up of God's everlasting kingdom. "The tenth part of the City," Rev. xi. 13; "The great earthquake;" "The slaughter of seven thousand," etc., explained to have "been strikingly fulfilled by the French revolution." This gave him more light; but did not bring out the grand conclusion of the whole story. With this light Bro. H. began to preach and expound prophecy, bringing out the idea of the earth restored, at the close of his subjects.

In 1842 Mr. Miller's lectures were put into his hands to read and give his opinion upon. He took the book hoping it would clear up some more of the difficulties which were yet in his mind; he was not surprised that the book taught that the Lord was coming about 1843, for, as he says, "I thought that the most of writers on prophetic chronology had terminated the periods between 1836 and 1866.

My mind had been greatly preplexed about symbolic prophecy, I dared not do as some did—tell what God *meant*; but here I got the key I had looked for so long. This book showed me that the Bible explained its own figures.

From this time the message was like fire shut up in my bones, I talked it and preached it, Christians loved it, calls came thick and fast, and the word was attended with the power of the Spirit; I preached three times in the week and four times on Sunday, with full houses; ministers who worked with me reported sometimes one hundred and fifty converts. Ministers were multiplied and the good work of God prospered."

He writes from Maniposa, Upper Canada, Jan. 1, 1842, that he is the only one openly preaching the advent of Christ near at hand, in that region. Bro. H. has been preaching the gospel for a long time. When the church and ministry became awakened upon the subject, and the doctrine was proclaimed as a distinct message, he sympathised with it and entered upon the specific work of sounding the midnight cry, and has continued in the work until the present. Being a man of sound and deep piety, with a heart controlled by the love and spirit of God, he has built up the church and gathered many converts to Christ. Active, zealous, critical, laborious and conscientious, his works have given testimony to his faith. His cry has been and yet is, "Behold he cometh!" Practical in his teachings and earnest in his prayers, his influence has been such as to induce piety, love, union and prosperity. On entering upon an examination of the claims which the Roman Catholic and modern Protestant churches make for the dogma of the immortality of the soul and eternal torture of the lost; he became convinced the Bible was not in their favor; but directly against such claims. Therefore he has preached the mortality of man; and Christ as a Saviour, through whom God has promised the gift of immortality and eternal life to all who are in Christ at the day of rewards. Bro. H. has for a long time labored successfuly in New York, Wisconsin, and other states, and is now in Iowa, cultivating that new field to gather sheaves for the garner of God. Though advanced in years his ardor and love for the work has not abated. The Lord is with him in spirit and truth, while he works, watches and waits for his coming in person and in glory.

UNCERTAIN SOUNDS OF THE WAR TRUMPETS.

Soon after the published lectures of Mr. Miller appeared, a copy fell into the hands of the editor of the "Boston Daily Times," and the most of the lectures were republished in that paper, and thus they obtained quite an extensive reading. Rev. Ethan Smith thought something must be done to counteract their influence, and furnished two letters, advocating that the 2300 days of Dan. viii. 14, ended in 1819, when the Greek revolution began its operations against the Mahommedans. He denied that the little horn of Dan. viii. was Rome, and applied it to Mahommedanism. He then denied the connection between the 2300 days and the 70 weeks. He was more logical than some, for if he allowed that the 9th of Daniel was an explanation of the 8th, then the little horn must be Rome, and not Mahomet, for it is clearly shown that the people of the prince who came after the Messiah was cut off, and "destroyed the city and the sanctuary," were the Romans.

Rev. David Campbell entered upon an effort and soon produced a book, which we have elsewhere noticed. He followed mainly in the track of Mr. Smith, but varied enough to demolish him, and give the trumpet an uncertain sound. Mr. C. contended that the little horn of Dan. viii. was Mahommedanism; and then adopted Dan. ix. as the key to Dan. viii. Mr. Shimeal, in a work since published, fell into the same singular inconsistency. All critical readers could see the folly of these men, and their efforts went for nothing, except among those who knew nothing of history. But this is a large class and easily acted upon by popular men.

The effort of Dr. Dowling followed, with a sound more strange still, and while it pleased the Roman Catholics and careless Protestants, who did not wish the Lord to come, and furnished counterfeit currency for editors and time-serving ministers to palm off upon their patrons; the work was laughed at by all careful scholars. He claimed that Antiochus Epiphanes, a Syrian king, was symbolized by the little horn of Dan. viii. He then reckoned the 2300 days as half days, and called them 1150 literal days, which he finally claimed to be literally fulfilled in about 55 literal days.

This work was briefly reviewed by Mr. Miller, and afterwards more fully by J. Litch, in pamphlet form, and widely circulated.

The efforts of Dr. Chase were reviewed by Eld. A. Hale, and will appear in another place. "The lectures" of Dr. Hamilton "on Millerism," the "two discourses" of Dr. Jarvis, the work of J.T. Hinton, of Prof. Stowe, D. D., of Prof. E. Pond (who said "Millerism is of the devil"), of Dr. Weeks, of Prof. Bush, and others, will be found noticed in a summary by Mr. S. Bliss, where it can be seen that these champions did a greater work of slaughter among themselves than among Adventists, each contradicting and refuting the expositions of their fellow-helpers. These writings and discourses, though wanting in facts and theological merits, and worthless to Bible scholars, had the tendency to abuse the minds and pervert the faith of the masses, who depend on their men of learning for information on all points which they are not supposed to be capable of understanding for themselves. And when their doctors of divinity, chief teachers in their theological schools, and most popular divines, scoffed, and turned into ridicule, the sublime, glorious (yet terrible to the wicked), and all important event, the coming judgment, calling the proclamation of it as an event soon to come, "a humbug," "a delusion," "the work of the devil," and other contemptible epithets, we are not to be surprised that prejudice and unbelief are prevalent.

Perhaps our readers should be permitted to see some specimens of the effort of the renowned teacher of Andover theology,—Prof. Stuart. His work to overthrow the theory that the Lord was about to come, (?) nay, that he is to return ever, is dead and out of sight, we believe. We will give a few extracts, with a part of

ELD. J. LITCH'S REVIEW OF PROF. STUART.

Mr. Litch says of the book, "While we acknowledge its excellence, in the general principles which it lays down, and which the author seems to have disregarded entirely, so far as the application of them is attempted, we cannot but regard it in its expository character, as utterly unworthy a Christian. One considerable objection to it, if there were no others, is this: The *date* which he gives to the book of Revelation, *destroys its character as a prophecy.* He has noticed (page 91), the charge of Porphyry against the prophecy of Daniel, that it was written *after the events took place.* If

17

Porphyry had preferred the charge against the Revelator, the Professor would have gone very far in sustaining the infidel, and in proving the truth of his charge. We do not refer here to the fact that the authorities most worthy of being considered, place the banishment of John under Domitian, and date the prophecy accordingly in A. D. 95—97, a fact which we should have supposed worthy of a "hint," at least, from one so remarkable for his "modesty" and concern for "the reproach of the church." But according to the Professor himself, "the *leading* and *essential* parts of the book" may certainly be as much history as prophecy.

Here is the clue to his date of the communication to John:—

> "It was only *after the Roman army was in Palestine, and had* BEGUN THEIR TASK, *that the time* (when Jerusalem was to be destroyed), *was* DECLARED TO JOHN. Rev. xi. 2." (P. 144.)

Was the Professor "inspired to explain" this item of the prophecy? or is it "conceit and conjecture?" or, further, a specimen of "theological romance?"

We may learn the more definite date from the following:—

> "The time when the imperial power of Rome, *i. e.*, Nero, made a formal declaration of war against Judea, and commissioned Vespasian and his son to execute his hostile determination, may be fairly taken as the *terminus a quo* of the Jewish war. . . . This commission appears to have been given *in the latter part of the winter of A. D. 67.*" (Page 117.)

How long "after" this, the communication was made "to John," the Professor does not inform us.

But "the great and leading event of the writer" of the Revelation, according to our Professor, was "the end of Nero's life and persecution," which, *i. e.*, the persecution he supposes to be "the sum of Rev. xi." and also of the 12th, 13th, and 17th chapters in particular (pages 115—129). This "great and leading event" is thus recorded:—

> "Turn we now to the pages of history, and we shall find that Nero commenced his horrible persecutions of Christians about the middle, or in the latter part of Nov. A. D. 64. All agree that this persecution ended immediately on the death of Nero; and this took place on the day that Galba entered Rome and was proclaimed emperor, *i. e.*, on the 9th of June, A. D. 68." (Page 127.)

As to anything that is said by John or the Professor, then, "the great and leading event" of the prophecy—"the end of Nero's life and persecution"—"was declared to John *after the Roman army was in Palestine, and* HAD BEGUN THEIR TASK;" (they were "*not ready to march upon Judea* from Antioch until some time in the month of May, A. D. 67"), and "the end of Nero's life" "*took place* on the 9th of June, A. D. 68."

But you may reply, "It is possible the book of Revelation *may* be prophecy, in 'its *essential* parts,' even allowing the matter to stand as the Professor has arranged it.—And perhaps our champion could show you that John had the parts of the book communicated to him at different times."

We do not deny that it *may be prophecy*, on his theory, but the Porphyrys of our day are not such "FIRST *of April men*" (see "Hints" p. 173), as to feel that there is any necessity for *them* to labor in undermining the argument from prophecy in favor of Christianity, when the argument is modified so much to their satisfaction by a learned defender of the faith. And that the Professor ever supposed that the different "parts," of the book were given "to John" at different times, it is not to be thought of for a moment. "All are agreed," at least, so far as we are concerned, that the book is "*The Revelation*." And you know he more than "hints" that his brother Duffield, for whose views, by the way, we have no particular sympathy, is half a "*barbarian*," because he "quotes this book by a new title, viz., *Revelation*" (p. 170). No, no. It is an "august drama," with its "prologue," and "epilogue," and "catastrophes," and "the person he introduces upon the scene," etc. It is "*The Revelation*," all given at one time, as John himself informs us (Rev. i. 10—12, seq.) in a manner so particular as to assure us, that if there had been any interruption he would have stated it.

Brethren, while we gladly and cheerfully grant that you believe *the prophets*, and that the only question in the case is, *what is the true interpretation?* we beg of you not to do us the injustice to expect that we shall be affected by any "Hints on Interpretation," which open the way for a suspicion that this portion of the word of God *is* prophecy.

But the difficulties multiply as we advance in the Professor's "straight and simple path." Admitting it to be possible, that he could, in his way, make it appear that "the *leading* and *essential* parts of the book" are "properly *prediction*," we confess we do not see, as the Professor appears to, such a wonderful adaptation of "the writer" to his design.

"It lies upon the face of the Apocalypse, from beginning to end, *that it was written in the midst of a bitter and bloody persecution of the church.* The writer himself is in exile, "on account of the word of God and the testimony of Jesus," Rev. i. 9; and the persons whom he addresses are exposed, or speedily to be exposed, to all the hardships, perils, and temptations, which result from persecution. Of course his object is to guard, to guide, to fortify, and to console Christians in such circumstances; and never did a writer cleave more fully to his purpose, or execute it more effectually." "The great and leading event, however, which the writer had particularly in view, viz., the end of Nero's life and persecution, was to take place *speedily.*" (Pp. 109, 129.)

Let it here be noted, 1. That "the writer himself is in exile." 2. That "the exact time" of "the end of Nero's life and persecution" was not "declared to John" until "after the Roman army was in Palestine and had begun their task, and that they were not ready to march from Antioch upon Judea, until some time in the month of May, A. D. 67; and, 3. That the end of Nero's life and persecution took place on the 9th of June, A. D. 68."

Now these queries arise:—Do the "facts of history" show that John was allowed to leave his "exile" in Patmos, to *deliver* his "book" before "the end of Nero's life and persecution," in order "to guard, to guide," &c.?—or that there was time, "after the Romans had began their task," for John to *send* his book to "the persons whom he addresses," before "the event," which "ended the persecution, took place?" If not, "must we involve John" or the Professor "in the charge of having failed to execute his purpose, or of having executed it in a feeble or unsatisfactory manner?" To us the view of the Professor is very "unsatisfactory," particularly when we call to mind that impartial witnesses testify that "the Romans" were extremely reluctant to "enter upon their task," and that the Revelation was not known to the church before A. D. 95—97; while in the case of your champion, as you must be fully aware, there is no concealment of *partiality*, and that his work is by no means to be considered any *better* than a "theological romance."

A still greater objection remains. This "beast" of a "Nero!" *Is* he dead, or is he *not* dead? "But, trifling apart (and in fact these matters are too grave to trifle with, when one can help it), what are we now to say?" For "if philology is to be trusted," and "the common laws of language are not to be set aside," it is just as certain as that Professor S. is right in his "interpretation" of "the beast," that the prediction of "the soothsayers" and "the Sibylline Oracles," to whom John is assumed to have accommodated his prophecy, were fulfilled, and Nero was alive and at his work of persecution *two years*, at least, after the above date of his death. "The beast" is thus interpreted:—

"Who this beast was, we cannot, after the explanations given in Rev. xvii., well doubt. *The persecuting power of imperial pagan Rome, and specially that power as exercised by* NERO, is, beyond all reasonable question, symbolized by the beast described in Rev. xiii. 3, seq. . . . Whenever the *beast* is distinguished from the seven heads, it then is employed as a *generic* symbol of the imperial power; but when particular and specific actions or qualities of a personal and distinctive nature are predicated of the beast, it designates the imperial power is individually exercised, e. g. by Nero: That Nero was in the exercise of his power when John wrote the Apocalypse, seems to be quite plain from Revelation xvii. 10. 'Five [kings] are fallen; one is; the other has not yet come, but when he shall come, he will continue but a short time. The *five fallen* are Julius Cæsar, Augustus, Tiberius, Caligula, and Claudius. Of course *Nero* is the sixth; and he is therefore the one *who now is*.' . . . But there are other things in the Apocalypse which serve also to characterize Nero, so as hardly to leave room for mistake. Thus, in chap. xiii. 3: '[I saw] one of his heads [viz. of the beast] as it were smitten unto death; and his deadly wound was healed. . . . It was PREDICTED by SOOTHSAYERS of Nero, early in his reign, that he would be deprived of his office, flee his country, go to the East, and there recover dominion, expecially in Palestine. . . In consequence of this, the great mass of the community, at that period, do not appear to have believed in the reality of Nero's death at the time when he was assassinated. . . . ***Passages in abundance are to be found in parts of the*** SIBYLLINE ORACLES, some of which were written about A. D. 80, and others early in the second century, which show most plainly how vivid the persuasion was, that Nero would again make his appearance, notwithstanding his apparently deadly wound. . . . If the reader is satisfied, with me, that John might describe Nero in this way, it will be easy to show him how well the description comports with the substance of the COMMON RUMOR. According to this, Nero was to be assassinated, and to receive a wound apparently deadly, and yet to recover from it. So says Rev. xiii. 3, 'One of the heads [i. e. Nero] was smitten as it were unto death, and yet his deadly wound was healed.' What can be more exact? . . . COMMON REPORT made Nero, after reigning a while, to disappear for some time, then to make his appearance again, as if he had come up from the regions of the dead, and finally to perish. So Rev. xvii. 8, 'The beast which thou sawest, was, and is not, and will come up from the abyss [the world of the dead, or the grave], and go to destruction.' . . . Enough to show the probability, I might almost say the certainty, that Nero is aimed at in this part of the Apocalypse. This supposed, all the difficulties of the writer's language appear to be solved, and everything moves on harmoniously." (Pp. 120—127.)

We mean to place the Professor's view in its true light, though we have not room to quote farther. And this, be it remembered, is the man who complains of other expositors in this language:—

"But the advocates of double sense have brought us into company with the interpreters of enigmas, charades, conundrums, and heathen oracles of *double entendre*, and invited us to keep pace with them."

But to return. If the Professor is right—and this beast was Nero,—he was alive after A. D. 68. In the history of the witnesses, Rev. xi., it is predicted, verse 7:—"And when they shall have *finished their testimony*, the *beast that ascendeth out of the bottomless* pit shall make war against them, and shall overcome them, *and kill them*." Who were these witnesses? Here is the "interpretation:"—

"The sum of Rev. xi., is, then, that the Romans would invade and tread down Palestine *for three and a half years*, and that Christians, *during that period*, would be bitterly persecuted and slain." . . . "Although the great mass of Christians fled from before them (the Zealot-party), and the Romans, so as to save their lives, yet all did not and could not retreat. Many remained in their country, faithful confessors of Christianity even unto death. Against these *witnesses* (see Rev. xi. 3) or martyrs, the great body of the Jews are represented as arraying themselves, in Rev. xi. 3—12, and as persecuting them unto death. For a while, the miraculous powers of some of the Christian teachers overawed their malignant enemies, Rev. xi. 5, 6. But at last the faithful witnesses were destroyed. *The period of consummating their destruction* is limited, however, *in the same manner as that of the subjugation of Palestine*." (Pp. 118, 119.)

When did this "period" terminate? Here is the "history."

"Let us now resort to history, and see what the result of an inquiry respecting *facts* will be. . . . If we *suppose* now that the former part of February, A. D. 67, was the month when war was declared, or the commission made out, we shall find that three years and six months elapsed between this period and the taking of Jerusalem and destroying it, on the 10th of Aug. A. D. 70." (Pp. 116, 117.)

Now this is a plain case. By all "*the common laws of language*," and keeping in view "the *generic*" and "the *specific*" properties of the beast, as defined by our Professor, "if his philology is to be trusted," this beast who slays the witnesses, *must be Nero*. And they were not slain, according to his own showing, until "A. D. 70." *Ergo*, was not Nero, who died A. D. 68, alive A. D. 70?

His "path is straight and simple," and "all moves on harmoniously," as he says; but to us there is an "*enigma*" somewhere. Is it to be ascribed to John or the "expositor?" Who can tell? If we suppose "the soothsayers, John," & Co. were right in their "predictions," and that Nero had ascended out of the bottomless pit, it would not only spoil the claim of the former to the prophetic character, but it would place them in a worse light than to call them "first of April men;" for, according to our author, they went on *pre*-dicting his return long after "A. D. 70." If we suppose he might here have had in mind "the great body of the Jews," of whom he speaks, as the beast, that would place him among "the *double sense* expositors." And Nero himself, with all the monsters of the Apocalypse, as abominations, in his estimation, are not to be compared with them. That would never do.

If we suppose, again, in violation of all "the rules of language" and "logic," that "the *genera*" may possess all the properties of *the species*, and that the Professor committed a slight fault in his zoölogical arrangement, still, "*the generic*" interpretation will not clear the "path." Because the "expositor" has not *assumed* nor *discovered* that the soothsayers or John predicted that "*the empire*" was to "go into the bottomless pit," which it must do in order to "*ascend* out of" it; nor is there any "history," "report," or "rumor" brought forward to show that any event of that kind "took place" at that time.

"What shall we say?" Is it to be said of this "*sober*" and "intellectual" "expositor" as he says of others, "where the reins are given without check to fancy and imagination, difficulties of this kind are *leaped over* instead of being removed?"

What then can be done? Not to commit the profanation of calling in the aid of "the interpreters of enigmas, charades, conundrums, and heathen oracles," is any help to be obtained from "philology—hermeneutics—exegesis—enlightened criticism—theological acumen—lexicons—grammars—vernacular power over language—*usus loquendi*—rationalism or intellectualism, as the *Supreme Court?*" Or must we set these all down as nothing more than

"GREAT SWELLING WORDS OF VANITY"

in the case? Or shall we, giving a "double sense" to his own words, allow that "the whole subject *is* at *rest?*" Yes, verily. For he has told us, and we fully believe it—"*No principles of hermaneutics* CAN BE SOUND, *which makes the Bible* CONTRADICT ITSELF."

It would occupy too much of our time and room to notice in detail, all the half quoted, and of course, unfairly quoted portions of the word of God in the Professor's work, with the "bold" and impious assumptions, in plain contradiction of the Bible, and of his own laws of interpretation, as applied when these assumptions are not in view. We must, however, notice one item in his "scheme of interpretation," which will show at once how readily his "taste" and "presumption" can "set aside" the testimony of God, where, as he confesses, the laws of interpretation forbid it. He says, p. 134:—

"The assumption so often made, that *the end of the world* is immediately to follow the overthrow of Gog and Magog, is by no means certain, nor even at all probable."

It is not improbable that our readers may here ask, Does the Professor consider it by any "means certain, or even at all probable," that "*the end of the world*" is *ever* to "follow the overthrow of Gog and Magog?" or to come at all. That is a difficult question to settle. We can tell you what *he says*, p. 181:—

"Paul puts the resurrection of saints at *the end of the world*, 1 Cor. xv. 24. 'Then *cometh* the end, when he shall have delivered up the kingdom to God, even the Father; when he shall have put down all rule, and all authority, and power.'"

Again, p. 169:—

"When the great period of man's probation and the process of redeeming sinners shall be completed—when (as Paul says) *the end cometh*—then all will be *restored*. A new heaven and a new earth will arise."

Now, keeping this in mind, mark "the period" which he asserts it is "certain" or "probable" is to "follow the overthrow of Gog and Magog," at the end of the Millennium.

"The thousand years of triumph to the church we have seen not to be strictly universal. *Numbers as the sand of the sea* are still in the regions of Gog and Magog. And shall one thousand years only, of the reign of Christianity thus limited, be allowed for the Redeemer's triumph, and more than *six* thousand for Satan's? Forbid it, all that is benevolent in the Godhead! Forbid it, dying love of Jesus! Forbid it, all the precious promises which the words of everlasting truth present." (P. 138.)

This, certainly, is as *bold* and *benevolent* as Peter's rebuke of Christ. We shall see presently if it is any better authorized by "what is written." He proceeds:—

"Whether we have respect to the millennium, usually so named, or to a more prosperous period still, near the close of time, the extravagant apprehensions so often entertained and avowed respecting this season of prosperity, seem quite unworthy of credit. The prophets have indeed employed most glowing language, in describing the future season of prosperity; and all they have said will doubtless prove to be true, in the sense which they meant to convey. But let him who interprets these passages remember well, that they are *poetry*, and are replete in an unusual degree with figurative language and poetic imagery. . . . . . . Are we to be told in earnest, that men will, at some future period, be born destitute of any taint, or free from any evil consequence of Adam's fall, and that they will be without sin, and need no regeneration or sanctification? . . . . . . A great diminution of evil of every kind we may well expect, when the latter day of glory shall come. But men will still be frail dying creatures, and undergo pain and decay. They will be imperfect in holiness, and will need admonition and correction." (Pp. 147, 148.)

This is "*to follow* the overthrow of Gog and Magog," and yet he repeatedly proves that "man's probation" ends with "the general judgment."

Now, to one who makes such solemn declarations, that he believes "*the Bible means what it says*," we should suppose it was made "probable," at least, if not "certain," that "the general judgment" is connected with "the overthrow of Gog and Magog." What says the Revelator? "And when the thousand years are expired, Satan shall be loosed out of his prison, and shall go out to deceive the nations which are in the four quarters of the earth, Gog and Magog, to gather them together to battle: the number of whom is as the sand of the sea. And they went up on the breadth of the earth, and compassed the camp of the saints about, and the beloved city: and fire came down from God out of heaven, and devoured them. And *the devil that deceived them was cast into the lake of fire and brimstone*, where the beast and the false prophet are, and *shall be tormented day and night forever and ever*." Rev. xx. 7–10. Will the Professor's "hermeneutics" show that the devil does not go with Gog and Magog, *finally*, at their overthrow, into the lake of fire? What can make it more *certain?*

When does this event "take place?" Hear Peter, who, in his argument to sustain the terrible prediction he had uttered in reference to the "false teachers," that "their judgment now of a long time lingereth not, and their damnation slumbereth not," says:—"For if God spared not the angels that sinned, but cast them down to hell, and delivered them into chains of darkness, to be reserved unto judgment." 2 Peter ii. 4.

The testimony of Jude is the same, verse 6:—"*And the angels which kept not their first estate, but left their own habitation,* HE HATH RESERVED IN EVERLASTING CHAINS UNDER DARKNESS UNTO THE JUDGMENT OF THE GREAT DAY." So also Matt. xxv., which the Professor himself applies to the general judgment: "The separation of the two parties—sheep and goats—is affirmed by Christ, to be complete, universal, and of eternal duration"—verses 32, 46." (Page 171.)

Then, "if" the word of God "is to be trusted," "hermeneutics" to the contrary notwithstanding, Christ will say to the wicked, "Depart from me, ye cursed, into everlasting fire, prepared for the devil and his angels;" and then, as the Professor and ourselves are agreed, "the separation of the two parties—sheep and goats—is to be complete, universal, and of eternal duration."

And is it, after all this, "by no means certain, or even at all probable, that *the end of the world* is immediately to follow the overthrow of Gog and Magog?" "What shall we say now to such argumentation as this?" It would be difficult to find in any or all the adventurous works on the prophecies which have hitherto made their appearance, anything which exceeds this, either in boldness of assertion, or in unfounded and presumptuous criticism and philology." Will he too "continue the connection of the sheep and goats for *centuries*, after a final separation is asserted by Christ" and himself "to be made?" Are we to have more than one "*final*" judgment? or is there to be "sin and death" after that, as also during the millennium? If the devil is to be cast into the lake of fire with Gog and Magog, and that is to take place in the judgment of the great day, and this is to be at the end of the world, what becomes of the Professor's *assumption* and *latter-day glory?*

"These are fair questions," it must be seen. Surely the Professor has given us "a new tune on the old instrument," that must place him fairly in competition with "Jacob Boehmen and Emanuel Swedenborg"—"sober and educated, in possession of his reason, and serious in its defence," as he appears to be. "He brings forward, and gravely and earnestly commends to the reception of the Christian public, fancies, extravagances, puerilities, contradictions—and these in respect to subjects of the gravest nature, too—even more improbable and more revolting to the simple-hearted reader of the Scriptures, than the *grain* or the *grape story* of father Papias." "Then our safety lies in adopting and *following out* the common, well-known, and well-established principles of interpretation."

We " have only to add, then, that a man may as well ask us " to trample under foot " the Revelation, " and with this a large portion of the New Testament also, as to ask us to believe in such a scheme of *interpretation.*"

"The one-half is not yet told—but enough." Enough to show that this champion of the anti-advent hosts, who has covered and led on and sustained the tumultuous clan of all sects and no sects, refined and vulgar, in their warfare of lies, and slander, and sophistry, and scoffing, and blasphemy, has given us nothing better instead of the doctrine he has thus assailed.

We might leave him here, but we may be pardoned for dwelling a little in such a case. Though we stand vindicated, as to this particular, the truth of God demands that we say a word in its defence. And what shall we say of " an author " who, " from one stage of development to another, moves on, now vehemently urging the absolute and indispensable obligation to construe every expression," as " bearing its *plain* and *primary sense*, unless *good reason can be given* why it should be tropically understood, and then winking everything of this nature entirely out of sight, or trampling it under foot ? " Out of his own mouth shall he be judged. "*I do not stop to argue with such expositors.*" " I protest against such an abuse of reason, of the holy Scriptures, and of all the established principles of language. That book is no toy for the sport of fancy and caprice."

He stands convicted of having violated every one of his own maxims, and falls under every censure he has pronounced.[1]

PROF. STUART REJECTS THE PERSONAL ADVENT OF CHRIST.

Before dismissing Prof. S. we should allow him to develop his unbelief in the Second Advent of Christ altogether ; he says:

"Christ himself *assumed a visible appearance* then (at his first coming), only that he might take on him our nature and disposition—Heb. ii. 9, 14. When

---

[1] Advent Shield, pp. 18, 28.

he appears the second time, there is no necessity of assuming such a nature; he will appear, *i. e.*, he will give manifest tokens of his presence, only for the purpose of salvation—salvation *spiritual.*

Again, the Prof. shows the regard he entertains for those who look for Christ's personal advent, when he alludes to "early opinions."

"Papias, whom Eusebius thinks to be somewhat *shallow*, seems to have been a pretty full believer in the visible coming and kingdom of Christ."

The feeling he manifests toward the doctrine of Christ's personal and glorious advent, and for those who looked for the event seems to be that of contempt. With a pure faith in the Bible how can we recognize such men as teachers of Christianity? We must be allowed to attend a school where Christ is honored.

ELD. CHARLES FITCH ASSOCIATED IN THE WORK.

We have already copied a letter from Bro. Fitch, in which he avows his faith in the immediate coming of the Lord. This was written while he was pastor of the Congregational church of Marlboro' street, Boston, in 1838. He had preached two sermons on the subject, giving the outlines of the arguments to his congregation; this produced much sensation in the community. The church were offended, and his ministerial associates treated the whole thing with so much contempt and ridicule, he lost his confidence in the system and relapsed into his former views of the world's conversion before Christ's coming. But his mind was not at rest; he was a very devoted, self-sacrificing man, and thirsted for the truth. In 1841–2 he entered again upon an examination of the doctrine of the Lord's coming, and came out a decided believer and advocate of the doctrine. He at once entered the field as a traveling lecturer, and became an efficient laborer in publishing the truth and exposing the fable of a temporal millennium. Being deeply pious, well educated, and a great lover of truth, he obtained an extensive influence in the cause of his Master.

In 1842 he visited Oberlin Institute, Ohio, where he proclaimed the message of the Lord's soon coming to the students and the faculty of the Institution and to the people in various other places in that State. While on this tour the Lord wonderfully blessed his labors, and gave him great favor in the eyes of the people. He was requested to move into that region and labor in Cleveland and vicinity; he did so, and their sowed the word, which was blessed of God to the salvation of many, and the awakening of many Christians to watch for the return of the Lord.

He also wrote some books, and contributed much to the columns of the "Signs of the Times;" "Midnight Cry;" and "Guide to Holiness;" but he was suddenly cut down by death in Oct., 1844, owing, probably, to excessive labors. His sleep is short, for he will come forth "in the resurrection of the just."

> " . . . . by small
> Accomplishing great things, by things deemed weak,
> Subverting worldly strong, and worldly wise,
> By simply meek; that suffering for truth's sake,
> Is fortitude to highest victory."
>
> MILTON.

"TRUST GOD AND NOT YOUR PHILOSOPHY"—MARTIN LUTHER TO MELANCTHON.

Melancthon, one of the Reformers, was timid, and took upon himself the burdens of the cause of the Reformation, becoming overwhelmed by every apparent reverse, instead of casting it on the Lord, who alone can defend his own cause and us while we obey his instructions. He was inclined to make concessions to the enemies of the gospel. He, like many others, reasoned from natural causes to natural results without recognizing that the Lord could control all events and cause "the wrath of man to praise him." When in great trial and frequently complaining in letters to Luther, that his "consternation is indescribable," Luther replies, "as for Melancthon, it is his philosophy that tortures him, and nothing else. For our cause is in the hands of Him who can say with unutterable pride, '*No one shall* pluck it out of my hand.' I would not have it in our hands, and it would not be desirable that it were so. I have had many things in my hands, and have lost them all; but whatever I have been able to place in God's, I still possess." On learning that Melancthon's anguish still continued, Luther wrote to him these precious words: "Grace and peace in Christ! in Christ, I say, and not in the world, Amen. I hate with exceeding hatred those extreme cares which consume you. If the cause is unjust, abandon it; if the cause is just, why should we belie the promises of him who commands us to sleep without fear? Can the devil do more than kill us? Christ will not be wanting to the work of justice and truth. He lives; what fear, then, can we have? God is powerful to upraise his cause if it is overthrown; to make it proceed if it remains motionless; and if we are not worthy of it, he will do it by others."

"I have received your 'Apology,' and I cannot understand what you mean, when you ask what we must concede to the Papists. We have already conceded too much. Night and day I meditate on this affair, turning it over and over, perusing all Scripture, and the certainty of the truth of our doctrine continually increases in my mind. With the help of God, I will not permit a single letter of all that we have said to be torn from us. The issue of this affair torments you, because you cannot understand it. But if you could, I would not have the least share in it. God has put it in a 'common place,' that you will not find either in your rhetoric or in your philosophy: that place is called Faith. It is that in which subsist all things that we can neither understand nor see. Whoever wishes to touch them, as you do, will have tears for his sole reward.

"If Christ is not with us, where is he in the whole universe? If we are not the church, where, I pray, is the church? Is it the Duke of Bavaria, is it Ferdinand, is it the Pope, is it the Turk, who is the church? If we have not the word, who is it that possesses it?

"Only we must have faith, lest the cause of faith should be found to be without faith. If we fall, Christ falls with us, that is to say, the master of the world. I would rather fall with Christ than remain standing with Cæsar."[1]

"The flinty soil indeed their feet annoys;
Chill blasts of trouble nip their springing joys;
An envious world will interpose its frown,
To mar delights superior to its own;
And many a pang experienced still within,
Reminds them of their hated innate, sin;
But ill of every shape and every name,
Transformed to blessings, miss their cruel aim,
And every moment's calm that soothes the breast,
Is given in earnest of eternal rest."

COWPER.

[1] Hist. of Ref., p. 494.

CHAPTER XII.

A DAILY RELIGIOUS PAPER—N. SOUTHARD—MESSAGE IN PHILADELPHIA, HARRISBURG, WASHINGTON, CINCINNATI—PROF. N. N. WHITING, F. G. BROWN—J. B. COOK—MILLER'S DEFINITE STATEMENT OF TIME—INFIDELS IN TROUBLE—GEO. STORRS—THE EXPECTATION 1843—THE GREAT TABERNACLE—DEDICATION SERMON—ELON GALUSHA—THE GREAT TENT, WEST AND SOUTH—THOMAS SMITH—BATH RESOLUTIONS—ECCLESIASTICAL TRIAL—L. F. STOCKMAN—NEW PAPERS—C. GOUD—ALEX CAMPBELL—WHO IS FOR THE LORD?—MRS. L. M. STODDARD—PROTESTANT PROSCRIPTION—PARSONS COOK—E. R. PINNEY—I. E. JONES—STATEMENT OF ABEL STEVENS, D. D.—LITCH'S REPLY—HALE'S REVIEW—LUTHER'S TIMES AND OURS—DR. N. FIELD—STRANGE UNION—A SUICIDAL MISTAKE—DR. N. SMITH—MILLER IN WASHINGTON—THE TIME PASSED—FUNDAMENTAL PRINCIPLES—MODES OF OPPOSITION—A BETTER CLASS—JOHN'S AND MARY'S—MR. MILLER'S TIME EXPIRES—HIS LETTER—O. R. FASSETT.

THE MIDNIGHT CRY—A DAILY PAPER IN NEW YORK CITY.

A paper was started at 36 Park Row, New York, Nov. 17, 1842, entitled "*The Midnight Cry*," to be published one month daily, by J. V. Himes. The interest had become such in that city it was thought duty to give the public the principle arguments and evidences of Advent views in a cheap form, and thus refute the public slander of the press and pulpit, and get the truth before the people. Eld. Himes engaged the services of Eld. N. Southard to assist in the editorial work of the paper. Ten thousand copies were issued daily for twenty-four days, the most of which were circulated gratuitously at the expense of the publisher. Many were sent through the post-offices to all parts of the surrounding country. Thousands were awakened, enlightened and embraced the views, who had never heard them preached. A new office for the circulation of books was also opened in that city; Dec. 23, "The Midnight Cry" became a weekly, N. Southard was employed by Bro. Himes, as editor-in-chief until April, 1843, and then he took full editorial charge until 1845; Eld.

Himes was the publisher. Bro. Southard was a man of great editorial talent and conducted the paper with much ability; there were many men of learning, talent and sterling piety, who contributed to its columns; a vast amount of gospel truth, with valuable criticisms on the errors and false traditions of the church, were brought before the people through that paper, which was a means in God's providence of correcting and reforming the theology of many ministers and laymen, whose labors or influence are yet in the church.

Professor N. N. Whiting contributed much to its columns and afterward became editor of the Morning Watch, which was its successor.

SKETCH OF ELD. N. SOUTHARD AND HIS LABORS.

Eld. N. Southard was a native of Lyme, N. H. In early life he was converted to Christ, and devoted himself wholly to the work of reform. Nature had endowed him with qualities for important work, and grace sanctified and directed them in the great work of instructing and leading his fellow-men in the way of righteousness. In 1830 he went to Boston. There he took a deep interest in the causes of Temperance, Anti-Slavery, and Education. He took great interest in children. For a time he was temporary editor of the Emancipator. Feeling impressed with duty to preach the gospel he entered upon that work. When the message of Christ's immediate coming was preached he was awakened to examine its claims, and he became convinced of its truth and began to proclaim it to the people. In 1842 he became editor of "The Midnight Cry," in New York, which he conducted with great ability until 1845, when failing health induced him to return to the hills of New Hampshire, where he taught school until his health was so far restored that he could again preach. He then moved to Providence, R. I., and took the pastoral charge of the Second Advent Church. But his health failed in 1850, and he was obliged to retire from the work of gathering souls to Christ, and submit to the enemy, death. He fell asleep Sept. 2, 1852, in the joyful hope of being soon raised from death's embrace at the coming of our Lord Jesus Christ. Mr. S. Bliss gave the following testimony of him: "In Bro. Southard we always had a kind and faithful friend and adviser. His intelligence and the judicious arrangement of his literary acquirements made his services very valuable. He was ever a firm believer in the Advent near, and adorned the doctrine by his life and Christian deportment. As a public man he was more powerful with his pen than voice, and we always regarded him as the best adapted to fill the editorial chair of any man entertaining our faith." [1]

---

[1] Editorial in Advent Herald.

THE MESSAGE IN PHILADELPHIA, HARRISBURG, WASHINGTON, PITTSBURG, AND CINCINNATI.

In the autumn of 1842 Bro. Litch visited Newark, N. J., and gave a series of lectures there, which continued each night for three weeks. The Lord blessed the word to the good of many souls. A company of believers was raised up as a beacon light in that city, who have since been waiting for the return of the Lord.

By invitation of Bro. J. J. Porter, he visited Philadelphia, and spent three weeks in publishing the Advent Message. This was the first effort to introduce the message south of New York. A company was raised up here also, to look for the Lord, and their light is not yet extinguished. After a few months Bro. Litch visited Philadelphia a second time, accompanied by Bro. Apollos Hale, where they found an open door of access to the people for a little time. But the message of Christ's soon coming was unwelcome news to the churches there. "After a short time," writes Bro. L., "the churches were all closed against us, and we were obliged to open a separate meeting or give up the enterprise. The friends interested in the cause came forward and secured a place for our meetings, which we commenced in the latter part of December, 1842, under the most encouraging circumstances. The beginning of January brought with it openings in the country, which were accepted, and the Lord blessed the labor to the good of many precious souls. The labors of Bro. Hale in Harrisburg, Pa., and vicinity, during the month of Jan., 1843, will be remembered by the people of that part of the country while thought or being last."

In Feb. of the same year Brn. Miller and Himes, visited Philadelphia and gave a course of lectures which were blessed of God, and an abundance of fruit appeared as results. The city was convulsed throughout with the influence of the lectures. Saints rejoiced, the wicked trembled, backsliders quaked, and the word of the Lord ran and was glorified." [1] This effort gathered a large number of believers, who united their interests to sustain the truths relating to Christ's coming and kingdom, and prepared the way for extending the message into the South and West. A book-room was opened in the city for the sale of publications on the Advent, and a small paper

---

[1] Advent Shield, p. 71.

was soon issued, by Eld. J. Litch, entitled the "*Philadelphia Alarm.*" About 50,000 copies of these were circulated within a few weeks.

About the same time an effort was made to carry this message into the states farther south, and two brethren went to Richmond, Va., but they found no access, and returned. Brn. Litch, E. Hale, jr., T. Drake, and J. J. Porter, visited the District of Columbia, and made an effort there. They obtained a hearing in the Methodist Protestant Church, at the Navy Yard, in Washington. The Lord attended the word with his blessing, and a few souls were converted. They then proceeded to Pittsburg, Pa. The Lord opened the way, and a course of lectures were given, which awakened an inquiry, and opened several churches for the word to be preached, and some embraced the faith. Others soon visited the West, proclaiming the *Midnight Cry* in several chief cities, and establishing many in the faith of Christ's immediate coming to judge the world and restore the earth, and the kingdom to Israel. The word was received in Cincinnati, and a class of believers raised up, which spread abroad the good news in all that section of the West.

Bro. Litch returned to Philadelphia again in March, and changing the title of his paper, published the "*Trumpet of Alarm,*" a paper containing the diagrams of the visions of Daniel and John, and a connected view of the Advent doctrine, gotten up for the express purpose of circulating in the West and South. Twenty-five or thirty thousand copies of these were circulated. During the same time the word was being preached by the ministers who had embraced these views, and by papers, books, and tracts, in all the Eastern, Northern, and Middle States. They traveled and worked day and night amid obloquy and reproach, with a zeal and energy which astonished their opposers, and electrified the masses. Just at this juncture, by the workings of God's providence and grace, three Baptist ministers, Prof. N. N. Whiting, of Williamsburg, Eld. J. B. Cook, of Middletown, Ct., and Eld. F. G. Brown, of Worcester, Mass., publicly professed and proclaimed aloud the message that Jesus the Christ was about to come in person to establish his eternal kingdom. These were men well known for deep piety, able ministers, and men of learning. They had "been through the schools." Prof. Whiting was master of several languages, had translated the New Testament, which was considered a superior version. The effect of these ministers' confessions was electrical. Many who had looked upon the subject as altogether beneath their notice, began to think it possible there was some evidence to indicate that the Lord was coming. This awakened many to investigate the subject, and careful investigation is sure to produce conviction of the truth of the doctrine. Thus the Lord worked graciously in spreading abroad these neglected, and, by many, hated truths due this generation.

SKETCH OF ELDER J. B. COOK'S EXPERIENCE AND LABORS.

He was born near Newark, N. J., Dec. 18, 1804, was begotten again by the incorruptible seed, the word of God, in 1826; was baptized after an earnest examination of Bible baptism, and having been profoundly sceptical, he became satisfied by "Leslie's Short Method," proving the authenticity of the Bible, that it is of God. Thus he was converted and baptized into a Bible faith—to take it and obey it in its integrity and divine authority. The life of faith and intelligent obedience thus begun, has been maintained on that line of light through forty-eight years. The brief outline is in his own words.

1. At my baptism, after seven months' inquiry, one deacon questioned me as to the divine decrees. The other answered for me, "The young brother has given a Bible reason for the hope that is in him, and that is enough! *The Bible is our standard!*"

2. On that basis I still stand, and at every stage of my advance in "the way, the truth, and the life," I have had a like caution, and a like certainty to my own mind, before I stepped forward to let my light shine.

3. After studying and preparing to enter the junior class in Brown's University (health not being good, and wanting to get into the gospel field), I was ordained in 1830, and made a missionary tour through the west, which resulted in a revival in about every place visited. Thence I went to the "Newton Theological Institution," Mass., where I studied and preached, and with my class graduated 1833.

4. Then, as my zeal glowed, and the call for missionaries was loud and earnest, it reached me. The Baptist Board appointed me to join Eld. Jones in Siam, with my wife, then Miss Susan L. Huntington, of Hartford, Conn.

5. Because of my wife's illness we were compelled to stay in our own country. My first settlement was with the First Baptist church in Cincinnati, Ohio. There I baptized about every week, or month, for years, till my health failed. After a few months' labors in Covington, across the river from C., where the Baptist church of ninety-three members was gathered, we came East. On my partial recovery, we went to Middletown, Conn. (1842.) The First Baptist church was revived; members were multiplied; a new church edifice was erected, and the whole city was moved.

6. Here, under a consuming desire to discharge the duties of my humble ministry, and see the gospel and grace of God triumph around me, and in all

the earth, I was enlightened to see what the preaching of the gospel is designed to accomplish,—to be "a witness to all nations," Matt. xxiv. 14, and "gather out a people to his name," Acts xv. 14.

Jesus *was* "the prophet greater than Moses." He *is* now our High Priest within the veil; he will "come *again*" as the "Blessed and only Potentate—the King of kings, and Lord of Lords," and in "*His times*" execute justice and judgment in the earth. John xiv. 3; Jer. xxiii. 5, 7; Ps. 72. This, in varied phrase, was promised to the patriarchs, set to music in the Psalms, heralded by the prophets, and proclaimed by the Son of God, and his apostles and people. All which is prefatory to the second coming, and great "Salvation," Heb. ix. 28. This "Salvation" is the decreed "deliverance" to man and earth! It is redemption from the curse (Gen. iii. 17) on all creaturehood—all creation! (Rom. viii. 19, 22.) It is "the Restitution of all things spoken of by all the holy prophets." (Acts iii. 19—21.) The mighty achievement belongs not to Christ, or his "called and chosen, and faithful" under the cross, nor in the present "TIMES of the Gentiles," but in "HIS TIMES"—when "he will take to himself his great power and reign!" "be king over all the earth!" Rev. xi. 17; Ps. xlvii. 2; Matt. xix. 28.)

The cross is the symbol of sorrow, and shame, and agony unto death throughout this age, or "times of the Gentiles," but *the crown* is the correlative of the kingdom "in the world to come." (Heb. ii. 5, 6.) He must reign and judge the world in righteousness, till he hath put all enemies under his feet, even to the last enemy—Death! Amen. (1 Cor. xv. 24—27.)

Having embraced and commenced preaching the Advent Message, and a portion of the church being opposed to its being promulgated, Bro. Cook resigned, and went out free to publish the gospel of the kingdom.

Referring to his resignation, Bro. C. says: "It had been a cherished principle of my Christian life, not to cause trouble to the church. But here was an unlooked-for state of things; and as I could not think of 'selling my birthright' at any price, I went out like Abraham, not knowing whither I went, only as I trusted that the Lord would provide, and guide, and do all things well for me and my family and his cause."

The principle which Bro. C. says he had cherished, "not to cause trouble to the church," is one of great importance, and should be carefully observed by all Christian ministers especially. How carefully Bro. C. has adhered to this since becoming an Advent minister is known to him who searches all hearts. We trust he is now seeking the good of all since recovering from the sad disappointment and bewildered state consequent upon the passing of 1844, when some were led to strange constructions of the word and of their experiences.

Mrs. Cook adds the following: "We gave up our home, and church, and income, and friends, and capital of some thousands—all that earth holds dear, —for the Lord's sake. Nay more, we have never taken them back. Thanks be to his name! His promise has been to us fully verified; and the light of truth has shone more and more, and will, we trust, unto the perfect day."

MR. MILLER'S STATEMENT OF TIME—MINISTER TROUBLED—INFIDELS CONVERTED.

"Mr. Miller had not been sufficiently definite respecting the time of the Advent, in the estimation of some who embraced his views. The expression 'about the year 1843,' they regarded as too general. As he was about to enter upon the long looked-for year, he prepared and published a synopsis of his views." [1]

These are stated in sixteen short articles, with proof texts appended, the last of which reads as follows:

"I believe the time can be known by all who desire to understand and to be ready for his coming. And I am fully convinced that some time between March 21, 1843, and March 21, 1844, according to the Jewish mode of computation of time, Christ will come and bring all his saints with him; and that then he will reward every man as his works shall be." [2]

He then addressed an affectionate letter containing wise counsel and caution to all believers, from which we extract the following:

ADDRESS TO BELIEVERS IN THE NEAR ADVENT.

"Dear Brethren:—This year, according to our faith, is the last year that Satan will reign in our earth. Jesus Christ will come, and bruise his head. . . . "And the God of peace shall tread Satan under your feet shortly. Therefore, we have but a little time more to do as our good brother Paul, was commanded, Acts xxvi. 18,—'to open their eyes, and to turn them from darkness to light, and from the power of Satan unto God, that they may receive forgiveness of sins, and inheritance among them which are sanctified by faith that is in me.' Let us then put forth our best energies in this cause; let every one of us try, by persuasion, by the help and grace of God, to get one, at least, of our friends to come to Christ, in this last year of redemption; and, if we succeed, what an army of regenerated souls may we not hail in the new heavens and new earth! I pray God, my brethren, that nothing may deter you from this work. Let scoffers scoff, and liars tell lies; we must not suffer ourselves to be drawn from our work. Yes, the glorious work of salvation, within a few short months, will be finished forever. Then I need not ex-

---

[1] Life of Miller, p. 170.

[2] Ib., p. 172.

hort you more on this point; you yourselves know the value of this great salvation.

"And another thing it is well for us to remember. The world will watch for our halting. They cannot think we believe what we speak, for they count our faith a strange faith; and now beware, and not give them any vantage-ground over us. They will, perhaps, look for the halting and falling away of many. But I hope none who are looking for the glorious appearing will let their faith waver. Keep cool; let patience have its perfect work; that, after ye have done the will of God, ye may receive the promise. This year will try our faith; we must be tried, purified and made white; and if there should be any among us who do not in heart believe, they will go out from us: but I am persuaded that there cannot be many such; for it is a doctrine so repugnant to the carnal heart, so opposite to the worldly-minded, so far from the cold professor, the bigot and hypocrite, that none of them will or can, believe in a doctrine so searching as the immediate appearing of Jesus Christ to judge the world. I am, therefore, persuaded better things of you, brethren, although I thus speak. I beseech you, my dear brethren, be careful that Satan get no advantage over you *by scattering coals of wild-fire among you;* for, if he cannot drive you into unbelief and doubt, *he will try his wild-fire of fanaticism and speculation to get us from the word of God.* Be watchful and sober, and hope to the end, for the grace that shall be brought unto you at the revelation of Jesus Christ.

"Think not, my brethren, that I stand in doubt of your perseverence. I know your faith, your love, and hope, to be rooted and grounded on the word of the Almighty; you are not dependent on the wisdom or commandments of men; many, if not all of you, have examined for yourselves; you have studied, and found true, what at first was only reported unto you; you have found the Bible much more precious than you had before conceived; its doctrines to be congenial with the holy and just character of God; its precepts to be wise, benevolent, and kind; and its prophecies to be clear and lucid, carrying conviction of the truth and inspiration of the Scriptures, by a harmony of manner and matter, from Genesis to Revelation. In one word, you have found a new Bible, and I hope and believe you have read it with new delight. I fear not that you can ever be satisfied with the views of our opponents; their manner of explaining Scripture is too carnal to satisfy the devoted child of God.

"Then let me advise to a continual searching for truth, both for faith and practice; and, wherever we have wandered from the word of God, let us come back to the primitive simplicity of the gospel once delivered to the saints. Thus we shall be found ready at his coming to give an account of our stewardship, and hear our blessed Master say, 'Well done, thou good and faithful servant; enter thou into the joy of thy Lord.' Every truth we get from the blessed book prepares us better for his coming and kingdom. Every error prevents us, in part, from being ready. Let us, then, stand strong in the faith, with our loins girt about with truth, and our lamps trimmed and burning, and waiting for our Lord, ready to enter the promised land, the true inheritance of the saints.

"The fathers before the flood, Noah and his sons, Abraham and his, the Jew and Gentile, all who have died in faith, of every nation, kindred, tongue, and people, will meet to part no more. This year! The long looked-for year of years! the best! it is come! I shall hope to meet you all, through faith in God and the blood of the Lamb. Until then, farewell. May God bless you, and sustain you in the faith."

In compliance with the wishes of Elder Marvin Eastwood and his congregation, in Waterford, N. Y., Mr. Miller lectured there from the last day of December, 1842, to the 8th of January, 1843. On the morning of the third day, the Congregational minister called on him, with a deacon of his church, and wished to ask him a few questions.

Five other gentlemen soon came in, and took seats in the room.

Mr. Miller told the clergyman that he might ask any question he pleased, and he would answer the best he could.

The minister accordingly asked him some twenty questions, each one of which Mr. M. answered by quoting a text of Scripture. He then thanked Mr. M. for his politeness, and acknowledged that he had answered him fairly.

Mr. M. asked him if he would answer three questions.

The minister replied that he did not come there to *answer* questions.

One of the gentlemen present then inquired of the minister why he would not answer.

He said he did not come for the purpose of answering questions, and did not choose to.

The gentlemen then said to him: "I have disbelieved the Bible, but have been one of your principal supporters many years; and, when Mr. Miller has answered so many of your questions, if you will not let him ask you three, I can pay you no more of my money." He added, "I have seen more evidence in proof of the truth of the Bible in the few lectures I have heard from Mr. M. than in all the sermons you have ever preached."

"Why," said the minister, "how does Mr. Miller prove the truth of the Bible?"

"By the fulfillment of prophecy."

"And do I not prove it in the same way? Do not I show how all the prophecies in reference to Christ were fulfilled in him?"

"Why, yes, you do that; but you have never shown that these prophecies were written before Christ; and it is very easy to write a history. But Mr. M. has shown us how the prophecies are being fulfilled in our own day; he has shown us how the history of Napoleon is a perfect fulfillment of prophecy; and I *know* that that prophecy was written before the time of Napoleon."

The minister and deacon retired. The gentleman then turned to Mr. Miller, and said that he and his four companions were infidels; that they had attended his lectures; had become quite interested; but had very curious feelings, and wished to know what ailed them.

Mr. M. inquired whether they would attend any more of his lectures.

They replied that they should lose none of them.

"Well," said Mr. M., "I think I will not tell you what ails you; but, if you will give close attention during the week, I think you will find out."

They attended his lectures, and, before the end of the week, with a number of others who had been infidels, were rejoicing in the goodness and forgiveness of God. At the close of his last lecture, one hundred and twenty persons voluntarily arose for prayers; a goodly number were soon rejoicing in the Saviour, and a glorious result followed.

On the 10th of January, 1843, Mr. M. began a course of lectures in the Presbyterian church in Utica, N. Y., where an interest was elicited which extended to surrounding places. Invitations were received from many of the neighboring towns, which could not be complied with. The meetings closed on the 17th, when forty or fifty were inquiring what they should do to be saved. A good work had been commenced, which continued for several weeks. The "Methodist Reformer," published in that city, announced that "many thoughtless sinners and cold professors were stirred up to duty by them;" and the "Baptist Register" said, "Mr. Miller's appeals were often very pungent, and made a deep impression on the audience, and many came forward for prayer."[1]

SKETCH OF ELD. GEO. STORRS AND HIS LABORS.

Elder Storrs was a native of New Hampshire; was born in Lebanon in 1796. At the age of nineteen years he was converted, and united with the Congregational church. He became interested in the preaching of the Episcopal Methodists, and being impressed that it was his duty to preach, commenced, and joined the Methodist Traveling Connection in 1825. In 1836 he "took the relation of a local preacher, but traveled more extensively than ever. For three years he spent most of his time lecturing and preaching on the subject of slavery, *in a time which tried men's souls*, as nearly the whole Methodist E. church was hostile to an agitation of that subject. As a result he withdrew from that church in 1840." Three years prior to this his mind was called to consider the subject of the final destiny of the wicked, by reading a tract written by Dea. Henry Grew, of Philadelphia, which advocated the entire extinction of the wicked in "the second death." In 1841 he so far embraced that view that he published *three letters* in pamphlet form, which he had previously written to a friend in advocacy of that view. In 1842 he prepared and preached *six sermons* on the subject in Albany, N. Y. During that year Bro. French visited Albany, preaching the Advent Message, and gave a course of lectures in the "House of Prayer," where Eld. Storrs was ministering. He became so deeply interested in the message as to send for Eld. Charles Fitch to "visit Albany and preach on the subject." A *tent* meeting was appointed, Bro. Fitch came "and labored unceasingly and with great power in preaching the coming of the Lord, and thousands came out to hear that holy man of God." During this meeting Bro. Storrs became settled in the faith that the Lord would soon come. "Under this impression, he left his stated ministry in Albany, to travel and preach; and for the next three months, in the fall of 1842, he preached to thousands on thousands in relation to the coming of the Lord."

Bro. S. continued to travel and publish this message for several years in many of the chief cities and towns, and at general meetings, with great suc-

[1] Bliss's Life of Miller, pp. 175, 176.

cess; many were awakened, edified, and built up in this blessed hope. Mr. Storrs possessed more than ordinary ability as a speaker and writer, with much zeal and activity, yet being subject to extremes he became over-heated in his zeal, and adopted extraordinary and unwise measures in the "time movement," which he afterwards heartily confessed with regrets, and took a separate position, distinct from the Second Advent body, though retaining his faith in the pre-millennial, personal, and soon coming of our glorious Lord. We shall therefore forbear further remarks on his views until we arrive at another department of our work, where we may proceed with items of his views, to do him justice before our readers.

THE TIME OF GREAT EXPECTATION.

Brother Fitch's mission in Ohio resulted in the establishment of a Second Advent paper in Cleveland, which has proved an instrument of great good to the cause in that section of the country.

Brethren H. B. Skinner and L. Caldwell, who spent the winter in Canada East, also commenced a paper there, devoted to the cause.

All the calculations of prophetic time were understood to end in 1843. What time, in that year, was a matter of uncertainty. Some supposed one point of time, some another. It was Mr. Miller's opinion that the 70 weeks ended with the crucifixion, in A. D. 33; consequently, the whole time would end with its anniversary, in 1843. But he was not satisfied as to the exactness of the calculation, and hence, from the outset, expressed himself "about 1843." The writer well recollects a conversation he had with Mr. Miller on the subject in 1839, when he remarked that he was not of the opinion that it would transpire in the Spring of 1843; he thought our faith would be tried; and added, I shall claim the whole Jewish year, until March 21st, 1844, for my time. It is due to Brother Miller to make this statement, because it has been said so frequently that he has changed the time. It is not so. True, he never publicly defined what he called 1843, until the winter of the year commenced, and so many fixed on its earlier parts as the terminus, that it became necessary to do so, in order to clear himself of their positions and responsibilities.

FEBRUARY—THE TAKING OF ROME.

The earliest date fixed upon by any of the Adventists as a probable time for the Lord's coming, was February 10th, forty-five years from the time the French army took Rome, in 1798. The next point, and the one which was thought the most probable, was the 15th of February, the anniversary of the abolition of the papal government, and the erection of the Roman Republic. Viewing this to be the termination of the 1290 days of Daniel xii. 11, they believed 45 years more would terminate the 1335 days of verse 12.

Accordingly expectation with many was on tip-toe, fully believing that the great day of the Lord would then break upon the world. Nor were such anticipations entirely without reason. The event which had marked that day, forty-five years previously, was of such a character as to warrant such an expectation. So far from condemning those who thus looked and expected the coming of the Lord, they are rather to be commended. Better, far better, to expect him, and be disappointed a thousand times, than to have him come in an unexpected and unprepared moment. 'Twas greatly wise, therefore, to expect and be prepared for the event, at the earliest possible point, where there was a probability of the ending of the periods.

Those periods came and passed with no unusual occurrence. As soon as they had gone by, a flood of scoffing, reviling and persecution burst forth, not from the infidel world, so much, but from the professed friends of the Saviour; the most idle and foolish stories of ascension robes, and going out into the grave yards to watch, going to the tops of houses, &c., &c.; these were repeated again and again, both from pulpit and press, until the public were, many of them at least, almost persuaded to believe them true.

How, or where they originated, except in willful falsehood, we cannot devise. Some of the reports of that character, we happen to know, originated with professed ministers of the gospel, who gave date and place, when there was not *a word* of truth in the whole story. Others must have originated in a similar way.

The effect of this disappointment on the believers in the Lord's coming, instead of shaking their confidence in the truth of the Bible, or the doctrine of Christ's speedy appearing, rather settled them in the belief, and rendered them less effervescent, but more confirmed and disposed patiently to watch. Few, if any, were so much shaken by the passing of that time, as to go back and give up the doctrine.

SECOND POINT—THE FOURTEENTH OF APRIL.

The 15th of February past, the next epoch which presented itself as a leading point of time, was the Passover, the season of the year in which the crucifixion took place. This was looked upon by many as being a strongly marked era,—1. Because it was on that occasion God delivered his people from Egypt, 430 years from Abraham's sojourn. 2. Because on that feast our blessed Saviour was crucified, and, as many believed, ended the 70 weeks of Daniel ix. 24. Hence, they argued, the 2300 days must terminate when the same feast arrives in 1843, and the Saviour will come.

The 14th of April was a point of time anticipated with the deepest solicitude by many. They had the fullest confidence that it would not pass without bringing the expected crisis. When it passed away, however, instead of sinking down in discouragement, the friends of the cause held fast their integrity, as a general thing, and continued to carry on the work with greater zeal than ever. Others looked forward to the season of the Ascension or Feast of Pentecost as being the most likely time for the Advent; and they, too, were disappointed. At this juncture, the enemies of Adventism supposed there would be a very general giving up of the faith. But in this they were as greatly disappointed as the Adventists were in not seeing the Saviour in his glory.

The month of May came and brought with it the Celebration of the great religious, moral and philanthropic anniversaries, in New York, Philadelphia, and Boston. Among the rest of the hosts, appeared the Adventists. These anniversaries were fully attended, both by lecturers and friends of the cause generally. The occasions were of deep interest, and gave a new impulse to the work.

The momentary reaction which resulted from the passing away of the month of May, was counterbalanced, and the brethren started on their summer tours with new zeal and courage. The door wase everywhere open before them, so that, notwithstanding the laborers had greatly multiplied, yet one half the calls for light could not be met and supplied.

As the summer opened, preparations were made for tabernacle and camp-meetings. East, west, and north, they were appointed and held; most of which were attended with the special blessing of God on the people, and greatly extended the knowledge of the Advent views. Nor did the presentation of the subject lose any of its power from the fact of the disappointment in respect to time. The same deep anxiety to hear on the subject, which has characterized the doctrine from its beginning, marked it still. Not only in places where it had gained a foothold, but in new places where it had never been proclaimed, the greatest anxiety to hear was manifested.[1]

THE GREAT TABERNACLE ON HOWARD STREET, BOSTON.

Although Chardon-street chapel, in which Eld. Himes officiated and the Second Advent church worshiped, was capable of convening a large audience, it became much too strait for the friends in Boston, and a Tabernacle, capable of seating five thousand people, was projected by Eld. Himes and his society. A lot on Howard street was leased, and the Tabernacle erected during the spring, which was opened and dedicated May 4, 1843. Between three and four thousand people were in attendance. Eld. Silas Hawley, jr., formerly a Presbyterian minister, but now an Adventist, preached the dedication sermon, from the text

"I will overturn, overturn, overturn it; and it shall be no more, until he come whose right it is; and I will give it him." Ezek. xxi. 27.

This was an able sermon on the prophecies concerning the kingdom of God to be established on the new earth under the personal reign of our Lord Jesus Christ.

EXTRACT FROM THE TABERNACLE SERMON.

"As Christ is the end of the law, so is he the end of prophecy, if all centres in him. This fact gives it its character, its interest, its importance, its glory. His work, as restorer of what was lost by sin, is the point to which prophecy directs and holds the attention. But the features of this work are only gradually unfolded; we have, first, a general and indefinite promise, an obscure hint, and then occasional predictions having no apparent connection or order; and, subsequently, others definite and connected, bringing out all the parts of the work, and giving order, system, and beauty to the whole; we have the rough outline, and then the filling up—the chaotic mass, and then the shaping of the whole into order, harmony, and beauty. Often, in the prophecy, great events, though different in character, and separate as to time, are grouped together and presented to view as though really connected. But increased light, arising from additional revelations, shows their true order. Sometimes we have the events properly arranged, without any clues as to the times and seasons of their occurrence. These, also, at the proper time and place, are furnished.

---

[1] Advent Shield, pp. 73, 76.

"But this method is only adopted in regard to the events of the distant future. All the light that is requisite at any one period, is abundantly furnished. The only light that could have been needed, in reference to the distant future, was enough to give form and direction to the faith, and to fix the hope of God's people. And this has steadily increased as the periods towards which the prophecy directed the eye, have approached. The first great promise made in Eden, contains in the smallest limits, the whole truth and history of redemption. The whole of its mysteries, its successes, its reverses, its conflicts, its victories, its glories are included in that single brief announcement. It comprises in miniature form, the most stupendous truths, the grandest displays of moral power, the most brilliant conquests, and the highest state of bliss and glory. The Bible is merely an expansion and illustration of that great promise. It will require an eternity to give us the idea in its fullness, richness, glory. But the truth it presented, like the shapeless and unorganized elements of the earth at their creation, was in a chaotic state. It was needful to give it form, order, symmetry. It was needful to bring out the means by which, and the times and seasons at which it was to have its fulfillment. This is the work of the Bible. But it was a gradual work. Its revelations became more clear, definite, and systematic. Its light grows brighter and brighter to its completion.

"We have now the full plan, in all its parts. We have the events and their order, the truths and their classification. But these are not given on one page, or always in the same connection; and yet, in many instances, they are presented in such succinctness, such order, as to make all plain to the careful reader.

"The text is a prophecy unfolding the order of the most important events connected with the great work of Christ. It is one of the prophecies relating to order. It stretches over a vast space of time, and fixes the mind upon two great crises or turning points that would occur during that period, and the state of things succeeding each. The first is, the entire subversion of Israel, succeeded by a long and gloomy period of desolation and dispersion; the last is, the coming of Christ to restore the kingdom, followed by the millennial state of bliss and glory. It involves, therefore, a fearful threatening and a cheering promise. The first is to have its full execution before the other is fulfilled. For how long a period the threatening has been in process of execution! More than two thousand four hundred years have passed since it commenced! But the work of vengeance is not yet done. The kingdom is yet in ruins. He, to whom it belongs, has not yet come. And to look for anything but overturning, change, desolation, and depression, until that time, is to disregard the Bible, and to cherish expectations most certainly to be disappointed. All this side of that point, will be, to God's people, a period of sorrow, darkness, affliction, and trial; for the mouth of the Lord hath spoken it, when he comes whose the kingdom is, their days of mourning will be ended, and the period of their joys and rejoicings will begin."

I. *The personal reign of Christ on earth.*
II. *The identity of the millennium with that reign.*
III. *The preparatory events of that reign.*
IV. *The privileges and enjoyments of that reign.*
V. *The evidences that that reign is about to begin.*

1. I propose to pass over this wide field of investigation, for two reasons: First, to correct, if possible, the common impression that the only thing that distinguishes the believers in the personal coming of Christ near, *is the time.* This impression has not been made without effort. The opposers of our views seem disposed to narrow down the matters of difference to this one point To this we strongly object. We feel determined that the real points at issue. between us shall be kept fully, and in their true light, before the public mind.

My second reason is, that I may set before the hearers the true grounds of our faith, and the real basis of our hope. Those who oppose us, either deny or disregard our premises; in most cases it is the latter. Where this is so we can look for nothing but opposition. We claim to have a faith that is founded on evidence; and we think we are not so irrational; not so far gone in fanaticism, as to not know that our conclusions are no sounder than our premises—that our faith is no better than the evidence on which it rests. If they fail, or are found unsound, the system must fail, if they stand, it will stand unharmed the fiercest and most desperate opposition. We wish, therefore, the question to be met on its merits, and to have a decision in the face of all the evidences. But a synopsis of these is all that I can hope to give in the present discourse. The point in order is:—

1. *The personal reign of Christ on earth.* This point is vital to the system we advocate. In the system it holds a central position; on it must turn the whole question; for though the question of time should be decided in our favor, there would then be ground for difference respecting the events to be expected. The character of the reign looked for, must decide the character of those events. If it be once admitted that Christ is to come to reign personally, we cannot see how our view of the character of coming events can be disputed. A personal reign implies a personal coming, and the events of such a coming all must admit to be such as we expect. But if Christ is only to commence a spiritual reign, our view of those events must be acknowledged to be wrong, and opposed to the Bible. To this point then, attention is invited.[1]

We would like to give our readers the discourse entire, had we room to do so. This sermon was published in a pamphlet and widely scattered, also bound up in the "library."

---

[1] Second Advent Library, Vol. 8.

SKETCH OF ELDER ELON GALUSHA AND HIS LABORS.

Elon Galusha was a native of Shaftsbury, Vt.; son of Jonas Galusha, for several years governor of that State. Elon obtained a good education and applied himself to the study of law. He was converted in 1810, and united with the Baptists, and soon felt that the gospel was of more importance to him than law. Being deeply impressed that it was his duty to preach the unsearchable riches of Christ; he entered upon the work and preached his first discourse in the old Meeting house, in his own town, among his acquaintances and neighbors. The Lord was with him and the immense congregation were melted into tenderness under the awakening power of the word. He became an able and successful minister in the Baptist denomination. A truly godly man, a profound reasoner, an interesting speaker, a careful and judicious worker in the Master's vineyard, conscientious and earnest, he won many friends to Christ, and gained much esteem from the household of faith. On meeting with one of his class-mates who was practising law, the conversation turned upon the difficulties of living a Christian life and being a lawyer. The friend remarked that he thought a lawyer could be honest. "Yes," replied Eld. G. quaintly, "I thought so and therefore abandoned the calling."

"In the autumn of 1843, Mr. Miller made a tour into Western New York; among other places he visited Lockport, N. Y., the residence of Eld. Galusha, so well known in the Baptist churches in the United States. He had been for several months more or less exercised on the subject of the coming of the Lord, and had given it a very candid examination; but had never fully committed himself to it until Bro. Miller's lectures in the church of which he had the pastoral charge. He, from that time, became a decided advocate of the doctrine,"[1] and continued to devote himself to its advocacy until his death, which occurred in 1855.

He was a man greatly beloved by his brethren and acquaintances; but as he faithfully preached the great truths of Christ's coming, the literal resurrection of the dead and the restitution of the earth, as verities, and traveled and preached them in the surrounding churches, they determined that it must be checked at least, if it could not be stopped. "Therefore the Baptist church in Perry, N. Y., where he was then pastor, expelled him from their communion;" this was overdoing the case. He took no notice of it but traveled and preached the more, for the doors were open for him. His extensive influence, as a man of God, and the knowledge of the rash act going abroad, brought much reproach upon that church. They became ashamed of their abuse of that servant of Christ, and of the gospel he preached, 'and rescinded the resolution of expulsion, and unasked, received him again into their communion.' "[2]

THE GREAT TENT WEST AND SOUTH.

Bro. Himes undertook the task of again sustaining *the great tent*, and going with it into western New York. This he, in connection

---

[1] Advent Shield, p. 78.

[2] Advent Herald.

ELON GALUSHA.— Page 288.

with other brethren, carried through; up to that time, no permanent interest had been created in that part of the country, but from the holding of tent-meetings in Rochester and Buffalo, the subject took a strong hold on the community through that region of country.

From Buffalo, the tent was taken to Cincinnati, Ohio, and a full exhibition of the Advent doctrines given to the people. Several courses of lectures, however, had been previously delivered in that city, and the people were thus prepared to improve the privilege of the tent-lectures. There had also been several camp-meetings in the vicinity of the city; so that a great interest prevailed in the country to obtain light on the subject.

In connection with each of the tent-meetings, an Advent paper was published, in which the main points of the Advent doctrine were given to the people, with great effect.

Another attempt was made, in the spring and summer, to carry the doctrine more fully into the south, by brethren Storrs and Brown. The former went to Norfolk, Virginia, in the month of May, but could get no hearing at all. The latter visited Washington city, Richmond, Virginia, and Norfolk, in June and July. In the first and last named places he gained a hearing; but at Richmond, no opportunity presented itself for a lecture. But little interest, however, was awakened at that time; and Brother Brown's health failing him, he was obliged to abandon the enterprise. Another effort was made by two brethren from Philadelphia, in the lower part of Delaware and eastern shore of Maryland, with good success.

As the autumnal equinox approached, the expectations of many were raised, that the Lord would come at the season of the Feast of Tabernacles. But that occasion passed by with no particular change; so that some took occasion to say, "every vision faileth, the days are prolonged." But the steadfastness of the faith of such as were looking for the Lord, showed that they had not believed the doctrine without investigation. They had made up their minds that the history of the world (as one brother expressed it), was not to turn round and go back again. They well understood that the prophetic history is filled up. There cannot be a long delay before the everlasting kingdom of God will come. Few, very few, were discouraged by the passing away of time.

We have not space for a full account of the numerous incidents which marked the labors of the summer and autumn of 1843. But it must be recorded, to the praise of God's glorious grace, that the work of the Lord went steadily forward, bearing down all opposition, from whatever source.

We were deprived, during the entire spring and summer, of the labors of our beloved Brother Miller, who was confined to his house, by a painful sickness, for a number of months. In the fall of the year, as his health improved, he again commenced his arduous work; first making a tour through New England, and then into western New York. During the eight weeks which he spent in the latter tour, he preached eighty-five times, besides all the other duties which devolved upon him, incidental to such a journey. Never were his labors attended with better results, or received with greater pleasure, than during that journey. "The good seed," "the word of the kingdom," still found good ground, into which it fell, took root, and brought forth fruit.

In the latter part of November, the writer, in connection with some friends, determined on another attempt to go into the south. We went to Baltimore, Maryland, and finding no place open to receive the message, the lecture-room of the Universalist church was rented for the purpose, and a course of lectures commenced. The attendance was small, and prejudice strong. After a few lectures there, the Odd Fellows' Hall was rented, lectures commenced, an interest excited, which continues to the present time. The effect of the success in Baltimore has been most salutary on the southern states. The prejudice has greatly given way, and an open door into the south now presents itself. The late visits of brethren Chandler and Brewer into Virginia, North and South Carolina, show that there is a hearing ear, and that, if time continues, the field will be one of importance as a scene of successful labor.

The labors and success of Brother I. R. Gates, in western and central Pennsylvania, are well known by the readers of the "Midnight Cry." The Lord eminently owns his labors in that section of the country, in planting the Advent doctrine, and bringing sinners to Christ.[1]

---

[1] J. Litch in Advent Shield, pp. 77, 78.

A SKETCH OF ELD. THOMAS SMITH AND HIS LABORS.

Eld. Smith had been an active and useful minister of Christ in the M. E. Church; was connected with their Conference twenty-four years. It was said of him that he had preached, visited, and prayed more, and gathered more members into the church than any other minister in "Maine Conference," during that time. He was prompt, deeply pious, a thorough disciplinarian; spent much time in prayer and study which others spent in sleep; Christ was his theme. Having obtained Mr. Miller's lectures, he carefully, prayerfully, and critically compared them with the Bible, until "thoroughly convinced," as he states it, "that those lectures contained, in the main, the true Bible doctrine concerning the immediate coming of our Lord Jesus Christ." Of the time argument he was not certain. He was a man of great caution, and very conscientious about adopting a point not demonstrated by full evidence. But his faith took hold of the main facts which showed the end was near, and his new experience quickened every faculty of his soul. He preached out the facts which he saw, in a modest and suggestive way, for this was his style. God added his blessing, and made the word effectual through the Spirit, and ninety converts were baptized by him and united to the church within the bounds of "Strong Circuit," where he was stationed in 1842. The next year he was stationed at Fayette, a hard circuit, and was under the restrictions of the "Bath Resolutions." Also, having great reverence for superiors, a strong sympathy for obedience to rulers, and being long time disciplined under Episcopal Church government, he was perplexed, distressed, and crippled. God was blessing his labors and converting sinners through his preaching, even while he was gagged. As converts were being multiplied the question came home to his conscience, Is it right for me to take in and pledge these converts to a church aud its rules, whose presiding officers prohibit, by a law, her preachers from preaching or teaching some of the most solemn and important truths of the gospel now due the church? He prayed and wept over it, and after many struggles, decided to surrender his credentials to the presiding elder, and absolve himself from responsibility to the conference for his future acts, and allow them to take such a course as they pleased with reference to him. He did so, and then baptized converts without pursuing the usual steps to initiate them into the M. E. church. The storm followed. The next conference brought the trial. Bro. S. was exhorted by his co-laborers, with sympathetic appeals, and touching references to past associations, usefulness, and blessings, to "give up the whole thing." He was threatened, by elaborate and ingenious descriptions of the results of leaving a large, popular, influential, powerful, and affluent church, whose supplies were full and at the command of their preachers while in service, and a reserve fund for them in sickness and old age,—to go out from all this into the world in the decline of life, with a dependent family, and be associated with an unpopular religious message, and a "deluded and unorganized people."

These are weighty considerations for the sympathies of a kind heart, and the natural inclinations of a mercenary mind. But the convictions of truth, which was at stake, and faith in a covenant-keeping God who could guide his confiding children, and feed the hungry thousands with a few loaves and a few fishes, triumphed over all worldly considerations. Bro. S. stood firm, and proposed to speak to the Conference in confession of his faith; but he was refused the privilege granted Paul in a Roman court, when a prisoner for a similar offense, to speak in defense of his faith in a doctrine "they called heresy." He could have said as truthfully as did Paul, "All our fathers instantly serving God day and night hoped" for the very things I believe and preach. He could not retract, but he could suffer meekly for Christ's sake, whatever the truth might require. He determined to stand "in defense of the gospel of Christ," and was discharged from the Conference, to go wherever the Lord might open the way, and publish the gospel, and its glad tidings of a soon-coming Saviour, and an eternal rest in his kingdom. This he has faithfully done, now more than twenty years, over a large part of Maine, and in various parts of Massachusetts. God has abundantly blessed him and his labors.

He became awakened upon the subject of man's entire mortality, and the gift of immortality through Christ, early in his advent history. This he studied prayerfully and cautiously, until he became fully convinced that man is unconscious in death; that immortality is the gift of God in Christ, to be received by the saints at the resurrection of the just; Also, that the wicked will utterly perish in the lake of fire after their resurrection. But he did not dogmatise.

Very many of the Lord's children were fed, strengthened, and much enlightened in the Scriptures, and built up in the Lord through his preaching and writing, and many sinners were converted. He wrote a great number of letters to friends, and they were always full of religious instruction. Too mild and peaceful to engender contention, too careful and prudent to strive and wrangle, too well instructed in Scripture and experience to be captivated by every new notion, and too systematic and Scriptural in his habits to be mixed up and fermented with disorderly and insubordinate clans and classes, he quietly did what he believed was his work for the Lord and went his way.

He is past labor, with faculties of action and thought nearly gone, sinking to the dust. But God is his trust, his hope, and support; under the care of a faithful, devoted, believing, though aged and feeble wife, who has, in the true sense, been to him "an help meet" for nearly sixty years. The Lord be with them to the last, and soon bring them, with all his saints, into the eternal rest.

We have been more minute and lengthy in speaking of this dear brother than of many others, not that he is more worthy, but because we have more intimate acquaintance with his experience and many incidents connected with it. Much which we have mentioned has been the experience of many of the faithful and true-hearted, God-fearing ministers who have been fellow-laborers in this work, and fellow-sufferers also. The message of the Lord's soon coming cut like a two-edged sword. The ministers who preached it seemed endued with a power of the Holy Spirit, which worked mightily upon the people wherever they preached. At the time when Bro. Smith was beginning to see and preach this stirring truth, during 1842 and 1843, about thirty ministers in the Maine M. E. Conference were also becoming interested and preaching it, and extensive reformations followed wherever they labored. Elds. Cox, Greeley, Atkins, Hopkins, Robinson, Palmer, Gay, Strout, M. Wellcome (brother of present writer), Shaw, Butler, Bailey, Higgins, and others whom we knew at the time, were among them, and the Lord set his seal to their faithful labors in proclaiming this message. Ministers of the several other denominations in Maine were also preaching it, and the same results followed. Many will not forget the labors of Elds. Frost, Hamilton, Horne, Chalmers, Spaulding, Hawes, and others, who for a time preached this message under the direct power of the Spirit of God. It was a time of general revival, East and West. God's spirit seemed poured out upon the people afresh, prayer-meetings were numerous, sinners were everywhere inquiring what they must do to be saved, and wanderers returning to God.

THE BATH (MAINE) RESOLUTIONS OF THE M. E. CONFERENCE OF 1843.

"1. *Resolved*, that every minister in the M. E. Church has virtually pledged himself and every Elder has emphatically pledged himself before God and his church, always to minister the doctrine and discipline of Christ, as the Lord hath commanded, and to be ready with all faithful diligence to banish and drive away all erroneous and strange doctrines contrary to God's word."

"2. *Resolved*, that the peculiarities of that theory relative to the second coming of Christ and the end of the world, denominated Millerism, together with all its modifications, are contrary to the standards of our church, and we are constrained to regard them as among the erroneous and strange doctrines which we are pledged to banish and drive away."

3. *Resolved*, that though we appreciate the motives of those among us who have been engaged in disseminating these peculiarities, we can but regard their course in this respect, as irreconcilably inconsistent with their ecclesiastical obligations, and as having an immediate and more particularly an ultimate, disastrous tendency."

"4. *Resolved*, that those who persist in disseminating these peculiarities, either in public or in private, and especially those who have left their appropriate work for this purpose, be admonished by the chair, and all be hereby required to refrain entirely from disseminating them in future."

ECCLESIASTICAL TRIAL IN PORTLAND, ME.—ARBITRARY POWER OF THE M. E. CHURCH VS. MILLERISM.

Brother Bliss:—If I can have the use of the columns of your paper, I will give a brief account of an ecclesiastical trial had recently in my case. Of this trial I should not speak, if it concerned only my own personal interests; but I think it involves an important principle of justice, in which every Christian, and especially every Methodist, should feel a deep concern. If ministers and members of the M. E. Church are to be unconstitutionally and unjustly deprived of their rights and privileges—if they are to be deprived of the common rights of all men of being governed by the laws of the constitution to which they have voluntarily subscribed, and that too for no other offence than believing and advocating the coming of Christ in a few months, it is time, I think, that we understand our position. Of the ground of these remarks, your readers can judge when they have read the facts as they occurred in the above-named trial. Being a member of the Maine Annual Conference, I, in common with others, at its last session, passed under the ban of the above anomalous resolutions, put forth by that body.

We would here remark, that the punishment contemplated in the last resolution was administered (and publicly reported through the country), contrary to the provisions of all judicious and equitable governments, viz., without attempting to prove those ministers guilty of any wrong. But of this I made no complaint, but went on my way, preaching as a matter of duty to God and the world, "Behold the bridegroom cometh, go ye out to meet him," until a few weeks since, when I was summoned before a council of preachers, by the P. E. of Portland district, to answer to the following charge and specifications:

"Charge.—Disseminating doctrines contrary to our articles of religion, as explained by our standard authors.

First Specification.—Teaching the doctrine of a spiritual millennium [or a millennium commencing at the personal appearing of Christ], in opposition to a temporal millennium, so called.

Second.—Teaching that the *time* of this millennium is revealed in the Bible.

Third.—Teaching that time to be 1843, of what you call Jewish time—ending March next.

Fourth.—Teaching two resurrections, one thousand more or less years apart."

Immediately after the opening of this trial, it was seen that those extraordinary resolutions were to be *sine qua non* in the case, and though passed by a non-legislative body, were pressed into the statutes of Methodism, to speak alone against "Millerism." The reason is obvious: the laws of Methodism are silent relative to the time of the second advent of the Saviour, and there must be some arbitrary appendage made, or nothing could be done. I here raised an objection to some of the committee, based on the fact that they had expressed their opinion strongly, that the sentiments which it was alleged I had disseminated, were contrary to Methodism. But it was replied that my objection could have no weight, for the question that "Millerism" is contrary to Methodism, was settled by the resolutions of our Conference, and the committee had only to determine whether or not I had preached the doctrine. To this decision I strongly objected, and appealed to the Discipline of our church as the only law by which I could be tried, and as I was charged with disseminating doctrines contrary to our articles of religion, I requested that an article of religion might be shown to which my doctrines were contrary, but the answer was that this question had been settled. The President here had his decision recorded, by the suggestion of one of the Committee, in the following language: "The Chairman decided that they should proceed to trial upon the grounds laid down in Discipline, as explained and applied by the Annual Conference as its acts define." *What* "grounds laid down in Discipline," upon which the trial proceeded, and *where* they could be found, we were not informed. But I suppose the Annual Conference had settled *this* also. The reference to Discipline in the language of this decision was merely *nominal;* for though I was solemnly accused of preaching "doctrines contrary to our articles of religion, as explained by our standard authors," and all our articles of religion are published in our Discipline, none was produced or referred to in any way whatever, nor any reference to our standard writings, either by reading, quoting, or otherwise.

The *charge says*, "doctrines contrary to our articles of religion, *as explained by our standard authors:*" the *decision says*, "proceeded to trial on the grounds laid down in Discipline, *as explained by the*

Annual Conference." Now every man must see the barbarous injustice of such a course, when he reflects that our Annual Conference has no right to make law; our General Conference being our only legislative body, and all the laws passed by the General Conference are embodied in our Discipline, which is the only authority to which any reference can be had (except to our standard writers, as explanatory of the same), in the government of our members, whether ministers or laymen. These resolutions must be regarded as a fifth wheel upon the coach, placed there for the express purpose of crushing "Millerism" and its advocates, and a reliance upon them as authority in such a case, supercedes entirely the necessity of any reference to our established rules, and is an assumption of arbitrary power, which, if carried out, would at least neutralize every principle of law, whether ecclesiastical or civil, and the rights of men be made to depend upon the despotic will of any organized body to which they were amenable, who might have power to carry their wishes into effect. If it be said that these resolutions were not regarded as law, but only explanatory of law, we reply, that an Annual Conference has no authority to *explain law* in case of trial, except when such case comes before *them* for trial, according to our Discipline. For, if they could determine the sense of Discipline in trial of a member some six months previous to such trial, then could they give its sense for any subsequent trial, if time should continue a thousand years. But, sir, if this were carried out generally in our church, what would become of her government? Our Quarterly Conferences would have equal authority to pass resolutions in reference to any who are responsible to such Conferences, and those resolutions, however conflicting with those of an Annual Conference, might, with as much propriety, be made the only and sufficient law in the intervals of these Conferences for the expulsion of such members. But it would be worse and worse, each Annual Conference having the same right, while one might resolve that "Millerism" was contrary to Methodism, another might resolve that it harmonizes perfectly with it; and as our church is a unit, and we should be obliged to be governed by the opinion of one Conference as well as another, we should indeed have laws many, and diverse one from another.

L. F. STOCKMAN.

ELD. L. F. STOCKMAN'S CASE.

Bro. Stockman was one of the arduous and faithful ministers who yet retained the activity and devotion which had characterized the primitive Methodist ministry. He had been one of the most successful workers in the Maine conference, and was highly esteemed wherever he preached, for his holy life and entire devotion to the work of Christ. He had embraced and preached that Christ was soon coming, and would probably come in 1843, as some *thirty others* of the same conference were also preaching, when the "Bath Resolutions" were passed. He was stationed in Portland, where he preached in 1843, until his health failed, when consumption seized him and closed his ministerial labors. While in this postrate and dying condition, confined to his house and mostly to his bed, he was "*tried,*" as above related, for heresy. At the close of the trial he was entreated to confess and retract; but he could not. He was then approached by the Presiding Elder with the intimidating threat that he would be turned out of the church if he did not recant, and, dying out of the church, his widow and orphan children would be deprived of the reserve funds of the Conference, for families of deceased ministers, which would be withheld from his family. This dastardly impious threat did not turn him; but it gave him the opportunity to give the ministers present a Scriptual lesson on Christian charity, which he improved. He was expelled, and within a few months after died in the triumphs of faith, with the joyous expectation of being soon raised "in the likeness of Christ's glorious body."

One of his Methodist ministerial associates wrote his obituary notice for Zion's Herald, giving him a noble Christian and ministerial career, "with the exception of this one dark blot upon his character," referring to his faith of Christ's immediate coming. The above trial was evidently produced as an intimidating example, to act on other ministers of the same views, and it had that result on many of them. They stopped preaching on the subject. Some located, and refrained from preaching at all, and turned to secular business. Those who felt strongly resolved, when they returned from their conference where the above "resolutions" were adopted, that they would "obey God rather than man," and were so stirred as to preach, on their first Sunday from "Whether it be right in the sight of God to hearken unto you more than unto God, judge ye," became quiet after this trial. One of the best preachers they had told the writer, three years after, that he had always had reformations on his circuits before, but had had none since, and that he was not allowed to preach on the subject which dwelt in his heart most,—the immediate coming of Christ. But there were a few who preached it without fear, and God abundantly blessed their labors, though they were obliged to leave conference and church, and go out where there was freedom to publish what they believed the gospel of Christ. We do not record these cases to complain, but to give a true account of the sufferings and obstacles which our brethren have met with in this glorious work. We trust many of the ministry and membership, who allow a few representative men to think and act for them, will not be charged with guilt. It was so in the Jewish Church. The Jews made and executed the laws, killed the prophets, crucified Christ, and cried out, "Men of Israel, help," when they imprisoned the apostles against law. The mass knew not what to do.

> "Then shall they seek to avail themselves of names,
> Places, and titles, and with these to join
> Secular power, though feigning yet to act
> By spiritual, to themselves appropriating
> The Spirit of God, promised alike and given
> To all believers; and from that pretence
> Spiritual laws by carnal power shall force
> On every conscience ——."
>
> MILTON.

A PAPER ENTITLED "THE SECOND ADVENT,"

Was published this year in Cleveland, Ohio, by Eld. J. V. Himes, which added much to the interest of the cause and work of spreading the good news of the coming kingdom, in all that region of country.

"THE GLAD TIDINGS."

A paper with the above title, was started in Rochester, N. Y., in June, 1842, by Eld. J. V. Himes, to publish the Advent Message. Eld. D. L. Fleming was engaged to edit it, which he did with much ability and propriety, until Bro. Himes transferred it to Eld. Joseph Marsh, giving him the paper to be continued for the advancement of the Advent cause. Eld. Marsh changed the title to that of "The Voice of Truth," when he began to publish it on his own account, and used it for a different purpose in several important particulars.

Bro. Himes also opened a book-room in the "Arcade," Rochester, which he sustained several years. Thus the work was prosecuted with commendable zeal in all parts of the country; and the Lord bestowed his blessing upon the people commensurate with their sacrifices and faithfulness.

"THE WESTERN MIDNIGHT CRY."

The above is the title of a paper published in Cincinnati, Ohio, in 1843, by Eld. J. V. Himes, to proclaim the Second Advent Message. He employed Eld. E. Jacobs as editor, while he sustained the paper. Eld. J. had been a Protestant Methodist minister; but professing to believe the views of the Adventists he took hold of the work with great zeal and did well for a while. He was a radical, earnest and erratic man. After the 7th month of 1844 passed Eld. Jacobs embraced the view (with some others), that the door of mercy was closed, and advocated what was called the "hope within the vail," with other gross errors and folly. After that idea died out, he joined the Shakers; he violated their rules and was cut off, after which he turned his attention to secular business with a theory of Spiritualism; having made shipwreck of his faith.

SKETCH OF THE EXPERIENCE AND LABORS OF ELD. C. GOUD.

In A. D. 1835, Bro. Goud listened to a discourse preached by Eld. A. Bridges, a Free Will Baptist minister, on "the thousand years" of Rev. xx., in which the two literal resurrections, and the personal reign of Christ on the new earth were clearly presented. This awakened an interest in his mind to study the subject, and the prophecies which related to the kingdom of God. Having a studious mind he was soon led out into the large field of study upon the rise, progress, and conclusion of the system of salvation by our Lord Jesus Christ. In 1842 he obtained and read Mr. Miller's lectures, which awakened in him a deep interest on the subject of the advent near, and he soon commenced advocating these great truths, which have since accomplished such mighty results in the salvation of sinners.

In 1843 Bro. Goud began to preach the gospel and proclaim the message of Christ's immediate coming, and was soon after discharged from the Free Will Baptist Church, in Topsham, Maine, of which he was an efficient member, and admitted to be one of the most devoted, faithful, conscientious, and efficient Christian teachers in their communion.

With little confidence in his own abilities, and great caution in the work of presenting truth, he has often refrained from the work to which the Lord had evidently called him. But he did not cease the study of the word, and during the last ten years he has been constantly in the work of proclaiming the good news of the soon-coming kingdom of our Lord. And though not extensively known, he is one of the deepest thinkers, most thorough Bible scholars, and profound reasoners in the land. Those who are favored with his preaching are constantly instructed in Bible truth; yet many wish for less scriptural argument and more rhetorical show and flourish than they find in his discourses. But the Lord has blessed his labors to the building up of many in the gospel faith. He was associated with the present writer in preparing the book entitled "The Plan of Redemption," a work of which four editions have been sold already, and those who have read it have seen in some chapters of it some of his Scriptural reasonings. Although once an advocate of definite time (1844), he has since learned more of the nature of Bible chronology, and of the impropriety of fixing with positive assurance upon any definite point for the end of the prophetic periods; while he is well assured that every department of testimony proves that the Lord will soon come, and he is rejoicing in this blessed hope.

A CHRISTIAN VIEW OF THIS SUBJECT BY REV. A. CAMPBELL.

The state of the cause at this time, and the state of mind produced by the belief of the advent near, was very truthfully and impartially depicted by Rev. Alexander Campbell, President of Bethany College, Va., in the following article, copied from the "Millennial Harbinger."

"As time advances, the doctrine of the Second Advent in 1843 gains new interest, and grasps with a stronger hold the minds of all who assent to its strong probability. This is just what we expected and predicted since first we heard its annunciation. Excitement keeps pace with every new convert, and consequently has not yet reached its proper height. The ardently pious and strongly imaginative proclaimers of the world's immediate end, in their untiring efforts to propagate the opinion in such a community as this, cannot fail to influence thousands, and to inflame their zeal to the highest enthusiasm. What topic more sublime, more soul-subduing, more delightful to the Christian, than that of the Lord's glorious return to judge the world, to reward his friends and punish his enemies? Talk they of sublime themes! Methinks the most sublime of all that earth and time afford are the veriest common-place compared with this.

"Many sincere and conscientious spirits are already enrolled among its advocates, and some of them are not only sincere, but pure, and noble, and amiable Christians. These are the great apostles of the theory, to whose virtues and excellences the cause is mainly indebted for its comparative success. Its temples are festooned with Christian charity. Its altars are covered with the garlands and wreaths of piety and humanity. Its priests wear the coronal of elevated sanctity, and its votaries are from necessity all more learned in the symbols of prophecy than those who oppose them.

"Everything in society is now favorable to the rapid propagation of the new theory. The prevailing ignorance of the Bible, and especially of prophecy, on the part of many who declaim against 'Millerism,' and the unfortunate essays of learned men in their zeal for old opinions, so far transcending the oracles of reason and the canons of common sense, have contributed no little to advance into public favor the doctrine of 'the Second Advent near.' Amongst these essays may stand first that of Professor Stuart, whose high attainments in biblical learning I highly appreciate. That essay, already trumpeted by a thousand voices, republished in various forms by distinguished preachers and writers from Boston to Cincinnati,—by the Colvers, the Stows, and the Mahans of this land,—has greatly aided 'THE SIGNS OF THE TIMES' and 'THE MIDNIGHT CRIES' of the new school of prophetic expositors.

"But more than any other individual cause have the profane scoffings, falsehoods, and caricatures of the religious and political press, in opposition to the doctrine of the 'Second Advent near,' contributed to confirming the minds of the initiated in the pleasing hope, and to the furnishing of their preachers with new '*signs of the times*' in arguing the certainty of their opinions. If Noah, Daniel, and Job had reappeared in the person of friend Miller, and uttered the oracles of the Lord, they would have been derided, slandered, misrepresented, and denounced as disturbers of the peace of the world's giddy dance, and troublers of the modern Israel in her one hundred and one fractions of orthodox proscription, just as Mr. Miller and his party have been.

"Another reason of the assurance of the faith in the minds of those who are true believers of the doctrine, is the delightful state of mind into which they feel themselves inducted through the new theory. Every righteous man must feel an exquisite pleasure in the strongly anticipated immediate return of his Lord. What possible event could be hailed with such overwhelming joy as the end of this sin-distracted and convulsed world, and the beginning of a new creation, in which, as Christians, all hope to participate? New heavens, illumined with an unsetting sun of ineffable glory, spangled with stars brighter far than our present sun; a new earth, surrounded with an immortal atmosphere, filled with unfading freshness, sweetness, and beauty, decorated with charms incomparably superior to those of Eden and its ancient Paradise, animated too with the presence of nature's eternal and immortal King and his celestial train, the eternal home of the saints, where 'sin and sorrow, pain and death, are felt and feared no more.' I say, who would not gladly exchange a sin-emaciated face, a shattered constitution, sown thick with the seeds of death, for a spiritual and immortal frame; a shipwrecked earth, filled with unquenchable fires, convulsed with interminable agonies, and covered with floods of water that have washed and drenched its deeply furrowed face with a thousand mountains and valleys, for a new earth never to be trodden by the profane foot of a solitary prodigal, nor marred by the unsanctified touch of a rebel hand, during the ceaseless ages of eternity!

"None on earth are more to be envied than those happy spirits who are wrought up, or have wrought themselves up, to the full persuasion that in one short year, a little less or more, and they shall most certainly realize all this. Methinks to such the year 1843 will pass along with dreams of felicity and sweet antepasts of blessedness, whose remembrance will, in years to come, be as the delightful oasis in a parched desert,—as the vision of a Paul caught away into the celestial Paradise, into the purer climes of the third heavens. And all this, too, without even the parting pang which nature feels when 'shuffling off this mortal coil,' and bidding a long adieu to those we leave behind. For in a moment, in the twinkling of an eye, perhaps during some prayer or song of praise, while in the midst of a monosyllable, one half uttered in time, the other in eternity,—the first accent from a mortal, the second from an immortal tongue, crystallized into a gem in less than time's shortest mark or minutest point,—we have passed the bourn of mortality, and are found dwelling not in houses of clay, founded in the dust, but in a house from heaven, spiritual, incorruptible, immortal, and glorious. And all this, too, I repeat, without the pain of parting from one we love. We cast *not* one 'longing, lingering look behind.' None are left we care anything about. Nature, flesh, and all earth's associations, are forever left without one single feeling that time or sense endear. What a mysterious, delightful, ineffable moment that in which mortality is swallowed up in life; in which we obtain beauty for ashes, joy for mourning, the garment of praise for the spirit of heaviness; in which we part from sin, and sorrow, and woe, and find ourselves at home in the presence of the Lord, in the bosom of his love, surrounded with all the sons of light, with the riches and glory of the New Jerusalem temple, thronged with the great hierarchs and kings of all the dominions of Eternity! Who, of the Christian family, would not rejoice with joy unspeakable and full of glory, that in a few months all this should transpire, and that without the least of all the agonies of death;—perhaps fall asleep some night, and awaken glorified in the presence of the Lord, hearing, with an immortal ear, the last echo of the grave-opening, body-reanimating, soul-transforming sound of the archangel's trumpet!

"No doctrine, then, more cheering than that of 'the Second Advent near;' no opinion produces a more delightful state of mind."

WHO IS ON THE LORD'S SIDE—WHO?

In times of contention and strife among religious parties, it is sometimes difficult to determine who is on the Lord's side. But in the work which our history covers it is shown to those who examine results impartially, who produces the fruits of Christian laborers. While many of the doctors and learned men of the churches were writing, preaching, and publishing their views respecting the Bible and what it did *not* mean, which quieted the consciences of sinners, and led many to think less and less of the importance of the Scriptures, and caused them to become, or to remain, at ease in Zion, those whom they were opposing, and generating deep prejudice against, were laboring to the extent of their ability to bring out the great and pungent truths of the Bible concerning Christ and his great salvation, and thereby bringing many sinners to the cross for mercy. They were everywhere showing the truthfulness of the Scriptures, thus convincing infidels and leading them to repentance. They were sacrificing ease, reputation, association, and all the means they could command, and with it laboring day and night to accomplish the duties of gospel ministers and Christian workers, without salaries or promises of remuneration, except the promises of the Lord. Truly could they adopt the language of the Psalmist, "If it had not been the Lord who was on our side, when men rose up against us: then they had swallowed us up quick, when their wrath was kindled against us." But the Lord had appointed this work to be done, and he will not forsake the servants he calls and qualifies to accomplish it.

During the summer of 1843, a vast amount of gospel work was done by the preachers, the laymen, and the printing press. None of the real believers were idle, and all were blessed. The great tent was pitched in many cities and towns, and many times filled with deeply attentive listeners. A great number were brought to Christ, who found pardon through faith in his blood, while very many Christians obtained light and knowledge on the true hope of the gospel, who had been surrounded by the darkness of false traditions, before.

The works of Miller, Litch, Jones, Ward, Hale, Bliss, Storrs, F. G. Brown, Whiting, G. F. Cox, Starkweather, Fleming, Fitch, Hawley, Himes, Sabine, and others, together with critical reviews of the chief opponents, were being extensively circulated throughout the American continent, in Europe and Asia, and to all missionary stations of the British and American missions, with which communication could be had. Vessels sailing from Boston and New York, for all foreign ports, were liberally supplied with publications to distribuce wherever they went. Tracts were published in French and German languages, bearing this message, and freely scattered among those portions of society in this country. The religious and secular papers did much to call the attention of the people to the subject of the Lord's speedy coming. Some allowed their patrons and friends who believed it, to state their views in their columns, while the majority referred to it in ridicule, and in relating fabulous stories and falsehoods, or in publishing "refutations," "explosions," "overthrows," and witticisms concerning it. Thus, as in Paul's day, "whether of good will, or of contention, Christ was preached," and his immediate coming was preached. Many an one has come to the faith by reading or hearing what was said to oppose it, and written out their experience on the matter since, telling how the opposing elements led them to study and find this blessed hope. Thus, "the Lord causes the wrath of man to praise him." The call for preachers and lecturers could not be complied with in but few of the places where desired. By the correspondence in the "Signs of the Times," and "Midnight Cry," we notice calls from Georgia, Virginia, South Carolina, North Carolina, Tennessee, Missouri, Florida, Indiana, and England. The interest was awakened in the hearts of millions to hear the arguments on this thrilling theme, who could not enjoy the privilege.

Although the work of the enemy and the evil influence of opposing teachers, together with the reaction on the disappointment or error of time calculations, have devoured much of the good seed sown, or choked and withered much of the crop, yet the good effect of the work is everywhere being felt throughout Christendom, and we doubt not that hundreds of thousands are enjoying more or less of its blessed light as a consequence.

SKETCH OF MRS. L. M. STODDARD AND HER PREACHING.

Mrs. S. was formerly Lucy Maria Hersey, a niece of Lewis Hersey, who was a writer of some note on the Advent views, and author of "A Clue to the Times," published in 1841 or 1842. She was converted in early youth and at the age of eighteen years, felt that the Lord had called her to publicly proclaim the gospel. She was a native of Worcester, Mass. While teaching a school in that city she was impressed that duty called her to a different work, and resigning her situation, she entered upon the work of preaching; associated with Miss Sarah J. Paine (afterward the wife of Dr. A. M. Higgins), who was the first female that preached in Massachusetts the Advent of Christ at hand, and she was successful in gathering souls to Christ. Sister Hersey began preaching in New Ipswich, N. H., where a good work commenced and sinners fled to Christ for mercy. Having attended several meetings in 1842, where the message of the immediate coming of the Lord was proclaimed, she embraced it. She soon accompanied her father to Schenectady, N. Y., to visit their friends; finding a believer there who was willing to open his house if her father, who was not a preacher, would talk to the people and give them the evidence of their faith. The people were so opposed to *female speaking*, the brother thought it would offend if the daughter should speak. The meeting commenced; but her father could say nothing. After long silence the brother remarked: "Bro. Hersey has a daughter here who talks some in conference meetings when at home in N. E., and if there is no objection raised by any one present, we would like to hear from *her*." She waited for objections, none were made, and she commenced speaking, the Spirit of God performed its work upon the people, they were melted in contrition. The court house in that city was soon obtained for her to preach to the people, many attended, reporters took notes and the morning papers published her discourses. The house and galleries were crowded and the meetings continued until the galleries settled by the weight of the multitudes. She continued to labor in Central N. Y. for some six months, preaching every evening and three times on Lord's day. Miss H. afterward married to Eld. J. C. Stoddard, and with him continued to proclaim the gospel of the coming kingdom, and Jesus Christ as the only Saviour, until his health failed; since then she has visited several States and continued to preach the Word. She has been the humble instrument of gathering sheaves for the kingdom of God, and is strong in the faith that Jesus will soon return to gather his scattered flock.

The late Eld. Jonas Wendall, and several ministers who are now proclaiming the gospel, state that their conversion to the truth, was through her preaching. This should encourage others, whom the Lord calls, to not refrain because they are females.

PROTESTANT PROSCRIPTION—COPY OF ROME.

"Rev. John Lillie presented (in 1843) his regular certificate of dismission, and recommendation from the classes of the school of the New York Presbytery. He passed the usual examination, which was '*entirely satisfactory.*' He adopted cheerfully the confession of faith of the church; but they then introduced a new rule, and proceeded to question him on a subject not named in the standards of the church. He avowed his belief in the pré-millennial personal advent of Christ, and the reign with the risen and changed saints at least one thousand years; but disavowed any connection or sympathy with the 1843 movement. After a labored effort of that august body, the majority vote rejected him for no other reason."—*Presbyterian Records.*[1]

YET ANOTHER CASE.

The association of Congregational ministers in Vermont passed a resolution in 1843, to prohibit all further teaching of the Lord's immediate coming.

They "enacted that no congregational minister shall preach or lecture on the subject (of the Lord's immediate coming), in any town where the minister is opposed, 'if all the church and people do wish to hear.'"[2]

ONE SPECIMEN OF MANY RELIGIOUS CURIOSITIES IN 1843.

"Whereas, Mrs. Hannah Dunning having embraced the doctrines lately preached in this city, concerning the 'Second Advent' of the Saviour, has been *immersed* by those preaching these doctrines, thereby gainsaying her *first* baptism (in her infancy), and has also communed with them and used their hymnody; and whereas, these are all contrary to the doctrines and practices of the Associate Reformed Church; Resolved, that Mrs. Hannah Dunning be, and she hereby is, suspended from church privileges, until she repent: and notice of this suspension be given her.

JAMES PRESTLY, *Moderator of Sessions.*

CINCINNATI, O., Oct. 18, 1843.

WAS REV. PARSONS COOK A TRUE PROPHET?

This watchman asserted in the "Puritan Recorder," of which he was editor, that "Mr. Miller's lectures were more demoralizing than

---

[1] Signs of the Times, Vol. 4.

[2] Letter of Rev. Lyman Lowell, Signs of Times, Vol. 4.

the theatre." If he meant that they would demoralize the temporal millennium theory and other fabled notions of the churches, the thing which he hath spoken has come to pass; but if he meant true Christianity he would appear to be one of the "false prophets" of the last days.

ELD. E. R. PINNEY, BAPTIST MINISTER, SENECA FALLS, N. Y.

Bro. Pinney heard the message in 1842 of the Lord's soon coming, he immediately examined its claims and heartily embraced it. He was a man of deep piety, a good preacher, a clear and forcible writer. He wrote much for the Advent papers; wrote and published several books, which were valuable, and proclaimed the good news faithfully the balance of his life, in Western New York. He finally died by a cancer in the face; but he died in the joyful hope of a part in "the resurrection of the just."

ELD. I. E. JONES, METHODIST MINISTER OF NEW YORK.

Bro. Jones embraced the faith in 1843 of the immediate advent of the Messiah, and entered upon preaching and writing on the subject. He was a good preacher, and became prominent as a lecturer, and at one time published a periodical in connection with Eld. D. I. Robinson, mostly devoted to the advocacy of the immortality of the soul and conscious state of the dead. He was a good man, but not finding success in his enterprise he joined the Baptists with whom he died some years since still holding to the view that Christ would soon return.

STATEMENT OF ABEL STEVENS, D. D., IN ZION'S HERALD.

In the autumn of 1843, Mr. Stevens, editor of Zion's Herald, in speaking of the causes of embarrassment of *their* missionary operations, gave as one cause, "the influence of Millerism." He says, "It has affected the whole public mind of New England." Again, "At the beginning, while yet but few decidedly received Mr. Miller's predictions, the whole public mind was interested in them. Those who would not hazard a word in their favor still feared they *might* be true. This vague anxiety showed itself in a general interest in religion. But now that the time is passing away, we behold a universal reaction. During fifteen years past there has not been another period of equal indifference in religion.[1]

"It would be useless to enter here into the arguments against the chronology of Miller. Christianity required 4000 years for its *introduction*, and has not yet been in operation 2000 years. Strange as it may seem, that God in

---

[1] This is certainly not correct, as to universality, because the records show that, in connection with the labors of the Adventists, there was a constantly increasing interest and reformation during that whole year and the next, with an increased number of conversions of sinners. That the interest should abate in those churches which had driven out or silenced these godly members is quite philosophical.

writing the book of time should make the preface twice as large as the main record itself; yet we know that no consideration can shake the confidence of those who with sincere hearts, though mistaken minds, are looking for the immediate appearing of their Lord.

"While with many who have not fully received the chronology of Mr. Miller, the vague apprehension of its truth has had the effect mentioned, a larger class, who have no respect for his chronology, have nevertheless received some of his collateral views, that cannot but dampen all missionary enterprise, and are the more pernicious because they will not pass away with the explosion of the rest of the theory. Many, contrary to the most obvious evidence, do not believe in the *actual* improvement of our race, have no confidence in the restoration of the Jews, no hopes of the future whatever, but look to the destruction of the world as the only relief to its sins and miseries. Alas, what a view of the providence of God and the mission of Christianity is this! And how slight the motives that remain with such for the *great plans* of modern Christianity. . . . We confess, that after all the new speculations on these and kindred subjects, we return to the old and clear-headed theologians of the Protestant Church with *unwavering confidence.* We still believe in the predicted triumph of Christian truth, and lament the recent novelties in opinion not only as theological errors, but as obstacles to the success of the church. Ministerial brethren, we *must revise these studies,* and remove from the public mind errors which strike at some of the strongest evidences as well as strongest motives of our religion. We believe the above to be one of the most effectual causes of decline in our missionary interests in the North. In respect to the first effect of it, time will soon come to our relief, and the second we hope will be corrected in the leisure of subsequent inquiries."

REPLY OF ELD. LITCH TO DR. STEVENS.

Eld. J. Litch wrote a candid but faithful reply to the above, for the columns of Zion's Herald, which the editor refused to publish. We find it in the "Signs of the Times," and here give the following extract:

"Bro. Stevens, I see in your paper of Nov. 22, in your editorial on 'Our Missionary Funds,' that among 'the causes of deficiency' you have given the prevalence of 'Millerism' a place. You say 'it has affected the whole public mind in New England.' This is true. You say that even a "vague anxiety showed itself in a general interest in religion.' All this is true. But it is more true that the direct efforts of those who have lectured and preached, and spread light on this subject have been the humble instruments of awakening thousands to a sense of sin, and led them to Christ. I ask, then, if that is a bad tree which produces this fruit? But it is not this interest of which you complain, but 'this apprehension of Christ's immediate coming, vague as it was, still neutralizes the public interest in most matters affecting the future labors of the church,' &c. I will not deny this. But I ask, has it neutralized their efforts for the present salvation of sinners? Have they not been as zealous and successful in their efforts, as willing to make sacrifices, as free from love of this world, and as eager after a heavenly inheritance, as their fellow-christians? Can you name instrumentalities which have produced greater effect on infidels, startled backsliders, aroused sinners, quickened the lukewarm, and exposed popery more successfully than Adventists with Advent doctrine? Did any doctrine ever produce more careful and diligent study of the Bible than this same doctrine? 'O, no, it is not any of these effects we deplore; but'—but what? But it affects the future labors of the church. Ah, that is the secret. It has exposed the heartlessness of the fable of a one thousand years of universal peace to the church before the Lord comes.

"That is a great concession you make, when you say, 'Ministerial brethren, *we must revise these studies*, and remove from the public mind errors which strike at some of the strongest evidences as well as some of the strongest motives of our religion.' Is it so, that after all your labors, all the efforts of doctors of divinity, doctors of medicine, theological professors and collegiate professors, learned ministers and learned editors,—is it so, that these studies must be revised? that they are all yet so loose and uncouth, that they must be revised before they are fit to be presented to the people? Yes, it is so.

"But, Bro. Stevens, I hope, in this revision, the first point to which you will direct your attention will be the solution of the following problem: 'If, with all the causes of death which have been operating ever since the flood, to lessen and keep back the increase of the population of the earth, that population has actually increased in 4,131 years (the vulgar reckoning), from eight souls to 900,000,000, now on earth, following the same ratio, what will be the number of earth's inhabitants at the end of a thousand years from now? How many persons would it be necessary to place on each square foot of the globe's surface, in order for them to have a place here? Now, don't run around this without looking it in the face. It is a simple problem, but it will show you a *physical impossibility* that we shall ever have a millennium on this earth while men are born and die.

All the men and learning in the world cannot prove a millennium of the stamp which has so ardently been expected. The Lord's coming is the only hope of deliverance from the curse under which creation groans; and it is the joy of my heart that his blessed word assures us that coming is near, even at the door. Do not then, my dear brother, do not lull a poor sinful world to sleep with the hope of the future, while the Judge stands at the door. Our faith, as Adventists, is in God's word, and was never more strong than now. And if your confession to me is true,[1] as I doubt not it is, you have good reason to be silent; that is, that you 'know nothing of the subject.' What a confession for God's minister and Zion's Herald.

Yours affectionately, J. LITCH."

"THEOLOGICAL ARTILLERY, PULPIT CAVALRY, THE PRESS MUSKETRY."

A review of Dr. Stevens, by a Methodist minister.—We here give an extract from a reply to Dr. Stevens' statement in Zion's Herald, from a minister of his own church; the article occupies thirteen columns in the "Signs of the Times." It is able and direct. We would publish it entire if space would admit.

He says: "As a minister of the M. E. church the writer of this article has felt as grateful for the privileges of that church, as he has felt obligated and honored to labor and suffer in its service and defense.

"As a believer in the second coming of Christ *about* 1843, he has been inspired with similar feelings of gratitude for joys and consolations of that faith, and impressed with as deep sense of obligation to labor and suffer in its behalf, though his labors and sufferings, in either case, are hardly worthy of mentioning.

"The history of the Advent cause presents a very similar chapter in moral history, to those which have been furnished by the contests of Christianity against the enraged and aroused legions of Judeaism and Paganism, Protestantism against Papery, to which the champions of the moral enterprises of our day feel as proud to point, as they feel grateful for their fruits, or obligated and encouraged to become the instruments of blessing their fellowmen by a similar contest and similar results.

"The analogies in the character of the opposition in our case, and the cases referred to above, as well as between our position and that of the faithful and fearless ones who have dared to stand up against the popular errors and frowning intolerance of other times, are so numerous that we often fall into reflections like the following: When prejudice officiates, truth must be the

[1] This confession was in a mutual conversation previously.

victim. When jealously presides, the innocent must bleed. In our case, as it was with theirs, the opposition is characterized by the same disregard of the acknowledged claims of truth, and right, and duty; the same folly which judges without hearing, and which constitutes sneers, and ridicule, and exaggeration, and falsehood, for decency, and candor, and charity, and truth; the same Jesuitical policy which invents the most glaring sophistries, as occasion demands, and denies the most self-evident truths, even those which itself asserts, and which consecrates the darkest features of depravity, or even applauds the most ill-disguised scepticism as piety.

"One of the most remarkable traits in the history of the opposition to the Advent faith is this: the members of the different branches of the professed church of Christ who have embraced the Advent faith, have had to meet, at least in principle, the same opposition from their brethren which the founders of the branches of the church met from the parent bodies with which they were originally connected, a circumstance which shows how little their own denominational history is understood by the anti-Adventists, or how ready they are to expose themselves to the same condemnation of the persecutors of their fathers."

Scarcely had this message of the Second Advent "begun to produce this 'general interest in religion' than the leading periodicals of every sect in connection with those which were of no sect, or opposed to all sects, commenced a sharp fire upon the 'fanatics' who were 'disturbing the churches' by devoting themselves as the humble instruments of promoting it. This was accompanied by a storm of nonsense, perverted truth, and denunciation from the heavier ordnance, mounted at the theological forts, which are now used for the manufacture and defense of 'modern Christianity.' To this running and random fire from the musketry of the press, and the artillery of the schools, was added the general charge by nearly the whole line of pulpit cavalry, bearing down upon the enemy in maneuvers often as ludicrous or imposing as if they were rallying 'the church' to a last 'mission' for the extermination of mad dogs or tigers.

"The *Orthodox* 'Puritan,' 'Observer,' 'Evangelist,' &c., in unison with the *Infidel* 'Investigator,' the *Baptist* 'Watchman,' 'Advocate,' and 'Secretary,' with the *Universalist* 'Trumpet,' 'Intelligencer,' and 'Tribune,' and a swarm of other kindred sheets—the grave *Episcopal* 'Churchman,' and 'Witness,' with the sparkling and profane 'Herald of Freedom,'—the patent *Methodist* 'Advocate,' with some or all of its branches in sweet concert with the nondescript 'Olive Branch,' and 'Zion's Herald,' with the infamous 'New York Herald;'—all these, with others which we must ask pardon for omitting, led the way and were followed up in the crusade by a series of wood-cut prints in *caricature* of scenes and events which are exhibited in the word of God, as of the most sublime and awful interest to the church and the world. What this 'strange' and unmerciful onslaught failed to accomplish, the schools and the pulpits, it appears, have completed.

"The honor of sustaining this *popular* movement by those who fill the Professor's chair in our theological schools, to say nothing of others who have proved themselves worthy candidates for the chair, is to be divided between Bangor, Andover, Newton, Middletown, Lane, and Oberlin. And who can wonder at the result, since their ill-directed fire has performed this surprising and complicated work? 1. Each battery has destroyed itself by turning the fire of one section upon another; 2. Each in turn, has demolished its neighbor and ally; and 3. All have exploded 'Millerism' and the word of God,—including, according to their own testimony, 'the general interest in religion.'

"If the world cannot sleep comfortably after so many D. D.'s and Professors have proved *in the same breath*, that the state of the world is both *too good* and *too bad* for 'the end to come yet'—that 'the prophecies cannot be understood until they have been fulfilled,' and then prove, from the same prophecies, that the world is to stand for a thousand years,—that it is 'horrible blasphemy! thus to dictate the Almighty,' as they declare Mr. Miller has done, in giving his opinion of the interpretation and termination of the prophetic periods, and then go right on and commit the same 'blasphemy' of telling us how these same periods have been fulfilled, or are to be fulfilled, though 'not yet.' . . .

"This idea of the preface being longer than the book, if Jesus comes soon, is from Rev. L. Dimick, in a book written by him, entitled, '*The end not yet.*' His course of reasoning would have the Lord remain away thousands of years yet, to fill up the book, that it be larger than 'the preface.' If all this has not 'overthrown the faith of' the church and given rise to 'this universal indifference and apathy in religion,'—we may bid defiance to earth and hell to put in operation a system of means which can produce these results: That the old prophetic Scriptures which speak of Christ's *Second Coming*, were fulfilled before he came *the first time;*—that Christ is never to return again to our earth, in like manner as he went into heaven,—and that the resurrection is past already.

. . . "If the effects of this war are not such as the Herald records, if the mischievous cause of the late 'interest in religion' has not been sufficiently 'exploded,' 'used up,' to be '*going down*' by this time, it must live for ever. And we can assure our brother that there are thousands who adopt the exulting language of the primitive church.—'*Thanks be to God who always causeth us to triumph in Christ,*' whose interest in religion has experienced no abatement by the 'reaction' or the 'passing of time.'

"We very much fear his sources of consolation will prove as 'fatal' to himself, as he fears our 'disappointment' will be to us. 'We can only pray that' he and his coadjutors 'may have grace to' prepare them for the worst. 'The effects of their' course are 'inevitable.' *Such* 'revolutions never go back.' What they have seen is but 'the beginning of the end,' even if we should be 'disappointed.' Signed, H."

That a slackening of religious interest and a wide departure from Christ, and the simplicity of primitive Christianity, had then begun to manifest itself in the churches, which has continued to increase with rapid strides and sad results, is true.

The strange interpretations of many Scriptures, the denial that many passages mean what they obviously state—the claim set up by several of these doctors and professors, that Christ would never personally return, and that the people were rewarded at death (as nearly all taught), together with the jesting, the scoffing, cant, and ridicule heaped upon the pious, studious, faithful ones, who were looking for the Lord and the judgment; opened the way for "modern spiritism" and all sorts of impiety. It is the epoch of church feasts, olios, levees, lotteries, and gamblings, which have since been such a great disgrace to the Christian religion, and caused "the love of many to wax cold." See Matt. xxiv. 11, 12, 48, 49; 2 Pet. iii. 4. It was just here that these disgraceful practices commenced to be prevalent, as all who are of sufficient age to remember can witness when they reflect upon it. The present writer calls to mind that the first church levee of which he ever heard was in 1842, and then the Methodist ministry preached against it as vehemently as they did against drunkenness and gambling. Has Millerism caused these sad departures? or is it the result of preaching "peace and safety," "my Lord delayeth his coming?" These are sad items to record, but the people should be reminded of them, and the rising generation be made acquainted with the causes of these evils which mark the last days.

THE ANALOGY OF LUTHER'S TIME AND OURS.

Those who have been long in the work of proclaiming the coming of the Lord, and met with the influences and ignorance of those who stood in opposition, can readily trace the analogy existing between these opposers and the Romish doctors and priests who opposed the Reformers. We give an item of their experience.

THE REFORMERS AND THEIR OPPOSERS.

Melancthon remarks: "We are well aware that Statesmen are averse from all innovation: and it must be confessed in this scene of mournful confusion (in time of the Reformation), which we call human life—controversies, however just the grounds from which they spring, are always chargeable with some measure of evil. Nevertheless it is necessary that God's word and his commandments should have preference in the CHURCH over every earthly interest. The everlasting anger of God is denounced against such as endeavor to suppress the truth. It was Luther's duty, therefore,—a Christian duty from which he could not escape, more especially as he held the office of a teacher in the CHURCH,—to reprove those pernicious errors which men were so shamefully engaged in diffusing. If the disputes engender many evils, as, to my great grief I perceive that they do, the fault rests with those who first propagated error, and with those who now, with diabolical malignity, attempt to uphold it."

But others charged Luther and his fellow-laborers, with all the evils which existed. He was overwhelmed with reproaches—the storm burst upon him from every quarter,—"He stands alone," said some; "He teaches new doctrines!" said others; "He causes divisions," "He preaches heresy," said others.

"Who knows," replied Luther, deeply conscious of the vocation he had received from on high, "who knows whether God has not called and chosen me for this very purpose, and whether they who despise me have not reason to fear lest they be found despisers of God himself."

"Moses was alone when the Israelites went out of Egypt; Elijah was alone in the time of King Ahab; Ezekiel was alone at Babylon. God has never chosen for his prophet either the high priest or any other person of exalted rank; he has generally chosen men of a mean and low condition,—in the instance of Amos, even a simple shepherd. The saints in every age have been called upon to rebuke the great of this world,—kings and princes—priests and scholars—and to fulfill their office at the peril of their lives. Has it not been so under the New Testament dispensation? Ambrose in his time stood alone; after him, Jerome stood alone. I say not that I am a prophet; but I say that they have the more reason to fear, *because* I am alone and they are many.

"Of this I am sure, that the word of God is with me, and that it is not with them."

"It is asserted that I bring forward novelties, and that it is impossible to believe that all other teachers for so long a time have been in error. No—these are not novelties that I preach! But I affirm that *the doctrines of Christianity have been lost sight of by those whose special duty it was to preserve them by the learned—by the*

NATHANIEL FIELD.—Page 315.

bishops. I doubt not, indeed, that the truth has still found an abode in some few hearts, were it only with infants in the cradle. Poor husbandmen and simple children, in these days, understand more of Jesus Christ than the Pope, the bishops, or the doctors."

I am accused of rejecting the holy doctors of the church. I reject them not, but since those doctors all labor to prove what they write, by the Holy Scriptures, it follows that the Scriptures must be clearer and more conclusive than their writings. Who would ever think of proving what is in itself obscure, by the help of something obscurer still? Necessity, therefore, obliges us to have recourse to the Bible, as all the doctors have done; and to test their writings by it,—for the Bible is our only rule and standard.—*D'Aubigne's Hist. of Ref. p. 172.*

SKETCH OF ELD. N. FIELD AND HIS LABORS—THE CAUSE IN INDIANA.

Dr. Nathaniel Field is a practising physician of the city of Jeffersonville, Indiana; having a population of about 12,000 inhabitants. He graduated at the Old Pransylvania Medical School, then located at Lexington, Kentucky. He was born in Jefferson County, Kentucky, a few miles from the city of Louisville, Nov. 7, 1805. His parents were natives of Virginia, and among the earliest settlers of that State.

Neither of Dr. Field's parents ever made any profession of religion; consequently when young he had no advantage from parental training in leading him to the knowledge of Christ. Notwithstanding the want of religious instruction, at a time most influential and impressive, he was from his youth a firm believer in the truth of Christianity; and when twenty years of age made a profession of faith in Christ and united with the Cumberland Presbyterian church in the Spring of 1825. This denomination was at that time quite numerous in Kentucky, Tennessee, and North Alabama. They are Aminian in sentiment but Presbyterian in government. It was under the ministry of Elder Robert Downell that Dr. Field professed religion.

He continued a faithful and zealous member of that church until the summer of 1829, when he espoused the theological views of the late Alexander Campbell. He withdrew from the Cumberland Presbyterian church and was immersed by Elder Zacheus Carpenter, who had also adopted the views of Alexander Campbell, in June, 1829, after which he commenced preaching. In the September following he located at Jeffersonville, Indiana, in the practice of medicine, ten miles from his native place, where he still resides. At the time he became a convert to the views of Mr. Campbell and commenced preaching, there was no organized church of his faith in the West, and the new doctrine was scarcely known in Indiana.

He was not long in Jeffersonville until he got into a laborious practice; but still he found time to preach, and on the first Lord's day in March, 1830, constituted a small church in Jeffersonville of eight members, the fruits of six months labor in the ministry. This small beginning became the nucleus of a strong church. By the year 1843 it numbered two hundred and fifty members. From its infancy the Doctor devoted all his spare time to its welfare, and previously having been regularly elected and ordained its pastor, with his aid they built a plain, commodious house of worship, which it was understood was to be a free house where the whole truth could be taught. It was the pride and glory of the churches of what was then known as the "Reformation," that they were free from all the trammels of Sectarianism. They advocated free thought, free speech, free pulpits and free presses. They courted investigation and claimed that every man had an undoubted right to read and judge for himself. They professed to be anxious to learn the whole truth and go on to perfection. In the summer of 1842 Doctor Field learning that a layman of the Baptist church, by the name of William Miller, was lecturing on the prophecies showing that the coming of the Lord would take place in 1843, procured some tracts and documents containing his views, which he carefully examined. He also subscribed for the Signs of the Times, published in Boston, by J. V. Himes. He soon became interested in the study of the prophecies. At the tent meeting in Cincinnati, in the summer of 1843, he formed the acquaintance of Joshua V. Himes, Geo. Storrs, J. B. Cook, and several other pioneers in the Second Advent cause. Several preachers of the Campbellite reformation were also in attendance, and seemed to be affilating with the Adventists. Walter Scott, one of the ablest among them, preached in the tent fully indorsing the doctrine and the time theory. But after the time passed he never afterward made it a pulpit theme. Not so with Dr. Field; he preached in the tent and has continued to preach the glorious truths of Adventism to the present time. While he believed it highly probable that the Lord would come in 1843 and urged all the members of his church to watchfulness and prayer and to be ready for it. Still he fortified against discouragement in case of disappointment by telling them our chronological calculations are not infallible; that while the event itself is certain the time is not. The result was when the time passed by without the realization of our hope, the faith of the church survived the disappointment.

But the failure of the time greatly intensified the opposition to the Second Advent doctrine. Everywhere the churches were closed against the Doctor, and finally after several years of fruitless effort to reconcile the minority in his own church to even the *right* to teach the coming of the Lord, the mortality of man, the end of the wicked, and other collateral subjects, he generously retired and gave them the house which he had helped to build, and in which he had largely invested, and on the first day of the week, the 29th of August, 1847, he constituted a new church composed of over forty of the members of the Christian church. Many others soon followed, and in a short time the old church was terribly depleted.

As experience had taught the Doctor that oral professions of freedom of speech, that right of private judgment, free investigation, etc., etc., were nothing but words and as unreliable as the winds, he resolved to guard against any betrayal of confidence, and another violation of the most solemn promises and pledges that individual rights should be respected, and therefore wrote out a definition of the position of the new church on the subject of Christian liberty, of which the following is an extract:

"They guaranteed to each other the right of private judgment and the liberty of speech, and firmly determined, under all circumstances, to maintain sacredly and inviolably these elements of Christian union and Christian perfection. They hold that freedom is secured to every son and daughter of the Lord Almighty by the word of God. That it is the germ of all mental and moral improvement; and without it there can be no progression in knowledge and righteousness. All efforts to restrain the liberty of thought and of speech, with a view to preserve uniformity in views and practice, they attribute to the spirit of popery, or a claim to infallibility, both alike repugnant to reason and Scripture. While they claim the right to judge for themselves and express their understanding of God's word, they concede the same right to others, subject to the order and decorum of the Lord's house. They consider it not only safe for all Christians to investigate the Bible, but it is their right and duty to do so; 'to prove all things and hold fast that which is good.' That it is their duty to receive each other to fellowship without regard to differences of opinion. That they shall bear with each other, cultivate a spirit of toleration towards all sincere and pious Christians though they may be in error. To persecute and non-fellowship a brother for a mere difference of opinion either held or expressed, they consider wicked and schismatical. The only certain and Scriptural remedy for error is the truth plainly and patiently taught. They consider a church built upon the proper foundation—having the one Lord, the one faith, the one baptism, the one hope, the one law, and the one loaf, with its Scriptural officers and organization—to all intents and purposes a church of God and the pillar and support of the truth in the place of its location, free and independent of all others: subject alone to the Great Head of the church. That no other church or preacher has any right whatever to prescribe their faith or interfere with their business. All human authority in religion, all ecclesiastical councils, conventions, and associations, claiming or exercising legislative power, they regard as the fruits of the grand apostasy and subversive of the peace and unity of the body of Christ.

"Confiding in the soundness of these views and the favor and support of the God of all grace, they gave themselves to him and to each other in the labor of love and the work of faith."

This is the church now meeting at the Christian Tabernacle of which the Doctor is now pastor. Its membership is about 120.

In 1845, he published 2000 copies of Geo. Storrs' Six Sermons, mostly for gratuitous distribution, besides other tracts.

In 1852, he held a four days' debate on the state of the dead, with Elder Thomas P. Connelly, of the Christian Church. The debate was held in Old Union Meeting-house belonging to the Christians, or, as they are sometimes called Campbellites, in the vicinity of Indianapolis. The church at Old Union numbered, at that time, largely over one hundred members. There were not more than a half-dozen who held our own views of the life and death question. This small element of Adventists—for such they really were—had been annoyed and challenged for a discussion from time to time. They finally consented to a debate, provided they could get a competent man to meet one of *their* champions. Arrangements were made between the pastors, and Dr. Field was selected by the Adventists. The sequel was a glorious victory for the truth. Nearly the entire church was converted, and came into co-operation with the Advent brethren. The house in which they meet, worth $2,000, was given up to our brethren by the minority, who withdrew from the church and reorganized elsewhere. The Doctor published 2000 copies of the debate, of 300 octavo pages, neatly bound in cloth. The debate being reported and the speeches revised by the parties before they went to the press. A second edition of the work has been issued recently from the press of the Advent Christian Publication Society.

In 1854, under the auspices of Dr. Field and through his exertions, the first Advent Christian Conference of Indiana was organized in the meeting-house where the debate was held. He wrote a definition of the position, aims, and objects of the association similar to that of the church at Jeffersonville, embodying the most liberal ideas on the subject of Christian liberty. After going on harmoniously and prosperously for several years, it was finally distracted and disorganized by the extreme views of the age to come. The Conference was generally attended more or less by men from other States, who took advantage of the Doctor's broad and non-sectarian principles, to privately inculcate their age-to-come sentiments, and ere he was aware of their ulterior designs, they threw off the mask and boldly demanded faith in their dogmas as essential to a valid baptism and to Christian fellowship. Finding that they had surreptitiously got possession of the Conference, he quietly gave it up to them. At the next annual meeting they passed a resolution declaring the Indiana Advent Christian Conference dead, and that its effects be willed to Dr. N. Field. In place of it they organized the Indiana Christian Association. They met two or three times afterwards and died out. Their meetings were characterized by contention and strife about points of doctrine respecting the age to come, about which no two of them seemed to agree.

After giving time for the wreck to drift away, the Doctor issued another call for a meeting of the few Adventists of the State whose minds had not been perverted by the Judaizing and age-to-come elements, to meet at Jeffersonville, for the purpose of organizing anew an Advent Christian Conference for the State. The meeting took place at Jeffersonville, May 5, 1870, and was a decided success. The Doctor was elected its president and still continues to preside over it. The Conference has for the last two years met at Colfax, near the center of the State. It steadily increases in the number of its ministers and its usefulness.

From his first connection with the Advent movement, the Doctor has been a decided advocate for order and system in our operations. He has written several strong articles against the anarchical and chaotic state of things which supervened in the failure of the '43 time theory. The confusion and disorganizing spirit that succeeded this memorable period, he regarded as the principal causes operating against the success of our ministerial labors.

Though the Doctor has been pastor of a church in Jeffersonville consecutively for more than forty years, and has seldom failed to occupy his pulpit every Lord's Day, yet *he has never had a salary for preaching!* He has waived his right to compensation and made the gospel free of charge to the people of Jeffersonville, supporting himself and family, in the meantime, by his profession. Occasionally his congregation makes him a present of something as a testimonial of their gratitude. He is now sixty-nine years of age, with a constitution unimpaired, and has all the activity and vivacity of one in the prime of life. He yet looks with ardent hope for the immediate and glorious Advent of the Messiah.

A UNION MORE STRANGE THAN THAT OF PILATE AND HEROD.

A Mr. Israel, professedly a Jew, and Hebrew scholar, published a pamphlet in 1843, the object of which was "to refute Millerism."

He informed the public that it was written at the earnest solicitation of many of the Protestant clergymen of different sects. Also that his subscription list showed that Protestant ministers were his most liberal patrons, some having purchased several copies of his work.

The "Christian Guardian," a Methodist Wesleyan paper, of Toronto, Canada, spoke very highly of the work, recommending "all to obtain it, as it is a complete overthrow of Millerism."

A person who had some curiosity for critical examinations, procured the book and put it into the hands of a critical Hebrew scholar, not an Adventist, who soon found it the work of an ignorant Jew, whose efforts were not only aimed at Millerism, but at Christ as an imposture, and the Christian religion as an imposition[1].

It was suggested that those clergymen who patronized this book, petition their Jew co-laborer to give them a comment on the 53d chapter of Isaiah.

ADVENT BOOK AGENCIES IN 1843.

We find offices established in the following cities as early as 1843, for the distribution of Advent publications: Boston, Mass., New

[1] Voice of Truth. Vol. 2.

York City, Albany, Rochester, Buffalo, Utica, N. Y., Philadelphia, Pa., Cincinnati, O., St. Louis, Mo., Louisville, Ky., Montreal, C. E., and Portland, Me.

During this year the Lectures, Addresses, and chief sermons of Messrs. Miller and Litch, with tracts, pamphlets, reviews of opponents, diagrams and chronology were bound up in 8 vols. of some four hundred pages each, and circulated in great numbers throughout the country.

A SUICIDAL MISTAKE.

Eld. G. F. Cox, a minister in the Methodist E. Church, and at one time editor of the Wesleyan Journal, a paper formerly published in Portland, Me., of which we have before spoken, was an able writer and preacher, and a devout man. He had heard and read Mr. Miller and others on the immediate coming of Christ. He was convicted of its truthfulness, and wrote some valuable articles upon the character of the Millennium, the Restitution, Signs of the Times, etc. But he neglected to preach out his full convictions. He pondered and weighed the influence and present results. At length he asked the Lord to give him the evidence of the correctness of the calculation for the 2300 days to end in 1843. This he believed he obtained by the direct witness of the Holy Spirit. He then preached it from March, 1842, to June, 1843, when the "Bath Resolutions" overtook him; and they did not fully silence him until he was convinced they would be put in execution. He was stationed in Orrington in 1842, where the Lord worked mightily through his preaching, and nearly *one hundred* souls were reported to have been converted. In the latter part of his circuit year he wrote a long and interesting letter for Zion's Herald giving his experience, and claiming that the Lord had given him, in March, 1842, "the witness of the Holy Spirit, that the 2300 days would end in 1843." He thought "the witness as clear or more clear than that of his sanctification years before." It is dated Orrington, Me., Apr. 6, 1843.

Zion's Herald had been closed against *arguments* on the subject for a long time, yet they published this letter, probably foreseeing the fatal results which it must produce (with those who believed in that *kind* of evidence for chronological data), in case the Lord should not then come. The letter was copied into the "Signs of the Times," but that kind of evidence and experience was decidedly disapproved of and rejected by Mr. Miller and the managers of the paper, and would not have been copied but for the hope of retaining the labors of a faithful co-laborer, and supposing no special harm would result in the little time yet to come before their *arguments* terminated the same period when *they expected* the event. They faithfully notified the people that their faith upon this subject rested on chronological calculations, and human applications of historical data to prophecy, that the position was not certain, though they believed the argument sound and reliable, yet they did not depend on, nor ask the Lord for the witness of His SPIRIT on such a point, when the SCRIPTURES furnish all the evidence promised. Had the Churches and the Conferences which passed their resolutions against the doctrine of the Lord's immediate coming, seen this letter and believed it a proper exponent of the views of Adventists, they might be exonerated for their course, and for the many references they afterwards made to it. But the men who were engaged in those resolutions had ample opportunity to know that it formed no part of the arguments or evidences which led them to their conclusions. But this false impression upon the mind of Bro. Cox, was suicidal to his confidence in the system of application of the periods, and he has never fully recovered from the shock it produced. Some others who trusted in such evidence were also bewildered; while opponents have used this circumstance to deter others from believing or examining the question.

DR. NICOLAS SMITH AND HIS LABORS.

Bro. Smith was a native of Maine. He was one of the first to enter upon the "Botanic Reform Practice" of medicine, and became one of the most successful physicians in Maine. Early in life he was converted to Christ and united with the Methodist E. church. His extensive business soon took his entire attention, and while he gave much of his money to the church and to the poor, his zeal and hope flagged, so that although he was called a good member, wise counselor, and strong friend of the church, his real piety, like many others, had departed; to use his own words: "I had a religion that did not save me." In this state, with a large "Infirmary" filled with patients, and several students under his instructions, in the city of Hallowell, he went to the annual Conference of the M. E. church, held in Gardiner, in the summer of 1842. Eld. J. Litch was there and lectured in an orchard on the coming of the Lord, to immense congregations. Bro. Smith being a man well known as a historian and Bible scholar, was asked by many, "What do you think of these lectures?" His reply was, "I know nothing about the subject; the preacher quotes much from the Bible and quotes history correctly; I intend to look into it." This he did faithfully, for months, until fully satisfied that the main parts of the doctrine were correct, and the time might be, no one could prove it not so. With a backslider's burden on his heart and a multitude of cares on his hands, more than any man ought to have, he was pressed down, and cried to the Lord for help. His decision was formed, he gave himself over to God with all he possessed; it was thorough work, and while in his bed at night a great blessing was bestowed. The next morning at the proper time he called his family—wife, two sons and five daughters—together, confessed to them that he had not lived as a Christian should, asked their forgiveness, told them his decision, which was "to be a Christian, if there was not another one in town," and asked his wife and children to join him; they promised, he read the Word and reared the broken-down family altar, and the Lord heard his prayers. His wife was reclaimed, his sons and daughters were soon all converted, though some of them have since wandered; the blessed results of that decision have not passed away. Bro. S. soon closed his Infirmary and attended only to outside patients, for he had *riches enough now*, and greater duties to do. He searched the Scriptures (the present writer has spent months with him in study and in meetings), and began to "reason out of the Scriptures," as he called it, both in private and in public. He preached, and read, and reasoned and became mighty in the Scriptures. Present salvation from sin, and the immediate coming of the Lord were his themes, "Twin Sisters" he called these two ideas. We have never been acquainted with his equal for a knowledge of the Bible. He preached the gospel and proclaimed the immediate coming of Christ until disabled by heart disease in 1858, much in company with the present writer, who with many others, received much instruction from him. He never fully adopted any definite time argument, nor any other that he could not give clear Bible proof for. After much effort to get this message before the church, of which he was an official member, and for which he suffered much persecution, he, with his family, quietly withdrew to enjoy that freedom of Christian action which the Scriptures allow every disciple of Christ. Though greatly belied and misrepresented by opposers, he bore it with Christian fortitude. For many years a prayer meeting was held in his house once or twice a week, in which some fifty souls were converted, and about as many more in our public meetings; and many of these went out to settle in various towns and states carrying this gospel light with them to sow among others, and good fruits resulted therefrom. Bro. S. died in 1861 in the joyous hope of being soon raised in "the first resurrection," to immortality and eternal life at Jesus' coming. He has been highly eulogized since his death, for his deep piety, Scriptural knowledge and Christian virtues, by those who bitterly persecuted him when living; good men are often abused when living and appreciated when dead.

MR. MILLER'S VISIT TO WASHINGTON.

It had long been in contemplation by Bro. Himes, in company with Bro. Miller, to visit Washington City, District of Columbia, and sound the alarm in the capital of the nation, but no opportunity presented itself for doing so until the past winter. Commencing in Boston, they lectured in that city, and from thence came to New York—delivered a course of lectures to a numerous audience; from thence visited Philadelphia, spent a week, and gave a course of lectures to an immense concourse of people, with very great effect. From Philadelphia he, in company with the writer, went to Washington, and commenced a course of lectures February 20, 1844. Two weeks were spent in different sections of the city, in presenting the doctrines of Adventism, and the evidences of the speedy coming of the Lord. The attendance was good, and the interest to hear deep. A greater revolution in public sentiment has rarely been witnessed in so short a time, than was brought about in Washington in reference to the Advent doctrine. It was during the time of these lectures that the fatal accident occurred on board the Princeton, by which so many prominent members of the government were swept away in a moment. The incident, probably, conduced somewhat to the interest which was felt on the subject of the coming of the Lord. But although the interest was great when the meetings closed, yet there being no one to stay behind and follow up what had been done, the influence soon passed away and was forgotten.

During our stay in Washington, besides the papers and books which were carried on from the north, a paper was commenced there, called the "*Southern Midnight Cry.*" Two numbers were published and circulated in Washington and vicinity, and another in Baltimore, while Bro. Miller was giving his course of lectures in that city. Thus ended the winter of 1843-4, and brought us to the point which had so long been before us,—the end of the Jewish year 1843.

THE POINT OF TIME REACHED AND PASSED.

As might be expected, as the crisis, the 21st of March, approached, there was a very general expectation of an entire overthrow of the whole system of Adventism. It was supposed that those who had embraced it, if the appointed time should pass, would yield the whole question. But they had not so learned the Bible. The doctrine does not consist in merely tracing prophetic periods, although that is an important part of the work. But the whole prophetic history of the world is given in the pages of inspiration, is recorded in history, and affords indubitable evidence of the fact that we have approached a crisis. And no disappointment respecting a definite point of time can move them, or drive them from their position, relative to the speedy coming of the Lord. There are, at present, some who falter, but comparatively few, however, who have given up the cause. Most stand unmoved amidst all the scoffs and jeers of a reviling world.

FUNDAMENTAL PRINCIPLES [1] ON WHICH THE SECOND ADVENT CAUSE IS BASED.

I.—The word of God teaches that this earth is to be regenerated, in the restitution of all things, and restored to its Eden state as it came from the hand of its maker before the fall, and is to be the eternal abode of the righteous in their resurrection state.

II.—The only millennium found in the word of God, is the 1000 years which are to intervene between the first and second resurrection, as brought to view in the 20th of Revelation. And the various portions of Scripture which are adduced as evidence of such a period in time, are to have their fulfillment only in the New Earth, wherein dwelleth righteousness.

III.—The only restoration of Israel yet future, is the restoration of the saints to the New Earth, when the Lord my God shall come, and all his saints with him.

IV.—The signs which were to precede the coming of our Saviour, have all been given; and the prophecies have all been fulfilled but those which relate to the coming of Christ, the end of this world, and the restitution of all things.

V.—There are none of the prophetic periods, as we understand them, that extend beyond the [Jewish] year 1843.

The above we shall ever maintain as the immutable truths of the word of God, and therefore, till our Lord come, we shall ever look for his return as the next event in historical prophecy.

---

[1] The above was written in the Jewish year 1843, which has now expired. According to the best chronologers, the captivity of Manasseh, the commencement of the seven times, or 2520 years of Levit. 26th, was B. C. 677; also, the captivity of Jehoiakim, the commencement of the Great Jubilee, or 2450 years, was B. C. 607; also, the decree to rebuild Jerusalem in the seventh of Artaxerxes, the commencement of the 70 weeks and 2300 days, of Dan. 8th and 9th, was given B. C. 457; and also the taking away of Paganism in Rome, the commencement of the 1335 days of Dan. 12th, was about A. D. 508. Reckoning from those several dates, the respective periods can extend only to about the Jewish year 1843. This being ended, our published time is now passed; and yet our faith is as strong as ever, that at the end of those periods the Lord will surely come; while we can only wait for his coming such time as human chronology may have varied from the exact time,—continually looking for, and momentarily expecting his appearing.

The foregoing principles have constituted the basis of Adventism, and the ground on which the friends of the cause, of all sects and parties, have labored harmoniously together. It has not been our wish in presenting these truths, to build up a sect, but to meet as Christians, with all sects, and if God in mercy bless our labors, leave those converted to God to unite and live in peace and love with the church with which they might be connected. But this could not be. Very few churches have been found which were sufficiently alive to God to be willing to hear of the coming of the Lord. A spirit of opposition to the introduction of the Christian's hope in social meetings, has almost everywhere been exhibited. The doors of churches have been closed against lectures, and every possible means used to prevent the spread of light on the subject. Under these circumstances, those who wished to hear were under the necessity of opening separate meetings for the lectures, or not have them at all. The same has been the fact with respect to social meetings. When forbidden to speak of their hope of seeing the King in his beauty, in the social meetings of the church, those who have been interested in the question could only go by themselves and enjoy the privilege. The fact has developed a very great and strange dereliction in piety in the various churches. What, profess to be the friends and lovers of Jesus, and yet be offended and disturbed at hearing the glorious tidings, "Behold, he cometh!" O, tell it not in Gath.

"But," it is answered, "we only object to your setting the time." It would do very well to make such a reply, if we did not happen to know that there is the same opposition against the doctrine of Christ's speedy coming, that there is to the time itself. But such is the fact.[1] Where there is a real love for the appearing of the Saviour, there is no trouble about the time. Such persons have no objection to learn all that the word of God has made known respecting the time of the Bridegroom's coming.

The unwillingness to hear on the subject, has *usually* originated in a want of readiness to meet the Lord *now*. Perhaps not a more

---

[1] We doubt not that many thousands of cases have occurred where the most pious, able, and unexceptionable ministers and members who never embraced any given year for the Advent, have been denied the privilege of preaching or speaking and singing of the coming of the Saviour, in meeting-houses and in social meetings: and have been as fully rejected as those who taught definite time; we have personally known very many instances.—EDITOR.

sure test can be given of a state of grace, than a real genuine feeling that we should like to see the Lord *now*. Reader, can you say thus in sincerity and truth?

MODES OF OPPOSITION.

It has usually been the fact that, as soon as the doctrine of the Lord's speedy coming has been presented in any place, the clergy, in the course of one or two weeks, would begin their attacks from the pulpit. The usual argument has been:

1. "Of that day and hour knoweth no man; yet these men profess to know the very time when the Lord is to come. Yes, they profess to know more than the angels, or even the Son of God himself."

2. "The Lord cannot come until after the millennium, during which the whole world is to be righteous, and the lion eat straw like the ox," etc.

3. "The Jews must be brought in, and restored to Palestine, before that day comes."

4. "It is to come as a thief, as a snare, etc., on all them that dwell on the earth. But now there are so many who are looking for it, that it cannot come as a snare."

5. "It cannot come now, because there are so many learned and holy ministers and Christians, that if it should come now, it would take them by surprise. The Lord will not come without their knowing it."

6. "The world is yet in its infancy; the arts and sciences are just beginning to come to maturity, and fit the world to live, and it cannot be that the Lord will come now and destroy it all."

7. "Then, again, there is so much waste land to be occupied in the western country, land which has never yet been cultivated at all, that it is not at all reasonable that the Lord should destroy it all, before it has been improved."

8. But the great argument, the one which has proved the most effectual, has been, that this vision of Daniel viii. has nothing to do with the coming of Christ, or setting up of God's everlasting kingdom. It simply refers to Antiochus Epiphanes, and his persecution of the Jews, and desecration of the temple, some 160 odd years B. C.

Thus we have the abomination of desolation spoken of by Daniel the prophet, for which the Saviour taught his people to look, about two hundred years before the instruction was given.

To the foregoing might be added a number more of the same class, *professedly* drawn from reason and Scripture, but none of them more formidable than those already recorded. Do you smile, gentle reader, at the idea of calling these, *arguments?* Yet, you may be assured that each of them in turn has been urged by grave men, calling themselves *Doctors of Divinity.*

But the most wonderful and overwhelming of all arguments which have ever been presented against the doctrine, is, "MR. MILLER HAS BUILT SOME STONE WALL ON HIS FARM!!!" But, I forget myself; I said the most wonderful; there is another quite its equal: "MR. MILLER REFUSES TO SELL HIS FARM!!!" *How, O! how* CAN *Christ come, when Mr. Miller will not sell his farm???*

But, this is not all; for the truth is, "MR. HIMES HAS PUBLISHED AND SCATTERED (a large part of them gratuitously) MORE THAN FIVE MILLION OF BOOKS AND PAPERS. HE MUST BE ENGAGED IN A SPECULATION; AND HOW CAN THE LORD COME?? *O! how* CAN *he come??*"

BUT THERE IS ANOTHER AND BETTER CLASS IN THE CHURCH.

We must say a word to and for them. With the Johns and the Marys we have had but little difficulty. Unlike Peter, they rarely become "bold" and impious theorizers; and never would they think of rejecting a plain promise of God, because it held out the prospect of a personal interview with their Lord. They would rather feel afraid it was too good news to be true, and "believe it not for joy."

They may not exhibit the most commanding development of the understanding, and of course they may err, but their love never fails to preserve the integrity of the heart. It may err in its manifestations, as we know it did when they would "embalm" the body of the Saviour, which was to see no corruption, although they had been so often told that he would "rise again the third day." And that error, it should be remembered, called forth the severest reproof they ever received from the Saviour's lips: "O fools, and slow of heart to believe *all that the prophets have spoken!*" But point out their errors, and they will always "rejoice in the truth."

It would be no wonder, since the false prophets who were to appear, should well nigh "deceive the very elect," if some of this class should be found under the influence of their "heresies." Indeed, one feature of their imposture is well adapted to deceive them. They are generally spiritually minded. The enjoyment of the Spirit is their chief consolation while absent from Christ.

Now these false teachers have given so many of the promises, which speak of Christ and his kingdom literally, a *spiritual* reference, that this spiritual meaning, as it is called, is all they think of, although Paul has plainly told us that the Spirit is only "the earnest" of the glorious reality.

"Yes," I hear them say, "that is just what we believe;" we have "the earnest" now, and when we die we expect the full glory of the "heavenly inheritance."

Very well. Do not lightly esteem "the earnest." We have no hope without that. But if the apostle is right, "the inheritance" is to be given to us, not when we die, but "*at the appearing of Jesus Christ.*"

Again you reply, "If we are to have a *heavenly* inheritance, must it not be *in heaven?*"

All that is made perfectly plain by "what is written." Abraham looked for, and is to receive "a heavenly country." If we ever possess the inheritance, it will be with Abraham. We shall "sit down with Abraham, Isaac, and Jacob, in the kingdom of God." And when we inherit that kingdom "we shall bear the image of the Lord from heaven."—"And as we have borne the image of the earthly, we shall also bear the image of the heavenly. Now this I say, brethren, that flesh and blood cannot inherit the kingdom of God; neither doth corruption inherit incorruption. Behold, I shew you a mystery; we shall not all sleep, but we shall all be changed, in a moment, in the twinkling of an eye, at the last trump: for the trumpet shall sound, and the dead shall be raised incorruptible, and we shall be changed. For this corruptible must put on incorruption, and this mortal, immortality. So when this corruptible shall have put on incorruption, and this mortal shall have put on immortality, then shall be brought to pass the saying that is written, Death is swallowed up in victory."—1 Cor. xv. 49—54.[1]

---

[1] Advent Shield, pp. 41—79.

The vernal equinox of 1844 was the furthest point of time to which Mr. Miller's calculation of the prophetic periods extended. When this time passed, he wrote to Mr. Himes as follows:

"LOW HAMPTON, March 25, 1844.

"MY DEAR BROTHER HIMES:—I am now seated at my old desk in my east room, having obtained help of God until the present time. I am still looking for the dear Saviour, the Son of God, from heaven; and for the fulfillment of the promise made to our fathers, and confirmed to them that heard him,—that he would come again, and would receive us unto himself; gathering together in one body all the family of the first-born in heaven and earth, even in him. This Paul has told us would be in 'the fullness of time.'—Eph. i: 9, 10.

"The time, as I have calculated it, is now filled up, and I expect every moment to see the Saviour descend from heaven. I have now nothing to look for but this glorious hope. I am full in the faith that all prophetic chronology, excepting the thousand years of Rev. 20th, is now about full. Whether God designs for me to warn the people of this earth any more, or not, I am at a loss to know. Should time continue longer than I have expected, I mean to be governed by the providence of him who will never err, in whom I think I have trusted, and have been supported by, during my twelve years of arduous labors, in endeavoring to awaken the churches of God and the Christian community, and to warn my fellow-men of the necessity of an immediate preparation to meet our Judge, in the day of his appearing. I hope that I have cleansed my garments of the blood of souls. I feel that, as far as it was in my power, I have freed myself from all guilt in their condemnation. . . .

"I feel almost confident that my labors are about done; and I am, with a deep interest of soul, looking for my blessed and glorious Redeemer, who will be king over all the earth, and God with us forevermore. This, I can truly say, is my chief desire. It is my meditation all the day long. It is my song in the night. It is my faith and hope. It consoles me in sickness, comforts me in tribulation, and gives me patience to endure the scoffs and taunts of the selfish and ungodly. My faith and confidence in God's word are as strong as ever, although Christ has not come in the time I expected. I still believe that the time is not far off, and that God will soon—

yes, too soon for the proud and scoffing—justify himself, his word, and the cry which has been given.

"This is the position I have now to take,.and what more work I have to do will be done in this manner.

"If God has anything more for me to do in his vineyard, he will give me strength, open the door, and enable me to do whatever may be his will, for his glory, and for the best good of men. To him I leave the event. For him I watch and pray: Come, Lord Jesus, come quickly. Amen! Even so come, Lord Jesus.

WILLIAM MILLER."

On the 2d of May he wrote as follows:

TO SECOND ADVENT BELIEVERS.

"Were I to live my life over again, with the same evidence that I then had, to be honest with God and man I should have to do as I have done. Although opposers said it would not come, they produced no weighty arguments. It was evidently guess-work with them; and I then thought, and do now, that their denial was based more on an unwillingness for the Lord to come than on any arguments leading to such a conclusion.

"I *confess my error*, and acknowledge *my disappointment;* yet I still believe that the day of the Lord is near, even at the door; and I exhort you, my brethren, to be watchful, and not let that day come upon you unawares. The wicked, the proud, and the bigot, will exult over us. I will try to be patient. God will deliver the godly out of temptation, and will reserve the unjust to be punished at Christ's appearing.

"I want you, my brethren, not to be drawn away from the truth. Do not, I pray you, neglect the Scriptures. They are able to make you wise unto eternal life. Let us be careful not to be drawn away from the manner and object of Christ's coming; for the next attack of the adversary will be to induce unbelief respecting these. The manner of Christ's coming has been well discussed. Permit me, then, to address you on the subject of

THE BURNING DAY.

"'This second epistle, beloved, I now write unto you, in both which I stir up your pure minds by way of remembrance; that ye may be mindful of the words which were spoken before by the holy prophets, and of the commandment of us, the apostles of the Lord and Saviour: knowing this first, that there shall come in the last days scoffers, walking after their own lusts, and saying, Where is the promise of his coming? for since the fathers fell asleep, all things continue as they were from the beginning of the creation. For this they willingly are ignorant of, that by the word of God the heavens were of old, and the earth standing out of the water and in the water; whereby the world that then was, being overflowed with water, perished: but the heavens and the earth, which are now, by the same word are kept in store, reserved unto fire against the day of judgment and perdition of ungodly men.'—2 Pet. iii: 1—7.

Following this Scripture quotation, Mr. M. gives a very forcible address, with many Scripture statements, which embody the Christian's hope; together with an outline of the revealed plan of salvation, the events connected with, and succeeding the second advent of Christ, the time of rewards and punishment, and concludes with the following:

"'Wait on the Lord, and keep his way, and he shall exalt thee to inherit the land; when the wicked are cut off, thou shalt see it.'—Psa. xxxvii. 34.

"And now, my brethren, I exhort you not to be led away from plain fundamental truths. Now is the time of danger. Satan has come down, having great power, knowing he hath but a short time. 'Behold, I come quickly; hold that fast which thou hast, that no man take thy crown.'—Rev. iii. 11.

"Low Hampton, May 2, 1844."

During the last week of May, the Annual Conference of Adventists was held in the Tabernacle at Boston. Mr. Miller was present, and, at the close of one of the meetings, in accordance with a previous notice, arose, and frankly confessed his mistake in the definite time at which he supposed the prophetic periods would have terminated. The following notice of this confession, written by a hearer, appeared in the Boston Post on the 1st of June following:

FATHER MILLER'S CONFESSION.

"Many people were desirous of hearing what was termed Father Miller's Confession, which, according to rumor, was to be delivered at the Tabernacle on Tuesday evening last, when and where a large concourse assembled, myself among the number, to hear the 'conclusion of the whole matter;' and I confess I was well paid for my time and trouble. I should judge, also, by the appearance of the audience, and the remarks I heard from one or two gentlemen not of Mr. Miller's faith, that a general satisfaction was felt. I never heard him when he was more eloquent or animated, or more happy in communicating his feelings and sentiments to others. Want of time and space will not permit me to give even a mere sketch of his remarks, which occupied more than an hour. He confessed that he had been disappointed, but by no means discouraged or shaken in his faith in God's goodness, or in the entire fulfillment of his word, or in the speedy coming of our Saviour, and the destruction of the world. Although the supposed time had passed, God's time had not passed. 'If the vision tarry, wait for it.' He remained firm in the belief that the end of all things is at hand, even at the door. He spoke with much feeling and effect, and left no doubt of his sincerity.

D."

SKETCH OF ELD. O. R. FASSETT AND HIS LABORS.

Eld. Fassett is a native of New York, was born of Christian and pious parents, March 30, 1817, in Penfield, Munroe Co., near Rochester. His parents were very strict in the moral and religious training of their children. His mother's death occurred in his seventh year, and his father's in his fourteenth year, leaving him an orphan in the world. He was converted in early youth, but did not unite with any church until at the age of seventeen years, when he connected himself with the Presbyterian church in Albion, N. Y. Bro. F. was early impressed with convictions of duty to preach the gospel, and at the age of eighteen years, entered upon preparatory studies which fitted him for college, when his health failed and his studies were abandoned. He then went to reside with a half-brother, Dr. D. D. Fassett, of Lockport, N. Y., where, after a dangerous sickness, voluntarily took up the study of Anatomy, Physiology, and Medicine, and through the aid of his brother's extensive library, practice, and funds, progressed until enabled to attend medical lectures of Jefferson Medical College, Philadelphia, in 1838–9 and 1839–40, graduating with the honors of the institution. Returning to Lockport, he entered upon the practice of medicine and surgery with his brother, and with him had a large and lucrative practice.

In 1841, he married Miss Elzira L. Armstrong, of Westfield, N. Y. In the winter of 1843–4, he heard Wm. Miller in a course of lectures delivered in Lockport, in the Baptist church then under the pastoral charge of Eld. Elon Galusha. Bro. F. soon after embraced the faith.

In a short time after this, Mrs. Fassett, who was a devoted member of the Presbyterian church, also embraced the faith of Adventism, under the labors

O. R. FASSETT.—Page 332.

of Eld. Thomas F. Barry, being absent from home when Mr. Miller lectured in their town.

Their view changed, gave them a new experience, new hopes, and new joys, and set them into gospel light and liberty, which they retain to this day, and which they determine, by the grace of God, to retain unto the end.

This conversion to the Advent faith revived Bro. Fassett's call to preach, as it has with many others who had neglected it, and he began to lecture, or rather to give Scripture readings in school-houses, in Niagara Co., on the prophecies and signs of the times, as opportunity offered. Pressing invitations from various quarters soon compelled him to leave his profession of medicine and preach the gospel of the kingdom, to quiet his conscience as to duty, and satisfy the demands of the public. His first labors were in Lewiston and vicinity, Niagara Co. Sister F. accompanied him and visited from house to house, while her husband lectured on the coming of the Lord. Revivals of religion in various towns and villages followed as results. The Lord set his seal to their labors.

They soon united in labor with Bros. T. F. Barry and E. R. Pinney, in camp-meetings and protracted efforts in western N. Y. After this they came East, to Albany, N. Y., Springfield, Worcester, and Boston, Mass., and became acquainted with the leading men of the Advent cause. By the urgent call of the Advent church in Providence, R. I., Bro. Fassett became their pastor in 1845, and retained his charge five years, while he also took the pastoral charge of the church in Bristol, R. I. Here also the Lord added his blessing to their faithful and judicious labors. Bro. F. attended the Albany Conference in 1845, and was associated in the council of eminent ministers who drew up that memorable "declaration of principles" which we shall give in another place, and which did much to unite the believers and still the raging elements, when aspirants, erratics, and fanatics were driving pet notions at the expense of truth and Christian fellowship, and threatened the utter demoralization of the cause.

Bro. F. was secretary of most of the conferences held in New York and Boston for many years, and reported business, speeches, and lectures, when the times demanded and called out the best and ablest talents of the church; which required much business, and many efforts that our younger brethren have not been at all acquainted with. Those were efforts which produced, with the Lord's blessing, a cause, kept it from ruin, and brought it down for these later reapers to find ready for harvest, without the sacrifices of those days.

Bro. Fassett was pastor of the Advent church worshiping in Hudson street, Boston, for a series of years; of the church in Hartford, Ct., two years; at Buffalo, N. Y., two years; Westboro, Mass., two years; Worcester and North Attleboro, two years; missionary in Maine one year; pastor in Poland, Me., one year; pastor at Sandy Hill, N. Y., three years; at Minneapolis, Minn., two years. In 1871, he, with his devoted wife, went to San Francisco, Cal., by the earnest request of the Advent church there. They have been laboring there and in several other towns on the Pacific coast, now two and a half years, and, with God's blessing, have accomplished much, under the most trying and afflicting circumstances, in building up believers in Christ and in his coming in glory. Sister F. has preached much of the time while in Minnesota and California, and is considered a logical, systematical, and able expounder of the Scriptures, and a faithful Christian worker. They both suffered much from the climate in California for a while.

Bro. F. is an able and pointed preacher, a critical expounder of the word, a zealous and active worker, a good adviser, and sound in the faith. Beside his pastoral labors, he has traveled and preached extensively in the New England, Middle, and Western States, as an Evangelist, has written several tracts, and much valuable matter for our papers. Sister F. has been a faithful co-worker with her husband from the beginning, and often supplying the desk to the satisfaction of large audiences, and working arduously in social meetings and in pastoral visits. In every place the Lord has produced fruits of their labors, and raised up numerous friends who remember them with much affection.

They sacrificed much of worldly prosperity and prospects to enter upon this gospel work, and have been constantly sacrificing since; but the Lord has been their portion, and, through this sanctifying and soul-purifying truth, has made them all they are, has accomplished through these "earthen vessels" all the good which has come of their labors, and will soon settle them in their eternal inheritance and beautiful home, with all the redeemed family of God, immortal, at the coming of our Lord Jesus Christ to establish his glorious kingdom.

CHAPTER XIII.

DISAPPOINTED, NOT DISCOURAGED—TWO CLASSES OF TEACHERS—C. P. DOW —ADVENT HERALD—MR. MILLER AND PROF. BUSH—DR. BUSHNELL'S CASE—COMING OUT OF CHURCHES—D. R. AND M. S. MANSFIELD—VARIOUS MINISTERS—KING HASTINGS—NOTICE OF OTHER MINISTERS—ONE GOOD CONFESSION—JONAS MARIAM—S. S. SNOW AND 1844—J. LITCH'S LETTER—LITCH ON 7TH MONTH—MILLER'S LETTERS—CLOSING WORK—A MORAL FEATURE—EXTRACT FROM BLISS—DOWLING—POSITION DEFINED—J. LITCH —PUBLISHING RESUMED—J. V. HIMES—GEO. STORRS—MR. MILLER—N. N. WHITING.

DISAPPOINTED BUT NOT DISCOURAGED.

As the several points of time passed which had been looked to with special interest for the ending of the 2,300 days of Dan. 8th, without bringing the Lord, and the resurrection, the believers were much disappointed, and much more ridiculed by unbelievers; but the leading and well instructed of the company were not at all disheartened.

They had examined, studied, and embraced the doctrine which they knew was based upon the prophetic Scriptures and calendar, which demonstrated the fact that they were living in the closing days of the Gentile times. These conclusions had fixed their minds on this fact quite as thoroughly as the crucifixion and resurrection of Christ fixed the faith of the apostles and their associates in regard to the opening and establishing the gospel dispensation.

Yet they were in a perplexed, tried state of mind; they were anxious to know why they had been mistaken. The question was not readily solved; they keenly felt their disappointment, and could not rest until they had some further instruction upon the matter. But there were others who had taken interest in this message and movement, yet had not seen enough of its foundation principles to keep them from vacillating. Many of these gave it up.

THERE WERE TWO GENERAL CLASSES OF TEACHERS AND BELIEVERS.

Mr. Miller and those who entered into the work with him after a careful, thorough, and lengthy investigation of the whole subject of prophecy, chronology, and history, who were capable of weighing candidly the intricate and uncertain points between sacred chronology and profane history, and of seeing the impropriety of claiming to arrive at infallible conclusions as to the ending of the prophetic periods, preached and wrote with becoming dignity and modesty when expressing their confidence that the end would be in or "about 1843." They used the "*if*" and the "*probable;*" they were far from being dogmatical; while several refused to accept time conclusions at all, they never allowed themselves to claim that their conclusions on these points of chronology and prophetic periods were positively correct. They considered their conclusions the *most reliable*, and asked opponents for better ones. These teachers and those who were led into the faith under such instructions, and who did not become wise above their teachers, were well fortified against the temptations of the adversary and the excesses which disappointments or defeat bring upon those who take too positive positions where there is possibility of being incorrect.

ANOTHER CLASS OF TEACHERS.

There was another class of teachers and believers of various grades, connected with this work, which it is our duty to here consider, not to censure or disparage, but to distinguish the principles which have manifested their fruits in all the history of this message since.

We refer to that class who readily embraced the message that the Lord was soon to come. As soon as they saw the leading evidences of the fact, they entered upon teaching it without that deep and thorough research and study of all the great principles which underlie and form the basis of the whole system, and which is required to arrive at ripe conclusions on so important a subject. They read and heard the main arguments and evidences which were presented on time, and accepted the conclusions as *positively* correct, or formed conclusions for themselves, after their own modes of thought, as *demonstrated* facts.

These were novices in the faith, and learned by experience what they had not by study. There were many of this class. The Lord blessed them and their labors, for they worked for him, and with him, for the salvation of souls, and the enlightening of the people of God on the gospel hope and the signs of the times. Yet some of them became positive and dogmatical. Their conclusions on time were formed without the "if" or "probability." Their conclusions were called "*facts* capable of demonstration," and the figures being set at such points, which, "*positively* belong there," the footing up was not difficult, the conclusion was "inevitable," and "*correct.*" It was "not possible to make it out any other way."

This class of teachers were sincere, earnest, and did much service in bringing the truth before the people, and in bringing sinners to Christ. They had much important truth which ministers of other churches did not see. They became very successful workers, but all this time they were gathering believers who were confident above what the actual truth would warrant. The time argument was not demonstrable, yet they considered it to be so, and often complained of more careful ministers because they did not preach the time as "*a positive fact.*" These complaints led some to become more positive, lest they should be too unbelieving.

Many of the ministers complained of Bro. Miller for allowing an *if*, and told the people that he was not definite enough, as we have already quoted; that he had some live spots, was not fully dead to the world. Sometimes they made assertions like the following: "If there is any truth in prophecy, the Lord must come in 1843." "If Gabriel told the truth," etc. "If the Bible can be depended upon," etc. These and other expressions of the same import were used to show their strength of faith in the time calculation; and not intended to put the Bible in jeopardy. Still, unbelievers so understood it, then exaggerated and added to it. Thus, the message and all concerned in teaching it were accused of teaching thus; whereas the more thoroughly instructed and riper scholars repudiated such positiveness, and often reproved it. But this teaching produced believers who were just as positive, when they had full confidence in their teachers, as were the teachers themselves. When the time passed, and the Lord did not come, this class of teachers and believers were less prepared to bear disappointment, less capable of seeing that they had believed an error, and yet the foundation of the system remained sound. With them, all rested on the *time calculation;* if that was an error the whole system was error. Thus reasoning, their dogmatism became a stumbling block to them and to others also. A large proportion of this class of teachers and laymen gave up the subject and went no more with us (while others framed theories to justify their credence and pervert their judgment). There were a plenty of teachers to help them believe it all a delusion, and to engage them with other hopes and other work.

But some of these positive ones had embraced too much Bible truth to give it up for the fables which they formerly entertained. Yet they had imbibed such views of time arguments, and such applications of certain texts of Scripture which involve time in a general sense, they were entirely perplexed, and many of them went their ways, to the farm, the mill, the gold mines, and other employments or side issues, until they should get more light on time. This unhealthful faith has been often acted upon since, by time messages, and always with similar results. Few of these have ever settled down thoroughly upon the great fundamental truths which form the basis of this message, and entered earnestly into the work with the body of Adventists for the advancement of the general cause of righteousness, and universal spread of this proclamation. Nor have they generally used their *influence* and *means* to aid in carrying on the great and glorious work which has been accomplished by the steadfast and faithful workers in the cause.

Had the Lord not sustained a class of believers more competent and ready to perform the work to be done, the "Second Advent Message" would have ceased to attract public attention long ago. But it lives because God lives. It will live until Christ comes, because it is his cause, and must be maintained by his faithful people until "he comes to be glorified by all them who believe in that day."

SKETCH OF ELD. R. HUTCHINSON AND HIS LABORS.

Eld. H. was formerly a Wesleyan Methodist minister. He was sent from England to Canada as a Methodist missionary; while pursuing his mission work there, he heard the message of Christ's immediate coming, and embraced it fully. From about 1842, we think, his history as an Advent missionary commenced. He was a good preacher and ardent lover of the Lord and his word, working with his might to promote the cause. He preached in various parts of Canada, published a paper entitled "The Voice of Elijah," to herald the message. Large quantities of this paper were sent to England for free distribution, which awakened some interest there. Many were circulated through the Provinces. In 1846 he went to England as an Advent missionary. Bro. H. was also much interested in the children, and for some time edited a child's paper. In 1861–2, in company with Eld. J. M. Orrock, he published a paper at Montreal, entitled, "Millennial News." He has since associated chiefly with the "Plymouth brethren."

SKETCH OF ELD. CHARLES P. DOW AND HIS LABORS.

Bro. C. P. Dow was a native of Vermont, born in Bakersfield in 1823, and a kinsman of the eccentric Lorenzo Dow. He was reared under the instructions of Universalism, and surrounded by its influence, yet his mind seemed intuitively to turn to the consideration of the true Christian religion, when but a boy. In 1836, he was brought under strong convictions of sin, and was converted among the Methodists. Believing he was called to preach the gospel, he began to appoint meetings, was licensed to preach, and entered upon the work of studying Methodist theology, with much ambition to become a Methodist traveling preacher.

In 1843, a copy of Eld. L. D. Fleming's "Reasons for believing in the speedy coming of Christ," was put into his hands. He read it; it left an impression on his mind which caused him to think; yet he soon concluded it could not be true, for he had imbibed the idea that the world must be converted before Christ could come. But he was not at rest until he examined the Bible to see if there was evidence of the world's conversion, when he found the idea a baseless notion. Bro. Dow then went to hear the Advent views as preached by Brn. Bates, Levi Dudley, D. B. Wyatt, R. Hutchinson, and others, and in 1844, while listening to a sermon based on the Abrahamic covenant, he considered the subject demonstrated, and concluded to preach it, which he commenced to do. Finding it afflicted his Methodist brethren he quietly withdrew, and went forth to sound the cry, "Behold, the bridegroom cometh, go ye out to meet him." Bro. D. says, "I adopted the argument, or assumed premise, without proper investigation, that is still held by too many, 'that the true church will go into the kingdom on time,' by which is meant, that although the time may not be known correctly now, it will be, for a time before the final end. With this opinion I do not now agree. I was for a few days '*a timist*'—in 1844. I will here say, although I am an Adventist, yet I deplore an excitement upon time, and believe every such excitement to be injurious. The providence of God was as manifest in raising up Wm. Miller to do his work as in raising up Martin Luther; and if any definite time-preaching has been in keeping with God's permission or will, his was; which explained the numbers and time indications of prophecy modestly, and concluded if he was right the end would come 'about the year 1843.'"

Bro. Dow further remarks, "A believer in the inherent immortality of the soul, of the conscious happiness or misery of the departed dead between death and the resurrection, as also of the eternal torment of the finally lost. I was not prepared to be a Bible Adventist, in the fullest and most consistent sense. I had been a very consistent *Methodist Adventist.* Not until the teachings of such men as Henry Grew and Geo. Storrs, of Philadelphia, Charles Fitch, of Ohio, supplemented by a host of other honored names, men of acknowledged ability and influence, that has made a lasting impression in religious teachings on these matters, did I doubt the correctness of my former position. But upon examination, patient and continual, with an earnest desire to know the truth, after years of suspense and indecision, I at length fully decided the matter for myself."

Since that time Bro. Dow has been earnestly and prosperously laboring in the Advent cause, in various towns and cities in New York, Vermont, Canada, and some in the west, also in Massachusetts. He has preached in many places where the Lord has converted souls and churches have been raised up. He has scattered many publications, and seen much good result from them. As an accurate hearer and reporter, Bro. D. is renowned. It was he who was Moderator and Reporter of the discussion between D. Chapin and Miles Grant, when we had "twenty-seven rods of printed matter in the Crisis, by actual measurement, on Universalism," and Bro. Grant said, "I am surprised at its correctness, our people are pleased with it." This, however, needed a recount, for the mass of readers did not choose to read it, and bleated for better food.

Bro. Dow now resides in Hatley, Canada, is a member of the Advent Christian Conference of the Province of Quebec, and is exerting a good and uniting influence in that Province, with other faithful younger preachers, believing and teaching that the Lord will soon come to judge the world and establish his everlasting reign, gather all his people into it, and make a final end of the wicked.

THE HOPE OF ISRAEL.

Early in 1844, a paper bearing the above title was issued in Topsham, Me., edited by Elders Joseph Turner and John Pearson, jr., to more extensively publish the message of the immediate coming of Christ, also to discuss the doctrine of man's entire mortality, his unconsciousness in death, the gift of immortality through Christ to believers, and the extinction of the wicked in "the second death." This paper served a good purpose for a time, having much truth for the people, but was, within a few months, perverted by fanaticism, and its name changed to "The Hope within the Vail," indicating more clearly the wild notions it promulgated while it was passing into ether to disappear.

The Hope of Israel was conducted in a manner which, while scattering seeds of truth, also published hurtful errors, which proved a source of much evil to those who imbibed them.

THE ADVENT HERALD.

In February, 1844, the title of the paper called "The Signs of the Times," was changed to that of "*The Advent Herald*"—the most appropriate title that has or can be applied to a paper bearing this message. It was then under the editorial management of J. V. Himes, S. Bliss, and Apollos Hale.

MR. MILLER AND PROFESSOR BUSH.

A lengthy discussion was published in the Advent Herald in 1844, commencing in March, between Mr. Miller and Geo. Bush, "Professor of Hebrew and Oriental literature, in the New York City University." Prof. B. admitted the probability that Mr. Miller was correct in his chronology, and use of the prophetic numbers, stating that he was sustained by nearly all learned protestant writers of the past. But he objected to the events which were expected. Although a Congregationalist at that time, he had so far departed from the faith as to reject the personal advent of Christ, the literal resurrection of the dead, and personal reign of Christ. During the great interest which was being everywhere awakened upon the subject of Christ's coming, Prof. B. canvassed the New England and Middle States, lecturing to large and popular audiences upon the prophecies. The public mind was prepared to listen, and be impressed, for they feared the judgment might be at hand; but they were informed by the papers, the ministers, and others, that Prof. Bush brushed it all away. He did so in the estimation of some. Churches and other institutions employed him to lecture, at $50 and $100 per evening, to tell them the prophetic Scriptures were nearly filled up, the periods of Daniel were about to end, the millennium was about to be introduced; but all this would take place without the personal advent of Christ. It was to be brought about by the increased influence of the Holy Spirit and the rapid increase of conversions to Christianity. Wars were to cease, universal brotherhood be recognized, and the good time inaugurated. When desired, he lectured in "review" of what was politely styled "Mr. Miller's theory," and he was constantly desired to do this. Then he modestly spiritualised, allegorised and metaphorised all the Scripture statements relating to the coming future; admitting all the while the periods of Daniel were about exhausted. This was saying "peace and safety" in a kind and gentle manner, and having large pay for his many predictions, of what has utterly failed of fulfillment, while the reverse in all points has been experienced. On the other hand, those who were proving from the Sacred Oracles, that war, pestilence, "distress of nations, with perplexity," with "abounding iniquity," were greatly on the increase, and would be removed only by the final judgment, were preaching and lecturing without pay, while crying, "Behold the bridegroom cometh, go ye out to meet him." And though he has not yet come, all the great events then preached, as preceding and impending, have been constantly fulfilling their calculations, showing they were on the track of truth; but were a little premature in their estimates of time for the final event.

Yet the great cry has filled the ears of the people, that these are the "false prophets of the last days," by which it is admitted that we are in the last days. But who has reproached Prof. Bush? Who has looked after his predictions? Who cries out that great mischief has followed his preaching and his strange views? And yet he became an apostate from all that is considered "Orthodox," went over to the Swedenborgians carrying about ten thousand Christian members with him. He then republished Swedenborg's writings, and others of his own, of the same nature, to furnish his quota of demoralizing religious literature, to turn away thousands of others from the gospel hope. But all this passes without noise, and was paid dearly for by the people. Thus now, as in the past, the human heart cries out for "smooth things," and the public mind smothers the gigantic errors of their chief teachers, while the truths of God are repudiated and the Lord's servants made odious by reproaches for the slightest errors.

THE CASE OF DR. BUSHNELL IS TO THE POINT.

As we have shown on a former page, Dr. Bushnell wrote a book in which he rejected, in the strongest possible terms, the personal advent of Christ, and with arguments, which if correct, negate the whole economy of salvation. This book was widely circulated, and lauded, especially by the Universalist press. The pill was not quite palatable, and must be sugar coated.

From the N. Y. Journal of Commerce, of June, 1853, we have the account of the performance:

"The alleged heretical sentiments put forth by Rev. Dr. Bushnell, of Hartford, Ct., in some of his recent publications, were brought before the General Association of Connecticut (Congregational), at its recent meeting in Waterbury. 'After an animated discussion, a resolution was adopted, almost unanimously, *condemning the sentiments which the complainants understood to be set forth in his publications.*' The resolution adopted was moved by the Rev. Dr. Bacon, of New Haven. It is so worded as to condemn the '*sentiments imputed to Dr. Bushnell by the complainants,*' without asserting, or even admitting, that they were rightly imputed to him. It hits the errors, but misses the man."

Since this quiet refusal to be responsible for the infidel dogma, which this eminent D. D. sent forth to undermine the foundation of Christianity, all things go on smoothly in relation to him. The church and world have not been told that his teaching, writings, and associations were dangerous, until he shall return to the doctrine of Christ. No advertisements, to be on guard, against his books. Why, then, should the faithful believers in the great fundamental truths of the Bible be held in such disrepute and covered with names and epithets to prevent the people from accepting Christ according to the Bible record which they are constantly teaching?

ON COMING OUT OF CHURCHES.

Eld. F. G. Brown, of the Baptist church, writes an article on this subject which is candid, and contains many valuable thoughts carefully expressed. We extract an item. He says:

"I have a sorrowful exhibition of the position which some churches are resolved on pursuing in relation to the Advent; many of them will not have it touched upon in their pulpits, however remotely. Others are determined on excluding those who imbibe the sentiments of Adventists, when the least pretext offers itself.

"At present I feel as though much might be said in favor of entirely withdrawing all connection from those sects or churches that reject the great Scriptural truth of Christ at the door. I can sympathize with those who have been cast out, or who have felt that their own peace and salvation call on them to dissolve their church relationship. And here arises a serious question: do we not by our continuance with those very sects that have proscribed our brethren, tacitly recognize and approve the course that has been pursued toward them? Do not the laws of friendship, aye, does not the spirit of Christ's declaration—'inasmuch as ye have done it unto one of the least of these my brethren, ye have done it unto me,' point out our duty under present circumstances. Brethren that are dear to us—some of Christ's most faithful servants—have been hastily ejected from those very churches to which some of us are now clinging. How can we cleave to those who are avowed enemies to those whom Christ loves? I must confess it requires great charity to fellowship such.

"But *again*, why should we wish to continue a union, which, after all, is *only nominal?* We are *virtually excommunicated* from these churches. Their hearts, their pulpits, and everything that constitutes union, are closed against us. Why, then, seek to preserve our connection?

"Again, if our doctrine be true, all hope of reclaiming to the truth the churches, as bodies, seems ready to be abandoned; they have had the truth blazing around them long enough to prove their inflexible determination to reject it; and our influence for good while among them seems quite cut off.

"Again, if we should all show our disapprobation of the course which the churches and the ministry are pursuing against the Advent doctrine, by forsaking them and leaving them to their own evil ways, would they not begin to see what and where they are? . . . We are in duty bound to be faithful to those who are slumbering, or crying peace and safety. . . . I feel that the subject requires a serious consideration. Let each one of us, with our Bibles in our hands, and with much prayer for guidance, try and ascertain our individual duty at this juncture of affairs.

For one, I desire to do right; I do not want to go too fast, nor too slow; I want to follow just such a line of duty as Jesus, were he here in person, would approbate, though it be attended with the loss of all things.

"Signs of the Times, Jan. 10, 1844. F. G. BROWN."

The treatment which the believers received from those with whom they had held the most intimate Christian association, made it impossible for them to worship in the same churches. Many were rudely assailed, taunted, ridiculed, shunned, tried for heresy, or dropped from church records without trial, while wanderers, worldlings, scoffers, and many who were known to be wholly destitute of Christian religion, were not dealt with, but allowed to control in the business of the churches.

While many of the most devoted, self-sacrificing Christians, both of ministers and the laity, were obliged to come out from their former church associations and form new ones. The Rev. J. Porter, D. D., who has since passed through searching trials under charges of being associated in the notorious frauds in the business of the "Methodist book concern," N. Y., felt it his duty to write a tract, entitled, "Come-out-ism," in which he made *mince-meat* of Adventists, Mormons, Mesmerisers, Infidels, and every grade of evil-doers, classing all who left the churches, as one stray herd out on the devil's common, and sure of perdition unless they returned and confessed.

SKETCH OF ELD. D. R. MANSFIELD AND MRS. M. S. MANSFIELD.

Brother Mansfield was converted in his early days. In 1842 he heard the message of the soon coming of Christ, investigated, and embraced it. Believing it his duty to preach the gospel, he entered upon the work with great zeal, proclaiming the message of Christ's coming, and calling on sinners to repent and be saved. The Lord crowned his efforts with success, and reformations followed. Miss M. S. Higgins, also a native of Maine, was converted and embraced the faith in 1844, through the labors of Brn. Wilder B. Start and D. R. Mansfield. And having the impression that she had a public duty to perform in the work of the gospel, commenced to visit the churches and exhort. Her gift of communication and logic, together with her earnestness and charming singing, soon caused her to become conspicuous. The Lord blessed her labors, and she had encouragement to continue in that work.

Bro. Mansfield and Sister Higgins were united in marriage in 1847, and mutually entered upon a life-work of proclaiming the gospel of the coming and kingdom of Christ. Souls were converted, Christians were instructed, and wanderers were reclaimed.

During several years they labored in the central part of Maine, and planted the truth in many towns. They traveled some in other New England States. In 1848 they embraced the views of "life and death," so called, i. e. of the entire mortality of man, eternal life through Christ, unconsciousness in death, and the final destruction of the wicked. In 1852 under a strong impression of duty to go West, they went to Milwaukee, Wis., where they were sick a long time, used up all their means, and were entirely destitute. The Lord heard their cry after he had prepared them for pioneer work, and led them to Indiana, where he gave them work, food and raiment. Then they were led to Michigan, where an open door invited their efforts. They worked, and the Lord worked with them, through privation, trial and poverty, for a while, and trial and opposition until now, but with the Lord's continual blessing they have accomplished much in his cause. Sister M. did not attempt to occupy the pulpit, or preach from a text, until they went to Indiana. The Lord fitted them for the good work, with faith and zeal equal to the difficulties, talents sufficient to meet any opposing elements of the times, Bible theology sufficient to correct or expose the errors of the day, eloquence and logic enough to command and interest the most extensive audiences; with music enough to charm and quiet the most obtuse and ill-disposed clans who might attend their meetings (for they rank among the first-class singers known in America). The Lord led them about and instructed them. New doors were constantly opened before them. Many sinners have been converted, Christians enlightened and brought into the faith of speedy redemption, scattered believers gathered and built up in Christ. They have organized over twenty churches, have held series of meetings in over one hundred towns, with reformations in nearly every place, have set on foot the building of nine meeting-houses, which have been completed. They have had the pastoral charge of a church in Ind., 6 years, and of one in Buchanan, Mich., 13 years, sustained a mission meeting in Chicago one year, with good results. They have been united in their labors, and thus the Lord has given them grace to accomplish more and do better than some husbands and wives who both enter upon the work of preaching.

The obstacles in the West when they went there were many and formidable. Christians were few, the people destitute, the country new and uncultivated. Also, several classes of teachers bearing the name "Adventist," had traveled over those States, teaching notions, visions and speculations, wholly foreign to our views of the Scriptures, and had thus greatly misrepresented our faith, and demoralized churches which were gathered. There were but few then to unite with them in faithful labor. They have preached in all the northwestern States. Others have been sent in to work with them, while the Lord has raised up many there to aid now in carrying on the good begun work. Brother and Sister M. now reside in Minneapolis, Minn., where the Lord is greatly blessing their efforts, and they are confidently hoping soon to see the Lord coming in his glory to gather his waiting people.

MENTION OF VARIOUS MINISTERS WHO ENTERED UPON THIS WORK.

Among the many whose names and work we have not mentioned, and have not space to notice, at length, are: Elders J. C. Bywater, who wrote many good things, and preached the message of Christ's soon coming, with much success and usefulness.

H. H. Gross, who gave himself chiefly to the study and advocacy of Chronology and definite time. He was an earnest worker.

C. B. Turner, a judicious preacher and useful man in the Lord's vineyard. We have had two of the same name; both good men.

B. Matthias, an erratic of good gifts, who run into strange novelties.

H. Buckley, one of the faithful preachers of the word of the kingdom.

Butler Morley, a very devoted, conscientious and useful minister of the gospel, whose labors were signally blessed in the salvation of souls.

Joseph Bates, an able speaker and writer, who was very useful in the work of Christ until he became a Seventh Day Sabbath advocate.

J. K. Bellows, who gave himself wholly to the work of promulgating this message and the salvation of men.

J. D. Boyer, a faithful and true worker in the Lord's vineyard.

Ira Fanchier, who devoted much of his life and efforts to preaching time.

L. Osler, who came from the South to New England, an able and zealous minister of the word; but who replies to me that he has

"Conscientiously refused any responsibility growing out of association with those who have brought the 'blessed hope' 'of the gospel into unnecessary disfavor by foisting upon it unscriptural, fanatical, and dangerous sentiments, tending to unseemly practices;' and adds, 'as limited as my influence may be, I cannot consent to sacrifice that little, by a *public endorsement* of those with whom I could not consistently coöperate in labor;' you will therefore please not use my name in connection with the book you speak of publishing."

Had we not mentioned this "conscientious" brother's name it would have been construed by many, as a want of fellowship with *him.* But as we give his *protest* we think he cannot find cause to complain. We hold him in good fellowship if he cannot us.

Geo. Needham, a critical, able, and good preacher and writer, who did good service in the cause until he conceived the idea that he should become more conspicuous, and attempted to move others out of the places he seemed to aspire to fill, which resulted in obscuring his lamp at noon-day.

Prof. J. P. Wethee, an able speaker and fair writer, who came from Ohio to New England, with the idea that he would soon become editor of the "Advent Herald;" preached well, exerted a good general influence, gained many friends, and aided in building up the cause until he became the tool of conspirators, to be made a leader of them, which did great injury and produced much division and alienation.

J. Lenfest, who wrote some valuable books adapted to sailors, and instructive to all, and published a paper; traveled and did much good in preaching, as an evangelist; but became entangled in some difficulties and turned his attention to secular matters.

N. Billings, a devout and stable Christian, good preacher and first-class singer.

Geo. Phelps, an earnest, zealous, critical thinker and devout minister.

P. Hawks, a stable and reliable man of God, a safe teacher, and faithful worker in the cause of Christ; a real lover of the truth.

SKETCH OF ELD. KING HASTINGS AND HIS LABORS.

Eld. Hastings was a native of Blandford, Mass. He was born in 1805. Of his early history we have no record, but that he was converted in early life, and became a minister of the gospel, many can gladly testify. He joined the Methodist E. church, and was for some time a preacher among them. It is said of him that he was one of the most devoted and laborious men known amongst the Methodists; a man of great faith, of daring undertakings, and a terror to evil-doers. He left the Methodist church on the Slavery and Second Advent agitation in the early days of the Advent proclamation. He embraced and preached the message of the Lord's immediate coming from 1842, until his death, in 1854. Great reformations attended his labors, and many incidents of deep interest are related of his work, but we have failed to obtain them in any form for our use. He was eccentric, attracting attention, aggressive in his efforts, daring in his attacks, and victorious in his engagements. Many were brought to Christ through his ministry. There is good reason to believe that his godly influence and instructions were not lost upon his son, Horace L., who has been made, through grace, an instrument of great service in the *Second Advent Message.*

Several attempts were made by mobs to break up his meetings, but without success. Once a young desperado gathered a company "of the baser sort," and entered a house where King Hastings was preaching with great earnestness to an attentive audience. He led his mob up to the front and daringly stared the preacher in the face. Eld. H. suspended his remarks, and cried out vehemently several times, *Amen!* AMEN! AMEN! The ringleader turned and ran out, with his posse, in great haste; the preacher followed to the door, shouting, time after time, "God Almighty chase him." He did chase him. The fellow ran to his home in great fright, and after several hours of distress under conviction for his sins, returned and sought the lodging place of Bro. Hastings, made known his errand, had him called up in the night to pray for and with him, till he found pardon in Christ to become a faithful servant of the Lord. King Hastings sleeps in death until Jesus comes to call his ransomed *from* death to immortality. Many revere his name and refer to him as the means of bringing them to Christ and the enjoyment of the blessed hope of eternal life when Christ comes.

NOTICE OF OTHER MINISTERS.

Charles Goodrich, an active, earnest, faithful preacher, formerly a Methodist preacher, who was brought into the faith through the preaching of King Hastings, and has continued in the Second Advent cause without wavering until this day.

I. H. Shipman, an ardent and faithful Christian minister who proclaimed the truth for many years, and built up many in the gospel faith and hope. He was a good teacher, writer and pastor. He died in the faith and at his post.

Brn. Bosworth, Bowles and Raynolds, who were faithful men in the proclamation of the Advent message, in leading sinners to Christ and building up the believers and churches in Christ.

John Howell, an earnest man with a good education, a devout and humble Christian, an able preacher; with eloquence almost equal to a Beecher, so active and zealous that he could never stop to rest until he rested in death; leaving a faithful and devoted Christian companion, and many friends to mourn his death.

Walter Pratt, an earnest and able minister, who sounded the cry long and faithfully with feeble health, until death cut him down to be lamented by a faithful wife and many devoted friends.

Edwin and G. W. Burnham, two brothers, who have labored extensively in proclaiming the Advent Message, and in leading men to Christ; but declined to respond to my request for items of their history. Edwin has been through "doubting castle" and joined the Baptists; but is doing a noble work as an evangelist among the churches, preaching as much of the message as he thinks they will bear. G. W. is yet among the "Evangelical Adventists," and a faithful minister; not ashamed, we believe, of the name we bear.

Elam Burnham, an eccentric, singular, devoted man of God, who loves the truth.

J. S. White, a reliable, faithful man, conscientious, devout, and an able preacher, a good historian, a clear and pointed writer.

S. Leavitt, who was a laborious and faithful servant of Christ.

Samuel Chapman, who traveled much in the Middle and Western States, and preached the Advent Message, always had reformations everywhere, organized a vast number of churches, and instructed them in the great truths of the Advent doctrine and practical Christianity.

J. G. Smith, who has worked faithfully and earnestly with the body, and for the up-building of the saints in the faith, from the early part of our history as a people.

J. W. Daniels, who was deeply interested and radical for a while, an able preacher; but made his way into the Baptist church, and we have never heard of any stir in that church on the subject arising from his labors.

Hermon Stinson, who was a Godly man and a sound and good preacher; educated at Bangor Theological Seminary, for a Congregational minister, but joined the F. W. Baptists, then became an Adventist, and a useful, safe man. He now sleeps in death.

Andrew Rollins, a good pastor and useful man, who embraced the faith and preached it thoroughly; but was over awed by his F. W. B. brethren to sign a confession and be re-instated; but he believed the truth and died in the faith.

Joel Spaulding, a F. W. Baptist, was earnest in proclaiming the Message and great numbers were converted and baptized by him; but he was persuaded to sign a confession and quit preaching it, and has done but little since.

Bro. Pease, of Exeter, Me., loved the Word greatly, and preached it with his might and lived it out among the people.

Israel Daman, one of the most noisy and unaccountable of men. Has labored much in word and has become especially conspicuous by shouting and jumping. But sinners have been converted under his labors.

John Pearson, jr., embraced the faith in Portland, under the labors of Bro. Miller, and soon began to preach it. Although for a while he was driven upon the sands and was in great jeopardy "between two seas," in the time movement, yet he got afloat, and has been an able minister and advocate of the *Advent Message*. He has been one of the officers and advisers of the American Millennial Association for many years.

Wilder B. Start, a young man of superior talents and deep piety, who was designed by his father for a Congregationalist minister, and while being educated in the Bangor Theological Seminary, became a believer in the Advent near, went out among the churches proclaiming it, was expelled from the Institute because of it, just before he was to have graduated. He traveled some three years proclaiming to all, "Behold, the bridegroom cometh, go ye out to meet him." An only son, rejected by the school of the prophets, denied a home and inheritance by a wealthy and formerly indulgent father; called insane by his former associates; he pursued the work he believed the Lord had appointed him, in company with Bro. D. R. Mansfield. The Lord wrought mightily through his labors, and many souls were brought to Christ. Though he died in 1846, many are now living in the service of God who were converted under his labors, while he rests in death awaiting the sound of the last trump.

Wm. M. Ingham was an humble and faithful Christian minister, traveling thousands of miles on foot through Maine, New Brunswick, and Nova Scotia, and preaching everywhere he found an open door, saying, "repent, for the kingdom of God is at hand," until, receiving an injury in the head by a swinging mainboom, on shipboard, while on a mission, his mind was ruined for further labor, and he is lost to the cause, but, we trust, ready for the kingdom of God.

E. Crowell, a minister of the F. W. Baptist church, who embraced the faith and preached it with good effects, bringing a large portion of the F. W. B. churches in Poland, Richmond, and several other towns in Maine, into the faith. He was a faithful minister for several years, but fell into sin, retired from the work rather than be made a public example, after which he advertised for work among the F. W. Baptists, abjuring Adventism, and they took him back, being ignorant of his fall. We hope he has done better, and may find his way into the kingdom of God by repentance and faith in forgiving mercy.

N. G. Reed, a good and direct practical preacher, a quiet and living Christian, always at work, and believes what he preaches.

A. Bridges, an able and faithful gospel minister, and proclaimer of the Second Advent Message. He moved west, and has since died.

M. Wellcome, who was a laborious worker with much success among the Methodists, preaching the coming of Messiah what they would allow, until checked by the Presiding Elder, and then came out and has faithfully proclaimed it in the Western States since, and yet enjoys the blessed hope of soon seeing the king in his beauty.

Benj. Spaulding, a godly man, who sacrificed ease and home society to travel and tell the story of Jesus' dying love and of his soon coming in glory, from house to house and in public; beginning in 1841 and going on thirty years, in Massachusetts, New Hampshire, Vermont, Connecticut, and Maine, and on many Islands off the coast, distributing tracts and instructing, in a quiet and humble way, thousands of men, women, and children, on some of the most glorious principles of the gospel, going on foot generally, and retired at about seventy years of age to his family and fine farm, being too feeble to pursue the mission longer, but strong in the faith of soon seeing Jesus coming in his glory. He keeps up an extensive correspondence in his advanced age.

Some of the above were timid, cautious, and doubtful in regard to the steps which should be taken in such difficult and trying times of controversy and distressing opposition; they were threatened and persuaded, until some signed confessions of errors, which had been prepared for the occasions, and which really embodied a fact, for the time—1843—had passed and proved them in error on that point, and thus they became restored to conciliatory standing among their former co-laborers. Others suppressed their convictions and were let alone. But they have never succeeded in accomplishing much for the churches since; for they were well persuaded that they were compromising great and important truths to keep peace and union with their churches. They were ever after suspected by their brethren as still secretly holding the great cardinal truths which distinguish the Adventists, and some have returned to the work anew. Yet the most of the above-named, and many others, who we cannot mention here, but whose names we trust are written in heaven, were firm in the faith. They could not be frightened, frowned, flattered, hired, nor bought off from the work of declaring constantly and ununmistakably, "Behold, thy salvation cometh." They could not suppress the great cardinal truths which they found to underlie the whole system of human redemption, nor hide their convictions that the grand consummation of the Christian's hope is about to be realized. They, with (in many cases) their faithful and believing wives and children, chose rather to sacrifice their church relations, salaries, comfortable homes, and delightful situations, worldly reputation, and fashionable society, than to sacrifice these sanctifying truths. They allowed themselves to be expelled, or quietly withdrew, that they might publish to all, the truths they believed due the people of this generation, and of great importance that they should hear. Their love for the truth and for the people, with their fellowship and interest for the professed people of God who bore fruits of righteousness, even when repelled and greatly misused by many of them, led them to endure great toil and privations to do them good, and bring them to the enjoyment of that hope which had been the source of great joy to themselves.

We acknowledge that some have been erratic, ever changing, teaching things they ought not. Some have been disorderly—opposed to all order except their own, and by false messages and false policy have done much more harm to the cause than all outside opposition could do. But as a class, those engaged in giving this message to the church and world, have been, by the blessing of God through the sanctifying power of his truth and spirit, as noble and faithful a company of men and women of God, as ever represented the church of Christ in this world since the apostles.

The above-named persons and experiences, toils, and trials, are but samples of thousands of similar cases throughout the States and Provinces of this Continent, from the early history of the message until now. Through the weaknesses of human nature, under the temptations of the enemy, and allurements of popular society, some have vacillated, changed, and foundered, several of whom righted again, and entered upon the work with renewed energy.

ONE GOOD CONFESSION—LETTER FROM BRO. EDWIN BURNHAM.

BRO. BLISS:—It is well known that about one year and a half ago I professed to believe in the second coming of Christ in, or about 1843. I preached it somewhat extensively, and was wonderfully blessed in my labors. Souls were converted and saints refreshed. But time passed on, and I began to doubt "the time." At length I entirely gave up the definite period of the "end of the vision:" I was disappointed, and felt very unpleasantly. From this time I began to sink in my feelings and became worldly and indifferent. Thus many of God's dear children were grieved, and those who loved not his appearing were glad. To be sure I did not give up the great truth that "Christ is at hand," but I did not feel interested in it as I did formerly; and therefore Satan took the advantage of me. Indeed, I slumbered and slept. I then began to hold those off who still contended for the time, to feel improperly toward them. Particularly, I could not, or rather would not associate with Brn. Himes and Cole, and others. I remember too of speaking of those brethren both publicly and privately in an improper manner. In this state of mind I went to Boston and preached to a portion of the Chardon street people, at the Melodeon. Of course I was arrayed directly against the Advent people at the Tabernacle. I was honest in this, but blind also—and knew it not. A part of that time I felt very unhappy and lonely, but did not see fully the cause. I was convinced that God was with the Advent people; and I daily saw them blessed, while I was doing comparatively nothing. Being thus discontented and unhappy, I left Boston as soon as convenient, and thought to travel. I visited Portland, New Bedford, and some other places; and endeavored to sympathize with the Advent people as far as I could in my then partial condition of mind. I thought I saw things among them that were wrong—perhaps in some instances I did—but in meddling with those things, I did some harm to those who were standing in the counsel of God. I remember of using strong language about the Advent people at the Lynn Convention—so called, and thought I was doing God service. I have recently been preaching at Haverhill, Mass., to the church that Eld. Plummer separated from, and thought I was preaching, and living just about right. I would not sympathize with Eld. Plummer and his friends, and therefore took sides rather against him. But after all this striving and slumbering the spell is at length broken. A few weeks ago while sitting in the Advent Tabernacle at Haverhill, about sunset, the Holy Ghost fell upon me as it never did before—and all my past life came into view, and O what a spotted life it appeared. The judgment scene opened before me, and I was broken to pieces. I cried to God—confessed, and found mercy. I felt that God would purify and make me whole. Amen, so let it be. Since that time no impure thoughts or feelings lodge in my mind. I am continually looking up expecting my Master. In future I wish to stand with those who are looking for Him, and are searching what, and what manner of time, etc. I ask forgiveness of God, and all men, for all my wrongs, and may I be kept unto eternal life. So come, Lord Jesus. Amen.

EXETER, N. H., Sept. 6, 1844.

SKETCH OF ELD. JONAS MERRIAM AND HIS LABORS.

Jonas Merriam was a native of Topsfield, Mass., a graduate of Bowdoin College, and formerly a faithful member of the Congregational church. When he heard the message that Jesus was coming soon, he entered upon a careful and critical examination of the Scriptures, with a prayerful heart, to learn the claims of this new thought. He was a very pious, conscientious and studious Christian, believing in the conversion of the world and a temporal millennium; but the light of truth soon revealed the fables which had formerly occupied his mind. Having seen the joyous truths revealing the true gospel hope, he turned his attention to the study of the prophecies and chronology, and in A. D. 1844, became a full believer in the views embraced in the "SECOND ADVENT MESSAGE." His joy was great; he appeared like a young convert, as his fruitful mind explored the precious truths, revealing the riches of God's grace in providing such glories and treasures as he had promised to all who would believe in Jesus Christ.

Although his constitution was broken so as to nearly destroy all prospects of future active labors, Bro. M. soon commenced to preach the unsearchable riches of Christ, and to proclaim that he was about to return to establish his eternal reign. His labors were retarded much by ill-health; but were blessed of God to the salvation of sinners and the up-building of many Christians in the gospel hope. Affectionate and kind to all, he made many friends who loved and revered him for his deep piety. He embraced the doctrine of immortality only through Christ, and of the final extinction of the wicked, and faithfully promulgated it in opposition to the immortality of the soul and eternal torture of the lost.

When the "World's Crisis" was originated Bro. Merriam was chosen editor of that paper, and continued to discharge his duties in that capacity until failing strength obliged him to retire. He then settled in Concord, N. H., where he remained under wasting consumption, joyful in hope, until death released him from all his sufferings in the spring of 1872.

A widow and numerous friends are left to mourn the separation; but they are consoled by the fact that he sleeps in Jesus, and that the life-giver is coming soon to bring back from death all the sheep of his fold to share immortality and eternal life.

PROPOSED MISSION TO EUROPE.

We propose, if time be prolonged, to go to England the middle of October next. Bros. Litch and Hutchinson will accompany us. We hold our first Conference in London, the first week in November. At this meeting, arrangements will be made for future operations in that kingdom, and in other portions of the world, as God shall give us time and opportunity.

We intend to bring before the groaning population of Europe, a hope of deliverance—a "blessed hope," a cheering prospect of a land of heavenly rest. A rest and blessedness found only in the kingdom of God,—in the New Heaven, and New Earth, that is speedily to be revealed by the Second glorious Advent of Jesus Christ.

If time be continued a few months, we shall send the *glad tidings* out in a number of different languages, among Protestant and Catholic nations, among which we shall not forget *Babylon, in Italy.*

A press will probably be established in London, and lecturers will go out in every direction, and we trust the word of the Lord will have a free course and be glorified. What will be accomplished we cannot tell. But we wish to do our duty. We ask the prayers of our brethren that we may be able to fulfill this ministry to the glory of God.

Some have suggested a desire to aid the mission. If it be of God, we have no doubt many will aid it by their prayers and contributions. Those who wish to assist, can send their contributions to J. V. Himes, 14 Devonshire St., Boston, or 9 Spruce St., New York. Or to Bro. J. Litch, 41 Arcade, Philadelphia, Pa. Or Bro. Hutchinson, who will attend the Camp-meetings in N. H. and Mass.

Nothing has been raised for the Mission as yet. It will be seen that the plan will require considerable means, if God gives us time to perfect it. Our trust and faith is in God. And here we leave the matter, knowing God will direct in all that is for his glory, and the salvation of men.

CLEVELAND, O., Aug. 10, 1844. J. V. HIMES.

The movement on definite time frustrated the work of this mission, and it was not carried out until two years later; as we shall show.

ELD. S. S. SNOW AND THE 1844 TIME MESSAGE.

The anxious suspense in which the Advent believers were placed after the last point to which they had looked passed can be realized only by those who had that experience. They were sure the end was near; in this they felt there could be no room for doubt. They had been confident that the definite time for the event was revealed in the Bible and that they had found the true date, but they were obliged to realize that their date was an error (though some novices declined). They were confident that a constant readiness, in a waiting position, was of all importance; the most of them came to the conclusion that they should not know the time more definitely than Christ had given it in Matt. 24th chapter, "Then know that it is nigh, even at the doors," yet a few, who had been more confident and positive in the message of 1843 than they were warranted in Scripture, still declared that the time would be understood by the church, definitely, before the Lord would come. This idea was pleasing to the disappointed, interested host, but it was received with general disfavor. The most of the leading preachers and writers, with all of the editors of the "*Advent Herald*" and the "*Midnight Cry*," declined to speak out with decision in its favor. They quoted Paul, "For yet a little while and he that shall come will come." Bros. Himes and Miller visited Rochester, July 23d and held a Conference. There they preached that we were in the space between the second and third woes, called "quickly," "a little while;" Bro. Miller called that "the scriptural and safe ground to occupy."

Eld. S. S. Snow had prepared an article of considerable length, in which he reviewed the whole argument and dates for 1843, and came to the conclusion that he had discovered an error of *one year*, which would extend the time on the same argument they had formerly used, one year later, to 1844. This article was published in the "*Midnight Cry*," dated Feb. 16, 1844; Eld. Southard, the editor, wholly dissented from its conclusions. It was republished in the "*Advent Herald*." The editors of that paper saw that Eld. Snow had fallen into an error in quoting Dr. Hales, making one year too much; this they pointed out, showing the error was in Snow, and not in the former arrangement. This correction, however, seemed not satisfactory to those who were in a state of mind ready to receive any solution of their disappointment; and some did not *see* the article which set the point right, others did not appreciate it. The subject was agitated, preached, written in letters of correspondence through the land, that the mystery was solved; that 1844, and not 1843, was the correct casting of figures. Those who did not have the books, or were not fully competent to adjust all chronological data, looked to those whom they supposed *were* qualified to do so. Added to this, Eld. Snow, while in deep meditation upon this subject, was casting in his mind the argument elsewhere mentioned, on types (which he had been interested in previously), in the typical law, the passover and wave sheaf of the first month after the vernal equinox, and the sacrifice of atonement on the seventh month; when he was suddenly impressed with the following thoughts. Mr. Miller's time expired in March. Some looked for Christ to come as the anti-type of "the wave sheaf," extended their expectations to April 18th (H. H. Gross and others), but they should have looked for Christ to come in fulfillment of the sacrifice of atonement, "on the tenth day of the seventh month." This is the tarrying time, "At midnight a cry was made." A prophetic day is one year, a night is six months; the tarry will be six months; the Lord will come on the tenth day of the seventh Jewish month this year. From this point Eld. Snow commenced to give, in an earnest spirit, what he called the *true midnight cry.* Others took the idea; it looked plausible, it was desirable, it relieved from suspense, and many were ready to accept it as truth. Eld. Snow had written an article which was published in the "*Midnight Cry*," of New York, dated June 22, 1844, in which he said, "About the first of last January I felt it my imperative duty to impart to the world, and especially to the Advent band, the light which my heavenly Father has given me, concerning the termination of the prophetic periods. . . It was necessary that a mistake should be made in regard to the ending of the days, and that this mistake should be general among the expectants of the kingdom, in order that their faith might be tried, and that a wicked world and a world-loving church might have ample opportunity to mock and scoff and manifest their hatred to our Lord's appearing, etc. . . . Had not such a mistake been made, there are some prophecies which could never have been completely fulfilled, such as Ezek. xii. 22, Hab. ii. 23, Jer. li. 45, Rev. xviii. 4.

"This was clearly unfolded to me. . . . I felt it my indispensable duty to the world, and especially to the dear brethren, to inform them that the periods could not terminate before the seventh month of the sacred year 1844." Thus it appears Mr. Snow did not accept the correction of his error in quoting Dr. Hales. Mr. Miller, the editors of the Advent papers, and other chief preachers were slow to accept Eld. Snow's argument as reliable. For this they were suspected as above receiving light from one of less note than themselves, that they dare not risk their reputation on another time argument. It was intimated that Miller, Himes, Litch, and others had done a good work, but as they would not advance with the light, God had committed his cause to other hands, and on Aug. 22, 1844, Eld. Snow issued a paper in Haverhill, Mass., entitled "*The True Midnight Cry*," to promulgate this *time message*. The paper was afterwards published in some city in New York. Eld. S. vehemently pressed this message, several others in various parts of the country joining with him. They urged it upon the editors of the Advent papers. It was the chief topic at the camp-meetings that season. The other papers began to publish the argument; all hoped it was true, many looked upon it with great anxiety. A letter which Mr. Miller had written a year and a half previous, suggesting that as the tenth day of the seventh Jewish month had been of great importance as the day of atonement, it might be that Christ would fulfill the type of the high priest in coming out of the "holiest of all" on the tenth of the seventh month when he should come, was republished. This greatly increased the faith of many who had confidence in Mr. Miller's opinions, though Mr. M. had not taught it as a doctrine, but gave it as a suggestion on May 7, 1843. Added to the above, Eld. Geo. Storrs, who had gained an extensive influence as a teacher, wrote an editorial in his paper, "*Bible Examiner*," of Sept. 24, 1844, in which he said, "I take up my pen with feelings such as I never before experienced. *Beyond a doubt*, in my mind, the tenth day of the seventh month will witness the revelation of our Lord Jesus Christ in the clouds of heaven." He then alludes to their disappointment in March, argues a "tarry" of half a year, then adopts the cry of Eld. Snow, accepts the argument on types, and adds, "I think the hour of the Advent will be in the evening of the tenth day (of the seventh month). I incline to believe that those who watch for the day and hour will understand both, before they arrive."

"*The Hope of Israel*" copied this and strongly advocated the tenth day view. The influence of this *time message* went forth like the released waters of a mighty river when the dam has given way. A good work had been in progress all summer in various parts of the land; meetings now multiplied; many gave up their secular business and congregated for the worship of God and the investigation of the Bible. Farmers left their crops unharvested; many seemed oblivious to all worldly affairs. Unbelievers noticed these movements with varied results. Some called the believers crazy, foolish, and fanatical; others were awed to reflections that these men were honest, rational, and devoted to the work of saving souls, *perhaps* they have the true light on the Lord's coming. Many unconverted men and women, who saw the sincerity and fruits of faith in the believers, really feared the Lord would come on the day designated. The movement rapidly gained strength. "The Voice of Truth," of Oct. 2d, states that Elders Marsh, Galusha, Peavy, and others had endorsed it. "The Midnight Cry," of Oct. 5th, yields to the argument. Oct. 6th, Mr. Miller accepts the argument as truth and writes his endorsement of it, and within a few days the most of those who held to the argument Mr. Miller had formerly used, that the definite time for Christ to come was revealed in the Bible, were brought under its influence. Those who did not have confidence in set times refrained from opposing it, but made some suggestions concerning their views.

LETTERS FROM BROTHER J. LITCH.

DEAR BROTHER BLISS:—The Lord is blessing our labors in this section, by awakening and converting sinners, and blessing his people. At our camp-meeting in Morrisville, the Lord was with us—quite a number professed to be converted—and a time of general quickening among Christians took place. The people of that section were deeply interested in the Lord's coming. Since we came home, we have had good seasons in the city. Some have been converted at Julian street, and two arose for prayers in the congregation at the Museum last Sabbath.

Brother Tullock returned yesterday from the camp-meeting, near Lancaster, and brings a most cheering account of the state of things there. There is a field from Lancaster to Chambersburgh, Pa., on the line of the Western Railroad, which promises a precious harvest if occupied. To morrow we commence a camp-meeting at St. Georges, Delaware, where we expect to meet our brethren from Baltimore. Yours in hope, J. LITCH.

Philadelphia, Sept. 3, 1844.

THE DELIVERANCE—THE SEVENTH MONTH.

DEAR BROTHER BLISS:—You speak of a great deal of interest existing among you on the subject of the seventh month. As I have already given you one article on that subject, I hardly know as it will be best to say more. And yet, I feel it to be of some importance that all the light which exists on both sides of the question should be brought out. I have strong fears that many will be injured by their confidence in the Lord's coming only at that time. I would do something if possible to help them. I love my Saviour, and long to see him, to be where he is, and to behold his glory. I would rejoice to see him in the seventh month. And if I could see any grounds for expecting him *then*, more than at any other time, I would hail it with delight. But I cannot see it.

1. *If* there is any season of the year pointed out by the types for the resurrection and deliverance to take place, it seems to me to be the passover, which is in the first month—for the following reasons:

The promise to Abraham of an eternal inheritance for him and his seed, Christ (see Gal. iii. 15—17), was in the first month. For it was 430 years to a day (Exodus xii. 40), from the sojourn of Abraham and his seed (I give it according to the Samaritan pentateuch), to that deliverance. That deliverance did take place on the 14th day of the first month. It is the most lively type of the resurrection and deliverance of the saints which exists in the Bible. At least, so it seems to me.

Again, it was the season of the year in which Israel went up from Babylon. Ezra 7th chapter. The next strong type of the resurrection of the just, was Christ's resurrection, which took place in the first month.

And finally, when Christ ate the last passover with his disciples, he said: "With desire have I desired to eat the passover with you before I suffer. For I say unto you, I will not any more eat thereof, until it be fulfilled in the kingdom of God." Is not that passover to have a fulfillment in the kingdom of God? And observe, this was the paschal feast, and not the Lord's supper.

"And he took the cup, and gave thanks, and said, take it and divide it among yourselves: For I say unto you, I will not drink of the fruit of the vine, until the kingdom of God shall come." Luke xxii. 15—18.

In view of this strong passage, I must repeat again, if there is any type set forth in the Bible, of the resurrection and deliverance of the church, it is the passover.

MY DOUBTS.

I say "If," because I have doubts whether in fulfillment of the types, the time of the year is to be observed—for the following reason:

The yearly sin-offering under the law of Moses was the type of the sacrifice of Christ. The Law required that offering to be made in the seventh month and tenth day of the month. Levit. xvi. 29, 30. Read also the whole chapter. Yet when the Ante-type came and the true offering was slain, it was the first month and the fourteenth day. The part of the type was fulfilled, but not in the time.

This circumstance, with others, produces a serious doubt in my mind whether the time of Christ's coming the second time is at any one of the great Jewish feasts. It is clear, that the general time of the Lord's coming is revealed, we may know it is near, even at the door—but I am firmly of the opinion that "of that *day* and *hour* knoweth no man." The Bible is full of such assurances of the uncertainty of definite time, and admonitions to WATCH. And I think that altogether the best way.

I do hope our dear brethren will pause and learn wisdom from the past, before they settle too strongly on the seventh month. Let them watch and pray, and live for God every day; but do not let Satan get an advantage over them. Yours, J. LITCH.

MR. MILLER YIELDS TO THE MOVEMENT.

We here give letters from Miller with an extract from his biographer, which show his position on this point:

"September 30, 1844.

"DEAR BROTHER:—I am once more at home, worn down with the fatigue of my journey, my strength so exhausted and my bodily infirmities so great, that I am about concluding I shall never be able again to labor in the vineyard as heretofore. I wish now to remember with gratitude all those who have assisted me in my endeavors to awaken the church and arouse the world to a sense of their awful danger.

"I pray God, my brethren and sisters, that you may receive a reward in this life of an hundred fold, and, in the world to come, eternal life. Many of you have sacrificed much,—your good names, former associations, flattering prospects in life, occupation, and goods; and with me you have received scorn, reproach, and scandal from those whom it was our soul's desire to benefit. Yet not one of you *to whom my confidence has ever been given*, has, to my knowledge, murmured or complained. You have cheerfully endured the cross, despised the shame, and with me are looking for and expecting the King in all his glory. This is to me a cause of gratitude to God. May he preserve you unto the end. There have been *deceivers* among us, but God has preserved me from giving them *my confidence* to deceive or betray.

"I found on my arrival here that my brethren had relinquished the meeting-house to a small minority of our church, who separated from us last spring, because the second coming of Christ was there preached—though they claim to be looking for him. Rather than contend with them, our brethren have peaceably relinquished the chapel to them, and will build, if time continues. . . .

"WILLIAM MILLER."

THE SEVENTH MONTH MOVEMENT—DISAPPOINTMENT.

For a few months previous to this time, the attention of some had been directed to the tenth day of the seventh month of the current Jewish year, as the probable termination of several prophetic periods. This was not generally received with favor by those who sympathized with Mr. Miller, till a few weeks previous to the time designated, which, on that year, following the reckoning of the Caraite Jews, fell on the 22d day of October. Mr. Miller had, a year and a half previous, called attention to the seventh month as an important one in the Jewish dispensation; but as late as the date of his last letter (September 30) he had discountenanced the positiveness with which some were then regarding it. On the 6th of October he was first led to favor the expectation which pointed to that month, and thus wrote: "If Christ does not come within twenty or twenty-five days, I shall feel twice the disappointment I did in the spring."

About the same time, also, the belief in the given day was generally received. There were exceptions, but it is the duty of the impartial historian to record the fact, that those who had embraced the views of Mr. Miller, did, with great unanimity, heartily and honestly believe that on a given day they should behold the coming of the King of glory.

The world cannot understand how that could be; and many who professed the name of Christ, have spoken contemptuously of such an expectation. But those who in sincerity love the Saviour, can never feel the least emotion of contempt for such a hope. The effect on those entertaining this belief is thus described by Mr. Miller, in a letter dated October 11, 1844.

"I think I have never seen among our brethren such *faith* as is manifested in the seventh month. 'He will come,' is the common expression. 'He will not tarry the second time,' is their general reply. There is a forsaking of the world, an unconcern for the wants of life, a general searching of heart, confession of sin, and a deep feeling in prayer for Christ to come. A preparation of heart to meet him seems to be the labor of their agonizing spirits. There is something in this present waking up different from anything I have ever before seen. There is no great expression of joy: that is, as it were, suppressed for a future occasion, when all heaven and earth will rejoice together with joy unspeakable and full of glory. There is no shouting; that, too, is reserved for the shout from heaven. The singers are silent: they are waiting to join the angelic hosts, the choir from heaven. No arguments are used or needed: all seem convinced that they have the truth. There is no clashing of sentiments: all are of one heart and of one mind. Our meetings are all occupied with prayer, and exhortation to love and obedience. The general expression is, 'Behold, the Bridegroom cometh; go ye out to meet him.' Amen. Even so come, Lord Jesus!

"WILLIAM MILLER."

The natural heart would be unable to realize that any emotion, but that of fear and dread, could fill the minds of those thus believing. But when the secrets of the great day shall be made known, it will be seen that the coming of Christ was ardently desired by them, and that their hearts were filled with a holy joy, while they were subdued by awe, as standing in the presence of the Governor of the Universe. The state of mind thus produced was a great moral spectacle, upon which those who participated in it will ever look back with pleasure, and without regret.[1]

CLOSING WORK OF THE ADVENT HERALD OFFICE.

On Oct. 16th an immense edition of the *Advent Herald* was issued for free distribution in all parts of the land, as its last work, containing lengthy articles in advocacy of the seventh month view;

---

[1] Bliss' Life of Miller, pp. 269, 270.

a long letter to Prof. N. N. Whiting, who had constantly been, and yet was, opposed to fixing upon set times; a sketch of the rise and progress of the time argument. From one of the writers we make the following extract:

THE PRESENT MOVEMENT.—ITS RISE, PROGRESS, AND CHARACTERISTICS.

After the passing away of 1843—the Jewish year, the great body of the Adventists settled down in the belief that we could henceforth reckon particular times with no degree of positiveness.—They believed that we were where our chronology points, as the end of all the prophetic periods, at the termination of which the Advent is expected, and that while we should have to wait only the *little while* that our chronology might vary from God's time, yet they believed that we could have no more clue to the definite time.

As early as May, 1843, Mr. Miller had called our attention to the seventh month, of the Jewish Sacred year, as the time of the observance of those types which point to the Second Advent; and the last Autumn, we looked to that point of time with much interest. After it had passed away, Bro. S. S. Snow, fully embraced the opinion, that according to the types, the Advent of the Lord, when it does occur, must occur on the tenth day of the seventh month; but he was not positive as to the year. He afterwards saw that the prophetic periods do not actually expire until the present 1844; he then planted himself on the ground that about the 22d of Oct.,—the tenth day of the seventh month of this present year, must witness the Advent of the Lord of glory. This he preached in New York, Philadelphia, and other places during the past spring and summer; and while many embraced his views, yet no particular manifestation of its effect was seen, until about July.

At first, the definite time was generally opposed; but there seemed to be an irresistible power attending its proclamation, which prostrated all before it. It swept over the land with the velocity of a tornado, and it reached hearts in different and distant places almost simultaneously, and in a manner which can be accounted for only on the supposition that God is in this matter. It has produced everywhere the most deep searching of hearts and humilation of souls before the God of high heaven.

This movement was perfectly legitimate from the elements producing it, though many failed to comprehend it. In cases which are recorded where singular phenomena have been witnessed in or about large cities, resembling the light of great conflagrations, the alarm bells were rung, cries of fire! fire! fire! were made in the streets, the rattle of engines on the pavements and the rush of the people in the direction of the light have awakened the interest and solicitude of those who had property in jeopardy, or who felt an interest in the general welfare of others, causing them to feel and act precisely as though there *was fire* when there was none. The results on all who have confidence in the signals are the same under an *error* as under a *true* alarm. This is seen in thousands of cases in life in both joyous and terrific messages or conceptions which prove to be incorrect.

A MORAL FEATURE IN THIS MOVEMENT.

Amid the unbelief, scepticism, and carelessness of the masses, this sympathetic movement was witnessed, and though not sympathized with, was made useful to many reflecting minds. Tens of thousands of believers in Christ at once abandoned every worldly pursuit, care, and interest, disengaged themselves from all parties and persons in business, in a faith so full as to manifest their entire confidence that their Saviour was about to visit them in person and take them to his eternal abode, thus demonstrating that there was a people who lived in such communion and fellowship with their judge that they were ready and anxious to see him. We here give an extract from Bro. S. Bliss on this point. He says:

"The time immediately preceding the 22d of October was one of great calmness of mind and of pleasurable expectation on the part of those who regarded that point of time with interest. There was a nearness of approach to God, and a sweetness of communion with him, to which those who experienced it will ever recur with pleasure. During the last ten days secular business was, for the most part, suspended; and those who looked for the Advent gave themselves to the work of preparation for that event, as they would for death, were they on a bed of sickness, expecting soon to close their eyes on earthly scenes forever.

"There were some cases of extravagance, as there have been in all great movements, and it would have been strange had there not been. But the published accounts of these were greatly exaggerated, and hundreds of reports had no foundation in fact. All reports respecting the preparation of ascension robes, etc., and which are still by many believed, were demonstrated over and over again to be false and scandalous. In the investigation of the truth of such, no labor and expense was spared; and it became morally certain that *no instance of the kind anywhere occurred.*

"The most culpable incident, which had any foundation in fact, was in Philadelphia. In opposition to the earnest expostulations of Mr. Litch and other judicious persons, a company of about one hundred and fifty, responding to the pretended vision of one C. R. Georgas, on the 21st of October went out on the Darby-street road, about four miles from Market-street bridge, and encamped in a field under two large tents, provided with all needed comforts. The next morning, their faith in Georgas' vision having failed, all but about a dozen returned to the city; a few days later the others returned. That was an act the report of which was greatly exaggerated. It met the emphatic disapproval of Mr. Miller and the Adventists generally, and its folly was promptly confessed by the majority of those who participated in it.

"The day passed, and the expectation of the Advent at that time was proved to be premature. The friends were at first quite saddened, but were not disheartened by the passing of the time. This was the *only* specific *day* which was regarded by intelligent Adventists with any positiveness. There were other days named by those whose opinions were received with no favor; but their unauthorized declarations should not be imputed to the body.

"The fact that many suspended their business for a few days was censured by opponents; but it was only acting consistently with their faith, opponents being judges. Dr. Dowling, a celebrated Baptist clergyman in New York city, in a review of Mr. Miller, used this strong language:"

> "Were this doctrine of Mr. Miller established upon evidence satisfactory to my own mind, I would not rest till I had published in the streets, and proclaimed in the ears of my fellow-townsmen, and especially to my beloved flock, 'The day of the Lord is at hand! Build no more houses! Plant no more fields and gardens! Forsake your shops and farms, and all secular pursuits, and give every moment to preparation for this great event! for in three short years this earth will be burnt up and Christ shall come in the clouds, awake the sleeping dead, and call all the living before his dread tribunal.'"

THE POSITIONS TAKEN AFTER THIS TIME MOVEMENT.

As the army of believers were thrown into disorder and seeming disaster, by this second and overwhelming disappointment, several different positions were taken by different leading teachers, some of whom gave novel interpretations of the movement and of certain Scriptures to sustain their several views of it.

As several of these positions and interpretations were divergent from the general principles of the body of Advent believers, as well as from each other, shaping and sustaining several parties bearing the Advent name until now, it is of some importance that our readers should know the real positions which were finally settled upon, by each class, when they had time for candid and considerate reflection, as also the evidences on which they placed their confidence. This becomes the more important because several vague, immatured thoughts of men in high position and influence among Adventists have been quoted to give influence and strength to the diverging views which the authors of the statements never settled upon, nor allowed themselves to be guided by the principles attributed to them, as their subsequent history shows.

AN EXTRACT FROM ELD. J. LITCH.

"As our time has thus passed by—the civil year having terminated last October, and the ecclesiastical with the new moon in April—we are now prepared to tell the world what we shall do,—a question which has often been asked. We intend to hold fast the integrity of our faith without wavering, and not cast away our confidence which hath great recompense of reward. We intend to continue to comfort one another with the words of the coming of Christ, who will come and will not tarry. We shall continue to believe God's word, in its literal acceptation, for not one jot or tittle of all that is written therein will fail.

"We shall continue, God willing, to proclaim, Behold the Bridegroom cometh! go ye out to meet him; and the hour of his judgment is come! and we trust we shall not fail to continue to cry aloud to the world and the church to arouse themselves from their songs of 'peace,' and to listen to God's overtures of mercy. We intend to continue waiting and watching for the coming of the Lord, believing that it is just upon us; and we hope to continue faithful to the cause of truth, ever ready to confess or forsake any errors, when pointed out, or to receive any truth in accordance with the word of God. By so doing, we believe we shall soon unite, when the Lord shall come, in that response when 'it shall be said in that day, Lo this is our God; we have *waited* for him, and he will save us. This is the Lord, we have waited for him, we will be glad and rejoice in his salvation,' those being blessed who *wait* and come to the end of the days.

"As our time has elapsed, and we have no other specified time in the future, but wishing to live, and induce others to live, in continual readiness and constant expectation of the Lord's coming, we shall know that all who oppose us for so doing have no sympathy for the Lord's return. With those who are looking for the Lord, or love his appearing, we have no controversy. But with those who put far off the day of the Lord, and say in their hearts my Lord delayeth his coming, or deny the resurrection of the body and a future judgment, we can hold no Christian fellowship; for those who assume such positions show that they have no love for Christ's appearing, and teach men contrary to the admonitions of Christ and his apostles, that we should take heed to ourselves lest at any time our hearts be overcharged with surfeiting and drunkenness, and so that day come upon us unawares."

THE PUBLISHERS RESUMED THEIR WORK.

Soon after the passing of Oct. 22d the papers, which had been supposed to have finished their work, reappeared to continue the proclamation of the Advent Message on a more scriptural basis, having learned some things by experience which they could not understand previously.

THE POSITION OF ELD. J. V. HIMES.

In resuming their work, Eld. J. V. Himes remarks, in a letter to Eld. J. Marsh, "We have now passed every point of *definite time* in which we looked for our blessed Saviour, and yet I do not give up the question; I only give up the point that our chronologies are to be depended upon for literal exactness, as to time. But we are in the circle of a short period, and may look now every hour for the advent."

The following extract from the *Advent Herald*, written by Eld. Himes, will more clearly show his views and objects:

IN THE FIELD AGAIN.

It was a bright and cheering hope we cherished in the seventh month of this Jewish year, when we ceased our public labors, and looked for the consummation and the endless rest of the saints, supposing we had finished our severe and arduous labors of public lecturing, controversy, and entreaty, and the intense and perplexing labors of the press. But the time has passed, and so far as the *exact* period of *time* is concerned in which we looked for the consummation of our hope, we were wholly disappointed. Our hope as to a point of time was cut off. But not so with the hope itself; this is still good, and will be revealed in the Father's appointed time, to the joy of all who wait and hope to the end.

Being still placed in a condition that requires labor in the vineyard, for ourselves and others, we regard it as our most imperious duty to gird up the loins of our mind, and engage afresh and with all our might in the work that God in his Providence has seen proper to lay before us. Hence, we have again put the Advent press in full operation; and to the extent of our means are scattering the light of truth with as much zeal and, so far as we can learn, with as much success as ever. Having put our accusers to shame, and lived down the hate and malice of opposers at home, we have resolved, as time may allow, to visit our brethren abroad; and, by the blessing of God, we intend to plead the Advent cause in *propria persona* to to the extent of our opportunities. The Advent question will never sleep. It will live and, by its mighty and irresistless energy, will keep the elements of opposition to the reign of our King in active commotion, "sorely afflicting" a time-serving *priesthood* and laity, and arousing the ire and demoniacal hate of a "wicked and adulterous generation."

We have counted the cost, and shall, to the extent of the means which God has or may give us, *agitate*, AGITATE, AGITATE, until the slumbering watchmen with their churches shall see the falsity of their position, or feel the full force of the truth, that the kingdom of God *is nigh at hand.*

Our position in relation to time has been fully given in previous numbers of this paper. We can count no exact time now from any data of human chronology, yet we believe that the Advent will take place within the few years of disputed time among chronologists. We are now bound to watch and wait continually for the coming of the Lord, as being at the door, that when he cometh and knocketh we may open to him immediately.—Luke xii. 36.

Our position as to labor is, fully to occupy until the Lord shall come. Our work now in this time of trial is to comfort the saints, to re-arouse the slumbering churches to a candid examination of the Advent doctrine, and once more publish salvation through a crucified Redeemer in its fulness and power. We must, as the ambassadors of Christ, seek to be filled with faith and the Holy Spirit. What little time remains we are to be more bold, faithful, and indefatigable than ever. May the God of Israel nerve us up to the work, and may we never hold our peace or cease from the conflict "until he make Jerusalem a praise in the whole earth." With these views we have once more entered the field.

THE POSITION OF ELD. STORRS.

He says, "After having been convinced that we were mistaken with respect to definite time or exact time for the Second Advent of our Lord . . . I remain fixed, at present, in the belief that the *exact time*—day, hour, or year—for the Advent is not revealed in the Bible. Those who think differently will still continue to make their figures, and give days, months, and years, but time will probably show, as it has done again and again already, that they 'labor in vain and spend their strength for naught.' The evidence to my mind is clear that we are now living under the pouring out of the sixth vial, Rev. xvi., and that therefore the Advent cannot be distant, but is 'nigh, even at the doors.' If any choose to call this 'not knowing *anything* about the time,' be it so; it is, however, knowing just as much as our blessed Saviour bid us *know*, and that is as far as I dare go, lest I come under the censure of adding to the prophecy. If others see their way clear to go further I judge them not, for we must all appear before the judgment seat of Christ, and every one of us must give account of himself to God."

MR. MILLER'S NEW POSITION.

After this second disappointment Mr. Miller wrote very cautiously at first, scarcely defining a position, only so far as to give some general statement of a few scriptural duties which should be observed for the strengthening of all, and then says, "Brethren, hold fast; let no man take your crown. I have fixed my mind on *another time*, and here I mean to stand until God gives me more light, and that is *to-day, to-day, to-day*, until he comes. . . . But, say you, time has shown us wrong. I am not so certain of that. Suppose that Christ should come before the end of this Jewish year, every honest man would say we were right; and if the world should stand two or even three years more, it would not, in the least, affect the *manner* of the prophecy but the time."

This statement does not agree well with the remark, which has been often stated in public and printed for the people, that Mr. Miller stated "if the Lord did not come in 1843 he would not come until 1873." But we will quote again: "I believe the ground we have formerly stood upon, as it regards the chronology of prophecy, is the only ground we can take, and if the defect is in human chronology then no human knowledge is sufficient in this age to rectify it with any degree of certainty, and I see no good that can be accomplished by taking a stand for any future period, with less evidence than we had for 1843–4. For those who would not believe, with all the evidence we have produced, we cannot expect will now believe with much less evidence."[1]

We here give an extract from the *Advent Herald* of Jan. 15, 1845.

THE SCRIPTURAL POSITION.

"Definite time has been one of the peculiar features of the Adventism of this country, while some in our own, and many in other, lands have been looking for the speedy personal coming of our Lord, without being united on the exact point of time for this event. Thus far we have supposed it possible to arrive at least within the circumference of a year of the time appointed for the Advent; nay more, we recently cherished the hope of seeing our Lord on a given *day*; but both of these periods have passed and left us disappointed. Our best efforts have been employed in order so to harmonize the prophetic periods as to bring their termination unitedly within a common circle. We have fastened upon events which we thought marked their rise, and which of course would lead to their conclusion. In a similar work, men of the most thoroughly disciplined minds, and of the purest hearts, both at home and abroad, both now and heretofore, have engaged but in vain. The fruitlessness of our own results, therefore, is not to us so much a matter of surprise. Having ascertained what we believed to be the true starting points for these periods, we have urged the correctness of our position on time with a positiveness which, at this point, may appear almost as strange to ourselves as it has been unaccountable to our opposers. In so doing, we now confess that we have honestly erred, and we trust that the past may so reflect wisdom upon the future as to teach us that it is as dangerous to be too confident as too sceptical, and that presumptuous belief deserves rebuke as well as sluggish incredulity. And we are heartily glad that we can now conscientiously yield to our friends on the other side some portion of the ground for which we have heretofore contended. Our conviction is that, for wise reasons, the divine mind has forever concealed the precise rise of those periods, at the end of which his Son shall be revealed from heaven; so that we believe it above the power of man to demonstrate either the day, the month, or the year of their consummation.

---

[1] Bliss' Life of Miller, pp. 277, 281.

"In making the above concession we have no intention of throwing ourselves back on the old ground of entire ignorance in relation to the chronological prophecies; the real truth in the case may be approximated, and our past labors have tended to this result. The system, therefore, as it has been styled, is as good now as ever, since it is not dependent for its existence on the expiration of one or more points of time. The historic prophecies are still to be credited and investigated. As intimated, we feel that we are not wide of the mark in our calculations and hopes. We therefore yield no portion of our former position, save the item of exact time. Our ground heretofore may have been too lofty, and we shall be rejoiced if, by descending a step or two, we can meet our honest opposers on a line more convenient and favorable for ourselves, and more likely to be beneficial to them. Nor should it be overlooked that one of the chief objections to our views is thus so far removed that we may hope to receive no small addition to our ranks from among all the humble and devoted who heartily love Jesus and his appearing, but whose faith has never been adequate to grasp a definite point of time for that event. We can but cherish the expectation that, for the future, the truth on this glorious subject, as we hope to entertain and present it, will operate as a test and extractor of the faith of all who really belong to Christ.

"The utility of definite time has always been urged in its favor, and the inefficacy of indefinite time has been as stoutly urged. It has been said that the church and the world make no objection to the position of indefiniteness; but this will not be found so when such time is presented with the above and other qualifications. We have ever maintained that the question before the religious world at this time is one which does not so much respect dates as it does the character of the events which are just before us. We are now in a favorable situation for proving the sincerity of those professors who have opposed time, and not the event itself of the Lord's coming, and we shall be extremely glad if now we may secure the sympathy and co-operation of such. But the point after all is not one of like or dislike, of utility or of inutility,—but what saith the Scriptures? If God has set the broad seal of his approbation on the proclamation of the coming of his Son within a specific time, it is equally as certain that, when we assume a ground yet more in accordance with his

Word, he will grant us equal manifestations of his favor. The experiment should first be made before an unfavorable conclusion be drawn. It has been made with signal success abroad, and very recently at home. During the period of what was known as the tarrying time converts were made to our faith, and souls were turned unto God. The present is not unlike that period, and may be safely relied on as a season in which, with diligence and prayer, God's blessing may be expected.

"It is urged that indefinite time induces a spirit of *slumber*. If this be true, then it does appear that our faith must be feeble on every point but that of time, when there is a great variety of evidence on which faith should be proportionately distributed. The legitimate tendencies of our present ground are highly unfavorable to sleep. Standing, as we do, where the prophetic numbers have disappeared from our view,—the natural and moral signs blazing out before our eyes, and the seventh trumpet liable at any moment to pour its heavy thunders into our ears,—this surely is no position for indifference or slumber. As well might the clime-burnt mariner sleep at his wheel, because his reckoning has run out without his being able to reach the long wished-for port; or as well might we relapse into indifference, because the usual moment for the arrival of the locomotive has passed by, and we are not pursuing our proposed journey. Every such passing moment should naturally increase our solicitude and awaken our watchfulness. So, now, as we have no means of estimating the precise hour for our Lord's Advent, our interest in that event should rise with every fleeting moment, and so far from taking advantage of such a delay, and of excusing ourselves for negligence in relation to this event, we should rather be grateful for the light that God has so condescendingly vouchsafed to us and let its every beam aid in guiding us to glory. More distinctness of time would have been granted, had infinite wisdom deemed it for our good and his glory. Let a trial be made of looking for the Lord *to-day*, TO-DAY, TO-DAY; let every morning and every evening be occupied in this service; let the conviction everywhere follow us that the Lord may come the present moment. Such a position will not only be followed by a highly blessed effect, as our own experience can testify, but it is a practicable position; it is one in which the Scriptures clearly sustain us. This position will impart constant fervor to our prayers, induce a spirit of abiding watchfulness over our thoughts and words, regulate our plans, and give nerve and activity to our religious actions. . . . And here, too, we think a danger may be avoided into which we are suspicious some may have fallen; we refer to that which probably has its foundation in the human mind,—a liability to suffer the mind, when it has fixed itself on a particular point of time, to become more engrossed with that mere abstract period than it is with the great work of a sufficient preparation to *meet* a distinct time. An indefinite period will open our hearts to us and test the nature of our faith as never before; yea, more, it will lift us above those fluctuations of feeling and hope which naturally result from coming and passing of stated periods.

"In this connection it may not be irrelevant to remark, that in taking the position of indefinite time, we thereby avoid an error of supposing (as some have), that the Holy Spirit seals upon the heart a definite period of time. It is not to be supposed that God has blessed us, as we have received and proclaimed time in the abstract, but having approximated the time of the Advent, as we have associated with our faith, corresponding watchfulness, prayerfulness, and true primitive zeal in the cause of Christ.

"The SPIRIT of God will never attest in opposition to the plain statement of Scripture. If the precise terminus of the chronological periods is, as we have reason to believe, purposely involved in obscurity, it is presumption to conclude that the Spirit of God reveals or bears witness to their exact beginning or ending. With the hearty reception of our Lord's immediate coming, we have received a greater or less manifestation of the SPIRIT: from this fact, we have, to some extent, drawn erroneous conclusions. We need not take the ground that we have reason to dispute the genuineness of our whole experience, because the time of the Advent, which might then have been associated in our minds with the general doctrines of it, seemed to have been as much set home to the soul, as the other truths of the system.

"Let these and all similar texts have their natural import, and be understood in a general sense, and then they may be quoted with propriety and effect. They certainly contain the doctrine of a general knowledge of time; they of course mean something, but not so much as, in our zeal for the truth, we might be tempted to make them.

"In relation to all such chronological terms, we may derive instruction, by carefully noticing the manner in which the New Testament writers invariably speak, when alluding to the coming of Christ. We instance them in this case, as we are accustomed to do in other cases, where both the Old and New Testament writers are understood to discourse on like topics, simply because the latter are more explicit and intelligible. Their most common method of presenting the doctrine of the end of the world, is not by numbers, but by events and signs: thus leaving us without the knowledge of the definite time.

"Let the past so far as it has its lessons of admonition, be ever under our eye, to check us from all unscriptural conclusions, and teach us to temper our confidence with humility and moderation; let it teach us the difference between the impulses of our own nature, and the operations of the Divine Spirit, and let it lead us to a more patient and thorough investigation of the plain testimony of inspiration."

To this position the Advent Herald and its chief supporters have adhered from that time until the present. Who can show it to be unscriptural? If scriptural, *all* should adopt it.

PROF. N. N. WHITING'S POSITION.

Prof. Whiting was a Baptist minister in Williamsburg, N. Y., who had embraced and taught the immediate coming of Christ, from 1842. He was a man of large experience, thorough education, and extensive reading in various languages. He was a regular contributor to the "Midnight Cry," "The Advent Herald," and became editor of the "Morning Watch." He was always opposed to fixing upon definite points of time, as were Elds. H. D. Ward, Henry Jones, and other eminent Adventists. We here give extracts from an article from him on Prophetic Chronology. After citing several important facts of Scripture history to show the "propriety and duty of searching prophetic Scripture and the chronology of prophecy for the benefit of all who do not prefer darkness to light." He adds:

"There is an important rule of interpretation applicable to all portions of Holy Writ, which demands attention from those who wish to learn the mind of the Spirit. It is this, that as God, in his communications to man, employs human language as a medium for those communications, he uses it in precisely the same manner as man would do. The circumstances of those whom he addresses are kept in view, such as their standard of scientific knowledge, their customs and habits of thinking. In short, Jehovah takes his stand as a man when he speaks to man, at least, so *far as language* is employed. It is well known that the sciences, which have been so much cultivated in later ages, were in a state of infancy, especially among the Hebrews, at the time when holy men of God spake as they were moved by the Holy Spirit. Hence, as the Jews supposed that the earth was a plane with four corners, the Lord speaks in conformity with their views when he mentions "the four corners of the earth." Material objects on earth and in the sky are described as they appeared to the eyes of the men whom he addressed. Hence, the sun and moon are mentioned as the two great lights of heaven, although modern astronomy has demonstrated the fact that many stars are of greater magnitude than the moon. Thus, as the Hebrews deemed the heart the seat of thought, no attempt is made to teach them physical or metaphysical science. God speaks of a wise and understanding *heart.* The only exception to this last case will be found in the book of Daniel, which was written in Chaldea, where science was much farther advanced than in Palestine. Hence, in this book, we find such expressions as "the visions of thy *head* upon thy bed."—Dan. ii. 28.

The principle which has just been noticed is applicable to the modes of computing time which were used by the Hebrews. From some examples that will soon be adduced it will be seen that there is a latitude often employed in estimating days and years which varies very considerably from the mathematical accuracy common in later times, especially among the nations of the west. Now, in attempting to interpret the Scriptures, in cases where there is reference to periods of time, it is obvious that we must adopt that mode of estimation which was common among the Jews, because the communication from God having been made to *them, their usage was the standard.* By looking at the Scriptures, we can ascertain what that usage was, and avoid any danger of mistake; but, on the other hand, had the Lord, in speaking to them, adopted a usage which was to prevail in a later age the communication would not have been adapted to their use, unless he had enlarged the range of revelation by teaching *natural* as well as *moral* science.

An examination of various passages where estimates of time are given in the Scriptures will convince the reader of the following facts, viz.: 1. In a period of years, the *first* and *last* terms of the series are often reckoned inclusive, although our usage would lead us to omit the *first* term. 2. There are cases where the Hebrews estimate years as we do, omitting the first term of the series. 3. There are also cases where both the *first* and *last terms* of the series are omitted when, of course, they would make the series exceed our estimate by nearly a year.

Illustrations of the first mode. 1 Kings xv. 1, 2, "Now in the eighteenth year of king Jeroboam, the son of Nebat, reigned Abijam over Judah. Three years reigned he in Jerusalem." Verses 8, 9, "And Abijam slept with his fathers; and they buried him in the city of David: and Asa his son reigned in his stead. And in the twentieth year of Jeroboam king of Israel reigned Asa over Judah."

It will at once be seen that we should estimate his reign at *two years*. Yet the Biblical computation makes the period *three*, by counting the eighteenth year, the first term of the series, as a *whole* year, and the twentieth, the last term, also, as a *whole* year. In this case, therefore, a portion of a year is regarded as an entire year.

1 Kings xv. 25, 28, "And Nadab the son of Jeroboam began to reign over Israel in the second year of Asa king of Judah, and reigned over Israel two years. Even in the third year of Asa, king of Judah, did Baasha slay him, and reigned in his stead." Here the *second* year of Asa and his *third* year are each estimated as full years, although we should say from the *second* to the *third* year there could have been but *one* year.

1 Kings xvi. 8, 10, "In the twentieth and sixth year of Asa king of Judah began Elah the son of Baasha to reign over Israel two years. And Zimri went in and smote him, and killed him, in the twenty-and-seventh year of Asa king of Judah, and reigned in his stead." This case is precisely like the last.

See also the notice of the time of Baasha's reign, in 1 Kings xv. 33, and xvi. 6—8; the reign of Jotham, 2 Kings xv. 32, and xvi. 1.

In 2 Kings xvii. 1, we are told that "in the twelfth year of Ahaz king of Judah began Hoshea the son of Elah to reign in Samaria over Israel nine years." Yet in verse 6 we read, "In the ninth year of Hoshea the king of Assyria took Samaria, and carried Israel away into Assyria," etc. Here the *current* year, the *ninth*, is reckoned as a *full* year.

1 Kings xxii. 1, 2, "And they continued three years without war between Syria and Israel. And it came to pass *in* the *third year*, that Jehoshaphat the king of Judah came down to the king of Israel," etc., to the end of the chapter.

Illustration of the second mode of computation. 2 Kings xv. 23, 27, "In the fiftieth year of Azariah (called also Uzziah) king of Judah, Pekahiah the son of Menahem began to reign over Israel in Samaria, and reigned two years." "In the two-and-fiftieth year of Azariah king of Judah, Pekah the son of Remaliah began to reign over Israel in Samaria," etc. In this instance, the two years of Pekah's reign are computed by omitting the first term (namely, the fiftieth year of Azariah, and counting the last term, namely, the fifty-second), precisely as they would be reckoned according to *our* practice.

Illustration of the third mode of computation. 2 Kings xv. 17, 22, 23, "In the nine-and-thirtieth year of Azariah king of Judah began Menahem the son of Gadi to reign over Israel, and reigned ten years in Samaria." "And Menahem slept with his fathers; and Pekahiah his son reigned in his stead." "In the fiftieth year of Azariah king of Judah, Pekahiah the son of Menahem began to reign over Israel in Samaria," etc. Now the modern estimate of Menahem's reign would be made thus:

50th year of Azariah,
39th do. do.,

11 years.

Hence the inspired writer has omitted both the first and the last terms of the series, namely, the 39th and 50th years, and hence he fixes the reign at *ten* years. So in 1 Kings xvii. 1, and xviii. 1, "And Elijah the Tishbite, who was of the inhabitants of Gilead, said unto Ahab, as the Lord God of Israel liveth, before whom I stand, there shall not be dew nor rain these years, but according to my word." "And it came to pass after many days that the word of the Lord came to Elijah *in the third year*, saying, go, show thyself unto Ahab; and I will send rain upon the earth."

From these two passages we should, perhaps, conclude that the famine continued two years and part of another, yet from Luke iv. 25, and James v. 17, we learn that this was not the period. "But I tell you of a truth, many widows were in Israel in the days of Elias, when the heaven was shut up *three years and six months*, when great famine was throughout all the land." "Elias was a man subject to like passions as we are, and he prayed earnestly that it might not rain; and it rained not on the earth for the space of three years and six months." The result of these examples is, that when the Hebrews computed a period of years, as seven, twenty, etc., there was a limited *range* of time within which they would regard the period as accomplished. To illustrate this, let it be supposed that, according to modern rules of computation, seven complete years would terminate on the thirty-first day of December. They would have reckoned any portion of the *current* year from January first, down to, or including, that day of December as the last of the seven years, or they would have used the same phrase, "seven years," during any part of the year *which followed* the 31st day. The range of time, then, for the end of the "seven years," would have embraced a space of about one year before and one year after the *exact point*, at which we should say, "the time is fulfilled."

Attempts to fix precise days, or even months, for the accomplishment of prophetic periods of years must, in view of this principle, be altogether conjectural. The uncertainty, which must result from these attempts, will be seen at once, if we recollect that the Jewish calendar having reference to the changes of the moon, and their year being of course about eleven days short of the solar year—an addition of a whole month is requisite, at least once in three years, to bring the lunar and solar time to a coincidence. It is singular that some learned men, overlooking this obvious difficulty, have told us that the death of the Saviour occurred four hundred and ninety years, to *a day*, from the date in which the command went forth to restore and rebuild Jerusalem. They seem to have forgotten that the nearest approach which can be made on *sure* ground to the period of issuing that command is furnished in the Scriptural history, Ezra vii. 9, "For upon the first day of the first month (Nisan or Abib) began he (Ezra) to go up from Babylon, and on the first day of the fifth month (Ab) came he to Jerusalem, according to the good hand of his God upon him."

It should not be forgotten that *moral* results have always especially been kept in view by our Creator in all that he has revealed to man. The Saviour, in view of his coming in the clouds of heaven to judge the world in righteousness, apprised his disciples of the signs which were to precede that stupendous event, and warned them in the most impressive manner that they should watch and pray because they could not know "the day or hour," although God could easily have made the very point of time known, and would have done so if it could have rendered them better prepared to meet him. He thus fixed their attention not on a point, but on a *space*, of time. The same principle I believe has an influence in reference to all events whose arrival the spirit of prophecy has connected with the lapse of time. Hence, while the precise moment for an event is fixed, in the Divine Mind, revelation throws its light not on *the point*, but on *a line*, within which the point is located. When we reach the beginning of that line the voice of Wisdom cries,—"Watch and pray!"

In reference to the time in which we now live, there is an appropriateness in the Saviour's counsel which secures the solemn regard of every reflecting man: "And take heed to yourselves, lest at any time your hearts be overcharged with surfeiting and drunkenness, and cares of this life, and so that day come upon you unawares. For as a snare shall it come on all them that dwell on the face of the whole earth. Watch ye therefore, and pray always, that ye may be accounted worthy to escape all these things that shall come to pass, and to stand before the Son of man."[1] N. N. W.

---

[1]Advent Shield, pp. 96–100.

CHAPTER XIV.

PHILADELPHIA ENCAMPMENT—DR. GORGAS—EXTREMES, MISCHIEF WITH—FALSE VIEWS—JOHN STARKWEATHER—FANATICISM—SECESSION—POWER OF GIFTS—UNION CONFERENCE—ABBY KELLY—A FALSE CRY—VOICE OF TRUTH—THE SHUT DOOR JOSEPH TURNER—ELLEN G. HARMON—DAY STAR—J. D. PICKARDS—ANOTHER BRANCH—VISIONS—THIRD ANGEL'S MESSAGE—WISE COUNSEL NEGLECTED—REPROOF BY MR. MILLER—A NEW RALLY—ALBANY CONFERENCE—ADDRESS—PACIFIC RESULTS—THE TIME OF LUTHER AND THE PRESENT—FANATICISM OF STORCH, STEBNER, AND THOMAS—ANTECEDENT CAUSES—CHURCH PARTIES, LEVEES, AND GAMBLING—SPIRITUAL FAMINE—MIDNIGHT CRY—COWPER—CHURCH ORGANIZATION—OBJECTIONS CONSIDERED—CREEDS.

In every great movement of reform, or advancement, of the church of God, either in doctrine or practice, the true and faithful have been obliged to meet and overcome the most serious obstacles from among themselves. External foes have sometimes been formidable: but when the "serpent is changed into an angel of light," and gains an influence over a portion of the family of believers, enlisting them in his service while they suppose they are doing the most important part of the Lord's work, the difficulty becomes terrible in its results. In such cases great evils become so connected with the work of Christian service as to cause much scandal and reproach before the dividing line is made sufficiently distinct for casual observers to discern "between the precious and the vile."

The history of the church in the days of the apostles, the days of Luther, of Wesley, and Whitefield, and of lesser reforms, show the same developments of evil under the disguise of good titles, with great professions of sanctity, seeming to be genuine fruits of the great reforms going on, but which proved to be the work of evil spirits, acting through the disordered brains of sincere but misguided disciples, or the agency of some unsanctified elements of the carnal mind, which "is not subject to the law of God."

The great reformation which has been produced through the proclamation of the *Second Advent Message* has been beset by the same evils. And while it becomes our duty, as an impartial historian, to record the chief evils, as well as the good work, accompanying this message, we are but copying the history of what has been enacted several times before, with slight variations of style, during the reformations above alluded to.

The adversary of God and man plays his greatest games against the church of Christ by using such persons as he can control and bring in collision with the saving truths of the gospel by counterfeit messages, newly coined terms, and strange exercises under Scriptural claims.

THE PHILADELPHIA ENCAMPMENT.

The disorderly movement in Philadelphia, in 1844, which was charged upon the Second Adventists, as a result of their views as a people, is shown to have had its rise from other sources. We give an extract of the account given of it in the Philadelphia daily papers, by Lewis C. Gunn.

He says: "Some of those worshiping in Julianna street were not looking for the destruction of the earth, nor for its complete physical renovation, at the present time; they looked for the introduction of the millennium by the personal coming of Christ to the earth; they think this will be the commencement of the promised restitution of all things, to be carried forward until all things shall be made new; they think that probation will close to those who have heard the gospel, but not so with the heathen and all those who have not heard of his fame; they think it will be the beginning of a new dispensation to the heathen, during which it will be emphatically true that the leaves of the tree of life will be for the healing of the nations. These were the published views of Geo. Storrs. . . In these views they differed entirely from Mr. Miller and the great body of Advent believers in this country, but agreeing with the Literalists of England (Millennarians). . . . *The Encampment!!!* It seems to be a common impression that this was the result of our doctrine. By no means. Only from one to two hundred, out of nearly three thousand believers (in this vicinity), were deluded by this. The others felt that they were not required to do anything of the kind, but saw that those favorable to it were led astray and were grossly perverting the Scriptures. Now for the origin of this movement. A Dr. C. R. Gorgas, of York County, Pa., pretended to have been inspired about three weeks ago, and that it was revealed to him that the Advent would take place at three o'clock in the morning of Oct. 22d. Charts to this effect were sent to Baltimore and to this city. The brethren in both places immediately opposed it.

Dr. Gorgas first went to Baltimore, but gained no converts; he then came to Philadelphia, and from that time the meetings have lost much of their solemnity and interest." "Several brethren slept with him, at the places where he visited, who were from abroad, some from New York, and were mesmerized by him so thoroughly as to readily accept his views. Now this total change in the feelings of so many, produced without argument, simply by being near him, and their opposition subdued, can be attributed to nothing but mesmeric influence. Eld. J. V. Himes, the chief publisher of Advent papers, strongly opposed Dr. Gorgas, as also Eld. J. Litch, a well-known Advent minister. Eld. Himes also went to New York and arrested the republication there of the doctor's chart, which the New York brethren before mentioned (as mesmerized) had commenced. . The five or six converts here were also distributing his charts freely, and the public therefore received the impression that these charts set forth the expectation of the Second Advent believers generally, who, on the contrary, rejected *in toto* the pretended inspiration. Now this Dr. G. professed to have a revelation of the destruction of the city as in the case of Lot, and that all who would be saved must flee from the cities. The influence he exerted over a few, and then theirs over others, led to the encampment—a most unhappy step—over which none can grieve more bitterly than the Advent preachers and Advent believers generally. It was the result of following a mere man. . . . Thanks be to God for his unerring Word, and thanks be to him also for keeping the great body of those who love his appearing from being led astray by such an unholy influence.

LEWIS C. GUNN."

Thus it is seen that though this was trumpeted through the land as the legitimate fruits of the Advent Message it is altogether another movement. But several similar movements have been made by *special time messengers* and fanatical classes, under the name of Adventists, yet always in opposition to them as a body.

TWO EXTREMES—WITH TRUTH BETWEEN.

After this, various questions began to be mooted respecting "the seventh-month movement." Some contended that it was all ordained and ordered of God; and others claimed that it was a work of Satan, to torment God's children by disappointment. The majority of Adventists took the position that the *time* was an error of human judgment; but that preaching the coming of the Saviour in connection with it, where it was attended with love to God, a desire to save men, and a love for Christ's appearing, was attended by the blessing of the Holy Spirit, not because of the *error* in the time, but because of their desire to do the will of God, notwithstanding the erroneous calculation. These did not deem it proper to make God responsible for their mistakes.

Those who ascribed the work specified to the devil soon apostatized, and walked no more with Adventists, some giving up all pretensions to religion. Those who ascribed it all to the Lord, or a majority of such, went into various fanatical views and practices, and imbibed a bitter spirit, which soon made a wide breach between them and those who were willing to admit their own imperfections and to confess their mistake.

To be consistent, those who ascribed that movement entirely to the Lord had to consider that some event, in connection with the fulfillment of prophecy, *did* transpire at that time. And, as they had taught that Christ would then come, they conceived the idea that he came invisibly and closed the door of mercy to the sinner, illustrating it by the parable of the Bridegroom's coming and shutting the door, after which the foolish virgins sought admittance in vain. Thus they contended that the work of preaching the gospel was ended.

It was an object of some importance to these to get from Mr. Miller some expression favoring their interpretation. It was known that he held that, for a period previous to the actual coming of Christ, he would cease to intercede for, and the Holy Spirit cease to strive with, sinners; and they were in hopes to convince him that that period had arrived. He was accordingly overwhelmed with letters asking his opinion on that point.[1]

Mr. Miller did not give them direct replies, as his own mind was not sufficiently settled to meet the case fairly. He wrote several letters to the believers, which were published in the *Advent Herald*, manifesting great care, and much affection for those who had fallen into grievous errors. He rehearsed the past experience, alluding to the peace and joy of anticipation which preceded the disappointment, and asked them to wait patiently the unfoldings of God's providence. As time passed on he soon learned more of the mischievous work which was going on under the spirit of fanaticism, and which had for some time been working its way up among a class of believers; he was also enabled to understand his own duty

---

[1]**Life of Miller, p. 294.**

more clearly. He then took a stand, with the leading men of the body, which developed that he and they did not approbate these errors, nor have any connection with them. They then did all they were capable of doing to restore these erring ones to a rational and Scriptural position, and to fellowship and union with the body of Adventists, to continue the work of the gospel for the salvation of men, and the proclamation of the Advent Message to awaken and strengthen the church.

POISON WATERS, FANATICISM, FALSE MESSAGES, DISORGANIZERS.

The most serious difficulties which have beset the *Second Advent Cause* came upon it as the turbid, poison waters from stagnant marsh pools ooze through the earth banks into the margin of the pure waters of a majestic river, which, while they are insufficient to defile the body of waters, continue to develop their turbid hue and poisonous qualities along the shoals and eddies, so distinct from the current as to be readily distinguished by the experienced eye. The experienced observer can readily perceive that the evil elements which were early introduced among the Advent believers, from foreign sources, have ever run along the margin of the cause, seeking the influence and strength of the current for support, now widening, then narrowing, but have ever maintained their qualities of foreign origin by a want of real union and co-operation in the great work of the body, and by peculiar exercises, distinguishing "gifts," and novel "messages," "stirring up strife and contention," like the shallow ripples and eddies of a river, which gather a heterogeneous mass of drift.

But in mentioning the opposing elements with which the cause has been retarded in its work we do not intend that *all* classes which have taken positions in opposition to the body are to be illustrated by the above simile. There are some exceptions to the rule.

THE JEW QUESTION.

"The first question that produced a distracting influence among the hitherto united Adventists was "Judaism," which taught the conversion and restoration of the natural Jews. A free and full discussion of this was permitted in the "Signs of the Times;" but after a long and wordy debate, the advocates of the Jews finding that they could not convince their opponents, and that the paper was not to be made subservient to their purposes, commenced the publication of the "American Millennarian," in Boston, in the summer of 1842. It was published here for several months, then removed to New York, and finally became defunct. Its advocates and supporters,—if what the mouth speaketh is any indication of the abundance that is in the heart,—became far more interested in the discussion of the Jew question than of the Advent, and with the decease of their organ many of them ceased to manifest any interest respecting the latter. They went out from us, and ceased to be of us. Their places were soon filled by many times their number, and it was soon forgotten that they had ever been with us.

FANATICISM.

The next trial the cause had to endure was of a much more serious nature than the first, and was more fatal in its consequences. In the autumn of 1842, the doctrine of the Advent had been embraced by John Starkweather. He was a graduate of the Andover Theological Seminary, and had obtained quite a reputation for superior sanctity. He had been a minister at the Marlboro' Chapel, in Boston, and at other places, but was at that time destitute of a charge. As Mr. Himes wished to devote himself more fully to preaching the Advent in other places than Boston, it was proposed to call Mr. Starkweather as an assistant pastor of his church. It was afterwards ascertained that, in most places where he had been located, he had contrived to embroil himself in a quarrel with some of his people, and to array one portion of them against the other. This feature in his character was unknown to the members of his new charge. He commenced his labors in Chardon street in October of that year. He soon afterwards remarked to a brother that from the first he foresaw that there must be a division there. He subsequently requested another, who was about leaving the city for a time, not to go, for he foresaw that there would be a division, and should need his services. He had not officiated at the chapel long before he demanded that the "Signs of the Times" and the issue of publications should be under the joint control of himself and Mr. Himes; this demand not being complied with, he from that time manifested a want of cordiality.

The personal appearance of Mr. Starkweather added greatly to his reputation as a man of superior sanctity. He was tall, well-formed, had a voice of great power, and not unpleasant tones, a long but retreating forehead, a solemn face, and an easy flow of tears. He had the ability to secure the confidence of his hearers who nightly thronged the chapel. His principal theme was the necessity of a preparation for the Saviour's coming. At such a time, no subject, seemingly, could be more appropriate. But Mr. Starkweather had embraced peculiar views respecting personal sanctification and, contrary to the understanding which had been had on the subject of sectarian views, he made his own notions not only a test of readiness for the Lord's coming, but of Christian fellowship, demanding the largest liberty for himself, and granting none to others. He taught that conversion, however full and thorough, did not fit one for God's favor without a second work, and that this second work was usually indicated by some bodily sensation. The losing of strength and other cataleptic and epileptic phenomena[1] now became manifested, and were hailed by him as evidences of the great power of God in the sanctification of those who were already devoted Christians. He denominated that "the sealing power."

Such manifestations were new to a majority of his hearers. Some looked on in wonder and awe, while others were suspicious of the new development, but feared to "offend against the Holy Ghost," as dissent from it was termed, and those who were favorably impressed were anxious to experience on themselves the "sealing power."

Those who were familiar with the history of fanaticism in past ages, who had read with pain the termination of the career of the eloquent Edward Irving in England, who knew the devastation caused by fanaticism in the time of the Reformation, of its effects in the early ages of Christianity, and of the results produced by it even in many portions of our own country, during the infancy of some of the sects among us, were filled with great pain when it was manifested among them. It was at first supposed that Mr. Starkweather was an innocent cause of this, and that he was ignorant of

---

[1]Dr. Pettigrew, in a lecture at the Collegiate Institution, Liverpool, stated that epilepsy is considered so catching that no one afflicted with it is allowed to enter a London hospital as an in-patient.

his strong mesmeric powers, by which he had obtained a sympathetic influence over some of his hearers. He was reasoned with on the subject, but to no purpose. His mind was bent in a certain direction, and pursue his course he would. His actual spirit was not discovered until one of the brethren publicly dissented from such exercises as any necessary part of Christianity. At this the uncaged lion was aroused, and it became evident what manner of spirit he was of.

The next day (near the close of April, 1843), it was deemed necessary to take a decided stand on the subject. A meeting had been appointed for the afternoon, and Mr. Himes, who had been absent during these occurrences, with judicious brethren, determined to endeavor to stem the current of fanaticism which had just commenced. In a calm and faithful manner he gave them the history of various movements which had been destroyed, or greatly injured, by fanaticism and, without intimating that evidences of such then existed, he exhorted them to learn from past experience, and see to it that they avoided the rocks on which others had shipwrecked. Mr. Starkweather arose in reply, and raved like a madman. His cloven foot was then entirely uncovered. His conduct was so vehement that Mr. Himes felt justified in again addressing the audience, exposing the nature of the exercises that had appeared among them and their pernicious tendency. This so shocked the sensibilities of those who regarded them as the "great power of God," that they cried out and stopped their ears. Some jumped upon their feet, and some ran out of the house. "You will drive out the Holy Ghost!" cried one. "You are throwing on cold water!" said another. "Thowing on cold water!" said Mr. Himes, "I would throw on the Atlantic ocean before I would be identified with such abominations as these, or suffer them in this place unrebuked!"

Mr. Starkweather announced that the "saints" would thereafter meet at Ritchie Hall,—showing that a place of meeting had been pre-arranged,—until further arrangements. He thus drew off a party, which at first was larger than the number that remained. He soon after removed his meeting to a hall in Washington street, to which, seven years after, Mr. Weethee, singularly enough, removed on *his* secession. Before this, and during the erection of the Tabernacle, it was ascertained that the contractor, Mr. Evans, who afterwards proved to be one of Starkweather's partisans, had arranged with the latter to put him in possession of the building on its completion, and that a private meeting of eight or ten had been held, at which Starkweather was chosen pastor of the Tabernacle. The committee, learning this, demanded that the contractor should deliver to them the control of the building, as a condition of their supplying him with funds for its completion. He declined to do this; the work on it was suspended for a time, which greatly delayed its completion. He afterwards complied with their wishes, and they completed it, so that it was dedicated the 4th of May, 1843. The dedication sermon was preached to an audience of some 3,500, by Rev. Silas Hawley, jr., and was one of the best digests of the Advent doctrine published.

As early as the dedication of the Tabernacle it was seen that Starkweather was organizing a party. He mingled with the brethren at the dedication, but made no public effort. Starkweather continued his separate meetings, but the honest ones who had gone with him were fast discovering his spirit, and were returning in crowds to the Tabernacle. He then determined himself to erect a tabernacle. The one who had previously contracted for the other volunteered to be responsible for the erection of one for him, and forthwith commenced the construction of one in a little court leading from near the foot of Winter street. Hastily thrown together, in the roughest manner conceivable, they were soon in possession, and from the various advertisements placarded around the streets a stranger would have supposed that that was the only Advent tabernacle, and they the only body of Adventists, in the city.

He continued there several months, his followers continually decreasing, till at length a quarrel arose between him and the builder respecting the control of the sums received by the collections, each claiming them as the result of his own services. It ended in the suspension of meetings there, and in the loss to the builder of five or six hundred dollars, from which originated the story of the loss by Mr. Himes, to a joiner on Tremont street, of five hundred dollars. (See the "Herald" of Nov. 6, 1844.)

Starkweather removed his meetings to a smaller place, and soon began to extend his labors to other places. Wherever he went the fanatical movements accompanied him, and these extended beyond the sphere of his presence.

On the 9th of August following, a camp-meeting commenced at Plainfield, Ct., at which Starkweather was present, and where some manifestations were exhibited which were entirely new to those present, and for which they could not account. Another meeting was held at Stepney, near Bridgeport, on the 28th of the same month, where the developments were more marked. A few young men, professing to have the gift of discerning spirits, were hurried into great extravagances. Elder J. Litch published a protest against such exhibitions, in which he said:

"A more disgraceful scene, under the garb of piety, I have rarely witnessed. For the last ten years I have come in contact nearly every year, more or less, with the same spirit, and have marked its developments, its beginning, and its result, and am now prepared to say that it is evil, and only evil, and that continually. I have uniformly opposed it wherever it has made its appearance, and as uniformly have been denounced as being opposed to the power of God, and as resisting the operations of the Spirit. The origin of it is the idea that the individuals thus exercised are entirely under the influence of the Spirit of God, are his children, and that he will not deceive them and lead them astray; hence, every impulse which comes upon them is yielded to as coming from God, and following it there is no length of fanaticism to which they will not go."—*Midnight Cry*, Sept. 14, 1843.

This fanaticism was the result of Starkweather's teaching that "gifts" were to be restored to the church. Even he seemed at first amazed at the results. As a specimen of the hallucination, a young man by the name of M—— imagined that he had power to hold the cars from moving on the railroad, by the mere effort of his will. As they were about starting he said, "Don't you go." The wheels of the locomotive made several revolutions before the heavy train started. "Now, go," said he, and it moved. "There," said he, "did I not stop the train?" Returning home, "Father," said he, "do you believe I have the power of God?" "Yes," said the father, who had been fascinated at the meeting. "Well, then, drive the horse on to that rock by the road-side," and he was obeyed, somewhat to their discomfort.

On the 13th of September another meeting was held at Windsor, Ct. The same spirit appeared there, and is described by Elder L. C.

Collins in the "Signs of the Times," Sept. 27, 1843. One female, believing that as Peter walked on the sea by faith, so she by faith might walk across the Connecticut river, resolved to make the attempt, but was prevented. They kept the meeting in confusion an hour or more, and would listen to no remonstrances.

Starkweather had been defeated in his efforts in Boston, those only continuing to adhere to him who have been foremost in every subsequent division. In the peculiar state of feeling then existing, it was impossible to speak out through the "Herald" to warn the brethren against him. Therefore, he told his own story, many believing him to be a holy, abused man, and took his part. It was deemed most advisable to keep steadily about the great work and leave the brethren to find him out for themselves. Most of them soon did so, and his influence became restricted to inconsiderable limits. He felt that his power was waning and determined to make another effort to maintain his existence. This effort was the calling of a

"UNION CONFERENCE"

at the Marlboro' Chapel, at which he designed to unite all the disaffected elements among the Adventists in the land. He did not offer to do this through the columns of the "Advent Herald," but an advertisement appeared in the "Boston Daily Times" of April 6th, signed by John Starkweather and others, inviting "the saints" to meet at the Marlboro' Chapel on the 16th of April, 1844. His Conference convened, and such a medley of discordant elements has not been often assembled. No two were of one mind. Each wished to lead off in his own direction. All organization of the meeting was scouted at, and each had liberty to do what was right in his own eyes. Some few who had been deceived respecting the nature of the meeting looked on as spectators. It was a perfect illustration of the no order, or rather disorder, system. At the opening of the meeting Starkweather took his seat in the desk, but his sitting there was objected to on all sides; they wanted no minister over them, they being, in their own estimation, "all ministers." He then took his seat in the front of the audience, but his offence in going into the desk had been so flagrant that his brethren would take no satisfaction until he took the back seat. He then sat there, pronounced the "minister dead," and affirmed that he should not again enter the pulpit till the Lord placed him there.

Silas Lamson, a man of a singular turn of mind, perhaps about seventy years of age, with a long white beard, who for some twenty years had dressed in white, even to his shoes and umbrella, and who rejoiced in the *sobriquet* of the "White Quaker," who had passed a large part of his time in the lunatic asylum, who had no sympathy for the doctrine of the Advent save to oppose, and who delighted to be imprisoned for disturbing meetings of every kind, commenced with a relation of his own history. His speaking was opposed by some, but the majority contended for "freedom of speech," and wished to have no "gag laws," and no "lording it over God's heritage." He managed to talk the greater portion of the day. They bore with him with exemplary patience, thinking that if they once heard him through he would be silent for the remainder of the Conference. The next day, however, he commenced again, and was as wordy as he was the preceding day. They remonstrated with him, but he met them with the plea that he only wished for equal liberty with others; they "all wanted to relate their experience, and he only wished to give the *whole* of his." One great object of this Conference being to "come out of Babylon," Mr. Lamson went into a full explanation of what he considered Babylon. It consisted of anything done to gratify what he considered pride and of no practical utility. "Thus," said he, "If you color your cloth it will not wear any longer; then why do you color it? to gratify your pride. So, if you shear your cloth it is not made better and will not wear so long; but it is done to gratify pride, and therefore all who wear cloth colored and dressed are in Babylon," etc. But his voice at length grew husky; he could talk no longer.

They now thought that their trials were over; but Abby Folsom, a female in every respect the counterpart of Lamson, excepting his beard and white raiment, was on her feet to fill his place, and when she was exhausted *he* was able to speak again; thus they relieved each other. Finding that they must endure these inflictions, the other would-be speakers had to seize on the unoccupied moments, or speak while Lamson or Abby was improving the time.

As the meeting progressed the confusion increased; altercation, crimination, and recrimination followed. By-and-by a Mr. Lemuel

Tompkins,[1]—who was subject to certain cataleptic exercises, usually commencing with a spinning whirl, like a top, accompanied with noises similar to those made by a frightened grunter, and ending in a fixed horizontal position on the floor,—professed to have had it revealed to him that Mr. Starkweather had a devil, while the latter professed that it had been revealed to *him* that Mr. Tompkins had a devil, both claiming the possession of the power to "discern spirits." Everything being thus in confusion, the members of the Conference concluded that, instead of escaping from Babylon, they had landed in the wilderness, and that it was their duty to pray that some Moses might be sent to lead them through the wilderness. Towards the close of the second day, a dignified stranger, apparently about fifty years of age, and about six feet two inches in height, with a Quaker-cut coat, broad-brimmed hat, and not unprepossessing in his appearance, presented himself in the Conference, and walked in a stately manner into the desk. Some of the members thought that their prayer was answered, and shouted, "Our Moses has come! he will lead us out of the wilderness into the land of promise." Their Moses, however, only added another to the would-be leaders of the meeting. Thus the turmoil continued, until the owner of the building, who happened to be passing at the time, hearing the rumpus, stepped in to ascertain the cause, and found Tompkins grunting and whirling on his toes in gyrations like a dancing dervish, Abby reading, at the top of her voice, from an old scrap-book, and Lamson from an autobiography of himself, which he called "The Flying Roll,"—their own ideas having ceased to supply them with words,—while Starkweather was making a speech, and several of the sisterhood were in mesmeric ecstacies. This was too much for the proprietor's sense of decency. Stepping up to Abby he told her to be seated. She inquired if he was not Deacon S——. He replied that he was. "Well," said she, "you are the rascal who once put me out of this chapel." "Then you shall go out now," said he. Abby prostrated herself on the floor amid cries of "no gag laws!" "Free discussion!" etc., and frustrated his efforts to move her. "Then you all shall go," said he. And thus ended the *first* "*union*" Conference

[1]The last time we saw this individual he was dressed in a Shaker's garb, mounted on a Shaker's wagon, loaded with brooms. A laudable calling withal, indicating an attempt to remove the dust.

held in Boston in opposition to the Advent cause. Their Moses was soon after advertised in the "Boston Daily Mail" as "A Wolf in Sheep's Clothing," as follows:

"A black-hearted monster in the shape of a man, by the name of Hull Barton, or as he now calls himself, Michael Hull Barton (pretending to be Michael, the angel, spoken of in Scripture), is now prowling about the country, dressed in a Quaker garb, with sanctimonious face, speech, and manners, seeking for prey, and making depredations among pious and unsuspecting women."

The above union of evil elements, accompanied by such ludicrous scenes in the name of religion, reminds us of the Roman Catholic ceremony of "Holy Fire," and the startling words of Ferdinand, "Hell is empty, and all the devils are here!"

After this, Starkweather effected but little. He got out a hymn book, issued a series of tracts, and a few numbers of a paper. He went from one error to another, and the last we heard of him he had embraced the Cochran doctrine of spiritual wifery, was separated from his family, and was stopping somewhere in Connecticut. The remains of the different societies that he had an influence over became hot-beds for the various fanatical views and exercises which have opposed and are now opposing the Advent cause, and will probably do so until Christ shall come to put an end to them.

DESTRUCTIVE ELEMENTS COMBINED FOR A PURPOSE.

Evil elements are usually antagonistic to each other, but "the prince of the power of the air, who worketh in the hearts of the children of disobedience," knows how to combine them to deceive the unwary children of God who do not observe the command to "try the spirits whether they are of God."

Here we find several classes of destructive principles, appearing as harmless as a lamb, as pious as Moses, as zealous as Jehu, and as deeply concerned for the cause of Christ as the angel Gabriel, combining to drive the plowshare of ruin through this precious cause of truth and righteousness.

In the summer of 1843 some, who had been repulsed, jaded, and derided by ministers and members of the churches, and who had not grace enough to endure it patiently for Jesus' sake, began to inquire more particularly into the *moral condition* of the churches. The

Anti-Slavery, Temperance, Moral Reform, and Second Advent questions, which had been agitated for some length of time, had made strange developments, and shown much evil and many startling sins in the churches. It was so admitted by many of their most faithful and reliable Christian members. This led some to suspect that the symbols or metaphors in Rev. xiv. 4, 8, represented the Protestant, as well as the Roman, churches. They were somewhat strengthened in this by a misapplication which some of the leading teachers had made of Rev. xiv. 6, teaching that the "angel flying through the midst of heaven" symbolized the Second Advent Message which began simultaneously in Europe, Asia, and America, early in the present century, whereas it had been more properly applied to the proclamation of Luther and his associates, and continued (with the two messages which immediately followed), and was re-announced by Mr. Mede, Dr. Goodwin, Mr. Faber, and others of the last century, and *now* renewed by this late announcement, with more conclusive evidence to prove the messages to be a Scriptural fact.

With this development of moral delinquency, and this false application of the above-named Scripture, they at once commenced the cry to all faithful Christians, "Come out of here my people," referring to all churches indiscriminately, and applying Rev. xviii. 4. When shown by their brethren, who understood the subject better, that it was the Roman Catholic church, exclusively, here called Babylon, they soon found by Rev. xvii. 5, that the woman, called Babylon, had daughters bearing the same character as herself. These, they concluded, represented all Protestant churches, and they continued the cry with unabated interest and consequent results. They taught with this cry that it was sinful to organize a church, and all who did so would "drink of the wine of the wrath of God."

A fearful crusade was made against all churches, and all sincere Christians who attempted to sustain and adhere to them. Many excellent Christians were greatly misguided and bewitched by this cry. It was affirmed by some of those engaged in this cry that connection with any church would peril one's salvation; some hold this mischievous idea until now. No countenance was given to this movement by the conductors of the Advent papers, Mr. Miller, or others who were pioneers in the work, but they faithfully expostulated, exhorted, and entreated these teachers to take a wiser course.

A paper called the "Voice of Truth," which commenced Jan. 1, 1844, published and edited by Eld. J. Marsh, and which struck out on a course independent of the general work of Adventists, affirming that "the object of the paper is the proclamation of truth as *we* understand it," yet claiming to be an Advent paper, came out on the 14th of March, 1844, fully committed to that view, and warned all to leave the churches, as Babylon, affirming that "all who remained there must inevitably be 'partakers of her sins, and receive of her plagues.'" The "Voice" continued during the ensuing season to be uttered against the churches, as Babylon, although it taught many good things and proclaimed the Advent message, which caused the more mischief to the Advent cause. Individuals went through the land, making the Babylonian cry their chief message. This greatly embarrassed the Adventists, closing the churches which were yet accessible against them, and preventing a hearing where till then they had admittance. Many came out of the churches under this cry who imbibed its theory and spirit, which has caused much disorder and opposition to Bible order and discipline among Adventists; but many others came out for better reasons, or were expelled for their hope, with better ideas of the duties and relations of the Christian church.

Being thus out, it became necessary to gather the friends into churches and to observe together the gospel ordinances. In the annual Conference of Adventists in May, 1844, at Boston, the Babylonish principle of interpretation was discountenanced. In their Address, after speaking of the danger of letting any church impose silence upon us in a question of duty, the Conference said, "The second form of danger is that of yielding to a spirit of revenge against the churches, on account of their injustice, and of waging an indiscriminate warfare against all such organizations."

The "Voice" recognized this as a discountenancing of *its* interpretation by the body, and remarked of the Conference: "What it said on the duty of Adventists in reference to the churches we consider has a particular bearing upon what *we have published* relative to the coming out of Babylon." "We regret our brethren found it to be 'very important' that we should express our views on several points particularly connected with the cause of God with which we are associated." [1]

The same paper also contained the following: "In reviewing the past we find for *convenience* sake we have, with others, contracted the unscriptural habit of expressing our *faith, hope, name,* etc., in words and phrases of human invention. 'Advent doctrine,' 'Advent faith,' 'Advent hope,' 'Advent Conference,' 'Advent meetings,' 'Advent books,' 'Advent hymns,' 'Advent message,' 'Advent Shield,' 'Advent Herald,' 'Advent brethren,' 'Advent lectures,' and worst of all 'Adventists,' and many other names have become of common use among us. We regret very much that we have not *wholly* avoided these things, and mean *in future to avoid them.*" Yet this same paper subsequently had its name changed to "Advent Harbinger."

---

[1] Voice of Truth, June 15, 1844.

We have been explicit relative to this paper because it is of importance to trace poisonous streams, which yet injure the body, to their fountains, and show thereby that they are foreign elements, foisted upon the Advent cause.

THE "SHUT DOOR" THEORY.

This notion originated with Joseph Turner, of Maine, and several others in various places, who simultaneously claimed to have it impressed upon them by the Holy Spirit, on "the tenth day of the seventh month." Oct. 22, 1844, Eld. T. proclaimed it at a campmeeting, in Woodstock, Me., while some penitent ones were being prayed for, repeating, "Every one to your tents, O Israel," and declaring that Christ had left the mercy seat. He soon worked the idea into a theory, which he and others began to proclaim throughout the Advent societies. It was readily accepted by some and was soon confirmed to them and others by visions of one Ellen G. Harmon, who traveled from town to town, where she was strangely exercised in body and mind, usually talking in assemblies until nature was exhausted and then falling to the floor, unless caught by some one sitting near (we remember catching her twice to save her from falling upon the floor), remaining a considerable time in the mesmeric state, and afterwards, perhaps not until another meeting, she would relate the wonders which she claimed had been shown her in spirit (these were subsequently called "visions"), among which was, that she had seen Christ in heaven, that he had ceased mediating, left the mercy seat, come out from "the holiest of all" and organized his kingdom, composed of his saints, including all who held fast to their experience in the 1844 movement. She also claimed to see that all those who gave up that experience, calling it an error, had their names blotted out of the book of life, they being "foolish virgins." Some had such confidence in her "visions" that they were thrown into great distress, nearly to despair, when she related that their names were "blotted out of the book of life."

We are aware that it has been, and is yet, denied in the most positive terms that the above-named woman ever proclaimed such views, but there is a true record in heaven, we are ready to abide that, as many of us, in New England, know the facts *when* and *as* they transpired. Later visions which contradict those do not prove them never to have been proclaimed, though it may militate against the reliability of either.

Eld. Turner was an impressive speaker, and had acquired considerable influence among the people. He now assumed that Christ had come spiritually as a Bridegroom, that the wise virgins had gone in with him into the marriage, and that the door was shut. He was a man of an active temperament, had rather a winning address, and a reputation for sanctity. He was also possessed of strong mesmeric power. He went forth on a mission to propagate his new views, and succeeded in deluding many into a partial, and others into a full, recognition of his fable. As early as Jan. 23, 1845, he writes from South Paris, Me.: "In every place I visited I found a goodly number, I think quite a majority, who were and are now believing that our work is all done for this world, and that the atonement was completed on the tenth day of the seventh month. Nearly all who heard me gladly received the message."[1]

Those who received these views immediately left the meetings of the Adventists, who admitted they had been in error in the time, calling them "foolish virgins," and set up private ones, *i. e.*, meetings for themselves only, calling themselves the "wise virgins" shut into the kingdom, as Noah and his family were shut into the ark, having lost their sympathy for those who did not embrace the message, as Eld. T. says in the same letter: "Such as receive this position have no sympathy with the indefinite movements of some of the brethren, who are trying to re-awaken a fallen church and a rejected world. They love them for their past labors, but their hearts are sorely pained in view of the sad effects of their present teachings. Such a course is like one's preaching in the tombs."

In the same letter he alludes to his visits to Boston, and to Portsmouth on Sunday, Jan. 10th. He also went to Lowell, Hartford, Worcester, and other of the principal places in New England, New York, and elsewhere. In most places where he lectured a division followed. On Sunday, Feb. 10th, he presented his views to the Adventists worshiping in Franklin Hall with seemingly overpowering success. S. S. Snow, who was then the pastor, embraced them in full, being convinced by Turner that he (Snow) had not been mistaken in teaching that the Lord would come on the tenth day of the seventh month, only that the *event* was different from what he had expected. He had been deeply engaged, as had Turner, in giving the cry "Come out of Babylon," applying the term to the Protestant churches. He immediately drew off a party and commenced meetings at the Medical College in Crosby street.

On the 13th of March Snow, in connection with B. Matthias, published the first number of the "Jubilee Standard," in advocacy of this theory. In his second number Snow says:

"The house of Israel is in the seive, and the seive is tremendously shaken. The congregation at Franklin Hall, to whom we have till recently ministered,

---

[1] Hope of Israel, Jan. 24, 1845.

has divided, and the portion that sympathize with our views have withdrawn and, with some of our dear brethren of the other congregations, have opened a meeting in the lower lecture-room of the Medical College in Crosby street."

Snow continued his separate meetings, went on from one gross error to another, proclaiming himself to be "Elijah the Prophet," "the Prophet like unto Moses," "the Messenger of the Covenant," "the poor wise man" who by his wisdom "delivered the city, yet no man remembered that same poor man," and assumed various blasphemous titles, as his advertisements in New York papers will show, and which have been copied in Germany as an evidence of fanaticism in America. The most fiendish imprecations have been uttered by him against all who reject his views.

About this time several new papers were started, advocating divers strange and discordant views, among which was the "Day Dawn," by O. R. L. Crozier. Some idea of these elements may be formed from what Mr. Miller related at the Albany Conference, that he had received seventeen different papers in one week, advocating opposite views, and all claiming to be Advent papers!

The "Voice" held a vibrating position on the "shut door" for a time, giving the largest liberty for all to present their notions through its columns, until perceiving that the tide had thus turned it finally went against it. The "Western Midnight Cry," which was originated at Cincinnati by Elder Himes, and placed under the editorial control of E. Jacobs, had its name changed by the latter to the "Day-Star," and committed to the promulgation of the "shut-door" notion. When Mr. Himes forwarded communications to the "Day-Star,"—his own paper,—they were withheld by Jacobs, so that he had no opportunity there to protest against its course; all works and publications were done without reference to legal forms or claims. But the "Advent Herald," and its faithful and able ally, the "Morning Watch," edited by Prof. N. N. Whiting, took a most decided stand against such fanciful and unscriptural teachings, and did all they could to stem the current which was sweeping over the Advent churches.

The Herald of February 15, 1845, under the caption "*Both Sides,*" says: "We shall next week, God willing, commence a series of articles exhibiting both sides of the question; whether the Bridegroom has come and shut the door."

In Feb. 26th that paper has an article of thirteen columns, devoted to a reply to the claim that the Bridegroom has come. And three columns quoted from the Morning Watch on the same. The evidence of the progress made by the adherents of the new views is seen in their letters.

In the "Hope of Israel," of April 4th, Eld. Turner says:

"No doubt remains in my mind but we have reached the hour of temptation." Feet-washing is also enjoined in the same letter.

He says: As we humble ourselves before God, and peform this duty, we are made in our degree, partakers of Christ's sufferings, and in our experience we feel the import: first, of the following Scriptures—Eph. i: 9—11; John xvii: 19—25; xiii: 35; and secondly, the following—Isa. xiii: 6—11 and xxvi: 12—21; Jer. xxx: 5—17 and v: 19—31; Hab. iii: 16; Psa. cxix: 119, 120; John xvi: 20, 21; Rom. viii: 22—25; Heb. xii: 5—10; Dan. xii: 1; Isa. liv: 5—10." Kissing followed as a matter of course. Turner soon became immortal, as he writes to Snow on the 24th of June following: "God is with us. He hears our cries, our sick are healed by the power of faith, and no Israelite has died among us since the seventh month, and we believe they may be preserved whole and blameless unto the coming of the Lord Jesus. Such things will be scoffed at by those who are fallen, but they are, nevertheless true."

In addition to the "shut-door" theory, some adopted other extravagant and fanatical views. Visions, etc., were had by some, and dreams by others. Feet-washing and kissing were generally held by them as gospel ordinances. To work was considered a great crime by the majority; and various mesmeric exercises prevailed, which were a subject of scandal.[1]

They taught it was sinful to perform manual labor, and "working not at all," they became "busy bodies," traveling from town to town criminating, as reprobates, those whose bread they ate; but the sisterhood were compassionated who were obliged to perform extra labor, to care for them, which they endured, as only faithful woman can, with more than Christian patience and fortitude; until some of them concluded if it was sinful to work they would prepare no more food for the table; and bringing this theory to a practical result they soon defeated the theorists and worked a cure in some cases.

A paper was started at Cleveland, O., by J. D. Pickands, entitled the "Voice of the Fourth Angel," teaching that Christ was then sitting on a white cloud (Rev. xiv. 16), and was to be prayed down. It would be an instructive chapter in the history of fanaticism to trace the history of this class in their progress, from one puerile notion to another.

We give these items for the especial benefit of the inexperienced, who are frequently brought under such influences, and spirits, and suppose it proceeds from the power of God's Spirit in his most humble children, and are bewitched thereby. Pickands went from the "shut-door" to "feet-washing" and "kissing," under the guise

---

[1] See Defense, pp. 7—20.

of Paul's injunction, Rom. xvi. 16. They then professed to have entered the kingdom of heaven and to have obtained immortality Soon after he renounced those things and commenced to advocate the infidel views of Andrew Jackson Davis, the Poughkeepsie mesmeric seer. E. Jacobs soon followed Pickands into the kingdom, and from there landed in Shakerism. He was afterwards expelled from among the Shakers for violating one of their principal rules.

ANOTHER BRANCH, ESTABLISHED WITH VISIONS.

The "door-shut" theory, after assuming several forms and phases, disappeared like a fog-bank evaporated by the heat of the sun; but it had generated a new form of error to succeed it, which would appear more plausible than any of the above; captivating and diverting the attention of more from the great central theme—the coming of the Lord. The most of those who had at first accepted the idea that the door of mercy was closed, soon saw it was a snare, a base fraud, and gave it up, confessing it an error, which they regretted accepting, and admitting that the movement was the result of a mistaken calculation and proclamation of time. But others were not ready to admit themselves in error, and these items of their experience the result of their sincere faith in what was not true. And out of this experience and persistency sprang, a new theory, which, if true, would justify the "whole *movement and experience:*" only a trifling error as to details of events.

This new theory after several changes from the Babylonian cry—no mercy for sinners—no organization of churches, has advanced to become of some note, and under it has been organized a church, or class of churches, with rules more stringent and autocratic, we believe, than any of the Protestant churches.

Eld. James White, a native of Maine, and member of the Christian church, a young man of much zeal and ambition, who had commenced preaching while in his own denomination, attended a meeting where he heard Elders Himes, Preble, and Miller preach in 1842, and embraced the views of the Advent near. He commenced preaching them with good success in several towns in Maine, where some were converted, and others awakened to examine the arguments and signs of Christ's speedy coming. He ran well for a season, though too positive on time arguments, but during the cry "Come out of her, my people," and the excitement which prevailed in the autumn of 1844, together with the great disappointment experienced by many on the passing of the time designated for the Lord to come, he passed under the cloud of that tempest of fanaticism which raged among the class who had been the most sanguine in their views. In the midst of the excitement and strange notions of that time he was captivated by fanaticism, receiving the views of Eld. Turner and the visions of Ellen G. Harmon, a native of Portland, and a wonderful fanatic and trance medium, as was supposed by those not under her influence, of whom we have already spoken. In her testimony in meetings she would speak with great vehemence and rapidity until falling down, when, as she claimed, wonderful views of heaven and of what was being transacted there were shown her. She claimed to have seen that Christ had left the office of mediation and assumed that of Judge, had closed the door of mercy, and was blotting out the names, from the book of life, of those who had not been faithful up to the tenth day of the seventh month, and of those who had believed the Lord would come at that time and subsequently confessed they were in error, that their experience was not all of God in thus believing. She claimed to see that "the Lord led his people out on that time," had "blessed them for believing and teaching it, that the prophetic periods had ended, and it was a great sin to deny their former faith and call it an error," etc. We saw her at Poland, Portland, Topsham, and Brunswick during the beginning of this career, and often heard her speak, and several times saw her fall, and heard her relate wonders which she said her heavenly Father permitted her to see. Her supernatural or abnormal views were not readily understood as visions, but as spiritual views of unseen things, which were quite common among the Methodists. They were soon after entitled "visions" by her friends.[1]

These visions were but the echoes of Eld. Turner and others' preaching, and we regarded them as the product of the over-excited imagination of her mind, and not as facts. Eld. White embraced these views and preached them a year or more; others taught them a longer time. It was denominated the "door-shut faith." All who confessed it an error and published the gospel of salvation to sinners, during this time, were called by them "fallen priests," if preachers,

---

[1] Since writing this article we have seen a statement, published in a scandalous sheet, over the name of one D. M. Canright, a teacher and defender of Mrs. White's visions, that "Eld. Wellcome never saw Sister White have a vision," also that he had "read a letter from Eld. Wellcome acknowledging that he had never seen her in vision," etc. Here is a grave statement. We will pay Mr. C. a large premium for a genuine letter of ours, in which such a statement is found written by us. He should read and remember the ninth commandment, as he claims to believe the decalogue binding. He should also remember that one of the six things which the Lord hates is "A false witness that speaketh lies and he that soweth discord among brethren."—Prov. vi. 19. The only escape for Mr. C. is, it was then Miss Harmon, when we saw her, *now* Mrs. White. It is said that a falsehood spoken by the Pope of Rome converts it into truth. We doubt whether Mr. C. has such prerogatives.

and all who professed conversion were denominated "strange children," "children of a month," quoting Hosea v. 6, 7, as proof.

We have seen it stated in a book by Eld. White "that Adventists were agreed that the door was shut." This is a specious statement. Some Adventists were agreed thus, but the great mass were *never* agreed to believe it. Again, he says, "It is vain for any man to deny that it was the *universal belief of Adventists*, in the autumn of 1844, that their work for the world was forever done." This is another specious statement. It can only be true by denying that the many who *did not* embrace the time calculation were Adventists; and it cannot be regarded as *true* of those who *did* fully believe in the time *only for a single day*, for as soon as that day passed without bringing the Lord the mass of believers concluded it an error which they had believed for truth. They at once began to plan and prosecute the work of the gospel, and to show those who had fallen into these strange views (as fast as they met them) that they were errors. But the great movement, the excitement, the experiences, the strange impressions which those had who had been too positive on time, and too unyielding to stubborn facts, when the time had passed, were overwhelmed and led by strange spirits, claiming that the Lord would "yet vindicate them in their belief." All these points were summed up, these arguments and experiences dwelt upon, and some concluded to believe that the Lord was revealing these mysteries to this devout young medium.

From the tenth day of the seventh month, 1844, Eld. White's preaching, experience, and associations changed to another channel, entirely distinct from the Second Advent people as a denomination, only as he could find access among them to teach his views and make proselytes to the views he promulgated. We were in company with him much of the time during the first four weeks of this mania, and during the first five days of it we were carried partially under the sympathetic influence. While attending a meeting in Portland with Eld. White, and hearing some singular experiences and strange messages, claiming to be direct from the Lord, our mind was brought under deep conviction that it was fanaticism; yet, as several were to be re-immersed that day, and we wished to be immersed also, we accepted that opportunity and were baptized by Eld. White, which we should not have consented to a few days later. But with a cautious, hesitating step and prayerful heart we marked and criticised every movement and new statement made, and within a day or two we saw clearly that it was a fanatical movement under a wild spirit, and we withdrew our sympathy wholly from it. The spell was broken while searching the Scriptures, and we fully realized that these brethren were ensnared by the spirit of fanaticism, and were being led into strange paths of the enemy. We at once abandoned the position we were being insidiously led into, announcing that it was "wrong;" that we had been believing an error; that the time calculation was of men. We then spent four weeks visiting societies and urging them to see and acknowledge it an error, and go to work for the Lord *and the salvation of men.* We earnestly besought Eld. White to take the same step, as the correct solution of our situation (though this confession subjected us and all who made it to these epithets, "foolish virgins," "false priests," etc.). He admitted to me one day, while walking a street in Brunswick, that he was "often tempted to think the *time* message an error, and felt inclined to go home to his father's to rest, and to study more upon Christian experience," of which he felt himself "deficient."

But he decided to do otherwise, and entered more fully upon relating, over and over again, the 10th day *experiences* of this class of believers and giving such expositions of certain Scriptures as to sustain them in their views, while he traveled through the country "to strenghen the little bands," as the companies were then called, confirming those who would listen, and convincing the waverings in the idea that it was all of God, the *time in particular,* and that the 2300 days ended in 1844,—the door of mercy closed—the church, i. e., those who continued in this confession were "shut in." Miss Harmon traveled with him much of the time in the New England and Middle States, and could witness to *all* with her "visions," which were said to be frequent, and impressive to some. It was under these circumstances, and during the early part of this experience (we think about the first of 1845), that they each embraced the idea that it was the duty of Christians to keep the ten commandments, not a new idea; but as they would have it, new light was shown them relative to the duty of the church at that particular time, to keep "the *fourth,*" which the Scriptures declare to be "the seventh day," and "the Sabbath of the Lord."

And although the whole decalogue was but a constitution of civil law, for the Jewish people—forever—during their nationality, yet but a small portion of the Christian church seem to have any good understanding of the distinctness of the Old Covenant from the New, and the entire abolition of the one to give force to the other; hence it was an easy matter to make proselytes among those who had found themselves in possession of many errors, which they had now abandoned, and in trial, on their disappointment, were ready to accept any plausible views presented by those who were *Adventists*, for Eld. W. and Miss H. retained this name, and too many thought *all* Advent teachers taught "the Bible doctrine." And there were "7th day Baptists" already, who, it was affirmed, had kept the 7th day, down through the Christian dispensation.

A little later, 1846 or 1847, Eld. W. found new light and strength in his position, from Rev. xiv. 9, and began publishing it with much zeal. This fourth command having been for a long time neglected, or rather, understood by the church to be observed in *effect*, by observing the *first* day of the week, must be made to assume *new* importance; consequently it was put in a *new* dress with a *new* title, for they now named their proclamation of the fourth commandment, or, the law of the Lord, as they would call it.

THE THIRD ANGEL'S MESSAGE OF REV. XIV. 9.

This was now backed up by assuming and teaching that the false cry which Eld. W. had assisted other misguided ones in proclaiming in 1843–4, viz., "come out of her my people," was truly applied to the calling of the saints out of Protestant churches. Eld. W. claimed that the Protestant churches with the Roman, constituted the Apocalyptic Babylon, and has since devoted twenty-five pages of a book to sustain it, in which he says, alluding to 1844 experience: "Everywhere among believers had been heard the solemn cry, 'Babylon is fallen, is fallen,' 'come out of her my people,' and these messages were clearly seen to be in the past." All will admit this to be in the past; but his reference is to the shameful and destructive work to which we have referred before, and which was proclaimed by certain ones in 1843–4.

Eld. White and others who taught the duty to keep the 7th day Sabbath claimed to be the true successors of those who made the former cry; this we shall not dispute. They next appropriated God's seal, or taught that the faithful observance of the 7th day secured the "seal of God," while those who *refuse* to observe it must "drink of the wine of the wrath of God." It *took* with many of the class who had been under the cloud of fanaticism, and with some others also, for changes in the theory opened the way for accessions from without.

After traveling together among the Second Advent Societies of New England for awhile enforcing these several peculiar and startling messages, confirming them with Miss Harmon's—God sent—visions, they were united in marriage.

The notion of the "door shut" was fast dying out, and they, with others who were teachers of the law, began to promulgate the doctrine that any and all who would now embrace *as truth* the *experience* of the church on time in 1844, and acknowledge that the 2300 days ended on the tenth day of the seventh month, that year, and receive the "third angel's message"—to keep the fourth commandment—or as they had rather be understood, "keep the law of the Lord," could be saved.

Eld. White had published several of Ellen's visions on small sheets for general distribution; but as time passed on the theology of her later visions was materially different from former ones, and they were suppressed to give place to those better adapted to enforce the new theological platform which was being framed for future operations. A small paper was started by Eld. White, in Middletown, Ct., called "Present Truth;" soon after it was issued in N. Y.; a little later the title was changed to "Advent Review," and was published at South Paris, Me., then at Rochester, N. Y., and finally at Battle Creek, an appropriate name for the work. Eld. White has shown much ability as a financier and theological manager, and has done much to build up an institution, now commanding a capital of about $100,000, while he is reputed to hold also, about $25,000 worth of property of his own, although he commenced without any capital. This was the process of generating and shaping a new system under the title of "Seventh-day Adventism," which by a new classification and application of certain Scriptures has been gradually maturing and being confirmed by frequent visions, with which Mrs. White was favored; but these visions as published now are greatly in conflict with those which acquaintances and witnesses in New England were accustomed to hear from her lips, after recovering from her clairvoyant state, or to read on sheets as published at first, by Eld. White. However, they are called by their adherents, "as true as the Bible." With these beginnings a sect has been founded, and through persevering efforts, and "visions," a system of dictatorial ecclesiastical government has been established for a class of believers in the Advent near, who have taken the name of "Seventh-day Adventists."

Many have joined them from other churches; they are quite numerous and have some able preachers and writers of their views, and many worthy Christian members, who would not believe the historical sketch we have given, "though a man declare it unto them," as their older teachers have insidiously labored to keep it from them and constantly denied these facts which we have recorded. We should have gladly passed over it could we have done so in justice to the cause we are tracing in history. Many of those who observe the seventh-day Sabbath, however, have repudiated the visions, after some experience, as an imposition, instead of acknowledging them of divine origin and authority for church government, while others never accepted them. Each of these classes are repudiated by the society in return. They have a large printing establishment, under a systematic arrangement worthy of imitation by the Second Advent body.

We find in Eld. White's "Life Incidents" a long and labored effort to *sustain* those who embraced the "door-shut" views, instead of commending them for confessing they were wrong. Then another labored effort, which he has been making for almost thirty years, to prove from "Scripture and *experience*" that the Lord Jesus Christ *did change* his relation to the church by an official act, on the tenth day of the seventh Jewish month, 1844, and that he *opened* the door and went in to the "holy of holies" to offer atonement for his people on that day. This argument alone is enough to show a disordered brain or a fanatical faith, without any other knowledge of him. According to the writings of Elder White, in his "Life Incidents," he claims for himself and followers to be the true progressive descendants of the original stock of Adventists; that while the great mass of believers *fell* from their position and "drew back toward perdition," in 1844, "in denying their experience" (but properly, admitting their errors), *he* and *his* have been going on to perfection on the old track!!! We think his claim almost as clear as Pius IX. can show to the chair of Peter and infallibility.

But really, the "Life Incidents" contains *much* of the *errors* of Adventists *glorified* as truths. A wonderful account of "fanaticism," by one who was as deeply in it as any in Maine, and who, with his consort, became *leaders in one of its chief phases.* His statement on this matter reminds us of the inebriate who staggered through the street badly intoxicated and then entered the complaint that every one in the street staggered; that the posts and trees ran against him. The book also contains many statements of "incidents" which appear, to many of us who knew them in their native dress and simplicity, very strange and singularly stated. Some of them remind us of Don Quixote, which we read in our younger days, while others appear like a woman in a full dress of modern style, so changed that the natural is lost in the artificial.

But we are reminded that in the course of singular events in history a book has been published to "vindicate" James and Ellen in their remarkable career. In this book much talent is displayed, greatly to their advantage in the eyes of *strangers to the actors.* Here we find it stated of Eld. White thus: "The fanaticism and strange delusions that arose during the confusion that followed 1844 he was disconnected from and opposed to. He is not, therefore, to be associated with, or held responsible for, anything of that nature." If this were true then the Christian people of Maine would need a new dictionary to inform them of the proper definition of fanaticism. As to the morals of Eld. W. and wife, their misstatements aside, we have nothing to say. The *Lord* knows; *we* make no pretensions. This would be changing the issue from fanaticism to morals. In another effort to *vindicate* Eld. White and wife from the charge of fanaticism, statements are profusely made, and *regularly* certified by a long list of names, that they were "*not* fanatics," and that they did much to avert and cure fanaticism in New England. The most of these signers were as deeply in fanaticism as themselves; some were leading ones. But signers who had *not been personally associated* in the fanaticism being scarce, to certify in these prepared papers, the names of two young ladies (perhaps more) are added, who, *at the time specified for the events,* were aged, respectively, nine and fourteen years. Prodigies in intellect and judgment, surely, or, perhaps, endowed with the "gift of discerning of spirits." But it is no difficult task to procure the names of partisans, associates, accomplices, their children, cousins, and aunts, to certify to one's rectitude, sanity, or orthodoxy. It is more safe and important, however, to have a good "record in heaven."

In the above historical sketch we make no attempt to show that it is not duty to observe the seventh day as Sabbath; that is a question we are not arguing here. With those who sincerely think it duty to do so we have no quarrel, although we think and teach differently, and may in another place show why, if we find room.

WISE COUNSEL DISREGARDED.

Had the following wise admonition of Mr. Miller been heeded by these young aspiring zealots, the above unpleasant events would have never been furnished for this chapter of sad occurrences. He had said in an address to all, "I beseech you, my dear brethren, be careful that Satan get no advantage over you *by scattering coals of wild-fire among you*, for, if he cannot drive you into unbelief and doubt, he will try his wild-fire of fanaticism and speculation to get us from the word of God. Be watchful and sober, and hope to the end for the grace that shall be brought unto you at the revelation of Jesus Christ."

"Not only Mr. Miller, but all who were in his confidence, took a decided position against fanatical extravagance. They never gave them any quarter, while those who regarded them with favor soon arrayed themselves against Mr. Miller and his adherents. Their fanaticism increased, and, though opposed by Mr. Miller and his friends, the religious and secular press very generally, but unjustly, connected his name with it,—he being no more responsible for it than Luther and Wesley were for similar manifestations in their day."[1]

DEFINITENESS OF PROPHETIC TIME.

"I had never been positive as to any particular *day* for the Lord's appearing, believing that no man could know the day and hour. In all my published lectures will be seen, on the title-page, 'about the year 1843.' In all my oral lectures I invariably told my audiences that the periods would terminate in 1843 *if* there were no mistakes in my calculation; but that I could not say the end might not come even before that time, and they should be continually prepared. In 1842, some of my brethren preached, with great positiveness, the exact year, and censured me for putting in an IF. The public press had also published that I had fixed upon a definite day, the 23d of April, for the Lord's Advent. Therefore, in December of that year, as I could see no error in my reckoning, I published my belief that, some time between March 21, 1843, and March 21, 1844, the Lord would come. Some had their minds fixed on particular days; but I

---

[1] Bliss' Life of Miller, p. 239.

could see no evidence for such, unless the types of the Mosaic law pointed to the Feast of Tabernacles.

"During the year 1843, the most violent denunciations were heaped upon me, and those associated with me, by the press and some pulpits. Our motives were assailed, our principles misrepresented, and our characters traduced. Time passed on, and the 21st of March, 1844, went by without our witnessing the appearing of the Lord. Our disappointment was great, and many walked no more with us.

"Previously to this, in the fall of 1843, some of my brethren began to call the churches Babylon, and to urge that it was the duty of Adventists to come out of them. With this I was much grieved, as not only the effect was very bad, but I regarded it as a perversion of the word of God, a wresting of Scripture.

"On the passing of my published time, I frankly acknowledged my disappointment in reference to the exact period; but my faith was unchanged in any essential feature. I, therefore, continued my labors, principally at the West, during the summer of 1844, until 'the seventh-month movement,' as it is called. I had no participation in this only as I wrote a letter, eighteen months previously, presenting the observances under the Mosaic law which pointed to that month as a probable time when the Advent might be expected. This was written because some were looking to definite days in the *spring*. I had, however, no expectation that so unwarranted a use would be made of those types that any should regard a belief in such mere inferential evidence a test of salvation. I, therefore, had no fellowship with that movement until about two or three weeks previous to the 22d of October, when, seeing it had obtained such prevalence, and considering it was at a probable point of time, I was persuaded that it was a work of God, and felt that, if it should pass by, I should be more disappointed than I was in my first published time.

"But that time passed, and I was again disappointed. The movement was of such a character that, for a time, it was very mysterious to me; and the results following it were so unaccountable that I supposed our work might be completed, and that a few weeks only might elapse between that time and the appearing of Christ. However that might be, I regarded my own work as completed, and that what was to be done for the extension of these views must be done by younger brethren, except an occasional discourse from myself."

In conclusion, he considered the

ERRONEOUS VIEWS CONNECTED WITH THE DOCTRINE.

"As time has progressed, I have been pained to see many errors which have been embraced, in different sections of the country, by some who have labored in connection with myself; errors which I cannot countenance, and of which I wish to speak freely, although I may lose the fellowship of some for faithfully doing my duty.

"I have been pained to see a spirit of sectarianism and bigotry, in some sections, which disfellowships everything that does not square with the narrow prejudices of individual minds. There is a tendency to exalt individual opinions as a standard for all to submit to; a disposition to place the results of individual investigation upon a level with solemn conclusions to which the great body of brethren have arrived. This is very wrong; for, while we are in this world, we are so short-sighted that we should never regard our conclusions as infallible, should bear with the imperfections of others, and receive those that are weak in the faith, but not to doubtful disputations.

"Some have an inclination to indulge in harsh and denunciatory remarks against all who do not agree with them. We are all liable to err; but we should avoid thus giving occasion of offence. We should instruct with meekness those that oppose themselves, and avoid foolish and unlearned questions, that gender strifes.

"There may be causes operating on the minds of others, of which we know nothing, that influence them contrary to the truth, as we have received it. We should, therefore, in all our intercourse with those we deem in error, treat them with kindness and affection, and show them that we would do them good, and not evil, if God, peradventure, will give them repentance to the acknowledging of the truth, and that they may recover themselves out of the snare of the devil, who are taken captive by him at his will.

"Some are disposed to lay a stress on the seventh-month movement which is not warranted by the Word. There was then a dedication of heart, in view of the Lord's coming, that was well pleasing in the sight of God. Desire for the Lord's coming and a preparation for that event are acceptable to him. But, because we then ardently desired his coming and sought that preparation that was necessary, it does not follow that our expectations were then realized. For we were certainly disappointed. We expected the personal coming of Christ at that time; and now to contend that we were not mistaken is dishonest. We should never be ashamed frankly to confess all our errors.

"I have no confidence in any of the new theories that grew out of that movement, namely, that Christ then came as the Bridegroom, that the door of mercy was closed, that there is no salvation for sinners, that the seventh trumpet then sounded, OR THAT IT WAS A FULFILLMENT OF PROPHECY IN ANY SENSE. The spirit of fanaticism which resulted from it, in some places leading to extravagance and excess, I regard as of the same nature as that which retarded the Reformation in Germany, and the same as have been connected with every religious movement since the first advent. The truth is not responsible for such devices of Satan to destroy it. I have never taught a neglect of any of the duties of life which make us good parents, children, neighbors, or citizens. I have ever inculcated a faithful performance of all those duties, enjoining good works with faith and repentance. Those who have taught the neglect of these, instead of acting with me, or being my followers, as they are called, have departed from my counsels, and acted in opposition to my uniform teachings; men have crept in unawares, who have given heed to seducing spirits and doctrines of devils, teaching lies in hypocrisy, denying any personal existence of Christ, forbidding to marry, and commanding to abstain from certain kinds of food, denying the right to pray for sinners, and commanding to violate our social duties, etc. With such things I have no sympathy."

THE PIONEERS RALLY ON THE MAIN PRINCIPLES.

Although many became disheartened and turned away in disgust while these new leaders and pretenders were seeking to guide them into their various schemes, yet the mass of believers waited in suspense, or were being more or less overpowered by the several messages and spirits which went abroad among them. We cannot better express the general situation than to quote from Bliss' Life of Miller upon this point:

"Some taught feet-washing and kissing as religious ceremonies bodily exercises and mesmeric ecstasies were regarded as religious experience; power to discern the spiritual condition of others was claimed, etc.; and they made no scruple in denouncing and consigning to perdition those whom they judged destitute of religion, according to their various standards and tests. Brotherly love gave place to contention and disputation, and the cause had to bear the reproach of those who had thus departed from the position occupied by Mr. Miller and the body."

Writing on the 7th of April, he referred to these things as follows:

"My Dear Bro. Himes:—I should utterly despair of the Second Advent cause, were it not evident, by its past and present history, that God is for us. You know, my dear brother, there was a time when you and I, with a few choice brethren, stood alone. . . We acknowledged our weakness, and claimed no superiority over our fellows. We provoked no one to combat, and made no attack on the prevailing or popular institutions of the day; yet they began to be alarmed. Why? Because, as the people began to hear the foolish reports of our enemies, they became more and more anxious to know what these things meant. . . .

"Among the many pious who took sides with us were some of those uneasy, ever-changing, unstable, insubordinate, and self-exalted spirits, who stood ready to jump on and ride into notice and power the moment they saw how the case would go. This kind of spirits have always seized the reins of government, are never satisfied with their present position, and will change every new moon. There are many of this class among us, if not of us, at the present time, who are trying to lead away followers after them.

"This is a peculiar time. The greatest variety of fanciful interpretations of Scripture are now being presented by new luminaries, reflecting their rays of light and heat in every direction; some of these are wandering stars, and some emit only twilight. I am sick of this everlasting changing; but, my dear brother, we must learn to have patience. If Christ comes this spring, we shall not need it long; and if he comes not, we shall need much more. I am prepared for the worst, and hope for the best. God will not forsake us, unless we forsake him. . . .

"'It is a small thing to be judged of man's judgment,' says the apostle; so that you need not fear man. I have often been consigned to perdition, and yet I have a blessed hope. I often think, when I hear a brother judging and condemning another, what an excellent Pope he would make. Therefore, fear them not; for if we judge and condemn our brother, we are making ourselves 'judges of the law, rather than doers of the law.' WM. MILLER.

"LOW HAMPTON, April 7, 1845."

In connection with the great variety of views received by those who adhered to the "Shut Door," there was issued a great variety of papers attempting to sustain them. These, being circulated in every direction, created great confusion, and made it difficult for those not initiated to understand the true position of believers in the Second Advent. This was illustrated by the following anecdote related by Mr. Miller:

The first person in his own parish who fully embraced his views was an old woman, an humble, praying Christian, and she continued steadfast in the faith on the original platform. She was in humble circumstances, and, not being able to take a paper, Mr. Miller sent her his papers when he had read them.

One week he received sixteen different sheets, all purporting to be Advent publications, but the most of them advocating contradictory sentiments. After he had examined them, he sent them to the old woman. It was not long before he had a special message from her, requesting his immediate presence.

He hastened to her house, not knowing but something important was the cause of the summons. On his arrival she began:

"Have you read all these papers?"

"I have looked them over."

"But are they all Advent papers?"

"They profess to be."

"Well, then," said she, "I am no longer an Adventist. I shall take the old Bible, and stick to that."

"But," said Mr. M., "we have no confidence in one-half there is advocated in those papers."

"We!" exclaimed the old lady, "who is *we?*"

"Why," replied Mr. M., "*we* are those who do not fellowship these things."

"Well, but I want to know who *we is.*"

"Why, all of us who stand on the old ground."

"But that ain't telling who *we* is. I want to know who *we* is."

"Well," said Mr. Miller, in relating the story, "I was confounded, and was unable to give her any information who *we* were."

In this dilemma it was considered very important to define their position, and to ascertain who did sympathize with their views. To determine this, a Mutual Conference was called, to assemble at Albany, N. Y., on the 29th of April, 1845.

MUTUAL CONFERENCE AT ALBANY—DECLARATION OF PRINCIPLES—PLAN OF OPERATIONS—ADDRESS TO THE BRETHREN.

On the 29th of April the Conference assembled at 9 A. M., at the "House of Prayer," in Grand street. After singing, and a prayer by Mr. Miller, it was temporarily organized by the choice of Mr. Miller, Chairman, and Mr. Himes, Secretary, who stated the objects for which the Conference had been called, namely, "to consult together respecting the condition and wants of brethren in the several sections of the country, that we may be better enabled to act in concert, and with more efficiency, in the promulgation of Gospel truths."

After the names and residence of members were ascertained, the Conference was fully organized by the choice of Rev. Elon Galusha, of Lockport, N. Y., President, and S. Bliss and O. R. Fassett, Secretaries.

A committee of twelve, consisting of William Miller, Josiah Litch, N. N. Whiting, J. V. Himes, Sylvester Bliss, L. D. Fleming, Erastus Parker, H. Caswell, I. R. Gates, I. H. Shipman, Prosper Powell, and Elon Galusha, were appointed to arrange business for the action of the Conference. While they were thus engaged the others were profitably occupied in listening to statements of the condition of things in different sections of the country. The committee reported, in part, on the second day, and in full on the third and last day of the session, as follows:

REPORT OF THE COMMITTEE TO THE CONFERENCE.

"Your committee, appointed for the purpose of taking into consideration the great principles upon which we can unite and act in advancing the cause of truth, for the edification of the body of

Christ, the salvation of souls, and the preparation of man for the near Advent of the Saviour, submit the following report:

"In view of the many conflicting opinions, unscriptural views, leading to unseemly practices, and the sad divisions which have been thereby caused by some professing to be Adventists, we deem it incumbent on us to declare to the world our belief that the Scriptures teach, among others, the following

IMPORTANT TRUTHS.

"1st. That the heavens and earth which are now, by the word of God, are kept in store, reserved unto fire against the day of judgment and perdition of ungodly men. That the day of the Lord will come as a thief in the night, in the which the heavens shall pass away with a great noise, and the elements shall melt with fervent heat; the earth also, and the works that are therein, shall be burned up. That the Lord will create new heavens and a new earth, wherein righteousness—that is, the righteous—will forever dwell, 2 Pet. iii. 7, 10, 13. And that the kingdom and the dominion under the whole heaven shall be given to the people of the saints of the Most High, whose kingdom is an everlasting kingdom, and all dominions shall serve and obey him, Dan. vii. 27.

"2d. That there are but two advents or appearings of the Saviour to this earth, Heb. ix. 28. That both are personal and visible, Acts i. 9, 11. That the first took place in the days of Herod, Mat. ii. 1, when he was conceived of the Holy Ghost, Mat. i. 18, born of the Virgin Mary, Mat. i. 25, went about doing good, Mat. xi. 5, suffered on the cross, the just for the unjust, 1 Pet. iii. 18, died, Luke xxiii. 46, was buried, Luke xxiii. 53, arose again the third day, the first-fruits of them that slept, 1 Cor. xv. 4, and ascended into the heavens, Luke xxiv. 51, which must receive him until the times of the restitution of all things, spoken of by the mouth of all the holy prophets, Acts iii. 21. That the second coming or appearing will take place when he shall descend from heaven, at the sounding of the last trump, to give his people rest, 1 Thes. iv. 16, 17, 1 Cor. xv. 52, being revealed from heaven in flaming fire, taking vengeance on them that know not God, and obey not the Gospel, 2 Thes. i. 7, 8. And that he will judge the quick and the dead at his appearing and kingdom, 2 Tim. iv. 1.

"3d. That the second coming or appearing is indicated to be now emphatically nigh, even at the doors, Mat. xxiv. 33, by the chronology of the prophetic periods, Dan. vii. 25, viii. 14, ix. 24, xii. 7, 11, 12, Rev. ix. 10, 15, xi. 2, 3, xii. 6, 14, xiii. 5, the fulfillment of prophecy, Dan. 2d, 7th, 8th, 9th, 11th, and 12th chapters, Rev. 9th, 11th, 12th, 13th, 14th, and 17th chapters, and the signs of the times, Mat. xxiv. 29, Luke xxi. 25, 26. And that this truth should be preached both to saints and sinners, that the first may rejoice, knowing their redemption draweth nigh, Luke xxi. 28, 1 Thes. iv. 18, and the last be warned to flee from the wrath to come, 2 Cor. v. 11, before the Master of the house shall rise up and shut to the door, Luke xiii. 24, 25.

"4th. That the condition of salvation is repentance toward God, and faith in our Lord Jesus Christ, Acts xx. 21, Mark i. 15. And that those who have repentance and faith will live soberly, and righteously, and godly, in this present world, looking for that blessed hope, and the glorious appearing of the great God and our Saviour Jesus Christ, Tit. ii. 11–13.

"5th. That there will be a resurrection of the bodies of all the dead, John v. 28, 29, both of the just and the unjust, Acts xxiv. 15. That those who are Christ's will be raised at his coming, 1 Cor. xv. 23. That the rest of the dead will not live again until after a thousand years, Rev. xx. 5. And that the saints shall not all sleep, but shall be changed in the twinkling of an eye at the last trump, 1 Cor. xv. 51, 52.

"6th. That the only millennium taught in the Word of God is the thousand years which are to intervene between the first resurrection and that of the rest of the dead, as inculcated in the 20th of Revelation, Rev. xx. 2–7. And that the various portions of Scripture which refer to the millennial state are to have their fulfillment after the resurrection of all the saints who sleep in Jesus, Isa. xi., xxxv. 1, 2, 5–10, lxv. 17–25.

"7th. That the promise, that Abraham should be the heir of the world, was not to him, or to his seed, through the law, but through the righteousness of faith, Rom. iv. 13. That they are not all Israel which are of Israel, Rom. ix. 6. That there is no difference, under the Gospel dispensation, between Jew and Gentile, Rom. x. 12. That the middle wall of partition that was between them is broken down, no more to be rebuilt, Eph. ii. 14, 15. That God will render to every man according to his deeds, Rom. ii. 6. That if we are Christ's, then are we Abraham's seed, and heirs according to the promise, Gal. iii. 29. And that the only restoration of Israel, yet future, is the restoration of the saints to the earth, created anew, when God shall open the graves of those descendants of Abraham who died in faith, without receiving the promise, with the believing Gentiles who have been grafted in with them into the same olive tree; and shall cause them to come up out of their graves, and bring them, with the living, who are changed, into the land of Israel, Ezek. xxxvii. 12, Heb. xi. 12, 13, Rom. xi. 17, John v. 28, 29.

"8th. That there is no promise of this world's conversion, Mat. xxiv. 14. That the Horn of Papacy will war with the saints, and prevail against them, until the Ancient of Days shall come, and judgment be given to the saints of the Most High, and the time come that the saints possess the kingdom, Dan. vii. 21, 22. That the children of the kingdom, and the children of the wicked one, will continue together until the end of the world, when all things that offend shall be gathered out of the kingdom, and the righteous shall shine forth as the sun in the kingdom of their Father, Mat. xiii. 37–43. That the Man of Sin will only be destroyed by the brightness of Christ's coming, 2 Thes. ii. 8. And that the nations of those which are saved and redeemed to God by the blood of Christ, out of every kindred, and tongue, and people, and nation, will be made kings and priests unto God, to reign forever on the earth, Rev. v. 9, 10, xxi. 24.

"9th. That it is the duty of the ministers of the Word to continue in the work of preaching the Gospel to every creature, even unto the end, Mat. xxviii. 19, 20, calling upon them to repent, in view of the fact that the kingdom of heaven is at hand, Rev. xiv. 7, that their sins may be blotted out when the times of refreshing shall come from the presence of the Lord, Acts iii. 19, 20.

"And 10th. That the departed saints do not enter their inheritance, or receive their crowns, at death, Dan. xii. 13, Rev. vi. 9–11, Rom. viii. 22, 23. That they without us cannot be made perfect, Heb. xi. 40. That their inheritance, incorruptible and undefiled, and that fadeth not away, is reserved in heaven, ready to be revealed in the last time, 1 Pet. i. 4, 5. That there are laid up for them and us crowns of righteousness, which the Lord, the righteous Judge, shall give at the day of Christ to all that love his appearing, 2 Tim. iv. 8. That they will only be satisfied when they awake with Christ's likeness, Ps. xvii. 15. And that, when the Son of Man shall come in his glory, and all the holy angels with him, the King will say to those on his right hand, 'Come, ye blessed of my Father, inherit the kingdom prepared for you from the foundation of the world,' Mat. xxv. 34. Then they will be equal to the angels, being the children of God and of the resurrection, Luke xx. 36.

ASSOCIATED ACTION.

"We are induced, from present circumstances affecting our spiritual interests, to present, for your consideration, a few ideas touching associated action.

"Order is heaven's first law. All things emanating from God are constituted on principles of perfect order. The New Testament rules for the government of the church we regard as binding on the whole brotherhood of Christ. No circumstances can justify us in departing from the usages established by Christ and his apostles.

"We regard any congregation of believers, who habitually assemble for the worship of God and the due observance of the Gospel ordinances, as a church of Christ. As such, it is an independent body, accountable only to the great Head of the church. To all such we recommend a careful examination of the Scriptures, and the adoption of such principles of association and order as are in accordance therewith, that they may enjoy the advantages of that church relation which Christ has instituted.

PLAN OF OPERATIONS.

"In the midst of our disappointed hopes of seeing the King of Glory and being made like him, and still finding ourselves in a world of sin, snares, and death, the question forces itself upon us, *what now is our work?*

"To us it seems clear that our first work is to make straight paths for our feet, lest that which is lame be turned out of the way. We are in duty bound to give the household meat in due season, and to build ourselves up in our most holy faith. While doing this we are to continue, in obedience to the great commission, to preach the Gospel to every creature; so long as the love of Christ dwells in us it will constrain us. We shall not be released, while in our present state, from our obligations to be 'workers together with God,' in saving those for whom the Redeemer died. It is evident that the duty, which of right devolves on every minister of the Gospel, of proclaiming the hour of God's judgment, is, if performed at all, to be done by those who are convinced of its truth. Shall we continue to do it, or shall it be left undone? And if we continue to work in this peculiar department of the Lord's vineyard, what system of operations shall we adopt for carrying forward our work? On this point we feel that we have need of great wisdom and prudence.

"In sounding the alarm through the length and breadth of the land, and awakening a general interest on the subject of the Lord's speedy coming and its kindred doctrines, our camp-meetings have been of incalculable importance, and, in many instances, have accomplished much good. But that peculiar work seems to have been performed, and a new aspect presents itself. What we now do must be done more by dint of persevering and determined effort than by moving the masses of community.

"We would, therefore, advise that our mode of operation, in this respect, be varied so as to meet the exigencies of the times, and are of the opinion that our camp-meetings, except in particular cases where the brethren deem it will advance the cause, should be dispensed with for the present, and our energies expended by visiting the towns and villages, and in some convenient place giving courses of lectures and holding series of conferences. By this we think our means could be better husbanded, and fewer laborers could carry on the meetings, and thus a wider field be occupied.

"We would also take the liberty of urging the importance of a wider circulation of our books and periodicals. These have been, and may still be, the means of great good to the community, and many may thus yet be reached who have not listened to the public lectures. Especially is it important at the present time to spread widely those which relate particularly to the personal appearing of Christ, the resurrection of the body, the return of the Jews, etc. . .

"Nor can we think ourselves justified in neglecting Sabbath-schools and Bible-class instruction. We would suggest to each congregation the necessity of opening a Sabbath-school for the benefit of at least their own children and as many more as can be induced to attend. If the beginning is small perseverance will accomplish the object.

"In all our labors we cannot be too deeply impressed with the sentiments of Paul, addressed to Timothy, his son in the Gospel. 'The servant of the Lord must not strive, but be gentle toward all men,—apt to teach, patient; in meekness instructing those who oppose themselves, if God peradventure may give them repentance to the acknowledging of the truth, and they may recover themselves out of the snare of the devil, who are taken captive by him at his will.'

"In conclusion, permit us to add the following resolutions:

"*Resolved*, That this Conference, while it sympathizes with every Scripture effort to save men from sin, and prepare them, by grace, for the kingdom of God,—and while it bids God-speed to the publication of the Gospel to every creature in the world,—yet it feels bound, by the most solemn considerations possible, to oppose, to the utmost of its power, that fatal and delusive doctrine of modern days, namely, that the Scripture warrants the belief, or even the hope, that, before the second glorious and personal appearing of Christ, to glorify his saints and renew the earth, the world, or even a majority of it, will be converted to Christ. And, 1st. We deem it *anti-scriptural*,—opposed to all that class of Scriptures which represents the church as in a state of warfare and suffering until her deliverer, Christ, comes,—all those Scriptures which declare the coexistence and the mingling of the righteous and wicked, even to the end of the world,—all those passages which represent the continuance of the Man of Sin, the little horn of the fourth beast in Daniel's vision, the great dragon power, etc., as existing till the personal advent of the Saviour, to destroy them that destroy the earth, and to reward his saints. 2d. We deem it dangerous to the eternal interests of men. It holds out to them the hope that a period more conducive to piety than the present is before them, thus inducing, however unintentionally, the sinner to defer immediate repentance, and encouraging professors to wait for a more favorable opportunity to expend their energies for saving sinners, both at home and abroad. And, finally, its direct influence is to put far off the second advent of the Saviour, and thus lull the world into a state of carelessness with respect to an immediate preparation for the event.

There can be no millennium until the first resurrection, the resurrection of the just.

"*Resolved*, That we consider the doctrine of the restoration of the natural Jews, as a nation, either *before* or *after* the second advent of Christ, as heirs and inheritors of the land of Canaan, as subversive of the whole Gospel system, by raising up what Christ has broken down, namely, the middle wall of partition between the Jew and Gentile. It contradicts those declarations of the New Testament which assert 'there is no difference between the Jew and the Greek;' that 'the promise that he shall be heir of the world was not to Abraham and his seed through the law, but through the righteousness of faith;' and that 'there is neither Jew nor Gentile, bond nor free, male nor female,' but that, 'if we are Christ's, then are we Abraham's seed, and heirs according to the promise.' For this Judaizing doctrine claims there *is* a difference between the Jew and the Greek; that the children of the flesh *are* accounted for the seed; that there still *is* the distinction of Jew and Gentile; that we *do* henceforth know men after the flesh, etc. We feel bound, therefore, as we value the fundamental principles of the gospel, to enter our most *solemn protest* against all such teachings; and in our public services we will endeavor to meet, in the spirit of love and meekness, this error, and expose its gross absurdity; while, at the same time, we will proclaim to all, both Jew and Gentile, the message found in the commission given by the Great Head of the church—'*He that believeth and is baptized shall be saved, and he that believeth not shall be damned*,' and 'WHOSOEVER calleth upon the name of the Lord shall be saved.'

"Whereas, in every great religious movement, there have been, among the wise and sober-minded advocates of the truth, others who have risen up, striving about words to no profit, but to the subverting of the hearers; making great pretensions to special illumination; indulging in many evil practices; creeping into houses, and leading captive silly women; laden with sins, led away with divers lusts, ever learning and never able to come to the knowledge of the truth; men of corrupt minds and reprobate concerning the faith, who will not endure sound doctrine, but after their own lusts heap to themselves teachers having itching ears; turning their ears away from the truth and turning unto fables; and who walk disorderly, working not at all, but are busy-bodies, for the cause of whom the way of truth is evil spoken of; and, *whereas*, in connection with the doctrine of Christ's near appearing, as in all previous religious movements, some of this class have risen up, calling themselves Adventists, teaching for doctrines that with which we can have no sympathy or fellowship, with many unseemly practices, whereby the word of God has been dishonored and the doctrine of Christ's appearing brought into contempt, therefore

"*Resolved*, That we can have no sympathy or fellowship with those things which have only a show of wisdom in will-worship and neglecting of the body, after the commandments and doctrines of men. That we have no fellowship with any of the *new tests* as conditions of salvation, in addition to repentance toward God and faith in our Lord Jesus Christ, and a looking for and loving his appearing. That we have no fellowship for Jewish fables and commandments of men, that turn from the truth, or for any of the distinctive characteristics of modern Judaism. And that the act of promiscuous feet-washing and the salutation kiss, as practised by some professing Adventists *as religious* ceremonies, sitting on the floor as an act of voluntary humility, shaving the head to humble one's self, and acting like children in understanding, are not only unscriptural, but subversive, if persevered in, of purity and morality.

"And whereas our congregations have suffered greatly from persons who have *called themselves* to the ministry and taught errors, and by smooth words and fair speeches have deceived the hearts of the simple and led them astray, therefore

"*Resolved*, That we recommend to our brethren to encourage those men only who give evidence that they are called of God to the work; who are of good behavior; who abstain from all appearance of evil; who are vigilant, sober, apt to teach, not greedy of filthy lucre, no brawlers, not covetous; men who will teach the unadulterated word of God, and, by manifestation of the truth, commend themselves to every man's conscience in the sight of God.

(Signed in behalf the Committee,)

WILLIAM MILLER, *Chairman*."

The above, after a full discussion and careful examination, was unanimously adopted, as was also, from the pen of Mr. Miller, the following

ADDRESS TO THE BRETHREN.

"The present state of our faith and hope, with the severe trials which many of us experience, call for much brotherly love, forbearance, patience, and prayer. No cause, be it ever so holy, can exist in this present world without its attendant evils. Therefore, it becomes necessary for all who are connected with this cause to exercise great charity, for charity covers a multitude of sins.

"The cause we advocate calls upon all men to read the Word of God, and to reason, judge, compare, and digest for themselves. This is certainly right and is the privilege of all rational members of the community; yet this very liberty may become a stumbling block to many and, without charity, be the means of scattering, dividing, and causing contention among brethren. Human nature is such that those who are governed by a desire to rule over others will seize the reins and think all must bow to their decision, while others will think such unfit for the station they assume. James foresaw the evils under which we labor, and gives us a caution in his third chapter, to which we shall do well to take heed. Our present difficulties arise more from the multiplicity of masters and leaders among us (some of whom are governed by carnal motives) than from any want of light. The Word of God affords light enough to guide us in all cases, 'that the man of God may be perfect, thoroughly furnished unto every good work.' But among the thousand-and-one expositions of Scripture, which are every day being palmed upon us, some of them, at least, must be wrong. Many of them are so weak and silly that they bring a stigma on the blessed Book, confuse the mind of the inquirer after truth, and divide the children of God.

"To remedy this evil, we must learn to judge men and principles by their fruits, and not be too hasty in receiving the expositions which may be presented by every pretender to wisdom and sanctity. Any exposition of Scripture which conflicts with other texts must be spurious. Any man whose object is to obtain followers must be avoided. Whatever produces envy and strife, brethren, is of the devil, and we must resist his temptations in their beginning. If God has been with us from the commencement of our illumination respecting the hope of his glorious appearing, shall we abandon the truth wherein our souls have been comforted, and our brotherly love established, for fables? We ought to be careful lest we grieve the

Holy Spirit. How did we receive this doctrine at first? Was it not by searching the Word of God and a careful comparison of Scripture with Scripture? Yes; our faith did not rest on the word of man. We then required chapter and verse, or we would not believe. Why should we leave our former rule of faith to follow the vain and changing opinions of men? Some are neglecting the lamp and seeking to walk by sparks of their own kindling. There is a propensity in many to make all prophecy apply to our time and country; others have split on this rock. Some of the best writers and commentators have thus erred. They have, in many instances, considered themselves, their sect, or their nation, as the peculiar favorites of heaven, and have, therefore, often failed to apply prophecy aright. An Englishman, writing on prophecy, will make the English territory the principal place of action; the Frenchman, France; the German, Germany, and an American, the United States. So is it with all sectarians. When minds are contracted by selfishness and bigotry they lose sight of the glory of God and his word, and seek only their own glory. On the other hand, they neglect, if they do not actually reject, such parts of the oracles of God as militate against their views, and rush headlong into error. If we are thus liable to be deceived by the cunning craftiness of men, we ought to be cautious how we are led by every fanciful interpretation of Scripture. Let us then be more wary, and, like the noble Bereans, search the Scriptures daily, to see whether these things are so. Then, if we err, we shall have the consolation that we have made a careful examination of the subject, and that the error was one of the head, and not of the heart. Christians should receive no evidence but the testimony of God as a ground of faith.

"We are commanded to be sober, and hope to the end for that grace which is to be brought unto us at the revelation of Jesus Christ. Our disappointment, as to the time, should have no effect on our hope. We know that Christ has not yet been revealed, and the object of our hope is yet in the future. Therefore, if we believe in God's word, as we profess, we ought to be thankful for the trial of our faith.

"We shall not have to wait long for the glorious appearing of Christ. Therefore, let us lift up our heads and look up, knowing that our redemption draweth nigh. We regret to see any impatience manifested among the friends of Jesus. God is now trying our graces. How solemn the thought that any should lose the crown when near the goal! Let us arise, shake off our dullness, redouble our diligence, let all the world know there is such a grace as Christian perseverance, and let all see that we are truly seeking a better country. Can it be possible, after we have run well for a season, loved the appearing of Jesus, come to a time when we must expect him, and should be ready to cast ourselves into his arms, that we shall go back, or again strike hands with a thoughtless world? May God forbid! Let us then go forward. It is death to go back; to go forward can be no more.

"We are pained to see a disposition to murmur against those who have been pioneers in the war,—who have sacrificed all earthly considerations to support a truth so unpopular as the second advent and personal reign of Jesus Christ.

"Brethren, shun such as cause divisions among very friends. Remember the admonition of James: 'Grudge not one against another, brethren, lest ye be condemned; behold, the Judge standeth at the door.' We see, by this rule, that when a brother loses his fellowship for the saints he is certainly in darkness. We must be careful not to follow what he may term 'light.' Love for brethren is a test of our interest in Christ, without which all gifts and works are like sounding brass and a tinkling cymbal. Let us cultivate, with peculiar care, this loveliest of all Christian graces, and frown on the man who attempts to cause division. 'Offences must needs come, but woe to that man by whom the offence cometh!' What can we say more to stir up your pure minds by way of remembrance?

"We would, therefore, recommend more study of the Scriptures, and less writing, and that we be careful not to submit to public inspection mere speculations until they are closely scrutinized by some judicious friend. Thus we shall avoid many errors. We should always be more jealous of ourselves than of others. Self-love is the strongest, most dangerous and deceitful foe that we meet in our Christian warfare. We have arrived at a period of deep interest and peril. It is interesting because the evidence of the Saviour being at the door is plain, so that no sincere student of prophecy can be at a loss to know that that day, for which all other days were made, is near. How interesting to live in expectation of the day which patriarchs, prophets, and apostles desired to see, but died without the sight! Persecution and death lose their sting in prospect of the coming Conqueror, who hath all power and who hath engaged to put all enemies under his feet. We need not murmur, for, in this our day, God will bring to pass this act, this (to the worldly man) strange act, for which all the weary saints, for six thousand years, have lived and prayed. We entreat you to hold fast the confidence which you have had in the Word of God unto the end. 'Yet a little while, and he that shall come will come, and will not tarry.' 'Here is the patience and the faith of the saints.' 'Be ye also patient; stablish your hearts, for the coming of the Lord draweth nigh.' WM. MILLER, *Chairman of Committee.*"

Thus harmoniously terminated a Conference, very fully attended, and congregated under circumstances of peculiar interest, in view of many conflicting opinions, with great forebodings as to the result. The best of feeling prevailed, and great calmness and patience characterized their deliberations. Everything adopted by the Conference was carefully examined in full meeting, and each separate item unanimously received, and then the whole without a dissenting voice.

Mr. Miller, in relating the story of his inability to convince the old lady who "*we*" were, remarked that he went to the Albany Conference with a heavy heart, fearing disunion and conflicting views; but was there cheered and strengthened anew by the unanimity and harmony that prevailed. And he was "rejoiced that so goodly a number had thus united in making known to the world who and what *we* were." He returned to Low Hampton, and the old lady referred to soon had an opportunity to read the doings at Albany. The first time she again saw Mr. Miller she grasped his hand and exclaimed:

"I have found out who *we* is, and I shall still be an Adventist and stand by the old ship."

"And I am glad," said he, in narrating it, "that you have told the world who you are, and if anybody wishes to know where I am, I wish to let them know that I am with you who approve of the doings of that Conference, and have told the world what you are."

The doings of that Conference gave great satisfaction to all of the consistent Adventists, but mortally offended those who had taken new positions and sought to lead away disciples after them. It was so much misrepresented and opposed that Mr. Miller, a few weeks snbsequently, came out, over his own name, in its defence.

THE EVENTS OF LUTHER'S TIMES SIMILAR TO OURS.

There is, in every great reformation, a similarity in the evils to be corrected, in the instruments by which they are to be corrected, and in the character of the opposition to the progress of truth. In reading D'Aubigné's History of the Reformation of Luther, we have been particularly struck with the number of coincidences which it presents to what we have witnessed in the progress of the doctrine of the Advent in our own day. It had the same humble beginning, encountered the same obstacles, was attacked by the same weapons, with the same spirit, and met with the same hindrances in its progress. These coincidences are so numerous that, with a change of names and places, we could almost fancy we were reading the history of the Advent doctrine.

We find that the great truths which were then about to be agitated had slumbered in the church so long that their existence was almost unknown, while the errors which prevailed, and which it was necessary to expose and eradicate, had so long been the prevailing belief that they had been supposed to have been the faith of the church from the days of the apostles. God chose an obscure monk —LUTHER—a man of great natural ability, as the first instrument in the great work which was then commenced. "An old wooden chapel, thirty feet long and twenty broad," was the cradle of the Reformation, in which it was first to any purpose preached, and a contemporary remarked that it might "be aptly compared to the stable in which Christ was born." Among the thousand cathedrals and parish churches with which the world was filled, not one was chosen for the glorious announcement of everlasting life.

"In a short time," says D'Aubigné, "the little chapel of Luther could no longer contain the crowds that flocked thither;" his doctrines astonished his auditors, his fame spread far and wide, and many flocked from distant places to hear. Luther obtained a profound knowledge of the word of God; he reasoned out of the Scriptures in a way that was new and astonishing to the people, and God raised him up friends. He then went forth, supposing the

DR. MARTIN LUTHER.—Page 428.

(Engraved from a Photograph obtained by H. A. King, in 1871, at Wartburg Castle, Germany, where Luther was imprisoned.)

church had only to hear the truth, to be shown the evidences of its authenticity, and she would receive it. His motto was,—"The writings of the apostles and prophets are more certain and sublime than all the sophisms of the schools." Multitudes listened to him with admiration, and marvelled that they had not earlier seen and acknowledged truths which he made so plain, and they compared his preaching to a new light arising after so long a night. Pious souls were attracted and penetrated by the sweetness of his doctrine. The firmness with which Luther appealed to the Scriptures gave power to his teachings, and his audiences acknowledged that he believed what he taught, and that his life corresponded with his precepts. The more men loved the Christian virtues the more they inclined towards him. As Luther continued his labors he saw more of the corruptions of the church and of the hopelessness of the expectation that she would embrace the truth. Those who wished to stand well with Rome and with society spoke of him as a proud fellow and an ignorant monk instead of meeting him with opposing arguments. For a time Luther's works were read in the theological schools with but little sensation; at a later period all gave ear to admire or oppose. He had no desire of becoming a reformer; he was distrustful of his own powers and moved only as God seemed to open the door for him. He sought not to please men, but God, and so followed where his Master called. He had no settled purpose; his only wish was that the watchmen of the church should arouse themselves and endeavor to put a stop to the evils that were laying it waste. But the princes of the church closed their ears to the voice of God, which was making itself heard in so affecting and energetic a manner by the voice of Luther. They would not understand the signs of the times; they were struck with that blindness which had been the ruin of so many. "But," said Erasmus, "I observe that the more irreproachable men's morals, and the more evangelical their piety, the less are they opposed to Luther."

All Luther's efforts might have been spent on the air; but the partisans of Rome prevented their ending thus. They fanned the flame instead of extinguishing it. Eager to crush the audacious monk, they raised a shout of indignation; they disputed with and reviled him. On one occasion Tetzel opposed Luther with a series of propositions, but they were overthrown by John Knipstrow—a boy of twenty; and yet Tetzel is made a Doctor as a recompense, and contents himself with hurling his anathemas at Luther. The priests raised a shout against the poor monk, and "Luther's name resounded from all the Dominican pulpits." "They stirred up the passions of the people, called him a madman, a seducer, a wretch possessed of the devil," and "his teaching was decried as the most horrible of heresies."

Luther saw the necessity of meeting his adversaries boldly; "but at the same time their weakness discovered to him his own strength, and inspired him with a consciousness of what it really was." Said he, "they are so ignorant, both of human and divine things, that it is humbling to have to dispute with them, and yet it is this very ignorance which gives them their inconceivable boldness and their brazen front." At Rome, for a time, they would not condescend to meddle with Luther's opinions; it is a "squabble among the monks," said Leo X., "the best way is not to notice it." But when a Roman censor sees fit to attack him he employs "ridicule, revilings, and threats."

Luther's fundamental proposition was,—"the word of God, the whole word of God, and nothing but the word of God." His opponents relied "only on the phrases and opinions of St. Thomas." They discovered more malice than argument. John Eck, a Doctor of Divinity, speaks of Luther as "his feeble adversary," "a pestilent man," "a heretic," "seditious," "insolent," "rash," "dull," "stupid," and "ignorant;" but this only gave Luther fresh courage, who shows in reply that he is not convicted of heresy, either by the Scriptures, or the fathers of the church, and only by mere opinions. The more Luther was opposed the more his opinions were read. To every objection the doctors made Luther always had a ready reply; "but," said he, "it is useless to talk to a deaf man; these doctors cling to their petty distinctions, though they confess they have nothing to confirm them but what they call the light of reason." When he appealed to the princes of the church some laughed at him; others turned a deaf ear; but Luther ever expressed his wishes that, if they were able from the Scriptures, they would convict him of error. When arraigned before the Legate of the Pope, he said, "Deign to inform me wherein I have erred." To the Elector of Saxony he wrote, "Let them bring forward their reasons; let them instruct me who desire to be instructed; let the Lord deprive me of his grace if, when I am shown a better doctrine, I do not embrace it." But all who attempted the task were obliged to retire in silence after a vigorous reply from the reformer. Many replied to him to advance their own fame, but injured their cause by so doing. When they attempted, by contemptible decretals of Roman Pontiffs, not four centuries old, to prove the primacy of the Roman church, he arrayed against this claim the credible history of the early church, the express declarations of Scripture, and the conclusions of the council of Nice,—the most venerable of all councils.

While the pulpits were all open to the enemies of the Gospel they were shut to those who proclaimed it, and "it was currently reported of Luther, in the meetings of the clergy, that he carried about with him the devil in a small box." Said Doctor Eck, "I am astonished at the humility and diffidence with which Luther undertakes to stand alone against so many illustrious fathers, thus affirming that he knows more of those things than the Sovereign Pontiff, the councils, divines, and universities; it would, no doubt, be very wonderful if God had hidden the truth from so many saints and martyrs till the advent of him." Luther replied, "The fathers are not opposed to me—St. Augustine, St. Ambrose, and the most eminent divines say as I do;" and he claimed that Eck "ran over Scripture without touching it." D'Aubigné says, that in Luther's controversy with Dr. Eck, the doctor "obtained the victory in the opinion of those who do not understand the question and who had grown grey in scholastic studies, but Luther in the judgment of those who have intelligence and modesty." They saw Luther relying on the word of God, while Eck took his stand on the traditions of men; and though defeated he "gave himself up to the intoxication of what he tried to represent as a victory;" and "the more he felt his weakness the louder were his clamors." At another time a princess inquired, "Who is this Luther? an ignorant monk; well, you are learned and so many, write against him; the world will surely believe a company of learned men rather than a single monk of no learning." But the learned found it easier to condemn and burn his writings than to reply. The Pope attempts to silence him by a *bull* of excommunication; Luther, in return, excommunicates the Pope. When overwhelmed with reproaches, and accused of standing alone, teaching new doctrines, he replied, "Who knows whether God has not called me for this very purpose? Moses was alone when the Israelites were led out of Egypt; Elijah was alone in the time of King Ahab; Ezekiel was alone at Babylon. God has never chosen for his prophet either the high priest or any person of exalted rank, but generally men of mean condition—like Amos, a simple shepherd. The saints in every age have been called upon to rebuke the great of this world, and they have more reason to fear because I am alone and they are many. Of this I am sure, that the word of God is with me, and it is not with them. They affirm that I bring forth novelties; but I affirm that they are not novelties, but truths which have been lost sight of. I am accused of rejecting the doctors of the church; I reject them not, but test their writings by the Bible. It is objected that I am censured; but the Scriptures show that they who persecute are in error, and that the majority are always on the side of falsehood."

Such was the manner in which the Reformation was ushered in. Who cannot see that it encountered the same elements which the reformation of our day has been called upon to encounter?

Failing of intimidating Luther, the church began to exert its influence over those who had embraced his doctrines. At the confessional the questions were, Have you read Luther's writings? and do you approve of his works? And if they would not renounce them they were anathematized. This expedient brought many under the yoke of the church, but it strengthened others in their faith. Luther bade his followers to adhere to the truth of God if it was at the expense of the "altar, the priest, and the church." And he proved from the prophecies of Daniel, John, Paul, Peter, and Jude, that the Papacy is the Anti-Christ predicted in the Bible; "and," said he, "may God hasten the day of the glorious coming of his Son, in which he shall destroy that man of sin." This caused the people to renounce their attachment to a church which appeared, in every particular, so directly opposed to the example of its Founder. A man of humble station, holding the word of God in his hand, had stood in the presence of earthly dignities and they had quailed before him. Learned divines and astonished theologians saw the weapons of their scholastic logic shivered in their hands. "Academicians, lawyers, nobles, the inferior clergy, many even of the monks, and vast numbers of the common people embraced the Reformation."

The Papists, in answer to Luther's arguments from the Scriptures, replied: "The Bible—it is like wax; you may stretch and mould it any way, and prove from it any doctrine you please." But they could not disprove from it Luther's doctrines. Their cry was, "He refuses to be set right;" "these Lutherans are a motley rabble of insolent grammarians, disorderly monks, and ignorant, misled, and perverted plebeians." Again, when seeing Luther's advantage, they would say, "Only give up" such and such points, which are unimportant, "and all will be well;" "we agree in all essential points—the only question between us relates to some secondary points."

When Luther visited Worms, at the summons of the Emperor Charles V., crowds flocked to see him, some of whom had conceived an idea of him as a prodigy of wisdom; others as a monster of iniquity; and yet, on hearing him, all were struck with the joy of his countenance and the wisdom of his discourses, which the Papists ascribed to the influence of the devil; and any one who manifested the least interest in his cause, was instantly cried down as a heretic. The enemies of the truth never failed to circulate inventions of pretended doctrines of Luther, and nothing was too absurd and silly for them to ascribe to his belief; but all those things only recoiled on their own heads. The Reformation, which only sprung up in the hearts of a few monks, spread abroad, lifted itself on high, and assumed a station of publicity. Like the waters of the sea, it rose by degrees, until it overspread a wide expanse. The Bishop of Constance complained that evil-minded persons were reviving doctrines which had been condemned, and that learned and unlearned men were alike everywhere irreverently discussing the most exalted mysteries. And the partisans of Rome, with that blind infatuation common to those who have long held power, were pleasing themselves with the thought, at every seeming advantage, that the Reformation was forever at an end. Many of those weak persons, who, when things were nearly balanced, were found on the side of truth, whenever their own interest was concerned were quite willing to take up again with error. When such left the cause the priests were ready to exclaim, "We have silenced him who troubles Israel." The most celebrated schools and professors gave their verdict against the Reformation, and pronounced the doctrines of Luther heretical; he, however, showed them that the heresy was in Rome and the schools, while the catholic truth was in Wittemberg.

When all the efforts of Rome to crush the Reformation had failed, and the frail bark, which had been tossed in every direction by so many winds, and been well nigh wrecked, had now apparently righted itself, it was called to encounter obstacles in another form. Says D'Aubigné:—

"Whenever a great ferment is working in the church some impure elements are sure to mingle with the testimony given to truth, and some one or more pretended reforms arise out of man's imagination, and serve as evidences or countersigns of some *real* reformation in progress. Thus many false Messiahs in the first century of the church were an evidence that the true Messiah had already come. The Reformation of the sixteenth century could not run its course without presenting the like phenomenon, and it was first exhibited in the little village of Zwickau.

"There were dwelling at Zwickau a few men who, being deeply moved by the events passing around them, looked for *special* and *direct revelations* from the Deity, instead of desiring, in meekness and simplicity, the sanctification of their affections. These persons asserted that they were commissioned to complete that Reformation which, in their view, Luther had but feebly begun. 'What is the use,' asked they, 'of such close application to the Bible? Nothing is heard of but the BIBLE. Can the Bible preach to us? Can it suffice for our instruction? If God had intended to instruct us by a book would he not have given us a Bible direct from heaven? It is only the SPIRIT that can enlighten! God himself speaks to us and shows us what to do and say.' Thus did these fanatics, playing into the hands of Rome, impugn the fundamental principle on which the whole Reformation is based, namely, the perfect sufficiency of the Word of God.

"Nicolas Storch, a weaver, publicly declared that the angel Gabriel had appeared to him by night, and, after revealing to him matters he was not allowed to divulge, had uttered the words, 'Thou shalt sit on my throne!' A senior student of Wittemberg, named Mark Stubner, joined Storch, and forthwith abandoned his studies,—for, according to his own statement, he had received immediately from God the ability to interpret holy Scripture. Mark Thomas, also a weaver, associated himself with them, and another of the initiated, by name Thomas Munzer, a man of fanatical turn of mind, gave to the new sect a regular organization. Resolving to act according to the example of Christ, Storch chose from among his followers twelve apostles and seventy disciples. All these loudly proclaimed, as we have lately heard it asserted by a sect of our own days,[1] that apostles and prophets were at last restored to the church.[2]

"Such preaching made a deep impression on the popular mind. Not a few devout persons were startled by the thought that prophets were again given to the church, and those on whom the love of the marvellous had most power threw themselves into the open arms of the eccentric preachers of Zwickau.

"But scarcely had this heresy, which had shown itself of old in the days of Montanism, and again in the middle ages, drawn together a handful of separatists when it encountered in the Reformation a strong opposing power. Nicholas Haussman, to whom Luther gave that noble testimony, '*What we teach he acts*,' was at this time the pastor of Zwickau. This good man was not led away by the pretensions of the false prophets. Supported by his two deacons, he successfully resisted the innovations Storch and his followers were seeking to introduce. The fanatics, repelled by the pastors of the church, fell into another extravagance; they formed meetings in which doctrines subversive of order were publicly preached. The people caught the infection, and disturbances were the consequence; the priest bearing the sacrament was pelted with stones, and the civil authority, interfering, committed the most violent of the party to prison. Indignant at this treatment, and intent upon justifying themselves and obtaining redress, Storch, Mark Thomas, and Stubner repaired to Wittemberg.

"Making sure of co-operation, they waited upon the University Professors to receive their sanction. 'We,' said they, 'are sent by God to teach the people. The Lord has favored us with special communications from himself; we have the knowledge of things which are coming upon the earth. In a word, we are apostles and prophets, and we appeal, for the truth of what we say, to Doctor Luther.' The professors were amazed.

"'Who commissioned you to preach?' inquired Melancthon of Stubner, who had formerly studied under him, and whom he now received at his table. 'The Lord our God.' 'Have you committed anything to writing?' 'The Lord our God has forbidden me to do so.' Melancthon drew back, alarmed and astonished.

"'There are, indeed, spirits of no ordinary kind in these men,' said he; 'but *what* spirits? . . . None but Luther can solve the doubt. On the one hand let us beware of quenching the Spirit of God, and on the other, of being seduced by the spirit of the devil.'

"It was not long before one who listened to these enthusiasts might have thought that there were no real Christians in all Wittemberg save only those who refused to come to confession, persecuted the priests, and ate meat on fast days. The bare suspicion that he did not reject, one and all, the ceremonies of the church, as inventions of the devil, was enough to subject a man to

---

[1] The Mormons.

[2] This effort has been several times made by fanatics claiming to be Advents, but always separated themselves from the Adventists.

the charge of being a worshiper of Baal. 'We must form a church,' they exclaimed, 'that shall consist of the saints alone!'

"Thus it was that doctrines were put forth directly opposed to the Reformation. The revival of letters had opened a way for the reformed opinions. Furnished with theological learning, Luther had joined issue with Rome, and the Wittemberg enthusiasts, similar to those fanatical monks exposed by Erasmus and Reuchlin, pretended to trample under foot all human learning! Only let Vandalism once establish its sway and the hopes of the world were gone, and another irruption of barbarians would quench the light which God had kindled among Christian people.

"It was not long before the results of these strange lessons began to show themselves. Men's minds were diverted from the Gospel, or prejudiced against it; the school was almost broken up; the demoralized students burst the bands of discipline, and the States of Germany recalled such as belonged to their several jurisdictions. Thus the men who aimed at reforming, and infusing new vigor into everything, had brought all to the brink of ruin. 'One more effort,' thought the partisans of Rome who, on all sides, were again lifting their heads, 'and all will be ours!'

"The prompt repression of these fanatical excesses was the only means of saving the Reformation.

"The evil, therefore, was gaining ground, and no one stepped forward to arrest its progress. Luther was absent far from Wittemberg. Confusion and ruin impended over the city. The Reformation beheld, proceeding, as it were, from its own bosom, an enemy more to be dreaded than Popes and Emperors. It was as if on the brink of an abyss.

"'Luther! Luther!' was the cry from one end of Wittemberg to the other. The burghers were clamorous for his re-appearance; divines felt their need of the benefit of his judgment; even the prophets appealed to him. All united in entreating him to return.

"We may guess what was passing in the Reformer's mind. The harsh usage of Rome seemed nothing when compared with what now wrung his heart. It is from the very midst of the Reformation that its enemies have gone forth. It is preying upon its own vitals, and that teaching which, by its power, had sufficed to restore peace to his troubled heart he beholds perverted into an occasion of fatal dissensions in the church.

"'If I knew,' said Luther, at an earlier period, 'that my doctrine had injured one human being, however poor and unknown,—which it could not, for it is the very Gospel,—I would rather face death ten times over than not retract it. And lo! now, a whole city, and that city Wittemberg itself, is sinking fast into licentiousness.' True, indeed, the doctrine he had taught had not been the cause of all this evil; but from every quarter of Germany voices were heard that accused him as the author of it. Some of the bitterest feelings he had ever known oppressed his spirits at this juncture, and his trial was of a different kind. Was this, then, he asked himself, to be the issue of the great work of Reformation? Impossible! he utterly rejected the doubts that presented themselves. God has begun the work—God will fulfill it. 'I prostrate myself in deep abasement before the Eternal,' said he, 'and I implore of him that his name may rest upon this work, and that if anything impure has mingled in the doing of it he will remember that I am but a sinful man.'

"Luther was aware that the ancient and primitive apostolic church must, on the one hand, be restored and opposed to that Papal power which had so long oppressed it, and, on the other hand, be defended against enthusiasts and unbelievers, who affected to disown it, and were seeking to set up some new thing, regardless of all that God had done in past ages.

"He set about his work in the spirit of an humble pastor—a tender shepherd of souls. 'It is with *the Word* we must contend,' observed he, 'and by *the Word* we must refute and expel what has gained a footing by violence. I would not resort to force against such as are superstitious, nor even against unbelievers! Whosoever believeth let him draw nigh, and whoso believeth not stand afar off. Let there be no compulsion. Liberty is of the very essence of faith.'

"The most noted of the prophets were not at Wittemberg when Luther arrived there. Nicolas Storch was on a progress through the country. Mark Stubner had quitted the hospitable roof of Melancthon.

"Stubner exhorted them to stand firm. 'Let him come forth,' interposed Cellarius; 'let him give us the meeting; let him only afford us opportunity to declare our doctrine and then we shall see.' . . .

"Luther had but little wish to meet them. He knew them to be men of violent, hasty, and haughty temper, who would not endure even kind admonitions, but required that every one should, at the very first summons, submit to them as to a supreme authority. Such are enthusiasts in every age. Nevertheless, as an interview was requested, Luther could not decline it; besides it might be doing service to the weak of the flock to unmask the imposture of the prophets. Accordingly the meeting took place. Stubner opened the conversation. He showed how he proposed to restore the church and reform the world. Luther listened to him with great calmness. 'Of all you have been saying,' replied he, at last, gravely, 'there is nothing that I see to be based upon Scripture. It is a mere tissue of fiction.' At these words Cellarius lost all self-possession. Raising his voice like one out of his mind, he trembled from head to foot, and striking the table with his fist, in a violent passion, exclaimed against Luther's speech as an insult offered to a man of God. On this Luther remarked, 'Paul declared that the signs of an apostle were wrought among the Corinthians in signs and mighty deeds. Do you likewise prove your apostleship by miracles?' 'We will do so,' rejoined the prophets. 'The God whom I serve,' answered Luther, 'will know how to bridle your gods.' Stubner, who had hitherto preserved an imperturbable silence, now fixing his eyes on the Reformer said, in a solemn tone, 'Martin Luther, hear me while I declare what is passing at this moment in your soul. You are beginning to see that my doctrine is true.' Luther was silent for a few moments and then replied, 'The Lord rebuke thee, Satan.' Instantly the prophets lost all self-command. They shouted aloud, 'The Spirit, the Spirit.' The answer of Luther was marked by the cool contempt and cutting homeliness of his expressions: 'I slap your spirit on the snout!' said he. Hereupon their outcries redoubled. Cellarius was more violent than the rest. He stormed till he foamed at the mouth, and their voices were inaudible from the tumult. The result was that the pretended prophets abandoned the field, and that very day they left Wittemberg.

"'The Sacred Writings,' said Luther, 'were treated by them as a dead letter, and their cry was, the Spirit! the Spirit! But, assuredly, I, for one, will not follow whither their spirit is leading them! May God, in his mercy, preserve me from a church in which there are only such saints. I wish to be in fellowship with the humble, the weak, the sick, who know and feel their sin, and sigh and cry continually to God from the bottom of their hearts to obtain comfort and deliverance.' These words of Luther have a depth of meaning, and indicate the change which his views were undergoing as to the nature of the church. They, at the same time, show how opposed the religious principles of the rebels were to the religious principles of the Reformation.

"The most noted of these enthusiasts was Thomas Munzer; he was not without talent; had read his Bible; was of a zealous temperament, and might have done good if he had been able to gather up his agitated thoughts and attain to settled peace of conscience. But with little knowledge of his own heart, and wanting in true humility, he was taken up with the desire of reforming the world, and, like the generality of enthusiasts, forgot that it was with himself he should begin. Certain mystical writings, which he had read in his youth, had given a false direction to his thoughts. He made his first appearance in public at Zwickau; quitted Wittemberg on Luther's return thither, not satisfied to hold a secondary place in the general esteem, and became pastor of the small town of Alstadt, in Thuringia. Here he could not long remain quiet, but publicly charged the Reformers with establishing by their adherence to the written Word a species of Popery, and with forming churches which were not pure and holy.

"'Luther,' said he, 'has liberated men's consciences from the Papal yoke; but he has left them in a carnal liberty and has not led them forward in spirit towards God.'

"He considered himself as called of God to remedy this great evil. The Revelations of the *Spirit*, according to him, were the means by which the Reformation he was charged with should be effected. 'He who hath the Spirit,' said he, 'hath true faith, although he should never once in all his life see the Holy Scriptures. The heathen and the Turks are better prepared to receive the Spirit than many of those Christians who call us enthusiasts.' This remark was directed against Luther. 'In order to receive the Spirit,' continued he, 'we must mortify the flesh, wear sackcloth, neglect the body, be of a sad countenance, keep silent, forsake the haunts of men, and implore God to vouchsafe to us an assurance of his favor. Then it is that God will come to us and talk with us, as he did of old with Abraham, Isaac, and Jacob. If he were not to do so he would not deserve our regard. I have received from God the commission to gather together his elect in a holy and eternal union.'

"The agitation and ferment which were working in men's minds were not a little favorable to the spread of these enthusiastic ideas. Men love the marvellous and whatever flatters their pride. Munzer, having inoculated with his own views a portion of his flock, abolished the practice of chanting and all the other ceremonies annexed to public worship. He maintained that to obey princes 'devoid of understanding' was to serve, at one and the same time, God and Belial; and then setting off at the head of his parishioners to a chapel in the neighborhood of Alstadt, to which pilgrims were accustomed to resort from all quarters, he totally demolished it. After this exploit, being obliged to leave the country, he wandered from place to place in Germany, and came as far as Switzerland, everywhere carrying with him, and communicating to all who gave ear to him, the project of a general revolution. Wherever he went he found men's minds prepared. His words were like gunpowder cast upon burning coals and a violent explosion quickly ensued.

"That moral agony which Luther had first undergone in his cell at Erfurth was, perhaps, at its height after the revolt of the peasants. On the side of the princes it was repeated, and in many quarters believed, that Luther's teaching had been the cause of the rebellion, and groundless as was the charge the Reformer could not but feel deeply affected by the credit attached to it. On the side of the people, Munzer and all the leaders of the sedition represented him as a vile hypocrite and flatterer of the great, and their calumnies easily obtained belief. The strength with which Luther had declared against the rebels had given offence even to men of moderate opinions. The partisans of Rome exulted, all seemed against him, and he bore the indignation of that generation; but what most grieved him was that the work of heaven should be thus degraded by being classed with the dreams of fanatics.

"This fanaticism broke forth in lamentable disorders. Alleging, in excuse, that the Saviour had exhorted us to become as little children, these poor creatures began to go dancing through the streets, clapping their hands, footing it in a circle, seating themselves on the ground together, and tumbling each other in the sand. Some there were who threw the New Testament into the fire, exclaiming, 'The letter killeth, the spirit giveth life,' and several, falling into convulsions, pretended to have revelations from the Holy Spirit."

The fanatics, unrestrained, ran into the greatest excesses; revolt was encouraged, blood was shed, and towns were pillaged, and the mercy of God alone preserved his cause. But the firmness with which Luther, and those whom God had made foremost in the work, met and protested against those delusions showed to the world that the Reformation was entirely distinct from the fanaticism of those spirits. Its character was distinctly seen, and it was demonstrated that its mission was to keep constantly a middle course between all extremes—remote alike from fanatical distortion and political disorders on the one hand, and from the death-like slumber of the papal rule on the other. The battle which the Reformation fought was not one but manifold. It had to combat at once several enemies, and after having protested against the decretals and the sovereignty of the Popes, then against the cold apothegms of rationalists, philosophers, and schoolmen, it took the field against the reveries of enthusiasm and the hullucinations of mysticism, opposing alike to these three powers the sword and the buckler of God's Holy Revelation. Says D'Aubigné:

"We cannot but discern a great resemblance,—a striking unity,—between these three powerful adversaries. The false systems, which, in every age, have been the most adverse to evangelical Christianity, have ever been distinguished by their making religious knowledge to emanate from man himself. Rationalism makes it proceed from reason; Mysticism from a certain internal illumination; Roman Catholicism from an illumination derived from the Pope. These three errors look for truth in man; evangelical Christianity looks for it in God alone; and while Rationalism, Mysticism, and Roman Catholicism acknowledge a permanent inspiration in men like ourselves, and thus make room for every species of extravagance and schism, evangelical Christianity recognizes this inspiration only in the writings of the apostles and prophets, and alone presents that great, noble, and living unity which continues to exist unchanged throughout all ages.

"The office of the Reformation has been to re-establish the rights of the word of God, in opposition, not only to Roman Catholicism, but also to Rationalism and Mysticism."

ANTECEDENT CAUSES.

The above mentioned elements were the same as those which have sought the destruction or perversion of the Second Advent Message. The sad picture we have been reviewing, in connection with the Second Advent cause, should teach all an important lesson. There are certain antecedents to these several excessive movements, and though erratic minds and fanatical persons have introduced and forced these disorderly elements into active and indiscriminate warfare against proper institutions and the best interests of society, bewildering and bewitching well-disposed persons and enlisting their sympathies in an evil work, yet there were producing causes which are not generally taken into the account by the common observer. We should always endeavor to seek the primary cause of all such evils, not to justify the actors in an injurious work, but to palliate, in some degree, the crimes which are charged upon instruments of such results, and to seek a remedy to remove the primary causes, or, at least, to avoid their re-occurrence. We have seen that the churches of Protestantism were classed with the Roman church and indiscriminately called Babylon, referring to that monstrous institution described in Rev. xviii. as "the habitation of devils, and the hold of every foul spirit, and a cage of every unclean and hateful bird." The thought strikes a thrill of horror through the hearts of all truly pious and well-disposed persons. The institutions which we have looked upon as sacred, and constituting the moral power of christendom, exerting all the influences of virtue, goodness, and piety which elevate us above heathen nations! can these institutions be thus assailed? Can men be so wickedly blinded and perverted as to make such charges? Who can have a trait of Christianity left and entertain such a thought? These are questions which arise in the minds of many true-hearted Christians. But should these persons become truly awakened to the sins of the age, and by the light of gospel truth see the importance of entering with all their energies upon the work of reform; should they see truths of the gospel which have been long buried out of sight of the masses, and which are of the greatest importance in working reform among men, and enter upon the work as reformers have; meet the opposition and hate, the contumely and intrigue, which they have met, matters would assume a vastly different appearance from what they now do. Yet they should learn to discriminate "between the precious and the vile." They should never lose that charity which recognizes the good and true hearts in all departments of society, and which sees the difference between a true principle, institution, combination, or doctrine and a perverted use and abuse of them. Here is where these men failed. They saw the enormous sins which were being sustained and practiced in high places in all christendom, by the direct sanction and aid of church combinations, such as the oppression in India by the English East India Company, the sustaining of idol temples, encouraging of pilgrimage, the opium trade, the poisoning of the Chinese nation to rob them of their wealth, the system of

American slavery, the anti-temperance efforts, with many other gigantic systems of public evil, together with the innumerable sins of a personal and more private character, which were winked at and shielded by a class of men who controlled the ecclesiastical affairs of the churches. On the other hand they saw that the faithful Christians of these churches who consecrated themselves to the work of reform, and had the courage to speak the truth and reprove iniquity, were treated with indignity, were reproached, defamed, oppressed, and sacrificed.

Added to all this and much more, when the light of truth, as they believed, broke in upon their minds upon the subject of Christ's immediate coming, and they in the earnestness of their faith and hope began to proclaim to their brethren that the glorious "Lord and Master" was coming to release them from woe and sorrow, sickness and death, and bring the blessed morn of immortal joy and the boon of eternal life, in an eternal home of blessedness, what did they meet? How did the churches commend themselves as the bride of Christ? While the common people heard it gladly and began to rejoice in the prospect, the rulers rejected, derided, scoffed, and ridiculed the idea. Some denied that such an event would ever transpire; others said it could not come yet; while others refused to hear, read, talk, or think of the subject. For a series of years these elements were being developed, as our record shows. Faithful, self-sacrificing men were doing the work of the gospel and meeting with signal success, even against all these opposing elements; but they were bearing reproach, contumely, ridicule, and shame for Christ's sake. Becoming wearied, jaded, and chafed by constant rebuffing, repelling influences, where they should have had sympathy and co-operation, until they lost patience, wounded charity withdrew from the field and a sterner principle took the lead. Comparing all these evil influences with the Scriptural account of Babylon, and contrasting them with the true characteristics of the church of the living God, they took the unjustifiable position, by mistaking the single point on which all turns. They put the rulers and chief actors in the place of the institutions under which they were acting. They failed to see that a few men were abusing the institutions which were good in themselves and worked properly in the hands of righteous men; but being prostituted to selfish, bigoted, and sectarian purposes, the church institutions became engines of oppression and a covert for evil doers, in too many instances (yet the laws of such institutions were directed against all sin), while the poor, humble, and faithful of the flock were starving for spiritual food and dying out as a result of such oppression. It should be mentioned also that just *here*, when the Advent Message began to go abroad among the churches, the worldly-minded, pleasure-loving, unsanctified members and ministers began their church parties, olios, feasts, levees, and gambling, much to the distress and dismay of the pious Christians among them. It was just at *this* point that ministers who opposed the doctrine of Christ's speedy return began to encourage these sins by aiding churches to get up these scenes of shame and acts of iniquity by preparing games, making, with their own hands, roulette and other gambling tables for their church members and the youth to sport and gamble with, and sometimes engaged in these chance games themselves. It was just *here* that this God-dishonoring, conscience-defiling, church-corrupting, moral-perverting, youth-destroying, law-defying system of church dissipation took root, in congenial soil, which has produced such abundant harvests of gamblers that grand juries, judges of courts, and governors of States have felt obliged to interfere, to save the youth of the country from these corrupting influences, by threatening civil prosecutions of church institutions for gambling if they continued these practices. These evils are but the fruits of unbelief, which have been taking the place of those noble acts of godliness and fruits of righteousness which marked the history of the church in former days. It is not to be so much wondered at that *novices* should conclude that the Protestant church was Babylon; she was in a deplorable condition. We give a specimen of these evils, which could be extended to fill a large volume, and many of them much more disgraceful than these, as my readers are aware.

A TEA PARTY AT LYNN, MASS.

Zion's Herald, of February, 1844, just after having charged Millerism with dampening the prospects of the church, in an editorial in large caps says:

"A tea meeting at Lynn, given by the ladies of the South Street Methodist Church in the town hall, which was filled with the most interesting assembly, including six clergymen, and its sociability was untrammelled. One of the speakers, who had been acquainted with the sainted founders of Methodism in Lynn, remarked, emphatically, that he believed their spirits were hovering with delight over this scene of Christian intercourse among their children. The tables were spread bountifully and elegantly; the hall was decorated with evergreens and portraits of our bishops and distinguished preachers." The bag received seventy-five dollars clear of all expenses.

ANOTHER.

"Grand festival by the ladies of the Sixteenth Street Baptist Church, in New York, Wednesday eve, Jan. 24, 1844, at Tivoli Saloon. Tickets may be had of S. Smith, also at Journal of Commerce, Tribune, and New York Citizen offices."

YET ANOTHER.

"UNPRECEDENTED ENTERTAINMENT at U. S. Hotel, New York, on Thursday eve, Jan. 25, 1844. The ladies of Nassau Street (Baptist) Congregation will commence their annual FESTIVAL, in the spacious saloons of the U. S. Hotel, at 7 o'clock and close at 11 o'clock. The windows on Pearl and Water streets will be brilliantly illuminated. Prof. Bronson, who, by a happy combination of extensive science, with commanding powers of oratory, is attracting multitudes in other parts of the city, has generously tendered his services for the evening. At suitable intervals he will deliver several of his most entertaining and instructive recitations; he will also give an exposition and explanation of *ventriloquism.* Prof. Nash, whose vocal powers will bear comparison with any musical performer in the United States, has also consented to be present. Several duets, solos, and other pieces may be expected during the evening. Tickets 50 cents. Sold at the U. S. Hotel, Pearl Street House, Waverly House, City Hotel, Howard Hotel, and Carlton House."

OLIO AND FAIR.

"A social olio and ladies' fair for the benefit of the Sabbath School will be held in the Congregational Church in Webster, on *Sunday,* Feb. 19th, at six o'clock P. M. For the entertainment of the evening, Messrs. Covert and Dodge, the celebrated temperance minstrels from New York, and John F. Cole, lecturer from Boston, are engaged to instruct and amuse with their temperance songs, glees, anecdotes, and speeches.

"Fruit, refreshments, etc., will be exposed for sale by the ladies of the society, and the social post-office will be in operation. Tickets for admission 25 cents.—Webster, Mass., Feb. 13, 1844."

CHURCH GAMBLING.

"One of the religious papers tells a story in relation to church gambling which contains a lesson worthy of repeating. A member of a church went to his pastor and entreated his personal intercession with his favorite son, who had become ruinously addicted to the vice of gambling. The pastor consented, and, seeking the young man, found him in his chamber. He commenced his lecture, but before he had concluded the young man laid his hand upon his arm and drew his attention to a pile of splendid volumes that stood upon the dressing-table. 'Well,' said the young man, 'these volumes were won by me at a fair given in *your church; they were my first venture;* but for that lottery under the patronage of a Christian church I should never have become a gambler.' "—*Advent Watchman.*

The grand jury of the city of Albany took action on the subject of lotteries in 1851. They presented the cause of certain merchants, as the fairs which had been held by different churches in that city, which they regarded as lottery operations in point of fact. The report stated that after its date the grand jury would be compelled to *present* any future violation of the statute upon lotteries. O what a scorching, withering rebuke to professed ministers of the self-denying Gospel of the meek and lowly Nazarene and his primitive followers!

The great object is to support modern and useless expenditures in proud and unnecessary church improvements and pay large salaries to ministers. Did they believe the Gospel they would be content to endure privation and, if need be, suffer, before they would consent to receive money obtained by such means.

CHURCH LOTTERY.

The Methodists of Huntville, Ala., have a lottery scheme under way, for the benefit of the Andrew Female College. Rev. John H. Caldwell is apparently the prime mover in the speculation. $110,000 is to be collected in $20 instalments (price per ticket), of which $75,000 is to be paid in premiums. It is expected to raise $30,000 for the college by this means. (1856.)

At some of these festivals and levees Dr. Dowling's book, entitled "Millerism used up for a Shilling," was sold, and the subject of the Lord's coming and the judgment ridiculed by these religious sporting mockers. But it should always be remembered that there were devoted Christians in these churches who wept tears of bitterness over these scenes of revelry, and who in some cases declined to attend services of these churches after these occurrences for very shame, lest the unconverted should suppose they supported such mischievous schemes.

A SPIRITUAL FAMINE IN THE CHURCHES.

Why should we wonder that those who were really interested in the advancement of real Christianity should, with sadness, make acknowledgments like the following:

Rev. R. Trumbull, missionary in Europe, says, in 1844,

"Everywhere, France, Italy, Switzerland, and Germany, a dead formality seems to prevail. The *heart* of religion has been worn out by speculation, or benumbed by iteration of mere forms and ceremonies, the consequence of which is that, in most places, it is nothing more than a hideous skeleton, hung up in *terrorem*, or exhibited to the people as a curiosity."

A letter about the same time, in a Congregational journal, remarks as follows:

"At a recent meeting of the Presbytery of Philadelphia, Rev. Mr. Barnes, pastor of the First Presbyterian Church in Philadelphia, stated that he had been in the ministry for twenty years, and never till the last communion had he administered the ordinance without receiving more or less to the church. But now there are no awakenings, no conversions, not much apparent growth in grace, in progression, and none came to his study to converse about the salvation of their souls. With the increase of business, and the brightening prospects of commerce and manufactures, there is an increase of worldly-mindedness. Thus it is with all denominations."

About the same period the PURITAN (Orthodox), of Boston, whose editor had said "Mr. Miller's lectures were more demoralizing than the theater," now informs its readers that "there has not been known such a state of coldness for twenty years."

"Zion's Herald made a similar statement, endeavoring to fix the blame on Adventism. We are informed also that at a protracted meeting held by Mr. Knapp, the great revivalist, at the Tremont Temple, Baptist (Mr. Colver's church), there was an entire failure, which was ascribed to the same cause." —*Advent Herald.*

The *Christian Palladium* says:

"In every direction we hear the dolorous sound, wafting upon every breeze of heaven, chilling as the blast from the iceburgs of the north, setting like an incubus on the breasts of the timid, and drinking up the energies of the weak."

Professor Finney said, in 1846, in speaking of the condition of the church:

"Every flash of light that breaks on our mind, revealing more and more the depth of this degeneracy, is painfully agonizing. All tells of the guilt and shame of Zion we love. We need not expand this painful subject. Suffice it that the evidence thickens and rolls heavily upon us to show that the *churches generally* are becoming SADLY DEGENERATE. They have gone so far from the Lord, AND HE HAS WITHDRAWN HIMSELF FROM THEM."

"GREAT SPIRITUAL DEARTH.—It is a lamentable fact, from which we cannot turn our eyes, that the churches of this country are now suffering severely on account of the great dearth—almost *universally complained* of. We have never witnessed such a general declension of religion as at the present. Truly, the church should awake and search into the cause of this affliction, for an affliction every one that loves Zion must view it. When we call to mind how few and far between cases of true conversion are, and the almost unparalleled impenitence and hardness of sinners, we almost involuntarily exclaim, *has God forgotten to be gracious?* OR IS THE DOOR OF MERCY CLOSED?

"Look again, and behold the spirit of the world—how it prevails in the church. Where is the pious man who has not been made to sigh on account of these abominations in the midst of us? Who is that man in the political crowd, whose voice is heard above the rest, and is foremost in carrying torch-lights, bellowing at the top of his voice? O he is a Christian! perhaps a class-leader or exhorter. Who is that lady dressed in the most ridiculous fashion, as if nature had deformed her? O she is a follower and *imitator* of the *humble* Jesus! O shame, where is thy blush? This is no uncommon picture, I assure you. Would to God it was. My heart is pained within me while I write."—*Circleville (Ohio) Religious Telescope.*

The following is from the *Christian Era* of May, 1862:

"Our churches at present are languishing. Their spiritual life ebbs, with little prospect of a turn in the tide. Devotional meetings do not attract the members by the marked presence of the Holy Spirit, and few unconverted persons are drawn within their influence. Little power accompanies the services of the Sabbath. Few houses of worship are filled. Few converts are gathered, and fewer of this small number have an apostolic zeal and earnestness.

"This is a sad picture to draw, but no doubt it is truthful. But then the contrast of condition and opportunity, advantages and results, makes this state of things exceedingly deplorable. We have the best of teachers, the best scholars, the best schools, the best pastors, the best church choirs, the finest church edifices and organs, and every other advantage to attract the people to the preaching of the Gospel and the services of the sanctuary, yet these forms of godliness have not the power accompanying them to draw sinners to Christ. The presence of the Holy Spirit is not there. The churches are languishing."

A DARK PICTURE.

Many good men begin to see the perilous condition of the mass of professors of religion in these last days. They have awakened upon the very verge of the cataract, and are nearly paralyzed at a sense of their awful condition. Most are sleeping in "slumbers most profound," from which, it is to be feared, they will not awake till the last trumpet shall sound. In a late article in the *Earnest Christian* it is said:

"Every discerning mind can but see that desolation reigns in Zion. Ichabod is the appropriate inscription—for 'the glory of the Lord is departed from Israel; for the ark of the Lord is taken.' Church members have gone after the world, and ministers and members, with a few exceptions, have gone to sleep. O what stupidity and infidelity in the church. How much formality and death everywhere. Sin abounds. Vice and crime are rampant as ever, and on the increase. Conversions are comparatively rare, and how few have a deep experience of salvation. Lukewarmness has taken the place of zeal for God. This sad state of things exists, and the fault must be somewhere. God has certainly provided for a far better state of society. The fault is not in a lack of professors of religion, nor in a want of wealth or learning, for these are all in advance of what they were in the past. The lack is in spiritual power, in humility, in simplicity, in plainness, and in secret wrestling with God. How little fasting, self-denial, groaning, and struggling for victory. How much conforming to the world, to its usages, opinions, and its pride. To what extent professors mingle with the wicked in parties of pleasure, in lodges, rides, amusements, and speculations!"

Ministerial improprieties, doubtless, have much to do with the above. They should unitedly lift up their voices against those existing evils. But alas! many of them have been guilty themselves, and as a stream cannot rise higher than the fountain, marvel that "*Like priest* like people." Here are some candid admissions of ministerial delinquency.

Says J. W. Hunnicutt, a preacher of the Gospel:

"We venture the assertion that there is as much ambition among the clergy of this generation and of this country to aspire to high offices and posts of honor and distinction in their respective churches as there is among politicians; and that there is as much secret plotting, wire-working, and clerical log-rolling, to work one party out or keep it down, and to exalt another party to power, as there is among politicians is a fact, which we presume no man of general intelligence will call in question."

Says the *Methodist*, when speaking of the ball given in New York to the Prince of Wales:

"Ministers of the Gospel of several different denominations—men who ought to be the nearest representatives of the Saviour of sinners—were there, as if to give the sanction of Christ's authority to the most monstrous earthly vanity. What now becomes of wholesome Christian discipline? What becomes of the line so clearly drawn by Christ between the church and the world? What of his command to deny ourselves of all ungodliness and *worldly lust*, and live soberly, righteously, and godly in this evil world? May the Holy Spirit himself intervene to restore the broken bulwarks of sacred discipline and to trace again the fading line between the aggressive world and the invaded church."

Speaking of the opposition to the doctrine of Christ's second coming, the editor of the *Prophetic Times* remarks in a late number:

"The church of our times has drifted away far from the apostolic and primitive method of dealing with this subject. A correspondent, in our issue of last month, testifies that in twenty years' regular attendance upon what is considered an evangelical and orthodox church, he never heard a single sermon on the subject, and rarely heard it alluded to in any way. We have ourselves taken up volume after volume of approved and widely-circulated modern sermons, in which the subject is entirely omitted. The apostles could not write even a short letter to a Christian friend without introducing it, and there is not a church address in the New Testament which does not repeatedly refer to it; and yet we may read dozens and dozens of pastoral addresses, pious books, and evangelical tracts of our day without being able to learn from them that there is any such idea among Christians as that the Saviour is to come again to this world! Well may our correspondent tremble at the condition of the churches which can thus expunge from their pulpits, their religious writings, their prayers, and their addresses all serious reference to one of the most prominent, powerful, and essential doctrines of the Christian religion, and whose ministers and members are ready to twit and stigmatize those who venture to say a word on the subject. It is dreadful."

We give below extracts from the annual returns from all the Methodist conferences. No denomination, probably, has been more successful in obtaining new members than the Methodist Episcopal Church. The report, as published in the *Western Christian Advocate*, says:

"There is a decrease of 45,000 in the membership of the church—about five per cent of the aggregate of last year.

"Of the forty-eight annual conferences all but six report losses, ranging from 5,172 to 51. Five of the six New England conferences show an aggregate loss of 3,046, while the East Maine gives a gain of only 64. Ratio of loss in the six New England conferences about three and a half per cent. The two New York conferences lose about 1,900, equal to a little less than three per cent. The two New Jersey conferences lose a little over three per cent. Troy conference almost holds its own, and Erie and Wyoming each lose very little, while East Genesee, after continuous losses heretofore, shows a gain of 401. The other two Central New York conferences—Oneida and Black River

—as in former years, lose largely, and Genesee, in the west end of the State, in a less degree. Philadelphia and Pittsburg, hitherto the gaining conferences, fall off largely—about six per cent of their large aggregates. The two Baltimore conferences report a less falling off than might have been apprehended—less than three per cent; there is reason to fear that their next report will be much more unfavorable; the same may be apprehended of most of the eastern conferences. Western Virginia loses at the rate of twenty per cent, and Kentucky only a little less, while Missouri and Arkansas fall off about two-thirds.

"An equal aggregate annual loss for twenty years would exhaust the entire church. These facts are startling, and ought to excite a lively and solemn interest throughout the church. If continued only a few years it will essentially detract from the church's influence and efficiency for good."

The above are but specimens of many similar confessions. Yet when those who were teaching that these were the last days, and showing it from various lines of prophecy, and, among other signs, citing the moral condition of christendom as now fulfilling such predictions as Isa. xxix. 11, 12, and Matt. xxiv. 12, 2 Tim. iii. 1, 5, 2d Pet. iii. 3, 4, they were thought to be not only great enemies to the church, but sadly blinded. They were told that the church was in a more prosperous condition than ever before, and they would soon convert all the inhabitants of earth; and although things have been constantly getting worse the same song of peace and prosperity is kept up, amid numerous confessions and developments to the contrary. Such are some of the sounds of the trumpets of watchmen. Do they not give uncertain sounds? These same religious papers teach general and universal progress in morals and righteousness to persuade the people that their temporal millennium, or golden age, is about to dawn.

THE MIDNIGHT CRY.

"In view of the facts, that the early Christians waited for the coming of Christ from heaven; that the epoch for which they looked passed without the establishment of the kingdom; that the tarrying or delay of the Bridegroom, beyond the period of his looked-for advent, had resulted in a general forgetfulness of his coming by the professed church; that the belief that prevailed in the tenth century on the subject was dictated by fear, and not by love for his appearing; that the faith of the Anabaptists had respect to a spiritual kingdom before the end, disconnected from the resurrection of the saints, and that the revival of the doctrine of the Advent near, under the reformers and their successors, was the first revival of the doctrine as preached by the early Christians, there is little reason to question that in these occurrences are to be found the likeness of the parable of the virgins, Matt. xxv. As light began to dawn on the prophetic Word, an early discovery was that of the year-day principle of interpretation."[1]

May it not be more in agreement with the movements of the church to apply the term "went forth" in the parable to the Lutheran reformation and expectancy, and the term "tarried" to the time intervening since, when the attention of the church was turned away by the false notion of the world's conversion? And may not the cry at midnight find its fulfillment in the Second Advent Message, which has been sounding these last fifty years? This looks very rational, yet we should locate the going forth to commence with the Gospel dispensation, and the "tarry" the remaining away of the Saviour until now, and the cry at midnight the advent message, which we have argued at length in our "Treatise on Matt. 24th and 25th chapters." But let us look at the general view of those who have been giving this message. We find in various communications, lectures, papers, books, and tracts, written and published during the rise and progress of the proclamation of the advent near, that Bros. Miller, Litch, Himes, Hale, Jones, Whiting, Bliss, and others of their co-laborers recognized (whether true or false) that their message was represented by the midnight cry in the parable of Matt. xxv. 6. That midnight darkness had rested upon the church upon the subject of Christ's return, that they had slumbered and slept while Christ had remained away, or tarried, is certain. But the signs having appeared, and the seals been removed from the prophecies, light had sprung up in the surrounding darkness, and their mission was to awaken the slumbering virgins by giving the cry, "Behold the Bridegroom cometh, go ye out to meet him." This idea will appear in many items of history we give in this work. It will also appear that while some of the writers and lecturers were very confident that the periods would end in 1843, and Christ then come, yet neither the chief of them nor the body of believers re-

---

[1] Thus reasons Mr. S. Bliss in The Time of the End, p. 45.

garded the specific *time* (unless it should prove correct) as properly constituting a portion or burden of the midnight cry. They did not feel themselves fully assured in the early part of their work, and some of them never, that 1843 was the true date for the ending of the periods, yet they continued with unwearied interest to cry, "Behold he cometh." We will give a few extracts on this point.

In 1840, Eld. Himes and his associate laborers published the "Signs of the Times," a large edition of Mr. Miller's lectures, and the works of several other writers, bearing on the question of the Advent. In a prefatory note in the second volume of the "Second Advent Library," Eld. Himes says:

"Notwithstanding the fears of many, esteemed wise and good, that the effect of this class of writings upon the community would be deleterious, we have, on the contrary, witnessed, as we expected, the most happy results. Their moral and religious influence upon all classes who have given them a candid examination has been most salutary. We are now induced to add a second volume on similar subjects, with a short memoir of Mr. Miller's life."

"On the question of '*prophetic periods*,' and of his laborious and learned chronology, we are not competent, with our limited erudition on the subject, to decide with such positiveness as on the other topics, having never given our attention to the critical study of the subject till within the last year. We, however, believe in the definiteness of *prophetic periods*, and feel satisfied that we live near the end of time. We have come to this conclusion by the *prophetic times* of Daniel and John, and not from the fact *only* that the kingdom has *always* been *at hand*. These 'times' (to which we might refer if it were proper in this place) are nearly accomplished, as all who believe in prophetic periods agree. Some have fixed upon the year 1866, some 1847, while Mr. Miller fixes upon 1843 as the 'time of the end.' We think he has given the more satisfactory demonstration of the correctness of *his* calculation. The advent is near. IT IS *possible* THAT WE MAY BE MISTAKEN IN THE CHRONOLOGY. It may vary a few years, but we are persuaded that the end cannot be far distant.

"With these views, we proclaim continually the Gospel of the kingdom at hand. And not being able with the voice alone, and our limited abilities, TO GIVE THE 'MIDNIGHT CRY' the extent which we think the subject demands, we have availed ourselves of the aid of the press. Accordingly, Mr. Miller's Lectures were put into the hands of a popular bookseller, who has in the last year circulated five thousand copies. In the meantime, fifty thousand numbers of the 'Signs of the Times' have been sent abroad in the United States and in Europe, and two thousand copies of the *full Report* of the General Conference on the Second Advent have just been issued from the press for distribution."

THEIR POSITION IN 1845.

The following is from an editorial column of the Advent Herald of July 8, 1845:

"If the cry was '*after* the *tarrying* time,' then the Herald is correct; but there is nothing but an *if* to prove this."—*Voice of Truth.*

"*While* the Bridegroom *tarried*, they *all slumbered* and *slept*. And at midnight there was a cry made, Behold the Bridegroom cometh; go ye out to meet him." *The Saviour.*

"That the midnight could not be the middle of a solar year is proved by time. It must, therefore, have reference to the condition of God's people. The tarrying time we understand to reach till the cry is made, Behold he cometh. This cry we have heard; and as that proclamation is always made till the Bridegroom comes, so we look for the cry that we have heard during the last few years to be continued until, and to be terminated any moment by, the Lord's coming."

We find Dr. Wolff, in Asia, and many of the writers and proclaimers of this measage in England, Scotland, Ireland, and elsewhere, holding the same view of the midnight cry. Some of them did not proclaim a definite time, and those who did gave a different point of time, and none of them seemed to recognize a date as a part of the cry, but as an opinion as to the point when the Bridegroom would arrive. The above is a safe and healthful position, and while the laborers occupied it, prior to the dogmatical teachings of some on knowing the precise time when the periods would end, or where it has been occupied from then until now, their influence and labors have been most salutary and serviceable in the work of spreading these distinguishing and vital Gospel truths through the world, and in the conversion of sinners to Christ so as to become rooted and grounded in the faith and to remain steadfast, and in building up Christian churches and societies which are sound in the faith, intelligent and Scriptural in their hope, and in watching and waiting for the Lord from heaven.

By the above we do not intend to criminate those who have been too positive in their teaching that they knew the time, but to admonish all that such teaching is not the burden nor the important part of the Second Advent Message, which has already resulted in so much good.

AN EXTRACT FROM THE ADVENT LIBRARY.

We here give an extract from Eld. J. Litch on the subject of the "*midnight cry.*" It was published, in 1842, in the "Advent Library:"

"The efforts of the Bible and Missionary Societies came into operation, and their success was great and excited the strong hope that the world would be converted and a long period of peace and triumph ensue. This syren song fairly put the world to sleep on the second advent. And most sweetly they slumbered; aye, and *dreamed* too! The expectation of the speedy coming of Christ, a few years ago, was scarcely named in the pulpits of this land.

"But '*at midnight,*' when sleep was most profound, '*a cry was made, Behold, the bridegroom cometh, go ye out to meet him.*' That such a cry has been made cannot be denied. That it came at a time when it was little expected by most is also true. It was about twenty-four years ago, 1818, that persons in different parts of the world, and entirely unknown to each other, made the discovery that the seventy weeks and 2300 days of Daniel's prophecy began together and, of course, that the 2300 days would end in 1810 years after the end of the seventy weeks. Some, thinking the seventy weeks did not end until four years after Christ's death, carried the end of the vision to 1847. Those who take the ground that the seventy weeks ended with the death, or, at most, the ascension, of Christ end it in 1843. Among those who, about the same time, saw this point and began to teach it, were Mr. Davis, of South Carolina, A. J. Krupp, of Philadelphia, William Miller, of New York State, David McGreggor, now of Falmouth, Me., Edward Irving and Rev. Mr. Way, of England, Joseph Wolff, the Jewish missionary, and a great many others of more or less note. So that, within the last fifteen or twenty years, the cry that is being made, '*Behold, the bridegroom cometh,*' has been most distinctly announced in both hemispheres. In Wolff's journal of his missionary labors we learn that he proclaimed it all through the east where he traveled, and awakened public attention to the subject. At most of the missionary stations in the east he preached the doctrine in 1831–2–3–4; had free conversation with most of the missionaries on the subject, as also with both Jews and Mahomedans; some of his discussions with the Mahomedans are very interesting. More than twenty years ago, as we learn from a missionary in Tartary, in a letter published in an English magazine, a Tartar priest discovered from the Bible that the prophetic times were nearly run out, and fixed on 1844 as the time. Within the last three years there have been sent from our office in this city second advent publications to nearly all the English and American missionary stations on the earth. They have been sent to China; to Burmah; to Hindostan; to the East Indies; to Persia, Egypt, Palestine, Syria, Asia Minor, Greece, Constantinople; into Africa, the West India Islands, the Islands of the Pacific; the Indian missions both sides of the Rocky Mountains. They have also been scattered broadcast all over these States, and in the Canadas, Nova Scotia, New Brunswick, etc. There are now probably five or six hundred ministers of the gospel in the United States who are engaged more or less in preaching the doctrine of the speedy coming of Christ, and a large number who are devoted entirely to the work. The doctrine has made more progress within the last four months than in all previous time. Is not this the midnight cry?

Then all those virgins arose and trimmed their lamps.' To trim a lamp is to put it in order to burn and give light. Has the world been aroused to the study of the Bible on the subject of Christ's coming? This is undeniable; the time never was when there was so universal a searching of the Scriptures as at present. All are at it, whether Christians or infidels, professors or profane. Are these things so? is the great inquiry; but some scoff.

"'*But the foolish said unto the wise, give us of your oil, for our lamps are gone out.*' Take a lamp with a wick and ignite it, and it will blaze for a moment without oil, but must soon expire. So with the unbelieving world; they hear and read what is preached and written, and are almost ready to yield to their convictions of its truth. It is the fact with a great part of the congregations who hear a course of lectures on the subject; but they go away, meet with scoffers, their unbelief sets in, and they lose all interest in the question and go into the dark. There is another class who have faith in whatever the Bible teaches; they are simple of heart, and willing to obey God. When they find it in God's book, however against their former opinions, they receive it; they are the wise virgins; they have oil as well as a lamp. 'Give us of your oil.' Nothing is more common than for believers to be accosted in this way. Not so; go to them that sell and buy for yourselves. Those who believe cannot give faith; it must be obtained of God.

"'*While they went to buy, the bridegroom came, and they that were ready went in to the marriage, and the door was shut.*' Some have concluded, from this text, that there will be no time for obtaining oil after the cry is made; but if so, why direct the foolish virgins to go and buy? There is time. But two difficulties are in the way of obtaining oil in season. First, they wait too long before they go to buy, and have not time after they start; the second is, they go to the wrong shop. Our citizens do not go to a hardware store to purchase dry and fancy goods. If some of the awakened virgins should happen to mistake Newton, Andover, New Haven, and other such schools of the prophets for the very place where they have the oil of faith to sell without money and without price, very likely while they are gone the bridegroom will come, go in, and shut the door. Reader, take care that this case be not yours. Go direct to Christ, and you may be sure you will obtain it in good time."—*Second Advent Library*, Vol. 4, pp. 165, 167.

It is true that Bro. Litch became very sanguine in his faith that 1843 would bring the end, but he did not conclude that the midnight cry or the proclamation that the Lord would come soon rested on that point of time, as his writings abundantly show, and as his labors subsequently fully demonstrate; for he and the mass of teachers on the subject have never ceased nor slackened their efforts in sounding the cry, from their first beginning until now, "Behold, the bridegroom cometh; go ye out to meet him." While several have located *their* cry on definite points, these have been giving demonstrative *proofs* that the Lord must come speedily, and exhorting all to be ready and to "watch, for in such an hour as ye think not the Son of Man cometh." This cry will continue until Jesus comes, and the believing will continue to awaken.

The venerated Joshua Spaulding, minister at the Tabernacle, Salem, Mass., in concluding one of his nine able and forcible lectures on "the coming and kingdom of Christ," published in 1796, after bringing forward the Scriptures in Daniel, Joel, Malachi, Matthew, and Revelation which speak of the events immediately preceding the coming of the Son of Man, such as the "blood and fire, and vapor of smoke," the "darkening of the sun and moon, the falling of the stars," "distress of nations with perplexity," "the roar of the sea," etc., follows with a historical sketch of the "northern lights," which made their first appearance Sept. 2, 1621. He next refers to their re-appearance in this part of the world, in the eighteenth century, and then says: "We have seen wonderful and alarming phenomena of darkness of the sun and moon, and in the earth there have been most sudden and surprising changes and revolutions of nations and kingdoms—'famines, and pestilences, and earthquakes'—strange commotions of the elements, 'the sea and the waves roaring;' whirlwinds have lately been driven over the earth in a manner the most wonderful and astonishing. We have heard nothing so much resembling the sound of the trump of God as these whirlwinds, and we have seen nothing so much resembling nature's final doom as the paths of these his chariots. The world appears

"'To toll the death-bell of its own decease,
And by the voice of all its elements
To preach the gen'ral doom. When were the winds
Let slip with such a warrant to destroy?
When did the waves so haughtily o'erleap
Their ancient barriers?—
Fires from beneath, and meteors from above,
Portentous, unexampled, unexplained,
Have kindled beacons in the skies; and the old
And crazy earth has had her shaking fits
More frequent, and foregone her usual rests.
The pillars of our planet seem to fail,
And nature with a dim and sickly eye
To wait the close of all.'

"But the philosopher, so called, will doubtless explain all these things fully to the satisfaction of an unbelieving world, for 'none of the wicked shall understand.' Means are ever at hand—a Magus, Jannes, Jambres, or Elymas—to blind the minds of the willingly ignorant—them that believe not. . . .

"To conclude; if the things we have noted be not the sign of the Son of Man that shall appear and give the warning to his people of his coming, what is? The sign of the Son of Man and the midnight cry, spoken of by Matthew, are doubtless one. When these things come to pass 'the wise shall understand,' and lift up their heads and look up. Therefore, is the time come to look for the final destruction of Antichrist, for the battle of that great day of God Almighty, and for the natural signs and omens of his second advent? Yea, do these things begin to come to pass? Then open the ear of wisdom and hear the cry at midnight, 'Behold, the bridegroom cometh.'"

APOLOGY AND DEFENSE.

Mr. Miller wrote a work after the disappointment of 1844 entitled "Apology and Defense," in which he gave a summary of his work, with references to the leading arguments on which he relied, and making a defense for yet expecting the coming of the Lord soon. Although his labors were not then closed, we give here a quotation from this pamphlet which will show something of the extent of *his* labors to that time, 1845.

FRUITS OF MR. MILLER'S LABORS.

After speaking of the commencement of The Signs of the Times, by Eld. J. V. Himes, he says:

"From the commencement of that publication I was overwhelmed with invitations to labor in various places, with which I complied as far as my health and time would allow. I labored extensively in all the New England and Middle States, in Ohio, Michigan, Maryland, the District of Columbia, and in Canada East and West, giving about four thousand lectures in something like five hundred different towns.

"I should think that about two hundred ministers embraced my views, in all the different parts of the United States and Canada, and that there have been about five hundred public lecturers. In all the sections of country where I labored, not only in the towns I visited, but in those in their vicinity, there were more or less that embraced the doctrine of the Advent; in some places only a very few, and in other places there have been a large number.

"In nearly a thousand places Advent congregations have been raised up, numbering, as near as I can estimate, some fifty thousand believers. On recalling to mind the several places of my labors, I can reckon up about six thousand instances of conversion from nature's darkness to God's marvellous light, the results of my personal labors, and I should judge the number to be much greater. Of this number I can recall to mind about *seven hundred* who were, previous to their attending my lectures, infidels, and their number may have been twice as great. Great results have also followed from the labors of my brethren, many of whom I would like to mention here if my limits would permit."—p. 22.

Notwithstanding the point of time, which Mr. Miller published to the world when he expected the advent of Christ, had passed, the masses were yet anxious to hear him preach, and continued to listen with deep interest to his discourses, as he could not refrain, when able to labor, from publishing the good news of salvation to the people, and warning them of the coming judgment.

"Come then, and, added to thy many crowns,
Receive yet one, the crown of all the earth,
Thou who alone art worthy! it was thine
By ancient covenant, ere nature's birth,
And thou hast made it thine by purchase since,
And overpaid its value with thy blood.
Thy saints proclaim thee King; and in their hearts
Thy title is engraven with a pen
Dipt in the fountain of eternal love.
Thy saints proclaim thee King; and thy delay
Gives courage to their foes, who, could they see
The dawn of thy last advent long desired,
Would creep into the bowels of the hills,
And flee for safety to the falling rocks.
The very spirit of the world is tired
Of its old taunting question, asked so long,
Where is the promise of your Lord's approach?
The infidel has shot his bolts away,
Till, his exhausted quiver yielding none,
He gleans the blunted shafts that have recoiled,
And aims them at the shield of truth again.
The veil is rent, rent too by priestly hands,
That hides divinity from mortal eyes;
And all the mysteries to faith proposed,
Insulted and traduced, are cast aside,

As useless, to the moles, and to the bats.
They now are deemed the faithful, and are praised,
Who, constant only in rejecting thee,
Deny thy Godhead with a martyr's zeal,
And quit their office for their errors' sake,
Blind, and in love with darkness! yet even those,
Worthy, compared with sycophants, who kneel,
Thy name adoring, and then preach thee man.
So fares thy church. But how thy church may fare
The world takes little thought; who will may preach,
And what they will. All pastors are alike
To wandering sheep, resolved to follow none.
Two gods divide them all, pleasure and gain;
For these they live, they sacrifice to these,
And in their service wage perpetual war
With conscience and with thee. Lust in their hearts,
And mischief in their hands, they roam the earth
To prey upon each other; stubborn, fierce,
High-minded, foaming out their own disgrace,
Thy prophets speak of such; and noting down
The features of the last degenerate times,
Exhibit every lineament of these.
Come then, and, added to thy many crowns,
Receive yet one, as radiant as the rest,
Due to thy last and most effectual work,
Thy word fulfilled, the conquest of a world."

—COWPER.

CHAPTER XV.

THE YEAR—DAY THEORY—PERIODS OF DANIEL AND JOHN—EPOCH OF A. D. 1836, J. A. BENGEL—JOHN WESLEY—EPOCH OF 1843-4, HANS WOOD—WM. MILLER—WM. CUNNINGHAME—MATTHEW HABERSHON—EPOCH OF 1847, R. C. SHIMEALL—JOSEPH WOLFF, F. SAUNDERS—EPOCH OF 1864-6, DAVID CHYTRÆUS—DAVID PAREUS—WM. WHISTON—THOMAS SCOTT—ALFRED BRYANT—GEO. S. FABER—JOHN CUMMING—EPOCH OF 1868, EDWARD BICKERSTETH—WM. C. THURMAN—EPOCH OF 1873, J. A. BROWN—N. A. BARBOUR—L. C. CUNNINGHAM—EPOCH OF 1880, WM. HALES—SYMBOLIC CHARTS—CHURCH ORGANIZATION—REVIVING AGAIN—LETTER FROM ENGLAND—R. GREENBACK—ALBION ROSS—CONFERENCE EFFORTS—SHORT DIALOGUE.

THE YEAR-DAY PRINCIPLE OF INTERPRETATION.

This is emphatically a discovery of the Protestant reformation. Says Mr. Elliott:

"For the first four centuries the days of Antichrist's duration, given in Daniel and the Apocalyptic prophecies, were interpreted literally as *days*, not as *years*, by the fathers of the Christian church."—*Horæ Ap.*, v. iii., p. 253.

From this period to the time of Luther there are to be found in the writings of expositors occasional mystical applications of the days of Daniel and John, in which they were enlarged from literal days, yet they seem to have had no clear or more than an occasional perception of the year-day principle of interpretation. Says Mr. Elliott: "The year-day principle scarcely broke on Luther's mind, and he once had a curious notion of a prophetic *time* being equal to thirty years. . . . But we find it hinted at by Melancthon, and the Magdeburgh Centuriators fully advocated the year-day principle and applied it to the Papacy, as also most Protestants afterwards." —*Horæ Apoc.*, vol. iii., p. 260.

So silently did this principle come into use, and so universally has it been acquiesced in by Protestant commentators, that Prof. Stuart says:

"It is a *singular fact* THAT THE GREAT MASS OF INTERPRETERS in the English and American world have, for many years, been wont to understand the *days* designated in Daniel and the Apocalypse as the *representatives or symbols of years.* I have found it difficult to trace the origin of this GENERAL, *I might say* ALMOST UNIVERSAL, CUSTOM."—*Hints*, p. 77.

He also says: "For a long time these principles have been so current among the expositors of the English and American world that scarcely a serious attempt to vindicate them has of late been made. They have been regarded as *so plain*, and so well *fortified* against *all objections*, that *most expositors* have deemed it quite useless even to attempt to defend them. One might, indeed, almost compare the ready and unwavering assumption of these propositions to the assumption of the first self-evident axioms in the science of geometry, which not only may dispense with any process of ratiocination in their defence, but which do not even admit of any."—*Hints*, p. 8.

And Prof. Bush, in writing to Mr. Miller, said: "I do not conceive your errors on the subject of chronology to be at all of a serious nature, or in fact to be *very wide of the truth.* In taking a *day* as the prophetical time for a *year*, I believe you are *sustained* by the *soundest exegesis*, as well as *fortified* by the high names of Mede, Sir Isaac Newton, Bishop Newton, Faber, Scott, Keith, and a host of others, who have long since come to *substantially your conclusions* on this head. They *all agree* that the leading periods mentioned by Daniel and John *do actually expire about this age of the world*, and it would be strange logic that would convict you of heresy for holding in effect the same views which stand forth so prominently in the notices of these eminent divines." "Your results in this field of inquiry do not strike me as so *far out of the way* as to affect any of the great interests of truth or duty."—*Ad. Her.*, vol. vii., p. 38.

"If the old established principle of the year-day theory is wrong, then, said Prof. Bush, 'not only has the whole Christian world been led astray for ages by a mere *ignis fatuus* of false hermeneutics, but the church is at once cut loose from every chronological mooring, and set adrift in the open sea, without the vestige of a beacon, lighthouse, or star, by which to determine her bearings or distances from the desired millennial haven to which she had hoped she was tending.'"

"It was quite impossible," says Mr. Elliott, "that Apocalyptic interpretation could go on without that question being considered and concluded on. Accordingly, we find that, almost immediately after Luther's publication of his Bible, it was discussed by the chief Protestant prophetic expositors that followed, and in most cases the *year-day* principle applied to explain them."

It then became a primary element with all such expositors in calculations of the probabilities of the future. As an element, however, in the unsealing of the book of Daniel, it should not be forgotten that

THE PERIODS OF THE APOCALYPSE WERE THE KEY TO THE TIMES IN DANIEL.

This position is sustained by the following extract from the writings of Joseph Mede, usually denominated "the learned Joseph Mede," who published his *Clavis Apocalyptica* in 1627. Mr. Elliott states that Mr. Mede "was looked on and written of as a man almost inspired for the solution of the Apocalyptic mysteries. The following is from a volume of Mede's Discourses," now belonging to Harvard College Library. Of the times in Dan. vii. 25, he says:

"Concerning these times thus found we will now further inquire, 1st. What durance they may be of. 2d. When they take their beginning, and by what mark their beginning may be known. For the first we will make no question but these are the self-same times whereof St. John speaks, telling us the church should be in the wilderness a time, times and half a time; the same with those two and forty months," etc., etc. "If therefore we can find the beginning and continuance we can find the end of them all. For the duration and length of them they must imply some definitive times, because the Scripture follows that use of speech, and useth no number indefinitely but those which the use of speech hath made such, as 1, 10, 1000; but mixed and compound numbers, as these, 3½, 42, 1260, are neither in Hebrew, nor, I think, in any other language, used indefinitely. Our adversaries would have them literally understood, as though it were a history, and not a prophecy; but, besides the use of the prophecy to reckon days for years, I think it would trouble any man to conceive how so many things as should be performed in this time should be done in three single years and a half."—*Apostase*, p. 72.

Mr. Elliott says: "As all know, the Millennium is construed by Mede like as by the oldest pratistic expositors,—Irenæus, Justin, Martyr, etc.; the first resurrection being the literal resurrection of the saints, fulfilled on Christ's coming to Antichrist's destruction."

Mr. Mede does not appear to have terminated the prophetic periods at any specific epoch, and one of the first who did so terminate them was David Pareus, D. D., who was born in Silesia, in 1548, and commenced the 1260 years in 605. This would terminate them in 1865 or 6,—a point within

THE HALF-CENTURY OF EXPECTATION OF THE CHURCH.

It is a singular fact in the history of prophetic interpretation that, in a majority of instances, the calculations of those who have attempted to penetrate the mystery of the prophetic periods have looked with interest to various epochs within the half-century extending from 1830 to 1880. These several epochs will be noticed, with the mode of computation by which they have been reached.

THE EPOCH OF A. D. 1836.

This epoch was regarded as a point of interest by Bengel, Wesley, and others; and, although it has passed, it may not be uninteresting to notice the chronological process by which they arrived at it.

JAMES ALBERT BENGEL,

Who was born in Wurtemberg, in Germany, June 24, 1687, was a learned writer on the Apocalypse, and is often referred to as terminating the periods in 1836. He wrote on this subject in 1740 and gave his views, not as articles of faith, but as things which would both admit of and require correction. Dr. Clarke says of him that "in him were united two rare qualifications,—the deepest piety and the most extensive learning."

In 1741, he published his "Ordo Temporum," in the preface of which he says:

"As the many numerical specifications found in Scripture have a peculiar claim to our attention, because they belong to Divine Revelation, so they have a mutual connection, which conducts us on to one great and important final point,—the day of Christ's appearing. That to this object the historical as well as prophetic books several-ly contribute, and that by attending to their intimations with simplicity, and a desire to learn, we shall find an agreeable path through the obscure labyrinth of their chronology."—*Memoir of Bengel*, p. 267.

He then proceeds to calculate the sum of the periods of the Hebrew text, which he estimates to amount to three thousand nine hundred and forty-three years from the creation to the Christian era, and says (*Ib.*, p. 278):

"The Bible divides the duration of this world's economy either into *two* parts, 'the *beginning*' and 'the *end*' (1 Sam. iii. 12, 1 Chron. xxix. 29), or into *three*, 'the *beginning*,' 'the *midst*,' and 'the *end*.' In the former case, the whole time of the New Testament dispensation falls within the second half, and is called 'the last time,' and 'the end of the world' (1 Pet. i. 20, Heb. ix. 26, 1 Cor. x. 11); but, in the latter case, Christ's first coming is in 'the *midst*' of this economy, fulfilling the prophetic petition of Habakkuk iii. 2. Now, by attending to the connection of these two expressions, the *beginning* and the *end*, we find incontrovertibly that the time of the *New* Testament dispensation must be shorter than the period of three thousand nine hundred and forty years, the duration of the *Old* Testament; consequently, the world would endure at furthest not beyond seven thousand eight hundred and eighty years;" the last two thousand of which, he claimed, would follow the commencement of the Millennium, which epoch would synchronize, in his scheme, with 1836.

What he considered the "key" to his system of interpreting prophetic time is briefly stated in a letter, in 1724, in which he writes J. F. Reuss:

"It is impossible for me to withhold from you a disclosure which, however, I must request you to keep entirely to yourself. By the help of the Lord I have found the number of the Beast. It is six hundred and sixty-six *years*,—from A. D. 1143 to A. D. 1809."—*Ib.*, p. 284.

A few days later he adds:

"It was with great pleasure I lately noticed Luther's remark upon Rev. xiii. 18, for I find that he, too, interpreted the number of the Beast as denoting six hundred and sixty-six years for the period of the Papal temporal domination; only, according to him, that period commenced under Hildebrand in A. D. 1013."—*Ib.*

He proceeds with an extended summing up of the various periods to his point, which he denominates the "end of the world and judgment." Speaking of the results of these calculations, he says:

"Should the year 1836 pass away without any such remarkable change in public affairs as I have anticipated, some fundamental mistake in the arrangement of my system must be sought after. Should even my exposition of the prophetic periods in general be ultimately found erroneous, still my practical application of the matters of those periods will stand good and be serviceable; and not less valuable in its place will be found, I trust, my exhibition of the *structure* of the Apocalypse; indeed, I cannot help thinking that the two inquiries, namely, into the structure of the subject-matters and into the determination of the periods, serve materially to illustrate each other, and my province is not so much to declare future events as to display the relative bearings of the Apocalyptical system. Perhaps I could tell the world more plainly than I am disposed to do in what manner a variety of future events will turn out; yes, how they will shape themselves in the course of the next century, as also how they will succeed one another. But men have warnings adequate to all necessary purposes; quite as adequate as if the events were rightly computed to an exact period or year.

"I have watched the condition of our times and am convinced that the art of political government is forming more and more methodically into a system from which all holy fear concerning the judgment of God is meant to be carefully excluded. And here, indeed, we outdo the ancients. *Their* governments had their religions, however false. Among ourselves also prevail sins, which the prophet complains of respecting Sodom, namely, pride, luxury, indolence, and contempt of inferiors. Those of lower ranks, who can by any means keep pace with the higher, are permitted to come up with them, and this permission is imagined to atone for everything else. Surely we cannot feel at home in such a world as we now find it; at best it is but as an inn upon the road, and the summons, 'Arise, and depart, for this is not your rest, because it is polluted,' surely cannot be unwelcome when it comes. For folly is practised exceedingly in our own days, because it is taken for granted that we can know nothing about futurity, and because, to superficial beholders of God's providence, all is at present uncertainty and suspense;

but when *the great breaking up* shall begin, what things are there of an awful and important kind that may not be expected to follow one another in quick succession!"—*Ib.*, pp. 316, 317.

As *mystical* as these calculations were, they had a great effect in calling the attention of Christians to the study of the prophecies, and were adopted by many distinguished divines. Among these we instance the name of

JOHN WESLEY.

This celebrated founder of Methodism was born in England in 1703. In 1754 he published his Notes on the New Testament, and, in interpreting the prophetic periods, he mainly followed Bengel. His conclusions may be very simply stated. In commenting on the text in Rev. x. 6, which he renders "There shall be no more a time," he says:

"That is, a time, a chronos, shall not expire before that mystery is fulfilled. A chronos (1111 years) will nearly pass before then, but not quite. The period, then, which we may term a non-chronos (not a whole time) must be a little and not much shorter than this. The non-chronos here mentioned seems to begin in the year 800 (when Charles the Great instituted in the west a new line of emperors or of many kings), to end in the year 1836, and to contain, among other things, the short time of the third woe, the three times and a half of the woman in the wilderness, and the duration of the beast."

Of the periods in the 12th chapter of Revelation he says:

"All the countries in which Christianity was settled, between the beginning of the one thousand two hundred and sixty days and the imprisonment of the dragon, may be understood by the wilderness, and by her place in particular. This place contained many countries, so that Christianity now reached, in an uninterrupted tract, from the eastern to the western empire. And both the emperors now lent their wings to the woman and provided a safe abode for her, *where she is fed*,—by God rather than man, having little human help,—*for a time, and times, and half a time.*

"In the year 1058, the empires had a good understanding with each other, and both protected the woman; the bishops of Rome likewise, particularly Victor II., were duly subordinate to the emperor. We may observe the one thousand two hundred and sixty days of the woman, from 847 to 1524, and the three times and a half refer to the same wilderness. But in the former part of the one thousand two hundred and sixty days, before the three times and a half began, namely, from the year 847 to 1058, she was fed by others, being little able to help herself; whereas, from 1058 to 1524, she is both fed by others and has food herself. To this the sciences, transplanted into the west from the eastern countries, much contributed; the Scriptures in the original tongues, brought into the west of Europe by the Jews and Greeks, much more; and most of all, the reformation grounded on those Scriptures.

"*But the earth helped the woman.*—The powers of the earth; and, indeed, she needed help through this whole period. The *time* was from 1058 to 1280, during which the Turkish flood ran higher and higher, though frequently repressed by the emperors, or their generals, *helping the woman.* The (two) *times* were from 1280 to 1725. During these, likewise, the Turkish power flowed far and wide; but still, from time to time, the princes of the earth helped the woman, that she was not carried away by it. The *half-time* is from 1725 to 1836."

And on the closing page of his Notes he assigns to the year 1836:

"The end of the non-chronos and of the many kings; the fulfilling of the word and of the mystery of God; the repentance of the survivors in the great city; and the end of the little time and of the three times and a half; the destruction of the beast; the imprisonment of Satan, chap. xix. 20.

"The loosing of Satan for a small time; the beginning of the one thousand years' reign of the saints; the end of the small time, chap. 20.

"The end of the world; all things new, chapters 20–22."

THE EPOCH OF A. D. 1843–4.

The simple argument for this epoch was based on a supposed connection of the seventy weeks of the 9th of Daniel with the 2300 days of the 8th, reckoning them from a common date. Beginning them with the decree of Artaxerxes Longimanus, in the seventh year of his reign (see Ezra 7th), the seventy weeks would terminate in A. D. 33–4; and, commencing the 2300 prophetic days at the same epoch, they would extend to 1843–4.

HANS WOOD, ESQ.

Says the Rev. Wm. Hales, D. D., the learned chronologer:

"This simple and ingenious adjustment of the chronology of the seventy weeks, considered as forming a part of the 2300 days, was originally due to the sagacity of Hans Wood, Esq., of Rossmead, in the county of Westmeath, Ireland, and published by him in an anonymous commentary on the Revelation of St. John: London, 1787, Payne, 8vo, whence I republished it in the *Inspector*, 8vo, 1799, and afterwards in the *Orthodox Churchman's Magazine*, 1803, and now, more correctly, 1809,"—in his "New Analysis of Chronology," vol. ii., p. 564.

WILLIAM MILLER.

This was the epoch to which the late Wm. Miller, of Low Hampton, New York, looked as that which should witness the second advent of Christ. The argument which Mr. Miller used in support of this point was based upon the literal meaning of the Hebrew word, which, in our version of Daniel ix. 24, is rendered "determined,"—*cut off* or *cut out*,—and the circumstances in which Gabriel appeared to Daniel, as stated in the ninth chapter, with the instruction given.

In the 8th chapter of Daniel is recorded a vision which was to extend to the cleansing of the sanctuary and to continue 2300 days. Daniel had "sought for the meaning" of that vision, and a voice said: "Gabriel, make this man to understand the vision." Gabriel said to Daniel: "I will make thee know what shall be in the last end of the indignation; for, at the time appointed, the end shall be;" and then proceeded to explain the symbols, but said nothing of their duration. At the close of the explanation Daniel fainted, and was sick certain days; and he says he "was astonished at the vision, but none understood it."

Three years subsequent to that vision, Daniel,—understanding "by books the number of the years whereof the word of the Lord came to Jeremiah the prophet, that he would accomplish seventy years in the desolations of Jerusalem,"—set his face unto the Lord to seek by prayer and supplications, with fasting, and sackcloth, and ashes. He proceeded to confess his own sins and the sins of his people, and to supplicate the Lord's favor on the sanctuary that was desolate. While he was thus speaking, Daniel says: "Gabriel, whom I had seen in *the vision* at the beginning, being caused to fly swiftly, touched me about the time of the evening oblation; and he informed me, and talked with me, and said: 'O Daniel, I am now come forth to give thee skill and understanding. At the beginning of thy supplications the commandment came forth, and I am come to show thee; for thou art greatly beloved; therefore understand the matter and consider *the vision.* Seventy weeks are *determined,*'" etc., "from the going forth of the decree to restore and to build Jerusalem unto Messiah the Prince:"—after which Jerusalem was to be made desolate "until the consummation."—Dan. ix. 20–27.

Dr. Gill, a distinguished divine and scholar, rendered the word "determined" *cut off*, and is sustained by good scholars.

Hengstenberg, who enters into a critical examination of the original text, says: "But the very use of the word, which does not elsewhere occur, while others, much more frequently used, were at hand, if Daniel had wished to express the idea of determination, and of which he has elsewhere, and even in this portion, availed himself, seems to argue that the word stands from regard to its original meaning, and represents the seventy weeks, in contrast with a determination of time (*en platei*), *as a period cut off from subsequent duration and accurately limited.*"—*Christology, of the Old Test.*, vol. 2, p. 301. Washington, 1839.

Gesenius, in his Hebrew Lexicon, gives *cut off* as the definition of the word, and many others of the first standing as to learning and research, and several versions have thus rendered it.

Such being the meaning of the word, and such the circumstances under which the prophecy of the seventy weeks was given, Mr. Miller claimed that *the vision* which Daniel was called on to consider, and respecting which Gabriel was to give him skill and understanding, was *the vision* of the 8th chapter; of which Daniel sought the meaning, which Gabriel was commanded to make him understand, but which, after Gabriel's explanation, none understood; and that the seventy weeks of years,—that is, four hundred and ninety that were *cut off*,—were cut off from the 2300 days of that vision; and, consequently, that those two periods must be dated from the same epoch, and the longer extend 1810 years after the termination of the shorter.

Mr. Miller also determined the 1335 days of Daniel 12th at the same epoch, commencing them in A. D. 508, when he claimed the last of the ten kings was converted to Christianity.

WILLIAM CUNINGHAME, ESQ.

The venerable William Cuninghame, Esq., an English gentleman and scholar, without any knowledge of Mr. Miller, had also arrived at the same conclusion from like premises.

MATTHEW HABERSHON.

The same view was advocated by several English writers. Mr. M. Habershon says: "In this conclusion I am happy in agreeing with Mr. Cuninghame, who says, 'I am not aware of any more probable era which can be selected for the commencement of the 2300 years than that which has been chosen by some recent writers, who supposed this period to have begun at the same time with the seventy weeks of Daniel, or in the year B. C. 457, and consequently that it will terminate in the year 1843.'"—*Hist. Dis.*, p. 307.

THE EPOCH A. D. 1847.

The argument in support of this date varied from that for 1843 in the commencement of the 2300 days and seventy weeks. Instead of reckoning them from the seventh year of the reign of Artaxerxes, the advocates of this epoch followed the chronology of Archbishop Usher, who varied from the canon of Ptolemy in the commencement of the reign of Artaxerxes Longimanus. He puts the death of Xerxes and the commencement of the reign of Artaxerxes nine years previous to that given in the canon, and, to harmonize it, he "takes nine years from the reign of Xerxes and adds them to the reign of Artaxerxes Longimanus, his son, contracting the former to twelve years, and enlarging the latter to fifty." (*Dr. Prideaux, Hist. of the Jews.*) Therefore, instead of commencing the reign of the latter in B. C. 464, he commenced it in B. C. 473; and so he reckoned the seventy weeks, not from the seventh, but from the twentieth, year of Artaxerxes (see Neh. 2d), which he synchronized with B. C. 454. Commencing the seventy weeks with that date, they would end with A. D. 36–7, Usher placing the crucifixion in A. D. 33, in the midst of the last week. Admitting the correctness of Usher's commencement of the seventy weeks, and commencing the 2300 days at the same epoch, they would terminate in A. D. 1846–7.

THE REV. R. C. SHIMEALL.

The Rev. R. C. Shimeall, Presbyter of the Protestant Episcopal Church in the Diocese of New York, in his "Age of the World," etc., published in 1842, argues that "*the great day of crisis*, both to the church and the world, would come in 1847," "and the finishing of the mystery of God in A. D. 1868."

Dr. Joseph Wolff, missionary in Palestine, also argued that the periods would end and the Lord appear in glory in 1847.

REV. FREDERIC SANDER.

The Rev. Frederic Sander, pastor of Wichl engshausen, in his work entitled "An Attempt at Exposition of the Revelation of St. John" (Stuttg., published by J. F. Slunkopf, 1829), briefly states his opinion that the number 666 of Rev. xiii. 18 are so many years, and mark the duration of the Papal power, commencing A. D. 1177, when the title of Pope Alexander III. was generally acknowledged, and ending with A. D. 1843. He then argues "that the millennial kingdom may be expected to commence in A. D. 1847, and not before."—*Memoirs of Bengel*, p. 350.

The next date which has been defended by any semblance of argument is 1864–6. But we must notice 1854 as we pass.

THE EPOCH OF A. D. 1854.

The year 1854 was designated by Jonathan Cummings and F. H. Berrick for the termination of these periods and the coming of the Lord. An interest was awakened upon the subject in the minds of those who confided in their wisdom; but no man who possessed a knowledge of chronology and history sufficient to be recognized as a teacher on these matters had ever seen any such an adjustment of these periods, or reasons for it, during the history of the church. Therefore, this arrangement had little or no influence on those who were well read on this important question.

THE EPOCH OF A. D. 1864–6.

Those who argue for this date arrive at it mainly by commencing the 1260 days of Daniel and John with the decree of Phocas in A. D. 606. The former number added to this would amount to 1866.

DAVID CHYTRÆUS, D. D.

One of the earliest expositors who referred to this date was David Chytræus, D. D., who published an Apocalyptic Exposition at Wittemburg in A. D. 1571. He said of the 1260 days, "If numbered from A. D. 412, when Alaric took Rome and overthrew its empire, the end will be in 1672; or if from the time of Phocas, A. D. 606, when the Pope's supremacy began, then the end may be expected A. D. 1866."

Foxe, the Martyrologist, according to Mr. Elliott, quotes Aretius of Berne, who died in 1574, as advancing the same idea.—*Horæ Apoc.*, vol. 4, p. 450.

DAVID PAREUS.

In the "Commentary" of David Pareus, which was the substance of lectures delivered in 1608 to the Academy of Heidelberg, over which he presided, and published in 1615, the 1260 days of the Gentiles treading the Holy City he inclines to reckon as 1260 years, beginning from Boniface's grant of the title of universal Bishop to the Roman Pope, A. D. 606, a period ending, says he, A. D. 1866. But he "leaves the *decision* of this point with God."

REV. WILLIAM WHISTON, A. M.

Prof. Whiston, the successor of Sir Isaac Newton in the Mathematical Professorship at Cambridge, Eng., in an essay published in 1706, according to Mr. Elliott, also dates the Papal supremacy from Phocas' decree in 606, and he quotes Archbishop Laud as affirming the same.

REV. THOMAS SCOTT, D. D.

Dr. Scott, the commentator, born in England in 1747, was a post-millennialist, but looked for the temporal millennium to commence at the end of the 1260 years. He commenced them in A. D. 606, which terminated them in 1866.

REV. ALFRED BRYANT,

The pastor of the First Presbyterian Church in Niles, Michigan, says:

"The chronological data which the prophecies give furnish intimations that the time is short when all that is predicted shall come to pass.

"One of the most prominent periods fixed for the termination of the 1260 years, so repeatedly brought to view in the prophecies of Daniel and John, is 1866. This clearly does not mark the time of the coming of the Son of man, for that time none can know; but, according to prophecy, within the limits of some four years from that time, preceding or succeeding, may be expected a great crisis in the political affairs of the nations, and great revolutions, which may dissolve the relation between church and state in Europe, and have a most important bearing upon the Jewish people, in preparing the way for their ultimate restoration in part to their own land.

"Precisely what course these political events are to take it would be hazardous to state, for it is not revealed; but there is clear intimation in prophecy that Russia is yet to gain an entire ascendency over continental Europe, and have all the powers thereof under its control, in accomplishing its vast schemes of ambition and war. And in its fully-developed form Russia will probably constitute the great Gog of Scripture,—Gog the prince of *Rosh* of Meshech and Tubal, who is described by Ezekiel, and who will be destroyed in the great battle of Armageddon as predicted. The present aspect of things in Europe looks suspiciously in this direction. But, whatever may be true in respect to these things, there can be no doubt that, according to prophecy, we are on the eve of vast political revolutions, in which probably blood will flow, as described in Apocalyptic vision. But these things, as they come to pass, will only hasten on the day of deliverance and salvation.

"The very general expectation upon the minds of most persons, that we are approaching some great crisis, is an indication of the coming Saviour."—*Views of Millennarianism*, pp. 224, 225.

REV. GEORGE STANLEY FABER, B. D.

Mr. Faber, Rector of Long-Newton, in the county of Durham, in his celebrated "Dissertation on the Prophecies," says of the commencement of the 1260 days:

"It will be difficult to pitch upon any era for the date of this sufficiently conspicuous act except *the year* 606; for in this and in the following year *the saints* were formally given into the hand of *the little horn*, and *the apostasy of individuals* became *the embodied and established apostasy of a spiritual catholic empire*, over which *the man of sin* presided.

"When *a spiritual universal tyrant* then was set up in *the church*, and when *idolatry* was (immediately upon his being thus set up) openly authorized and established by him, the afflicted woman, *the true church*, seems to have fled into *the wilderness* from the pollution of the *holy city* by the new gentilism of Popery, and *the witnesses* appear to have begun to prophesy in sackcloth, or to profess the fundamental truths of the Gospel in a depressed and afflicted state. Accordingly, as Bishop Newton well observes, and afterwards satisfactorily proves, 'there have constantly been *such witnesses* from the seventh century (the century in which *the apostasy*, considered as *the open act of a community under its proper head*, commenced) 'down to the Reformation, during the most flourishing period of Popery.'

"Thus it appears that the tyrannical reign of *the fourth beast's little horn*, and consequently *the prophetic period of* 1260 *days*, are most probably to be computed from *the year* 606, and will, therefore, upon such a supposition, terminate in *the year* 1866."

Mr. Faber says: "Bishop Newton seems to hesitate between *the year* 727, when *the Pope* and *the Romans* finally broke their connection with *the Eastern Emperor; the year* 755, when *the Pope* obtained *the Exarchate of Ravenna; the year* 774, when he acquired by the assistance of Charlemagne the greatest part of *the kingdom of Lombardy*, and *the year* 787, when the worship of images was fully established and the supremacy of *the Pope* acknowledged by the second council of Nice; of these different dates, however, he is inclined to prefer the first. Now, upon examination, not one of them will be found to answer to the tests furnished by the prophet. In none of these years, except the last, were *the saints* given into the hand of *the papal horn*, and as for the acknowledgment made by the council of Nice, it was only a repetition of the grant already made by *the sixth head of the beast;* in none of them was any *Eastern revolt* completed that was in any way connected with *a little horn of the he-goat*, and none of them will bear to be checked by the larger number according to any one of its three readings. There is yet another date fixed upon by Mr. Mann, which *prima facie* was more probable than any of the preceding ones. About *the year* 533 or 534, the Emperor Justinian declared *the Pope* to be *Head of all the churches.* Hence, it seemed not unlikely that *the* 1260 *years* ought to be computed from that era, because *the saints* might be considered as having been then formally given into the hand of *the little horn.* That such a title was conferred upon *the Pope* about that time may be very true, but I am much inclined to think that Mr. Mann has greatly mistaken the nature of Justinian's grant, and that no authority was then given to the Bishop of Rome which at all corresponds with the idea of *universal episcopacy.* Phocas declared *the Pope* to be at once *Head of all the churches,* which is a title of precedence and dignity, and *sole universal Bishop,* which is a title of authority, because he forbade all the other Patriarchs to assume it; whereas, although Justinian conferred upon him the first of these titles, yet at the very same time he styled the Patriarch of Constantinople *Head of all the other churches.* A comparison is accordingly drawn very judiciously by Brightman between the grant of Justinian and the grant of Phocas, in which he states that the former merely gave *the Pope* precedence of all his episcopal brethren, but that the latter exclusively constituted him *universal Bishop,* assigning to him the whole world for his diocese. That this was really the case any person may satisfy himself by consulting the *Novellæ.*"—*Ib.*, pp. 287–300.

REV. JOHN CUMMING, D. D.

The eloquent Dr. Cumming, minister of the Scottish National Church, Crown Court, Covent Garden, London, says of the second advent:

"I know not the times and the seasons; he comes at an hour men think not. The periods of prophetic chronology are all rapidly converging. The great epochs of Daniel, the grand eras of the Apocalypse, as has been shown, all terminate about the year 1864. Reader, do no take up the idea that we assert that Christ comes in that year. All we allege is, that the great prophetic epochs converge just about that time, and, according to Clinton's chronology, in his 'Fasti Hellenici,' the most able adjustment of the chronology of the world that has issued from the pen of any, he demonstrates, not guesses, that the six thousand years of the world terminate about 1863, and then, that 1864 or 1865 begins the seventh millennary of the world. Now, the Jews looked to the seventh thousandth year of the world as the great sabbatic rest of the people of God. Account for it as we like, it is singular that the great epochs of prophecy should all converge at that time. Do any say that before prophecy is fulfilled great things are to be done? It is true. Let any person notice the difference between the way in which things are done now and the way in which they were done thirty years ago,—let him note the speed with which events rush on compared with the sober pace with which they moved in stately procession many years ago,—and he will see that events are now consummated in years which it took centuries to ripen before. It is as if the wheel revolved more rapidly on its axle before it came to the bottom of the hill. It seems as if everybody moved by *express* and believed they should not be able to finish their mission before that night comes when no man can work. The omens and auguries of an approaching crisis are so thick, and so vivid, and so remarkable, that there is not a distinguished thinking statesman in Europe that does not feel afraid to look into that unsounded but opening future that is before Europe, our country, and mankind."—*Benedictions,* pp. 181, 182.

THE REV. E. B. ELLIOTT, A. M.

Mr. Elliott, late Vicar of Tuxford, and Fellow of Trinity College, Cambridge, in his Horæ Apocalypticæ (London, 4 vols.), gives the arguments on which Dr. Cumming bases his opinions, and which will be found on another page, under the head of "Our Present Position in the Prophetic Calendar." He looked for the Lord in 1875.

THE EPOCH OF A. D. 1868.

The Rev. Edward Bickersteth, Rector of Watton, Herts, England, in his "Practical Guide to the Prophecies," published in London in 1836, says:

"It may be useful to refer the reader to CERTAIN SPECIFIC DATES which have been SUPPOSED TO BE NEAR THEIR CLOSE. The circumstance of so many scriptural dates having probable terminations about the same time, and the possibility that these terminations may be near, both calls for attention, and, in proportion as we see they have a real foundation, they are well calculated to impress our minds and increase our watchfulness. Yet the author would be far from dogmatizing on such dates.

"1260 *years.*—Rev. xiii. 5. This date occurs frequently, and in three different forms. Dan. vii. 23–25, time, times, and dividing of a time; Rev. xii. 6, 1260 days; Rev. xiii. 5, forty-two months. All, after the length of the Jewish year and month, point out 1260. This date refers to the duration of Popery.

"If we take its rise in 533, it reaches to 1793, when Popery began to fall. If we take its fuller establishment (Rev. xi. 2; xiii. 8) in 608 to its final fall, it reaches 1868. The interval is seventy-five years."

Elder Wm. C. Thurman, of Virginia, arrived at the same results in his "Sealed book of Daniel opened," but by a different process, which he claimed to demonstrate by astronomical events.

THE EPOCH OF A. D. 1873.

This is an epoch assigned for the termination of the 2300 days of Daniel, by J. A. Brown, in his "Even Tide," 2 vols., published in London in 1823. He commences the period referred to, with the second visit of Nehemiah to Jerusalem, which he places in B. C. 428.

Reckoning them from that point, he would terminate them in 1873, where he also ends 1290 years of the Mohammedan Hegira. He, however, reckons lunar instead of solar years.[1]

THE EPOCH A. D. 1880.

This is the epoch of the Rev. Wm. Hales, D. D., the distinguished chronologer, and is based, like that of 1843 and 1847, on a supposed connection of the 70 weeks and 2300 days. The argument of Dr. Hales is as follows. Speaking of the vision in the 8th of Daniel, he says:

"And he was astonished at the vision; but '*none understood*' how the daily sacrifice should be taken away, or when the period of 2300 days should begin or end.

"Three years after, a further insight into the last mysterious vision was given to the prophet, immediately after his admirable prayer and confession of his own sins, and the sins of his people, and supplication for the holy mountain

---

[1]Dr. N. A. Barbour in his recent effort terminated his time argument at the same point, but by a different mode of reckoning, in some respects. He had been a believer in the closing of time in 1843.

of his God; that *his people* might be restored from the *Babylonian* captivity, now drawing to a close, and *the city* be rebuilt; 'yea, while I was speaking in prayer, even the man *Gabriel*, whom I had seen in the foregoing vision (viii· 16), *flying swiftly*, touched me about the time of the evening oblation, and informed me, and spake to me, and said:

"'O *Daniel*, I am *now* come forth to give thee understanding and information.

"'At *the beginning* of thy supplications, THE ORACLE came forth; and I am come to tell thee [His response], for thou art greatly beloved. Therefore consider the matter and *understand the vision*.

"'THE PROPHECY OF THE SEVENTY WEEKS.

"'*Seventy weeks* are determined upon *thy people* and upon thy *holy city; to complete the transgression* and *consummate sins; to expiate iniquity* and *introduce everlasting righteousness;* and *to seal up vision and prophecy,* and ANOINT THE SAINT OF SAINTS.

"'*Know*, then, and *understand:*

"'From the going forth of THE ORACLE to restore (thy people), and to rebuild *Jerusalem*, until MESSIAH THE LEADER, shall be *seven* weeks and *sixty-two* weeks.

"'*Thou shalt return* [and *thy people*, at the end of the vision of 2300 days], and *Jerusalem* shall be *rebuilt;* both *the street* and the *breach* [of the wall], even in straitness of times.

"'And after *the sixty-two* weeks shall MESSIAH be cut off; *and* [*thy people*] shall *not* be *His; a people of* THE LEADER TO COME shall destroy both *the city* and *the sanctuary*, and its end shall be in a deluge. And until the end of the war *desolations are decreed.*

"'But *one week* shall establish a [*new*] *covenant* with *many*, and *half of the week* shall abrogate the [*daily*] *sacrifice* and *oblation.* And upon the pinnacle [or battlement of the temple shall stand] *the abomination of desolation,* even until the consummation [of the 2300 days]; but then the decreed [desolation] shall be poured [in turn] upon *the Desolator.*'

"This *chronological* prophecy (which I have attempted to render more closely and intelligibly, supplying the ellipsis necessary to complete the sense of the concise original) was evidently designed to explain the foregoing vision, especially in ite *chronological* part of the 2300 days; at the end of which the predicted '*desolation* of the *Jews*' should cease, and their '*sanctuary be cleansed,*' or their temple finally be rebuilt, by determining a certain fixed point or epoch within it,—namely, the destruction of the city and temple of *Jerusalem* by the *Romans*, A. D. 70; for, counting backwards from thence seventy weeks of days, or $70\times7=490$ years, we get the beginning of the period, B. C. 420; and, this being known, the end of the period, also, A. D. 1880; for $420+1880=2300$.

"The destruction of *Jerusalem*, therefore, divides the whole period into two unequal parts; the former, consisting of 490 years, beginning B. C. 420; the latter, of 1810 years, ending A. D. 1880.

"I. The former part and its divisions, noticed in this vision, are first to be considered.

"1. The seventy weeks, or 490 years of which it consists, are *historically* divided into 62, 7, and 1 weeks; and the one week subdivided into a *half-week*. At the expiration of 62+7=69 weeks, or 483 years, MESSIAH THE LEADER was to send forth '*his armies* (the *Romans*) to destroy those *murderers* (the *Jews*) and to burn the city,' (Matt. xxii. 7). And, accordingly, the *Jewish war* commenced in the last or seventieth week B. C. 65, during the administration of *Gessius Florus*, whose exactions drove the *Jews* into rebellion, according to *Josephus*, Ant. xx. 10, 1.

"2. '*After* the 62 weeks,' but not immediately, "the MESSIAH was *cut off;* for the 62 weeks expired A. D. 14; and the *one* week, or *Passion week*, in the midst of which OUR LORD was crucified, A. D. 31, began with his public ministry, A. D. 28, and ended with the martyrdom of *Stephen*, A. D. 34 (see the Articles of THE MINISTRY OF CHRIST and GOSPEL CHRONOLOGY, vol. i., pp. 199–206, in which is given the luminous account of the *Passion* week, in reference to *Daniel's* prophecy, by *Eusebius*). The *Passion* week, therefore, began two weeks after the sixty-two weeks, or at the end of sixty-four weeks; and there were five weeks, or thirty-five years, after the passion week, to the destruction of *Jerusalem*. So that the seventy weeks must be *chronologically* divided into sixty-four, one, and five weeks. For the *one week* in the prophecy is evidently not the last week of the *Jewish* war, and cannot, therefore, follow, in the order of time, the sixty-two and seven weeks.

"The magnificent opening of the prophecy itself seems to blend the fortunes of the *Jews* and of *mankind* together in the important period destined, —1. 'To complete the transgression, and consummate the sins' of the *Jewish* nation, 'when their transgressions should come to the full,' or they should 'fill up the measure of the iniquity of their forefathers (Matt. xxiii. 32), by rejecting and 'cutting off' THE MESSIAH (Isa. liii. 8; Acts ii. 23; iii. 13–15; v. 30, 31). 2. 'To cover, or expiate the iniquity' of the *human* race, by the voluntary sacrifice of himself (Isa. liii. 4–6; 1 Pet. i. 19; Heb. ix. 26; John i. 29, etc.); and also 'to introduce everlasting righteousness.' And 3. 'To seal, or close *prophetic vision*,' when the grand scheme of Divine economy, in the *Patriarchal*, *Mosaical*, and *Evangelical* dispensations, should be sufficiently revealed to mankind by OUR LORD and his *apostles*, before the end of the seventy weeks; after 'THE SAINT OF SAINTS should, on his resurrection, be anointed,' or 'invested with *all authority* in *heaven* and earth' (Matt. xxviii; Rom. i. 4, etc.).

"'The decree of THE ORACLE for restoring the *Jews* and rebuilding *Jerusalem*,' could not refer to their return from the *Babylonish* captivity, which was now past, and the city rebuilt by *Nehemiah*, long before the commencement of the prophecy, B. C. 420, in the fourth year of *Darius Nothus;* it must, therefore, relate to the *final* restoration of the *Jews* and rebuilding of their city, after the long-continued desolation which was to follow the *Roman* captivity, and to end with the period of 2300 days. Then follows a parenthetical apostrophe to the prophet himself, foretelling his (and his people's) final return, at 'the end of the 2300 days,' or 'resurrection of the just' (Dan. xii. 13; Luke xiv. 14, etc.), analogous to the parenthetical remark in *Nathan's* prophecy to the same effect (2 Sam. vii. 10), and the rebuilding of the city (Isa. lx. 10; Ezek. xlviii. 30; Zech. ii. 4).[1]

"When the *Jews* should reject and cut off THE MESSIAH, they should also be rejected by him, and 'no longer *his*' peculiar people, as expressly foretold by *Moses* (Deut. xxxii. 5, more correctly translated), and by the *prophets* (Hosea i. 9, etc.), until their final adoption (Zech. viii. 8); and 'the *Roman armies*' were to be sent, as 'people of MESSIAH TO COME' in judgment, in order to be the executioners of indignation against that 'wicked and apostate generation' of the *Jews* (Matt. xxiii. 35, 36).

"'*The abomination of desolation*' were the *desolating* standards of the *Roman* armies, which were held in *abomination* by the *Jews*, on account of the *idolatrous* worship paid to the images of their gods which they displayed. The phrase occurs in the same sense afterwards (xi. 31; xii. 11); and its signification is ascertained by OUR LORD himself in his reference to, and citation of, this very prophecy of *Daniel* (Matt. xxiv. 15), as explained of 'the Roman *encampments* besieging *Jerusalem*' (Luke xxi. 20). This testimony of OUR LORD himself is decisive to prove that the seventy weeks expired with the destruction of *Jerusalem*, A. D. 70, and, consequently, that they began B. C. 420. And the fourth and last vision of *Daniel* is also decisive to prove that the joint beginning of the 2300 days and seventy weeks, was in the reign of *Darius Nothus* (xi. 1, 2)."—*New Anal. Chron.*, pp. 559–566.

The 1290 and 1335 days of the 12th of Daniel, Dr. Hales commences with the literal taking away of the daily sacrifice, by the destruction of Jerusalem, in A. D. 70. The former he terminates in 1360, the epoch of WICKLIFFE, who "began to make a noise in 1360, by strongly opposing the attempts of the monks, who, under color of their exemptions, violated the rules and statutes of the University of Oxford" (*L'Enfant Concile de Constance tom.* 1, p. 201). And the latter he terminates in A. D. 1405, quoting from the same writer,—"JOHN HUSS rendered himself very famous in 1405 by his preaching in Bohemia," etc. Dr. Hales says: "The author of *Sacræ Heptades*, or a Treatise on *Daniel's* seventy weeks, cited by the learned *Whiston*, in his Treatise on the *Revelation*, in 1706 (p. 240), explains it in the same way.

---

[1] We give this extract from the learned author that our readers may have all that can be said on this period and prophecy; but we think the critical, logical readers of these days will readily see the impropriety of dissecting the seventy weeks as above in order to make out a chronological chain, when no rule exists in Scripture or elsewhere to so divide and compute fractions of any given statement of time, yet the author gives many valuable ideas worthy of notice. What is asserted on the rebuilding of Jerusalem and the final adoption of the Jews we leave for our brethren to explain who believe that view.—*Editor*.

"This simple and obvious solution, adopted by *Whiston* above a hundred years ago, has been strangely overlooked by succeeding commentators, down to the present time; *arbitrarily* assuming that the 1290 and 1335 days began along with the 1260. Hence, *Faber's* perplexities, and new coinage of '*the afterhood* of the times.'"

The 1260 days of Daniel and John, however, he commences in A. D. 620, and terminates them in 1880. Speaking of the period in the 7th of Daniel, he says:

"A *time*, in the Chaldee language, frequently signifies a *year;* and is so understood by *Daniel* himself (iv. 25–34); and in the phrase 'at the end of *the times*, even of *years*,' which is paraphrased in the English Bible, 'after certain *years*' (xi. 13); the period, therefore, denotes *three years and half*, or forty-two months, or (allowing thirty days to the primitive month) 1260 days, as this mysterious period is explained in the Apocalypse (Rev. xii. 14; xi. 2, 3; xii. 6). This woeful period of persecution is to expire along with the grand period in A. D. 1880, 'after which, the *holy people*, or *saints*, are to be delivered.' Therefore, counting backwards from thence, we get A. D. 620 for the time of its commencement; which corresponds, as we have seen, with the *Bangorian* war in *Britain*.

"It is truly remarkable that the *Mahommetan* power in the East sprung up the very same year; for '*the false prophet*,' as *Mahomet* is styled in the Apocalypse, in A. D. 620 or 621, broached his celebrated journey to heaven in company with the angel *Gabriel*, which was so ill received by his countrymen at first, that he was forced to fly from *Mecca*, A. D. 622, whence the *Arabian* era of the *hegira* ('flight') commenced; upon which he published his commission from God, in the *Koran*, to persecute *infidels*.

"The joint persecutions of the Eastern and Western *apostasy* are foretold in the Apocalypse, chap. 13, as will be shown in the sequel.

"This commencement of the 1260 days, analytically deduced, by a chain of reasoning from the context, is surely preferable to A. D. 606, adopted by Bishop *Newton*, *Faber*, and others, upon the hypothetical ground that this was the year in which the title of *Universal Bishop* was conferred on the Pope by the usurper *Phocas;* and the same year, also, in which *Mahomet* retired to his cave in Mount *Hara*, to fabricate his imposture."—*Ib.*, p. 567.

The foregoing are the epochs which have been advocated, by able and gifted minds, as those which should witness the ushering in of the Millennium. We have presented them, with the chief reasons given in their support. The most of them are past, and the others are approaching.

A careful and critical examination of these dates and the chronology of the events to which they apply has been of great advantage to the Christian students generally, who have engaged in them, and the masses who have been privileged with their instructions have become by the blessing of God the most faithful, intelligent, and useful members of the church of Christ. Being more permanently established in the reason for their hope—the fundamental principles of Christianity, and the proper uses to be made of the Scriptures in instructing the unbelievers and in building up believers in the faith of the gospel.

It is worthy of special notice, that the chief of these students above cited never dogmatized, as have some of our less wise American students of prophecy. They simply gave their views and best deductions from their careful investigations, leaving others to accept them or to differ, without crimination or denunciation. Let us all seek to imitate their worthy example, and the study will be productive of good to us.

SYMBOLIC CHARTS AS TEACHERS.

As instruction in some branches can be much more readily and accurately conveyed to the mind through the eye, therefore maps, globes, charts, diagrams, and pictures have been of great service to the world in educating the human mind. The Bible abounds in geographical, historical, and prophetical statements associated with symbols, such as Man, Woman, Beasts, Reptiles, Birds, Trees, Trumpets, Vials, etc.

Early in the history of the Advent Message the idea was conceived of a symbolic chart to assist in illustrating the prophecies. This idea was encouraged by the passage in Hab. ii. 1, 2, "I will stand upon my watch, and set me upon the tower, and will watch to see what he will say unto me, and what I shall answer when I am reproved. And the Lord answered me, and said, Write the vision, and make it plain upon tables, that he may run that readeth it."

A large chart was drafted and duplicates printed containing horizontal lines with chronological dates from the time of creation to the birth of Christ, the cross, and onward to A. D. 1843. The metalic image of Daniel, 2d chapter, was presented with the several segments in divers colors, chronologically arranged; then the several beasts and horns of Daniel, 7th and 8th chapters; then the beasts, horses, riders, and trumpets of Revelation, 6th, 8th, and 9th chapters, the woman and the dragon of the 12th, the beasts of the 13th, the angels of the 14th, the vials of the 16th, and the woman upon the dragon of the 17th chapters. These were printed upon cloth charts of large size to suspend upon walls of houses or lecture rooms. They were accompanied by dates to designate what point in the history of the world each were supposed to have acted its part, and all filling up the space of time allotted to this world in the mortal state, and footing up in numerals A. D. 1843. These charts were used, generally, by lecturers and ministers who were engaged in publishing this message. They served a great and useful purpose in conveying to the minds of audiences, readily, with short historical explanations, some of the most sublime and important features and intentions of the prophetic Scriptures, yet some of the chronological data being incorrect probably produced some hurtful impressions upon concentrative and sanguine minds, which were not easily eradicated after abundant evidence proved them inaccurate, for some novices got the date on the brain and declared, after they had passed the point, that the end would be in 1843 if it did not come for twenty years. But this only develops the mischief of dogmatizing, and not that it is wrong to use dates in chronology. By these charts hundreds of thousands who had not known what these symbols referred to were permitted to see and understand them. Many who had never known that they were in the Bible were awakened to study the Scriptures and learn something about them. Ministers and other educated Christians would look upon these charts *with surprise* and ask, "Where do they find such things as these?" Some ministers in the desk have called them "the Millerite's Caravan," being ignorant of the fact that it was the Lord's panoramic description of this world's history, and that themselves were occupying "the seat of the scornful," and among the "last-day scoffers."

These symbols and diagrams were also arranged in form to publish in papers, books, tracts, and sheets, with explanations, to be sent out among the millions for the instruction of the masses who might study them. In this form much important information has been communicated to the people on these great prophetic truths.

As 1843–4 passed without bringing the desired event many received new views, consolation, and strength from various passages which exhorted to patience, and especially from Hab. ii. 3, "For the vision is *yet* for an appointed time, but at the end it shall speak, and not lie: though it tarry, wait for it; because it will surely come, it will not tarry." Much stress was laid upon the word "*yet* for an appointed time" in this text. The vision had been "written," had been made "plain upon tables," but it was *yet* for a time appointed. "It will surely come." This was all true, and the application made was an ingenious and comforting one to a company of disappointed ones in deep anxiety. But whether this was a correct use of this Scripture in the *first* and *last* case is not yet settled. Several charts have been published in England; some of the same, and some of other, chronological dates. As time passed on some of the students of prophecy fixed upon 1847, a point which had been made by European and American writers in earlier days, which we elsewhere mention. A new chart was arranged by Eld. John Pearson, jr., and published with the periods adjusted to correspond with that date. This was adopted by some as "the fourth watch," using 1836 for the first, 1843 for the second, 1844 for the third watch. It was supposed that the vision mentioned by Habakkuk was *now* plainly written; but this time also passed and the Lord did not come.

In this state of disappointment there was everything to encourage and strengthen those who were well established in the main arguments on which the Advent Message or Midnight Cry is based, for events were transpiring constantly in fulfillment of prophecies connected with the last days, and light was steadily increasing upon the sacred Word; but some are always in search of extra supports, and often overlook the most reliable arguments while they seize upon some Scripture which has no reference to their case, and make an application of it which relieves their minds and fortifies them against temptation. It may be a providential gift. In this case such minds resorted to the following with other texts of equal relevancy: "Son of man, what is that proverb that ye have in the land of Israel, saying, The days are prolonged, and every vision faileth? Tell them, therefore, Thus saith the Lord God; I will make this proverb to cease, and they shall no more use it as a proverb in Israel; but say unto them, The days are at hand, and the effect of every vision."—Ezek. xii. 22, 23.

Neither the visions of Habakkuk nor of Ezekiel had been written on these charts, but the visions of Daniel and John, and though these are a part of "every vision" yet they form no part of every vision referred to by Ezekiel. While the most of the believers in the advent near had decided that the periods could not be so located as to form a reliable date for the event, yet a few were determined that the time would be known definitely, and they computed the periods from other points and fixed upon another date.

A new chart was arranged and published, by Eld. J. C. Bywater, with the figures adjusted to terminate the periods in 1850. This was urged by *time* brethren as the true "midnight cry," the "fourth watch," after the "tarrying time," etc. Perhaps one in five hundred of the Second Advent believers took an interest in this point. All wished it true, but did not see proof of it. Some located and published on 1851, others on 1852, but without charts. These points having been passed another was sought by those who still held to the idea that "the definite time for the Lord to come is revealed in the Bible." A few made a new calculation which ended the 2300 days in 1854. To illustrate this, a new chart was designed and published by Eld. Jonathan Cummings, with the symbols and chronology arranged to correspond. This was called "the midnight cry," after the "tarry," "the fourth watch," etc. Perhaps one in *fifty* of the body of believers became interested in this message. All examined it, we presume, but saw no good proof of its truth. This having failed to be the true adjustment, some of the leading "time brethren" became doubtful as to the whole theme, and the most of these turned their attention to secular employments, while others became convinced that the position occupied by the main body of Adventists was the Scriptural one, viz., that the consecutive fulfillment of prophecy shows conclusively that we are in the closing days of "the gentile times;" that the prophetic periods are given to corroborate this fact, and their commencement marked sufficiently definite to prove it beyond doubt, yet sufficiently indefinite to keep the faithful believers in the waiting, working, and watching position which Christ instructs us to be in, because "ye know not when the time is."

A few, however, were determined they were warranted in seeking *the time*, or they would not be wise, and became interested in several other periods. The year 1866 having been fixed upon by many eminent English standard writers and commentators, some were sure that year would bring the Lord and his kingdom. All hoped it might, but could not rely upon it. But others had already fixed upon different dates. Some decided that 1867 would end the periods and bring the long-desired conquering King. This was the date Mr. Wm. Cunninghame, of Scotland, had fixed upon for the advent of Christ. A new chart was arranged to illustrate that view and published, together with a paper and books. This was called the "midnight cry," "the fourth watch," etc., by the class calling themselves "timists," using the same texts and making the same applications as had been done before. But Eld. Wm. C. Thurman, from Virginia, had come to New England, with a new adjustment of chronology and interpretation of certain prophecies, ending the 1335 days, bringing the resurrection of the saints, the commencement of "the great jubilee" in 1868, all of which was "demonstrated by astronomy." A new chart was prepared and published with the dates adjusted to this arrangement. A small portion of the Advent believers became deeply interested in each of these last-named dates, but the body of the denomination were convinced that the position taken by "time expositors" of modern days was not sufficiently sound to recognize as a *foundation for faith*, however much they desired to see the Lord and enter into the eternal rest. It might be proper to entertain an opinion upon such deductions, but not consistent to call it a "Bible doctrine," "proved," "demonstrated." All these proved incorrect adjustments of the prophetic periods, as the Lord did not verify either of them by his glorious advent, which is to take place "at the end of the days."

Another epoch which has gained the attention of some able scholars in this department of chronological data is 1873. When arriving near that point some few of our "time brethren," as they are now designated, became deeply interested in the calculation and very dogmatical; their efforts enlisted a small number of the body of Adventists, mostly of the younger class, in that view. But very few really believed it among the number who were engaged in the movement, but it was published in book, tract, and paper, and the public charged it upon *the* Adventists. This epoch has also passed, and Jesus has not yet returned, but his coming does not at all depend upon the contingency of time arguments, although he has a time to come, and "at the time appointed the end shall be."

These few "timists" yet persist in the application they have made of the text in Dan. xii. 10, "the wise shall understand," viz., that it teaches the wise shall understand the definite point of the ending of the 1335 days. They have now adjusted the periods so as to teach the end in A. D. 1875, and are proclaiming that the Lord will come then. A new chart is prepared bearing this date, and the leading author of this adjustment, Wm. C. Thurman, declares the time for Christ's advent to the exactness of an hour and minute, demonstrated by astronomy. But it should be more thoroughly understood that *the people* known as Second Adventists, as a body, or as several bodies, of believers in the immediate coming of Christ, have no special connection with these time messages, though they are more lenient to those brethren than others. As a proof of this statement, it is a well-known fact among those who have given heed that each time movement, or each excepting 1843 and 1868, have had special "time papers" published, distinguished from the standing Advent papers, to publish these specific messages, because the Advent papers would not publish them with their dogmatism without reviewing their arguments and showing the body that they were only *conjectural* and *not demonstrated* positions. All the above-named make eight different adjustments of time "made plain upon tables," published upon charts (beside six other times published on sheets), each believed by their advocates to be the true writing of the vision, each called the true "midnight cry," and each, except 1843, called the "fourth watch," and each claimed to fill certain Scripture types or prophetic declarations, and tenaciously persisted in as the correct adjustment, which all ought to see, and all honest minded *Christians would see* and believe. Yet each of these, excepting the last mentioned, has proved incorrect. No one, excepting the Lord, knows whether 1875 will come and pass without the return of our adorable Lord. We wait with anxious interest to see him coming in his glory. We see no cause why he should not come as soon as 1875. Perhaps he may come before then. He may intend to rebuke those who *persist in being positive* on a point which he has not definitely revealed to his church. We are sure "the wise will understand" all he *has* revealed, but we do not know *his time.* That those who care for none of these things, and those who manifest *no* wish to know *anything* about their Lord's return, *need* reproof, and stand in danger of being cast off as "unfaithful servants," appears palpable.

While we do not believe in "being wise above what is written," or positive on what is not proved, yet it is safe and important to be interested, anxious, and confiding in all the Lord has revealed, though we are not justified in rashness, presumption, dogmatism, and censoriousness, nor can we repair the injury done to the weak of the flock of Christ in such a course, or avert the reproach it brings upon the truth.

CHURCH ORGANIZATION.

It has been already stated in several forms that the preachers of the advent near, had no thought of ever establishing a sect, or church organization. Their only object being to arouse the existing churches to a realization of the fact that the Lord was about to come to establish his reign; and also to warn sinners to turn to the Lord and seek a preparation to inherit eternal life. But as circumstances worked such changes in various localities as to cause large numbers to be dismissed from the churches which would not tolerate them with their views, it became a necessity, as we have before stated, for them to organize themselves into churches to maintain the ordinances and discipline of the gospel. This they did generally, as cases required. In Chardon street church, Boston, a minority rejected the Advent views, and left the body ready organized. The same occurred in several other places. Where it was otherwise, and minorities were obliged to leave the churches, they organized anew, but generally in a more scriptural and simple form, as they considered, yet in various places they neglected any formal organization, believing time too short to need any other regulations than were mutually consented to for the time being. In other instances they had been infected by the cry, "Come out of Babylon," and were led to think the organization of a church was very sinful. Hence they not only neglected to organize, but often misused those who did. And as no great amount of good could be accomplished by a host of believers scattered through the land in a disorganized state, with a general disregard for the ordinances and discipline of the gospel, it became no small part of the work of faithful men to bring about a better state of society in this respect. For those who were orderly and knew the importance of gospel order, would show but little respect for, much less unite in labor with, those whe ignored or persistently neglected it.

This has been one of our chief hindrances to prosperity as a denomination until the present time. The pioneers in the cause made a good effort toward order and system at the Albany Conference in 1845, as the report and the following statement shows:

"The doings of the Albany Conference were unanimously ratified by the annual conferences subsequently held in that year, in New York and in Boston; and the 'important truths' there inculcated were often unanimously re-affirmed, so that they have become the settled principles of those known as Adventists. Others, dissenting from the position taken by that conference, but agreeing in unimportant points, and yet claim to be Adventists, should never be recognized as representing the body properly bearing that name, though they may be believers in the advent. It has come to pass that many who stoutly opposed the doings of the Albany Conference, and particularly objected to their calling it a conference of Adventists, or using that name, have adopted the name, under which they wish to be recognized, though they do not at all represent the general principles or interests advocated by that conference.

There were those who had become demoralized by false views and false messages to that degree that everything done in a collective or united capacity seemed to afflict them. They had formed views for themselves which were so sacred that they could not endure to have the body of believers express any views which conflicted with theirs. Thus they had each a creed which they would not yield to save the whole body of believers from anarchy. Consequently they were very jealous of a conference which would transact any business for united action. When the conference had closed and the report was published these zealots were greatly disturbed, and filed their objections about among the different societies where they went, in these forms.

OBJECTIONS CONSIDERED.

The name "Adventists" was objected to as a sectarian name; and it was claimed that instead of being called an Advent church, we should be called "The Church of God." It was replied, This is a misconception of terms. The conference at Albany made no provision for calling churches by any distinctive appellation. They merely expressed themselves as regarding "any congregation of believers who habitually assemble for the worship of God, and the due observance of the gospel ordinances, as *a* church of Christ." They designed to prefix or affix to it no appellative whatever.

"All true churches are 'churches of God,' 1 Thess. ii. 14; 'churches of Christ,' 1 Cor. xi. 16; 'churches of the saints,' 1 Cor. xiv. 33. They are thus called in the Scriptures; but they are not thus called as distinctive appellations; neither have we the right to choose either of those as a specific term. And if we wished to select either of those terms, by which to be designated, which should we select? The Winebrennarians of Pennsylvania call themselves '*The* Church of God,' as a denominational term. If we were also to be known as such, we should be confounded with them. But we have no right to take a name that belongs generally to the whole family, and apply it exclusively to a branch of the family. If a branch of the family wish for a distinctive appellation, they must apply to themselves a term significant of what they are.

"*A* church, according to the Scriptures, is a religious assembly, selected and called out of the world, by the doctrine of the gospel, to worship the true God according to his word. *The* church must include all the elect of God, of what nation soever, from the beginning to the end of the world, who make but one body, whereof Jesus Christ is the Head.—Col. i. 18. 'The church' in any certain place must include all the faithful who are wont to assemble in such place for solemn worship.—Rom. xvi. 5. We thus have in the Scriptures not only 'churches of God,' 'churches of Christ,' and 'churches of the saints,' but we have 'the church at Jerusalem,' Acts viii. 1; 'the church which is at Nymphas' house,' Col. iv. 15; 'the church at Babylon,' 1 Pet. v. 13; 'the church in the wilderness,' Acts vii. 38; 'the church at Antioch,' Acts xiii. 1; 'the church of Laodicea,' Col. iv. 16; 'the church of Ephesus,' Rev. ii. 1; 'the church that is in their house,' Rom. xvi. 5; 'churches of Galatia,' 'of Asia,' 1 Cor. xvi. 1, 19; 'churches of Judea,' Gal. i. 22; 'churches of Gentiles,' Rom. xvi. 4, etc., etc. The above are sufficient, to my mind, to establish the position that a church should be simply called a 'church,' so described that its characteristics may be understood.

"Words are the symbols of ideas. All bodies of men have their peculiarities and characteristics. It is, therefore, necessary to distinguish them as such. Thus God has divided mankind into peoples, kindred, tribes, nations, and tongues. Those of the same peculiarities have an affinity for each other, and naturally associate together. All these branches of the race are known by their distinctive names, and all acknowledge the convenience of their being thus known; it enables us to designate those we wish by an intelligible term. Thus the Israelites of old were known as belonging to the tribes of Judah, of Joseph, of Dan, etc., as the case might be. To call men sons of Jacob was sufficient to show that they belonged to the nation; but even then it was found necessary to know their tribe, their family, and their household; and even the different members of the same household must have different names to distinguish one from the other.

"While all Christians in the days of the apostles were known as Christians, yet if they had had no other distinctive appellations there would have been as much confusion as there would be in a city, if all its inhabitants were known by the name of John and Mary; or as there would be in a family, if there should be twelve children with no individual names,—call one, and all would run; or as it is at the present time, none would regard the call; they would not know which was meant. Therefore, we find the apostles writing, now to the Hebrews, then to the Romans, and again to the Ephesians, and Galatians, etc., etc. If, therefore, it was right for Paul to speak of the 'churches of the Gentiles,' Rom. xvi. 4, it may not be so very wrong for us to speak of the churches of the Adventists, or the churches of the Congregationalists, etc.; while, at the same time, it would be unscriptural to call an association of churches *the* Advent church, *the* Methodist church, etc., etc.

"It is again said that we have no right to be called Adventists, because there are others who believe in the pre-millennial advent, and that to apply it to ourselves is arrogancy. To this we reply that it cannot be arrogancy if no others claim it but ourselves. We do not claim it belongs to us exclusively. All have a right to it who wish thus to be designated. But those who repudiate the name have surely no right to find fault with our use of it; such can have no claim to it. Neither do we, when we call ourselves Adventists, say that we are the only Adventists, any more than we say, when we call ourselves Americans, that we are the only Americans. It should, however, be understood that words are entirely arbitrary and that custom alone establishes their use. Was the term Adventist in use ten years ago? No; it is not in the dictionary; it is a newly-coined word, made by appending an affix to the word advent. In the use of the word it has been only applied to those of like precious faith with ourselves, and by its use the community understand who, and who alone, are intended. The coiners of the word are entitled to it, and those who associate with them; but let it be distinctly understood that, at the Albany Conference, the question did not arise whether we should adopt that name. It was already upon us, and the only question that arose respecting it was whether, when speaking of some fanatics who call themselves Adventists, the word should be permitted to remain in that connection. But, says one, why is that Conference called a 'Conference of Adventists?' It is not so called by vote or direction of the Conference; but as an Adventist is, in accordance with the use of the term, one who believes in the immediate coming of Christ, and as all those who thus assembled professed thus to believe, it was in truth a conference of Adventists. What's in a name?

"'The rose would smell the *same*,
If called by *any* name.'

Another objection to that body is that they told the world some things which they believed the Scriptures teach, and some things which they believed they do not teach. Let us look at this objection. Has not a man a right to tell the world what he does or does not believe? O, yes, certainly. Then have not five, or ten, or fifty men the same privilege? Most certainly. Then, wherein, pray, is the objection?

TOO MUCH LIKE A CREED.

"O, says one, it looks too much like a creed, and I object to all creeds, either *oral* or *written*. But what do you mean by a creed? If you mean by it a test of Christian character, we agree with you, and the Conference expressly voted that they had 'no fellowship with any of the *new tests*, as conditions of salvation, in addition to repentance towards God, and faith in our Lord Jesus Christ, and a looking for and loving his appearing;' but if you mean that a man or body of men have no right to speak or write what they believe, we must dissent from you. The objector replies, we want nothing short of the entire Scriptures for our creed; that alone is sufficient. And that alone is sufficient for us. But while we receive the entire Word of God according to our understanding of its teachings, and while different men draw different and opposite conclusions respecting its teachings, have we no right to inform the world what we conceive to be the truth it inculcates?

"To say that we believe the Bible, and that alone, is to say the same that all denominations say. It is, therefore, meaningless as far as any distinctive idea is conveyed; it is truth in general, meaning nothing in particular. And with that view, why should we stand aloof from all others who claim to believe the same? Theodore Parker, the rationalist, claims to stand on that ground, and yet his constructions of Scripture are so *anti*-scriptural that even the Unitarians repudiate him. Can there, then, be no line of demarcation between what we believe to be the truths and errors which are alike claimed to be based upon the Word of God? Have we no right to tell the world which of opposite doctrines we believe are therein contained? If not, we have surely no right to disfellowship Theodore Parker and his adherents; and nothing can be rejected, and nothing received. And if so, those who told us to come out of Babylon, because the churches rejected their creed, which was their understanding of the Scriptures, did wrong.

"We wish here to say that, in proclaiming the coming of Christ to the world, nothing was further from our thoughts than to form a separate, distinct body of Christians; it never came into our hearts. We thought to benefit all; but, by a combination of circumstances within and without, over which we had no control, we find ourselves as we are. We have been called out of the churches and thrust out of the churches; the churches have refused to fellowship us, and what shall we do? We cannot go back and give up our blessed hope, and all we can do is to find what the gospel teaches and act accordingly.

"The fact is, there is no man living without his distinct creed, for a creed is nothing more or less than (*credo*) a belief. When a man makes his belief, or a body of men make their belief, the test of other men's salvation, they act as bigots; they usurp God's prerogative. But when he or they allow to others the same liberty of thought and speech that they ask for themselves, making them only responsible to their Maker, they do not transgress the 'golden rule.'

"What a man believes is his creed. The creed of the infidel is, 'I believe in all unbelief.' The creed of another is, 'I believe we have no right to write out our belief.' Another's creed is, 'I do not believe in any creed except the New Testament.' And the creed of another is, 'I believe we have the right to write out and undeceive the world as to our understanding of Scriptural teachings.' Now, shall the man whose creed is, 'I believe we have no right to have an *oral* or written creed (belief),' make that creed the standard to which all men must submit? If he does, he is himself a bigot. A man who thus believes has no right to speak or write; for, if he speaks what he believes, he has an '*oral* creed,' and if he writes what he believes, he has a '*written* creed.' If, therefore, he speaks or writes he puts forth his creed, unless he speaks or writes what he does *not believe*, and then he is a hypocrite. A man who thus believes can write for no periodical; he can preach no sermon; every thought he gives utterance to is a violation of *his* creed; it is a departure from it, or in confliction with it. And while thus continually violating his *own* creed, he has surely no right to oblige all others to submit to it.

"Those who cry the loudest against creeds, and disclaim the strongest, are the very men who require others to submit to their *ipse dixit*; they require the largest liberty for themselves and allow the least to others, and if others are not ready to comply with their fancies, ever varying as they are, they are ready to consign them to perdition. For shame on such absurd inconsistencies!

"The aim of all our writings has been to show the church and the world what we believe to be the great truths the Bible inculcates. We have had a right so to do. These truths have had a mighty influence on the community. To bring discredit on them, and thus to weaken our labors, the adversary has connected with them, in the mind of the public, various odious extravagances. When we, therefore, set ourselves up as teachers, all have a right to demand of us what we believe, and what we teach. Says the apostle, '*So* we preached, and *so* ye believed.' We must, therefore, be ever ready to tell *how* we believe, *what* we believe, and *why* we believe. If, therefore, we have no fellowship with any of the abominations so rife among us, we have the right to tell it to the world. And if a large company of 'like precious faith' have the same views on these points, they have an equal right to unite in thus proclaiming it to the world. Those who have sympathy with those things, or who will unite with none who avow to the world their belief, have the same privilege to dissent from them. And if any prefer to stand alone, rather than to unite with a body who do not act in every respect in accordance with their individual creed, who seek to get up a party that do, let it be so understood, that all may act accordingly and understandingly.

"But what has the Albany Conference done? Why, it has committed the crime of informing the world of some of the important truths which the members of it believe the Bible inculcates, with the reasons therefor; and some things which they believe are not therein contained! No Advent lecturers or writers can consistently object to that; for in so doing they would condemn themselves. 'Thou, therefore, which teachest another, teachest thou not thyself?' 'Thou that abhorrest idols, dost thou commit sacrilege?'

SCRIPTURAL ORGANIZATION.

"Another objects to the doings of that Conference because they recommended organization. Indeed! And what did they recommend? Why, they recommended to all 'a careful examination of the Scriptures, and the adoption of such principles of association and order as are in accordance therewith, that they may enjoy the advantages of that church relation which Christ has instituted.' It is left to each church to judge of their own association for themselves. Those who would object to this would surely object to the recommendation of the Scriptures as a rule of faith and practice. Those who would object to this would have objected had they recommended all to fear God and give glory to him.

"Another objection is, that they passed *resolutions* expressive of their sense of truth and duty. This is a great sin, truly. It is said, a resolution can prove nothing; and that it would be absurd to resolve that light is light, or that God reigns. That may all be; and yet it may be perfectly proper to resolve that we will walk in the light, or that we will submit to the rule of God. Every soul does this at conversion; and what may be done individually may certainly be done collectively. To bring forward, as an absurdity, the use of a thing to which it is never applied, as an argument against its being applied to other uses, is to set up a man of straw which cannot stand alone, and, in knocking it down, take to one's self the credit of having overturned an immutable principle, of which it was only an effigy. Resolutions serve the two-fold purpose of showing our true position to the public, and of nerving up our hearts in defence of such position.

"Another objection is, that they have expressed themselves with regard to the intermediate state of the dead, respecting which there is a difference of opinion among Adventists. To this we reply, that that question did not arise at the Conference. No allusion was made to it either in their doings or speeches. They expressed, what all Adventists believe, that the time of the entrance of departed saints into their inheritance is at the resurrection. But the question, whether the intermediate state of the dead is a conscious or an unconscious one, was not even mooted there. This shows the necessity of great cautiousness in stating objections against what is not perfectly understood.

"Another objection is, that the proceedings 'look like doing something in the future;' 'seem like aiming at something which we shall not approve.' Well, as those are not objections to what was there done, and are only fears of what may be done, arising out of the jealousy of the human heart, we shall not spend any time in replying to them; for all magnanimous minds are content with pointing to actual transgressions, and never allude to future fancied ones, unless they are very desirous of finding something to find fault with, in accordance with their pre-judgment.

"The above are all the objections we recollect to have heard or seen advanced against the doings of the Albany Conference; and those have been by a very few. We are happy to see that the doings there give such general satisfaction. What weight such objections are entitled to, all must judge of for themselves. It must be evident, that unless we come out of the BABYLON into which we have been thrust, God will not bless us.

"The question then comes home to each one of our hearts, Shall we continue in the anarchy in which we have been, or shall we take gospel measures to restore gospel order, that, at the Master's coming, we may be approved of him? It must be evident to all, that without union we can do nothing; and if there are no 'important truths' in which we are united, all can see that there can be no union among us. 'How can two walk together except they be agreed?' We can only unite on those points in which there is union. The great doctrine which has called us out is the nearness of Christ's Advent. To persuade men to repent, in view of the coming King, we should all be willing to lay aside the unessentials of our belief, which are at variance with such union.

"All union consists in a sacrifice of individual prepossessions for the common good. Those who love the peace of Zion more than they do their private opinions will be prompt thus to unite. Those who love self more than they do the general good will contend for their own selfish ends. Any doctrine, however plausible to the human mind, which tends to divide true Christians, cannot be of God. We cannot be the disciples of Christ unless we love one another and faithfully labor to keep the unity of the Spirit in the bond of peace. And, therefore, those who seek to produce disorder and confusion, contrary to the doctrine of Christ, cannot be true friends of the cause.

"The union that prevailed at the Albany Conference was what should ever characterize the children of God. They laid aside their prejudices and acted for the general good, and the Adventists, as a body, approve of their doings. What, then, shall we think of the efforts of any who seek to undermine the counsels which there prevailed? Shall we not look upon them as endeavoring to divide the children of God? Shall individuals set up their own individual creed as the criterion to which a united and harmonious body shall come?

"Let all ponder these things well. We live in an awfully dangerous moment of time, when we are beset with foes without and foes within. Let us, therefore, take heed to our ways, to all our thoughts, and to all our doings. Let us have no enemies in disguise among us, professing to be friends. Let all who have no fellowship with the principles we inculcate manifest it. But let all who are willing to contend earnestly for the faith once delivered to the saints not be afraid to tell the world what they believe the Scriptures teach, and fight manfully the good fight, for they will soon win the race."

Such as have followed the principles and rules above advocated have found the Lord to approbate their course and bless their work. And by such means the Second Advent cause has been saved from entire ruin. But it is to be greatly regretted that many have stood

32

aloof from all Bible rules of order, yet claiming to be Bible men, and have had, and led others to have, disorder, derangement, and the destruction of very much of their own and others' arduous labors and means.

REVIVING AGAIN.

It has appeared very strange to those who do not recognize the hand of God in the work of proclaiming this judgment message, that after the doctrine had been "confounded," "confuted," "exposed," "exploded," "refuted," "demolished," and "overthrown," so many times as had been advertised and reported, it should be yet alive and steadily advancing. It was often condemned by the high and learned as a bad cause; had been reported as arraigned before the court of truth, found guilty, sentenced, and executed, time after time. On the strength of such published reports and claims, thousands of the common ministry preached "funeral sermons of Millerism," and really appeared gratified in hoping the subject was dead; while the inconsiderate, careless, slumbering virgins, who were not yet awakened (enough to understand the warning), were sometimes as jubilant as the participants of an "Irish wake."

But it always turned out that this subject was yet alive, and not convicted, by proper authority; that the coffin and shroud at those funerals did not contain the real body, but an imaginary one; that only one side of the testimony had been given them, and that generally from incompetent witnesses,—men who did not believe, did not know, did not care to know, did not believe anybody else could know, and did not wish to know anything about the case. These would be poor witnesses in a court of justice. All this time and labor was lost to them, yet not lost to the cause of this heavenly message, for the Lord overruled these efforts to the opening of many minds to study and pray and learn the truth on this glorious hope. Thus all things, through God's directing care, are made to preach and teach that the Judge of all the earth is soon to appear in his glory and establish a kingdom in righteousness. There is something grand, glorious, and powerful in this blessed hope which these men were not acquainted with. But those who believed the literal truths of the Word, though they were in error in some things, were not easily "moved away from the hope of the Gospel by the error of the wicked."

And although the enemy had changed the base of attack by sowing "his wild-fire of fanaticism" within the camp, and made a breech in the ranks, yet the main army had begun to rally anew under the old standard of truth. The year 1845 was one of rallying the believers to renewed action in the work of the gospel, of seeking to correct the errors into which some had fallen, and of setting our true position and work fairly before the public mind, which had become bewildered and abused by the constant reports, from the press and pulpits, of the basest and most shameful falsehoods, a sample of which we shall give in another place. One specimen is in place at this point.

LETTER FROM BRO. R. HUTCHINSON.

"DEAR BRO. HIMES:—Various are the means which the devil is employing to check the progress of 'the present truth.' As its foes utterly fail to meet it with fair argument, they resort to maligning its adherents. Thus the way of truth is evil spoken of. The following extract of a letter from my parents in England furnishes a specimen: 'R. Greenbank has written to James Buck that the day the Advent believers expected the Lord to come it was awful to see their proceedings; that many families were quite distressed and turned out of doors by giving all they had, and that they *put an end to their lives in various ways!!* Therefore the people here think you are the wickedest upon earth. Some say you want burning and others say you should be shot. The Superintendent (Methodist preacher) says that if he had ten or fifteen souls he would forfeit them all if this world was not standing a thousand years after this. However, here are many who have received your papers and have read them carefully, and say they have received *more light and understanding of the Bible through them than by all the sermons they ever heard.* We receive the Advent Herald from Boston.'

"R. Greenbank is a minister of the Methodist Episcopal Church in the States. About a year ago I received through the same medium a similar misrepresentation of his. I suppose the Adventists in the States put an end to their lives in various ways at the time that *you were* in *jail* and I *hung myself*, as published through the States and this Province. R. HUTCHINSON.

"Waterloo, Canada, March 17, 1845."

Advent Conferences were held in New York and Boston, during the usual anniversary weeks, which were fully attended, and were seasons of great interest to the faithful veterans and the younger members of the body. During the year many conferences, camp, and other protracted meetings were held, by the leading ministers in the cause, in which many were encouraged and strengthened to continue the work of sounding the cry, "Behold, the bridegroom cometh," while many others were reclaimed from the false notions which they had imbibed during the reign of fanaticism in several localities. At these meetings many new converts assembled who had never heard much preaching of the Advent message, excepting what they had heard on time the previous year. The chief points of the faith were now brought before them in a form to instruct and confirm them in the fundamental principles of the gospel hope, and show them that there were points connected with this message of far greater importance than a mere time arrangement. On these occasions many attended *just to hear* what these deluded people could say on the subject after the whole matter had been exploded by the passing of their time. Some of these were made to hear and see the gospel as they had never before seen it, and they felt obliged to believe and unite with this despised and degraded truth. In many places, where there were believers enough to maintain public worship, churches were set in order in the simple form of apostolic custom, by "ordaining elders in every city" or town, and deacons, also, to maintain order, public worship, and the gospel ordinances. Many were stoutly opposed to this gospel work, and from several causes. They had seen exhibitions of arbitrary church power in opposing the truth, in abusing and expelling the faithful of the churches, and in exalting and sustaining wicked and unworthy members for sectarian purposes. This had become so fixed in the minds of some they had decided, *without* a Scriptural examination, that the Bible furnished no rule for *such arbitrary* government, and finally, *no* government at all; thus one extreme produced another. Others had been perverted and their mind strangely abused by the false cry, "Come out of her, my people," and dare not recognize church order for fear of becoming "Babylon." There were yet others who had practiced so much under the spirit of insubordination, using their liberty to say and "do what seemed right in their own eyes," allow-

ALBION ROSS.—Page 501.

ing no one to question their claims, that they determined to maintain that "independent position." Thus they preached, and thus their admirers believed, that none but God united believers to his church; none but God severed unfruitful branches from it; none but God should decide who was right or who was at fault, *e. g.*, there is no discipline to be exercised in the body by its members. This last mentioned has been the most difficult of all classes of unorganized persons; others can be made to see the New Testament rules of organization, but these are above wholesome government; they "despise dominion and speak evil of dignitaries," and some of them "defile the flesh." Their morals, frequently, are such as would place them out of the church of Christ if brought under the authority of New Testament rules of church discipline. They *are*, of course, out of Christ's church now, but so long as they refuse to be amenable to any body of Christians they can denounce all reports or charges against them, "persecution," "and by good words and fair speeches deceive the hearts of the simple." But the faithful and judicious laborers in the cause persevered against all opposing influences, and the Lord blessed their untiring efforts. The word of life took effect, and the mass of believers began to take on "the form of sound words" and united action.

SKETCH OF ELD. ALBION ROSS AND HIS LABORS.

Bro. Ross is a native of Maine, born in 1825, and converted to Christ in 1842, in the town of Skowhegan, where he united with the Free Christian Baptist Church. That church and their minister were at that time interested in the message of the immediate coming of Christ. Bro. R. believed the doctrine as it was then preached. Being soon impressed that it was his duty to preach the gospel to his fellow-men, he commenced to speak from the Scriptures in 1846. He has preached nearly every Lord's day from that time until now, and a great many times, perhaps an average of twice a week, on other days also. During the first years of his ministry he traveled much on foot, calling on the people from house to house, conversing with them about Christ and his salvation, exhorting all to believe on him, and praying with and for them. He appointed meetings wherever he went, and called the people together to speak to them of Christ and his work. These efforts were blessed, and many sinners were turned to the Lord. Christians were awakened and instructed in the way of truth more perfectly, and many wanderers were reclaimed. While Bro. Ross believed Jesus was coming soon, he made it a practical theme in all his efforts to strengthen the churches and save sinners. He believes the dead sleep until Christ comes and that the wicked will utterly perish in the second death. Bro. R. preached on several of the chief islands in Penobscot bay and off the coast of Maine, where much good resulted through the blessing of the Lord. His deep piety, great conscientiousness, and faithful labors have won for him many strong friends wherever he is known. In 1856 he left Maine to take the pastoral charge of the church of Adventists in Lowell, Mass., where he remained several years. Since then he has traveled as an evangelist much of the time, in Massachusetts, New Hampshire, Vermont, and Maine. Bro. R. is studious, deep in research, able in theology, clear in his thoughts, eloquent, modest, bold and direct in his preaching. He deals in profound, simple gospel facts, and disregards speculative, sensational notions; thus the hearts of the people who listen are educated in sound doctrine, and strengthened in the faith of the gospel of Christ. He is a sincere friend, a good adviser, a cautious worker, and conscientious believer of what he teaches. Bro. R. has baptized about five hundred believers thus far during his ministry; he is yet deeply engaged in the Master's work, believing time is short, and that the Lord will soon come in all his glory to gather the sheaves, when all the redeemed ones who sleep, together with those who are awake, will put on immortality to enter upon eternal life in the kingdom of God.

CONFERENCE EFFORTS.

Bro. H. Osler sends to the Advent Herald a report of an important conference of Advent believers in Baltimore in 1845, which Brn. Himes, Galusha, Litch, and Fleming attended. The Lord blessed the effort, and a good work was accomplished. Bro. Himes visited Canada East and reported good meetings, reformations, and progress generally; also northern New York and Vermont, where the believers were generally engaged in the good work, with reports of conversions of sinners in several places. Brn. Litch. Hale, Miller, Jones, Osler, Fassett, and others sent cheering reports, from various

States, of healthful, united efforts among the believers for the salvation of souls. As the cause was seen to be reviving, while opposers had supposed it was dead, new and mighty efforts were made to crush it out. Many ridiculously false reports were forged and put in circulation, and many otherwise respectable journals and ministers published them, some of whom refused to correct them when fully assured they were false. This course had been pursued for several years, the result of which had been to stir up the passions of "the baser sort" to produce mobs and other violent means to break up meetings and commit various indignities upon the person and houses of believers. It was fully ascertained in several instances that church members were associated in mobs and in breaking windows of meeting-houses and dwellings where meetings were being held. This was the same course they took against our divine Master and his apostles. Our Saviour referred to the treatment his church would receive in the closing days of probation in the following language, "For if they do these things in a green tree, what shall be done in the dry?" The most eminent ministers and exemplary Christians were often treated with great insolence and impudence. We will here give a sample of clerical impudence, if not ignorance, under the head of

A SHORT DIALOGUE IN 1846.

Between an Advent Lecturer and a Presbyterian Minister in Canada.

P. M.—Are you a minister of the gospel?

A. L.—Yes, sir.

P. M.—How long have you been a minister?

A. L.—About ten years.

P. M.—To what denomination do you belong?

A. L.—Not any at present.

P. M.—That's a bad sign.

A. L.—I suppose it appears so to you.

P. M.—To what denomination have you belonged?

A. L.—The British Wesleyan Methodist.

P. M.—And what are you now? a Mormon, Christian, or a Millerite?

A. L.—They call me a Millerite.

P. M.—You are the first Millerite preacher I ever saw.

A. L.—I suppose the sight is a great curiosity.

P. M.—I would advise you never to mention the Advent again while you live, for the doctrine does more harm than good.

A. L.—I should not be very apostolical in my preaching were I to adopt your advice.

P. M.—What kind of a Bible do you Millerites use?

A. L.—You can see it (here the Advent lecturer handed his Polyglott Bible to the clergyman).

P. M.—I perceive it is one of our regular Bibles. Can you tell me the meaning of the word Polyglott? (This insulting interrogation was designed to show the listeners that the Millerite preacher was an ignoramus).

A. L.—Do you allow the principle that exchange is no robbery?

P. M.—Yes, to be sure.

A. L.—If you will translate me the following (here the Advent lecturer repeated a Latin stanza from Horace) I will tell you the meaning of Polyglott.

P. M.—That is Latin, is it not?

A. L.—Yes, and if you will translate it for me I will tell you the meaning of Polyglott.

With this the clergyman walked away, receiving the reprehension of the listeners!

These faithful servants of Christ felt that they could appreciate and fully adopt the statement and prayer of the 123d Psalm:

"Unto thee lift I up mine eyes, O thou that dwellest in the heavens.

"Behold, as the eyes of servants *look* unto the hand of their masters, *and* as the eyes of a maiden unto the hand of her mistress; so our eyes *wait* upon the Lord our God, until that he have mercy upon us.

"Have mercy upon us, O Lord, have mercy upon us: for we are exceedingly filled with contempt.

"Our soul is exceedingly filled with the scorning of those that are at ease, *and* with the contempt of the proud."

CHAPTER XVI.

THE QUESTION OF IMMORTALITY—THE MYSTERY NOT SOLVED—HENRY GREW—ORIGEN—AUGUSTIN—POPE PIUS VI.—COUNCIL OF LATERAN—MARTIN LUTHER—WM. TYNDALE—ANOTHER APOSTASY—BIBLE EXAMINER—GEO. STORRS' SIX SERMONS—THE QUESTION AT ISSUE—D. T. TAYLOR—ROMANISM—THE MOTHER OF GOD DEAD.

All careful readers will readily recognize the fact, by our mere allusion to it, that throughout this history thus far the believers in the advent near have manifested an interest in the theme as one of the greatest importance, one which involves the final destiny of the race of man. The writers and speakers advocating this cause have constantly declared or implied that until Christ returns the saints are in a state of captivity in death, are unrewarded; that the wicked are unpunished. In short, as expressed in their declaration of principles and often reaffirmed, "that the departed saints do not enter their inheritance or receive their crowns at death; that there are laid up for them and us crowns of righteousness, which the Lord, the righteous Judge, shall give at the day of Christ to all that love his appearing." On the other side of the question, it as clearly appears, in all our quotations and extracts from opponents, that they regard the second personal advent of Christ and the resurrection of the dead as of little or no importance to the church or world. Several of them, and among the most learned in the schools of the church, regard the doctrine as untrue, unphilosophical, conflicting with the progress of religious thought, and contrary to certain principles held as most vital and sacred points of the Christian system. We refer to Professors Stuart, Bush, Sanborn, Dr. Bushnell, and the class they represent. It is well known to all that these opponents and the Christian church generally, at that point when this controversy began, believed in the dogma of the inherent immortality of the soul; that the soul being immortal is indestructible, is the intellectual part, and is really the man proper. It has, therefore, been extensively taught that the soul-man resides in a tenement of clay for a while, and at death the man leaves the tenement and goes to his reward, according to his class, either to heaven or to hell.

Many labored and learned efforts have been made to harmonize this view with the plainly declared Bible doctrine of the resurrection of the dead, a future day of judgment and rewards; but it has always proved that the greater the effort the more prominent the antagonism of the two ideas has appeared to careful thinkers. Therefore, to avoid the accumulating difficulties to a reconciliation of these points, they have usually been quietly bridged over with the word "mystery." It was called one of the mysteries of God. As a result, the doctrine of Christ's second coming, the resurrection of the dead, and the restitution of the earth has been for many years ebbing out of the faith of the church, while the dogma of man's inherent immortality has been made constantly more prominent to keep pace with the advancing principles of "man-worship," while death has become deified as a friend who opens the prison-house of the saints to release the soul-man that he may go to his blissful abode in heaven. The Advent believers were also involved in the same views, and while teaching the doctrine which distinguished them they were meeting this counter doctrine at every step, which often led them to diligent research to extricate themselves from the illogical situation. The Bible furnished abundant and unequivocal testimony that Christ is yet to come, and that when he comes he is to raise the dead and judge the world, restore the earth and reward his people with "eternal life," and the wicked with "the second death." On this testimony they planted themselves; to this point their attention was directed; for this purpose they were sure Christ was to visit the earth. They also saw that Christ had shown that no home was yet prepared for the church, but that this earth restored was promised as their eternal abode. The process of the change and restoration and the epoch for its accomplishment were also clearly revealed truths. On examination of ecclesiastical history they found this had been the almost universal faith and hope of the church through the Jewish and Christian ages, a few mystics excepted. They, therefore, as has been shown, embraced the same as their hope, and when opposed they could readily show a thoroughly

Scriptural foundation for their faith and easily win a decided victory. But the mystery involved in the two antagonistic doctrines continued to urge investigation. The mystics (or "Spiritualists" Prof. Bush chose to denominate them, meaning those opposed to literalism, which was in reality the embryo state of modern spiritism), such as Professors Stuart, Bush, and Sanborn, with Dr. Bushnell and others of their class, urged the new views, teaching man's immortal nature, his going to his reward at death, the impropriety and inconsistency of the advent of Christ and the resurrection of the body, a doctrine so unphilosophical and inharmonious with the fundamental principle, as all considered it, viz., the immortality of the soul. Therefore, to successfully overthrow the Advent faith in a kind and effectual manner, Prof. Bush wrote his learned and candid work, entitled "Anastasis, or the Doctrine of the Resurrection of the Body, Rationally and Scripturally considered." This was, perhaps, the most able effort ever put forth to *disprove* the Bible doctrine of the resurrection of the dead and to *prove* what is known as Swedenborgianism true. Mr. Bliss gave this work an able Review, thoroughly refuting many of the points advanced, and clearly defending the Scriptural doctrine of the resurrection of the body.

THE MYSTERY NOT SOLVED.

But the mystery of "the immortal soul," considered the responsible agent, the real man, being separated by death from the body, to live on in "fulness of joy" or in "untold agonies" for a time, and then compelled to come back and enter a new, resurrected body, to be brought to judgment and then returned to its respective place of happiness or misery, was not solved. Nay, this theory seemed more illogical and produced a more complicated difficulty than before. These circumstances impelled many careful students of the Bible to enter upon a thorough re-examination of the whole subject of man's nature, his original component parts and structure as he came from the hand of his Creator, the nature of the penalty pronounced upon Adam for sin, the results of its execution, the nature of death, the necessity and results of the plan of atonement, the principles involved in Christ's nature, death, and resurrection, the significance of his promise to give eternal life to his followers, and the nature of the penalty of the New Covenant against sin, which is declared to be "the second death." Such an investigation soon brought a flood of light from the Word of God on this subject, disclosing great and ludicrous deformities in the general views entertained upon these points of doctrine, yet they were not easily disposed of. The habits of thought and modes of expression were deeply rooted in the mind. Theologians, in their efforts to reconcile the differences between the statements of Scripture and their "traditions received from their fathers," had established rules of reasoning and coined expressions of thought which often buried the simple statements of Scripture far out of sight. But the light increased, and some learned to unshackle the mind from habits of "leading strings" and exercise the full strength of their own intellects, which brought out views clearly expressed in simple Bible language and in great harmony with all the points of hope already cherished. But this was met by the Orthodox guardians with the declarations, "This is new doctrine." "It is contrary to the ancient faith of the church." "It is heresy." "If it was a Bible doctrine would not the learned men of former generations have seen it?" This led to an investigation of the controversies of the church in former days on these subjects, as we shall hereafter show, with some of the results. The first arguments which came among the Advent believers in a tangible form, on the doctrine of the entire mortality of man, were from

DEA. HENRY GREW, OF PHILADELPHIA, PA.

He was a devout and critical writer, whose works on this theme were circulated about A. D. 1835, or a little later. Some of them fell into the hands of men whose attention was called to compare them with the Bible.

In 1837 Eld. Geo. Storrs read one of these pamphlets, while a Methodist preacher, which led to his adoption of the views it advocated and prepared the way for his memorable "Six Sermons" "on the inquiry, is there immortality in sin and suffering." These sermons were first preached in Albany, N. Y., in 1842, where Eld. Storrs was ministering the gospel, and were soon after published for general circulation. Many thousands of these were circulated among the Adventists. Eld. Calvin French, also, wrote a work, advocating the same views, which was widely scattered. Eld. Charles Fitch soon embraced this doctrine and began to preach and write upon it, as also several other able ministers. It was very acceptable to many of the believers whom we have already described as much perplexed upon the inharmony which appeared between two points of doctrine they had supposed were equally true. They had supposed the terms, "immortal soul," "never-dying soul," "immortal spirit," were to be found interspersed through the whole Bible, but when called upon to find them, to defend the views called in question, they were, both ministers and laymen, much surprised to find that no such expressions, nor any analogous to them, were to be found there; they were in hymn books, commentaries, sermons, theological books, and school books, but not in the Bible. As we have already stated, a flood of light from the Bible disclosed great deformities in the general views of the Christian church upon this subject; but reforms in doctrine, as in morals, proceed slowly and with many stumblings. Some were soon convinced that the Scriptures fully prove man to be *wholly* mortal; having sinned and been separated from "the tree of life" he *wholly* dies under the sentence, "Thou shalt surely die . . . unto dust shalt thou return." This view showed an absolute necessity of the atonement which Christ offered for man, to redeem him from under the dominion of death, and "as Christ died for all, then were all *dead;*" as he promised immortality and eternal life to those who believed they did not possess these by nature. This opened a wide field for investigation, as we shall hereafter show, but it met with strong opposition of feeling on the part of many of the leading Advent teachers. Mr. Miller was opposed to it, yet he said but little, except to give caution. Elders Litch, Himes, Hale, Brown, Galusha, Whiting, Bliss, Jones, Osler, Gunner, Bonham, Gates, Chapman, and others concluded it was an innovation, and sought to avert the discussion of it. They had fought, or were yet in the engagement of, a mighty battle against modern innovations, such as the world's conversion, the spiritual reign of Christ in the millennium, the return of the carnal Jews to Palestine, the reward of the saints in heaven at death, and they did not feel like entering upon the discussion of this "new question" among themselves, although it would have greatly assisted them in their work had they adopted it. But some of them, knowing it must be brought into recognition soon (for it was rapidly gaining adherents), consulted the standard works of the Protestant church, which contained certain writings against these views, written in a summary manner and covering the subject with criminating epithets which retained all the odor of the Vatican. These brethren honestly decided that this was a pestilent error which had afflicted the church in former days, and instead of being *new* it was an old battered heresy. This is not strange when we reflect that during this period they had taken little thought concerning the great amouut of superstition and Papal corruptions that had been brought out of the Roman into the Protestant church on this subject. Nor had they carefully traced the influx of pagan superstition and heathen dogmas which entered the early church in the days of Constantine, on the same theme, and the accumulation of new furniture and new codes to prepare the way for "the whore of Babylon" (Rev. xvii.) to keep house, to multiply, and manage her numerous family of strange children by seducing the nations during the long night of Papal tyranny, during which the all-important truths of the gospel were perverted, tortured, or banished to give place to the reign of popes and purgatorial superstitions.

This apostasy began to develop strangely in the days of Origen, as the following will show:

"During the reign of Emperor Alexander Severus, who also was a member of the Oriental apostasy, Origen lent the whole weight of his talent and influence to aid the emperor in his design to unite all creeds in one at Rome, and with a view to this end he prevailed upon the emperor to add the name of Christ to the number of his gods. He then immediately changed his own name, originally Admantus, adopting that of Origen.

"From that moment the distinctive doctrines of the gospel ceased to be taught generally. The atonement was no longer spoken of; the second advent of Christ and his future kingdom were denied; the resurrection of the body was explained away. The conspiracy triumphed under Pope Damascus (about A. D. 381), who declared the millennium had already commenced and *expelled from the church,* as heretics, *all who looked for Christ's second advent and kingdom.*"—*Church History.*

This stem and bud of the Papacy grew from the root of heathen philosophy.

"All this," says Dr. Duffield, "was the genuine offspring of the *allegorical system and Platonic philosophy of Origen,* who made *the church on earth the mystic kingdom of heaven.*"

Coleridge tells us, "The pastors of the church had gradually changed the light and life of the gospel into the very superstitions they were commissioned to disperse, and thus paganized Christianity in order to christen Paganism." And in the words of Mosheim, in his Church History, "The new species of philosophy, imprudently adopted by Origen and many other Christians, was extremely prejudicial to the cause of the gospel and to the beautiful simplicity of its celestial doctrines."

AUGUSTINIAN INTERPRETATION.

All apostasies in the church of Christ have grown out of the spiritual or allegorical principle of interpretation; never from the literal; and from the fourth century, onward through the dark ages of superstition and tyranny, an allegorical interpretation of the Scriptures and of the teachings of the early church prevailed, teaching what is called "the Augustinian view of the reign of Christ and the saints," which reign was that of the spirit in the church, and the reign of the church in the spirit, without the personal Christ. Dr. Elliot remarks that "this view prevailed from Augustine's time down to the Reformation."

Great would have been the blessing to the church had it never revived since the Reformation. Augustine was born A. D. 354, and became one of the chief writers in the church and commentators on the Scriptures; he adopted Origen's views, of whose principles of interpretation Dr. Adam Clark says, "According to the plan instituted by Origen the sacred writings may be obliged to say *anything, everything, or nothing*, according to the *fancy*, peculiar *creed*, or *caprice* of the interpreter."

In the midst of this kind of progress the Council of Nice assembled, A. D. 325, and decreed what has been called "the Apostles' Creed;" but it was far from the doctrine of Christ's Apostles.

Pope Pius IV. drew up a summary of the dogmas of this Council,[1] with additions and perversions, which was sanctioned by the Council and promulgated as "APOSTOLIC." Let us notice some of the items.

CREED OF POPE PIUS IV.

First. "I most steadfastly admit and embrace apostolic and ecclesiastical traditions, and all the other observances and constitutions of the same."

Second. "I also admit and embrace the Holy Scriptures according to the sense which our holy mother, the church, has held and does hold, to whom it belongs to judge the true sense and interpretation of the Scriptures. Neither will I ever take and interpret it otherwise than according to the unanimous consent of the fathers."

---

[1] Cumming on Popery, p. 87.

Here we learn that all who would enter the church, from that time onward, must "*steadfastly embrace ecclesiastical traditions*," while they only nod *assent* to the Scriptures, and that only as the church shall interpret them.

But what "ecclesiastical traditions" were they to steadfastly admit and embrace?

Were they not those teachings of Platonic Origen, Augustine, and others of their school?

Who composed the church and the fathers who are here admitted to be the judges of the true sense of interpreting Scripture?

Plainly, such as agreed with the dogmas of popes and councils. All others were heretics. All traditions which could not be interpreted to suit *their* cause were suppressed as heresies, and those who promulgated or defended them were anathematized or martyred.

Third. "I constantly hold that there is a purgatory, and that the souls therein detained are helped by the suffrages or prayers of the faithful."

The view of Plato was, "that the soul of man was a spark from Deity, hence eternal; and that it existed independently of the body."

It will be seen that this tenet in the creed of Pope Pius IV. constitut "go-between" to unite the Platonic view to Christian doctrine.

Fourth. "Likewise I believe that the saints, reigning with Christ, are to be honored and invoked, and that these saints offer prayers to God for us, and that their relics are to be held in veneration."[1]

This tenet opens a wide door for the reveries of superstition and priestly speculation, which has been zealously improved, to both impress creeds and get cash.

Fifth. "I believe it duty to worship the pictures of Christ, the Virgin Mary, and of other saints, and of the cross."

We will trace this turbid stream a little further and we shall learn where our Protestant commentators and theologians obtained their ideas of the soul's immortality, rewards at death, and intermediate state, which has caused the church to drift into such carelessness and unconcern about Christ's return, or to reject it altogether.

THE COUNCIL OF LATERAN. A. D. 1513.

This council, held under Pope Leo X., decreed as follows:

"Whereas in these our days, some have dared to assert concerning the nature of the reasonable soul, that it is MORTAL, or one and the same in all men; and some declare this to be true. We, with the approbation of the Sacred

---

[1] Parisiis, 1837, p. 416.

Council, do CONDEMN and REPROBATE all those who assert that the INTELLECTUAL soul is MORTAL, or one and the same in all men, and those who call these things in question; seeing that the soul is not only truly, and of itself, and essentially, the FORM of the human BODY, as is expressed in the canon of Pope Clement V., published in the General Council of *Vienne;* but likewise IMMORTAL, and, according to the number of bodies into which it is infused, is singularly multipliable, multiplied, and to be multiplied; and we strictly inhibit all from dogmatizing otherwise, and we decree that all who adhere to the like erroneous assertions, shall be shunned and punished as heretics."[1]

Tyndale, Luther, and others took this stand, and with the blessing of God, in the name of Christ, and with his Spirit, did nobly for the truth. They conversed, preached, wrote, and published the great truths of the Bible, which, when brought out, exposed the fabrications, traditions, perversions, corruptions, and usurpations of the Catholics.

MARTIN LUTHER'S ANSWER. 1520.—In Luther's Defence of the Propositions condemned by the bull of Leo X., proposition xxvii., he replies:

"It is certain that it is not in the power of the Church or the Pope to establish articles of faith or laws for morals or good works." . . . "But I permit the Pope to make articles of faith for himself and his faithful, such as *The bread and wine are transubstantiated in the sacrament. The essence of God neither generates, nor is generated. The soul is the substantial form of the human body. The Pope is the emperor of the world, and the king of heaven, and God upon earth.* THE SOUL IS IMMORTAL. With all those monstrous opinions to be found in the Roman dunghill of decretals, that such as his faith is, such may be his gospel, such his disciples, and such his church; that the mouth may have meat suitable for it, and the dish a cover worthy of it."[2]

Again, he says, "All souls lie and sleep until doomsday." Duke George, in writing to Duke John, October 15, 1521, says: Some deny the immortality of the soul. All this comes of Luther's teachings." The reformers were also charged with stating: "All which had been said about the immortality of the soul was invented by Anti-christ for the purpose of making the Pope's pot boil." In the celebrated *Historical Review*, published in London in 1772, it is recorded that Luther taught that souls "lay in a profound sleep, in which opinion

---

[1] Caranza, p. 412.

[2] Luther's Works, vol. 2, fol. 107. Wettemberg, 1562.

he followed many fathers of the ancient church." It adds, "The doctrine was held by the first Reformers."[1]

Sir Thomas More, a zealous Catholic, wrote a book to refute the doctrine taught by the Reformers, in which he assails the teachings of Luther, and in bad philosophy asks,—

"What shall he care how long he live in sin, that believeth Luther, that he shall after this life feel neither good nor evil in body nor soul until the day of doom [judgment]?"

To this book of More, William Tyndale, the man whose translation of the Scriptures was the first ever published in the English language, replied thus:

"Christ and his Apostles taught no other, but warned to look for Christ's coming every hour, which coming again, because ye believe will never be, therefore have ye forged that other merchandise [Purgatory]."

"And ye, in putting them [souls] in heaven, hell, and purgatory, destroy the argument wherewith Christ and Paul prove the resurrection. If the souls be in heaven, tell me why they be not in as good a case as the angels be? And then what cause is there of the resurrection?"

The above extracts show which class followed heathen philosophy, and which followed the teachings of Christ.

God signally blessed the people in their effort to honor his word, and nearly all Europe was revolutionized, religiously and politically, in consequence; and the best of all, the Bible has been given to the nations of the earth to give them the knowledge of Christ.

But the power of tradition, which controlled the masses, and was taught in all the schools, pressed heavily against the reformers, producing

ANOTHER APOSTASY.

Archdeacon Blackburn remarks, "Among Protestants the honor of condemning such as dissented from Plato and Socrates was reserved for our English Reformers in 1552, whilst on the continent, where four years afterwards the second Helvetic Confession was published, under the title, 'The Creation of All Things; of Angels, the Devil, and Man,' it is solemnly announced, after a description of the qualities of the soul, as well as those of the body, 'that we condemn all who scoff at the immortality of the soul, or bring it into doubt by subtle disputation.'"

---

[1] London Historical Review, p. 3416.

This is a great remove from the teachings of Luther, Tyndale, and their fellow-laborers in the Reformation, and from Bible doctrine.

It will not be difficult for the reader to see that on the revival of the doctrine of Christ's second advent the questions should arise with much pertinence, by those who hold the above views, What is he coming for? What is the necessity of his coming? To attempt the answer of these questions would at once produce discussion relating to the state of the dead, and that would involve the question of the nature of man—the soul, and the wages of sin. All of which is now being discussed throughout Christendom as among the more important questions connected with the Christian's hope.

It was thought by many of the Advent believers that this question concerning the nature of the soul, of death, and the reward of the wicked, would divert the attention of the people from the great and all-important theme of Christ's coming. But instead of that it has produced a three-fold interest in that question, and in a more direct and logical form. For when presented to the masses in a clear and Scriptural light so as to convict those who believe the Bible (and yet hold the soul to be immortal—and that it leaves the body and goes to reward at death), that the Scriptures teach the soul to be mortal and dying, and wholly dependent on the resurrection for future life, and wholly dependent on the Lord for the gift of immortality through faith in Christ; it at once shows them *the necessity* of Christ's return to bestow that gift, or man remains eternally dead. The issue of the argument, or proclamation of Christ's second coming, is now turning upon this point throughout Christendom, though all have not yet come to it.

BIBLE EXAMINER.

The above is the title of a periodical issued by Eld. Geo. Storrs, New York, Dec., 1842. Its motto was—"No immortality, or endless life, except through Christ alone." This paper was devoted to the proclamation of the immediate advent of Christ, and the doctrine of immortality through Christ alone, with such other views as probation after the Advent, a mixed millennium of mortals and immortals. It was not recognized as properly an advent publication. Mr. Storrs labored much as an advent preacher for a time, as we have already shown, but he has proved to be very erratic and radical. He published this paper on his own account, and advocated what he judged to be truth. Some of his teaching has been very servicable to the cause of truth, while much of his work in later years is considered by most Adventists as well as other churches to be very detrimental to the progress of truth and sound doctrine, on several points. His "Six Sermons" as first published on the question of immortality were his best. Fifteen thousand of the first number of the Bible Examiner, containing the six sermons on the inquiry, "Are the wicked immortal?" were published and circulated; after which the sermons were published in pamphlet form.

"THE QUESTION AT ISSUE, OR POINT IN DEBATE."

Eld. Storrs entered upon the inquiry in his introductory sermon, thus:

"The question is not whether *man can* be immortal, nor whether the righteous *will* be immortal. These points are admitted and abundantly proved by the Bible; but the question is—Will the wicked, who live and die in their sins, continue eternally, or without end, in a state of conscious existence? Or, once more—Is the punishment God has threatened to sinners an *eternal state of suffering and sin?* This involves the question of immortality. For if all men can be proved to be immortal, it seems to follow from the Bible that the finally impenitent will be left in a state of endless suffering and sin.

"The arguments in proof of man's immortality are mainly three, viz.: First—The desire all men feel for it. Second—That the soul is immaterial, uncompounded, *indivisible*, hence *indestructible*, and *therefore immortal*. Third—That God *wills* the immortality of all men."

Mr. Storrs critically and candidly considered and thoroughly refuted these arguments, and fairly vindicated the opposite view by the Scriptures. About the same time that Mr. Storrs published these sermons, Mr. H. H. Dobney, a Baptist minister of Bristol, England, wrote and published a candid and able work of several hundred pages, on "*Future Punishment*," advocating the same views. Mr. Edward White, a Congregational minister of England, also published a work—"*Life in Christ*," taking the same ground. Dr. Lees, of Leeds, Eng., published on the same side of the question. Archbishop Whateley, of Ireland, published an able work on the same, entitled, "Man's Future State." William Glenn, Moncrieff, a Congregational minister, Scotland, published a critical work advocating the same views. J. Parton Ham, a Congregational minister, Bristol,

Eng., published the same views; also several others. Eld. Pritchard and Dr. Lee, of North Carolina, Dr. N. Field, of Indiana, Dr. Pope, of Missouri, and several others entered upon the same work, about the same time, publishing that there is no immortality for man out of Christ, and that the penalty of the New Covenant against sin is death in its fullest sense,—*extinction of being* by "the second death." In the Bible Examiner of May, 1844, we find a letter from Eld. Charles Fitch, from which we extract. He says:

"I have received a long letter from Bro. L——, touching the state of the dead, the end of the wicked, etc. It would be exceedingly pleasant to me to be able to please him, and the dear brethren who agree with him, for I love them all, and could rejoice to concede anything but truth, to be able to harmonize with them in my views. But there is a friend who has bought me with his blood, and I take more pleasure in pleasing him than to please all the world besides. I never preached my views touching the state of the dead and the destruction of the wicked, until fully convinced that I could no longer withhold them without displeasing my blessed Lord and Master. Most sincerely and truly can I call God to record upon my soul that I have never been influenced in this matter except upon the full, solemn, and irrepressible conviction of duty, to him who died that I might live. I held my peace most gladly, I can assure you, just as long as I dared to do so, and when I felt that I had no more right to be ashamed of God's truth on one subject than another, I bowed to his will and consented, henceforth to believe and teach that when a man is dead, he *is* dead, and that when a man is cast 'into the lake of fire and brimstone, and burned up, root and branch,' and 'utterly consumed with terrors,' he cannot after that be eternally alive."

In a short time a large number of the Advent ministry embraced the above views, and commenced preaching and writing them; among whom were Elders Brewer, Cook, Fassett, Howell, T. Cole, Crowell, J. C. Smith, T. Smith, N. Smith, Goud, Reed, Meriam, J. S. White, W. S. Campbell, Bellows, Allen, Lenfest, Couch, Jones, M. Wellcome, Chandler, Ladd, Munger, Damon, Pease, Edwin Burnham, and others, and the number has continually increased, until perhaps seven-eighths of the body now believe them.

These views added much strength to their faith and hope, as it greatly expanded the doctrine of atonement and brought the Scriptures into harmony much more fully than they had seen before. They now taught that man is wholly mortal, and if any obtain immortality it must be a gift through Christ and obtained at the resurrection of the just; that all probationers must *seek it in* Christ or never obtain it; that the dead are asleep, and not in heaven nor gehena; that all who die in their sins will be raised mortal and experience "the second death" as the wages of their sins, and that they then cease to be, as beings.

This was a step in advance, or a step aside from the Bible track. Most christians thought it the latter. We are not to advocate either here. Certain it is that its advocates have had much easier work in harmonizing Scripture than before, or than the opposite classes, and have an immense amount of plainly-stated, direct texts to sustain their views, and none to conflict with them, except by inference; it has also given them much greater success in their gospel labors. But it awakened, as might be expected, much controversy among the brethren, and sometimes strife of words and unkind feelings. This should not have been, yet while we are human such events will occasionally occur, from desire for the mastery. It soon resulted, however, in a universal admission, we think, among the Advent believers that the soul of man is *not immortal,* the Bible proof being entirely wanting, and its statements so unequivocal, that God *only* hath immortality, that we are called upon to seek it, and that the righteous are to put it on in the resurrection. This was admitted; still many could not admit that the soul dies or sleeps. In the researches upon this theme it was found that many before our day had located the soul, during the death of the body, in an "intermediate state." Wesley calls it a "sort of anti-chamber;" he repudiates the idea of teaching that the saints are now in heaven. But we reserve the argument for a future chapter, and then shall give it only in part, for that is not our work in this book. It has been seen that the declaration of principles at the Albany Conference states the belief that the saints do not receive their crowns until the second advent of Christ, yet it was believed by Mr. Miller and others that the souls of the dead saints were in heaven, for they taught thus when speaking of them. As the controversy went on they took the position, generally, that they were not in heaven, nor the wicked in hell—gehena, but in an "intermediate state," separate from the body. This seemed to be wanting Scriptural proof. Some could see *no* proof but inferential, and that illegitimately drawn. They consequently taught that the souls of the righteous went to heaven, and those of the unrighteous to hell, at

DANIEL T. TAYLOR.—Page 519.

death, while others who saw the Scriptures clearly teaching that they were asleep, unconscious, so taught.

When brethren who differed from this view expostulated with these for so teaching, they wished to know what they were desired to teach, and were told, "teach that they are separated from the body and in an intermediate state in paradise." Josephus was usually cited as giving the orthodox views of the Jews on that point. But, these replied, "we can find no Scripture for an intermediate state, and no paradise except in the new earth, Rev. ii. 7, xxii. 1, 2, unless you show that Paul's statement of a man 'caught up into the third heaven, into the paradise of God,' locates paradise in heaven. If so, and the saints are there, then they *are* in heaven, which *you* do not admit yourselves. Again, your author, Josephus, locates paradise in 'the under world,' a 'cavern in the earth.' *You* do not believe that." It was found too crooked a theory, at every attempt to make out the case, for these who had seen such beauty and harmony in the Scriptures on this subject."[1] And from that time onward until now there has been a continual and rapid increase of these views, not only among those called Adventists, but throughout christendom, more of which will appear hereafter in the forms of argument, discussion, and experience.

SKETCH OF ELD. D. T. TAYLOR AND HIS LABORS.

Bro. Taylor is a native of New York, born at Rouses Point, in 1823; was converted to Christ and joined the Methodist Episcopol Church in 1841. In the winter of 1843, he first listened to the preachers of the pre-millennial advent of Jesus, and became a believer that our Saviour was "at the door," which he yet believes. In 1844, he dissolved his connection with the M. E. Church and stood identified with the general body of Advent Christians, and has remained in this capacity since that time. In 1846, the Lord called him to preach the gospel of the grace of God and coming kingdom. During the two preceding winters he taught a district school in the State of Vermont,

---

[1] On this point Mr. Bliss, editor of the Advent Herald, although a firm advocate of the conscious state, gave the following answer to a correspondent, in the Herald of Jan. 27th, 1847, on the question, "Is the 'right hand' of the Father in the third heaven?" Answer.—We think not, if you mean the third heavens to which Paul was caught up. Although when the third heavens shall have been created, we suppose it will be. God filleth immensity with his presence. Dr. Campbell says that the *original* of the phrase "*caught up*" expresses not the direction of the motion, but the suddenness of the event, and the passiveness of the Apostle. It is claimed by some, that the *third* heavens, to which Paul was caught, and of which he had a vision, were not the third heavens in point of *elevation*, but in point of *progression;* and that it is spoken of in distinction from the *first* heavens, which "were of old," before the flood; and the *second* heavens, which "are now," and which with the earth "are reserved unto fire against the day of judgment, and perdition of ungodly men." The *third* heavens, they claim, are the "*new* heavens," which are to be created with the "new earth, wherein dwelleth righteousness;" and that as Moses was permitted to have a view of earthly Canaan from Pisgah's top, so Paul, after being carried to the place of the departed in Paradise, was carried forward in spirit to the prospective new earth—the third heavens and earth from the creation.

where a revival continually accompanied his labors and a score of persons, many of them his scholars, were converted. When called to preach he did not long resist the summons to give himself to the ministry of the Word and the work of saving souls. He commenced preaching in Canada, where he labored two years in association with Eld. Levi Dudley.

He was ordained July 1, 1848, in Clarenceville, Canada, by Elders J. Litch, R. Hutchinson, H. Buckley, and C. P. Dow. During a period of twenty-eight years Bro. Taylor has preached about 4,000 sermons, in various places in New England, New York, and Canada. He has been several times pastor of churches, varying from one to four years. He has labored much of the time as an evangelist. He has had good success in winning souls to Christ and leading inquirers into the truth on the nature of the gospel hope and the evidences of Jesus soon coming. Bro. T. has immersed one hundred and sixty believers, and united one hundred couple in marriage. But he has written more than he has preached. During the years 1852–5, Bro. T. prepared his "Voice of the Church" on the coming and kingdom of our Lord Jesus Christ. It is a masterly work, and was first published by H. L. Hastings, in 1855. It has now reached its eighth thousand, and ought to be more extensively advertised and sold. But few books now published contain such a vast amount of truth which the Christian church should read as this volume. It has already led a large number from the fable of a temporal millennium to a knowledge of the Scriptural doctrine of the personal reign of Christ. Beside this, Bro. Taylor has written several other valuable books, viz.. "The Coming Earthquake," "Few Saved," "Voice of Warning," "New Heavens and New Earth," "Science of the Resurrection," "The Burning of Rome," "The Age of Murder," published by H. L. Hastings, Boston, Mass.

Bro. Taylor has also written many valuable articles for the Advent papers; has been, during several years, a paid correspondent of the Boston Journal, furnishing that paper many important historical, statistical, and scientific articles, one of which has been published and copyrighted by S. Hawes, entitled "The Black Year," without giving the author credit for his labors. Eld. T. is, perhaps, the best historian connected with the Second Advent people at the present time, relating to the Christian Church, Roman and Protestant, its theories and its authors. He has a work now prepared for the press, containing full title pages of 700 pre-millennial Advent publications, with notes appended. It ought to be published. Bro. T. says: "I became an Adventist from a thorough conviction, upon good and abundant evidence, of the instant coming of our blessed Lord. I was persuaded, and still am, that there is an abundance of solid proof to show that the end of this age and coming of the Bridegroom is at hand, and to be witnessed irrespective of the passing of fixed dates that seemed likely to bring that day. I have not been a real timist since 1846, though not adverse to sober investigation in that line. I preach everywhere as I am able. I love to herald Christ's coming to earth to reign. It is good business, and in whatsoever pulpit I present myself, whether Congregational, Presbyterian, Methodist, or Baptist (and I often do in them), it is as an Adventist, an unworthy, but hoping, expectant of Jesus."

Eld. Taylor has also a poetic talent, and has furnished some very sublime and excellent hymns. We here copy one which we think will be read with pleasure by those who have not seen it.

"Lift your glad voices in triumph on high;
Shout, for the day of redemption is nigh;
Sing, for the Lord will appear in his glory;
Mountains and valleys repeat the glad story,
Tune every lyre,
Lift the strain higher,
Far o'er the ocean the tidings shall fly.

"Lift your glad voices ye nations and sing;
Let the high anthem re-echo and ring;
Sing, for the bright One that slept in the manger
Comes, and the earth, that once pillowed the Stranger,
In rich adorning,
Hails the glad morning,
Blossoms to Eden, and welcomes her King.

"Lift your glad voices, he conquered the grave,
Jesus, Immanuel, Almighty to save;
Shout to the tyrant, 'Thy chains are all broken;'
Sing, for the voice of Jehovah hath spoken.
Open the portal,
Ransomed immortal,
Life shall endure with eternity's wave.

"Lift your glad voices, your banners unfurl,
Sin, death, and hell shall to ruin be hurled;
Christ shall come down in his chariot of fire,
Bethlehem's beauty and Israel's Messiah;
Prince, ever glorious,
Strong and victorious,
Lion of Judah and King of the world.

"Lift your glad voices, he cometh again;
Sound out the tidings o'er earth and o'er main!
Sing, for the dark days of evil are ending;
Shout to the Bridegroom with angels descending.
Bride of Jehovah
Welcome thy Lover;
Sing, for he cometh, he cometh to reign.

"Lift your glad voices wide under the sun;
Sing of his power who the vict'ry has won;
Strong is the arm that the strengthless defended,
Saved us from hell, and the warfare hath ended.
Hallelujah, again,
Hallelujah, Amen!
Shout, for the work of redemption is done." [1]

---

[1] Jubilee Harp, p. 368.

THE STRAYED RETURNING.

During the years 1845–6, while the faithful and stable believers were seeking to "strengthen the things that remain," by publishing the word of life and salvation, as before, many minds were reached by the arguments embraced in the doctrine of the Advent near which had not been moved before. They came into the faith under calm and thorough investigation, free from the excited feelings which accompanied specific time preaching. Those who had been turned aside by false messages and fanaticism, had taken time for sober reflection, and some allowed themselves to carefully examine the steps they had been led to take. This soon showed them their error, and they made healthful and proper confessions of their fault, of following false impressions, which led them to strange views. These were received with open hearts and good faith. Several of the ministers and female speakers and writers, who were endowed with superior gifts for teaching, had gone astray. The most of these returned and united in the work of the gospel as before, which step opened the way for many of the laity to see their error and return also.

EXPOSURES OF ROMANISM.

We have thus far said but little of what the Advent preachers and writers published on Romanism, because that is a subject so universally talked of in these times. But when they commenced the proclamation of the Advent near there was comparatively little written or preached by the Protestant churches of this country in relation to the matter. Some there were who saw and wrote of their rapid increase in America and the dangers which threatened, but the mass were quietly dozing over the idea that Protestantism was converting the Catholics, and soon they would all come round right, thinking they were very docile and harmless in their principles. But when the prophecies of Daniel and of Revelation were brought out and their fulfillment traced in history, to show *where* in the prophetic calendar we were living, it brought the character and position of Paul's "man of sin," the "little horn" of Daniel 7th, and "the two horned beast," "scarlet colored beast" and its rider clearly before the considerate portions of society. This gave great offense to the Catholics, of course, and they often found much sympathy among certain Protestant teachers who were ready to give any other application to these prophecies than accept the legitimate ones, because if they admitted such as the Reformers and the Adventists gave it would be an admission that Christ must soon come to fill up these prophecies. So obstinately determined were some of them to shut their eyes to all facts that favored such conclusions they denied that the prophecies made any mention of the Papacy. Prof. Stuart took this position, as we have already seen. By thus doing they were not only unfaithful stewards of the word, but unfaithful to themselves, and more so to the benighted Catholics, who are ignorant of the word of God relating to the system of religion which their popes and cardinals impose upon them. Under the faithful preaching and writing of the advent believers many hundreds of the Catholics have been led out from their superstitions to embrace the truths of the gospel and to lay by their idolatry,—saint worship,—and wait for Christ from heaven. Several Catholic priests have become "obedient to the faith." What so well calculated to reach and convert them from image or saint worship as to show them that the doctrine of the immortality of the soul is false; that the saints of past ages are neither in purgatory nor heaven, but sleeping in death, awaiting the coming of the Lord.

THE MOTHER OF GOD DEAD.

We once spoke to a lady who had been trained up a Catholic but loved the Lord: "Well, sister, you now pray to Christ instead of the Virgin Mary." "Ah, and I pray to Christ and the Virgin Mary too," was the reply. "But the Virgin Mary is dead," we rejoined. "Dead, dead, the mother of God dead! Who told you?" We explained a little from the Bible on death, for she had begun to read and believe the Protestant Bible. "Well," said the good woman, "I suppose she is dead, but I never heard any one say so before, and I never thought the mother of God could die, but she must be dead."

We have heard it remarked by those competent to judge, and not Adventists, that the Second Advent doctrine had given more light on Catholicism than all other Protestant teaching in America.

CHAPTER XVII.

THE MESSAGE IN EUROPE—WM. CUNNINGHAME—BEN EZRA—SCHOOL TO STUDY PROPHESY—EDWARD IRVING—LIGHT AMONG THE TARTARS—THE MESSAGE IN RUSSIA—THE MILK EATERS—THE MESSAGE IN SMYRNA—HOLLAND—GERMANY—PROF. S. R. L. GAUSSEN—SANDWICH ISLANDS—EFFORT IN ENGLAND—ADVENT HARBINGER--LETTER FROM LONDON--LETTERS FROM TIVERTON—LETTER FROM LIVERPOOL—E. BICKERSTETH—EUROPEAN MISSION—ELDS. HIMES, HUTCHINSON, AND BROWN—THE WORLD'S EVANGELICAL ALLIANCE—A RAY OF LIGHT ON IMMORTALITY—TRUE AND FALSE ANTICIPATIONS—HUGH M'NEILE—DR. JOHN CUMMING—DOOM OF THE PAPACY—DR. E. B. ELLIOT—DR. H. BONAR—LONDON JOURNAL OF PROPHECY—GEORGE MULLER—M. B. CZECHOWSKI—MISSION IN SWITZERLAND AND ITALY—ANOTHER STANDPOINT—AWAKENING ON THE NATURE OF MAN—DR. WM. LEASK AND THE RAINBOW—HENRY CONSTABLE—SECOND ADVENT CONFERENCE IN LONDON—ENGLISH LITERATURE—REBUKING THE NATIONS.

THE SECOND ADVENT MESSAGE IN EUROPE.

Although we have a great amount of matter and much of special importance relating to the publishing of the message in Europe during the last fifty years, that Christ is soon coming personally to reign on the throne of David, and with his church forever, in the earth restored and filled with the glory of God, yet we shall devote space for but a small part of it. Portions of it are interspersed through much which we have already written, where many English, Scotch, Irish, and German authors and teachers are quoted. There has existed much more of the doctrine of Christ's second coming in the European Protestant churches from the time of Luther, than in the American. Yet there have been many hindrances to a free and full development of it in as specific a form as in this country since the clear light has shown believers that the event was even at the doors. The complications of the union of Church and State, the controlling influence of government-appointed and regulated clergy, and the poverty of the masses of the people, prevent such free independent evangelization enterprises as are afforded in this country. Preaching outside of the regularly established order of churches can rarely be had, because of the expense incurred, yet open air, or out of door preaching, is practiced to some extent among the poor classes.

EARLY EXPECTATIONS OF THE CHURCH.

During the French revolution in the closing part of the eighteenth century, and the startling events which resulted in nearly taking away the dominion of the Papacy soon after, there was considerable interest awakened in the minds of careful students of prophecy concerning the immediate coming of Christ. They recognized these events as fulfillments of those prophecies of Daniel and the apocalypse which speak of the "taking away his (the little horn's) dominion," the "slaying of the witness," and as sure precursors of the coming end. From that point until the present we find that prophetic studies have constantly increased. Among the pioneers in these studies and the proclamation of the Advent near, may be mentioned the name of

WILLIAM CUNNINGHAME, ESQ.

The late Rev. William Cunninghame, of Lain Shaw, Scotland, was an eminent student of prophecy. In his youth he spent some time in India. While there his attention was awakened to the study of the prophetic Scriptures, which he began as early as A. D. 1800. The first edition of his "Dissertation on the Seals and Trumpets of the Apocalypse" was published in 1813, the fourth in 1843, which contained 550 8vo. pages. Previous to this he had written on these views for the religious magazines. During his studies he has published several valuable works, one of which is on Chronology, based on the Septuagint version. Mr. C. was a man of great candor, simplicity, and piety. Through his writings and teachings he did much to mould the thoughts of those who are now teachers. Dr. John Cumming, of London, may be considered as his successor as far as prophetic interpretation is concerned.

In 1812, "Ben Ezra" (Lacunza) published his "*Veuida Sequnda de Messias eu gloria y Majestad*," in Cadiz in South America. This was considered a work of great importance on the prophecies and the coming of the Lord. Lewis Way, of England, Pere Lambert, in France, Faber, Frere, and others, also wrote works on the subject.

A SCHOOL TO STUDY PROPHECY.

A notable epoch was the assembling of about fifty persons—clergy and laity, learned and pious, at Albury, England, for the express purpose of studying the prophetic Scriptures, Mr. Cunninghame being one of them. These meetings continued five years—1826 to 1830—results of their researches were published as "Dialogues on Prophecy," in three volumes. During this time Edward Irving published a translation of "Ben Ezra," and several volumes of his own writings on prophecy. These writers, with many others, considered the evidence conclusive that the Lord of life and glory would soon appear. Mr. Cunninghame also took a deep interest in children, and about 1820 he established a Sunday-school for poor children, and thus was among the pioneers of *ragged;*—if not of Sunday schools, yet his was not a *ragged school*, for he *clothed* the scholars by giving them work-day clothes.

At this time he was in the communion of the Established church of Scotland. With some of his teachers he was arraigned for the heresy of "teaching that Jesus Christ tasted death for *every man.*" This was contrary to Calvinism, and they were *cast out* of the church fellowship. This led to the formation of the Congregational church of Stewarton, the Sunday-school furnishing the nucleus. This was in 1837. Mr. C. wrote over twenty books on the Scriptures and chronology.

In 1834 his work entitled "*The Political Destiny of the Earth*" was published. In this we find a thrilling appeal to the ministry on the duties of the times and the subject of Christ's immediate coming to cleanse and restore the earth and establish his reign. He refers to the signs, the exhausted state of prophecy, the wasted condition of the Papacy, the parable of the ten virgins, the midnight cry, arguing that all go to show the Lord must soon appear in his glory. Mr. C. took a deep interest in this subject, and constantly watched for Christ's advent. In his chronology he ends the 1335 days of Dan. 12th chapter, in 1867, yet he thought the Lord would appear sooner, and looked for his return in 1843. But he never dogmatized. This good man died in 1849, greatly beloved by numerous friends, having been engaged in the study of prophecy over fifty years.

THE SPECIAL AWAKENING.

The first effectual awakening in Europe in a direct and impressive form concerning Christ's immediate coming was produced through the labors of Dr. Joseph Wolff and Edward Irving, in England and Scotland. Of Mr. Wolff's labors in Asia we have already given a sketch in another chapter. Mr. Irving began to preach it with great earnestness in London, about 1825, and continued with much success, exerting an extensive influence for good during five or six years, when his labors became disastrous to the cause he was so anxious to advance.

EDWARD IRVING, MINISTER OF CALEDONIA CHAPEL, LONDON,

Was considered one of the most brilliant and able preachers of that great city. He was sometimes called "the lion of London." He preached and wrote much on the immediate advent and the prophecies. But the enemy captivated him with a fanatical spirit, which brought great reproach upon the cause of truth. He avowed special sanctity, superior gifts by the Spirit, among which was the "gift of tongues." He was thus turned out of the path of usefulness in the midst of his most promising days; and as a result a "Catholic apostolic church," whose leading members were fascinated by his fanatical views and spirit, remains in London, to perpetuate his memory, and "the gifts," as a warning to Christians to try the spirits before following them.

Rev. Dr. Sprague, of New York, remarks, "I was fortunate enough to see and hear Edward Irving, a little before the dispensation of tongues opened upon him. His appearance impressed me, at once, as most extraordinary; and my wonder, instead of having abated, rose to a higher and higher pitch till the close of the service. His voice was bland and musical. His prayers were uttered with great solemnity, and even pathos; but they were scarcely suitable prayers to be offered by sinners. I could have easily imagined myself in a congregation if not of angels, at least of those who had grown into perfect persons in Christ. His sermon was worthy, I had almost said, of a splendid maniac. His subject led him to speak of the construction of the person of the Saviour, and, so far as I could understand him, I could not but be startled at his presumption. I had, of course, no idea of what a few months would bring forth, but the sermon which I heard from him left me with no doubt that he was on his way to some higher point of extravagance than he had yet reached; and when I heard of the "tongues" I felt that that was only the legitimate result of the wonderful words which I had heard him utter, and the no less wonderful works (taking into view the writhings of his body and the contortions of his countenance), which I had seen him perform.

"I was favored with a personal interview with him at his house. He met me with so much kindness that I had not the least feeling of being an intruder. He was familiar and affable in conversation. He seemed deeply and solemnly impressed with the great interests of religion. I could not doubt there were the actions of a genuine faith and of a truly humble and devout spirit, amid some of the wildest religious demonstrations I had ever witnessed."

GOSPEL LIGHT AMONG THE TARTARS.

"A Tartar priest being introduced to an Irish missionary asked him when Christ would come the second time. He made answer that he knew nothing at all about it. The Tartar priest expressed great surprise at such an answer from a missionary who had come to teach them the doctrine of the Bible, and remarked he thought every one might know that had a Bible. The priest then gave his views, stating that Christ, he thought, would come about A. D. 1844. The missionary wrote home this statement of facts, which was published in the Irish Magazine in 1821." Thus in the dark corners of christendom the Lord has some disciples who have studied his promise to return and gather his church to himself, and are waiting with great interest to see him and share his glory.

THE MESSAGE IN RUSSIA.

"A Russian gentleman informed a traveler on the lakes that Christ's second coming and the end of the world had been preached throughout Russia, but was received only by the lower classes." Yes. This is the estimate which this sinful world's proud children set upon God's "precious jewels," his "blood-bought" and cleansed sons and daughters. So thought the carnal Jews of the disciples of Christ in their day. "Have any of the rulers believed on him?" they derisively reasoned. But we have an item further on these "lower classes" of Russian believers. We have *seen* a more full statement of their faith in the immediate advent of Christ, showing that this was one of their special points of doctrine, which made them obnoxious to the Greek church, but it is not now in our possession.

We give below a candid and interesting statement concerning them, which shows that they meet the same intolerant spirit in Russia which the faithful believers meet here, and in a worse form, for the church and State are one in that country. The readers of the following will notice that this banishment took place about 1840, just when the Advent Message began to awaken the people in America.

BELIEVERS IN THE ADVENT IN RUSSIA.

The following article is taken from the Christian News, published in Glasgow, Eng., June 5, 1848:

Shores of the Baltic, May, 1848.—I have recently obtained some intelligence respecting a Russian colony, of considerable extent, singular origin, and very uncommon attainments, of which, though prevented by reasons affecting its political security from quoting all the sources of my information, I may convey to our readers some very interesting particulars.

Although, doubtless, the name of temperance societies was never heard of in the wide Steppes of Russia, the thing itself is not unknown to a simple and true-hearted community of dissenters from the Russian Greek Church, whose continued existence, and even increase, during many years of persecution, seems to have borne some resemblance to Israel's experience in Egypt, while their present comparative tranquility in the land of their banishment equally displays the power of divine grace, and the truth of the declaration, "that when a man's ways please the Lord, he will make even his enemies to be at peace with him." The first detailed account which I saw of the Molokaners, or Milk-eaters, was contained in a letter from the Rev. Mr. Roth, one of the Bastle missionaries, whose station, Helenendorf, may well be described as situated on the utmost verge of Christendom.

In the course of a missionary tour to Schamachi and its environs,—a journey in which the gospel messenger is exposed to dangers similar to those rehearsed by St. Paul, 2 Cor. xi. 26,—Mr. Roth met with a venerable member of this singular community, and he details the interview in the following words: "It was in the middle of October, that in one of those nearly impassible and wholly indescribable roads, with which nothing in Germany can be compared, that I again fell in with one of those Molokaners of whom I have before made mention. With this aged and highly interesting disciple I was happily enabled to converse for some considerable time, as our several roads lay in the same direction, and one of my companions was capable of acting as interpreter between us. Before, however, entering on the chief subject of our discourse, it may be well to give a short account of the rise, past history, and present extent of this long despised and severely tried people.

"The Milk-eaters separate themselves from the Greek communion, avowedly, on account of the invocation of saints, the various masses, the worship of pictures and relics, the prescribed use of the sign of the cross, and similar superstitious observances, insisted on by the Greek Church. In short, they took conscientious exception against every part of the public worship of that church, excepting the sermon, which, however (more especially in the country parishes), is almost always omitted as superfluous. After enduring in their birth-place, which was situated in the interior of Russia, unspeakable hardships and oppressions, and seeing, year after year, many of their leaders exiled to Siberia, as obstinate heretics, it was matter of thankfulness to them when the Russian government came to the determination, some eight or nine years since, to banish the whole of this pestilent sect to the Schamachian district in the province of Grusia. This punitive measure was no doubt meant for their hurt, but God turned it to good, as, like Israel of old, the more they were oppressed the more they multiplied and grew. The Russian government may well have felt surprise at the amount of immigration to which this sentence of banishment gave rise, and there now exist in that wild region from sixty to eighty villages, containing many thousand families. The norm of their faith is simply the Scriptures of the Old and New Testaments; their hymns are the Psalms of David, and the Bible knowledge possessed by both men and women among them may be justly termed extraordinary. Their public worship commences with the singing of a psalm; then follows an extempore prayer of one of the elders, who afterwards reads and expounds a chapter of the Bible, much in the manner, it would seem, of our Wirtemberg Scripture readers. . . . The children of both sexes are, generally speaking, instructed by their own parents, although, where a person fitted for the task can be found in a village, a regular school is maintained. But, however accomplished, the result is a most happy one, since not one child above twelve years of age can be found among this people who does not possess a complete knowledge of reading and writing, as well as a rich store of Scripture passages committed to memory. In respect of morals, they are so exemplary, that few denominations of German Christians may bear comparison with them. When, for example, a dispute arises between two Molokaners (which is said to be a very rare occurrence) they feel bound in conscience to so literal a fulfillment of the apostolic admonition, 'let not the sun go down upon your wrath,' that they make a rule of seeking out each other and shaking hands before sunset. A liar or a drunkard is unknown among them; indeed, the majority of them drink no species of fermented liquor (although the use of such is not forbidden) and hence the application of Milk-eaters, by which they are now generally known. Whether this name was at first assumed by themselves, or given in derision by others, I am unable to determine. Such being the character given of this singular and estimable sect, by persons on whose testimony I feel warranted to depend, I return to my old fellow-traveler and the conversation which passed between us. You may imagine my surprise when, after some general remarks on religious topics, he addressed me as follows: 'I should feel greatly obliged if you will give me your opinion whether we Molokaners are right in thinking that the coming of the Lord Jesus cannot be far distant.'

"After stating to him my conviction that, according to Scripture, we were bound to mark the movements of the nations, and especially the progress of the gospel proclamation, as the finger-posts which should guide our judgment as to 'times and seasons,' but that, notwithstanding this, the prophecies of Scripture could only be safely pronounced upon after their fulfillment, and that, therefore, in my mind, no mortal man was empowered or entitled to decide, with authoritative certainty, when the coming of the Son of Man would take place; I proceeded to impress upon, to the best of my ability, the present duty to which we were all called, that of watchfulness with prayer, since our Lord himself compared his coming to that of a thief in the night, or to a flash of lightning, which may at any moment dazzle our astonished vision from the most unexpected quarter. The old man seemed satisfied with my answer, saying that was his own opinion too, and that it afforded him great pleasure to find their views on this question were shared by other Christians. I then observed that in Germany several very pious men had given much diligence to the examination of all that could throw light on the interesting questions connected with the twelve hundred and sixty years, and yet had never been able to satisfy even their minds so fully upon it as to fix the time of our Lord's second coming. 'Among others,' continued I, 'a very thorough search was made into this matter many years ago, by a distinguished man named Bengel; even he has found it too high for him to reach, and its depth too great for him to fathom.' On the mention of Bengel's name the old man's countenance lighted up, and he exclaimed with animation, 'O! I know him, I know him well!' and farther converse proved him indeed no stranger to Bengel's sentiments. You may imagine my astonishment. Can it indeed be possible that Bengel's Apocalypse or his Sixty Discourses have been translated into Russ? And yet, how else could this Russian become acquainted with his name and writings? Luther, too, appears to be a familiar name among the Molokaners, who sometimes, indeed, call themselves simply Lutherans, in opposition to the Russian Greek Church. But what a glorious hope does this excite as to the disclosures which the great day shall make! What extensive good may we not then find has been accomplished by believing authors and preachers compared with what either they or we ever dreamed of! And how large may be the accession to the 'white-robed multitude,' which shall then stand at the right hand of the Judge, from places of the earth deemed by us as dark only because they were to us unknown! Lastly," concluded Mr. Roth, "my old friend informed me that, but a very few weeks since, a fresh detachment, comprising several hundred families, had just joined them from Russia, now no longer exiled by government, but coming of their own free will to enjoy the liberty of faith and worship granted to their co-religionists in their far, but now not desert, home."

FROM SMYRNA, TURKEY IN ASIA.

A missionary writes to the "Signs of the Times," Sept. 25th, 1841, stating that he had arrived East, and presented Mr. Miller's Lectures and Litch's Address to the Clergy to Rev. H. G. O. Dwight, missionary at Constantinople, Rev. Daniel Temple, at the head of American missions in Smyrna, Rev. Mr. Reed, Rev. Mr. Calhoun, at the same place, Rev. J. Perkins, missionary at Oroomiah. Also to the United States Consul, who had become interested in the doctrine of Christ's soon coming. He says the anxiety is great in the East to obtain these publications. Signed, J. A.

THE ADVENT MESSAGE IN HOLLAND.

Mr. H. Hentzepeter, of Holland, wrote and published on the immediate advent of the Lord. Two of his pamphlets printed in the language of that country, on the subject, one in 1830, the other in 1841, were sent to the office of the "Midnight Cry," New York.

In the "Signs of the Times," of 1842, we find the following letter from the above-named gentleman, with an introductory note by Eld. Himes, who says:

We have just received a packet of books and papers from M. H. Hentzepeter, keeper of the Museum at the Hague, with the following pertinent note. Among the works sent are one of his own, in the German language, and two letters, by *Johann Ronge* (the modern Luther, in Germany).

To my beloved brother in the Lord, J. V. Himes, at Boston:—

I was much gratified by the testimony of Christian regard you have sent me in the bountiful collection of books which accompanied the Midnight Cry. All these annunciations, like the cry, "see the Bridegroom cometh," give strength to my hope and faith in the great and joyful event that is near at hand.

Our Almighty Father before pouring out his judgments has ever warned the wicked. Noah warned the first world; Abraham and Lot, Sodom; Jonas, Nineveh; and Jerusalem was warned of the destruction that awaited her—and in like manner the Lord may have appointed you and others in America to announce the approaching judgments of this world—following the coming of Christ, and the restoration of all things, Acts iii. 21. But you know, my dear brother, that in the last days mockers shall say, Where is the day of his coming? all things remain as they were, 2 Peter iii. 3, 4. But this shall not prejudice us; let us have our lamps burning and await our Lord's return.

I believe we are in the evening of the Saturday of the great week of this world, and that what has yet to happen before the Sabbath day of 1000 years, is found in Isa. ii. 10, 21; Isa. xliii. 1, 6; Daniel ii. 35; Daniel vii. 12, 26; Rev. vi. 12, 17; Rev. xi. 15, 19; Rev. xvi. 13, 21; Rev. xvii. 16, 17; Rev. xix. 19, 21.

I have sent the Midnight Cry to Germany, with some of the other papers, after sending them to Capadore and other christian friends at the Hague.

Hoping this will find you in good health, I remain, in christian love,

Yours truly.

Prof. S. R. L. Gaussen, of Geneva, Switzerland, being a Pre-millennial Advent believer, a profound scholar, an eminent teacher, and well-known writer on the Scriptures, and on the prophecies relating to the papacy, has exerted a healthful influence in the churches in Germany on the coming and kingdom of Christ.

In Wirtemburg there is a colony numbering hundreds who look for the speedy Advent of Christ.

While in London, Eld. J. V. Himes received the following letter from Prof. Gaussen, which shows an item of his interest in the subject of the Lord's return. His reference to a typographical error in his "small discourse" relates to tract No. xlvi., in the "Second Advent Library," entitled, "The German Rebuke of American Neology," being a discourse delivered by him "to the theological students, at the opening of the course of lectures in October, 1843." It was written in French, and translated into English by American Adventists.

To Rev. J. V. Himes.

Dear Sir and Brother in Jesus Christ,—I have just received the interesting books that you have had the goodness to send me in the month of August. I made haste to peruse them, and I could appreciate them. The small tract on the chronology of the Bible appeared to me very well written, both as it respects clearness and solidity. I am grieved to see that in your America some doctors have appeared so contemptuous of the authority of the Scriptures as your Prof. Bush. Your review of "Anastasis" shows him in a very unfavorable light. God guard your churches from that spirit of temerity and innovation which has made such great ravages in Germany! I would like to know what is thought in America of the chronology of Dr. Jarvis. Is his book in circulation in England?

I will read with attention your "Advent Herald." I am endeavoring to enlighten myself again on the question of the *future*, for it is principally, and almost exclusively, on the prophecies *already fulfilled* that I have studied Daniel, Ezekiel, and St. John.

They speak very highly in some papers of the recent work of Dr. David Brown "on Christ's Second Coming," in which this author seems to sustain a view contrary to yours. Did you read it, and was it refuted?

I have been traveling for the three months past, so that I am a stranger in Israel to the recent publications. As to myself, I could not understand the Scriptures otherwise than announcing the return of our Redeemer *before* the

Millennium; but I have nothing published on that question which is explicit.

In the translation of my small discourse on Dan. 7th there is an important typographical error to correct; they printed (page 28, line 25) "Trent" instead of "Toulouse."

The enterprise of the American Adventists to enlighten their European brethren on a question so grave as that of the second appearing of Christ is very commendable, even though it were only on the ground of charity and Christian union. Your enterprise is even justified by the importance of the subject.

It is certain, also, that several of those who throw obscurity on the second coming of Christ do this to avoid the testimonies of the Word of God against the Man of Sin.

I then invoke, with all my heart, the aid of the Holy Spirit on your holy enterprise, which is certainly according to the mind of God; he shall certainly bless it.

Your XLI. No. ["Age to Come," etc.,] has appeared to me very solid. That which proves that (Matt. xxiv. 34), *e genee,* signifies not *the present generation,* is the parable which follows, viz., the fig tree.

Farewell, dear sir and brother; receive my hearty good wishes and respects.

Eld. Himes appends the following note to the above in the Advent Herald: "When in London, we understood from ———, of Geneva, that Prof. G., in consequence of his devotion to the study of prophecy, is regarded in the same unfavorable light with all others who in England and America are in like manner employed. Great talents, learning, station are no security against the sneer and scorn of those who think it folly to 'read and observe the sayings' of the prophecies of the word of God. It may, therefore, be a consolation to our brethren in America to learn that, in this respect, no trial has befallen them but such as is common to all their brethren everywhere."

LETTER FROM THE SANDWICH ISLANDS.

My Dear Brother:—I have but a few short moments to scribble a line to you. I am just informed that a vessel is to sail soon for U. S., and I cannot let the opportunity pass. We were made twice glad on receiving your letters, bearing date March 15th, and Nov. 6th, 9th, and 18th, 1843. The letters, books, and papers all came per brig Globe, which had an uncommonly long passage. We received them on the 25th of July. We have for a long time been very anxious to hear from you and the Second Advent cause. I have thanked you a thousand times for the books and papers you sent in the fall of

1842; they have led me to great searchings of heart, as well as Scripture. I am a firm believer of most of the Second Advent doctrine. My faith is not the least staggered because 1843 has passed. Your time has passed; but God's time is at hand. A number of the missionaries have received Second Advent publications; but few, if any, have Second Advent faith; the doctrine is repugnant, or I would say it has been repugnant to the hearts of some who are *now quite inclined to search after the truth.* Is it not astonishing that men in our enlightened land will take the word of erring men for a rule of faith, in preference to the word of God? How fully did I once believe in a temporal millennium. The return of the Jews, etc., etc. And why did I so believe? Because it was so *preached!* I did not think of examining the word of God to see if these things were so. The Bible has been my *study* for a year past—not merely my reading book, as it formerly was.

These we presume are your days of trial. Scoffers, perhaps, have grown more bold; and those whom you hoped were Christians have cast off the little fear they may have had, and now wear triumphant looks. This is the Christian's day of trial; no better day can he expect in this sin-cursed earth.

I hope you will write us often, as our souls are much cheered by your letters. We feel revived when we have such testimony that we still have friends, though separated by land and sea.

I have this moment received the Signs of the Times of Nov. 29th. Where it came from we cannot tell; but suppose it must be from you. We are very much interested in the papers, and hope to see more, should time continue. I remain your affectionate brother.

S. Bliss. CHARLES BURNHAM.

Koloa, Aug. 8th, 1844.

AN EFFORT IN ENGLAND.

In 1840, an attempt was made to open an interchange between the Literalists of England and the Adventists in the United States; but it was soon discovered that they had as little fellowship for our Anti-Judaizing notions as we had for their Judaism, and the interchange was broken off.

In 1842, Robert Winter, an Englishman by birth, and a primitive Methodist by profession, fell in with the Adventists in this country and embraced the doctrine. In the fall of the year he resolved to return to England and proclaim the coming of the Lord. He did return and commenced the work. God owned his truth, it took effect, and many have been raised up to join with him in spreading the light through these islands of the sea. Last summer, camp or field meetings were held in different parts of England with great success.

Books and papers to a large amount have been sent to England and scattered abroad through the country, and several books and papers have been re-published in that country with great effect. The British Provinces, adjoining the United States, have been visited and furnished with the light. Our beloved brother, Hutchinson, in Montreal, has published a large amount of matter in his paper, "*The Voice of Elijah*," and sent it over the United Kingdom.

THE ADVENT HARBINGER, BRISTOL, ENGLAND.

A paper with the above title was published in Bristol, in 1844, by Elders Winter and Bonham, from which we find the following from Eld. Wm. Burgess. He says:

"We began the midnight cry and to visit as far as possible the surrounding country; the truth is finding its way among all classes and every sect. Some of the ministry embrace and preach it, but many denounce us and the subject as fanatical, crying 'peace and safety' to the people. Those who embrace these views talk of possessing a new Bible, or the old one better understood.

"We have sounded the midnight cry in London, Hull, Knotingly (Leeds, in what is called the Second Advent chapel three weeks), Bradford, Wakefield, Nottingham, Sheffield, Manchester, with Brn. Dealtry and Wilson, in Isle of Man, Lancaster, Carlisle, New Castle, and other places, in chapels, halls, in the market to a thousand people, on commons, in streets, lanes, squares, and to great congregations in Stockport and Liverpool; have scattered 2,000 copies of published lectures on the prophecies of Daniel and many of '*The Voice of Elijah.*'"

Eld. E. Micklewood also traveled and preached it. Great reformations followed. Eld. M. immersed over 1,700 believers in about three years. Edmund Bickersteth's "Practical Guide to the Study of the Prophecies" is a thrilling cry at midnight, or thorough showing that this mortal state is about to cease to give place to the coming and kingdom of our Lord Jesus Christ.

It is now asserted that more than one thousand ministers of the

Church of England have united in the general work of preaching the immediate coming of the Lord. But it is proper to remark in this connection that their preaching on this theme is usually connected with the idea of the return of the Jews, and they frequently make the remark that when the Jews begin to gather to their land Christ may be expected soon. They teach that one of the sure signs to precede the Advent will be the gathering of the Jews to Palestine. But as the prospects of the return of the Jews are growing less favorable, or rather it is becoming very evident that they, as a people, have no intentions of returning, the faith of many stands still. They measure the argument for the Lord's return by the indications of the Jews' return. This is evidently one of the principal causes which has acted against a more active faith and general movement in Europe on this great and important theme, for very many works have been published there on this subject and very many able and influential ministers have preached much upon it. It will be seen by the correspondence of several ministers, which we proceed now to give, that some take the view on the Jew question that the Adventists of America do.

LETTER FROM LONDON.

DEAR BROTHER HIMES,—I have sent these few lines to inform you that I feel much disappointed by your non-arrival here, as do many of the dear brethren and friends, from different parts of England, who expected to meet in London to hold the Conference. But for my part I feel resigned to the will of God, and I would say, in the language of my blessed Redeemer, not my will, but thine be done. It appears to me that if the Midnight Cry is to be sounded in London the American brethren must come and give it. Although the cry has been sounded in many parts of England, yet there are thousands in London that never heard or read on the subject. This is, surely, a modern Babylon, and if time continue something should be done immediately. I have been lecturing in the streets and commons for six weeks past, and I trust some good has been done; but to hire places to lecture in I have not had the means, and sorry I am to say that very few that have feel inclined thus to use them. Surely, when the Son of Man cometh shall he find faith on the earth?

I intend, God willing, should the vision tarry, to sound the cry in doors and out, as the way may be open this winter in London, etc.; and I beg an interest in your prayers that the Lord may open my way to sound the cry, "Behold, the Bridegroom cometh; go ye out to meet him." It is now about fourteen months since I left New York for my native land, and I have lectured at most of the large towns in the South of England, and likewise in

Norfolk and Suffolk, and the Isle of Wight. I have lectured in chapels among different denominations, and given hundreds of lectures to large and attentive congregations. Many have been awakened, and, I trust, hopefully converted, and many of them say they have to bless God that ever they heard the Midnight Cry, and are now looking for that blessed hope and glorious appearing of our great God and Saviour, Jesus Christ. I feel much obliged to you for sending us publications to assist us in publishing the glad tidings of the kingdom. These have been a great blessing to thousands of souls, and likewise have assisted us in sounding the cry. I have never taken up a collection to pay my expenses. I have sometimes met with friends that have assisted me, but generally the English people are not so liberal as they are in America; besides thousands can hardly get their daily bread. The poor in England are miserably poor. I see them every day in the streets of London, destitute of clothing, and in a state of starvation, as they are not allowed to beg. This makes me cry, Come, Lord Jesus, and come quickly.

I have had some conversation with Brothers Winter and Roturn. They both send their love to you, hoping to see or hear from you, as we are kept in suspense respecting your coming to England; and I am requested to say, if you cannot come to let us know the particulars by the next steamship, as we are all anxious to know the result. I think there are several in the churches who would come out and assist in spreading the cry if you were here. We have got places open to commence in, but we want an efficient lecturer to take the lead and start a press, etc. But I must leave the subject with you and your God, and may his blessing attend it. Amen.

The dear friends all join in love to you. Brother and Sister Lloyd are still strong in the faith and have a desire to see you. Bro. Winter is at Maidenhead, and is publishing a paper called the Advent Harbinger. Brother Roturn is traveling with him. Bro. Burgess is in Bedford. Bro. Dealtry is at Bristol. I send my love to all the dear friends in America. I often think of the blessed meetings we had in New York and Brooklyn. I have sat by the rivers of Babylon and wept when I have remembered Zion.

I remain yours, in hope of a better country, viz., an heavenly one, wherein dwelleth righteousness.

William Barker,

No. 11 Lion Street, New Kent Road, Borough, London.

Jan. 2, 1845.

LETTER FROM BRO. C. DEALTRY.

My Dear Bro. Himes,—Although I have been long silent, neither yourself, nor the rest of the brethren whom I loved and esteemed in America, are forgotten. My confidence in the correctness of the principle upon which we interpret the prophecies is strong, not only with regard to the nature of Messiah's kingdom and character of his reign, but also the time of its establishment. I am determined, God's grace assisting me, to wait patiently, watch closely, and labor faithfully until our Lord does appear.

There is a sad want of Second Advent preachers in this country, and a greater want of co-operation amongst those who are here. *No effectual good can be accomplished without union.* In order to carry weight with the great truths we advocate in this country it is *essential* that the lecturers should be able and *educated* men. However good or strong in faith the opposite class may be, they cannot command an audience unless prepared at all points. If yourself, with Bro. Litch, will write and say that you will visit us in the spring, I do not doubt you will find encouragement. Do let me urge it upon you. The people here are very, very dark. You are aware that this is a stronghold of *Judaism,* and so long as they read the Scriptures with that veil before their eyes they never will see the Advent as near as we do. I am surprised that people who profess to read their Bibles cannot see it. There is too much reason to fear that if our Lord were on the earth now he would address professing Christendom in the same language he once addressed Pharisaic Jewry: "O ye hypocrites, ye can discern the face of the sky, but can ye not discern the signs of the times."

The year is opening with appalling prospects; war, pestilence, and famine are clearly seen in the distance. Parliament opens early in January. How Sir Robert Peel, who has again taken office, will steer the state vessel through the stormy sea before him I cannot tell. Distress and perplexity are the characteristic features of the nation and government. "The sea and the waves roaring" is true, understanding it either figuratively or literally, while the next verse, "men's hearts failing them," etc., is *most fully* accomplished at this moment. Oh! how blind are the people!

I leave this place for Devonport to-morrow, to give a second course of lectures. I anticipate good congregations. I have had a large chart painted, eight feet broad by nine long, illustrating Daniel's visions, and also have had printed some thousands of tracts (one of which I send you), with which I hope, with God's blessing, to wake up the people to a sense of their position, —slumbering beside the fire God's wrath has kindled to devour them.

Write to me, dear Bro. Himes, if you have time. And with my love to yourself, and all who love the Lord in truth and sincerity, believe me affectionately yours, C. Dealtry.

Tiverton, Eng., Dec. 29, 1845.

LETTER FROM BRO. W. BURGESS.

My Dear Bro. Himes,—It is with feelings of the deepest gratitude that I address these few lines to you, and thank you for your very kind letter and papers which you sent us. I am pleased with the letters in the papers, as they relate the experience of many brethren who are looking for the Lord. I am also delighted with the Christian spirit in which most of the articles are written.

We believe that we shall soon see our blessed Redeemer revealed in all his glory, who will change these vile bodies, and "fashion them like unto his glorious body, according to the working whereby he is able to subdue all things unto himself." This blessed hope kept us bound together in the bond of love to God and man. We have no language to express the joy this blessed hope affords. (1 Pet. i. 3-13, 1 John iii. 1-3.) I well remember the effect this doctrine had on my mind when Bro. Winter first laid it before me. I was convinced that this earth would soon be dissolved, and a new one created which will be inhabited by God's people forever, even forever. I then felt it my duty to proclaim it to my fellow-men, that they might be made the partakers of like precious faith; but as soon as I mentioned it to some of my best friends they very much opposed it, and asked, "What will you do if you give up your situation?" (for which I was receiving £100 a year.) My only reply was, "That the apostles of Christ went out without either purse or scrip, yet they lacked nothing, and God is the same to-day as ever." With these views before me, I made a full surrender of myself and all that I had to God, to spend and be spent in this glorious cause. I then experienced what the two disciples felt on their way to Emmaus. They said, "Did not our hearts burn within us while he talked to us by the way, and while he opened to us the Scriptures." This burning love I felt, and very soon it kindled in me a love and pity for my fellow-men, and they became the subject of my prayers and tears. I saw that there would be no return of the Jews, no conversion of the world, no millennium before the coming of the Lord. I also knew that the mass of the people were in darkness on this great and momentous truth. I could not rest, day nor night, until I commenced to give the Midnight Cry, and I bless God that I ever engaged in this work. It is three years since I engaged in this cause, and the hundreds of letters I have received testify that my labors have not been in vain in the Lord. The Lord has not suffered me to engage in a warfare at my own charge, but in almost every place he has raised up friends to help me, and many thousands of books and tracts have been printed and scattered over a great part of the country. But a great work remains yet to be done, and there is but little time in which to do it. The harvest truly is great, but the laborers are very few.

We want a centre of action in this country. Is it not possible for you and Bro. Litch to come over in the spring and edit a paper? This would unite the brethren and do an immensity of good. I am quite sure that it would be well supported, for there are many that love the Lord that have this world's goods, who, if they could have the evidence before them that Christ would speedily appear, would act in accordance with their faith and help to spread this truth. Dear brethren, do come, if possible, for your presence is much desired and needed. There is much darkness on the minds of the ministry here as well as the people. I will give you one specimen, among many, which came under my own notice. A minister in T. said to me not long since, "You must not preach Christ's coming to judgment, you will frighten and alarm the people and make them ill; you must preach death to the people, for it is certain they will all die." "Surely those that love the Lord will not be frightened or made ill to hear that the Lord is coming to set them free," I replied. Said he, "There are some so weak in the faith that all their life-time they are subject to bondage through the fear of death." "Well, sir," I replied, "I would deliver them from that fear by telling them if they are alive when Christ comes they shall never die. 'Behold I show you a mystery, we shall not all sleep (that is, we shall not all die), but we shall all be changed, in a moment, in the twinkling of an eye, at the last trump,' etc. (1 Cor. xv. 51.) 'Jesus saith unto her, Thy brother shall live again. Martha saith unto him, I know he shall rise again in the resurrection at the last day. Jesus saith unto her, I am the resurrection and the life; he that believeth in me, though he were dead, yet shall he live; and whosoever liveth and believeth in me shall never die. Believest thou this?'" (John xi. 23–26.)

My kindest love to all the brethren and sisters that are looking for the Lord. Let us all be strong in the faith, giving glory to God, "for yet a little while, and he that shall come will come, and will not tarry."

Yours most affectionately, WILLIAM BURGESS.

Tiverton (Devonshire, Eng.), Jan. 1, 1846.

EXTRACT OF A LETTER FROM BRO. J. CURRY.

I do rejoice at the prospect of your coming to England. I am sure great good will result from your visit. The people are fast asleep and need arousing. The visit of a stranger will effect good, as a hearing will be obtained. Surely, "a prophet hath no honor in his own country." I would like well to correspond with you by each steamer from Liverpool to Boston, and will furnish you with a file of the Liverpool newspapers regularly by every packet.

The people of England generally are swallowed up in speculation, "laying up treasures for the last time." The few who are looking for the coming One are denominated fools, and I am about to be silenced in the church to which I have long been attached because I preach the doctrine of Christ's second coming at hand. Let the will of the Lord be done in this respect. I have endeavored to be faithful, and by God's help will never cease to sound the alarm until the Saviour comes. There are singular movements going forward which will shortly shake the kingdom to its centre.

With love to all the brethren, I remain yours, affectionately, in the blessed hope, JOSEPH CURRY.

Princes Place, Fleet St., Liverpool, Jan. 3, 1846.

"SIGNS OF THE TIMES," BY REV. E. BICKSTETH.

The above is the title of a book written by Mr. B. in 1845. He was an extensive writer on the prophecies and on chronology. His chronological deductions we have already given in another place, ending the periods in 1868. In his "Signs of the Times," he says:

"Even political men have pronounced from common sagacity and foresight of what is coming. In December, 1826, the late Mr. Canning testifies in the house of commons, 'I fear the next war that shall be kindled in Europe will be a war not so much of armies as of opinions, consequent of letting loose of passions, at present chained and confined, would be to produce a scene which no man can contemplate without horror.' Such are the views of a most ripe defender of divine truth, who states his opinions thus: 'Of this in general I am satisfied, that the next coming will be a coming to precede and usher in the millennium. I utterly despair of the universal prevalence of Christianity as the result of a pacific missionary process under the guidance of human wisdom and principle, but without slackening in the least our obligations to help forward this great cause. I look for its conclusive establishment through a wider passage, through desolations and judgment, with the utter desolation of our civil and ecclesiastical structures.'

"Pious men on the continent are awakening to these Scriptural views."

Mr. R. T. Birks, a very eminent minister of the church of England, has written several able works on the prophecies and the immediate Advent of the Lord. Mr. Brock and Mr. Brooks have also furnished valuable works on the same theme, each of whom are among the more prominent ministers in England. Rev. Wm. Thorp also has furnished many able works on this theme, which are among the numerous pre-millennial works of English literature.

THE EUROPEAN MISSION.

The American Adventists had from the beginning been desirous to extend the proclamation of the "midnight cry" to all parts of christendom, as the way might open for it by publications or living preachers. Some had arranged to go to Europe on a mission in 1844, but the special time movement of that year diverted them from the effort, as we have already noticed.

In 1846, the way appeared to afford opportunity for such an effort. The calls were numerous and urgent, from England especially. Consequently, at the general Conference of Adventists, assembled in New York, May 12–15, 1846, a committee, consisting of Elders J. Litch, L. Kimball, A. Hale, T. M. Preble, and I. E. Jones, was chosen and instructed to consider and report the necessity and practicability of this mission. Said committee made the following report, which was unanimously adopted:

Whereas, many urgent calls from our brethren in Great Britain have been made for assistance in spreading the great principles of our faith in that country, and thus to arouse the church and the world to a sense of their danger, and influence them to prepare for the Lord's speedy coming;

And *whereas,* that field of labor seems to us a most important one; therefore

Resolved, That we believe the time has come when we are imperiously called on to put forth an effort in this cause, and in the name and strength of the Lord to lend all the assistance in our power to assist those already in that field.

Resolved, That in view of the work to be done in that country, of lecturing, and publishing books, tracts, and periodicals, we deem it important, if we do anything, to have an efficient mission in the field, and that less than three would not be sufficient for the work. In looking for laborers for such an enterprise, we are fully of the opinion that our beloved brethren, J. V. Himes, R. Hutchinson, and F. G. Brown, are the men who can better attend to and accomplish this mission than any other brethren among us; we earnestly recommend them to the work.

And *whereas,* "no man goeth a warfare at his own charge," and the Scriptures declare that the "laborer is worthy of his hire," therefore

Resolved, That we invite the pecuniary co-operation of all who love the glorious appearing of our Saviour and feel an interest in the spread of light on this grand question. And we trust that all who have this world's goods will seriously inquire what part they have to perform, as God's stewards, in carrying forward this enterprise.

The general conference adjourned to meet in Boston, May 26th. At the Boston session this mission enterprise met the hearty approval of the representatives of the Advent cause assembled. An "Address to Believers in the Lord Jesus Christ in England, Scotland, Ireland, and elsewhere" was prepared and ordered by the conference to be printed as an expression of the views and objects of American Adventists, and an appeal to the Christian church to awake and labor and watch for the return of the Nobleman. It is a valuable document, and we would gladly publish it had we space. It should be published in pamphlet form for general distribution. We hope to be able yet to do it.

June 1st Brn. Himes, Hutchinson, and Brown sailed for England, arriving in Liverpool the 13th, where they were welcomed by glad hearts who had waited for them. They entered at once upon their work. Eld. Himes soon issued the "European Advent Herald," which was published for one year. The first number contained the elaborate Address of the General Conference of American Adventists, signed Elon Galusha, President, O. R. Fassett, Secretary. These missionaries also announced to the public in the first issue their readiness to preach on the following topics: The blessed hope, first resurrection, the five kingdoms of Dan. 2d, the seventy weeks, the little horn, the vision of Dan. 8th, 2,300 days, Dan. 11th and 12th chapters, Matt. 24th chapter, and the signs of the times. They visited such parts of England, Scotland, and Ireland as was in their power and proclaimed the gospel of the kingdom to multitudes. Eld. Himes took over a large lot of books and tracts which were widely circulated with the European Herald. He was assisted by Dr. Hutchinson and Eld. J. W. Bonham, with other faithful brethren.

Many testimonials show that much good resulted from this effort, with the united aid of many believers in England. But this special mission was closed up in 1847, as there were not then men and means to effect an organization to continue the work in an efficient manner.

These missionaries were also appointed delegates to "The World's Temperance Convention" and "The World's Evangelical Alliance," to be held in London during the coming summer. As those great conventions, composed of delegates from all parts of Christendom, to confer upon matters of vital interest, relating to man's present necessities, these ministers of the gospel of the coming and kingdom of Christ met with them. Eld. Himes remarks that he

"Feels that much has been accomplished by the lectures and papers. Nor has our work been retarded by a faithful discharge of our duties in the World's Temperance Convention and the Christian Alliance. As our views of the 'Advent' became known, we were frequently inquired of in relation to our past, present, and future position, so that we were afforded with the opportunity of scattering our papers and works in very desirable and extensive directions, and of disabusing the minds of many in relation to us and the cause we advocate. . . . Many members of the Alliance are strong advocates for the pre-millennial doctrine. Some of the most forward of its members are of that class, among whom are Messrs. Bickersteth, Birks, and Campbell. The latter gentleman, who is one of the principal secretaries, and was one of the original movers in the Alliance scheme, distinctly stated to the Conference that he 'regarded this great movement as one of the signs of the times and as preparatory to the coming of the Son of Man in the clouds of heaven.'"

During the work of organizing this Alliance, and defining principles as its basis, Eld. F. G. Brown moved that an amendment of one of the articles be made by adding the clause "his blessed coming." Mr. Bickersteth replied that "this point was implied in another part of the basis." Their attendance and active services in this Alliance informed all the members of that meeting that there was an interest on this continent in the speedy return of our Lord and King.

A RAY OF BIBLE LIGHT IN THE ALLIANCE.

The report of the organizing of the Evangelical Alliance and of its doings has some items of special interest to Adventists. We quote the following item from the report on forming the "*Basis of the Alliance*."

"Another article, making nine in all, was added to the 'basis' of belief, at the suggestion of Dr. Cox, of New York, and runs as follows:

"The Immortality of the Soul, the Resurrection of the Body, and the Judgment of the World by our Lord Jesus Christ, with the Eternal Blessedness of the Righteous and the Eternal Punishment of the Wicked.

"Bro. R. Hutchinson moved that the phrase 'the immortality of the soul' be rescinded from the theological basis; he showed, with great freedom of speech, that the word immortal, or immortality, is never used in the sense intended; that these terms are only used six times in the Bible, and are applied exclusively to God, to Christ, and to the saints when made like him at his coming. The Rev. T. Binney, of London, seconded the amendment, assigning as the reason, 'that the "immortality of the soul" savors more of heathenism than of Christianity.' The Rev. Mr. Kuntye, of Berlin, supported the amendment and said that 'the phrase "the immortality of the soul" is not used by the evangelical ministry in Germany, as it is one of the gods which the Rationalists of that country worship.' Many of the distinguished and thinking voted in favor of Bro. H.'s proposition, yet the majority were on the other side."

This action showed that the majority of that representative body were yet under heathen superstition in regard to the nature of the soul of man and its ultimate destiny. Although there were many good men of sterling piety connected with this great representative body of all Christendom, and some grand objects before them which led to the effort of calling and organizing such a body, yet the majority of them were evidently impelled to the interest they have taken in its doings by the delusive, unscriptural hope of the world's conversion and a temporal millennium.

This object, being made very prominent by frequent statements and declared intentions, has kept many of the most clear-sighted and devoted Christian ministers from uniting in it, as a matter of conscience. Bro. Himes, after a few preparatory remarks, gives an illustration of this as found below:

Brethren, let us arouse ourselves and enter upon our work with a renewed and determined purpose. Let not a moment be lost; our time is precious, it is short. What we do we must do quickly. Let holy zeal fire our hearts. Let prayer, deep, fervent, and incessant, go up to Almighty God for his blessing upon our labors in this last and most glorious work assigned us. We are happy to know that our brethren in this country have done well for the cause, yet much remains to be done. Your dear brethren in America are looking to you with confidence and hope. Yea, your Divine Master has committed to you a most sacred trust, and he looks to you to guard and preserve it unto his coming. Never had a religious system better ground on which to rest than that we advocate, and never one so calculated to bless and enrich the souls of God's beloved people, or to awaken and save perishing sinners. Then let us gird up our loins and unitedly enter the field with new courage, faith, and hope.

TRUE AND FALSE ANTICIPATIONS.

Large bodies of professed Christians are looking for this world's conversion unto God; money is employed, and many lives are laid upon the altar of this enterprise; rich and admirable machinery is employed and propelled to this end; many warm hearts and strong hands are giving it motion; still there is wanting proof that the object sought is to be gained. True, the scheme is brilliant, but will the result be equally so? We are apprehensive that neither sound reason nor Scripture authority have been made to bear as they should on this question. If the Word of God presents the ground for such expectations from such plans, then all is right and well. If not, then, though good may be accomplished to a limited extent, at which we ought to rejoice, yet, as the end looked for cannot be attained, disappointment, at least, will be the result. Every Christian, therefore, who is not engaged in efforts to convert the world ought to be able to give his reasons for withholding his co-operation. On the other hand, every one thus engaged ought to be able to give his authority for his labors and anticipations, and, in both cases, the Bible should be called in to settle the respective positions. Hence, the importance of studying the prophetic Scriptures, in order to ascertain what are true and what are false anticipations respecting the world's conversion.

This is only a solitary illustration of the great practical value of a consideration of those portions of Scripture which refer to "the consummation." We have before us the third edition of an excellent sermon by Rev. Hugh M'Neile, on "The Manifested Oneness of the Church of Christ, with some reasons for not joining the proposed Evangelical Alliance," which we may notice more fully at another time. We subjoin from the appendix the following paragraphs:

"Suppose a man who is habitually anticipating the conversion of the world, by means of the preaching of the gospel and the manifested unity of the Christian churches of all denominations! Such a view of 'things to come' will strongly incline him to favor any project which professes to aim at the accomplishment of those things.

"Suppose another man, who is habitually anticipating the coming of our Lord Jesus Christ to the salvation of his church chosen out of the world and to the destruction of the ungodly! Such a view of 'things to come' will strongly incline him to reject, as an ensnaring delusion, a project which aims and teaches men to aim at the conversion of the world. The question, then, is deeply and vitally practical. Which of these men is anticipating according to the Word of God, and which in opposition to it?

"The next question, of course, is, what saith 'The Word' on this subject?"

Mr. M'Neile answers the question by introducing plain and unequivocal passages from the mouth of our Lord and the pens of his apostles. Regarding the world's conversion, the main object which "the Alliance" has in view, as radically defective, being sustained by no authority from the Scriptures, he cannot give it his approbation and support. And we must say that his objections are worthy of deep consideration. One vital question, therefore, presents itself at the very threshold of this magnificent project,—Is the object of the Evangelical Alliance likely to be realized? Now is the time to take special heed to the sure word of prophecy; the future is dark, but the Word of God may dispel the darkness, and thereby enable us to give a wise and efficient direction to our plans and efforts as members of the Church of Christ, and thus save us from inflicting upon Christ's body much mischief and otherwise injuring his holy cause. Are our anticipations to be realized? The Bible must answer the question. Shall that and that alone answer the question at issue? Or shall we dare to plunge forward, heedlessly and recklessly, with no reference to the revealed purposes of heaven? If so, the consequences must fall on our own heads. The Great Teacher said, "Take ye heed; behold I have told you all things." Saul persecuted the saints of God "ignorantly." The Jewish Church and the princes of this world murdered the Lord of life and glory "through ignorance." And may not the Christian Church be in danger of committing crimes quite as atrocious through a criminal neglect of what God has spoken? Who of us would be found opposing the world's conversion, providing this be a Scripture truth, or the doctrine of the speedy termination of this age and the immediate appearing of our glorious Deliverer, if indeed that be a Bible truth? On one or the other of these sides we are each arranged; on which side is the Word of God? We are all indulging our warm and confident expectations. Which are true, and which are *false?*

AN ENGLISH OUTSIDE VIEW.

By the following correspondence it will be seen that the same ignorance and blindness prevails among the literary worldlings in

England as in America, and the same fear to hear anything about the coming of the Lord. This writer is evidently unacquainted with the Lord, his word, and his ministers. We quote his letter because it gives a ray of historical light. "The prudent" will see its bearing, while "the simple will believe every word."

ADVENTISM IN ENGLAND.

The following is copied from the Foreign Correspondence of the Philadelphia "Saturday Evening Post:"

PROPHECY.—How much misery has spread through the world, in all ages, by pretended prophets,—to what serious, and even fatal, results have their allusions tended,—and how frequently have their innocent victims fallen under the hands of keepers of mad-houses, or been imprisoned, tortured, and even put to death by the agents of despotic governments.

A fanaticism of this kind has been recently gotten up in Wales (a fanatical and somewhat superstitious part of the kingdom, by the way), caused chiefly by one "Prince" who, with two or three eccentric clergymen of regular churches, have been "touring it," through the counties of Glamorgan and Caermarthen, and preaching sermons predictive of the end of the world and of the final fires, all of which are about to occur. Their congregations are called together by hand-bills, headed "The Lord is at hand," "Behold, he cometh!" etc. Of course the attendances at these preachings have been numerous, and many who went to ridicule became terrified. These false prophets, however, have made no great impression as yet, but their followers are on the increase. Unlike your notorious Father Miller, they abstain from naming the exact day, and content themselves with declaring that it is *at hand.* Turn we, however, from these to a delusion of a more serious character, because backed by a great name,—a name respected in all parts of the Protestant world, I mean Martin Luther. Well, then, publications are going the rounds to the effect that we are to have the end of the World about April next,—that it had been foretold by Martin Luther. The vaticination is drawn from "*Luther's Divine Discourses,*" written in February, 1516; and the great Reformer begins by predicting a "great crash and downfall" in the spiritual world in 250 years from that date, which prediction is said to have been fulfilled by the denial of Christian Revelation in France. And he foretells "*the last Day of Judgment*" to be within 300 years. And again, in the 55th chapter of the aforesaid book, he hints that "*about the time of Easter, in April,*" will the last day come. It is really probable that much anxiety and alarm will be produced by the revival of these ideas, dug up, as they are, from an age full of enthusiasm, excitement, change, and even terror, so deeply tinctured with these emotions that it is fair to presume that Luther himself was not free from their morbid inspirations and influence. Be that as it may, these things are not given to finite and frail man to foretell. They belong alone to the Infinite. "Of that day and hour knoweth no man," and I mere-

JOHN CUMMING, D.D.—Page 549.

ly introduce the singular correspondence as one of the signs of the times, which are now more than ever full of excitabilities. Is it not strange that in these days of education such fancies should prevail? Yet so it is. Even in Germany, ever noted as a land of deep and gloomy sentiment, of prophecy, ever aspiring to the spiritual, and therefore to the unattainable, I observe that in the public schools, according to recent statistics, there are 6,000,000 of pupils. Still, superstition and fanaticism prevail, and will, it is to be feared, to the "last syllable of recorded time."

During these years of expectancy and of toil on the part of the believers the Lord has continued to manifest his awakening power in the fulfillment of certain prophetic Scriptures, which has aroused many minds, heretofore indifferent, to the study of those portions of the Word which describe the events of the last days, and accessions have been constantly made to the company of waiting ones who desire and expect soon to see the Lord coming in his glory. The preaching and writings of those who have continued in the work have been crowned with much success. We proceed to notice several of the most noted among them, such as John Cumming, D. D., Horatius Bonar, D. D., E. B. Elliot, Hugh M'Neile, with others.

SKETCH OF JOHN CUMMING, D. D.

We will give a few extracts from "John Ross Dix's pen and ink sketch of Rev. John Cumming, D. D., of the Scotch Church, Crown Court, London."

After describing the place where the house of worship is situated in which Dr. C. preaches, the immense congregation in attendance, the members of parliament and other noted personages who attend upon his ministry, and the singing, which he says is "beautiful exceedingly,"

"There is no organ, but it is evident that the choir requires not the aid of that king of musical instruments. Never have we heard better singing than at Dr. Cumming's; all may join in it, and indeed all present did, at least so it seemed to us. Dr. Cumming's prayer was a model of its kind. The preacher is of the middle height, perhaps rather above it; but, attired in his clerical robes, one is apt to be deceived in such a matter. Dr. Cumming's face is a remarkably fine one. A glance at it might convince any ordinary observer that it belongs to one whose mind is not of the common stamp. . . Opening a little Bible, which he holds with both hands, Dr. C. commences his discourse by reading from it his text. Very clear and musical is his voice; although by no means loud, it can be heard with the utmost distinctness in the most distant part of the church, and consequently, as there is no shuffling and leaning forward to catch the sounds, the most perfect stillness reigns. Without a single preliminary 'hem,' or a moment's pause for the purpose of collecting his ideas, he at once commences the elucidation of his theme, and before he has uttered half a dozen sentences it is evident enough that all his matter has been carefully arranged beforehand. There is not the slightest hesitation; his words and ideas flow forth like a clear, continuous stream, and they are as transparent too. Perhaps there is not a firmer or more fearless preacher than the doctor, a fact which has been proved over and over again of late, as his Romish antagonists have found to their cost.

"Often have we heard Dr. Cumming, but never without having noticed that he referred either to the Apocalyptic mysteries or to Papacy. These are his two great topics. His 'Sketches' on the former subject must be familiar to every reader of Scriptural literature, and therefore it will be needless for me to add anything on this point further than that by many able persons it is considered Dr. Cumming is mistaken in many of the predictions which he utters, and that his great abilities are wasted on mysteries which, after all, are unfathomable by mortal mind. With respect to the Roman Catholic Church, he has long been known as one of its most vigorous, consistent, and uncompromising foes. As a controversalist he is truly great. No man can dissect Popery so fearlessly, so mercilessly as he. There is not a web of sophistry, however artfully woven, which he cannot disentangle, and his profound learning, great sagacity, and extensive acquaintance with his subject render him the most dangerous enemy which Cardinal Wiseman has in these realms."

Dr. Cumming is a very voluminous author, but we cannot, in this place, more than generally allude to his writings. The sale of his works is prodigious. It would be difficult for one not at all acquainted with the religious views of Dr. C. to realize from Mr. Dix's sketch that he has for some forty years made the second personal and immediate advent of Christ a special theme. This is what Mr. Dix calls "his predictions" and the "Apocalyptic mysteries."

Dr. Cumming's books, which number some fifty volumes, are chiefly his reported sermons, written out by a reporter as he preaches them, and submitted to his inspection and correction. They are of a very practical character, yet all based on the great doctrine of Christ our Sacrifice, Advocate, and soon coming Judge, to reward every man, restore the earth, fill it with his glory, and reign on the throne of David forever. Probably no one man's writings, of this faith, have had so wide a circulation among the popular class of readers of religious works as those of Dr. Cumming. The influence of his views on the immediate coming of Christ has been felt so strongly that the public press of Europe and America have often resorted to falsehood to counteract it, by reporting that he had fixed upon a certain year for the catastrophe, and at other times reporting that Dr. C. had "found an error of a hundred years," or "a thousand years" (once they reported it a million years), in his calculations. Shallow and careless ministers have echoed it to the churches to allay their interest in the subject. We have circulated over 1,000 copies of Dr. C.'s books in Maine, and seen much good result from their influence. We have possessed thirty-three different volumes of them in our own library.

In 1848, Dr. John Cumming, in lectures delivered in Exeter Hall, London, before five thousand people, said:

> "The sixth vial, I have told you, is already poured out; its effects are now in action. Nations feel it. The seventh is ready to be poured out; or, if not already pouring out, we are upon the very verge of its being so. It trembles in the hand of the angel. The effect of its action, the moment it is poured out, is that the *air of heaven*,—the symbolic air mainly, I believe, though the *literal air*, according to others, may be included also,—will be affected, or darkened, or tainted, in some way, by its influence. Certainly, we gather from this prophecy one fact, at least, that the action of this vial will not be like previous ones, local, but universal. *The air* is the most universally present element we have or know.
>
> "So we may expect here that this *tainting of the atmosphere* is, primarily indeed, a moral and social influence; but, secondarily and subordinately, a literal and actual influence on the *atmospheric air*. We may, therefore, expect the physical air will be tainted as well as the moral one."

Dr. Cumming then proceeded to specify influenza, cholera, miasma, etc., as being the effects of this vial, and appealed to all the medical men in the house if it were not the fact that there was *a taint in the atmosphere.* He then instanced aerial changes, miasmas, political and church confusion, strange notions of divine truth, awful heresies, new and extraordinary schemes, rocking thrones, subverted dynasties, trembling among the rich and poor, dislocation and disintegration of things, all to be magnified a thousand fold when these calamities were at their height, as being at the door. How this calculation has been verified in the *convulsions* and remarkable changes going on for over twenty years *in the air*, and noticed by scientific men generally, every careful reader can readily perceive. In a more recent lecture on the prospects of the Papacy and of the Church, Dr. C. made the following statements on the

DOOM OF THE PAPAL HIERARCHY.

"The Papacy is to be destroyed finally by a miracle; I appeal for evidence to the prediction in the Thessalonians, 'Whom the Lord shall consume with the Spirit of his mouth, and destroy by the brightness of his own personal appearing.' We shall succeed in consuming and wasting it, but the great skeleton, awfully corrupt and overshadowing, will still survive to be swept away by the brightness of Christ's appearing. If persons say we do not see the appearance of it now, we answer, everything is going on exactly as it was predicted. Romanism, broken and shattered, is making its last and most desperate effort to regain a foothold in Europe, and in this country it has influence. But the present struggle of Rome, instead of being discouraging, is the reverse, for it forebodes dissolution. When was it that the handwriting came forth on the wall and wrote, 'MENE, MENE, TEKEL, UPHARSIN—thou art weighed in the balances and found wanting?' Just when Belshazzar was in all his glory, with his golden cups stolen from God's people, feasting with his counsellors and mocking at the name of God. Then was it that ancient Babylon passed away, its gates burst open, its rivers dried up, and the Mede and Persian thundered at the doors of its palaces; and similarly, just when Nebuchadnezzar, in all his pride and glory, was saying, 'Is not this great Babylon that I have built by the might of my power, and for the glory of my name?' at that very moment the kingdom was taken away from him. And so will it be with the antitype. Just while Papal Babylon is boasting and blaspheming it will go down like a millstone into the depths of the sea, and the voice of the bride, and the bridegroom, and the harper, and the musician shall be heard in it no more at all. And afterwards will follow the descent of the New Jerusalem as a bride prepared for the bridegroom, and the paradisiacal state of the world in its last times."

OUR PRESENT POSITION.

Rev. E. B. Elliot, of England, wrote much valuable matter on the prophecies of Daniel and the Apocalypse. Many have considered his elaborate work entitled "*Horæ Apocalypticæ*" the most learned and thorough exposition of the Apocalypse ever published. In his closing chapter, written some twenty-five years ago, he remarks:

"With regard to *our present position*, we have been led, as the result of our investigations, to fix it at but a short time from the end of the now existing dispensation and the expected second Advent of Christ. This thought, when we seriously attempt to realize it, must be felt to be a very startling as well as solemn one. Can it be that we are come so near to the day of the Son of Man that the generation now alive shall very possibly not have passed away before its fulfillment; yea, that perhaps even our own eyes may witness, without the intervention of death, that astonishing event of the consummation?"

REV. HORATIUS BONAR, D. D.

Mr. Bonar, of Kelso, Scotland, is author of the well-known "Kelso Tracts," a very valuable series. Several books of his writing have also been widely known. "Night of Weeping," "Morning of Joy," and "Eternal Day" are among them. Mr. B. is a man of deep piety and simplicity. During the last twenty-five years he has published one of the most valuable periodicals known, "*The London Quarterly Journal of Prophecy*." This journal has filled an important place in English religious literature, and has been instrumental in leading many to study and understand the prophetic Scriptures and thereby to look with ardent hope for the immediate coming of the Lord. In 1873, Mr. Bonar closed up his work of publishing this periodical. We extract the following from his farewell address in his closing number:

OUR LAST.

"In October, 1848, we published our first number; and now, in October, 1873, we publish our last.

"We were smiled at when we began our work, as re-attempting what had been often tried but never succeeded, and what never would succeed. The adversaries of prophetic study, and especially some of our post-millennial friends, began to prophesy concerning us, and to fix dates, predicting that in two years at furthest we should be no more.

"By the good hand of God upon us, we have survived the predicted period considerably, and have disappointed our opponents by upwards of twenty years, having published no less than one hundred and one numbers, or twenty-five volumes, while during this period we have seen several similar periodicals go down.

"Our circulation has not been very large, but it has been sufficient to enable us to go on so far without loss to any one. Various reasons, however, into which we shall not enter, incline us to close and to bid our readers farewell.

"We trust that we have been in some measure useful, both in maintaining truth and exposing error,—not prophetical truth or error only, but theological as well. We trust that we have done something towards resisting the torrent of strange doctrines so vehemently and so variously overflowing us in these last days."

GEORGE MULLER'S VIEWS.

Mr. Müller is extensively known as "the man of faith," having founded several orphan houses and brought up thousands of orphans with means received of the Lord, in answer to the prayer of faith, without ever soliciting aid from any human being.

His "Life of Trust," as republished in this country is a very interesting book and shows some of the most remarkable workings of the "guiding hand" of God in using this man of faith to accomplish great ends. But Dr. Wayland left out much of what is published in the English edition on the theological views of this man of God. Perhaps it was more than he wished the American readers to know, that George Müller was a thorough pre-millennial Adventist. This is the fact clearly stated in the English edition. He constantly teaches the doctrine of the Lord's immediate advent to restore all things. He has religious services connected with his orphanages, where those under his charge are in attendance upon the preaching of the word and the Sabbath school. He also has a school especially for the study of Scripture theology, and the preparation of those who are called to the work of the ministry or mission labor. Many have gone out from these orphan houses, enriched by the grace of salvation from sin and the joyous hope of a home, with plenty, in the coming kingdom of God, to preach the unsearchable riches of Christ and his soon coming in his glory.

One of these orphans attended a meeting which the writer was holding in the mission tent, a few years since, and at the close of the sermon arose to witness to the truths he had heard, and added: "I am one of the orphans from Mr. Müller's orphan houses in Bristol, Eng. He was the first man I ever heard preach about Christ's coming. He preaches it as you do and believes he is coming soon." After the services were ended we had an interesting interview with this orphan. He informed us that Mr. Müller instructed all his pupils in the doctrine of Christ's soon coming and of the restitution of the earth as the final abode of the saints. He believed this was one of the causes of his great success, through the abundant blessing of God.

A SECOND EUROPEAN MISSION.

In 1865, Eld. M. B. Czechowski, a native of Poland, and formerly a Roman Catholic Priest, but converted to Protestantism and to the Second Advent faith while in America, felt strongly impressed with the duty of going to Europe to proclaim the Advent Message. He received encouragement from the New England General Conference of Adventists, who recommended him to Christians abroad and contributed money, raised as a "European Mission Fund," to sustain him. He was an intelligent, educated, and pious man, well fitted to travel among strangers with such important tidings as the message of the Lord's immediate coming, being able to speak several languages. He visited Switzerland and Italy, preached in many towns, publishing and scattering tracts as he went. The Lord blessed his efforts, and several churches of believers were gathered, and many Christian hearts received the word with readiness of mind, also several ministers embraced the faith. The reports which he gave of his labors, for some two years, from those parts of Europe which he visited, were very interesting and encouraging. We suppose he is still in that country as he has not returned to this, but we have heard nothing from him of late. Having become a Sabbatarian, and allowing that theme to absorb his special interest, it had neutralized his efforts and cut off his usefulness in the great work which led him into that important field. This has proved the same with some others. When those enlightened upon the subject of Christ's soon coming turn their attention to preaching some other theme except repentance and faith as a preparation their labors usually cease to be of benefit to the church or world.

THE LIGHT DISCOVERED FROM ANOTHER STANDPOINT.

We have already mentioned in another chapter that Messrs. Dobney, Ham, Whateley, White, Moncrief, and other eminent ministers of England, Scotland, and Ireland, had come to the decision, after much investigation and critical study, that the dogma of the soul's immortality was a heathen superstition and contrary to the teachings of the Bible. They wrote and published the results of their researches, showing that the Scriptures promise immortality to believers in Christ, and the final destruction of not "the man of sin" only, but *all sinners who continue in sin*, at the coming of Christ as the appointed Judge of mankind. As this view awakened discussion on a class of Scriptures which of necessity turned the attention to the coming of the "Life Giver" to bestow the reward and to "render to every man according as his work shall be," they who embraced the doctrine became interested to know whether this day of universal reward was remote or at hand. This led them to the study of prophecy, and thus an interest has sprung up upon the subject of Christ's coming from another quarter and is taking a wide range and destined to produce a much more direct and Scriptural interest in the theme than has before been produced, but not without much opposition. We will here quote an article from the editorial columns of "The Christian World" (Congregational), London, England, written in 1868:

"The many books and pamphlets that have been published of late upon the subject of the future punishment of the wicked confirm the conviction, to which we gave expression a few months ago, that a great number of the most devout and thoughtful persons in our churches are deeply exercised regarding it and anxiously desirous of ascertaining the real teaching of Holy Scripture thereupon. To those who have had no doubts upon the subject, this questioning of the current teaching in our pulpits and religious books may seem alike unnecessary and absurd; but, as a matter of fact, the momentous theme has come up for reconsideration and cannot be repressed by mere dogmatic assertions. And while recognizing the fact, it would be well for all of us to be fully assured of this, that the rejection of the doctrine of eternal torment does not necessarily imply the giving up of a single essential doctrine of the gospel, and that, therefore, there ought to be no calling of names. 'Sceptic,' 'heretic,' 'infidel,' and the like are wholly out of place and should never be used in such a controversy, for it happens that a considerable number of our unquestionably evangelical ministers, both Episcopal and Nonconformist, have avowed their disbelief in the creed that satisfied a former age, and themselves also, in bygone days. It would be well, moreover, to remember that whatever opinions may prevail the real truth will remain the same; that the future will not be altered to us, or to a single human soul, in consequence of any man's opinions. People are often apt to forget this very manifest truth in a time of theological debate, but the recollection of it will do much towards keeping our minds calm, even when the very foundations of our faith may be assailed. . . .

"It is not a little startling to find the extent to which this opinion is spreading in our evangelical churches. Several well-known ministers, whose orthodoxy on other points is as firmly fixed as ever, have ventured to brave the opposition, sure to arise, by writing boldly and earnestly in support of this new reading of the many declarations of the New Testament, to the effect that life and immortality come only by accepting the Gospel of Christ. These names include a Baptist, the Rev. William Miall; Congregationalists, the Rev. E. White, Rev. Dr. Leask, and many others; and it is stated that one of the rising leaders of this section of Nonconformists is about to issue a book on the same side that will certainly arouse the attention of the whole church to which he belongs. Of the Episcopalian clergy, quite a host have declared themselves on this side of late. The Rev. William Ker, M. A., Vicar of Tipton, has published a very elaborate argument, and more recently the Rev. Samuel Minton, M. A., minister of Eaton Chapel, Eaton Square, has

WILLIAM LEASK, D.D.—Page 557.

penned a powerful letter to Mr. Robert Baxter, reviewing the whole controversy, and declaring explicitly for the views set forth by Mr. White, whose communication to us may be regarded as an epitome of the facts and arguments relied upon by this growing party in our Christian society."

Since the above article these great gospel truths have been rapidly gaining among the real believers in the Bible.

REV. WM. LEASK, D. D., AND THE "RAINBOW."

Dr. Wm. Leask is among those now engaged in the theological reform going on in Europe on the faith of the gospel, relating to Christ's soon coming and the nature of rewards and punishment. He is editor of "The Rainbow," a monthly magazine of Christian literature, with special reference to the *revealed future* of the Church and the world. The Dr. has written some important papers on the nature of future punishment, the gift of eternal life, and the coming and kingdom of Christ.

We will here give an extract from a notice of Dr. L. and the Rainbow, by Eld. W. Kelleway, an English correspondent to the World's Crisis.

"You are so well acquainted with the *Rainbow*, and have so often published precious articles from its pages, that the name of this excellent monthly will not be strange to you. On Saturday, Bro. Brown and myself had the pleasure of meeting its able editor and conductor, according to appointment, at his residence in Sandringham Road, and spending with him an hour in conversation on the state and prospects of the truth in England. We found in the Dr. all that cordiality, energy, and emphasis we expected, and when we left his house did so hoping that the future, although as we believe short, would witness our friendship and mutual efforts for the cause of Christ advance, deepen, and strengthen. I think some facts concerning the Dr., and the magazine he pilots, will be of interest to you. I shall, therefore, presume to give them.

"A few years ago, while I was carrying on the business of printer and publisher in a fashionable watering place in the south of England, and was scattering from the press with full and bountiful hand the seeds of truth, it was one day told me that an established monthly, of good reputation and sterling ability, had declared on the side of truth which we espouse, and had made its appearance for the current month with a trenchant article on *Immortality.* I lost no time in procuring a copy, and when I opened it, sure enough, there it was, a long dissertation by William Maude, covering some pages of the magazine. Of that article I may say, it was scarcely what we should consider affirmative, in the sense of taking a position on the point. It was simply suggestive in its construction, limiting the possible falsity of the commonly-received opinions touching endless sin, torture, and woe. But one very good feature of it was, it declared the principal arguments in favor of eternal life through Christ only.

"Against this gentle pressure of the theological pulse of the readers of the *Rainbow* arose a secret, dastardly, and decided opposition. Threats of discontinuance of patronage of the *Rainbow* were poured in, and the sales and subscriptions ran down to an alarming extent, till it appeared as if the *Rainbow* must suspend publication. But God showed that he was not depending on man, and where he chooses and appoints a testimony he will sustain it for his name. No matter though its sales were smaller than formerly, and its subscription list had thinned, and its old and enthusiastic admirers had anathematized it and consigned it to 'annihilation,' the Lord prospered it sufficiently, so that, if it did not command a popular circulation, it lived, and still preached the gospel of the kingdom of God, and the sister truth of eternal life alone through Christ.

"Vain are the 'bulls' of indignant Protestants when God wills to bless altogether! Who can curse what God has not cursed? And so it lived, and did not bite the dust, dying a foul death by strangulation.

"At this time the *Rainbow* was not 'committed' to the truth, in the sense of being an exponent and defender of the faith; discussion was freely admitted in its pages, and many well-known authors and teachers wrote, according to their various predilections and views, discussing the subject up for consideration. The first aspect of the controversy appeared in the part played by those who held to the old dogma of the soul's natural immortality. They wrote in an affected and lordly manner, trying to overthrow the glory of revelation,—that eternal life is a *gift* of sovereign grace and divine goodness,—to erect in its place the heathen notion of the necessary and eternal being of a conscious and separate soul. As you will think, their arguments fell through; for, from being futile, they became scarce, till they finally ceased and were no more seen. The effect, however, of the articles written with the force and in the authority of infallibility was that it brought out hundreds who have embraced the 'truth,'—'truth' that eternal being is not of our own natures, or an entailment of our constitution, but a great gift of divine and peerless mercy to all believers.

"However, there has been a great conflict for the *pure* and *whole* truth. Many had been so refinedly spiritualistic that it is easily imaginable that one stride would scarcely make them wholly real in faith. And so many modified their faith so far as to accept the fact of the ultimate ending of the sinner and his life, but they still retained many strange incongruities prejudicial to the interests of truth. Instead of making clean work of the error, and washing their hands of the last defiling stains of this spiritualistic dogma, they held on to the soul as a distinct, inside, separable, spirit-entity, self-conscious, and divisible from the body at death. They held on likewise to its conscious intermediate life between death and the resurrection, and some contended that, though it would be finally destroyed, yet it might take a thousand years or even more to make a full end of it.

"One great hindrance to these brethren's acceptation of the whole truth, inclusive of the unconsciousness of the dead, has been found in a name, which many have feared to have applied to them; I refer to the term 'materialist.' In England this is an epithet of great reproach, and one called by this name is considered almost as bad as an infidel,—a kind of next kinsman, or as one but a step away from infidelity.

"But there have been many men who, fearing nothing, and none but God, and not despising any cross for Christ's sake, have committed themselves to a confession of the old and true Hebraistic faith without reserve, committing their dead in unconsciousness to the care and memory of God in Christ, cherishing for them the good old hope of a resurrection of the dead. These, of course, believe in no separable, conscious part, distinct from the body, and so teach that when men die they are dead, their thoughts cease, their feelings vanish, their consciousness and knowledge alike perish, till God rebuilds them and calls for the breath to re-enter them that they may live.

"Mr. Constable was selected to write articles on *Hades.* They were very ably commenced, and gave great promise for the interest of truth, when all at once they stopped. It was a pity, for his lines were as the track of a stream of sunlight. Some readers wished to know *why* they were discontinued.

"It seems that in consequence of Bro. Constable's articles the *Rainbow* was again dwindling in circulation. In a month or two it had fallen by hundreds, and in order to save the magazine for the main subject,—the coming of the Lord,—it was considered wise to withhold the remaining articles on *Hades*, at least for a time. What was the effect? The very next month the magazine rose again, and has been rising ever since.

"Mr. Constable and others take the view of their Advent brethren of America. The editor is with us and is known to be a believer in this simplest of problems,—'When a man's dead he *is* dead.'

"If rumors are true, these intermediate-state friends will soon issue a monthly of their own, when you may expect the worthy Dr. and editor of the *Rainbow* will be pressed to take a decided and defined position in his monthly. I think Dr. Leask is no trimmer or man-pleaser; but he likes to give a chance and hearing to all. I know the arrangement between the Prebendary and the Dr. has been made for the best of purposes and for the ultimate and permanent gain of the cause."

Rev. Henry Constable, referred to above (late Prebendary of Cork, Ireland), is now Chaplain to the City of London Hospital. His "Articles on Hades," now published in book form, are in the market. It is, probably, the most able and convincing work ever published on that subject, excepting the Bible. It is the Bible *argued.* The English "Church Messenger" says of it:

"It is characterized by his usual vigor of thought and clearness of expression. To all sincere lovers of truth, rather than of tradition, we cordially commend the treatise."

Mr. Constable has also written several other works, among which is one entitled "The Duration and Nature of Future Punishment." This is a work of 330 pages, and is perhaps the best work ever published as an argument thoroughly sustained on this point. *The Nonconformist*, of the English press, says:

"Mr. Constable has, in a series of works, devoted much labor and research to establish from Scripture and other sources the real nature of the future state. His argument is supported by no little learning, a keen logic, and a clear and available style. There is a good deal to be said for the general doctrines propounded."

Thus it is manifest that while the enemies of the truth are multiplying, yet there are some true friends of the Bible, and they are studiously engaged in bringing out its rich treasures from God's treasury and clearing them from the heathen dogmas which have done so much to disparage and degrade the Christian religion. While time continues this discussion must continue between Spiritism and Bible Materialism, or the dogma of the immateriality of the soul and its spirit existence without a body, and the doctrine of man's entire mortality, with the offer of immortality, through faith in Christ, at the resurrection.

SECOND ADVENT CONFERENCE IN LONDON.

An important measure was adopted by some of our Advent brethren in Europe in 1873. After some consultation with a few of the friends of the cause, a call was published in the leading religious organs of the land for a "Second Advent Conference, to be holden in St. George's Hall, London, May 5th to 10th." This Conference was numerously attended by interested believers and was a season of much interest. Some of the chief men in high stations attended and took active part in the services, and several made speeches.

Lord Shaftsbury was chairman of the meeting, and by solicitation made a speech on the importance of the subject of Christ's return and the duty of constantly watching for him and being in readiness to meet him. The subjects discussed were, "The Man of Sin," "Papacy," "The Second Advent of Christ," "The Signs of the Times," and "The Practical Duties of the Church at the Present Time." The chief speakers were R. W. Dibdin, Dr. Nolan, W. Haslam, C. Skrine, Mr. Dalton, S. A. Blackwood, Canon Frevor, R.

Baxter, D. C. Marston, Lord Shaftsbury, Right Hon. the Earl of Cavon, Mr. John Jones, Rev. S. A. Walker, Lord Radstock, General Alexander, Rev. G. E. Tate, Rev. H. Atkinson, Rev. J. R. Jagoe, Rev. G. W. Stratton, Rev. W. Kelleway, and Col. Lavie.

The report of the Conference, by Eld. W. Kelleway, shows it to have been a meeting of much interest and importance in calling the attention of the public to this glorious theme. Every such gathering sounds out the news that some of the friends of Jesus are looking and longing for his return. This gathering of the believers in conference is to become a yearly institution in England while time continues. This will greatly advance the interest of the cause. There is no distinct sect or body of Adventists in England, but many members in all the churches are much interested in Christ's immediate advent. Although there are many of different views, there is not that malignant opposition and hatred manifested against it as in the American churches. The Established Church has the subject of Christ's advent, the resurrection, and judgment clearly stated in their articles of faith, and many of their ministers preach much more upon these themes than ministers in America do. Their literature constantly directs the attention of the reader to it as a subject of much importance, though often mixed with various absurdities. The Plymouth brethren preach much upon Christ's soon coming, but they mix so many crotchets with their teachings it nullifies the doctrine. The Christadelphians and Disciples also preach that Christ is soon coming. There are three or four local churches of Second Adventists where the Advent Message is distinctly proclaimed.

The literature of Second Advent views is very extensive in Great Britain, but it is mostly mixed with the idea of the Jews' return; yet many of the works are very valuable. There are also many able ministers in that country who are bold and decided advocates of the pre-millennial and immediate advent, but are too narrow in their views to take in the light, as yet, on the subject of immortality and eternal life as the special gift of God in Christ. The religious papers of England and Scotland are of a very different tone from those of America on these subjects. Those of the Established Church publish much on the Second Advent. The Free Scotch Church and other sects mentioned do the same. There are several undenominational monthlies, "The Hebrew Witness," "The Rainbow," "The Signs of our Times," and "The Last Vials." These make the immediate advent a prominent theme and argue the evidences of it. These mighty truths of God's word cannot be buried, banished, nor kept out of sight. Our God revealed them to feed the faith and hope of his Church, and to awaken and enlist the attention and move the hearts of sinners towards him, and he has shown that these truths would be especially needed in the closing days of probationary time, to meet the exigencies of the times and resist the tide of error which would encumber the Church. The faithful of the flock of God will continue to awake and study, and compare the startling events of our times with the sure word of prophecy. The light will break in upon their faith and awaken their hope until they too will sound the cry, "Behold, the bridegroom cometh; go ye out to meet him," and "Behold, thy salvation cometh. His reward is with him and his work before him."

Every year which passes brings new and interesting cases of men of mind, of piety, of learning, of influence, becoming deeply interested in this great fact, the Lord is soon coming. Men who have buried their minds in other themes, taxed their brains to the fullest capacity in other studies, and who have thought this subject forbidden, hidden, and of no use to the Christian teacher, have felt called upon, finally, to look at facts which often stared them fairly in the face, and then turn to the Scriptures and learn the meaning of these things. Mr. Spurgeon, the minister of fame, as a great teacher in the gospel, has now declared his faith that the Lord will soon appear in his glory and judge the world in righteousness and establish his everlasting reign on the throne of David. Amen, even so, come Lord Jesus.

REBUKING THE NATIONS.

Divine legislation is indispensable to the welfare of men, and that legislation to be effectual must be enforced by divine power. The law of Sinai and the gospel of Calvary, both divine, have been long in this world; but "the prince of this world," who hates both, is still at large and, without difficulty, gets his multitudinous subjects to trample on the one and reject the other. For proof look around you! Take all the states, and kingdoms, and empires, all the islands and continents of the broad earth, and say whether the evidence is not overwhelming that some desperately evil and malignant power is constantly at work through the agency of men. Satan, the adversary, the devil, the prince of the power of the air, the god of this world, is untiringly active as a liar, a spoiler, a murderer, a destroyer. It is vain to talk of improving and blessing humanity, and bringing in the reign of universal brotherhood by education, and science, and commercial interests, while this awfully evil being is lord of the kingdoms. He said to Christ that the kingdoms are in his power, and he was not contradicted! Our Lord speaks of him as the prince of this world. This gigantic foe of God and man is not to be cast down from his dark supremacy by any wisdom of statesmen or work of ecclesiastics. He is too wise and too strong for them. A stronger than he must do that, and the honor is reserved for him whom saints delight to honor, the Anointed of Jehovah, the Man of God's right hand, whom he hath made strong for himself. . . . Some time ago a gentleman quoted, for our benefit, as a proof that the church is destined to convert the world to Christ, the following words: "Ask of me, and I shall give thee the heathen for thine inheritance, and the uttermost parts of the earth for thy possession."

"Pray proceed," said we. "What is the result?"

"Their conversion to Christianity, of course."

"Well, no; the next sentence is, 'Thou shalt break them with a rod of iron; thou shalt dash them in pieces like a potter's vessel.' And such will be the terrible experience of the Lord's enemies when he riseth up to the long-delayed battle."

"You astonish me!" said our friend, after a long pause.

"I! What have I to do with it? They are the words of inspiration regarding the King that Jehovah will set upon his holy hill of Zion; has set in 'decree,' will set in fact; and, as a Christian man, you will surely agree with me in thinking that we are bound to believe them."

"Well, but, sir, our minister—"

"Hush! not a syllable, if you please. Your minister is an excellent man, whom I love, both for the sake of his work and his character; but I am profoundly impressed with the conviction that it is high time for us all to take up the Bible and see for ourselves what God has really said to us."

Christians, living, as they do, under the dispensation of grace, are too apt to forget that a time comes when the sword of justice will be drawn from its sheath to execute the long-delayed judgments of heaven. "For, behold, the Lord will come with fire, and with his chariots like a whirlwind, to render his anger with fury, and his rebuke with flames of fire. For by fire and by his sword will the Lord plead with all flesh; and the slain of the Lord shall be many." Isa. lxvi. 15, 16.—*Rainbow.*

A NEW INTEREST IN THE CAUSE.

Bro. Moody, of Chicago, Ill., the leading man in America among the "Young Men's Christian Associations," and who has accomplished much under God in gathering souls to Christ, has long been a believer in the speedy advent of Christ, although he has not made it very prominent in his teaching until recently. He is now in Europe and great reformations are reported in the papers as attending his labors there. From English papers we have the following:

"Sunday morning, March 15, 1874, at the early hour of nine o'clock, Mr. Moody gave an address in the City Hall, Glasgow, Scotland, to one of the most distinguished audiences which it has been his privilege to address since he and Mr. Sankey landed in England. The meeting was advertised for "Christian young men" especially, and was presided over by John Burns, Esq., the principal owner of the Cunard line of steamers. Nearly two hundred of the leading gentlemen of the city were on the platform, including the Lord Provost, while the body of the hall was crowded with upwards of 3,000 people. Mr. Moody's subject was 'Daniel,' and occupied about an hour in delivery. His audience was deeply interested. In reviewing the life of the prophet he made reference to Nebuchadnezzar's dream.

"Mr. Moody explained that the prophetic image represents the history of the four Gentile empires from Nebuchadnezzar's time down to the future end of this Gentile dispensation and the Second Advent of Christ."

He is reported as giving a clear exposition of that portion of prophecy, stating that the stone represents that Christ at his coming who will overturn and destroy the kingdoms of this world, which will then "become the kingdoms of our Lord and his Christ." Mr. Moody adds:

"I don't think the day is far distant when the Lord will return. 'As the days of Noe were, so shall also the coming of the Son of man be. For as in the days that were before the flood, they were eating and drinking, marrying and giving in marriage, until the day that Noe entered into the ark, and knew not until the flood came and took them all away: so shall also the coming of the Son of man be' (Matt. xxiv. 37–39). Just as the judgment overtook Belshazzar, carousing at his feast, so will judgment come suddenly and swiftly upon the world revelling in its sins."

"At eleven o'clock the same morning," says the London "Christian," "Mr. Moody preached in Finnieston Free Church, taking up the subject of Christ's Second Coming. With his usual power he showed what a mighty motive this doctrine is to all who are winning souls. He himself had found it rousing him to tenfold more effort to save all that could be rescued from the coming wreck."

CHAPTER XVIII.

West India mission—I. C. Wellcome—Unabated interest—J. M. Orrock—Theological and Literary Journal—Wm. Sheldon—Death oe Mr. Miller—H. L. Hastings—The Advent Watchman—The Watchman—Pnumatologist—Spiritism—Miles Grant—New York Conference and Judaism—Revivals—The World's Crisis—Advent Christian Association—A strange saying—C. F. Hudson—American Second Advent Missionary Society—American Millennial Association.

WEST INDIA MISSION.

In the latter part of 1846, Eld. L. D. Mansfield and wife, then of Cleveland, Ohio, sailed for the British West India Islands, on a mission, to proclaim the message of Christ's immediate coming. They arrived in November and entered upon their work, sowing the gospel of the kingdom of God as the Lord opened the way; but they found the ministry and church guardians, generally, opposed to the message, as they were in most cases throughout Christendom, yet "the common people heard" and read "gladly," as in the case of Christ's own ministry. We will give a few extracts from Bro. Mansfield's letters of correspondence to the Advent Herald. He says:

"On the second Sabbath after our arrival, being 'Advent season,' the 'Venerable Archdeacon' Holberton preached upon the subject of our Lord's coming, and took occasion to say that 'it was peculiarly his duty to admonish the flock in reference to that subject, advise them of the truth, and especially at that time, as he had been informed of the arrival of persons from the United States, who fixed the time for this event, and who were proved, by the failure in their expectations, to be *fanatics;*' and also descanted upon the evils which had been brought upon many in America on account of this fanaticism.

"On the following Monday I sent him a number of publications, among which were a report of one of the early Conferences, a copy of the addresses contained in the Supplement to the Herald, Hale's chronology, the Herald Extra, etc. I also enclosed nearly the same works to the Presbyterian, the

Wesleyan, and the Moravian (or, as they call themselves, 'United Brethren') ministers. The people, having heard we would distribute tracts and papers from our residence, flocked in great numbers to our doors, so that for several days we were thronged much of the time by applicants for papers. It was astonishing with what avidity the publications were sought. We have been visited by many intelligent persons,—Wesleyan clergymen and official members of that church,—with whom we had much interesting conversation, and to whom we gave publications."

After fully testing the unchristian spirit of the ministry of the place, and not finding any house in which to preach, Bro. M. appointed meetings and preached in the open air to good and attentive audiences. This awakened the feelings of one Christian gentleman, a Mr. Ick, to realize the disgrace which the ministry were bringing upon Christianity, among the heathen, by shutting their meeting-houses against a faithful gospel missionary who had come to labor for the salvation of his fellow-men. He expressed his mind upon this matter, and, being president of the "Mechanics Institution," came forward and gave Bro. M. the use of its rooms, which he occupied for meetings, free of charge, for several months, until the Lord opened a larger and better hall.

He gained access to the hearts of many and was permitted to see such fruits of his labors as to show that his mission was not in vain. After speaking of the immorality of the masses in those islands, and of the testimony of Christians that it was rapidly increasing, he says:

"Alas! the church is in an alarming state. Its outward machinery is but a poor substitute for inward purity and zeal, and its sectarian, proselyting spirit but a hypocritical semblance of holy benevolence and ardent love for the souls of men. I was particularly struck with a remark upon the Wesleyans, in the 'Correspondence of the English Mission,' that 'they were more opposed to the Advent doctrine than any other class, and that they were aspiring to a seat by the side of the English Church.' So it is evident that the church, which has made the greatest professions of holiness, is now wanting in the most palpable evidence of piety, 'a love for Christ's appearing.' I must confess there is a great discrepancy between Paul's testimony that 'We who have the first fruits of the Spirit do groan within ourselves, waiting for the . . . redemption of our body,' and the testimony of those who profess to be so full of the Spirit, and yet are quite indifferent about redemption and wish to hear nothing about the Saviour's coming. There are, however, some Wesleyans here who love the doctrine of the Saviour's coming, and are willing to advocate it at the expense of their sectarian reputation. There are

ISAAC C. WELLCOME.—Page 567.

new cases recently where interest is awakened. Last Sabbath we had a most solemn meeting, and many persons arose to express their determination to forsake all for Christ. I baptized four persons in the public bath, and administered the supper to about forty persons, or perhaps more. There is no cause of discouragement in this field, and I feel anxious to have the tidings of the Kingdom spread to other islands, and hope the door may soon be opened by the coming of some brother to my assistance. L. DELOS MANSFIELD.

St. Johns (*Antigua*), May 10, 1847."

This mission was closed up after Bro. Mansfield concluded it his duty to return to the States, as there were no others to enter the field without means to sustain them, and there was not sufficient mission interest to furnish funds for it. But the work which had been done was not lost. We trust some fruits of it will be gathered in the great harvest. On returning to Syracuse, N. Y., 1849, Bro. Mansfield published a paper for a season entitled "The Adventist." It was a good sheet, containing cuts of the symbols of the prophecies of Daniel, and circulated, as tract matter, free.

SKETCH OF ELD. I. C. WELLCOME AND HIS LABORS.

Isaac C. Wellcome is a native of Maine, born in Minot, May 8, 1818. His parents were poor, and during his minority not Christians. His father was, however, a thoroughly read and zealous believer in Universalism, and possessed a large amount of that kind of literature. In his early boyhood they removed into the interior of the State, where he was almost entirely deprived of a school education, but having a desire for information he read almost everything which he could obtain, excepting novels; those he detested from childhood, but worried through two volumes to gratify his comrades. He was obliged to work hard at farming and lumbering constantly and do his reading while others slept. His mother was one of the best and most exemplary of women, and taught her children good morals and industry, by precept and example. Isaac became sceptical early in life, and being almost wholly deprived of hearing gospel ministers, or associating with any who professed Christianity, he thought but little of it. Having an opportunity he read infidel works and, like many others, soon became "a fool" by denying the existence of any God but nature.

At the age of 18 years he became disturbed by the conversion of several associates, and soon after by the conversion of his elder brother. He resorted to the Bible to see what it meant, and soon became perplexed with the doctrines of the New Testament. He next resorted to his father's library for help from books which he had already perused, such authors as John Murray, Thomas Whittemore, Hosea Ballou, C. C. Burr, A. C. Thomas, Belfore, Winchester, and other Universalist ministers. These he had read for entertainment; he now became deeply interested in their doctrines, as they argued away conversion, bridged over the duty of repentance, philosophized away the doctrine of sin and the promise of forgiveness, dissipated the doctrine of rewards and punishment, whittled the doctrine of atonement down to a myth, and advocated the immortality of the soul, claiming it was a part of God and must be eternally holy and happy. He read while others slept or sported. These specious reasonings captivated his mind, and he soon became a confirmed, praying Universalist, in which he continued four years, when through a well-directed train of God's providences his heart was opened, little by little, until he saw himself a great sinner, though strictly moral, and then the Lord opened his mind to see mercy and pardon promised through the blood of Christ. This he sought and obtained, in 1840, through tremblings, tears, and prayers, and before he ever had any church privileges. That year he went to Hallowell, Me., where he became associated with the Methodist Episcopal Church, which he joined, and was an active, living, working member for nearly five years, being at times chided for feeling as united and free to work with the other churches as with his own, and lastly for loving to talk, sing, and pray about Christ's coming to bring the promised kingdom and eternal rest.

In 1842 he read Mr. Miller's lectures and heard several sermons preached on the immediate coming of Christ. He was delighted with the prospect presented and greatly enjoyed the spirit manifested by the believers; but being wholly ignorant of the subject of prophecy and of the real meaning of the promises which relate to the future life, for his ministers never gave any theological instruction on these points, but generally asserted views entirely the reverse of what he now heard, he could only say, "It is a beautiful thought and an excellent hope these men teach. It seems too good to be true, too real to believe." But he "searched the Scriptures daily," or rather nightly, believing he could learn what they taught on this subject. After two years prayerful study of the subject and of listening to and reading the scandal, scoffing, and blackguardism offered in opposition to it, he was constrained to acknowledge that the Bible fully sustained the general views taught by Adventists, excepting the time. This was a subject he considered too deep for him then. He had neither the books nor the ability to decide that the Lord would come on any given year. He was much beloved by the church, and they persuaded, entreated, and flattered; they denounced the system and reviled it and its advocates; they made efforts to intimidate him by referring to the treatment others were receiving,—being dismissed from the churches, refused the right to preach in their meeting-houses, class leaders having their papers taken from them, private members refused the privilege of speaking of this hope in their meetings, etc. But their efforts only confirmed his former convictions that, if Christ's plain truths and his most faithful and humble followers were being turned out of the church, it was time for him to "come out" and share persecution with them, and suffer for Christ and truth's sake. Accordingly, he asked and obtained his dismission, September, 1844, from the church in which he had experienced much real happiness, strong fellowship, and mutual joy in Christian worship and labor, and which still contained many devoted Christians. But truth and duty were esteemed of more value than a social relation which could be no longer retained except at the price of their sacrifice.

He now associated fully with the Advent believers and found his faith and hope greatly increased by the new light which the Scriptures afforded on the return of the Saviour and the eternal abode of the saints in the earth renewed. But he soon came under the influence of those who were preaching with positive assurance that the Lord would come on the tenth day of the seventh Jewish month (Oct. 22d), 1844, and while he wished this might be true he was not competent to decide the argument conclusive. Some urged that all "the wise" would understand it, and all honest hearts could see it. This brought a great trial; he was conscious of being honest with God and his truth, but was not capable of deciding that this time argument was true. After several weeks of careful study and full attention to all the arguments brought to sustain it he came to this decision: These teachers are faithful men of God; they are educated, thoroughly read in history and chronology; they claim to know, they ought to know, what the Lord has revealed on this great subject; they interpret that "the wise shall understand" *the time;* they must be right or they would not be so positive. I will trust *their* conclusions. I believe *they have* the true time. This decision brought great joy, as he ventured to believe he would see the Lord of life and all the redeemed in immortality at a certain time within a few days. He went on growing stronger in this view, as enthusiasm increased, until time proved the argument untrue, when great disappointment was experienced, and during five days he was under a strange cloud. He soon saw, as all may see, that this faith on time was based upon man's wisdom and understanding, and not upon the word of God. Thousands of time believers have been led to take the same course of reasoning he had and believed *their teachers knew the truth,* and have exercised faith in the conclusions of their *teachers* while they thought their faith was resting on the word of the Lord.

When the results of this disappointment had sufficiently passed to allow of careful re-examination, he, with others in the same state of mind, spent several months in as thorough investigation of chronology of the prophetic periods and definite time conclusions as he was capable of, when he decided that while we have arrived at correct conclusions as to the general scope and epochs of chronological data, and a right general use and understanding of the prophetic periods and consecutive prophecies, by which we are assured we are in the closing portion of the Gentile times and near the point of time for the second advent of Christ, yet the Lord has not revealed the events which date the exact starting points of the prophetic periods sufficiently clear to enable the church to determine accurately at what precise point they end.

This decision gave him a settled and unshaken confidence that the Lord is soon to come, and the proclamation which had been and was being made concerning it was a dispensational truth of God, and must continue until Jesus appears in the clouds of heaven. While he has examined all the time arguments which have since appeared, and kept a close watch of the many singular events which have occurred in fulfillment of prophecy, this decision has been constantly strengthened, and he has given his life and energies to do what he could to promote this cause.

It was during this thorough investigation of the Scriptures relating to the failure of time calculations that his attention was called to the Scriptural account of the nature of man, of death, and of the final reward of the wicked. When he embraced Universalism it was by adopting their arguments for the immortality of the soul. When he was converted to Christ the change was great and miraculous to him, and finding he had been so unwise as to accept the views he formerly held he now decided to accept the teachings of Christian men, and concluded what they asserted concerning the dead being in heaven or hell and the wicked suffering eternal pain must be true, as they were teachers of the gospel. When he took his Bible and concordance and drew out every passage on life, death, soul, body, spirit, heaven, hell, punishment, judgment, eternal life, destruction, perish, and their equivalents, he was obliged, against his previous views, to accept the clear, unequivocal, and universal testimony of the Scriptures that man is wholly mortal; that death suspends all power of action and thought of body and soul; that the spirit is not an entity, but the principle of life; that man is wholly dependent on Christ's death for a resurrection, and on the return of Christ and "the first resurrection" for eternal life; that the wicked will rise in the second resurrection and receive the wages due them, which is to "utterly perish" in "the second death." In all his subsequent studies and readings of the discussions which have become so prevalent, and the many criticisms offered upon this subject in the past and recently, he has been more fully confirmed in these views, as the revealed mind of God in Christ, and the only view in true harmony with all parts of the Scriptures.

Early in his Christian experience he was called of God to preach the gospel, but feeling incompetent for such a work he declined, deciding to do all he could to promote the work of Christ by prayer and exhortation in public meetings and elsewhere and the use of his earnings to help others preach; but the Lord's calls are imperative, and he does not excuse from duties he appoints. The first stroke of the rod of chastisement produced a broken constitution and loss of health; the second, the loss of all the property he had accumulated and a heavy debt incurred beside, by "becoming surety for another." In this crippled condition the duty to preach haunted him seven years while trying to be faithful in every other duty. He pleaded ignorance, lack of gift, ill health, and finally that it would be a disgrace to Christianity to preach while owing his fellow-men what he could not pay, and promised the Lord he would try to preach when the way opened to pay his debts. His health soon so improved that he could do more labor; friends came without being asked and offered means to do business with; a plenty of business and success followed, and his debts were soon cancelled.

In 1848, he commenced in much weakness to proclaim the gospel of the kingdom of God as an expounder of Scripture. In 1850, he was ordained, in Boston, Mass., at the General Annual Conference of Adventists. The Lord has been his "shield and buckler" and constant help, until this day, amid trials and afflictions many and blessings innumerable. He cannot speak of having done any good; if good has been done through his labors the Lord has done it. He has given him access to the people, and made him instrumental in opening meetings and proclaiming the Advent Message in about two hundred new places and in preaching to the people in about three hundred towns and districts in Maine; some in several other New England and Western States.

He has never been admired as a preacher, has made no converts to himself, formed no party cliques. He has made it a rule never to send an appointment to a church until he knew they wished him to, and never to preach to a church when he knew that a portion of them were opposed to it; but in new fields he has preached everywhere he found an open door.

During this period he has earned, when in business, several thousands of dollars which he has used in tract and mission work. And while preaching from 100 to 200 discourses and traveling, at his own expense, from 2,000 to 4,000 miles a year, he received during the first nine years an average of $43.44 per year for preaching. This was mission work, in a mission field, and the labor was not in vain. He has seen many souls converted to Christ by the gospel and the Holy Spirit, and a large number of Christians brought to see and embrace the gospel hope and to rejoice in the prospect of Christ's soon coming to give them eternal life. He was at one time elected and served a term of one year on the editorial committee of the World's Crisis. Also, elected and served four years as one of the "Board of the Advent Christian Publication Society;" has been elected twice since, but declined serving. He has been chosen secretary of the Maine A. C. Conference nearly every year and has served about twenty years. He has purchased over ten thousand bound books, and more pamphlets, on the Advent faith, and tracts without number, and circulated them as the Lord opened the way, either by selling or giving (he has served as mission and tract agent many years), and much good fruit has resulted from them. In 1854, he wrote his Treatise on Matt. 24th and 25th chapters, which has gone through six editions. In 1862, he wrote his Pamphlet on War, which has passed through five editions. In 1863, he wrote his Christian Baptism, which has reached its sixth edition. In 1866, he wrote the Plan of Redemption, which has passed through four editions. In 1869, he prepared the Berean's Casket; the first edition is nearly sold. He has published fifteen thousand books of his own and four thousand of Eld. S. S. Brewer's, with over two million pages of tracts of his own writings and selections from others, the most of which have gone on their mission, preaching portions of the gospel.

In 1863, the Lord healed him miraculously of a disease in the spine, caused by an injury, which had worked the ruin of his health for four years, and has blessed him abundantly for eleven years since with physical health and strength, plenty of work, and much spiritual enjoyment; has kept him from overmuch vanity and presumption, and given him prosperity, in a moderate degree, in all his undertakings since he consented to preach the gospel. And although he is wholly unworthy, and has made but poor work and little progress in the divine life, he is enjoying "the blessed hope" of seeing Jesus coming in all his glory during this generation, and through his righteousness to obtain eternal life and enter the eternal inheritance with all the blood-washed throng.

UNABATED INTEREST.

Those who understandingly embraced the views of the advent near, and who consecrated themselves to the work such a faith obligated them, and who had no other interest to serve, have known no abatement of interest in this cause. They have been constantly impelled by the stupendous facts that teach the judgment nigh, and attracted by the blessed hope of soon "seeing the King in his beauty;" and while others vacillated and faltered because of disappointed hope and sullied reputation, or glittering temptations, these kept at the work they believed the Lord had assigned, and trusted him to care for results; this he has graciously done. Elders Himes, Hale, Litch, Burnham, Jones, and others continued to travel and gather the masses under the "big tent," where many thousands were glad to hear and learn the gospel of the Kingdom, the prophecies and history of their fulfillment, the signs of the times, and proximity of the judgment. Bro. Miller, though infirm and health fast failing, responded to numerous calls and gave many lectures in various towns and cities, and was listened to with as profound attention as ever. His "Apology and Defence" was a work which in most respects was well calculated to disarm all candid readers of their prejudices and to convince them of the great truths he had been promulgating to the church. His continued, unabated interest in these truths and his ability to defend them, with the earnest and loving spirit he manifested in doing it, after all the efforts of the chief scholars of the churches and schools, who had exhausted their ingenuity and wit in seeking to explode the doctrine, had failed, added great force to the conviction which many already felt that the message was true, though the specific time was an error. A large number of ministers were constantly holding conferences, camp and protracted meetings, to the extent of time and ability, throughout the Eastern, Middle, and Western States, Canada East and West, and the Provinces of New Brunswick and Nova Scotia. But little access was gained to the churches of the Southern States, because all the ministers of the Second Advent faith were either well-known "anti-slavery" men or opposed to the system, and although they were not disposed to make that subject the point of their efforts, not meddling with politics at all, as they were fully occupied in proclaiming the advent of the great Emancipator of all slaves, black or white, if they believed in him, yet the people who controlled society South had but little desire to have such a class of men among their slaves and the non-slave-holding portions of society, fearing they would sow abolition principles. The Lord in mercy to them all has now broken down that barrier by heavy judgments upon the nation for allowing it to continue so long. Adventists have certainly been in error in their expectations on this point; they had not looked for the abolition of American slavery until Jesus should come to effect it. It is always a relief to confess an error, especially so in this case. The South is now calling loudly for this message. The general call from the thoughtful and pious for preaching and reading matter on the subject of the immediate advent of Christ has been continually augmented by the prevailing coldness and deplorable worldliness manifest everywhere among the great religious bodies. Added to this, crimes in all forms were seen and felt to be constantly on the increase. The faithful and humble followers of Christ wept and prayed over the demoralized condition of their respective churches and the degenerate state of piety which was exhibited, and desired the true gospel of Christ and real reformation. The Advent believers who had continued in the work and those who had rallied to it after being for a time bewildered by the strange vagaries which followed the time movement, together with new recruits which had been converted among them from time to time, and Christians who had embraced the hope, were actively and constantly laboring for the conversion of sinners, the reclaiming of wanderers, the strengthening of believers, and in exposing and reproving the sins of the age, in church and out, by preaching repentance and publishing the great truths of Christ's coming to judge the world in righteousness, to give eternal life to the true Christians, and to destroy all workers of iniquity. And although many of the ministry and other sectarians opposed them, as formerly, and did what they could to shut them out from all opportunities to reach the people, using slang phrases, opprobrious epithets, telling fabulous stories of glaring inconsistencies of Adventists, giving perverted statements of their views and relations to society, to which the managers of the press gave their general influence by publishing them and inventing puns to please their patrons, and in republishing old and exploded falsehoods about them, yet the Lord in his Word and faithful servants was more mighty than all these obstacles. The message continued to awaken attention and gain the faith of candid listeners and readers, and the work of reform has followed. Sinners were thoroughly converted from sin to Christ, and professors of religion, who had been captivated by a worldly, popular religious spirit, were brought to see and realize their lack of genuine piety and to consecrate themselves anew to God and Christian labor, while the Lord bestowed upon them the riches of his grace and gave them an enlarged hope which embraced the things he had promised to those who believe in Christ.

Many who had been taught that the world was nearly converted, and were hoping to live to see the fabled millennium in mortality, began to feel the force of the prophet's words where he describes a similar state of things in former days:

"None calleth for justice, nor *any* pleadeth for truth: they trust in vanity, and speak lies; they conceive mischief, and bring forth iniquity.

"They hatch cockatrice' eggs, and weave the spider's web: he that eateth of their eggs dieth, and that which is crushed breaketh out into a viper.

"Their webs shall not become garments, neither shall they cover themselves with their works: their works *are* works of iniquity, and the act of violence *is* in their hands.

"Their feet run to evil, and they make haste to shed innocent blood: their thoughts *are* thoughts of iniquity; wasting and destruction *are* in their paths.

"The way of peace they know not; and *there is* no judgment in their goings: they have made them crooked paths: whosoever goeth therein shall not know peace.

"Therefore is judgment far from us, neither doth justice overtake us: we wait for light, but behold obscurity; for brightness, *but* we walk in darkness.

"We grope for the wall like the blind, and we grope as if *we had* no eyes: we stumble at noon-day as in the night; we *are* in desolate places as dead *men*.

"In transgressing and lying against the Lord, and departing away from our God, speaking oppression and revolt, conceiving and uttering from the heart words of falsehood.

"And judgment is turned away backward, and justice standeth afar off: for truth is fallen in the street, and equity cannot enter.

"Yea, truth faileth; and he *that* departeth from evil maketh himself a prey: and the Lord saw it, and it displeased him that *there was* no judgment."—Isa. lix. 4–15.

It often occurred to reflecting minds that these persecuted ones might, after all, be doing the work of the Lord. The sound had gone out that the harvest was ripening, that evils would increase until the judgment, that the Lord was soon to come to set up a righteous kingdom and to put an end to sin. Those who were opposed had scoffed at or ridiculed it, or stigmatized those who taught it, and the masses had heard in some form about this people and some items of their views, but in fragmentary or perverted forms; many were impressed by facts continually developing that the Advent Message might have some important truth in it, and they wished to hear and to read (many secretly seeking opportunities), and thus calls have been constantly made, "Come over and help us." New doors have been continually opening where the message had been forbidden. New converts to the faith have been constantly adding interest and strength to the work. Eminent ministers, who had, through prejudice, tradition, and false report, refrained from examining the claims of this subject, have been brought to consider them and to accept the doctrine and publish it. Scholars of all grades, from the learned professors of various branches of education down to the common herdsmen, have become united in the belief that the Lord will soon return to produce the glorious restitution promised. But this has been done through the self-sacrificing and untiring efforts of faithful workers in the Master's vineyard, who believed these truths and gave themselves and all they possessed to the work, God adding his blessing and making the work effectual in producing results.

SKETCH OF ELD. J. M. ORROCK, EDITOR OF THE ADVENT HERALD.

John M. Orrock is a native of Scotland, born near Edinburgh, July 15, 1830. His parents removed to this country and settled in Canada when he was but a boy. At the age of fourteen years he professed faith in Christ and became an active, studious Christian, noted for his critical study of the Bible.

In the early part of 1845, the Rev. John Borland, a Methodist Missionary from England to Canada, preached a sermon on Dan. ii. 44, to refute the doctrine of the Lord's soon coming and to teach the conversion of the world by taking "the stone which smote the image upon the feet" to illustrate the work of the gospel in converting men. The Christian youth, John, read this sermon in print and was so impressed with its absurdity that he wrote a refutation of it, reviewing the main points and giving a Scriptural exposition of the text. It was a thorough explosion of the great man's puny effort, modestly done in a kind and unassuming spirit. Some of the Advent believers in Canada published this review in a *pamphlet* and sent a copy of it to the Advent Herald office. Mr. Bliss, its editor, in noticing it spoke of Mr. Borland as being refuted by a boy fifteen years old. This notice fell into the hands of the Elder and brought upon him such grief that he wrote to the editor claiming reviewer to be older, and offering to discuss with Mr. Bliss in the columns of the Herald. This was accepted and resulted in fully demolishing the Elder's theory. While this discussion was proceeding Eld. B. made use of the following language in reference to Dr. Hutchinson and the youthful reviewer: "Another gentleman, to realize an object dear to him, speaks of a certain youth as 'fifteen years of age,' when he knows, or certainly ought to know, that he is nearer twenty!" This was considered a tacit confession of defeat and a wish to make it appear that the boy was older. To this Mr. Bliss quaintly replied in a note as follows: "As for the 'youth of fifteen,' we presume 'our author' would rather have had his arguments handled in that manner by a boy of twenty; but we know of even younger youths who would not hesitate to disprove them from the Word. By the way, we learn by a correspondent from Canada that this youth, since his victory, is known by the cognomen of 'Jack, the giant-killer.'" It was thought best by his friends to put Mr. B. to the fullest point of reflection as to his wisdom "in the things of the kingdom of God," and they proved John M. Orrock's age, by his parents, to be less than fifteen years, which brought the Elder to the following proper confession: "By the certificate, signed respectively by the father and mother of John M. Orrock, I perceive that my impressions concerning his age were erroneous. I beg therefore to recall the language I used so implicatory of the character of Mr. H., and to apologize for its use."

Bro. O. commenced preaching at the age of eighteen years (being licensed in July, 1848, by Elders J. Litch and R. Hutchinson, in connection with the church of Adventists in Melbourne, P. Q., Canada), and was ordained at the General Annual Conference of Adventists, in Boston, June 5, 1851. He has been studious, judicious, and safe as a preacher and writer. He aided in organizing the Canada and Vt. Conference in 1852 and was its secretary nineteen years. Much of his time has been spent in preaching in Canada, until 1867, chiefly in the capacity of pastor of churches in Shefford, Magog, Waterloo, and Stanstead, with good success. Churches were instructed and strengthened, and sinners awakened and brought to Christ, while the great fundamental truths of the gospel of the kingdom, the fulfillment of prophecy, and signs of Christ's immediate advent were constantly kept before the people. Beside pastoral labor he traveled occasionally as an evangelist, and attended the general meetings in the Province, and aided in promulgating the glorious truths of the coming reign of Christ, in many parts of the Provinces and New England States, as the doors were opened for this message. He also published several pamphlets and tracts, of a very excellent character, and was associated with Eld. R. Hutchinson and Bro. Stephen Foster in publishing a paper, in Montreal, in 1861, entitled "Millennial News." This was filled with valuable matter for the household of faith, and was circulated chiefly in Eastern and Western Canada and Vermont.

Jan. 1, 1867, Eld. Orrock took the editorial charge of the Advent Herald, Boston, Mass., by choice of the Publishing Board of the American Millennial Association, which charge he has held over seven years, giving more than ordinary satisfaction to the publishers and readers of that excellent paper. He was also editor of the "Youth's Visitor," an illustrated child's paper, eight years, published by the same society. As an editor he has but few superiors, of his age, being well stored with knowledge, having a special care for accuracy in history, a good degree of moderation and candor, a clear discrimination between sensational matter and reliable facts, a sound judgment in selecting Christian literature to instruct, strengthen, and build up the believers in Christ, and a good gift to write and teach. In many respects he follows closely in the line of Bro. Bliss, one of the former editors of that paper, and produces a valuable religious journal for the times, although not fully up to our idea of Bible theology on the nature of man, of death, and future punishment. But each must walk in the light as he sees it and reflect it upon others as it shines upon him. We expect "the watchmen will see eye to eye when the Lord brings again Zion," and that day will soon arrive. Then we shall know as we are known.

THE THEOLOGICAL AND LITERARY JOURNAL.

A high-toned and valuable journal with the above title was issued by Franklin Knight, New York, July, 1848, David N. Lord, editor. Mr. Lord had been a prosperous merchant in New York, but seems not to have worshiped mammon. He had a study fitted up in his business establishment, furnished with a library, where he spent much of his time in searching the Scriptures and such other works as made him a thorough Biblical scholar prior to his undertaking of directing the Theological Journal. He had given much attention to the study of prophecy, and became familiar with prophetic figures and symbols. We give an extract from his introduction:

"While Evangelical Protestants acknowledge the whole of the Scriptures as the word of God, and hold it to be the duty of those in the sacred office to master all their teachings and expound them to the people, they still, with few exceptions, from the difficulty of their exposition, give to a part of them a slight attention and assign to them but an inconsiderable value. The last great communication, especially, which God has made to man, in which he asserts his attributes, his right as moral governor, announces the principles on which he conducts his present administration over the Church, exhibits the great actors which have appeared in it and in the political world, perverted his truth, usurped his throne, and persecuted his true worshipers, and foreshown Christ's interposition at length to establish his Kingdom on the earth and redeem the race from the thraldom of sin, they almost totally neglect; not indeed as not presenting anything which it is desirable to know, but as couched under signs so mysterious and equivocal as to render it impossible, satisfactorily, to determine their meaning. That book, accordingly, which presents a larger disclosure of his designs than any other, and the understanding of which is, perhaps, more essential than that of any other to the just conception of the great aims of his government and a comprehension of the past and future, is excluded, in a large degree, from their study and debarred from its legitimate influence on their views, their faith, and their hope.

"Not one in a thousand of the expositors of the word, in discussing the great questions, What are the grounds on which God founds his claims to the homage of men? What are the principles on which he administers his government? What are the aims of his peculiar providential dispensations towards the church? What are his great purposes in respect to the future? What are the means by which truth is at length to be made victorious in its struggle with error? How is the race to be rescued from the bondage of evil? What is to be the destiny of our world? consults, as it seems to me he ought, the great oracle in which these themes are treated and invested with a noon-day light. A portion of the prophecies of Ezekiel, Daniel, and Malachi are in like manner much neglected and excluded from their proper influence on the faith and expectations of the church.

"Is this neglect, however, of the symbolic Scriptures justifiable and wise? Can it accord with the ends for which God made those revelations? Is it consistent with the principles on which Protestantism, as well as religion itself, is founded? If those books are a revelation from him, have they not all the claims to attention with which his authority invests the other parts of his Word? If they treat of the most important questions that teach his designs and the destiny of our race, have they not a title to our consideration proportioned to the interest of those themes? If they present new and peculiar revelations, or throw a clearer light on what is but dimly disclosed in other predictions, is not a knowledge of their teachings requisite to a certainty that the views we have drawn from the other parts of his Word are correct? How can we tell but he there announces new and higher truths that must advance us beyond our former knowledge? How can we be sure but he there indicates purposes that must greatly modify the views we had formed, from other parts of the Scriptures, of his future administration over the world? How do we know but that he there calls us to act in a sphere and fulfill duties essentially unlike those we should otherwise suppose he had assigned us?"

The intelligent reader can at once perceive that this layman sees a meaning in the prophetic Scriptures which but few of the ministry seem to consider, and that these opening questions are to be answered in future numbers of his journal. They *were* answered, giving much sound matter to his readers and sounding out the message of the soon coming and kingdom of our Lord. Several valuable books of "Prophetic Expositions" and "Laws of Figures," all of the pre-millennial stamp, were published in connection with this periodical, much to the edification of many. The Theological and Literary Journal was published, we think, some ten or twelve years, and greatly aided in the general work of arousing the church to the fact that Christ is soon coming to commence a reign of righteousness.

SKETCH OF ELD. WM. SHELDON AND HIS LABORS.

Of the early life of Bro. Wm. Sheldon we have no history, only that he was converted to Christ and became a probationer of the Methodist Episcopal Church on a six months' trial. He embraced the Advent faith in 1842, commenced preaching in 1849, and was ordained to the work of the gospel ministry in 1851. Several of his first years in the ministry were spent in Northern and Western New York. He has preached more or less in eighteen of the States and some in Canada. Since 1857 he has labored mostly in the Northwestern States; he has made one tour in the South with good results. As a preacher, he is direct and clear, generally ready for any occasion which offers an opportunity for the Word. His labors have resulted in bringing many into the faith of the Lord's soon coming and of immortality in Christ alone, while many of the unsaved have been brought to Christ. He is an earnest speaker and a ready writer, and is author of many tracts on the "Life and Death" theme, among which are Gospel Vindicator, Key of Truth, Man's Future State, Immaterialism, Ghostology, Life and Death Theory, Death and the Dead, Life Beyond Death, Going to Heaven at Death, The Disembodied State. Beside these he has written tracts on Prophetic Time, Reign of Messiah, Next Dispensation, The King of Glory, Symbolic Prophecy, The Coming Judgment, Christ's Kingdom, The End of the World, and a book entitled "Adventism." Some of these have been extensively circulated, reaching over 50,000 copies on the free distribution list; others from 5,000 to 10,000. They have accomplished much good service in bringing the gospel hope and signs of Christ's soon coming before the people, and leading many into the truth. Bro. Sheldon was several years corresponding editor of the "World's Crisis;" is now one of the editors of the "Bible Banner," and during 1873 was editor of "The Advent Christian Times," Chicago, Ill. Having resigned that office he has returned to Broadhead, Wis., where he has resided several years in the past. He is an earnest worker in what he undertakes, an original thinker, and doubtless makes some mistakes and imbibes some errors. Who does not? But he has been instrumental in the hand of the Lord of getting much light and truth among the people, and we hope he may be guided in the path of righteousness and gain the eternal rest when Jesus comes and gathers his flock.

MR. MILLER'S DEATH.

Mr. Miller continued to travel and preach at intervals, as his failing health would permit, with his usual earnestness and success up to the spring of 1849, when he wrote to the brethren assembled in the Annual Conference in New York: "My multiplied infirmities admonish me that the time of my departure is drawing nigh." During the following summer he was visited by very many of the ministry and laymen to enjoy their last interview in mortality with that faithful man of God. On the 20th of December he "fell asleep" in the joyful hope of being soon awakened to eternal life by the coming of the Lord for whom he had so confidently waited and faithfully labored. The religious, political, and secular papers, throughout this country and in Europe, gave extended notice of the good man's death, and appended many comments, according to their fancies, prejudices, or judgment, of the character of the man and his work. We append a few as illustrations of the popular mind:

"WILLIAM MILLER.—The celebrated Wm. Miller, distinguished as the founder of the sect known as '*Second Adventists, or Millerites,*' recently died at his residence in the State of New York, at an advanced age. Mr. Miller was one of the remarkable men of the age, and his character, acts, opinions, and ministrations are destined to live and be canvassed by this and succeeding generations. That he was a sincere, devoted, and a good man, we have not a shade of doubt. But in his views he embodied that which was really in advance of much of the learned theology of the day."—*Christian Repository.*

"FATHER MILLER DEAD.—Mr. William Miller, familiarly known as 'Father Miller,' and as 'Miller the Prophet,' died at his home in Hampton, Washington County, on the 20th inst., aged about sixty-eight. Mr. Miller was a native of Pittsfield, Mass., and during the last war with England served as a captain of volunteers on the northern frontier. He began to speak in public assemblies upon the subject of the Millennium in 1833, and in the ten years which preceded the time which he had set for the consummation of all prophecy he labored assiduously in the Middle and Northern States, averaging, it is said, nearly one sermon a day for more than half that period. He was uneducated, and not largely read in even the common English commentaries; his views were absurd and supported but feebly; yet he succeeded in building up a sect of some thirty or forty thousand disciples, which disappeared rapidly after the close of the 'day of probation,' in 1843, after which time Mr. Miller himself did not often advocate or defend his views in public."—*N. Y. Tribune.*

In reply to this a correspondent sent the following, which appeared in the *Tribune* of Dec. 29:

"THE LATE WILLIAM MILLER.—Sir: I saw in your paper of Tuesday a short, incorrect notice of Mr. Wm. Miller, which I presume you will correct, on better information, as you wish others to do so to you when misrepresented.

"You call him 'the Prophet.' In the usual sense of the term he was not, nor ever pretended to be. The only grounds for it was his explaining the prophecies, historically and chronologically, which Bishop Mede, Vitringa, Daubuz, Wesley, Fletcher, Clarke, the Newtons, and some scores of other able, pious, and learned divines of the Episcopal and dissenting churches of England and America have done, with nearly the same manner and result; *i. e.*, they show the prophecies mostly fulfilled, and the chronological periods to terminate near this time, and the Millennium begin. And many, as Dr. Duffield, Dr. Lord, President of Dartmouth College, and President Weethee, of the United States, and Dr. Clinton, Elliott, Birks, Brooks, Cunningham, Noel, etc., of England, that it is in this generation or age they terminate, and the Lord personally comes at the Millennium. Are their views absurd?

"You say 'he was not well read in commentaries,' etc. This is a mistake. In his early life, for many years, he had a great thirst for reading, and had access to several large libraries, as Hon. Matthew Lyon's, Judge James Witherell's, and Alexander Cruikshanks', esq., and in commentaries and history few men were better read. To grammar and the exact sciences he made no pretensions.

"You say he drew for a time 30,000 or 40,000 followers, but they soon disappeared. There were more than 100,000 a while; there are about 50,000 now.

"You say his views were absurd. They appear so to most, we admit, and so do yours on Fourierism, but does that make them so? You call to the test of reason; he to the Scriptures."

"DEATH OF WILLIAM MILLER.—From the manner in which some of our contemporaries, religious as well as secular, notice the departure of this distinguished advocate of the Advent doctrine, we must think they have little of the delicacy of feeling which inclines most men to 'tread lightly on the ashes of the dead.' They speak of him sneeringly as 'Miller the Prophet.' They say he was ignorant, fanatical, feeble, etc., etc. To say such things of a dead man, even though they might be true, would be no proof either of courage or of good taste. But in this case they are not true. Those who knew Mr. Miller knew that, however limited may have been his early educational advantages, he was by no means an ignorant man. He was neither fanatical nor feeble. As a strong and sober reasoner, he proved himself not inferior to many who had enjoyed far greater facilities of mental culture. As to the prophetic character, he never made any pretensions to it. True, he sought earnestly to obey the divine injunction, 'Whoso readeth, let him understand' (Matt. xxiv. 15), and to secure the blessedness pledged to 'him that readeth, and to them that hear the words of the prophecy, and keep the things written therein.—Rev. i. 3. After diligent efforts to discover the significancy of the prophetic numbers, he believed, and hesitated not to declare his belief, that the point indicated by them as that of the second Advent was 'about the year 1843.' But when the passing of that point had proved him to be in error, he was equally frank in acknowledging his mistake."—*Western Christian.*

THE ENGLISH STATEMENT.

Bro. C. A. Thorp writes from Leeds, England, Jan. 24, 1850:

"Bro. Bonham continues to labor very successfully. Not only are the members of the churches where he preaches instructed and edified, but sinners are converted under his ministry. I think it would be well if he would send you an account of his labors and their fruits for publication in the *Herald.*

"I have received the *Heralds* containing the account of Father Miller's death. I can sympathize with you in this bereavement. We feel it as such here. The world, and the Church generally, have not rightly appreciated his labors. But he is now beyond the reach of their malice. O what consolation there is in that blessed assurance that 'he sleeps in Jesus!' We sorrow not for him as those without hope.

"The following unmerited comment appears to be going the round of the papers here. It appeared last week among the *Miscellaneous* of the *Leeds Mercury* and *Leeds Times:*

"'The notorious American fanatic, generally known as "Father Miller," who predicted the destruction of the world and the second coming of Christ in the year 1843, and formed a sect of some 40,000 disciples, died on the 20th of December, at the age of sixty-eight.'"

SKETCH OF ELD. H. L. HASTINGS AND "THE CHRISTIAN."

Horace L. Hastings, son of Eld. King Hastings, was born Nov. 26, 1831, and was brought up in a rural town in Massachusetts, on a farm. But his mind was on books, and he cared more for what he might learn than what he could earn. He was converted to Christ when very young, and made the Bible his special study. When about seventeen years of age he commenced preaching the gospel. His father had become a believer in and preacher of the advent near, and Horace was deeply interested in the message and in the gospel hope. We find his letters in the Advent papers, when but a youth, full of interest and instruction on various themes connected with the subject. His mind was given to study and to writing. In a short time he produced several important tracts on The Church not in Darkness, The Three Worlds, The Last Days, Plain Truths, Outline Coast of Man, Scripture Searchers, Future Punishment, Destruction, Intermediate State, Destiny of the Wicked, Will all Men be Saved? and several others. After publishing and scattering several editions of these, the plates were purchased by the "Advent Christian Publication Society," and hundreds of thousands of them have been sent out to instruct the readers in the great gospel truths they contain. Shortly after these he wrote books,—Pauline Theology, or, The Christian Doctrine of Future Punishment, a work of which many thousands have been circulated. Then, Old Paths; then, The Signs of the Times, 416 pp.; The Great Controversy between God and Man; Thessalonica, or, The Model Church; Reasons for My Hope; Retribution, or, The Doom of the Ungodly; After the Resurrection of the Dead; Just and Unjust; Looking Forward; The Prospects of the Church. These books and some others are from the pen and heart of Bro. Hastings. They have had an extensive circulation and ought to be yet more widely known, as they contain much of the most able, candid, and useful Scriptural literature and theology now in circulation among the churches of Advent believers, and should be put into the hands of Christians generally. In 1861, Eld. Hastings was elected President of the Advent Christian Publication Society, and served with much ability, sound judgment, and economy, in advising and in prosecuting the work committed to his charge four years.

Being discharged from that office, and feeling oppressed with responsibility to do what he could while time yet remains, and urged by the conviction that the Advent societies were not doing as much work with the press as ought to be done to reach the masses and save the lost, he opened an office in Lindall St., Boston, started a monthly paper entitled "The Christian," and established the "Scriptural Tract Repository," at the commencement of 1866. From that time, until burned out in 1872 by the "Great Fire," he issued an enormous number of papers, tracts, and books, filled with light and truth, and well adapted to instruct, admonish, correct, excite to duty, induce activity, feed the famishing, encourage the timid, strengthen the weak, build up believers, and lead the perishing to Christ. The only estimate which approximates the amount of publications he has printed is by the printing paper used, which is about one hundred and twenty-five tons. He commenced without any funds, and has never begged (except of the Lord) or called for help from the people, neither received the support of any society or mission funds, only as persons or parties have voluntarily given. He acknowledges no denominational name but *Christian.* When the war closed, opening the door for mission labor and other acts of mercy in the South, he and his faithful wife, who is as devoted and godly as himself, opened mission schools and repositories in several of the Southern States, where Sister Hastings, with other faithful Christian women and men, taught the liberated slaves to read, and distributed among the destitute large amounts of food, clothing, seed to plant, and reading matter to guide them in the way of peace and instruct them in the gospel hope, and also preached to them the gospel freely, many faithful hearts and hands contributing to the work.

"The Christian" is a gem which but few who form its acquaintance are willing to part with, and all denominations take it. It now has a circulation of over thirty-five thousand copies; it is replete with spiritual food. As a preacher, Eld. H. is able, forcible, clear, and fearless. Many sinners have been brought to Christ and believers instructed and strengthened through his faithful ministry. He works for Christ and finds in him all the support needed, while he hopes for a permanent home and eternal rest when Jesus comes to give rewards and restore the earth. But few persons have a variety of superior gifts for the leading duties of life. In Eld. H. are found the talents of preaching, writing, gleaning, projecting, and prosecuting business with financial tact, all largely in advance of common minds.

THE ADVENT WATCHMAN.

In 1850, a new paper with the above title was issued in Hartford, Conn., W. S. Campbell, editor, David Crary, agent. This paper advocated the immediate coming of Christ, the sleep of the dead, the destruction of the wicked, no personal devil, and the thousand years of Rev. xx. 5, 7, to have been fulfilled in the past. This drew the attention and interest of a class, and formed a new center of action. This Association meant business, in a new line, to promote the interests of the Advent Message. In its first number was published a circular of a "Missionary Association," stated to be "the first movement of this character," signed by Miles Grant, S. G. Matthewson, S. C. Chandler, committee. If this meant that it was the first missionary society among Second Adventists, it was a singular error; but if "the first of this character," referred to a different work from that which had been going forward, it might be all true.

There were many faithful ministers associated in it, and a good work was prosecuted by them, while a door was opened, inconsiderately, to circulate some of the errors which had been repudiated previously by the body, but which have since continued to spread and embarrass the work originally entered upon. Eld. Joseph Turner, of whom we have before spoken, had recovered from fanaticism, as was supposed, and was laboring with the Adventists, but with some personal views of doctrines which were not generally received by Adventists, and being a special leader, among a class, gathered some special disciples of his views of the thousand years past, no personal devil, and no leadings or gift of the Holy Spirit. He became a leading writer for that paper, and in A. D. 1852 became an associate editor. He was an original thinker and ready writer, and produced many good things in a clear form, with some grievous errors, dressed in an ingenious style, making them look more like truth than any other writer, we ever knew, was capable of doing. In 1854, he became chief editor. In 1855, its name was changed to "Christian Reformer," and being in a bad condition financially soon closed, when its friends found a heavy debt to pay. This last was directed especially by Eld. Turner. It was to be "a free paper," *i. e.*, "free from all sectarianism and to advocate all truth." Such papers have been very scarce.

THE WATCHMAN.

Such was the title of a paper issued in Oswego, N. Y., in 1850, by Elders J. C. Bywater and Jonas Wendall, started specially to advocate that the Lord would make his second advent in 1850. The other papers of the Adventists published the writings of these believers, but also gave their reasons why the arguments were not to be relied on as proved. This did not meet their approval, and they started a separate enterprise to teach this argument in a form that should not be criticised. This was not the style of 1843 advocates; they allowed the most rigid and thorough criticisms. But this time sheet produced results, and a small class endorsed the argument as a fact which none could refute. The public were told through press and pulpits that the Adventists had set another time, leading many to suppose setting time was their chief business. The main body were exerting a wider and better influence, however, and planting the great fundamental truths of the gospel system in the hearts of many, while the Lord was adding his blessing to the good work and thousands were becoming believers in these gospel truths of Christ's soon coming to establish his everlasting kingdom on the earth made new. Also the subject of man's nature, the sleep of the dead, and the final destruction of the wicked were awakening public attention and leading many to see the absolute necessity for Christ's return and the resurrection of the dead, in order that the church might gain eternal life. This was opening the way for the preaching of the prophecies and signs of Christ's speedy coming as nothing else could; but many of the Adventist did not see it in that light, and some thought it duty to show it to be error, and a paper called "Bible Inquirer" was started in New York, April, 1850, edited by Elders I. E. Jones and D. I. Robinson, chiefly to defend the doctrine of the immateriality of the soul, the conscious existence of the dead, and the eternal pain of the wicked, against the "Materialists," as they termed those who believe in the mortality of man and the utter destruction of the wicked. In the same month, Eld. J. Litch issued a monthly entitled "The Punmatologist," Philadelphia, devoted to the same work. The first of these did little work to effect and soon passed without smoke; the last contains many curiosities on the existence of spirits, ghosts, and pre-vision, which we intended to make quotations from, but our space will not permit. We will give an extract from his introduction:

"Tullius remarks, 'If I am wrong in believing that the souls of men are immortal, I please myself in my mistake, nor while I live will I ever choose that this opinion, wherewith I am so much delighted, should be wrested from me; but if at death I am to be annihilated, as some minute philosophers imagine, I am not afraid lest those wise men, when extinct too, should laugh at me for my error.'—*Addison's Evid.*, p. 184.

"It will be the aim of this publication to establish, by all legitimate means, the doctrine of man's spiritual existence after death till the resurrection, when soul, spirit, and body will be re-united to receive their final retribution.

Our appeal will first be to the Scriptures of truth to establish these doctrines; but, in addition to their direct testimony, we shall avail ourselves of all the collateral evidence within our reach. We frankly avow our entire confidence in the faith and confession of the Pharisees, in the fact of the resurrection, and existence of angels and spirits.—Acts xxiii. 8. . . . We hope to be able to present to the public a work which will be read both with interest and profit.

"The progress of materialism is a subject which should awaken lively and energetic efforts, on the part of all evangelical Christians, to counteract its influence. If it is true that there is an intelligent spirit in man, which survives in consciousness the death of the body, it is important that all should understand it and act in reference to it. No one can wish to die in a state of deception and awake in another state to find their mistake. Finally, the whole question of man's final destiny is involved in this. If it can be proved from Scripture and facts that the spirit of man does exist in consciousness after death, then the terms *die, perish, destroy, consume, etc.*, being all used in reference to temporal death, when the spirit does survive, do not prove the final extinction of the conscious being of the wicked."

The above monthly was published some two years. Those who have read the theological arguments of Eld. Litch, on other subjects involved in the Second Advent doctrine, are ready to admit that he is a strong man, whether they agree with him or not, a man of much ability as a logician and reasoner; but those who read "Punmatologist" at once conclude that he misunderstands the position of his opponents, and also has engaged to do a work to which his tools are not at all adapted.

These puerile efforts of men of strong intellects and thorough research only added fresh collateral evidence for the materialists that their views of the Bible account of man were correct. For as they tested these efforts by the Scriptures they found the arguments of the immaterialists rested on inferences drawn from strange phenomena of spirit manifestations, histories of ghosts, with inferences drawn from certain Scriptures which did not give any certain proof of what was claimed, while the united testimony of all the plain declarations of the Bible was on the side of materialism in the proper (not the odious) use of that term. It was at once noticeable that although our immaterialist brethren tenaciously believed the Bible they were nevertheless playing into the hands of the Spiritists, though unintentionally. And while they declared against *modern* Spiritism, and tried to show it was from evil agencies,—spirits of wicked dead men,—they were constantly quoting historical accounts of spirit phenomena of former times to prove man's spirit existence after death which modern Spiritists were themselves quoting to sustain their manifestations as the work of the immortal souls of the dead.

DEFEAT OF MODERN SPIRITISM.

It is a well-known fact that modern Spiritism is based wholly on the doctrine of the immortality of the soul; this they claim in all their theological writings. They declared in the beginning of their public efforts that this new phenomena had "appeared to prove to mankind the doctrine of the immortality of the soul." They then used the portions of Scripture much from which inferences were usually drawn to prove such a view. They challenged the Christian ministry to meet them in debate as to the spirit manifestations being revelations of the souls or spirits of the dead, and as often as those ministers met them in oral or written discussion they were either defeated or their positions badly damaged, for they were found agreeing with the Spiritists in the fundamentals of their claims, that the soul is immortal and exists in a more active state after death; but when those called materialists entered the arena of debate they came in open conflict at the first step. Man is wholly unconscious in death; the soul is mortal and is unconscious in death; the spirit is not an entity, not an intelligent being *separate* from man, but is the life-principle which, when in man, causes *him* to live and *think* and *act;* your spirit manifestations and communications, when real, are from demons, and demons are fallen angels under the guidance and control of Diabolas, the devil; your teachers are antagonists of Christ and the holy angels, and counterfeits, deceivers, and liars; your claim for the immortality of the soul is of heathen origin, of Papal adoption, and Protestant admission, but is thoroughly refuted by the Bible. With such propositions backed up with the proof, which was at hand, always defeated the Spiritists. They soon admitted that they could defeat all classes of Christians except the Adventists, meaning those who are called materialists. And they soon ceased claiming the Bible as teaching the immortality of the soul, refusing to admit it as a source of evidence in discussion. It seems as though the Lord has mercifully caused this truth of man's

MILES GRANT.—Page 589.

entire mortality to be exhumed from beneath Roman rubbish to defeat the purposes of the devil in seeking to destroy the faith of the Church in the return of her Lord by this attempt to establish, by spirit miracles, the false hope that "death is the gate to endless joys," is a friend which releases man that he may go to enjoy eternal felicity without a resurrection and judgment.

SKETCH OF ELD. MILES GRANT AND HIS LABORS.

Eld. Miles Grant is a native of Connecticut, born in Torringford, December 13, 1819. Until twenty-one years of age he spent most of his time in hard farm labor, excepting winters when at school. At the age of eighteen he commenced teaching school in Winchester Centre; afterward in Walcottville and Winsted, Conn., with excellent success. He was also employed for some time as a teacher at Armenia Seminary and at Jonesville Academy, N. Y.

Early in life he had religious impressions, but drove them off and became a sceptic. As such in December, 1842, he went to hear H. A. Chittendon lecture on the prophecies of Daniel, in the Methodist Church in Winsted. Those lectures convinced Mr. Grant of the truth of the Bible. He was converted and became very active in Christian exercises. He continued in the business of teaching until the spring of 1850, when he felt it his duty to commence preaching the gospel of Christ, and especially the message of his soon coming and kingdom, in union with the Second Advent ministry of Connecticut. In the same year we find his name as one of a committee of a Second Advent Mission Society. From that time until now he has been a successful preacher among this people, generally as an evangelist. During the years 1855 to 1858 he was pastor of the church of Advent believers, in Boston, worshiping in Lowell St. In 1856, he was elected editor of the "World's Crisis and Second Advent Messenger." In this capacity he labored until 1860. Soon after his conversion Bro. Grant became a believer in the unconscious state of the dead and the destruction of the wicked, which he has advocated very extensively until now.

He has accepted many challenges to discuss the questions of "the immortality of the soul," "the conscious existence of the dead," "the eternal torture of the wicked," "the universal salvation of the race," "modern Spiritism," and the "seventh-day Sabbath," and has held over fifty debates with various ones who affirmed these positions while he denied. In the most of these he has been very successful according to the "Reports" which he and others of his views, and also those who were neutral, have given of the several debates. Several of the opponents whom he has met were quite distinguished as disputants and considered able speakers, while many have been renowned only as being wordy tricksters in low witticisms and slang blackguardism, without good social standing as men of moral worth, and some of very *low* morals. It has been a matter of doubt on the part of many friends of truth whether these cases have resulted in any real good to the communities or the parties, though much truth was elicited by the discussions. Eld. G. has become quite an expert in debate, with much experience in all the windings and subterfuges which errorists employ to cover their weak points. He is open, frank, easy in his manner, direct in his aim, clear in his statements, positive in his assertions, forcible in his declarations, gentlemanly in his bearing, self-possessed, calm and collected in his thoughts, and perfectly cool under the most severe attacks of his opponents, whether they use arguments, sophistry, opprobrium, or slander. These important qualities of a disputant are well combined in his mental composition. These constitute his real forte in debate, while he deals out the truths or views he possesses against what he considers error.

The chief or most important debate he has ever engaged in was with Dr. J. Litch, in Music Hall, Boston, four evenings, 1858, on the question, "Do the Scriptures teach the eternal conscious suffering of the wicked?" Dr. L. affirmed; Eld. G. denied. Eld. Litch is a scholar, a gentleman, and admitted, generally, to possess much stronger mental powers than Eld. Grant, and he proved the most formidable opponent he has ever met; but lacking the essential part of a debate,—the Bible proof of his proposition,—Eld. Grant and the Bible gained a decided victory, as we think those who read the published report, mutually corrected, must feel convicted of, whether they all admit it or not.

In November, 1861, Eld. Grant was elected again as editor of the "World's Crisis," associated with Eld. P. B. Morgan, and has been re-elected every year since, either as sole editor or associate. And although he has done but little editorial work, compared with some (for his is a preaching rather than a writing and selecting gift), he has traveled and preached very extensively in all the New England, Middle, and most of the Western States, beside several mission tours to California and several to the Province of Quebec, and many have been converted under his labors, and many enlightened in the gospel truths he preaches. Some have been surprised that he could preach so much and not break down. This he attributes largely to his diet. He uses no meat, butter, tea, coffee, or tobacco. This may be one cause of his physical vigor. He has a sound constitution, and pays special attention to keeping it so; he is very methodical, eating only such food as he has proved to be beneficial to him; he has a set time for each department of his work, and scrupulously adheres to it. What wears the life and constitution of many of our laborious ministers is the adapting themselves to all modes of travel and all common habits of living, lodging, and association, *i. e.*, constantly traveling by steamers, packets, barges, first or second class cars, or even on freight trains, by stage coach, family carriage, lumber carts, or on foot, to save time and economize their scanty means and get the gospel before the perishing; then visiting from house to house instructing, comforting, conversing, and praying with the people, often until midnight; then preaching in hot kitchens or parlors, school-houses, log huts, in bad atmosphere, in open barns and groves, often without receiving money enough to pay traveling expenses, and sometimes none, while a family must be cared for and bills paid, the pressure of family cares and debts weighing them down. These are among the causes of broken constitutions and young ministers looking old; these accomplish *a great amount* of labor. Bro. Grant's method shields him from all this. He usually stops and sleeps at one house, while in one town, visits little, keeps his talk for the public assembly, his thoughts and strength also, and his time for study and mental culture. He receives a full support and is kept free from the embarrassments of accumulating bills for rents, fuel, food, and clothing, travels by pleasant and speedy conveyances, and is fresh to enter at once upon his prepared work. With such care he is able to preach *fifteen times* a week without being weary. He is ever at work, and always ready to preach or debate. The Lord has made him very useful in the interests of the Advent cause, although he ignores the denominational name, *Adventist*, and chooses to be called only a Christian.

Within the last few years Eld. Grant has become specially interested in the Methodist view of sanctification, and devotes much of his time in its advocacy and gains many converts to that view. But as the Adventists, generally, believe that a person is truly sanctified when truly converted, and as ready for the kingdom of God as the penitent thief (though if he lives a holy life he will continually grow in grace and spiritual power), they believe that view unscriptural; consequently, much inharmony has been arising therefrom, which seems likely to increase, as has generally been the case among the Methodists themselves when that point has been urged as a work after conversion and necessary to secure the believer's salvation. This is working extensive disunion in the Methodist Church at the present time, but we trust the Lord will overrule this matter for the good of his cause, and soon bring the full knowledge of what we now see only in part, when the watchmen and all the saints will see eye to eye, and rest together in our eternal home.

NEW YORK CONFERENCE.

Tuesday morning, May 7th, 1850. The Business Committee presented the following preamble and resolution:—

Whereas, our position as believers in the Advent at hand, and its relative Scriptural events, still appears to us to be as fully in accordance with the Word of God, and of as great practical importance as ever; and whereas, there are serious indications of defection from this position among those who profess the Advent faith; and whereas, there are cheering encouragements to constancy in our testimony for the truth, in the interest with which many sincere minds, who are dissatisfied with prevailing errors, turn to the sure word of prophecy, as we understand it, it becomes us, from a sense of duty to ourselves, a desire to warn our brethren, and to benefit our fellow-men, to RE-AFFIRM the leading features of our faith as Adventists; therefore,

Resolved, That the Conference appoint a committee, whose duty it shall be to prepare an address, which shall embody the principles of the Advent question, and be *particularly* adapted to the dangers of our brethren, for presentation at the Boston Conference.

This resolution called out a lively and useful discussion on the great questions at issue, and which distinguish Adventists as a people: Elders J. V. Himes, A. Hale, I. E. Jones, E. R. Pinney, L. Osler, Edwin Burnham, Joseph Marsh, H. H. Gross, and others participating in it. One of the chief innovations being then introduced to nullify and subvert the believers was Judaism, which had been constantly rejected; but was now being published anew by Eld. J. Marsh, in his paper, yet stated he had not endorsed it as truth.

On this subject Elder Himes remarked, that no man ought to set himself up to teach until he had fairly settled in his mind what to teach. He will then be able to instruct and establish others in the truths, or sentiments, he teaches. When we first began in this glorious cause, we took nothing upon trust. We did not believe the doctrine of the Advent because Father MILLER, or any one else, taught it; but because the Bible taught it;—and the main doctrines that constituted our faith in the beginning I believe to-day. In respect to the Judaizing notions that prevail, we have battled the whole church, and now shall we turn our backs, and give up the whole ground gained? I have always been happy to associate and counsel with my brethren on the best means to promote this great cause. To this end I called the Boston Conference in 1840. I go for acting as a body of brethren, and not for the standing aloof, or excommunicating every brother that does not see in all points with me. I want brethren to be heart and hand in the main questions of our faith, and co-operate together, and then something can be done. But I cannot associate with a brother who will never define his position. We speak of defections from the Advent views. Yes, there are, and serious ones too. Judaism is being taught. If brethren do not mean to teach it let them tell us so and not teach this under the cloak of Adventism. Judaism and Adventism are two different things. The former we have been battling from the beginning, and whenever our brethren have embraced it it has perfectly bewitched them. It did the Galatian brethren; for says the apostle, 'Who hath bewitched you?' 'I marvel ye are so soon removed from the hope of the gospel.' There is a sort of bewitching influence about this Judaism which is seen everywhere, where its foot-prints can be traced. This is evident from its effects in Albany, and elsewhere, where no good, but evil, was the result of its promulgation. I want to act with a body of brethren who are true in the faith, and which will act unitedly and harmoniously in the great work that we have so long been enlisted in. I go against the *one-man power*. If there are fifty men only who are going to proclaim the Advent faith, we are capable of acting together. I want to work with such an army as will be true to the faith. I would re-affirm the main principles of our faith. Judaism we have repudiated from the beginning, and I make an eternal and open repudiation of such a faith. A man, said Bro. H., must have a heart as hard as adamant, to see the whole Advent body distracted and torn by the suggestion and enforcing of extraneous views, and still presist in such a course, and constantly be getting up something new to feed the excitement. If a man knows not what he is teaching, he ought not to teach. What great principle of our faith has not been attacked?—and that, too, by the professed friends of the cause. I feel an interest in this cause. I have been engaged in it in its darkest hours, and my heart has never faltered. I hope to help sustain it to the end.

The above resolution passed and resulted in giving the public an address which set this subject in a Biblical light, that all, who prefer the gospel *leveler* to Jewish fables, might see if they would study thoroughly the gospel plan.

REVIVALS CONTINUE.

Our records show an almost constant work of conversion of sinners in nearly all parts of our country where the Advent Message has been faithfully preached. We give an occasional lettter like the following to show samples of the work. Other sects have become friendly and unite in the work.

Bro. L. E. Bates writes from Pompey, Onondaga Co., New York, Feb. 7th, 1850:—"We are enjoying an interesting revival in this place.—The minds of the mass for miles around, are stirred, and moved to their very depth; a more solemn and deeply interesting state of things I think I never witnessed. I shall attempt no estimate of the number converted, reclaimed, and benefited by the truth. Seventy have already followed Christ in baptism, and others are expected to go forward soon. I was invited to this place by the Church known as Disciples, and a more cordial reception and hearty co-operation I have never witnessed on the part of any people, and though they have been distinguished as a Bible people, yet they were willing frankly to acknowledge their ignorance in relation to the beauty and harmony of the Scriptures touching the second speedy coming of the Son of man, the doctrine of the saints' inheritance, etc., and have applied themselves with increased interest to the investigating of that blessed volume, and the result thus far has been, that many have become fully persuaded of the divinity of these great truths."

Prof. J. P. Weethee writes from New York the 11th inst.:—"Since I wrote last, the work has been progressing. New cases every night, and conversions. Between sixty and seventy have professed religion. The reclaimed and converted number nearly one hundred and twenty. The interest is spreading to the churches. Truly it has been to me a feast. I have not retired to rest before about midnight for three weeks. My days are spent in visiting the seekers, and in conversing on the Advent, and my nights in preaching. I have done all the preaching since I have been here, having delivered thirty-four discourses. I have been wonderfully sustained. Yesterday was a day long to be remembered. About 12 o'clock, after preaching, we proceeded to the East

38

River to attend to the ordinance of baptism. A dense crowd had collected. I baptized twenty-two; among them were twelve young ladies, five or six young gentlemen, and the rest were married persons."

THE WORLD'S CRISIS AND ADVENT CHRISTIAN ASSOCIATION.

There are many believers now connected with this Association who know nothing of the history of its origin, and but little, except incidentally, of any other Advent Societies besides this and the Western A. C. Association. It would be quite improper to neglect such a prominent point in the history of an institution so important as this has now become because it had a rude beginning and the task is unpleasant. In 1852, Eld. Jonathan Cummings, one of the ministers of the Advent body in earlier days, claimed to have obtained "new light on the commencement and terminus of the periods of Daniel." He was ambitious, aspiring, erratic, with a good degree of eloquence, an air of knowledge and self-sufficiency, and a very defiant, dogmatic spirit, well calculated to gain disciples. He began to teach that the 1260, the 1290, and 1335 days commenced A. D. 519, by a union of Church and State under an edict of the Emperor Justin; consequently, that the 1260 days terminated in A. D. 1779, the 1290 days in 1809, and the 1335 days would end and bring the resurrection in A. D. 1854. Those who had long looked and anxiously waited for the return of their Lord, and the many who had, through their constant labors and God's developments of signs of the impending judgment, been brought to unite in the same expectation, were interested in any argument which seemed to give evidence as to the time of deliverance and final redemption. A large proportion of them had never gone through a "time movement," or thoroughly examined a "time argument," and but a limited number were competent to decide such a matter after they had heard all that could be said upon it. But the fact that they had ears to hear and hearts anxious to learn what they could about the return of the Lord is highly commendatory to their affections for Christ. They "loved his appearing," but this fact should not justify any one in tantalizing them with unreliable testimony as to the time of his coming, nor should it deter any faithful teacher from dissuading them from relying upon such evidences as are without foundation. In the Advent Herald of Nov. 2, 1852, we find the following from Eld. Cummings:

"Bro. Himes having ascertained the point beyond which the coming of the Lord cannot be extended, I wish to extend the truth of it to all. I therefore send you a little sheet containing a part of the light on the subject. . . . Napoleon declared the civil power of the Pope ended May 17, 1809, because he would not fight England. The Pope was made a prisoner the same year. The 1290 days cannot go later. I feel certain the 1335 days will end before the spring of 1855, and hope to be ready."

Then follows a congruous argument with badly applied historical sketches to sustain it, and a diagram with the figures so placed as to end the periods in 1854, without any good evidence why they should be so placed. To this the editor replied:

"As it is proper to express an opinion on what is published in the Herald, we feel constrained to say respecting the above that there is no evidence presented in connection with it that justifies the positiveness with which the writer speaks. We know not what future light may be given on the termination of the prophetic periods, but we greatly deprecate this drawing conclusions with such positiveness on a question of so much moment on evidence which, compared with that for 1843, is but a rushlight to the sun. We feel that it is tantalizing our brethren with assumptions for which the evidence presented affords no just grounds. It is very easy to make straight lines, to extend them to this point or that, but it is not so easy to show why they should be thus terminated. To do this it is necessary to consider certain characteristics which here pass unnoticed. We shall be ever ready to present any light that is light, but at the risk of being again denounced as backslidden, etc., etc., for not receiving as light all that is presented, we feel bound to thus speak our honest convictions."

This greatly offended the correspondent and some of his associates, but other articles were furnished and admitted, during all the succeeding year, from him and others who embraced these views. They were candidly and thoroughly reviewed, however, by the editor, who was competent to the task, and by other experienced students of prophecy, and shown from well-attested and reliable facts that the arguments of these brethren were unreliable, as their historical citations and applications were not sound and did not prove what they claimed for them. In their efforts to establish what they thought to be evidence to prove this time argument true they departed from some of the rules of interpretation and of application of history and prophecy which were well known by eminent expositors as demonstrated facts. They had instituted applications which outraged good sense and ignored some of the plainest Scripture statements, and some of the brethren who then adopted them have been misled and perplexed with them until now.

Eld. F. H. Berrick, another of the former ministers of the body, a young man of considerable ability, a fluent speaker, who had traveled and preached extensively and gained many friends, embraced the argument as truth, and wrote a book entitled "The Lord soon to come," 383 pp., to demonstrate it. From the preface of this book we extract the following:

"According to the faith which we have publicly professed and advocated, we are now approaching a momentous crisis in human affairs, and if the Author and Finisher of our faith has so highly favored us with the communication of his Spirit and grace that we are enabled to understand the point of prophetic chronology at which the world has now arrived, we feel under infinite obligations of gratitude to God for such high and distinguishing gifts, and under corresponding obligations to exert every energy of our entire being to diffuse this sacred light, by sounding an alarm in God's holy mountain."

It is thus shown that these two leaders in this movement were positive beyond the possibility of doubt; the last believes the Lord had bestowed upon them this *high and distinguishing gift of understanding the definite time*, for this was his point. Men with such views teach as infallible guides. What they teach must be true, for the Lord has given the distinguishing gift and sent them to announce a *divine fact*, and such were their feelings and the authority with which they taught. The following are some of their sayings: "This is the second writing of the vision, Hab. ii." "The 'one taken and the other left,' Luke xvii. 34, relates to those who believe this time and are 'taken' from work in the field, mill, etc., quitting business while the unbelievers are 'left' at work." "God is in the '54 time movement and not outside of it." "This is God's truth, it is as true as the Bible." "There is no possibility of a mistake in this time." "Those who reject this light will be lost." "Those who do not accept this argument are backsliders," etc. The mass of Advent believers could not endorse such statements nor the arguments on which they rested, and they were obliged to use caution, as they were called to constantly reply to the inquiring brethren and give the reasons why they could not believe thus. A great ferment and disunion set in among all the societies where these views were promulgated, because most of the brethren could not say they were correct. The time brethren concluded it was not right for them to continue their communications in the Advent papers where they were constantly criticised and their evidences damaged by more able and experienced writers and historians. They therefore called a mass meeting of time believers to convene in Lowell, Mass., in January, 1854. A large number of brethren assembled; counsel was had; contributions were freely made to start a paper which should be devoted to the interests of the Second Advent cause, but especially to the advocacy of the 1854 time argument, and so managed that no opposing argument, no counter testimony, should be allowed in its columns. On this basis "The World's Crisis" was issued in March, at Lowell, as "a free paper, supported by contributions, to be sent to all who wished it, whether they gave to support it or not." This shutting off criticisms, free investigation, and interchange of thought and research was so unlike the spirit of Protestantism, and so far removed from the practices of the pioneers of Adventism, that the brethren were quite unwilling to believe such a principle could have been adopted by these leaders. We did not feel ready to give credit to it until we wrote to the editor and received from him a confirmation of it.

A time paper conducted on this principle had the result to cause all believers who had not seen the other Advent papers to conclude the time argument unrefutable, and as they saw no efforts to disprove it in their paper, and were constantly reading assertions that it was demonstrated, and no one had or could show it incorrect, the tendency was to confirm many of the brethren in its favor, even of those who did see counter arguments, for they made many positive assertions where there is no means of showing whether true or false. When a statement is made that the Lord will come at a certain time no one can *prove* he will not, though they see no real proof that he will, while there is much collateral evidence indicating that he may.

During this movement a line of separation between the time brethren and the main body was becoming very visible, although it had previously commenced with some on the life and death question. But the Lord blessed the truths which the time brethren believed and taught with the time message, and made use of the faithful labors and sacrifices of the true and humble believers, and many were converted, and many Christians brought to believe the general principles of Adventism. Thus the Lord often turns the errors and enthusiasm of men, as well as "the wrath of man, to his praise." There was much truth preached, but it was not all truth. The time passed and brought great disappointment to a large number and *apostasy* to these two leaders and many others who had become fully positive they were correct.

Eld. Cummings became the leader of several hundreds whom he gathered into communities, on the "common interest" principle (he controlling the bag), in Fairfield, Me., Providence, R. I., and one in some town in Canada, where some twenty to forty thousand dollars were abstracted by expenditures or the extravagance and duplicity of the leader, who managed to control their property and them for a time, under the claim of establishing "the apostolic order of the church," while he drove fine and fast horses. Himself and two others being ordained apostles, promised that the other nine would yet be developed. "Signs followed, and the gifts" were bestowed, especially "the gift of tongues," either by the Lord or some other spirit. But the spell was finally broken, and the most of these brethren and sisters were sufficiently chastened by the Lord, for following men, to return to his service and directions, while a few apostatized. Eld. C. retired to farm life in a rural town. Eld. Berrick became sceptical and for some time staggered between the Bible and infidelity, telling the writer on one occasion that he had been powerfully tempted to give up the Bible, "for," said he, "we proved that those periods ended in 1854, if the Bible is reliable, yet I do not say the Bible is not true." He vacillated several years, then studied law, went West, preached some, made sad work in a sad life, studied medicine, and became a practising physician. We wish to cast no reflections, but record these sad facts of history with the hope that some may carefully ponder them, and remember that while they have been published to the world as "the views and conduct of the Adventists," they have been adopted and practised in opposition to and against the remonstrances of the leading organs, pioneers, and more advanced students and experienced portions of the body.

ADMISSION AND CONFESSION.

In the World's Crisis of May 29, 1855, we find the following admission and confession:

"We now frankly admit that the time argument, as it has been viewed the past three years, has proved a failure, our only apology for preaching it is, we believed it. We were fully convinced it would be so, and we governed ourselves accordingly. . . . We wish to say that we have been both disappointed and mistaken.—F. H. B."

In the same number of the paper is a confession, as follows:

"We frankly confess that time has proved our *argument* of the prophetic periods defective. We confess that some of us have been rather denunciatory in our overheated zeal on time."

From this point the "Crisis" began to assume a more healthful tone. The ambition which originated it had departed, the confident spirit was softened and the mass of minds which had been centered upon that organ as their medium of correspondence and communication needed a new focal point to combine the scattering and unsettled elements, which had been produced by another disappointment, and to guide the many young converts and other believing Christians, who had united with them during this movement, into the knowledge of the gospel faith and to united action in the future work of proclaiming the truth and gathering others to Christ.

They had become so separated from the main body by their positiveness on the time argument and sensitiveness because it was not generally received by the body as really true; together with the inharmony which had for some time existed on the doctrine of man's nature and the destiny of the finally lost (for as a class they were believers in the entire mortality of man), that they were not inclined to again enter upon united labor with the original body, at the cost of what they considered one of the cardinal principles of the gospel—immortality and eternal life through Christ alone—for the Advent Herald had already published the following notice:

"OUR FINAL DECISION.

We wish to say to our friends and subscribers in regard to the controversy on the intermediate state of the dead and final destiny of the wicked, that we shall not make these questions prominent in the *Herald*. We desire every one who writes on them, to speak what he believes in respectful language. No one will be cramped in this respect. But we cannot permit either party to be assailed, or their *motives questioned*, for their honest faith."

There was a general feeling among these brethren, that the views they held upon this subject were vital, and especially demanded to meet and overthrow the gigantic errors into which the Protestant church had fallen, by which the doctrine of Christ's coming, the resurrection and judgment was being ignored and modern spiritism strengthened: they saw it must be made prominent, and they were not ready to go back, although courteously invited through the Advent Herald to do so.

THE GENERAL CONFERENCE OF ADVENTISTS

Was advertised in the Advent Herald to meet in Boston, on June 5, 1855, and the managers strongly hoped the "time brethren" would come into union with them; but they soon appointed a Conference at Worcester, Mass., to convene on the same day. Each of these bodies met at the places appointed, and transacted business for the future promotion of their work, and the separating line became fully developed.

Who has the wisdom to decide that this separation was not permitted for a good end. We had no part in it, but regretted it at the time, although we have since felt obliged to unite with those with whom we could labor in harmony on the gospel hope which we cherished. But inasmuch as it was not possible for the believers in immortality through Christ alone, to teach fully and freely that view among those who recognized it as heresy, it is far better to stand on a basis known and understood, where others may unite or not, and only themselves be responsible for it. Let every class which has a central truth stand upon it independently, but yet in full fellowship with all other Christians.

As each body became more zealous in promoting their views on the subject of man's nature and the future destiny of the finally lost, the believers in man's entire mortality, who were with the original body, have been continually coming over to the body which teaches that view, also, many who held to the conscious state, and eternal pain, have been constantly giving it up and coming over. As those who are managers of the original body consider this view heterodox and are now throughly opposed to it, they have reorganized under the name of "Evangelical Adventists," to be distinguished from those whom they call "Materialists."

In February, 1856, "The World's Crisis" office was removed from Lowell to Boston, by its managers. Its publishing committee was H. V. Davis, John Couch, Miles Grant, and Geo. T. Adams. At that point there was no regularly organized society to own or control it. All that was done was allowed by common consent. June 4th, 1856, Eld. Grant became editor. In the Crisis of Aug. 20th, we find a synopsis of the Second Advent faith, under nine heads, written by Elder Edwin Burnham. It is a clear and Scriptural statement.

From the time of its location in Boston it assumed a healthful and regular Scriptural tone, compared with its beginnings, and continued to improve for several years, gaining a subscription list of about 3000. It had several reverses under unhealthful handlings. Eld. R. Wendall become editor and retained the chair six months; but the patient nearly expired under the treatment. At this juncture another mass meeting of the friends of this cause was called, to meet at Worcester, Nov. 6, 1861. The attendance was large at that meeting, and

THE ADVENT CHRISTIAN ASSOCIATION,

was organized; also, the "Advent Christian Publication Society;" of the last-named Eld. H. L. Hastings was elected president; Eld. J. D. Brown, secretary; H. V. Davis, S. S. Brewer, J. G. Hamlin, I. C. Wellcome, Solomon Hovey, publishing committee; H. L. Hastings, D. T. Taylor, H. F. Carpenter, editorial committee; Miles Grant, editor; P. B. Morgan, assistant.

From that time onward the World's Crisis has been a denominational paper, the organ of the great majority of the Second Adventists in New England, the Middle States and of many West and South, for the Materialists have greatly outgrown the Evangelical class, as they now embrace about one thousand ministers and some thirty State and sectional annual Conferences. And by the efforts of its managers, the constant solicitations of several hundreds of faithful ministers and many more patrons, it has arisen to about nine thousand subscribers, and with the Lord's blessing, has accomplished a vast amount of good, in awakening and bringing souls to the gos-

PROF. CHARLES F. HUDSON.—Page 601.

pel hope through Christ, and in bringing thousands to see and realize the fact that time is closing and Jesus is soon coming to judge the world; it has also fed many famishing souls with the bread of life.

It has been a good family paper. It should have been better; but the imperfections must be overlooked, and improvements made as the Lord gives wisdom to do so.

As to the work of the society in other departments, we shall speak under the head of missions and publications.

ANOTHER STRANGE STATEMENT.

Prof. Sanborn of Dartmouth College, Hanover, N. H., read a paper before the Congregational Asssociation of that State, and at their request it was published in the Andover Bibliotheca Sacra, for July, 1855. In the opening of the Essay is found the following strange statement:

"The meaning of unfulfilled prophecy is not a proper subject of human inquiry. Only scheming theologians attempt to penetrate its dark arcana. The most worthless writings that have been preserved are those which have been written on this subject; and it would be better for the world could every vestige of them be destroyed—serving as they do only to bewilder."

The Essay is an admixture of infidelity and Christianity, in relation to the leading truths of the Bible, contradicting many of its clearest and most precious promises. And yet a representative class of teachers in a great Christian denomination, vote for it, and give it publicity to the world through a Biblical Journal.

SKETCH OF PROF. C. F. HUDSON AND HIS LABORS.

"Charles Frederick Hudson, son of Timothy and Catherine Hudson, was born in Wardsworth, Medina Co., Ohio, May 18, 1821. His parents shortly after removed to Medina, the county seat, where he received the elements of a common-school education.

"After suitable preparation he entered the Western Reserve College, and was graduated among the foremost of his class. Having in early life devoted himself to the service of the Saviour, and believing that he was called to the work of the gospel ministry, he pursued the course of study prescribed at Lane Theological Seminary, receiving his certificate under the hands of Lyman Beecher, C. E. Stowe, and D. H. Allen, June 9, 1847. After spending some years as pastor of the Congregational Church in Sycamore, Illinois, certain changes in his opinions regarding the nature and destiny of man led to a dissolution of his eclsiastical connections, and being released from pastoral responsibilities he was free to employ his time in study and in writing, preaching meanwhile wherever an open door was set before him, without regard to denominational lines or connections.

"During the latter part of his life he traveled extensively, visiting libraries and consulting with literary men, and some of the fruits of his patient research were given to the world in an elaborate volume entitled 'DEBT AND GRACE, as related to the Doctrine of a Future Life;' which was followed by 'CHRIST OUR LIFE, The Scriptural Argument for Immortality through Christ Alone;' 'HUMAN DESTINY, a Critique on Universalism,' and other minor publications on kindred topics. His last years were spent in the vicinity of Cambridge, Mass., and were devoted to these and other literary pursuits. The Critical Greek Concordance was the crowning labor of his life.

"As a controversialist, Mr. Hudson was candid, patient, calm, and courteous, indefatigable in research, and temperate in expression. As a preacher, he was sober, diffident, and deliberate, yet instructive to the patient hearer. As a man, he was generous, cautious, honorable, self-reliant, and modest, even to bashfulness. As a Christian, he was circumspect, reverent, conscientious, and of good report. In person, he was tall, slightly stooping, of light, though swathy, complexion, having rather a thin face, and prominent nose, high, full forehead, and brown hair. His health was never robust, but his powers of execution were considerable. Mr. Hudson never married. He is buried at Haddonfield, New Jersey, where he died May 26, 1867, aged forty-six years and eight days." [1]

Prof. Hudson became associated with the Adventists about 1860, from which time until his death his writings and wise counsels were of much service to the cause. He was, during several years, a member of the Board of the Advent Christian Publication Society, and, until his feeble state of health prevented, was a critical and instructive correspondent of the "World's Crisis." His books have been extensively read by ministers and other scholars, and have exerted a wide influence in leading thinking minds out of the traditions of the soul's immortality and the eternal pain of the wicked, into the Bible doctrine of immortality through Christ, for all believers, and the final destruction of the wicked. He sleeps in death, awaiting the morn of the resurrection of the just at the return of their Lord.

THE AMERICAN SECOND ADVENT MISSIONARY SOCIETY.

At a convention of Adventists called and held at Providence, R. I., May 18, 1854, Henry Tanner, of Buffalo, N. Y., was called to the chair, and D. I. Robinson, was appointed secretary.

A constitution was reported, which had been prepared by a committee of the conference, which was adopted.

---

[1] Preface to Critical Greek and English Concordance, p. 10.

PREAMBLE.

Whereas, The great events of prophecy are being rapidly fulfilled, and the coming of the Lord evidently drawing nigh, we deem it a solemn duty, as believers in the glorious personal advent and reign of Christ over a redeemed world, to adopt more efficient measures than have of late characterized our efforts, to make known these great truths both to the church and world. And as a part of our system of labors, we agree to form a Missionary Society, and adopt the following

CONSTITUTION.

ART. 1. This Society shall be called the American Second Advent Missionary Society, whose object it shall be to raise and disburse funds for the support of missionary labor, in any field, either at home or abroad, where a door is opened, and a field promising usefulness presented.

The above society has continued its existence and prosecuted some mission work, by partly sustaining several evangelists to supply churches destitute of pastors and to labor in new fields, as doors have opened for such a message.

During 1865–6 it collected and disbursed some funds in aid of the European—or rather, Italian Mission. It also sent two or more missionaries into Tennessee during the civil war—Elders I. I. Leslie, and G. H. Child, who were obliged to conform to the rules of the Christian Commission for a time. They labored among the Freedmen and established several schools and meetings. The correspondence shows a good work begun; and reformation followed. Very interesting accounts were published in the Advent Herald, of their work.

THE AMERICAN MILLENNIAL ASSOCIATION.

This association of Second Adventists, was organized in Boston, Mass., Nov., 1858, and is composed mainly of those ministers and churches of the original body of Second Adventists which adhere to the doctrine of the conscious state of the dead, and the eternal conscious suffering of the wicked, and those of the same views, who have since united with them. It publishes a paper and some tracts, its publications have dwindled to a trifle, compared with former times. The society is divided in feeling about their name, many of them wish to be called the Messiannian Church and have carried the point so far that their class have the Advent Herald published for them, bearing the title "Messiah's Herald." The paper with each title has a circulation of about three thousand copies. They have, until recently, published a juvenile paper—Youth's Visitor—which is discontinued for lack of support. Several years ago this society, feeling unwilling to be recognized as members of a common body of Advent believers, the great majority of whom believe in the sleep of the dead and the destruction of the wicked, adopted for themselves "Evangelical Adventists," as a denominational name, to distinguish them from the main body, which has been, until recently, considered *un*-evangelical. But that thought is being played out, so far at least that some of the savants of the church have decided that the other class is evangelical, and have opened the "evangelical gate" to both classes in many instances. This shows a decided improvement in Christian understanding and fellowship. The "Evangelical Adventists" claim to adhere to the views of Mr. Miller, on the nature of man and future punishment, while the others do not; but as these views formed no part of the distinguishing features of Adventism in its early history, nor in its declarations of principles in its several chief conventions, neither should they now. All *Christians* who adhere to the great leading *facts* which were taught as distinguishing features of the Advent Message, and which gave a distinctive position to that class of believers are Evangelical Adventists; but as the term, like orthodoxy, is self-appropriated, it is not worth contending about.

We quote from their declaration of principles the "Reasons for their distinctive Denominational Existence," which we trust the Advent Christian Churches can as readily adopt, and with equal propriety.

REASONS FOR A DISTINCTIVE DENOMINATIONAL EXISTENCE.

The justification for the maintenance of a distinctive denominational existence lies:

1. In the real value placed upon the great event of Christ's return to the world.

2. In the rejection of all theories which inculcate the notion of a Millennium prior to the second coming of Christ, or that puts in the far distance the time of the advent. And

3. In tenets not now found embodied in any of the prevailing systems of Christian belief.

As the principal object of all prophecy was to prepare the world for two comings of the Messiah; and as there is more said, in the New Testament

Scriptures, concerning Christ's coming the second time than of any other doctrine, this event should be regarded, especially by the professed people of God, as one of stupendous and overwhelming importance. The manger—the cross—the tomb—the resurrection—the ascension and the intercessory throne are presented to us as so many onward, stately steppings of the glorious Redeemer toward the accomplishment of the grand work of salvation, an event which introduces the final judgment, when the fate of every individual will be decided for eternity and this globe be reduced to a fiery chaos, thus closing up the present dispensation of mercy, cannot be treated otherwise, by inspiration, and certainly should not be by any believer in revelation, than a subject infinitely solemn, important and grand.

The popular notion of the world's conversion has become a vail before the vision of many, and faith in the coming again of the Lord has become greatly obscured. As a legitimate sequence, instead of watching for and waiting His return, it has become an almost universal belief that He comes not again for a long, long time. Nay, a system of spritual or mystic interpretation is being accepted by the church, which questions the ancient faith of a personal and visible advent of the Son of man, hence we now hear much about a "spiritual coming"—a merely "providential coming"—that is a "figurative event"—that "Christ comes at death." The same principle of intrepretation that denies the personality and visibility of Christ's second advent will surely undermine faith in the literality of the resurrection of the dead.

The purification of this sin-stained world by fire,—the forming out of its ashes a new earth,—after its regeneration becoming the everlasting inheritance of the saints—the "rectified and beautified" world and the ransomed millions to constitute the kingdom of Christ in its state of perfection over which he will reign in person,—are doctrines which were held by the primitive church, and by the Reformers as cardinal in the Christian system, and which are cherished by this people as being essential to the integrity of the divine plan of human redemption.

And believing that the visible church has discarded some of the most blessed doctrines of the gospel—that although she is the professed Bride, yet she no longer looks, and longs, and waits for the coming of the Lord—that the present period is pregnant with indications of the speedy coming of the second Adam to inaugurate the new and endless dispensation of righteousness and peace, may not this people feel justified in the maintenance of a distinctive denominational interest, in order to the more effective defense and propagation of their faith?

The history of the past is replete with evidences of Jehovah's ever watchful and jealous care over, not only the Scriptures in their entireness, but the preservation in their original purity, of each doctrine of his written word. To this end, at different times, when the exigency of the case demanded, the great Author of the Bible has, in his infinite wisdom, selected his own human agencies to defend and keep alive the truth imperiled.

CHAPTER XIX.

ANNUAL CONFERENCES—OTHERS MORE TOLERANT—H. F. CARPENTER—WESTERN A. C. P. ASSOCIATION—VOICE OF THE WEST, ADVENT C. TIMES—YET IN DARKNESS—FEARFUL STATE OF SOCIETY—A. A. PHELPS—HOME MISSIONS, AMERICAN ADVENT MISSION SOCIETY, STAR OF HOPE MISSION, UNION FEMALE MISSION ASSOCIATION—WM. L. HIMES—ERRORS EXPOSED—TENT AND CAMP-MEETINGS—SUNDAY SCHOOLS—J. H. WHITMORE—REVIVAL OF GIFTS—FRENCH PROPHETS—P. G. BOWMAN—PUBLICATIONS—BOOKS AND PAMPHLETS—PUBLICATION SOCIETIES—C. C. MARSTON—GOOD TIDINGS—WATCHMEN AWAKING—RESULTS.

STATE ANNUAL ADVENT CONFERENCES.

In the beginning general conferences were held annually, usually in Boston and New York, but as believers multiplied, and the interest became too widely spread to be properly represented and provided for by these gatherings, the societies began to feel the necessity of united action in carrying forward the work of extending this message into all communities by combining the influence of the ministry and the churches in local parts of the country. It seemed advantageous to such a work to organize annual sectional conferences. This has been done as the number of believers multiplied and the cause seemed to demand.

Such a conference was organized in Maine, in 1848, the first annual State Conference, we believe, that was organized. At that time many were confused by the spirit of disorder resulting from the cry, "Come out of Babylon." Some were warring against all church organization, and the opposition which these few ministers put forth and encouraged others to put forth was so violent that after three yearly meetings the present writer moved to disorganize the Conference. It was voted to do so with the hope that it would pacify the no-order party and prevent open disunion. This proved to be a bad measure, as the object was not realized, and it re-opened the door to those who had felt checked by the united elements to run riot with their wild and destructive, speculative, new notions, to produce confusion and discord among the infant churches and societies, and to bring discredit and disgrace upon the truth and those who taught it. After several years of experimenting, without any concert of action, during which every man did and taught what seemed right in his own eyes, the believers were in such a confused state that nearly all cried out for some system, some line of action, by which it could be known who were building on Christ and who were working ruin to his cause. Accordingly, in 1854, a conference was called, after consulting every Advent minister in the State, which resulted in organizing the Maine Annual Advent Christian Conference, which has continued its sessions until now, greatly to the advancement of the cause of truth and the benefit of the churches and ministry.

Annual Conferences are now organized by the Adventists believing in immortality and eternal life through Christ only (embracing the societies which sustain the "Advent Christian Publication Society," Boston, Mass., and the "Western Advent Christian Publication Association," Chicago, Ill., and the "American Advent Mission Society") in Maine, Massachusetts, New Hampshire, Vermont, Rhode Island, Connecticut, New York, Pennsylvania, Ohio, Indiana, Michigan, Illinois, Wisconsin, Minnesota, Iowa, Kansas, Missouri, Arkansas, Tennesee, and in the Provinces of Quebec (Canada), Nova Scotia, and New Brunswick. Perhaps some in other of the Southern States, as the message is being received there.

"The Evangelical Adventists," represented by the "American Millennial Association" (who believe in the conscious state of the dead and the eternal torture or pain of the wicked), hold annual sectional Conferences in Massachusetts, New Hampshire, Pennsylvania, Province of Quebec, Vermont, and Province of Ontario. They own a camp-ground of eleven acres in Hebron, Mass., fitted up with a chapel and cottages, where they hold an annual camp-meeting. They also hold annual camp-meetings in the Province of Quebec, and in Cameron, Clearfield, and Centre counties, Pennsylvania.

Besides the above the Seventh-Day Adventists hold annual conferences in several of the States, but we do not have the means at hand to give any representations of them.

OTHERS MORE TOLERANT.

The divine favor has been so manifest in connection with the Advent Message, the cases of genuine conversion so numerous, the reform so thorough, the piety so deep in most cases, together with the fact that eminent ministers are constantly embracing the faith, that a large class of brethren of other denominations, who have opposed the faith and been unwilling to associate with the Adventists, are now very tolerant and ready to fellowship them, and in numerous cases to unite with them in worship and in work for the salvation of souls. The truth exemplified in the lives of those who profess it will always commend itself to the consciences of men, and will ultimately beget sympathy and union with all true Christians. Much of the opposition manifested by true Christians against the doctrine of the Advent has arisen from ignorance and prejudice, while in many others it has come from sinful hearts which were unprepared to meet the Lord.

SKETCH OF ELD. H. F. CARPENTER AND HIS LABORS.

Bro. H. F. Carpenter was converted to Christ in the Park Street Methodist Church, Worcester, Mass., in the early part of 1854, and became a member of that church, with which he continued two years. He was convinced before his conversion that Christ was coming soon, and embraced the doctrine of immortality through Christ alone at the time of his conversion, and maintained that view during his connection with the M. E. Church. Believing the Lord had called him to preach the gospel, and being urged to that duty by his Methodist brethren in 1856, and finding that he could not labor harmoniously with them while holding his faith in the Bible doctrine concerning man's nature and destiny, he took a letter of dismission from them and united with the Adventists in publishing the gospel message of Christ's immediate advent. Bro. C. commenced his ministerial labors in company with Eld. H. L. Hastings, in Peacedale, R. I., and was ordained to the work soon after, at a camp-meeting in Wilbraham, Mass., by Elders Hastings, Edwin Burnham, and S. G. Mathewson. Eld. C. has been an active and faithful workman in the Master's cause, careful and stable in the work of the gospel of the kingdom. He is an able minister, "a workman that needeth not to be ashamed, rightly dividing the word of truth." Many have been brought to Christ and built up in the faith through his labors. He has been a constant correspondent of the Advent papers, has been secretary of the "Advent Christian Association" for several years, and is the author of "The Scriptural Question Book," one of the best books ever prepared for Sabbath School scholars. He is now an associate editor with Eld. A. A. Hoyt, of the "Biblical Messenger," Plainfield, Vt., a professedly neutral monthly. The object of

HENRY F. CARPENTER.—Page 608.

the paper is to publish the doctrine of Christ's soon coming, the obligations of the Christian religion, and the exceeding riches of Christ. We hope they will give the trumpet a certain sound that their patrons may be warned faithfully of the speedily coming judgment.

WESTERN ADVENT CHRISTIAN PUBLICATION ASSOCIATION.

In April, 1860, Eld. J. V. Himes issued a paper in Boston entitled "The Voice of the Prophets," which he published quarterly for three years. During this time he gave up his views of the immateriality of the soul, and embraced what is called the "life and death" views. We give an item of his statement of it in his "Apology:"

"I have said that up to 1860 I was not impressed with the importance of the so-called *Life and Death question* as a vital issue in Christian theology. It was, I think, in that year that I was led to commence an earnest re-examination of the subject, as the result of a deeply interesting conversation and discussion with Dr. O. R. Fassett, who was then residing in Westboro, Mass. . . . . . . And thus I was led to, I believe, a candid and thorough re-examination of the entire subject, as presented in the Word of God, which I recognized as my only rule of faith in regard to this, or any other doctrine. I would bow to the sacred Word; but I must re-examine its utterances on the doom awaiting, perhaps, the larger portion of mankind.

Immediately other influences began to affect me. As a public teacher I had long stood opposed to the doctrine of the sleep of the dead and destructiou of the wicked, and I must now meet a large circle of companions and friends, endeared by many ties in the past, who had received the views I now questioned from both my lips and pen; who looked to me for a sturdy defense of a doctrine the truth of which I was fairly beginning to doubt. They had learned of me, taken my counsel in upholding the Orthodox views, and opposing the "annihilationists, as they were, and are popularly called. . . . My mind is now settled. The arguments which have forced me, as an honest man and a Christian, to take a decided stand, and exert a vigorous opposition against the views I once held, will be forthcoming."

In 1863, the Illinois State Conference passed a resolution inviting Eld. Himes to remove West and give his aid to the cause in that extensive field. In January, 1864, a conference of believers was convened at Jonesville, Mich., and organized the Michigan and Northern Indiana Advent Christian Conference. In their report we find the following Resolutions were read, discussed and adopted.

RESOLUTIONS OF THE ILLINOIS CONFERENCE.

"*Whereas,* The Advent Christian Conference of Illinois, at their last session in Iowa, passed a preamble and resolution, inviting Eld. J. V. Himes to this western field, to aid us in our work of spreading the knowledge of the coming kingdom, and building up the Advent cause generally, therefore

Resolved, That we thank our brethren of Illinois for this act of theirs, in advance of us; and now, in our first public meeting, in Conference, do cordially adopt their resolution inviting Elder Himes to labor with us in the West, as also to establish his press and print his paper,—weekly, if possible; if not, as often as he can do so, with the means afforded.

Resolved, That we will give him our full and hearty support, both as a general evangelist and publisher, and call on all the friends of the cause to aid us in this matter.

Resolved, That we are pleased with and approve of the action of the Advent Christian church in Buchanan, in inviting Eld. Himes to locate in that place, as it will be central, and he will have the sympathy and support of the community in the enterprise, and be better sustained than in any other location at present known to us.

We are yet weak and few in this State; and so we are in all the Western States. Our churches and Conferences are yet in their infancy in this great field. But with united and vigorous action, we cannot fail to become a strong and efficient people.

Eld. Himes being present, and giving encouragement that he would enter upon the work in the West, and publish a weekly paper entitled "The Voice of the West, and Second Advent Pioneer," they passed the following resolutions:

Resolved, That a fund of $1000 be raised by subscription, to aid Elder Himes in the publication of the *Voice of the West, and Second Advent Pioneer,* and also to publish such tracts as shall be needed the coming year, to spread the light we profess to enjoy on the Lord's speedy coming.

The question here came up, as to whether the paper should be published by an Association, or by Elder Himes. He proposed to have it published by an Association, so soon as one could be formed. But the Conference was of the opinion that the paper would be more efficient, and better serve the great cause in the West, for him to conduct it independently, and call to his aid such help as would best advance the great objects in view. Whereupon, Elder Babcock offered the following resolution:

AN INDEPENDENT PRESS.

Whereas, an independent press is the life and support of the cause of liberty, progress, and reform; and whereas it is equally valuable in the cause of Christ; and whereas Elder J. V. Himes is about to publish a paper, entitled the *Voice of the West,* at Buchanan, Mich., therefore

Resolved, That it is the voice of this Conference that we encourage Bro. Himes in this enterprise; and also in publishing books and tracts, and such other matter as the wants of the cause demand. We have full confidence in his ability and wisdom to do this work; and now that he is *free*, we do not wish him to be trammeled or hindered in this work, to which God in his divine providence, has called him.

Pursuant to the above, Eld. Himes issued the paper proposed, now the "Advent Christian Times;" its first number bearing date Feb. 13, 1864, Buchanan, Michigan.

It appears that Eld. Himes conducted the office and paper through the year as the Conference had proposed, until a general Western Conference could be convened, which was effected at the close of the same year.

THE FIRST GENERAL ADVENT CHRISTIAN CONFERENCE OF THE NORTHWEST.

This conference met at the office of the *Voice of the West*, Friday morning, Dec. 9, 1864.

The time was occupied in social worship, addresses, reports, and suggestions as to the state of the cause and the demand for efficient efforts, until Monday.

Conference met Monday A. M., Dec. 12, at the office of the *Voice of the West*, and after reading of the Scriptures and prayer by Eld. P. B. Hoyt, proceeded to business.

The minutes of the previous meeting were read and accepted.

The Business Committee then submitted the following:

RESOLUTIONS.

Resolved, That an Association be organized, to be called the Western Advent Christian Publishing Association, to constitute the legal business organ of the Advent Christian Conferences of Ohio, Michigan, Indiana, Illinois, Wisconsin, Iowa, Minnesota, and other Western States and Canada.

Resolved, That this Association shall, in accordance with the proposition of Eld. J. V. Himes, take in charge the publication of the weekly paper now entitled the "Voice of the West," and the publication of all books and tracts that may be thought important for the advancement of the interests of the Advent cause.

Resolved, That this Association, in order to become an effective organ of the body, shall procure, so soon as possible, a press, type, and furniture to constitute an efficient printing, book-binding, and publication office.

The above resolutions were taken up separately, freely discussed during the morning and afternoon sessions of the Conference, and were unanimously adopted.

The Secretary then read the Constitution of the Association, as proposed by the committee on a plan of association. It was then freely discussed and approved, section by section.

Adjourned.

The day following, the Association was legally incorporated under the law of Michigan. Eld. J. V. Himes was unanimously chosen editor, and the paper and office appendages transferred to the Western Advent Christian Publication Association.

From this small, but resolute beginning, the cause was greatly blessed with help and general prosperity, through the abounding grace of God, and the faithful, self-sacrificing, unceasing efforts of its servants. Though they have passed through several strait places, the country new, the believers poor and far between, money scarce and ministers few, the Lord has worked mightily, and a vast amount of gospel labor has been accomplished, and thousands of souls awakened and brought to Christ, and thousands of believers have accepted the glorious message of Christ's immediate coming.

Subscriptions to the paper came up to over four thousand. It was enlarged and improved. Many tracts have been issued and widely circulated. Eight thousand of the "Doctrine of Immortality," by Whittemore, have been published and circulated. Several thousands of "Adventism," by Sheldon, were also published and circulated. Several thousands of L. C. Collins' "Address to the M. E. Church," "Hades and Sheal," "Faith of St. Paul," have been published. The Minstrel, a small hymn-book, with an Appendix—containing a synopsis of the Adventist's views with the scriptural reasons, has been published, and many thousands circulated. The "Second Advent Quarterly" was issued two years, and much other work done which constantly added to the spread and growth of the infant cause in the West. Eld. J. V. Himes was elected from year to year, as editor, who, with his son, Wm. L., superintended the work until after the office was removed to Chicago, Ill. (which had been for some time contemplated), and better located, and appeared fair for more and better work than ever. At this juncture, the representatives of the Association carried a majority vote to change the base of management of the publication society, which gave a new (and as they thought better), plan of operations, but which has proved disastrous to the publishing interest West. Eld. J. V. Himes resigned the office of editor, and Wm. L. Himes was elected editor in the fall of 1872, and served until the spring of 1873, when he also resigned; since which, Eld. Wm. Sheldon was elected, and served until June, 1874. Eld. Sheldon having resigned, Eld. Frank Burr, a faithful minister, was elected through Elder Sheldon's recommendation. There are causes which have been for some time changing the condition of this Association, preventing its prosperity and working disunion; the Association is greatly embarrassed financially, and now unable to do much work. The primary causes of these evils are not yet sufficiently investigated and developed to record in history. We pray the Lord may correct the evils and give prosperity to the work of publishing the glorious message of the soon coming Christ, to deliver his groaning church.

YET IN DARKNESS.

In the midst of an alarming state of morals, which should turn every heart to the Scriptures and their author, to learn whether the Lord is not about to come to harvest the world, we read of the assembling of the "Massachusetts General Conference at Northampton (1866), with the First Congregational Church," when Rev. Dr. Hopkins, President of "Williams College," read an essay on "*The Pouring out of the Spirit in the Latter Days*," after which a spirited discussion on the subject was participated in by five doctors of divinity and six other eminent clergymen. But what was their light? The chief point of the essay and the remarks which followed were:

"There are at the present time remarkable providential preparations, such as have never been known or approximated before for a rapid diffusion of truth, and so for bringing *all men*, through the truth and by the power of the Spirit, into sympathy with each other, and into subjection to the will of God. *Many passages* of Scripture favor this view, and according to it, *the pouring out of the Spirit in the latter days is yet to come, and is to result in universal peace and righteousness.*"

Dr. Marvin, who followed him, said that "the general views brought out in the essay were those *generally* held, and that *the world is to be subdued to Christ* by the power of truth, *as administered by the Spirit.*"

If the doctor is correct, then Peter was in error in his sermon on the day of Pentecost, Acts ii. 14–21; Paul was in error when he wrote to Timothy that "in the last days perilous times shall come." Do the following facts indicate that these doctors understand the "many passages of Scripture" they speak of? Can ye not discern the signs of the times?

A Fearful State of Things.—The *New York Tribune* has the following in 1866: "The telegraph wires bend under their weight of woe; the old earth quivers with throbs of agony from the centre to the pole; cities are shaken down, countries are engulfed, fair domains are overflowed with red-hot lava; wife is arrayed against husband, mother against child, son against father; a hecatomb is sacrificed on one railway, half as many on another, and on still another the width of a hair stands between a thousand and sudden death. In social life, our newspapers are smutched all over with reports of divorce and separation trials, of infidelity and disgrace, of gigantic crimes undertaken, half accomplished or completed. What shall be the end of these things?"

LAST CRISIS.

That we are living in the last crisis, or last generation, is now a fixed fact, proved by every fulfillment of prophecy, and believed in by all classes, skeptics as well as believers. It is evidenced by the thousand and one reports we are having continually from every kind of source, all going to show that we are living in an unparalleled age in the commission of crime, without we except the days of Noah and Lot, as the following extracts will show. The Portland *Advertiser* of Jan. 4, 1866, says in an article headed "Murders and Executions," quoting from the *Philadelphia Age:*

"The highest of all crimes is frightfully on the increase. . . . It is startling to compare the number of murders and executions during the past year, and to see with what ease the criminal is permitted to escape. . . . In 1864 there were in the United States 682 murders,—not accidental killing, but real murders. And how many executions followed? Just 98. . . . And things have naturally been growing worse and worse every year since."

Says the *Independent,* "The present times bid fair to be distinguished preeminently as a period of crime. . . . The progress of the grosser forms of wickedness are facts frightful to observe and more frightful to ponder. Every newspaper is laden with the records of such. They make the staple news of the day. They load and darken the columns of all journals till one trembles to take up the morning paper, is afraid to have it read in the family, and lays it down with a sense of heart sickness, . . . a keen apprehension of what is to be expected in the future. It is not those who are avowedly worldly and godless in their lives. . . . Teachers, physicians, lawyers, ministers, the young not only, but the aged, in well nigh equal measure. All seem to be smitten with the foul contagion."

Says the *Christian Press,* of Cincinnati, Ohio: "Brethren, the

A. A. PHELPS.— Page 615.

crisis of the world is come. Are we prepared for it? Can we resign all the interests of an earthly life, and identify ourselves with the will of God and spiritual excellence? Can we stand in the whirlwind, talk with the thunder, and look calmly on heaven when God looks forth in indignation on a guilty world? Are we prepared with serene joy and holy confidence to unite in the song of Moses and the Lamb, when the plagues of heaven shall fall on the wicked, and the earth shall be filled with wailing and blasphemy?

"Before me lies the programme of the concert given at the Maine Wesleyan Seminary, in 1867, and judging from the name of the institution we should judge that the programme might have been filled with selections from the Oratorios of *The Messiah*, *David* *The Creation*, etc., but true to the description given by Paul of the form of godliness, the programme stood thus:

"Part first. 1. Overture, *Caliph of Bagdad.* 2. Polka. 3. Declamation. 4. Berlin Waltz. 5. Polka. 6. Polka. 7. Lily White Quadrille. 8. Polka.

"Part second. 1. Waltz. 2. Duet. 3. Wedding March. 4. Irish Polka. 5. Johnny Schmocker. 6. Hanover Waltz. 7. Gallop. 8. Quadrille Polka.

"I wonder if John Wesley were alive now if he would know his followers. I do not think you would find him listening to Irish Polkas. It fulfills Scripture,—'Departing from the faith.'"

Rev. T. L. Cuyler, in the *Independent* of Sept. 7, 1865, says of lukewarm Christians, "I would not exchange the prayers and power of a single servant girl, that I have in my Brooklyn Church, for five hundred of these petrified professors sitting around the communion table in meaningless mockery of a crucified Master. . . . Put a score of lukewarm professors into a prayer-meeting and it becomes an ice house. . . . Terrible to contemplate the mischief which these lukewarm professors make in the church and in society. Over such as these sinners stumble into perdition. . . . To avoid such a state, go back to your secret closet again; ask the Spirit to help you. To-morrow you may be in your shroud."

SKETCH OF ELDER A. A. PHELPS.

A. A. Phelps was born in Monterey, N. Y., Feb. 28, 1836. His parents were poor, and his childhood was interwoven with toil and privation. His mother died when he was thirteen years of age, and he went out into a world of strangers and of sin, to brave its storms all alone. Having promised his dying mother that he would seek the Lord and lead a Christian life, he set about the matter with an honest and earnest heart. At the age of fourteen he felt a satisfactory assurance that he was a child of God. He was immersed on the 3d day of August, 1851, and was received into the Methodist Episcopal Church, at Lawrenceville, Pa.

The conviction soon fastened upon him that he must preach the gospel. The thought of assuming such solemn responsibilities almost overwhelmed him. The contemplation of such a life-work supplied a mighty motive for earnest activity in seeking the necessary preparation. His constantly increasing desire for knowledge led to very studious habits, and he spent all his earnings in acquiring an education. Advancing through various stages of student-life in the public school, the academy, and the seminary, he entered Genesee College in 1856, and graduated in the regular course June 21, 1860.

Meanwhile he was not an idler in the Master's vineyard. In the fall after he was sixteen he commenced holding meetings, and soon gained the distinguished title of "*boy preacher.*" On the 10th of December, 1853, when seventeen years old, he was formally licensed to preach.

Religiously, he was of the radical type. He saw enough of empty forms to make him feel the importance of striking for a spiritual religion. Early in life he took his stand against a superficial, policy-working piety, and committed himself on the side of plainness and purity. These views and feelings had something to do in adjusting his subsequent church relations.

He was married on the day of his graduation, and entered upon the life of an itinerant minister. The troubles that had been brewing in the M. E. Church for years, in some sections of the country, and especially within the bounds of Genesee Conference, were just then culminating. Antagonistic elements were at work and a square issue was inevitable. On the one hand, fashion, formalism, festivals, freemasonry, pro-slavery, and worldly policy were sapping the very life-blood of the church that was professedly raised up "to spread Scriptural holiness over the land." On the other hand, there was a large minority who still loved the simplicity of the gospel and were willing to make any sacrifice for the promotion of earnest Christianity. He narrowly watched the measures adopted by the majority for crushing out the very elements that once made the Methodists a "peculiar people, zealous of good works."

When persecution waxed hot and drove several of the most earnest preachers from the conference, and hundreds of the best members from the churches, it became a serious question what those proscribed brethren ought, under the circumstances, to do. In August, 1860, a goodly number of the scattered saints came together and organized the *Free Methodist Church.* The subject of this sketch was secretary of that organizing convention. Having cast in his lot with those whom he regarded as "persecuted for righteousness' sake," he acted as secretary of their largest Annual Conference during the eight years of his connection with them.

It was a great satisfaction to feel that what little influence he had was thrown upon the side of an uncompromising Christianity. He formed the acquaintance of a large number of devoted Christians, whom he still regards with tender feelings. But the time came when the dearest ties must be sundered. To make the trial doubly severe, he must go out under the imputation of having become a *heretic*, an *infidel*, and a *hopeless apostate from the faith!*

Several years before this painful culmination, he had promised himself a re-examination of the doctrine of immortality. At length he set about the work, being especially interested in the question of *future punishment*. Carefully and prayerfully he pursued the investigation, anxious to know the exact truth of the Bible, before whose authority he bowed in deepest reverence. The fear of imbibing dangerous error made him very careful in weighing evidence and very slow in arriving at new conclusions.

He read the ablest works he could find on both sides of the question, diligently comparing the arguments with the Bible. He also published an extended series of "Notes, Queries, and Objections," bearing on the state of the dead and the doom of the ungodly, to see how formidable an array of evidence could be presented.

In August, 1867, while residing in the city of Lockport, N. Y., he received an invitation to preach for the Adventist brethren in Rochester, to which he responded. He enjoyed much liberty in meeting the aforesaid engagement, but the act stirred up no small breeze among his Methodist brethren, and he began to be strongly suspected of heresy. He was closely catechized at the ensuing Conference, but his character passed and he was stationed in Rochester, N. Y.

The year was a laborious one. In addition to his regular pastoral work, he spent considerable time in editorial work on *The Free Methodist*, a paper with which he was officially connected. Nor did he abandon the investigation which he had commenced, although repeatedly urged to do so by his friends. As he was gradually outgrowing sectarianism, he frequently attended the meetings of those who were especially interested in the Lord's coming, and on one occasion he joined with them in a communion service.

Another Annual Conference at length arrived, and his case was the subject of much discussion, in the course of which the following resolution was offered and passed:

"*Resolved*, That the course pursued by A. A. Phelps, in fraternizing and communing with a sect called Adventists, who deny the natural immortality of the soul, is condemned by this Conference."

He had no disposition to complain of this resolution, for it was the expression of honest convictions. But it served to indicate the path of duty, as he could not conscientiously cramp himself into the narrow limits prescribed for him. Therefore, in good faith and good feeling, he presented the following paper of withdrawal:

TO THE GENESEE ANNUAL CONFERENCE OF THE FREE METHODIST CHURCH.

DEAR BRETHREN:—Since I espoused the cause of Christ I have endeavored to maintain my integrity as an earnest, consistent Christian. Beginning at the early age of seventeen to herald the tidings of mercy to perishing men, I have tried to be God's faithful mouth-piece during the fifteen years that have succeeded—seven years as a local preacher in the M. E. Church, and eight years in the Free Methodist itinerancy. In both Christian knowledge and Christian experience I trust I have not remained *in statu quo.* I have an ardent love for truth, liberty, and goodness, wherever I find them. Much of the bigotry of other days has been replaced in my heart by that gospel charity which "rejoices not in iniquity but rejoices in the *truth,*" by whomsoever promulgated. Since all cannot see exactly alike, I believe Christians ought to incorporate in their platform as much liberty as we find in the words of an ancient writer: "In essentials, unity; in non-essentials, liberty; in all things, charity." An application of this rule would banish from the churches that narrowness which cramps the conscience and divides the Christian world into so many partisan cliques and clans. Much of the mischief, doubtless, results from the substitution of human creeds for the New Testament of our Lord Jesus Christ. Tradition is often largely interwoven with those creeds, and too much stress is laid upon a perfect agreement in *doctrine*, as a condition of church membership. I believe that Christian *experience, character, and conduct* should constitute the test of membership in any ecclesiastical organization. The church belongs to *Christ*, and *every Bible Christian has a right to a place within her pale.* Head religion will do to make bigots, but it takes heart religion to make Christians. "If *thy heart* be as mine, give me thy *hand.*"

A careful and prayerful study of the Scriptures has led me to these conclusions:

1. *Men will be judged before they are rewarded or punished.*
2. *Jesus Christ will come the second time before men are judged.*
3. "*The wages of sin is death; but the gift of God is eternal life through Jesus Christ our Lord.*"

The discrepancy between the views herein expressed and those entertained by the Free Methodist Church, and the unwillingness you feel to have anything said in the direction above indicated, suggest the propriety of my withdrawing from your connection. It should also be stated, as an additional reason for taking this step, that there are several things in the polity and administration of the Free Methodist Church which I cannot fully endorse.

In taking my peaceful departure let me say that there are some principles and many persons connected with your movement for which I entertain a profound respect. I shall still advocate those principles and love those brethren with whom I have stood shoulder to shoulder in fighting a common foe. Should you ever invite me to occupy your pulpits, there is nothing in my views or feelings that would cause me to refuse. Should any of you, on the contrary, feel it your duty to treat me coolly and suspiciously, and to cripple my influence with the poisoned arrows of slander, I shall try to love you still, and pray that God will "not lay this sin to your charge."

I go out, "not knowing whither I go." I have no definite plans for the future. I mean to *be* good and *do* good, according to my ability, and the opening of a kind Providence. *Eternal life* is the blissful goal for which I am running. As God has graciously saved me from the spirit of sectarianism, I desire to be recognized hereafter simply as a CHRISTIAN. May I share, with you, the fadeless glories of immortality, when all the saints get home! "Finally, brethren, farewell!"

When the denominational ties were fairly severed, his former brethren seemed to feel sacredly bound to close their pulpits against him and to treat him "as a heathen and a publican." But the Lord set before him "an open door which no man could shut." Invitations to preach began to pour in from various States, and he soon found himself traveling a much larger circuit than ever before!

It was about six months before the last fog-bank was dissipated by the light of heavenly truth. On the 17th of March, 1869, he made the following entry: "The chains are severed at last. The clearing-up shower descended a few days ago, while on my knees pleading with God for light. I am fully convinced that the devil and all his works will yet be *destroyed*, and the universe of God, so terribly marred by sin, will rise up out of the smoke and ruin, free from every element opposed to purity and love! O enrapturing thought! Transporting prospect! Glorious consummation! Eternal triumph! The plan of redemption will yet be a grand success. Millions of redeemed ones will be crowned as trophies of amazing grace, and all who would not come into the glorious plan will be accounted useless rubbish, and cleared out of the way by the raging fires which God will kindle in the day of the sinner's doom! *Praise God for being such a God!* Praise him for devising such a wondrous plan of recovering mercy! The Bible possesses new charms. Harmony is restored. The last spot is removed from the shining face of the sun. Hallelujah! I shall henceforth be a happier man."

Nearly six years have now elapsed since he walked out upon an independent platform, taking the Bible for his creed and the world for his parish. He has had time to review his course and to take a sober "second thought." His present testimony is, that all the emoluments of the world could not tempt him back into the traditional, creed-bound theology of other years. He has had plenty of work to keep him from rusting, and plenty of trials to keep him from self-exaltation. A considerable amount of his time and energies have been devoted to the *Bible Banner*, New York, of which he has been the conducting editor since it originated. He is fully determined to *work on*, and, if necessary, to *suffer* on, until his heavenly Master shall bring the crown of immortal life which he hopes to wear.

Bro. Phelps is now proprietor and principal editor of the *Bible Banner*. This is an ably conducted and valuable monthly paper. His residence and address is Vineland, N. J.

HOME MISSIONS.

The proclaimers and supporters of the Advent Message have been engaged in mission work constantly in developing and teaching these portions of the gospel to the masses who were ignorant of them. But in addition to this general work, several missionary societies, besides those already mentioned, have been organized, and special missions sustained by them, among which are the following:

THE AMERICAN ADVENT MISSION SOCIETY.

This society was organized on Mount Wilbraham, Mass., August, 1865, and was intended to "embrace in its membership and operations, brethren of the whole land, East, West, North, and South, uniting in one Society, and bending all their energies to the accomplishment of the work to be done, and having special reference to missionary efforts among the freedmen."

Its officers were:

Eld. Joshua V. Himes, President, Michigan.

Eld. S. G. Mathewson,	Vice-President,	Vermont;
Eld. D. T. Taylor,	"	New York;
Eld. I. C. Wellcome,	"	Maine;
S. P. Clark,	"	Rhode Island;
Eld. John Couch,	"	New Hampshire;
Eld. William Sheldon,	"	Wisconsin;
Sidney Hall,	"	Connecticut;
Eld. O. R. Fassett,	"	New York;
Eld. H. K. Flagg,	"	Massachusetts;
Eld. J. D. Brown,	"	Pennsylvania;
C. S. Sherman,	"	Vermont;
Dr. P. B. Hoyt,	"	Ohio;
Eld. William McCullock,	"	Illinois;
N. W. Wait,	"	New York;
Randolph E. Ladd,	"	Massachusetts.

Wm. B. Herron, Corresponding and Recording Secretary.

George T. Adams, Treasurer.

Solomon Hovey, Auditor.

Eld. J. V. Himes, Eld. Miles Grant, Solomon Hovey, George T. Adams, Eld. A. W. Sibley, Eld. L. T. Cunningham, and William B. Herron, Executive Board.

The above society raised one thousand dollars at their beginning, and at once entered upon work in Memphis, Tenn., and St. Louis, Mo. Eld. Himes went there to open the missions, establish schools, and build a house of worship for the freedmen. Eld. I. I. Leslie, who was already in the South, and a faithful missionary, acquainted with the work among the colored people, was engaged; and, with sisters Butler, Bywater, and others, conducted several schools and meetings in Memphis and adjacent towns. The Lord blessed this effort and much good resulted and several churches of believers were gathered. Bro. L. F. Cole and wife, from Maine, spent two winters in that mission, and the reports of their work show that it was not in vain.

Eld. H. K. Flagg was employed in the mission among the freedmen at St. Louis, Mo., and, in connection with the labors of Sister M. K. Prescott, a resident there, and a faithful Christian lady, a good work was accomplished. But the state of southern society, the need of schools to first educate the people to read, together with the strong prejudices existing against the people of the north, requires more money, and more laborers suited to southern work, than the Adventists can well furnish to prosecute a vigorous and extensive mission among them. Yet the Lord will have the southern people warned of the speedy judgment, and faithful men and women have continued to carry the Message either by missionary aid or individual effort.

Eld. P. A. Smith has carried the Message into Florida, and the Lord has made it effectual in leading some to Christ, and in building up a goodly number in the faith.

In 1867, John B. Wardsworth, of North Carolina, came to New York on business, and was directed to the "Big Tent," then pitchad in Rochester, N. Y. This was a mission tent, and meetings were in progress, he was attracted to it. He says of it: "This was something I never heard before, and, through curiosity, was drawn to the meeting, though under the impression it was a speculative affair, or some Yankee scheme for making money."

He was soon converted to Christ and to the Message of his soon coming. His first impulse after being baptized was, to try to win souls to Christ by distributing tracts. He made this known to the ministers, and was soon supplied out of the Tract Fund; and returning, commenced at Baltimore, Md. From thence he *walked* to all the principal cities South, distributing tracts bearing the Advent Message, or parts of it, with other practical truths of the gospel. His work was blessed of God. He has published a pamphlet entitled "A Colporteur's Notes," giving some accounts of the work, and narrating a discussion he heard in Louisville, Ky., between a Baptist and an Adventist. This work is one of much interest, and has been scattered through the South.

In 1867, Eld. P. G. Bowman, a prominent Methodist minister of S. C., then preaching in North Carolina, was sent to the Northern States to obtain aid for their churches. He obtained more aid than some of them were willing to accept.

While in New York, he met with an Advent believer, who set him to thinking of new themes. At Boston he visited the World's Crisis office, and obtained books and the paper. He was soon brought into the faith, and has since become an efficient Advent missionary in South and North Carolina, Georgia, and other States. Much good is thus resulting from the "aid" he obtained in the North. Many and wonderful have been the singular providences which have attended this Message, in opening ways for its proclamation where all human wisdom and device had failed, and where all human efforts and plans of misguided ones had been applied to keep it out.

In 1868, Eld. L. C. Collins, of Minnesota, whom we have before mentioned as being engaged in this mission in Massachusetts in 1842, having relaxed his efforts and continued within the scope of Methodism, until re-awakened by the subject of man's nature and future destiny, was brought to see and fully embrace the doctrine of immortality through Christ alone, and to re-enter upon the work of proclaiming the message of the soon coming of Christ. Being dismissed from the Methodist E. church, he has become an efficient laborer in pulpit and press, in the Second Advent cause, and many others of that church have been led to see the truth on these subjects through his labors.

We have good news from Alabama. The following is clipped from the "New Era," of Stevenson, Ala.:

"Shortly after the war a ripple of excitement blew over the religious waters in this section, caused by some religious tracts circulating, which proclaimed the speedy coming of the Saviour to earth; soon after this Adventism began to be preached, a worthy Baptist minister, Rev. J. J. Smith, being among its earliest advocates, obtaining thereby the title of 'Prophetic Smith.' The dreams of Daniel and the mysteries of the Book of Revelation were simplified and explained to a nicety. Tracts almost innumerable, and religious papers, edited by brilliant and emphatic rhetoricians, well versed in the Scriptures, were in every household."

The editor next refers to Eld. H. Davis, one of our missionaries, and Mrs. Hattie Hastings, with the large tent called Bethel, in which they preached, and adds:

"Recently, Rev. John A. Cargile, a native Alabamian, a worthy son of a worthy farmer of Jackson, Co., became a prominent proclaimer of these doctrines, having two debates with two different ministers." Brethren Smith and Cargile are now publishing the message extensively in Alabama and Tennessee. They are able and influential. The Lord is with them and many are being converted.

Eld. Cargile has published a work—"Truth and Error Contrasted"—being a review of several sermons preached against his faith. It is a masterly work, and shows him fully competent to the task. It is being circulated South, and will enlighten many on the gospel hope.

Eld. J. C. Smith, formerly of Maine, who has labored successfully in the Southern mission field, is meeting with signal success in mission work in Kansas, where he has labored since 1871. The Lord has raised up others to help, and given him a faithful missionary wife, who is with him in the work, and extensive reformations are resulting from the mission labors in that new State.

Eld. D. D. Reed and his faithful wife are prosecuting a prosperous mission through Oregon, bearing his own expenses and seeing good results of their work. These are but samples of many cases which we cannot record, where this message is moving the hearts of the Lord's children in the churches, to see that the judgment is soon coming, and the work is not ended, the calls are constantly increasing: "come over and help us." The A. A. Mission Society has aided the brethren in South Carolina in building three good houses of worship, and sustained or aided missionaries in North and South Carolina, Georgia, Virginia, Maryland, Tennessee, Kentucky, Florida, Texas, Missouri, Kansas, Nebraska, California, and other States and Territories. They have also sent out an immense number of tracts.

During 1866 this Mission Society raised and expended in the *Home Mission* field, $3,017.57; for the *European Missions*, $683.-65; for free distribution of *Tracts*, $2,176.62; for the *Poor Fund*,

$361.36; total, $6,239.20. Since that time the yearly contributions have varied but little. In 1873 the total contributions were $6,139.23. Beside this, State Mission Societies have raised funds and disbursed them, for Missions and Tracts. During 1872–3 "The Maine Scriptural Publication Society" circulated over $1000 worth of tracts, and the "Maine Mission and Tract Society" circulated over $200 worth in the Southern and Western States.

THE STAR OF HOPE MISSION.

Sister Anna E. Smith, one of the female preachers who has been engaged in city mission work among the poor and degraded classes in Philadelphia and New York much of her time from her childhood, opened a mission in New York City in 1866 or '67, hired a building as a home or hospital for the sick, employed others to assist, and furnished a home for others who volunteered to help. This mission was sustained partly by the liberality and energetic labors of that noble-hearted Christian lady and liberal contributions of Christian friends throughout the country. Sister S. and her co-laborers visited cellars, garrets, and lanes, and ministered to the wants of thousands of the poor and the fallen of that corrupt city, providing food, clothing, and medicine, holding meetings, preaching, reading, and praying with them, and holding regular religious services at the home and at other points, and distributing tracts freely. Along with this work, which was continued for several years, a mission was sustained in Hackensack, N. J., a neat chapel erected and kept open for schools and preaching among the colored people.

A large amount of good has been accomplished and several hundreds of souls converted through these unrequited toils and sacrifices. Several thousands of dollars were contributed and expended. In addition to the above, Sister S. visited Virginia, projected a mission, and had school-houses erected, where other faithful believers taught the Freedmen to read, and preached to them the gospel of Christ, resulting in the conversion of many and the improvement of society generally.

The mission work projected and prosecuted by Brother and Sister Hastings, with their faithful helpers, has been merely alluded to in a biographical sketch of him. A large amount of mission work was done through their agency, and great results will, we trust, appear in the harvest day. Eld. F. H. Burbank established a "Wanderer's Home," in Philadelphia, Pa., where, for a time, he sustained a city mission among the poor of the colored race and the orphans who had no homes. Good results followed that work of mercy, and through the blessing of God fruits will be gathered unto eternal life.

UNION FEMALE MISSIONARY ASSOCIATION.

In 1866, a female mission society, with the above title, was organized in New England, including the female preachers and public laborers associated with the Second Advent Message throughout the land. We have not the minutes of the original organization. We give the names of the officers chosen at their Annual Meeting in 1867, at Mount Wilbraham, Mass.: President, Mrs. E. S. Jennings; Vice President, Mrs. Anna E. Smith; Secretary and Treasurer, Mrs. M. McKinstry; Assistant Secretary, E. P. Hobbs. Some twenty preaching women became members of this society, who have been actively engaged in mission work throughout the Eastern, Western, and Southern States. They also organized a "Woman's Christian Association," including all Christians who wished to coöperate with them in this mission work and would become members. This Association published a paper entitled

"WOMAN AND HER WORK."

The paper had been previously started by Mrs. A. E. Smith, in New York City. It was subsequently enlarged and published at Concord, N. H., and edited by Mrs. T. F. Sargent one year (1870–1), after which it was published in Rochester, N. Y., and edited by Mrs. E. S. Jennings. It was well adapted to the work for which it was originated, but after several removals and changes of managers it was given up, in 1872, for lack of pecuniary aid.

Mrs. C. Tuller, a pious and devoted Christian lady, has established a mission school at West Point, Ky., for the colored people, where through great perseverance and unrequited toil she has, during several years, been very successful in educating many, and in teaching them the gospel of Christ and its blessed hope of the Lord's soon coming. The A. A. Mission Society and Christian friends contribute voluntarily in aiding her in this noble work.

SKETCH OF ELD. WM. L. HIMES AND HIS LABORS.

William Lloyd Himes is a native of Boston, Mass., born in 1839. His early training by Christian parents, the constant association with Christian society and the Advent ministry, who visited with the family, were not lost upon him. He was thoroughly instructed in the great principles of the gospel, its duties and hope, the prophecies and the signs of the advent and kingdom of Christ. He was converted to Christ in 1856. He had served in the "Advent Herald" office in such work as he was capable of doing in his boyhood. When his father, J. V. Himes, removed to Buchanan, Mich., and started the "Voice of the West," now "Advent Christian Times," of Chicago, William went with him and entered upon the work of journalism and the proclamation of the Advent Message, with which he was already familiar. Although not the editor of the paper he did much of the editorial work from its beginning, and labored incessantly in overseeing the general business and interests of the office, as well as performing much of the hard labor required to prosecute such a work.

His heart glowed with the precious truths of the gospel, and his ambition knew no bounds but impossibilities in seeking to promote the work of spreading these truths far and wide. His natural abilities for such work are superior, and experience, with his deep interest, impelled him to the fullest extent of his physical strength, which resulted in helping to make that paper one of the best of all the Second Advent weeklies ever published in this country, and also in projecting and helping forward the publication of many valuable tracts and books, healthful and instructive, by which the Second Advent cause in the West has been greatly extended and strengthened. There are numerous friends in the West who appreciate these labors.

In 1868, he commenced preaching, and was ordained for the work of the gospel ministry, which he has since been pursuing with commendable zeal and good success.

In 1869, he commenced the "Second Advent Quarterly," and associated with him Eld. J. H. Whitmore in the editorial department. This we regard as being the most able and thoroughly Biblical periodical ever published among the Second Advent believers in America. It was published two years, and discontinued for lack of support when it ought to have been raised to a list of 20,000 paying subscribers, and sent out free to 10,000 ministers of this country to acquaint them with the views it advocated.

In the fall of 1872, Bro. W. L. Himes was elected, by the Board of the Western A. C. P. Association, to the editorial office of the "Advent Christian Times," in fact, while he had long served as such in connection with his father, who traveled extensively as an evangelist. During the term of his editorship the paper was the best religious journal we had ever taken among over thirty different ones. But circumstances connected with the association, together with disunion arising out of various causes, led him to resign the office in March, 1873, and to accept a call to become the pastor of the Second Advent Church in Castleton, Vt., where he has been preaching until now, and has received a unanimous call to remain another year. He is looking with deep interest for the return of the Lord, and labors with earnestness to lead sinners to prepare for a home in the coming kingdom.

ERRORS EXPOSED.

Editors and reporters often strangely mix matters with which they are not acquainted, and thus mislead their readers.

The N. Y. Tribune in a late issue declares:

"The majority of the Second Adventists, at their late General Convention in Springfield, Mass., agreed on the general doctrine of the second coming of Christ *soon*, but concluded to give up trying to fix the time. They hold unanimously to another doctrine, which is gradually pervading all the evangelical sects, that the saints only are immortal, and that the wicked utterly perish, soul and body, at death."

The majority of Second Adventists agreed long ago on the general doctrine of the Second Advent of Christ *soon*. They also concluded to give up trying to fix the time long before the abovenamed Convention; but such agreement and conclusion were arrived at individually without mutual consultation.

That they hold unanimously that the saints only are immortal is *not* true. They hold unanimously that the saints only will put on immortality when Christ returns. That this doctrine is gradually pervading all the evangelical sects is true; but that the Adventists believe "that the wicked utterly perish, soul and body, at death" is *untrue*. Not one in a hundred hold to such a view.

About 1848, Mr. John T. Walsh, then an associate editor with Eld. Geo. Storrs, of the Bible Examiner, commenced teaching that the wicked would never be raised from death, that their remaining dead was the penalty for sin. He was not associated with the Adventists. Some Adventists read his writings. After Mr. W. began to deny the resurrection of the unjust, Eld. Storrs published in the Examiner the following Scriptural and sensible article on the subject of

THE NON-RESURRECTION THEORY.

"We have no intention of spending our time for a year and a half in discussing so fruitless a topic, and one which we are clearly satisfied is opposed both to the spirit and the letter of the Bible. If any man can give us as plain a text that men are immortal by creation as we have that—'*all* that are in the graves . . . *shall come forth* . . . they that have done good . . . *and they that have done evil*,' then we will confess our error in ever having preached or printed the 'Six Sermons.' Here we leave the topic of the non-resurrection of wicked men, and little children; for, the theory we oppose denies the resurrection of infants, *except possibly the infants of believers.* According to it, there is a bare *possibility,* nothing more, that our sleeping children 'shall come again from the land of the enemy;' and it is quite *uncertain* whether to them, '*Jesus is the resurrection and the life.*'

"The method of interpreting Scripture on which this theory depends, unsettles all faith in the Bible, and saps the foundation of Christianity. Prophetic Scripture is made by it to speak of events past at the time. Because the prophets speak as if God had *already done* what he will finally do, it is inferred there shall be no resurrection of the wicked. For example, the Psalmist says —'*Thou hast* destroyed all them that go astray from thee'—W. says, 'there is no intimation of a resurrection . . . for the characters are utterly consumed and destroyed.'

"The question here all turns on *time.* *When* are 'all that go astray destroyed?' If he is correct in his theory, David lived in a *happy time;* all the wicked *had been* destroyed—not one was *then* left; for David says—'Thou *hast*' done it;—not, thou *wilt* do it. Thus the truth of God is turned into a fable, and Christianity is a falsehood. Do you ask how so? We answer—Several centuries before the birth of Jesus of Nazareth, Isaiah said, 'Unto us a child is born . . . the government shall be upon his shoulder,' etc. Now, says the Jew, 'It is plain the Messiah was born long before Jesus of Nazareth; Jesus cannot therefore be the Messiah of God.' Again, the same prophet said of Messiah, seven hundred years before the birth of Jesus, 'He *is* despised, . . . we *did* esteem him smitten of God, . . . with his stripes we *are* healed, . . . the Lord *hath laid* on him the iniquity of us all, . . . he *was* oppressed,' etc. Hence, it is as plain a matter of fact, to a Jew, that Jesus cannot be the Messiah, as it is to the author of '*Anastasis*' that the wicked will have no resurrection from such *texts* as that in which David said—'Thou *hast* destroyed all them that go astray from thee.' And we think the argument of the Jew is as well founded and as forcible as that of him who contends there is no resurrection of the wicked because their future and final destruction is spoken of as already past. To us it seems clear that 'blindness in part has happened to' the authors of such interpretations. 'God calls things that be not as though they were,' on account of the certainty of the accomplishment of his purposes; thus he said—'I have made thee a father of many nations,' when as yet he had no child.

"This principle nnderstood and applied subverts all the fine-spun theory of non-resurrection of the wicked, and shows that what is spoken on the subject of their being destroyed, and not rising, in the various texts relied upon, to support the Pharisaic doctrine of the non-resurrection of the wicked, relate to their final destruction *after* the 'judgment of the great day,' unto which the wicked are '*reserved;*' when as Job says—' The wicked *shall be brought forth to the day of wrath;*' and he affirms, they are '*reserved unto the day of destruction;*' Job xxi: 30; and Jesus Christ says, they '*shall come forth from the graves'* to condemnation or 'damnation;' after which, the testimony of John the apostle is, they shall be 'cast into the lake of fire:' surely that is '*the day* of destruction.' Let men beware of deluding their souls with the vain fancy that they will lie in their graves in a state of insensibility to the judgment and the awful execution of the sentence that is to follow; vain hope; *strong delusion.*

"We have called the doctrine of the non-resurrection of the wicked '*a Pharisaic doctrine.*' Our authority for this assertion is Josephus and the 'Cyclopedia of Biblical Literature, by John Kitto, D. D., F. S. A.,' an English work of great research. The Pharisees maintained that those who had 'lived virtuously,' and they '*only* have power to *revive and live again.*' This fact is worthy of serious attention, as the advocates of the non-resurrection of the wicked, who have recently come up, try hard not only to destroy the force of Christ's words (John v: 28, 29), but to make Paul's words (Acts xxiv: 14) to mean only, that the Pharisees *allowed* there would be a resurrection of the just and unjust, while the apostle did not. The truth is, the Pharisees 'allowed' there would 'be a resurrection of the dead,' but *denied* that it embraced the '*unjust.*' Paul affirms his *expectation*—for that is all the Greek word *elpida,* translated *hope,* in this text necessarily means—'that there shall be a resurrection of the dead *both* of the just *and of the unjust;*' thus agreeing with the testimony of Jesus, that '*all* in the graves shall come forth—good and evil;' and the 'two witnesses' strike down the Pharisaic doctrine of the just *only* being raised from the dead."—*Bible Examiner, Vol. V. pp. 43—44.*

Mr. Walsh, after driving this Pharisaic notion against the views of the Adventists and all other Christians, for some time, made another theological shift, and embraced a system of immaterialism which no Adventist would accept, claiming that the spirits of the wicked were alive in *Sheol-Hades* and would, at the day of judgment, be sentenced and be cast, without bodies, into the lake of fire and suffer eternal punishment, meaning eternal misery. Thus Mr. Walsh goes out of his pet theory; but Mr. Storrs now goes in. After the above plain Scriptural statements of Eld. S. against this system of unbelief, strange as it may appear to those not acquainted with him, Mr. S. himself embraced this "Pharisaic view," a view held by a portion of the Pharisees. He advocated it thoroughly for a few years and made a few disciples, then abjured it, and now teaches the theory of Mr. Dunn, of England, an almost universal salvation of the race, in a day of probation after the Second Advent and resurrection. We have before spoken of him as an erratic; though a man of much talent he is given to constant change. This denial of the resurrection of the unjust is a square contradiction of the plain testimony of the Bible.

Eld. H. L. Hastings, in a pamphlet, Retribution, thoroughly exposed the fallacy of the view, also in a tract on the resurrection. Eld. C. C. Marston has a published sermon on the resurrection which clearly refutes the notion with all who will give due credit to Scripture statements. Those in doubt should read these. Eld. D. T. Taylor wrote a series of articles in the World's Crisis which fully met this system of negation. We subjoin a few extracts:

TO LIVE, OR NOT TO LIVE.—BY D. T. TAYLOR.

"I like your name, 'The World's Crisis,' that is to say in the Lord's words, 'The Judgment of this World.' You believe there is to be a judgment for all men, not for some men, and some dust scattered through *hades;* you believe a critical point in the world's history is at hand. And so you exist to warn all men that, whether they live till that solemn time, or die before it comes, they must, nevertheless, stand at that bar. Be faithful to your mission, and consistent with your name, dear 'Crisis.' Walk in the old paths. So shall ye prosper. When you become the organ of a people who write 'No Resurrection' on the coffins of sinners, then change your name, my dear 'Crisis.'

"*Apodidomi*, in the Greek New Testament, is variously rendered, and means —to give, to render, to pay over to, to reward. See the following: 'The Son of man shall come in his glory—and *then* shall he *reward every man* according to his works.'—Matt. xvi. 27.

"'Who *will render* to *every man* according to his deeds.' When? 'In the day of wrath and revelation of the righteous judgment of God.'—Rom. ii. 5, 6.

"'Who *shall give* account (*logos*) to Him who is ready to judge,' etc.—1 Pet. iv. 5.

"'*Shall give* account (*logos*) thereof in the day of judgment.'—Matt. xii. 36.

"These passages teach that when our Lord comes it will be pay-day for all. THEN, and not before, shall each and all be rewarded for their deeds, whether good or evil. The non-resurrection theory contradicts these passages, and says the wicked dead *are* reaping their reward,—gone to sleep, never to awake; that's all. Then their going to sleep must be the day of wrath and revelation of God's judgment! . . . The non-resurrection theory says, in effect, that *hades* is the place of punishment of evil men. They die, go to *hades*, and that is the end of them. I read of another place, viz.: *gehenna.* Read Matt. v. 29, 30; x. 28; and Mark ix. 43, 45, 47, where the word is rendered *hell* and *hell-fire.* Now, *gehenna* is not *hades.* The latter is never set forth as the final place of punishment for sin, but all the learned admit the former is. To say the wicked dead will never come out of *hades* alive, is to confound the two places. Now, God can and will destroy both soul and body in gehenna-fire, which is no doubt John's lake of fire. But how can he do it, if the man never comes out of *hades?* Eh? Who are those having 'two feet, two hands, two eyes,' and a 'whole body,' and a 'soul' to boot, that are some day 'to be cast into gehenna-fire?' These texts are so plain, that my opponents are 'reduced to the extremities of solution' to dispose of them. Accordingly, the plow-share of ruin is got out, and Mr. False-Criticism hitches on his hobby-horse, and drives it through the Book. The passages only mean —a few million of sinners, who live to see our Lord come; or, it may mean—some dead corpses will be flung into gehenna! That's all.

"The "first resurrection" is next assailed. It don't mean *first*. Why? O, that would imply a *second*, and that second might, peradventure, be of the wicked; and, if so, then the second death might have some 'power' over them, to actually kill them. Accordingly, *protos* is made to mean,—not *first*, which would imply a *second*, or a series, of which that of the good is number *one*, but—'*chief*.' Now, for the benefit of those who do not own a Greek Concordance, I will here say, that *protos* is found in the original one hundred and sixty times, and, in one hundred and forty places out of the one hundred and sixty, it is rendered '*first*,' and could be rendred first in the other twenty places without doing the least violence to the sacred text. Such is the *usus loquendi*, or general usage of the word. It means first, numerically; and a first implies a second.

"As to the idea that the wicked will have their bodies gathered into human form, and come forth out of their graves—dead corpses; stand up—dead corpses; appear at Christ's bar—dead corpses; render their (*logos*) account—dead corpses; go away into everlasting punishment—dead corpses; be consigned to gehenna—dead corpses, etc., it is a view unworthy of any public teacher, and too absurdly silly to waste more words about. But, I dare say, some will be found to believe it. 'How it is,' says Cicero, 'I know not, but there is nothing can be mentioned so absurd as not to have been said by some one of the philosophers.' Christians are often compelled to divide this reproach with the ancient philosophers. Unhappy Adventists!—I pity you. Disappointed in your expectations, hated by the world, persecuted by the devil, opposed by the church, every man's hand against you, and your hand compelled to be against every man, overrun with new messages, bestridden with theorizers and schismatics—some of whom are as hard to get rid of as it is to get away from a March wind;—how my heart aches for you! I am anxious to know what whim or notion is next to be thrust upon you; what strange error is next to be hung upon our generally beautiful system, till, in the eyes of the good, the whole fabric, daubed with untempered mortar, becomes a stench in the nostrils. . . . And when this comes to pass, and you have succeeded in forming schisms, sects, parties, and in creating havoc and division among all peaceable churches where you set your foot,—Satan, who from the beginning has watched your career with intense interest, will

'Grin horribly a ghastly smile.'

"I dissent entirely from some brethren in allowing even the eternal sleep of the people of Sodom and Gomorrah. The 'all' of John v. 28, and the 'every man' of Rom. ii. 6, covers even them. These later New Testament evidences refute all opposing inferences that may be drawn from Genesis. . . .

Death to the wicked an eternal sleep! A very pleasing consideration this for incorrigible sinners. Death an eternal sleep! So infidel and blasphemous France once said of the whole race. Who, in 1843, ever imagined the time would come when a part of the so-called American Adventists would affirm this of even a part of the race; and call the first French Infidelity, and christen the second the Gospel of God! But need anybody's brains get puzzled in estimating the difference between six and half a dozen? All the old, long-established doctrines of a future judgment and gehenna-fire for living, guilty sinners, are thrust aside, to give place to a notion of yesterday's birth, now persistently pressed upon our churches. The judgment, the grand Scripture motive to repentance, the nailing up to which made Felix tremble, is virtually sought to be overthrown;—salutary fear is destroyed. . . . It is also declared that the dead, speaking in general terms, shall live again, no distinction being made of character, the good and bad being both included. 'God is—the God—of the living; for ALL (will) live unto him.' *Boothroyd*, 'ALL live to him.' *Campbell*, 'ALL are alive to him.' *Thompson*, 'To him, they are ALL alive.' *Newcome*, 'For ALL live to him;' and the last named translator adds, 'Who regards the future resurrection as if it were present.'—Luke xx. 27–38.

2. "God who quickeneth *the dead*, and calleth those things which be not as though they were." Rom. iv: 17.

3. "*The dead* shall hear the voice of the Son of God, . . . and shall live." John v: 25.

4. "The Father raiseth *the dead*, and quickeneth them." John v: 21.

5. "God who quickeneth *all* things." 1 Tim. vi: 13.

6. "As in Adam all die, even so in Christ shall *all* be made *alive*." 1 Cor. xv: 22.

7. The unholy "dead *lived* not again until the thousand years were finished." Rev. xx: 5.

Many more passages of similar import might be added. Let these suffice for my purpose.

On the sixth one quoted, Wakefield, Boothroyd, Thompson, Macknight, and others, render it "by Adam," instead of "in Adam;" also "by Christ," instead of "in Christ." This is better. Only the good are ever "in Christ," or can awake in him. The evil are to "hear his voice" and live, but not in Christ, not to immortality or eternal life. But be it remembered that the *all* who are to come to life by Christ, is the exact *all* who died by Adam, *i. e.*, the whole race. C. Thompson's translator has it, "For as by Adam all die, so by the Christ all shall be brought to life." Let God be true!

Of the seventh and last passage I have quoted, it is worthy of note that the same form of the Greek verb *anazao*, used here to set forth the re-living of the unholy and unblessed dead, is rendered "revived" in the following passage, where it refers to the resurrection of Jesus;—"Christ both died, and rose, and *revived*, that he might be Lord both of the dead and the living." Rom. xiv: 9. Let God be true again!

Is it any wonder that the advocates of the "non-re-living of the wicked" want to get rid of this passage in Revelation? "It is hard for thee to kick against the pricks." Christ *revived;* the good will *revive* at his coming; the wicked will *revive* a thousand years after. Truth inherits the eternal years of God. . . . . .

I look upon this view as being the most serious defection from the true faith that has ever obtained among us since we first had an ecclesiastical existence;—a view most obnoxious to the evangelical portion of the church, and one that saps the very foundations of the doctrine of a "judgment to come" and retribution for sin;—a view which, once received by the ungodly, who place no value on eternal life, would lead them recklessly to say, "Let us eat and drink, for to-morrow we die." Behold the tree, and its legitimate fruit.

It is claimed to be exceedingly strange that the second death, if it ever prove a fact instead of a fable, is never spoken of anywhere but in the book of Revelation. Yes, and, we might add, it is equally strange, that the millennium, the hidden manna, the white stone, the two-horned beast, Armageddon, and twenty other important things, are nowhere mentioned but in Revelation. Isn't God to be believed, when he says a thing only *once?*

COLLATERAL EVIDENCE.

We consider the following facts the best collateral testimony that could be furnished that the doctrine is baseless and pernicious. Mr. Walsh, an able author, who first brought it forward in this generation to give it ventilation, abjured it and embraced immaterialism. Eld. Geo. Storrs, the second pioneer, a man of acknowledged superior abilities, sifted and abjured it, and teaches a system of probation after the advent and resurrection, which is nearly analogous to Universalism. Eld. J. T. Curry, the third in the scale of natural and acquired abilities and in leadership, closed his religious career, as Elijah, the forerunner of *Yahvah*, in the shameful case of his *socialism* in the late Georgia "community." Eld. Rufus Wendall, the fourth in the scale of ability, pioneering, and influence, sifted and abjured it and materialism with it, and went over to Methodism. We might carry this testimony of apostasy much further, but we forbear. These *four* were editors, authors, chief writers, pioneers, representatives of the view. What has it done for them? Their present positions give the answer. We do not mention these cases to reproach them nor the class they have led, but to awaken serious consideration. There are some excellent men of talent, learning, moral and religious worth among them; men we highly esteem in the society called "Life and Advent Union." They believe in and proclaim the immediate coming of the Lord, and publish a paper entitled "Herald of Life and of the Coming Kingdom," which is ably edited. We speak of the circumstances attending their representative men as a strong indication that the theory has a deleterious influence upon its advocates. We freely admit that all classes and sects of religionists have met with seeming misfortunes from members, able, leading, representative members, apostatizing. That, in the common range of fallen humanity, is not strange; but when *all* the pioneers and original able and chief producers and defenders of a cause apostatize, it should lead the younger and later disciples to pause and ponder the cause of it.

TENT AND CAMP-MEETING EFFORTS.

In prosecuting the mission of proclaiming the good news of Christ's immediate advent, enlightening the people upon the subjects of prophecy and signs of the times, and in bringing sinners to Christ, every means which was considered practicable has been employed. Large tents of canvas, capable of convening congregations of from 1,000 to 4,000, have been constructed and conveyed from place to place, pitched in towns and cities, where the masses could come and listen to the thrilling truths which the faithful messengers were publishing. Sermons, lectures, and social meetings are the order of services, and from one week to four weeks usually spent in a town in these services. Hundreds of thousands of people have been thus brought to listen to this stirring and soul-searching message. Many thousands who never attend upon religious services at houses of worship have been attracted to these tent meetings and have heard the gospel published in a manner which awakened in them an interest for their salvation, and a very large number of these have found mercy and hope in Christ. There are now some twenty or more such tents owned and in use in the summer seasons by the Second Advent people.

Camp-meetings have been another means which has proved of great service, with God's blessing, in prosecuting this work. Annual camp-meetings have been held in nearly all the Eastern and Western States for many years. In some of the New England, Middle, and Western States two or three have been held annually in each. Beside these, several larger centers have been formed for general camp-meetings. Camp Wilbraham, Mass., has proved a Bethel to many souls. An annual meeting was held there for more than twenty years, at which from ten to twenty thousand people of all religions and no religion were in yearly attendance, where they heard many of the most sublime and important truths of the gospel of salvation, in its various parts, together with the signs of speedy redemption, preached by some of the most able ministers of this generation, whose hearts were aglow with the love of Christ and his return, and whose minds were burdened with the deepest solicitude for the salvation of their fellow-men. Many have found Christ, at these meetings or subsequently, as their Saviour. In 1867, a new plot of ground was fitted up in Springfield, Mass., for a National Second Advent camp-ground, which has been occupied now six years with general good success. For the last ten years or more a mammoth camp-meeting has been held annually at Alton Bay, N. H. This being a great center of travel by rail and boat, multitudes attend the meetings who would not at a less feasible point. From twenty thousand to thirty thousand people have been in attendance during the last few years.

This spot, too, has become sacred to hundreds of believing disciples, who found mercy and pardon either at the meetings or subsequently. It is true that there are evils connected with such gatherings, as there are many in attendance who have no interest in anything good, and these often become a nuisance to the good and respectable. There are inconveniences, privations, expenditures, inconsistencies, and not a little gossip, at these places, causing many to feel that it is unwise to hold such meetings. But what effort has ever been made to save men which has not had more or less of evil connected with it? Where is there a spot or an institution from which the devil and wicked men have been debarred? These evils will exist until Jesus comes. Until then the saints should keep the most vigilant watch that evil does not get the lead and become the ruler of their camp-meetings.

At these meetings many who come wild and wicked, thoughtless and gay, return home subdued and converted, thoughtful and praying. Many who belong to other sects come just to have a ride and see their acquaintances, or the place, without the least idea of believing what these deluded teachers preach, but go home under convictions of the truthfulness of this mighty message, and never feel right again until they acknowledge they believe the Lord will soon come, and get prepared to meet him. Many come to these meetings weighed down with doubts and enveloped in the darkness of theological mist, having reasoned and pondered, enquired and prayed over the complications of the theories they once took on trust as all right, but which time and experience have put out of all logical form; these often return home full of light and peace and hope such as they never expected to find in this life, and their Bible is a new book to them, developing great and precious treasures, soon to be possessed, which they had never before supposed were revealed.

We will give here a few extracts from an account by an orthodox minister of his first visit to Alton Bay camp-ground, and published in the "Congregationalist," Boston. He has since attended the meetings every year, we believe, and brought some of his church brethren with him.

AN ADVENT CAMPMEETING.—BY REV. A. H. QUINT, D. D.

At the southernmost point of the long and narrow arm which the beautiful Winnepesaukee thrusts southward, in a small, natural amphitheatre a few rods west of the railway station, were the seats for the three thousand people who were just gathering for the forenoon sermon. The first impressions were to the effect that, in a place of great natual beauty, the tents and rough board buildings around the circle of seats, had been dropped pretty much by accident, and not to good effect; that the area was very carelessly kept; and that the benches were extremely uncomfortable.

The next impression was that those people could sing to perfection. One of the wild, weird, touching songs of the Advent people was floating on a sea of melody, as much superior to any quartette of any church as God's free forests are to a pile of boards.

By and by, the impression is that these people are tremendously in earnest. They believe what they profess. Most of the real people of the meeting have, without an educated and cultured look, a look of intelligence, and an unmistakably firm and decided expression. There is energy in that throng, physical, mental, and spiritual. They are not to be laughed out of their notions; and, to argue with them, you will soon find, requires a very careful study of the Bible. They know the language of the prophecies by heart, and each man and each woman is a concordance.

Stay for a day and a night, and a candid man, who will look underneath the Advent peculiarity, will find a genuine faith in the Lord Jesus, an implicit reliance on the power of the Holy Spirit, and a simple Christian experience. To me, naturally enough, some of their peculiar views did not seem well judged; their Scripture not always well applied; their experience not always well regulated. But any one who denies the Christian element in this strange body, will make a great mistake. The opening prayer was one of fiery earnestness. I was a little surprised, however, when the praying minister told the Lord, regarding the one who was to preach, "Lord, thou knowest he isn't much of a preacher. He is only an earthen vessel, and nothing but poor crockery at that. He is nothing but a farmer's boy." But it was done to magnify their need of the power of the Holy Spirit. Then was sung the old hymn, "When I can read my title clear," to a tune whose chorus, rolling up from thousands of voices, not boisterous, but mild, was well calculated to fascinate. They ignore written creeds, and embrace an immense variety of views on some points. They addressed the Lord Jesus and the Holy Spirit in prayer, apparently as freely as the Father. "We are not Trinitarians," said one of their ablest leaders to me, "nor Unitarians. We believe in the divinity of Christ, and exalt him more than you. But we do not state absolutely things which the Scriptures leave incomprehensible."

There is a multitude of these believers. Their preaching is bold, direct, and plain. They are throughly skilled in stating and defending their views. They are powerfully in earnest. To them Satan is a personal enemy. They are in actual contests. Their probation is a literal strife with the beings of darkness. They spiritualize nothing in the Bible which seems to be material. Their future paradise is a literal city, four square. Their future heaven is the earth purified. They look for the personal reign of Jesus Christ.

They *believe* these things. In the belief that in a few years, at the farthest, the trumpet shall sound; that most of those now living shall see the Lord coming out of the skies; the graves opened, the earth and the sea giving up their dead, is a thought of awfully fascinating power. The dwelling in the heavenly city, the tremendous scenes of the judgment day, the great final battle of Satan's hosts with the Lord, the fiery overthrow of the wicked, the lightnings and earthquakes of the earth's regeneration,—are beliefs which stir the soul. Ridicule will not move men whe believe that next year Jesus Christ shall come again. They act as men who believe that in a few months the destinies of all men will be eternally decided. It becomes thinkers and scholars to show the errors in their already extensive literature. Who will do it?

I left the spot with the feeling that I had witnessed intense convictions and zeal. I left it with a deepened impression of the vast importance of so serving Christ, that we shall not be afraid to meet him.

September 9, 1867.

SUNDAY SCHOOLS, BOOKS AND PAPERS FOR THE CHILDREN.

When it became an established fact that the churches would not tolerate the Adventists as fellow-worshipers and laborers with the privileges the gospel allows, and that they must occupy a separate position and become a sect, it became a matter of importance with them to learn the most proper course to pursue with their children that they might be trained in the fear of the Lord and the proper knowledge of his word. There were Sunday Schools, question books, and S. S. libraries and papers in abundance. Their children and youths were as intimately associated with these institutions as their parents had been with the churches. But to continue the children in the schools of churches where themselves were not allowed to worship the Lord and believe the gospel according to the dictates of their own consciences, and permit their children to be taught the incipient principles of false theology from which they were just clearing themselves, and to give them free access to S. S. circulating libraries made up of heathen mythology, Roman Catholic superstition, and Christian truth, interspersed and elaborated by an enormous amount of novel literature, much of which is a low grade of silly fiction, seemed quite inconsistent. But as, in many towns, the believers were few, the children have been usually sent to these schools or instructed at home. Where churches of Advent believers exist they have usually established and maintained Sunday Schools, some very prosperous ones. And in many country places where there were a few believers and no church, and other churches were not interested enough to maintain schools, these few have rallied the people, got up schools and Bible classes, and have thus done great good in leading many in the way of truth and in opening the way for the true gospel to be preached to the people afterward. Several papers have been published for the children, such as the "Children's Advent Herald," "Youth's Visitor," "Young Pilgrim," "Little Christian," etc. Some excellent question books have recently been published and a few good reading books, but it is a lamentable fact that the interest of the various publication societies has been far less than it should be in this matter. With proper attention to the work of preparing books and of sustaining the papers now published, our schools might be readily furnished, and many would be induced to organize schools where there are none now.

While time continues we should take special care to instruct our children in the true knowledge of God and his Son Jesus Christ and the true gospel hope, and thus teach them the way of salvation. The Sunday School, properly conducted, is a great instrumentality in this work, and parents as well as children ought to attend the schools, and be benefited and instructed themselves while they help instruct the children, when it is practicable to do so.

SKETCH OF ELD. J. H. WHITMORE AND HIS LABORS.

James H. Whitmore was born at Almont, Mich., June 30, 1838. When he was twelve years old he went to live at East Shelby, N. Y., where his parents still continue to reside. When about sixteen years old he was converted to Christ and joined the Methodist E. church. He received an academic education, and engaged in school teaching for a time, in which he was so successful that on his 24th birthday he received a State Certificate.

In May, 1852, he began the study of law in the office of John H. White, of Albion, N. Y. In 1863, he entered the Albany law school, and graduated with his class in 1864. He had previously been admitted to the bar, after passing an examination at General Term of Supreme Court, held at Albany, in Feb., 1864. In the fall of 1864, he enlisted as a private soldier in the 17th N. Y. Battery Light Artillery, army of the James, then before Richmond, and immediately went to "the front."

He served till the close of the war, and had the satisfaction of being present at the surrender of the army of Northern Virginia, at Appomattox Court House, April 9, 1865.

Leaving the army in June, 1865, he soon after opened a law office in Lockport, N. Y. In the summer of 1867, while visiting his uncle, Mr. Michael Nowlin, then of Dearborn, Mich., now of Ypsilanti, he became converted to the doctrine generally held by the Adventists, and at once abandoned his profession of the law, and exchanged Blackstone and Kent for Paul and John. His uncle was an earnest and very intelligent Adventist, and he found at his house the books that had most influenced his mind. (He was not converted by reading definite time arguments, but by reading the works of Hudson, Hastings, Grew, Blain, and other writers on the immortality question.) He now threw himself with all his energy into the work which he believed was so necessary to be done.

For the next two years he remained mostly at his uncle's, engaged in studying, writing, and lecturing. It was during these two years that he wrote "The Doctrine of Immortality." That book has enlightened thousands on this subject, and led them to thank the Lord for its publication. Eight or nine thousand copies have been circulated, and it ought to be more extensively advertised and sold. There is no work among us better calculated to elicit light on this important subject.

Bro. W. having given himself wholly to the work, he was ordained in the summer of 1869, as a minister of the gospel, by the Michigan Conference. He soon after accepted a call to preach his new faith in his boyhood home, and spent the next two years as pastor of the Advent Christian church of East Shelby, New York. In 1870, he became associated with William Lloyd Himes, in the conduct of the "Advent Christian Quarterly," an able and valuable periodical, which should have been placed in the hands of thousands of the ministry. This publication was continued two years, and contains some of the most able articles from the pen of Eld. W., that have ever appeared in our periodicals.

In 1871, he became the pastor of the A. C. church in Rochester, N. Y., where his labors were much blessed, as they were in Shelby, also, in gathering and building up the believers in Christ, until, in 1873, the time believers obtained a hearing there, and worked alienation and division among them, just as they were contemplating the erection of a house of worship, which they much need. Eld. W. accepted a challenge and held a debate with Dr. C. C. Barker, on the question "Is the definite time of the Second Advent revealed in the Holy Scriptures." This debate is published in pamphlet form, and those who read it with candor will readily see the ability and wisdom with which he argued the negative, and developed Bible truth on this vital question. There is, perhaps, an occasional error, and some severity of expression, but we are confident that his general position there taken will stand the test of time, and commend itself to the wise in Christ.

REVIVAL OF THE GIFTS.

Many times during the Christian dispensation, when great reformations were in progress, certain persons have been strangely exercised by some spiritual agency, causing singular phenomena, uncommon exercises of body and mind, speaking in unknown tongues, claiming to discern the state of heart of others, even of strangers, and claiming divine wisdom by the Spirit beyond that of Christians in general. These powers they claim are by the Holy Spirit, "restoring apostolic gifts," which they say have been lost by the Church through unbelief. These gifts are considered sure tokens of the divinity of the views these persons entertain, whether the Roman Catholic, Mahommedan, Reformers, Shakers, Irvingites, Methodists, Mormons, or Adventists; but *this* claim has proved false many times. The Adventists have such persons among them occasionally, and strange scenes have sometimes been witnessed. We do not intend to controvert these claims, though the Adventists repudiate them. We fully believe "the gifts" are with the Lord, and he can and does bestow them upon any person to accomplish any work he designs to be done in that manner. The healing gift he has bestowed upon many through all the dispensation of the gospel. The writer has himself experienced its blessed effects. But this gift is not bestowed upon the religious attendant, but upon the sick patient. When men claim the healing gift and give out that they have healing faith there is danger of some imposture.

We have often heard "the tongues" and the interpretations. Many of them, according to the interpretations, bore false messages. We never learned any important ideas by them, nor have we heard of any good arising since the days of the apostles, when the gospel of Christ was *confirmed;* but much reproach and scandal and many bad impressions have resulted. Should the Lord bestow the gift of heathen languages to the missionaries among them, we should begin to believe such a gift was useful to the church in these days; but we think when Christians get the Scriptural idea of the Lord's use of the apostolic gifts they will not look for them to be bestowed here. We have written enough to introduce the following historical illustration of fanaticism, from among many others, to acquaint those who do not know what to think of such exercises when they witness them, also to show the subjects of such views and exercises that they are neither new nor of divine origin:

THE FRENCH PROPHETS.

We find in Ecclesiastical History, many accounts given of Enthusiasts who have arisen, and pretended to be under the immediate inspiration of God, and to have the gift of tongues, discerning of spirits, etc., as in the Apostles' time. Among those who have made the greatest figure in modern times were the *French Prophets*, who first appeared in Dauphiny and Vivarais in France. In the year 1688, five or six hundred Protestants of both sexes, gave themselves out to be prophets, and inspired by the Holy Ghost. They were people of all ages and sexes, without distinction, though the greatest part of them were boys and girls from six or seven to twenty-five years of age. They had strange fits which came upon them with tremblings and faintings, as in a swoon, which made them stretch out their arms and legs, and stagger several times before they dropped down. They struck themselves with their hands, they fell on their backs, shut their eyes, and heaved with their breasts. They remained awhile in trances, and, coming out of them with twitchings, uttered all which came into their mouths. They said they saw the heavens open, the angels, paradise and hell. The least of their assemblies made up four or five hundred, and some of them amounted to even three or four thousand persons. When the prophets had for awhile been under agitations of body, they began to prophecy. The burden of their prophecies, was, "Amend your lives; repent ye; the end of all things draws nigh!"

In the year 1706, three or four of these prophets went over to England, and carried their prophetic spirit with them, which discovered itself in the same way and manner, by ecstatics, agitations, and inspirations under them, as it had done in France; and they propagated the like spirit to others, so that before the year was out, there were two or three hundred of these prophets in and about London, consisting of men, women and children; who delivered four or five hundred warnings. The great things pretended by their spirit, was to give warning of the near approach of the kingdom of God, and accomplishment of the Scriptures, concerning the new heaven and new earth, the kingdom of the Messiah, the first resurrection, the new Jerusalem descending from above, which they said was now even at the door; that this great operation was to be wrought on the part of man by spiritual arms only, proceeding from the mouths of those, who should by inspiration, or the mighty gift of the Spirit, be sent forth in great numbers to labor in the vineyard; that mission of his servants, should be witnessed by signs and wonders from heaven, by a deluge of judgments on the wicked, universally throughout the world, as famine, pertilence, earthquakes, etc. They declared that all the great things they spoke of, would be manifest over the whole earth within the term of three years.

These prophets pretended also to have the gift of languages, of discerning the secrets of the heart, the gift of ministration of the same spirit to others by the laying on of the hands and the gift of healing.

SKETCH OF ELD. P. G. BOWMAN AND HIS LABORS.

Peyton G. Bowman is a native of Virginia, born in Shenandoah County, Sept. 15, 1809. He was converted to Christ June 21, 1828, and joined the Methodist E. church. In 1832, he went to South Carolina, where he was licensed to preach, the year following, and was received into the South Carolina Methodist Conference in Jan., 1834. From that time until 1871, he did all the work of an itinerant preacher from the mountains to the sea-board, and during these years of toil and travel, he saw thousands of souls converted and united with the Methodist E. church. For seven or eight years before the late civil war, he was appointed and served as missionary to the colored people on the rice plantations of S. C., preaching every Sunday to, perhaps, 1500 to 2000, and during the week visiting the plantations, catechising the children, visiting the sick, the aged, and infirm, distributing Bibles, Testaments, and hymn-books to such as could read; doing the work of an evangelist.

The war having broken up all the missionary operations with the colored people, he was again thrown out into the regular itinerant field, in which he was a successful and arduous laborer.

In 1867, the church in Morganton, N. C. (which was then in the S. C. Conference), of which he was then pastor, sent him to the Northern States to raise money for church purposes. He did more than that, for he collected truths worth more than all the money North and South. While in New York, he made the acquaintance of a pious and intelligent young man, named Driggs, a member of the Methodist E. church; he denied the dogma of the immortality of the soul, and the eternal misery of the wicked, and gave Bro. B. a book entitled "What is Man?" written by Dr. Morris, of Philadelphia. A

PEYTON G. BOWMAN.— Page 642.

careful comparison of the contents of this book with the Bible convinced him that he and his church were all in error on the nature of man and the end of evil.

From New York he went to Boston, where he visited the office of the World's Crisis. Here he obtained other works on this subject, and on the immediate coming of the Lord, and from that time the World's Crisis made its weekly and welcome visits to his home.

He now began prayerfully and earnestly to review the whole ground which he and all the churches in the land had occupied on these great questions. He soon found that he could bring neither reason nor Scripture on *his side* to confute those on the other. He then felt it his duty as an honest man, however reluctantly, to make a final and total surrender. He did so, and then commenced preaching publicly his new views. Some of the preachers objected, and said it was "heresy," etc., etc. But this did not move him. The Lord was with him, and he had taken this position understandingly, and determined to teach the truth of God. The opposition continued until Aug., 1871, when his Presiding Elder, W. H. Fleming, had him arraigned before seven Elders, to answer to the charge of *heresy*. Specifications:

1st. "For preaching that from death to the resurrection all is unconscious sleep."

2d. "For preaching that the wicked at the final day will be annihilated from all conscious being forever."

He plead guilty to the charge, but stated at the same time "that there was nothing in the word of God to condemn him, and that his views were not in conflict with the twenty-five *articles* of religion in the Methodist Discipline." It was replied "that he was not arraigned for going against the Bible or the Discipline, but for opposition to Watson's Institutes and Dictionary, Wesley's Sermons and Notes, and the Hymn Book." This whole movement was maladministration and believed to be without precedent in the South, yet it has been several times enacted in the North. Most Methodist ministers who *study* theology do not agree with the above-named authors on several points; but this faithful man, deeply engaged in publishing the gospel and successful in gathering souls to Christ, was pronounced "a *heretic*," and suspended from all the rights and benefits of the Methodist ministry.

But before his trial proper before the next annual Conference, he decided to send in a formal withdrawal from that church in which he had lived and toiled for forty years. This was well. The Lord wanted an evangelist in that field who could sound the message of the coming of the Lord and tell the people what he is coming to do.

Bro. B. was a chosen vessel, and we can admire the wisdom and providence of God in opening his eyes to these truths due the people at this time, and in freeing him from other bonds that he might preach them.

In September, 1871, he united with the Adventists, since which he has been constantly and extensively preaching the speedy coming of the Lord, a literal resurrection of all the dead, the gift of immortality to the saints of God, and an eternal end of all evil in the destruction of the wicked. And God owns and blesses the truth in the midst of the most determined opposition on the part of the ministry. In the county where he resides three substantial and commodious houses of worship have been built through his energetic efforts and the aid of the A. A. Mission Society, and some seventy believers, in covenant fellowship, have been brought into this blessed hope, and enlisted to aid in bringing others to Christ. Among them are some of the most pious and best men in the land. Bro. B. has carried the message into Georgia, North Carolina, and other parts of the South.

As a preacher he is able, eloquent, forcible, and thorough. And although stripped of his property and home by the civil war, he is blessed with a family united in the faith and hope of the Lord's soon coming to give them an eternal home and rest in the earth renewed.

PUBLICATIONS ON THE SECOND ADVENT.

A great variety of papers have been issued by believers in the immediate coming of the Lord, many of which contain much crude and unprofitable matter, written by those whose minds were not disciplined nor adapted to theological teachings, and much more by those whose views were in incipient stages, and their writing often illogical and subversive of what they have since arrived at as truth.

But the staple and current publications of this people are among the first-class of theological writings of the Christian church. They contain the ripe thoughts of deep thinkers, and critical investigations and deductions of sound minds on the most sublime and important themes of the Bible. Some are from eminent scholars, others from minds competent to communicate Scriptural facts to their fellow-men in an intelligible manner, impelled by strong faith in the Bible, and a deep sense of the magnitude of the Message they were communicating to others.

We have mentioned but a few of the many periodicals published, as it was not important.

At the American Antique Library, Worcester, Mass., we found a volume of specimens collected, on a fly leaf of which was written:

"This unique specimen volume is collected and presented to the American Antique Society by the undersigned. It comprises the good and the indifferent—Orthodoxy and heterodoxy, fact and fancy—mingled with truth and error, together—with divine and human. 'He that hath a just eye will discriminate.' This collection embraces seventy-two varieties of Advental papers, and includes nearly every sheet that has been printed in America on that subject. D. T. TAYLOR."

The above volume was made up some ten years ago. We recalled to mind ten other papers not in this volume, and several have been issued since. The whole number will exceed ninety varieties.

We should not neglect to mention "The Prophetic Times," an able monthly, edited by Rev. J. A. Seiss, D. D., and several other Lutheran ministers, published in Philadelphia, Pa. This work, although differing from the Adventists on some points, has faithfully proclaimed the message of the immediate personal advent of Christ and the restitution. "Waymarks in the Wilderness," by J. Inglis, N. Y., is the title of another very valuable monthly, which taught the same message, during ten years, until the death of its editor.

BOOKS AND PAMPHLETS.

We cannot give the number and variety of books and pamphlets which have been issued in America on this theme, but are confident that they number nearly one thousand. Many of them contain much valuable matter which is mixed with time arguments, chronological tables, and speculative theories based on fanciful interpretations of certain prophecies, which time has proved unsound, hence unfitted for circulation. This manner of writing books has been a great detriment to the influence of Advental literature, and to its present circulation. This fact led us to once write one of our publishing societies our opinion that it was best to publish only such works as would be of value to circulate until the Lord shall come. We think most sound-minded Adventists will now agree with this opinion.

There are many valuable works among us of this character, and such will preach their parts of the truth until books are no longer needed. We have named the titles of many. A few others will be in place here. "The Saint's Inheritance," by H. F. Hill, which has reached its tenth edition, is very valuable. "The Destiny of Man," by Wm. Erwin, is also a very important work on man's nature and destiny. These are written by two ministers yet in the Methodist church.

"The Bible Doctrine of the Soul," By Prof. C. L. Ives, of Yale College, should be circulated by tens of thousands.

PUBLICATION SOCIETIES.

Publication societies should publish the books needed to advance the interests of the society, but the most of our books have come otherwise. We confess there has been great prodigality in this work. It may be considered unavoidable. We admit that individuals obliged to do their own publishing could not avoid it, but we think that past experience should have corrected the evil. But as it has not we shall venture a thought for contemplation. Publication associations have been organized and much work done, but book publishing has scarcely been considered a matter of sufficient importance to engage the attention of these associations (the Western Association excepted). Authors generally are without money; the most of those who have written works on the questions connected with our mission have been ministers, who have neither salaries nor hoarded means. They have been obliged to get their publishing done on credit, at outside publishing houses, and in small editions, then compete with the extensive book trade in prices, with an unpopular Message. These books, thus published, have cost the proprietors from 20 to 30 per cent more than the same would cost a good publishing house, yet must be sold as low as other books. Thus by each one being obliged to publish single handed, and buy all the work and material at nearly retail prices, many thousands of dollars have been lost to the cause, while the publishers made nothing on their books, and probably not more than half as many books sold as could have been by a live publication society with a knowledge of the business. A living, active, enterprising publication society, or individual, with experience and means, who should own the plates of all books especially desirable to be circulated in this mission, when such can be purchased, and who will accept and pay for manuscript for new works considered worth publishing, and keep a good stock of such English and American works as they cannot publish, would be of great service in the work of spreading abroad the grand and glorious truths which the Second Advent Message includes. So great is the want felt of such an institution that several brethren with means have recently proposed to put in $1,000 each, when $10,000 can be raised to establish, in some central city, a publishing house, to issue, and keep for sale, a full supply of Advent publications. "But do these brethren believe the Lord is coming soon?" many will ask, and will answer their own question, "If they did they would not contemplate such a work as this." Perhaps they would. They *do* believe the Lord is soon coming, and believe in working to the best advantage to accomplish the most until he does come, and they wish to be found at their post and in this work when the Lord comes, and to hear him say "well done."

SKETCH OF ELD. C. C. MARSTON AND HIS LABORS.

C. C. Marston is a native of Massachusetts; born in West Medway, June 5, 1849. He was converted and baptized in December, 1861, and united with the Winebrennarian denomination.

At the age of sixteen years and six months he preached his first sermon; July 23, 1865. His ministerial labors have been confined to Iowa, and Illinois, where he has traveled as an evangelist, and labored in the gospel with good success. In 1870 his brethren charged him with heresy, for "teaching the sleep of the dead," and "the absolute mortality of man previous to the resurrection of the dead." He plead guilty to the charges specified; but not guilty of heresy. He was discharged from their church, and united with the Adventists in 1871. This opened a wide door of usefulness for him, and he has been preaching the Advent Message with other gospel truth incessantly since and his labors have been crowned with much success in gathering souls to Christ and in building up the believers in sound doctrine. As a writer he has superior abilities and with practice will be classed as an able writer. He has already written several excellent pamphlets, among which are, "Modern Spiritism," and "Will the wicked be resurrected?" He has prepared a volume of sermons which he proposes to publish within a few weeks. We do not doubt it will be a valuable work.

In March, 1874, Bro. Marston, in connection with Eld. L. C. Collins, by the advice of many brethren in the West, issued a weekly paper entitled "Good Tidings," Chicago, Ill., devoted to the interests of the Second Advent Message and the Church of Christ. It is an independent paper, breathing the true gospel spirit, and will, we think, find a good degree of success, with the blessing of God. Eld. Marston is its chief editor; Bro. Collins is an associate editor. He is yet young in years and in experience; but endowed with gifts suited to give him great success, if he honors the Lord with them by using them to publish this dispensational truth and all gospel truth for the salvation of men.

THE WATCHMEN AWAKING.

Dr. James Carlyle, of Dublin, has written a work entitled "The First and Second Advents," and another, "Latter Day Pamphlets." Dr. Capadose, of Amsterdam, in a Free Church General Assembly, recently recommended that the doctrine of the personal reign of Christ be woven into the church creeds, confessions, etc. In "The Watchman," a periodical established in Paris and devoted to the subject of prophecy, the editor said, a few years ago, that many in that place had embraced the pre-millennial view, and mentions a society of about one hundred, living in Paris, who were looking for Christ's second coming to establish his personal reign on earth. Mr. Fox, a Scottish Missionary to the Teloogoo people, was a believer in Christ's soon coming. James McGregor Bertram, a Scottish Missionary of the Baptist order, at St. Helena, has sounded the midnight cry extensively on that island, making many converts to the faith; he has also preached it at South Africa, at the missionary stations there.

The old "Presbyterian," a paper widely circulated, is awakened to the subject, and admits of stirring articles in its columns on the signs of the times and the immediate coming of Christ. The Christian Era pertinently asks, "Is it not time that we came back to apostolic practice, and thought of, and rejoiced in, and spoke of our Lord's second coming?" Some of the organs of the Methodists are also speaking in tones which show that some of their watchmen see the signs of the Lord's coming and are beginning to speak out upon the subject.

At the Methodist ministers' meeting, held in Boston Mondays of each week, a discussion, continuing nearly through 1873, on the saints' inheritance, resulted in the radical conversion of several of the ministry to the fact that the Lord is coming to renovate and restore the earth. Rev. J. H. Brookes, D. D., of St. Louis (Presbyterian), is alive to the subject, preaching and writing upon it. In 1871, he called a ministerial conference at St. Louis to examine and discuss the subject of the Lord's immediate coming. While the subject is taking deep hold of many minds, it is alarming the mere sectarians who labor for worldly show, and if a man is found looking for the coming of Christ the second time, and his heart is so set on the return of his Master as to cause him to talk, sing, pray, and preach concerning the second advent of Christ, he is classed among the infidels, sceptics, and crazy lunatics.

In the Central Christian Advocate (Methodist), of Nov. 26, 1873, in an article headed "Plan of Union," for the uniting of all Methodists in one body, to be known as the Methodist Episcopal Church of God, I find in the fifth resolution,

"That we appoint able, spiritual minded men to preach on doctrine, and expose the errors of infidelity, rationalism, scepticism, spiritualism, and *fanatical Adventism*," etc.

As well might they attempt to prevent the shining of the sun as to stop the advancing light upon the coming of the Lord. They can close their eyes and shut their ears and harden their hearts, but the people will be warned and the Lord will come.

RESULTS.

The results of Christian labor and sacrifice are of secondary consideration. To know the work of the Lord and follow his leadings is of the first importance. Duty, at any sacrifice, is ours; consequences, the Lord's. Yet, it is duty to watch results, that we may be assured we are working with the Lord, and especially when multitudes of the Lord's children tell us we are wrong. What have been the results thus far of this message and mission? The extent of results none but the Lord knows. We know, however, from history and observation, that less than fifty years ago, when the mass of the Christian Church, ministry, and membership were drifting far from the gospel hope, fascinated by dreams of the world's conversion and a temporal millennium; while Neology and Mysticism were alluring the chief of the clergy, and permeating the literature, and the multitudes were listless concerning the return of Christ and the day of judgment, one man on this continent, and he "an herdsman," and a few in other lands raised their voices so as to attract public attention with the cry, "Behold, the bridegroom cometh; go ye out to meet him." "Behold, thy salvation cometh, his reward is with him and his work before him."

This message met those and other errors in the field of contest, and with awakened, enlisted, accumulating numbers, who took the sword of the Spirit—the Word of God—it has unmasked this fiction of Satan, destroyed the beauty of his armor, turned back the tide of these deceptive errors, and sent a gleam of light through the darkness of night that was settling down upon this generation. It has awakened, convinced, and restored to several thousands of the Lord's ministers, the ancient and Scriptural faith and hope of the Church, and greatly modified, corrected, and improved the theology of thousands of others. It has enlisted hundreds of thousands into active and joyful service of the Lord, who were in a lukewarm or cold state of religious profession. It has gathered hundreds of thousands of sinners from "the broad way," "the highways and hedges," into the peaceful fold of Christ, to await his return. It has sent forth millions of pages of Scriptural literature (not free from errors, of course), to neutralize, check, and avert the pernicious influences of the gigantic errors before mentioned (which have constantly increased), together with their legitimate offspring—modern spiritism, and to instruct and lead men to Christ; to comfort and strengthen and prepare a people for the coming and kingdom of the Lord.

And while errors abound, and sin abounds, and the love of many waxes cold, the voice is now sounding from thousands of faithful watchmen in all parts of Christendom, "Behold thy salvation cometh," "The Lord is at hand." Although we have given more particular account of the Adventists as a society, yet we remember with gladness the many associated with other churches who see the great truths which animate our hearts, and who, observing the signs of speedy redemption, are seeking to awaken others to the same sublime, awful, yet glorious fact that the Lord is coming soon. The work of awakening and preparation will go on amid the darkness, unbelief, scoffing, and ridicule, until the final hour when our Redeemer shall come with the suddenness of the flood upon the ante-diluvians, and of the fire upon the Sodomites, and the terrific word is pronounced, "It is done." Then the most joyful word which ever saluted the human ear will reverberate through all the earth, "Come ye blessed of my father, inherit the kingdom prepared for you from the foundation of the world."

Watchmen, see! the land is nearing,
  With its vernal fruits and flowers!
On! just yonder, O how cheering,
  Bloom forever Eden's bowers.

CHAPTER XX.

THE BIBLE AND ITS TEACHINGS—CHRONOLOGY—GREAT GEOLOGICAL MISTAKES—HABAKKUK'S PROPHECY—KNOWLEDGE SHALL INCREASE—THE FOUR UNIVERSAL MONARCHIES—THE KINGDOM OF GOD—DANIEL'S VISION OF CHAPTER SEVENTH—THE FOUR BEASTS—THE HORN WITH EYES AND MOUTH—THAT MAN OF SIN—CHRIST'S COMING—THE VISION OF 2300 DAYS.

THE BIBLE AND ITS TEACHINGS.

It will be seen in the foregoing history that those who are looking for the Lord have manifested a positive and unremitting faith in the Bible. We now proceed to give a sketch of some of the chief points of doctrine which the main body of believers in the immediate personal advent of Christ teach as included in the true foundation of the Christian faith and hope, together with expositions and applications of several prophecies and promises which have engaged their attention and led them to the position they occupy, which distinguishes the most of them from other churches in this closing period of the gospel age.

We shall also present in this department some Scriptures, with expositions, selections from discussions, sermons, and articles of eminent writers, on the nature and destiny of man, as understood by the great majority of Adventists, and by many ministers and members of other churches, and now gaining the attention of, and working conviction in, a large number of believers throughout Christendom.

We shall not attempt to mould these theological themes into a denominational creed, or platform of faith, but shall select and present, as our space admits, such matter from able authors as comes within the general scope of the faith and hope of those classes of believers our book is intended to represent.

As the Word of God is claimed by us as the only true and reliable standard of Christian doctrine, we implicitly bow to its inspired voice, and accept its teachings in the most literal sense, governed, of course, by its laws of tropes, figures, symbols, and parables, admitting, also, that there are words of wicked men and of devils in the Scriptures. And that there are errors (of minor importance) in the translations we admit, yet we are captivated by the

ASTONISHING ACCURACY OF THE BIBLE.

"An astonishing feature of the Word of God is that, notwithstanding the time at which its compositions were written, and the multitudes of the topics to which it alludes, there is not one physical error, not one assertion or allusion disproved by the progress of modern science.

None of those mistakes which the science of each succeeding age discovered in the books of the preceding; above all, none of those absurdities which modern astronomy indicates in such great numbers in the writings of the ancients, in their sacred codes, in their philosophy, and even in the finest pages of the fathers of the church, not one of those errors is to be found in any of our sacred books. Nothing there will ever contradict that which, after so many ages, the investigations of the learned would have been able to reveal to us on the state of our globe, or on that of the heavens.

Peruse with care our Scriptures, from one end to the other, to find such spots; and whilst you apply yourself to this examination, remember that it is a book which speaks of everything, which describes nature, which recites its creation, which tells us of the water, of the atmosphere, of the mountains, of the animals, and of the plants. It is a book which teaches us the first revolutions of the world, and which also foretells its last; it recounts them in the sublimest strains of poetry, and it chants them in the charms of glowing song.

It is a book which is full of oriental raptures, elevation, variety, and boldness. It is a book which speaks of the earth and things visible. It is a book which nearly fifty writers, of every degree of cultivation, of every condition, and living through the course of fifteen hundred years, have concurred to make. It is a book which was written in the centre of Asia, in the sands of Arabia, and in the deserts of Judah, in the courts of the temple of the Jews, in the music schools of the prophets of Bethel and of Jericho, in the sumptuous palaces of Babylon, and the idolatrous banks of Chebar, and finally in the centre of the western civilization, in the midst of the Jews and of their ignorance, in the midst of polytheism and its idols, as also in the bosom of pantheism and of its sad philosophy. It is a book whose first writer had been forty years a pupil of the magicians of Egypt, in whose opinion the sun, the stars, and the elements were endowed with intelligence, reacted on the elements, and governed the world by a perpetual alluvium.

It is a book whose first writer preceded, by more than nine hundred years, the most ancient philosophers of ancient Greece and Asia, the Zalucses and the Pythagorans, the Xenophons and the Confuciuses. It is a book which carries its narrations even to the hierarchies of angels, even to the most distant epoch of the future, and the glorious scenes of the last day.

Well, search among its fifty authors, search among its sixty-six books, its 1,189 chapters, and its 31,173 verses; search for any one of those thousand errors which the ancients and the moderns committed, when they speak of the heavens, or of the earth, of their revolutions, of the elements; search, but you will find none."

CHRONOLOGY.

The Chronology of the Bible shows that six thousand years have not yet expired since the Lord formed the world we dwell in. Many and mighty are the efforts of some of the enemies of the cross to prove by the guesses of geology, by Chinese fables, by Grecian fiction, by Egyptian exaggeration and many other ways that the Bible chronology is not true; and if that is untrue the book is spoiled, the Mosaic account of the Creation must be false; as well as the account of the flood. For the benefit of those who may be attacked by these enemies of the Bible, we give the following historical extracts from standard historians and chronologers:

CHINESE CHRONOLOGY.

"Nearly all the eastern nations have legends of times when gods ruled on the earth for many thousands of years, giving way to demigods, and these to men; but these claims are considered by chronologists to be underserving attention, and to have arisen simply from the difficulty of conceiving an abrupt commencement to the existing order of human events."—*New Amer. Cyclo.*, vol. 5, p. 202.

"It is . . . manifest that the high antiquity of the Chinese empire must be deemed little better than a fiction."—*Universal History*, vol. 20, p. 7.

"Their original . . . savors strongly of fable, as does also the history of several of their first emperors."—*Universal History*, vol. 20, p. 109.

"In fine, that the Chinese annals cannot be depended upon, may be inferred even from Confucius himself, who more than hints at the inaccuracy of them; nay, that many of the oldest materials for such annals had been destroyed before he wrote."—*Universal History*, vol. 20, p. 155.

"In the memoirs concerning the history, arts, etc., of the Chinese, extracted from the grand annals, and lately published by the missionaries of Pekin, it is asserted, that all the relations of events prior to the reign of Yao, or You (as differently pronounced by different writers), which they date B. C. 2057, 'are fabulous, composed in modern times, unsupported by authentic records, and full of contradictions. And that neither the *Chou-king*, or *Xu-king*, their most ancient and authentic record, nor the book of *Confucius* (who died B. C. 479), or of his disciples, make mention of any genealogies, or princes, before *Yao*. It is also proved, that the origin of the *Chinese* empire cannot be placed higher than one or two generations before *Yao*."—*Dr. Hale's Chron.* vol. I, p. 296.

GRECIAN CHRONOLOGY.

"A little after the death of Alexander the Great, they began to set down the generations, reigns, and successions, in numbers of years, and by putting reigns and successions equivalent to generations, and three generations to an hundred or an hundred and twenty (as appears by their chronology), they. have made the antiquities of Greece three or four hundred years older than the truth."—"*Chronology of Ancient Kingdoms*," *by Sir Isaac Newton, p. 3.*

EGYPTIAN CHRONOLOGY.

"The priests of Egypt told Herodotus that Menes built Memphis and the sumptuous temple of Vulcan, in that city, and that Rhampsinitus, Mæris, Asychis, and Psammiticus, added magnificant porticos to that temple. And it is not likely that Memphis could be famous before Homer's days, who doth not mention it, or that a temple could be above two or three hundred years in building. The reign of Psammiticus began six hundred and fifty-five years before Christ, and I place the founding of this temple by Menes, about two hundred and fifty-seven years earlier; but the priests of Egypt had so magnified their antiquities before the days of Herodotus, as to tell him that from Menes to Mæris (who reigned two hundred years before Psammiticus), there were three hundred and thirty kings, whose reigns took up as many ages; that is eleven thousand years, and had filled up the interval with feigned kings, who had done nothing. And before the days of Diodorus Siculus, they had raised their antiquities so much higher, as to place six, eight, or ten new reigns of kings between those kings, whom they represented to Horodotus to succeed one another immediately."—"*Chron. of Ancient Kingdoms,*" *by Sir Isaac Newton*, p. 6.

The Egyptians held that on the account of the rich "soil, the first men were formed in Egypt," or grew up out of the ground.—*Diodorus Siculus*, vol. I, p. 18—19.

"From Osiris and Isis, to the reign of Alexander the Great, who built a city after his own name, the Egyptian priests reckon above ten thousand years, or (as some write) little less than three and twenty thousand years."—*Diodorus Siculus*, vol. I, p. 29.

How did they make out so many years?

"In their fabulous stories, they said that the most ancient of their gods reigned twelve hundred years . . . apiece." The Egyptian priests, in their computation of time, do reckon above three and twenty thousand years from the reign of Sol to the passage of Alexander the Great into Asia."—*Diodorus Siculus*, vol. I, p. 32.

It is said they had *lunar years* of thirty days each.

Diodorus Siculus says:—"The priests have fabulously reported" that "the gods and demigods reigned in Egypt for the space almost of eighteen thousand years." "Afterwards, they say, that men reigned there for the space of fifteen thousand years, to the one hundred and eightieth Olympiad, at which time I myself came into Egypt, in the reign of Ptolemy, who took upon him the name of Dionysius the Younger."—*Diod.*, vol. I, p. 50.

GREAT GEOLOGICAL MISTAKES.

Sir William Thompson, in the *North British Review*, says:

"If you go back ten thousand million years ago—which I believe will not satisfy some geologists—the earth must have been rotating more than twice as fast as at present, and if it had been solid then, it must be now something totally different from what it is. Now here is direct opposition between physical astronomy and modern geology as represented by a very large, very influential, and I may add, in many respects, sound and philosophical body of investigators, constituting, perhaps, a majority of British geologists. *It is quite certain that a great mistake has been made—the British popular geology at the present time is in direct opposition to the principles of natural philosophy.* Without going into details, I may say, it is no matter whether the earth's lost time is 22 seconds, or considerably more or less than 22 seconds, in a century; the principle is the same. There cannot be uniformity. The earth is filled with evidences that it has not been going on forever in its present state, and that there is a progress of events toward a state infinitely different."

Profs. McChesney and Andrews, from Chicago, both visit the Tiber for the same purpose. The former arrives at the conclusion that the drift-beds, containing bones of extinct animals, covered with peat twenty-five feet thick, must have required ages to accomplish.

The latter finds bones and flint implements of men in the same drift-beds, and thereby shows they lived contemporaneously with those animals. He shows that the Tiber has been many times larger than now, and that boulders of ice and frozen ground of tons weight have been buried in the sand before the ice had chance to thaw, making the drift-beds rapid instead of gradual. The peat-beds above-supposed to require one hundred years to form an inch, are proved to have been formed much more rapidly, as there are stumps of trees three and four feet high in these beds, requiring a deposit of more than four feet in a century, or the stumps of any tree would have rotted by exposure.

Hence the geological argument that is going the rounds, that there was an age of birds and another of beasts before the creation of man, is disproved by the fact that man's bones are intermingled with the bones of these extinct species.

The Rev. Edward Hitchcock, D. D., remarks:

> "Hitherto the Bible has never been proved to come into collision with any scientific discovery, although many of its books were written in the rudest and most ignorant ages. It does not, indeed, anticipate scientific discovery. But the remarkable adaptation of its language to such discoveries, when they are made, seems to me a more striking mark of its divine origin than if it had contained a revelation of the whole system of modern science."

Starting, then, with the Bible as a foundation invulnerable, a standard perfect, its Author the fountain of all wisdom and knowledge: we accept its teachings as literal truths, concerning the creation of the worlds and of all living creatures. We accept its laws as of divine authority; its history of the introduction of sin by the volition of law, and of the penalty which was executed upon the offender, and the curse which fell upon our world, introducing the train of evils which have affected all animate and inanimate nature, causing "the whole creation to groan and travail in pain together until now."

We accept its statements of the divine administration and the conduct and destiny of a fallen and depraved race, under God's dispensations of mercy. We accept the promises, prophecies and history of the plan of grace and redemption through the offering of the Son of God; the sufferings, death and resurrection of our Lord Jesus Christ, which, when completed, shall result in the recovery of the race of man from the death experienced through Adam's sin; the immortality and eternal life of all who are the children of God by adoption in Christ, and the restoration of the Earth to its Edenic perfection, and filled with the glory of God, to be possessed and enjoyed by Christ and his blood-washed Church eternally.

We accept its precepts and its covenants as the rules of life, and its threatenings of "judgment and fiery indignation, which shall devour the advesaries" and "utterly consume the wicked, that they be no more" as evidence that there shall be no more rebellion and no more curse in the world.

Arguments and evidences that the Gentile times are about closing and the Lord soon to come the second time and establish his eternal reign, have appeared in much of our foregoing history, for several portions of which we refer the reader to pages 98, 131, 159, 460, but we shall yet say more upon this point.

HABAKKUK'S PROPHECY.

"I will stand upon my watch, and set me upon the tower, and will watch to see what he will say unto me, and what I shall answer when I am reproved (or argued with, margin). And the Lord answered me, and said, Write the vision and make it plain upon tables, that he may run that readeth it. For the vision is yet for an appointed time, but at the end it shall speak and not lie: though it tarry, wait for it; because it will surely come, it will not tarry."—Hab. ii. 1, 3.

This remarkable passage, with the Lord's command to the prophet, indicates the development of a message of truth for those who will read. It has been regarded by learned students of the Bible as a prophecy of what would afterwards be written, for the instruction of the church, rather than what Habakkuk was himself to write. And as the visions of Daniel were given and written since the prophecy of Habakkuk, and the subject seems to be the same, the inference may be legitimate.

Daniel did "write the vision," and more than one; it has been "made plain upon tables;" some who have read it have "*run to and fro.*" The vision written relates specially to the symbols of kingdoms and events, in chronological succession, and closing with the second advent of Christ, the resurrection of the dead, the judgment, and the setting up of the kingdom of God, rather than to numerals to express the exact points of time, on the scale, when these events would occur. We do not deny that symbolic time accompanies the vision, but the definite time upon the tables has not been plain. Bishop Lowth comments thus on Habakkuk, 2d chapter.

"God commanded the prophet to write the contents of this vision in such legible characters as were used in public tables, that were hung up in temples and market places, that every one might have cognizance of them. 'Though it tarry.' There are two different words in the Hebrew which our English expresses by that one word, *tarry*. Though *he* tarry, *expect him;* because he that cometh will come, he will not go beyond the appointed time, but will make good the promises of deliverance given to your fathers."

Dr. Gill remarks upon this passage, "The vision concerning the coming of the Messiah, and the destruction of the enemies of the church and the people of God. 'And make it plain upon tables,' *i. e.*, engrave it in plain legible letters, 'that he may run that readeth it.' May run through the whole without difficulty; that a man might run it over at once, with ease, or even read it as he was running. 'For the vision is yet for an appointed time,' which were the limit determined and appointed time for the Messiah's coming, the fullness of time. 'But at the end it shall speak and not lie,' or rather, he shall speak, and so the apostle has taught us to interpret it for a person and not a thing, Heb. x. 37, that is, at the end of the time appointed the Messiah shall appear, at the end of the world.

"'Though it tarry wait for it,' or though he tarry wait for him. Not that he would or did tarry, but might seem to do so, not coming so soon as expected or desired. And sometimes the saints would be ready to give it up, and their hearts ready to sink or faint because it was seemingly delayed. But he that is to come will come, and not tarry beyond the appointed time.

"'Behold, his soul which is lifted up is not upright in him: but the just shall live by his faith.' Here is a point to such as are incredulous, that disbelieve his coming, whose hearts are like bubbles, blown up, full of wind; whose souls are swelled with pride and vanity, and a high conceit of themselves, of their merits and worth, of their holiness and works of righteousness, and trust in themselves and in their own righteousness to the great neglect of the true righteousness of the Messiah. He has no right notions of God and of his holy law, nor of Christ, nor indeed of himself. 'But the just shall live by his faith,' his own faith and not another's. Such live by faith upon a promising, or by faith of Christ promised to come in the preceding verse, by that faith of which he is the object, author, and finisher."

KNOWLEDGE SHALL INCREASE.

"But thou, O Daniel, shut up the words, and seal the book, even to the time of the end: many shall run to and fro, and knowledge shall be increased."—Dan. xii. 4.

In the above passage the assurance is given that at the "time of the end,"—a space just before the end,—there would be a search for a knowledge of these things, and some would obtain it. We give the following comments on this subject. Dr. A. Clark's note reads:

"Many shall *run to and fro.* Many shall endeavor to *search out* the sense; and knowledge shall be increased by these means. This seems to be the meaning of this verse, though another has been put upon it, viz.: 'Many shall run to and fro, preaching the gospel of Christ, and therefore religious knowledge and true wisdom shall be increased.' This is true in itself; but it is not the meaning of the prophet's words."

Matthew Henry comments freely on the passage, and among other things says: "They shall read it over and over, shall meditate upon it; they shall *discourse* of it, talk it over, *sift out* the meaning of it, and thus knowledge shall be increased."

The French translation, published by the American Bible Society, renders the passage following "the time of the end" thus: "When many shall run all over it (or through it), and to them knowledge shall be increased."

The old English Bible, printed by Barker in 1580, has this marginal note: "Many shall run to and fro to search the knowledge of these mysteries."

Dr. Gill says: "*Many shall run to and fro, and knowledge shall be increased;* that is, towards the end of the time appointed, many shall be stirred up to inquire into these things delivered in this book, and will spare no pains or cost to get a knowledge of them; will read and study the Scriptures, and meditate on them; *compare one passage with another,* spiritual things with spiritual, in order to obtain the mind of Christ; will carefully peruse the writings of such, who have gone before them, who have attempted anything of this kind; and will go far and near to converse with persons that have any understanding of such things; and by such means, with the blessing of God upon them, the knowledge of this book of prophecy will be increased, and things will appear plainer and clearer the nearer the accomplishment of them is, and especially when prophecy and facts can be compared; and not only this kind of knowledge, but knowledge of all spiritual things, of all evangelical truths and doctrines, will be abundantly enlarged at this time."

"The word translated *run to and fro* is metaphorically used to denote investigation, close, diligent, accurate observation,—just as the eyes of the Lord are said to run to and fro. The reference is not to missionary exertions in particular, but to the study of these Scriptures to find out their meaning."

The above work has been going on in a special manner the last forty years, as all will admit. It has been a common saying: "The Adventist's Bibles always open at the book of Daniel." A visitor at one of our camp-meetings remarked: "I perceive your boys and girls are all theologians." This is not strictly true. We wish it was more fully so. The angel informed Daniel, not only that knowledge shall be increased, but that "the wise shall understand."

Understand the nature and scope of these visions, what they teach, and "what shall be the end of these things." They will know when they are near the end, and what is to take place in the closing scene, and will watch, while the wicked will do wickedly, scoff or disbelieve and "not understand." Paul says, to the living Church, "But ye, brethren, are not in darkness, that that day should overtake you as a thief."

THE FOUR UNIVERSAL MONARCHIES.

The kingdom of God is a subject occupying much space in the Scriptures of the Old and New Testaments. From the time Adam was cut off from the right of dominion of the earth, in consequence of his sin, until John heard voices in heaven, under the sounding of the seventh angel, saying: "The kingdoms of this world are become the kingdoms of our Lord and of his Christ," the Scriptures direct our attention to the great fact that God has purposed to establish an everlasting kingdom of righteousness on the earth. For a clear description of this kingdom see pages 181 to 200.

We now purpose to present the outlines of the succession of the universal kingdoms of the Gentiles, and introduction of God's kingdom as shown to the King of Chaldea, and explained by the Lord through his servant Daniel.

Visions and dreams are among the most ancient methods of divine communication. "If there be a prophet among you, I the Lord will make myself known to him in a vision, and will speak unto him in a dream." (Numb. xii. 6.)

It was not directly to the king that the Lord revealed this matter, but to Daniel, "that the king might know there is a God who maketh known his secrets to his servants, the prophets."

It is characteristic with the Scriptures to record the censurable actions of men, even the best of men; but in the case of Daniel there is an entire omission; showing that he was a man, though not perfect, yet of the highest moral excellence. Hence says the angel to him: "O Daniel—thou art greatly beloved." (Chapter ix. 22, 23.) It was because of this that the Most High revealed through him the future history of the world and the *time* of the two advents of his Son.

Daniel was a Hebrew captive under Nebuchadnezzar. The king dreamed and forgot the subject of his dream. (Dan. ii. 1.)

The period of the dream was, "In the second year of the reign of Nebuchadnezzar" (v. 1.), B. C. 603, Nebuchadnezzar reigned conjointly with his father, Nabopolasser; after his death, "the second year" of his single reign he had this dream.

"His spirit" being "troubled" because of the dream, and yet it having gone from him so that he could not recall it to his memory, he commanded the astrologers, and the sorcerers, and the Chaldeans to show him his dream." Thus summoning into his presence those whose business professedly was to interpret dreams and visions of the future in ancient times. They could do nothing for the king in this matter, and confessed that "none other except the gods whose dwelling is not with flesh could show the thing." We will here observe that symbols and hieroglyphics were in common use in ancient times to convey ideas. They were the first attempts at writing, and have also been much used since the art of writing was invented. Sculptured and painted pictures and hieroglyphics as symbols are found on all ancient monuments and relics.

The Lord observed this custom in giving the king his dreams, that the impression might be the deeper when the matter is explained. Daniel is allowed time for a prayer meeting with his brethren, after promising to "show the king the interpretation." (Dan. ii. 15, 16.)

When the Lord had answered his prayer, he came before the king to explain.

Thou, O king sawest, and behold a great image. This great image, whose brightness was excellent, stood before thee; and the form thereof was terrible. This image's head was of gold, his breast and his arms of silver, his belly and his thighs of brass, his legs of iron, his feet part of iron and part of clay. Thou sawest till that a stone was cut out without hands, which smote the image upon his feet that were of iron and clay, and brake them to pieces. Then was the iron, the clay, the brass, the silver, and the gold, broken to pieces together, and became like the chaff of the summer threshing floors;

and the wind carried them away, that no place was found for them; and the stone that smote the image became a great mountain and filled the whole earth. "This is the dream; and we will tell the interpretation thereof before the king." "Thou, O king, art a king of kings: for the God of heaven hath given thee a kingdom, power and strength, and glory. And wheresoever the children of men dwell, the beasts of the field and the fowls of the heaven hath he given into thine hand, and hath made thee ruler over them all."

Thou art this head of gold.

And after thee shall arise another kingdom inferior to thee.

And a third kingdom of brass, which shall bear rule over all the earth.

And the fourth kingdom shall be strong as iron; for as much as iron breaketh in pieces and subdueth all things; and as iron that breaketh all these, shall it break in pieces and bruise.

And whereas thou sawest the feet and the toes, part of potter's clay and part of iron, the kingdom shall be divided; but there shall be in it of the strength of the iron, forasmuch as thou sawest the iron mixed with miry clay. And as the toes of the feet were part of iron and part of clay; so the kingdom shall be partly strong and partly broken. And whereas thou sawest iron mixed with miry clay, they shall mingle themselves with the seed of men; but they shall not cleave one to another, even as iron is not mixed with clay.

And in the days of these kings shall the God of heaven set up a kingdom, which shall never be destroyed; and the kingdom shall not be left to other people, but it shall break in pieces and consume all these kingdoms, and it shall stand forever. Forasmuch as thou sawest that the stone was cut out of the mountain without hands, and that it brake in pieces the iron, the brass, the clay, the silver, and the gold; the great God hath made known to the king what shall come to pass hereafter; and the dream is certain, and the interpretation thereof sure.

The Metallic Image seen by Nebuchadnezzar, composed of four different metals—symbolizes four successive ages or empires, according to ancient rules of symbolization.

"Hesiod, who lived about two centuries before Daniel, characterizes the succession of ages (four) by the same metals—gold, silver, brass and iron." And from this and Nebuchadnezzar's image, the ancients drew their fabled four ages of the world: "the golden, the silver, the brazen, and the iron age." The world has now had its four fabled and symbolized ages. "The golden age," has long been in the past, and is not a thing in future prospect, unless "the Image" and "the Ages" are to be repeated in their history backwards.

"The Stone" symbolizes the kingdom of God, which succeeds the present governments of the world, and is to stand forever.

The entire Image is demolished together, and driven away, which can only be when the history of the world is complete—and at the appearing and kingdom of Jesus Christ to judgment. Then all human governments will be destroyed together, to make way for God's everlasting kingdom, which is to stand forever.

The stone that smote the image, became a great mountain (kingdom), and filled the whole earth. The stone of itself, and not by the adhesion of the fragments or dust of the image.

This interpretation is perfectly simple and intelligible. The Assyrio-Babylonian kingdom, which was considered one by the ancient authors Herodotus, Xenophon, Strabo, and others, of which Nebuchadnezzar was the representative head, constitutes the first kingdom symbolized.

This kingdom was founded by Nimrod. (Gen. ch. x. and xi.) It was fitly represented by the golden head from the exceeding greatness and wealth of the kingdom, and the grandeur and magnificence of its capital. Babylon is called, "The golden city"—"The glory of kingdoms, the beauty of the Chaldee's excellency"—and "Abundant in treasures."

Those who builded and founded the cities of Babylon and Nineveh designed them to surpass all the cities that should ever be built after them. Babylon was a perfect square, having a distance of 15 miles on each side, and was 60 miles in circuit. Its walls were 87 feet in thickness, and 350 feet in height. The tower of Belus, its principal temple, was 630 feet high. The Palace of the Kings occupied an area of 8 miles in circuit. The city was furnished with magnificent hanging gardens, which would support the largest trees. It had 100 gates of brass, 25 on a side, and the streets crossed each other at right angles. The wisdom, power, grandeur, and beauty of this city has never been excelled, and Babylon as a kingdom for extent of empire and wealth takes its place as the first of the kingdoms.

THE BREAST AND ARMS OF SILVER.

"And after thee shall arise another kingdom inferior to thee."

These symbolize "another kingdom," and one to succeed Babylon. The kingdom symbolized must be that of the Medes and Persians, as all history and every chronological canon shows this.

Josephus says, "The two hands and shoulders signify that the empire of Babylon should be dissolved by two kings." These were Darius the Median, and Cyrus the Persian. "The kingdom here referred to," says Mr. Barnes, "was undoubtedly the Medo-Persian, established by Cyrus in the conquest of Babylon, which continued through the reigns of his successors until it was conquered by Alexander the Great. This kingdom succeeded that of Assyria, or Babylon, 538 years B. C., to the overthrow of Darius Codomannus, 331 B. C.

A part of the hand-writing on the wall of Belshazzar, the last king of Babylon, as interpreted by the prophet Daniel, is conclusive proof upon this point. "Peres; thy kingdom is divided and given to the Medes and Persians." The sacred history confirms this fact. "And Darius the Median took the kingdom." (Dan. v: 31.) After the death of Darius his uncle, Cyrus issues a proclamation, declaring that "The Lord God of heaven hath given me all the kingdoms of the earth." (Ezra i: 2.) Thus prophecy uttered its oracles, and both sacred and profane history confirm the truth of them.

THE BELLY AND THIGHS OF BRASS.

"And another third kingdom of brass, which shall bear rule over all the earth."

These symbolize, according to Daniel's interpretation, "another kingdom;"—a "third," in successive order, which should "bear rule over all the earth." The Macedonian or Greek empire founded by Alexander the Great is referred to under this symbol.

Alexander having quelled the insurrection in Macedon, after the death of his father, Philip, proceeded in his conquests toward Greece, and conquering them he united Macedon and Greece in one dominion, of which he was the head. With an army composed mostly of Greeks he subjugated the Persian empire, and Europe, Asia, and Africa yielded to the sway of the Greco-Macedonian kingdom. That Alexander bore rule over all the known earth is evident from the fact that "he wept because there was not another world for him to conquer." And "he ordered himself to be called the king of all lands and of all the world." "At which time," Diodorus Siculus says, "he received ambassadors from all countries; and legates came to him from almost the whole habitable world." Michael says to Daniel (ch. x. 20), "And now will I return to fight with the Prince of Persia: and when I am gone forth, lo, the Prince of Grecia shall come." Alexander is here designated, for he was appointed generalissimo of the Greek forces at the time of this conquest of Persia."

This kingdom is called a "kingdom of brass." The Greeks were famous for their brazen armor, and hence the appellation in the days of Homer: "The brazen-coated Greeks." The Grecian government, under Alexander and his successors, is symbolized by the "belly and sides of brass."

THE LEGS OF IRON.

"And the fourth kingdom shall be as strong as iron," etc.

The "legs of iron" denote a "fourth kingdom," that should subjugate all that remains of its predecessors.

The Roman empire, which succeeded the Grecian, and conquered the world in the days of Julius Cæsar, and over which Augustus Cæsar ruled with unrivalled authority and peace, must be designated by this symbol. All ancient Jewish, and the early Christian writers agree that this "fourth kingdom" was Rome. Mr. Mede says, "That the Roman empire was the fourth kingdom of Daniel, was believed by the church before, and in our Saviour's time—by the disciples and the whole Christian church for the past 300 years." Porphyry, a heathen and an infidel, was the first to deny this universal testimony—and undertook to prove that the visions of Daniel were written after the fulfillment of his prophecies. Some Christian authors in modern times have followed in his wake, so far as the application of the prophecy is concerned, in order to avoid the inevitable conclusion, that the kingdom of God is still future, and nigh at hand. Prof. Stuart leads the van. But little headway can be made against the truth of God. Mr. Gibbon unwittingly concedes the fulfillment of this prophecy in the history of Rome, in the following remarkable language: "The arms of the Republic, sometimes vanquished in battle, always victorious in war, advanced with rapid steps to the Euphrates, the Danube, the Rhine, and the Ocean; and the images of gold, or silver, or brass, that might serve to represent the nations and their kings, were successively broken by the *iron* monarchy of Rome." We are willing to leave the testimony here, proving by this prince of historians, who cared nothing for divine revelation or the Christian's hope; but whom God has raised up to write his remarkable history confirming his prophetic word.

Of Rome, under the leadership of Julius Cæsar, prophecy declares, "He shall do according to his will, and none shall stand before him." (Dan. xi. 16.) And of his successor, Augustus Cæsar, it says, "Then shall stand up in his estate a raiser of taxes in the glory of the kingdom." (v. 20.) And by turning to Luke's gospel, ch. 2: 1, we learn the fulfillment in the following language, "And it came to pass in those days, that there went out a decree from Cæsar Augustus, that all the world should be taxed."

Thus Rome under the dominion of the Cæsars, constitutes the "fourth kingdom" symbolized in the image seen by Nebuchadnezzar.

THE FEET AND TOES.

"And whereas thou sawest the feet and toes, part of potter's clay and part of iron, the kingdom shall be divided."

The "fourth kingdom," or Rome, according to this symbolization, is to "*be divided*"—instead of being given to another supreme power, or make way for another universal kingdom. The history of the "decline and fall of the Roman empire" confirms the interpretation of the prophet given 3,000 years ago! Rome has been broken up and divided into fragments as symbolized by the feet and toes of this image. And among the divided fragments there *have been ten distinct kingdoms within the bounds of the fourth or Roman government.* The first ten kingdoms originated within that government, were as follows: (1.) *The Huns, in Hungary, established A. D.* 356. (2.) *The Ostrogoths, in Mysia, A. D.* 377. (3.) *The Visgoths, in Pannonia, A. D.* 378. (4.) *The Franks, in France, A. D.* 407. (5.) *The Vandals, in Africa, A. D.* 407. (6.) *The Sueves and Alans, in Gascoyne and Spain, A. D.* 407. (7.) *The Burgundians, in Burgundy, A. D.* 407. (8.) *The Heruli, in Italy, A. D.* 476. (9.) *The Saxons and Angles, in Britain, A. D.* 476. (10.) *The Lombards on the Danube, in Germany, A. D.* 483. This list of kingdoms, as the first ten, is given on the authority of Marchiaval, a historian, and Dr. Hales and Bishop Lloyd, chronologers. It may perhaps be objected, "the above are not the only ones which have existed within the old Roman empire." True, they are not; but if they are the first ten established there, they answer the description given by the prophet. For it was *three of the first horns* which were to be plucked up by the roots. Besides, we are to take the events of the government as they transpired, and when the event predicted is exactly answered, we have done with it on that point. It matters not what other kingdoms have existed subsequently.

CHARACTERISTICS.

1. "There shall be in it the strength of the iron, forasmuch as thou sawest the iron mixed with miry clay."

The old Roman iron continues intermingling its strength among the divided kingdoms, and will to the end. And Rome, the capital city, still exists, under the appellation of "The Eternal City."

2. "The kingdom shall be partly strong and partly broken." (Margin—brittle.)

Such is the character of Rome to this day: not only of the kingdom of Rome proper, at its capital, but of the fragmentary kingdoms.

3. "They shall mingle themselves with the seed of men."

Romans, and subjects of the dominant power at Rome, are found among all people.

4. "But they shall not cleave one to another, even as iron is not mixed with clay."

This is true of the subjects of Rome, who are the faithful adherents of the Roman Pontiff. In whatever nation or clime they are, they are a distinct people under the dominion of the power at Rome, and at the beck of his will; and oftentimes are in sworn hostility to the governments.

The fragmentary divisions of the old Roman empire will never be united or consolidated into one kingdom of universal dominion, as the four which preceded them. Near fourteen hundred years of history have proven this feature of the prophecy true. Efforts have been made to accomplish this end by ambitious men and governments, but all in vain. Alaric, the Pope of Rome—Charlemagne, Napoleon I, who declared as he coronated himself with the crown of Italy, "I shall inherit Cæsar's power," with others, all have failed; and will fail to the end. No person on earth can disannul this purpose of the Most High: "They shall never cleave one to another." The arm that attempts it will be palsied, as was Alexander's when he attempted to rebuild the doomed city of Babylon in the face of God's prophecy; and the men who have endeavored to reach universal empire through seas of blood, fight against this sure decree of Heaven![1]

THE KINGDOM OF GOD.

The kingdom of the stone is constituted of Christ, and the saints of the Most High. Christ is "the chief" and "precious stone," and he is the king of the kingdom. "The saints" of all ages are also symbolized as "precious stones," and are to "possess" and "inherit" the kingdom of God. Inasmuch as the kingdom "shall never be destroyed," but "stand forever," it is evident that it belongs to the immortal state.

"Therefore God has already immortalized the king of the kingdom of God." (Acts, 2. 30, 31.) "And is to immortalize his saints." (1 Cor. 15. 50, 54.)

This kingdom given to Christ and his saints will be possessed by them eternally: it "shall not be left to other people." For God will

---

[1] Many of these facts are quoted from an article by Dr. O. R. Fassett.

not dethrone a righteous ruler, and his Son; nor disinherit his saints, made immortal.

The epoch of the setting up of this kingdom, is when the history of worldly kingdoms is complete, as symbolized by the image. For the stone kingdom was not seen until the image stood complete before Nebuchadnezzar (v. 34.). And is at the demolition of the fragmentary portion of the fourth kingdom (v. 34); and not before the fourth kingdom is "divided" as some affirm. It is also at the contemporaneous destruction of all the governments symbolized by the whole image: for they are "broken to pieces together" (v. 34). Therefore it must be at the end of time. And the kingdom of God must occupy the earth, for, "the stone that smote the image became a great mountain and filled the whole earth."

Then will be fulfilled the promise recorded in the second Psalm:

"I will declare the decree: the Lord hath said unto me, Thou art my Son; this day have I begotten thee. Ask of me, and I shall give thee the heathen for thine inheritance, and the uttermost parts of the earth for thy possession. Thou shalt beat them with a rod of iron; thou shalt dash them in pieces like a potter's vessel. Ps. ii. 7, 9.

"The second woe is past; and, behold, the third woe cometh quickly.

"And the seventh angel sounded; and there were great voices in heaven, saying, The kingdoms of this world are become the kingdoms of our Lord, and of his Christ; and he shall reign forever and ever. . . . And the nations were angry, and thy wrath is come, and the time of the dead that they should be judged, and that thou shouldst give reward unto thy servants the prophets, and to the saints, and them that fear thy name, small and great; and shouldst destroy them which destroy the earth." Rev. xi. 14, 18.

These Scriptures state the subject so plainly that the conclusion is unavoidable that the kingdom of God is to succeed all earthy, i. e. mortal kingdoms, and it will occupy the territory which the preceding kingdoms had. Other Scriptures positively prove this to be so.

DANIEL'S VISIONS.

We shall now present the chief features of Daniel's visions upon the same subject, with the symbols shown him, and the angel's explanation of them, with his statement of the location of the kingdom of God.

"Daniel spake and said, I saw in my vision by night, and, behold, the four winds of the heaven strove upon the great sea. And four great beasts came up from the sea, diverse one from another."—Dan. vii. 2, 3.

"The first was like a lion, and had eagles' wings; I beheld till the wings thereof were plucked, and it was lifted up from the earth, and made to stand upon the feet as a man, and a man's heart was given unto it."—Dan. vii. 4.

This Babylonian kingdom, in its pride and glory, is represented by the king of beasts. But as that kingdom was humbled in the person of its proud monarch until he had manhood enough to acknowledge the God of heaven, a symbol of that humiliation is presented to Daniel. See Dan. iv. 24, 34.

"And, behold, another beast, a second, like to a bear, and it raised up itself on one side, and it had three ribs in the mouth of it, between the teeth of it: and they said unto it, Arise, devour much flesh."

This *second* is the Medo-Persian kingdom, represented by the silver metal, and here by the bear. The Medes were in the lead in conquering Babylon, but the Persians were joined with them, and gaining the ascendency, and raised the kingdom higher by its arms. For proof see Dan. v. 25, 31; viii. 3, 20.

"After this I beheld, and lo, another, like a leopard, which had upon the back of it four wings of a fowl; the beast had also four heads; and dominion was given to it."

This symbolizes the Grecian kingdom; the same as that represented by "brass" in the second chapter, and by "an he goat" in the eighth.

Please read the whole vision. Daniel was "grieved" and "troubled." But the Lord, who designed instruction, sent Gabriel to explain this vision. What does he say it means?

"These great beasts, which are four, are four kings (or kingdoms), which shall arise out of the earth. But the saints of the most high shall take the kingdom, and possess the kingdom forever, even forever and ever."—Vs. 17, 18.

Though these great beasts, or kingdoms, are to occupy the earth in succession for a while, yet the saints are to eventually obtain the kingdom, and then occupy it eternally. This is the angel's assuring promise. These are the same as the four represented by the metallic symbols, chapter 2d. But these symbols will give not only the succession, but indicate the characteristics of these kingdoms.

Media and Persia, constituting the second universal kingdom, was conquered by Alexander, son of Philip of Macedon, who commenced the Grecian monarchy B. C. 331. He went to Susa and sat on the throne of Darius, B. C. 330, and established the third kingdom, which continued 300 years, in various forms. The leopard and the wings represent velocity of movement. See chapter viii. 5. Mr. Rollin says of Alexander:

"The very thought of sitting still fatigued him, and the great vivacity of his imagination and ambition would never suffer him to be at rest; nay, could he have conquered the whole world, he would have sought a new one to satiate the avidity of his desires."

The four heads of the leopard represent the division of this kingdom into four parts. We shall remark upon this point under the symbols of Daniel 8th.

"After this I saw in the night visions, and behold a fourth beast, dreadful and terrible, and strong exceedingly; and it had great iron teeth: it devoured and break in pieces and stamped the residue with the feet of it: and it had ten horns. I considered the horns, and, behold, there came up among them another little horn, before whom there were three of the first horns plucked up by the roots; and, behold, in this horn were eyes like the eyes of

man, and a mouth speaking great things. I beheld till the thrones were cast down, and the Ancient of days did sit, whose garment was white as snow, and the hair of his head like the pure wool: his throne was like the fiery flame, and his wheels as burning fire. A fiery stream issued and came forth from before him: thousand thousands ministered unto him, and ten thousand times ten thousand stood before him: the judgment was set, and the books were opened.

"I beheld then, because of the voice of the great words which the horn spake: I beheld even till the beast was slain, and his body destroyed and given to the burning flames."

This fourth beast and the horns, especially the last one, which waxed great, and spake great words, fixed the attention of the prophet, and he asked an explanation and obtained the desired information.

"Thus he said, The fourth beast is the fourth kingdom upon earth, which shall be diverse from all kingdoms, and shall devour the whole earth, and shall tread it down, and break it in pieces."

This fourth kingdom is the same as that symbolized in chapter second by the legs of iron, and in the eighth chapter by "a little horn, which waxed exceeding great, toward the south and toward the east, and toward the pleasant land." This is the Roman kingdom, which succeeded Grecia. It attained the supremacy about 30 B. C.

"And the ten horns out of this kingdom are ten kings (kingdoms) that shall arise:"

Here again we have the same ten divisions of the Roman kingdom as symbolized by "ten toes," given in a new symbol because another feature is to appear which could not be given in the former.

"And another shall rise after them; and he shall be diverse from the first, and he shall subdue three kings (kingdoms). And he shall speak great words against the Most High, and shall wear out the saints of the Most High, and think to change times and laws: and they shall be given into his hand until a time and times and the dividing of time. But the judgment shall sit, and they shall take away his dominion to consume and to destroy it unto the end. And the kingdom and dominion, and the greatness of the kingdom under the whole heaven, shall be given to the people of the saints of the Most High, whose kingdom is an everlasting kingdom, and all dominions shall serve and obey him. Hitherto is the end of the matter."

This little horn with "eyes and mouth," according to Gabriel, was to perform the same work and occupy the same relation of "that man of sin, the son of perdition," mentioned by Paul, 2d Thes. ii. 3, 8; the same, also, as the mouth of "the leopard beast," and as the "two horned beast" of Rev. xiii. 2-17. Facts of history show conclusively that each of these symbols was given to represent the same power, and that power was papal Rome.

After the Roman empire lost its unity, by being divided into fragmentary kingdoms, the ministry of the Christian religion having greatly apostatized from the faith of the gospel now began to seek the secular power, which was finally attained when the church became a politico-ecclesiastical government.

Three of the ten kingdoms were subdued to prepare the way for the papacy to assume the exercise of power declared to be given this horn. This horn was to have supremacy over times and laws, and the saints, for 1260 years. This the papacy has had. It was to speak great words against the Most High. This the papacy has constantly done. It was to wear out the saints of the Most High. The papacy through its civil power has put to death some sixty millions of the saints. "They (the kings or kingdoms) were to take away his dominion, to consume and to destroy it unto the end." This has been done to the papal power. It was wasted by Napoleon I. It was cut down to small dimensions and there limited by the Holy Alliance in 1815. It received its death wound by the Italian revolution under Mazzina in 1848. Its last vestige of civil power was taken away by Victor Emanuel in 1870. We have not space to elaborate these facts. The reader can find them in full detail in other works. But what is the next item in this prophetic explanation? Paul says of "that man of sin," "he shall be destroyed by the brightness of Christ's coming." He also says, "Christ shall judge the quick and the dead at his appearing and kingdom."—2d Tim. iv. 1.

Daniel says, "I beheld, and the same horn made war with the saints, and prevailed against them; Until the Ancient of days came, and judgment was given to the saints of the Most High; and the time came that the saints possessed the kingdom." Gabriel explains that when the little horn is consumed, "the kingdom and dominion, and the greatness of the kingdom under the whole heaven, shall be given to the people of the saints of the Most High, whose kingdom is an everlasting kingdom, and all dominions shall serve and obey him."

This gives the chronology of the kingdom of God, and shows it to succeed all mortal governments. It states its locality, "*under the whole heaven.*" It is declared to be "an everlasting kingdom." This is the kingdom and dominion lost by Adam, which Christ recovers from the usurper, and declares:

"When the Son of man shall come in his glory, and all the holy angels with him, then shall he sit upon the throne of his glory. . . . Then shall the King say unto them on his right hand, Come, ye blessed of my Father, inherit the kingdom prepared for you from the foundation of the world."—Matt. xxv. 31, 34.

THE VISION OF THE 2300 DAYS.

In the eighth chapter of Daniel is recorded another vision of the prophet and an explanation by Gabriel. The prophecy of the future kingdoms had been partially given by the former symbols and explanations; but there were other features, not given, and the Lord favored the Church with a new class of symbols which, with Gabriel's explanations, affords a clear light upon the path of the just "until the perfect day."

Nebuchadnezzar had "made Daniel a great man," in a worldly point of view, by giving him "many great gifts," and appointing him "ruler over the whole province of Babylon, and chief of the governors over all the wise men of Babylon." (ch. ii. 48.) Such was his wisdom and sagacity in counsel that he continued the Prime Minister of State, or in influence and authority, at different times, during the period of the whole of the seventy years captivity. (ch. i. 21.) And when Babylon was conquered by the Medes and Persians he was appointed the Premier of the new empire. (Dan. vi. 1–3.)

"And I saw a vision; and it came to pass, when I saw, that I was at Shushan, in the palace, which is in the province of Elam; and I saw in a vision, and I was by the river of Ulai."

"Then I lifted up mine eyes, and saw, and, behold, there stood before the river a ram, which had two horns; and the two horns were high; but one was higher than the other, and the higher came up last." v. 3.

Gabriel explains: "The ram which thou sawest having two horns are the kings of Media and Persia." v. 20.

"And I saw the ram pushing westward, and northward, and southward:

so that no beast might stand before him, neither was there any that could deliver out of his hand; but he did according to his will and became great."

Daniel had been deeply interested in the former visions, for they each related to the future history of the Church and her final deliverance with the establishment of the kingdom of God for their eternal home. The scenes of this vision begin during the increasing strength and extension of conquest of the Medo-Persian kingdom.

The Medo-Persian kingdom became great by conquering all the provinces about it, "doing according to his will." It was said to the bear, which represents the same, "Arise, devour much flesh." It raised the largest military force that ever marched into the field of battle. The army of Xerxes was two million nine hundred forty-one thousand and six hundred fighting men; his attendants and all who accompanied him swelled the army to over five million. But God had determined the bounds of this kingdom and declared it should be succeeded by another, of brass.

"And as I was considering, behold, an he goat came from the west on the face of the whole earth, and touched not the ground; and the goat had a notable horn between his eyes. And he came to the ram that had two horns, which I had seen standing before the river, and ran unto him in the fury of his power.

And I saw him come close unto the ram, and he was moved with choler against him, and smote the ram, and break his two horns, and there was no power in the ram to stand before him, but he cast him down to the ground, and stamped upon him: and there was none that could deliver the ram out of his hand." v. 7.

"And the rough goat is the king (kingdom) of Grecia, and the great horn that is between his eyes is the first king." v. 21.

It is a well-known fact of history that Alexander the Great conquered the Medo-Persian kingdom. Greece and Macedonia (both being the Biblical Grecia) were subject to Alexander B. C. 335. He commenced the invasion of Persia by crossing the Hellespont in the spring of 334 B. C. and winning the battle of Granicus. The decisive battle of Arbela was gained B. C. 331, which put an end to the reign of Darius Codomanus, the last Persian king.

"Therefore the he goat waxed very great: and when he was strong the great horn was broken, and for it came up four notable ones toward the four winds of heaven." v. 8. Explanation,

"Now that being broken whereas four stood up for it, four kingdoms shall stand up out of that nation; but not in his power." v. 22.

After conquering the east as far as the Indus, Alexander returned to Babylon, where he died in the summer of the year B. C. 323. His kingdom was divided between his four generals. Ptolemy had Egypt, Cassander took Macedonia, Lysimachus had Thrace, Seleucus took Syria.[1] "But not in his power," said the angel. Alexander's brother, his mother, his three wives, and two sons were murdered. "So that fifteen years after his death not one of his posterity were left."[2]

These four parts of the Grecian kingdom, represented by the four heads of the leopard beast, and the four horns of the goat, continued to govern the chief nations of the world about 300 years. Syria and Egypt became rivals and were for some time the chief controlling powers.

"And out of one of them came forth a little horn, which waxed exceeding great, toward the south, and toward the east, and toward the pleasant land; and it waxed great, even to the host of heaven, and it cast down some of the host and of the stars to the ground, and stamped upon them, yea he magnified himself even to the prince of the host, and by him the daily sacrifice was taken away, and the place of his sanctuary was cast down; and an host was given him against the daily sacrifice by reason of transgression, and it cast down the truth to the ground; and it practiced and prospered."

---

[1] Rolen, vol. ii., book 17.

[2] See Clark on Dan. xi.

Although Gabriel did not inform Daniel that this little horn represented the next universal kingdom, nor give its name, as he had the two previous ones, yet with the explanation he did give, and with the history of imperial Rome before us, we could ask no clearer information to prove that power to be here symbolized. The effort has been made by Catholic writers, and endorsed by some Protestants, to apply it to Antiochus Epiphanes, but without proof and much opposed to facts. The effort seeks to break the prophetic chain which proves that Christ is soon to come. This little horn was to come forth out of one of the four, or from one of the four winds of heaven. Moses predicted, concerning Israel's chastisement, what Rome was sent to perform. Deut. xxviii. 49. "The Lord shall bring a nation against thee from far, from the end of the earth," or from one of the four winds of heaven. This came to pass at Jerusalem's destruction. This horn was small in its beginning, but waxed EXCEEDING great. The angel explains:

"And in the latter time of their (the four horns) kingdom, when the transgressors are come to the full, a king of fierce countenance, and understanding dark sentences, shall stand up. And his power shall be mighty; but not by his own power: and he shall destroy wonderfully, and shall prosper, and practice, and shall destroy the mighty and the holy people." Moses said of the Romans, "a nation whose tongue thou shalt not understand, a nation of fierce countenance."

Rome did "come from far," from one of the four parts of Grecia, and "waxed exceeding great." Antiochus did not come from one of the four horns; he was a king of one of them—Syria—and the eighth in a regular line of twenty-five kings. This little horn was a *fifth*, and was to come "in the latter time of their kingdom." Rome did, and became universal B. C. 31. Antiochus destroyed 80,000 of the Jews, but Rome, in a single siege, destroyed ONE MILLION ONE HUNDRED THOUSAND of that nation. This little horn was to "stand up against the prince of princes." Rome gave sentence to crucify Christ, persecuted, condemned and executed his apostles.

Gabriel said, "Behold, I will make thee known what shall be in the last end of the indignation: for at the time appointed the end shall be."

He declared that this little horn should "destroy the city (Jerusalem), and the sanctuary; and the end thereof shall be with a flood, and unto the end of the war desolations are determined . . and for the overspreading of abominations he shall make it desolate, even to the consummation." Dan. viii. 19, ix. 26, 27.

Rome invaded and overrun Judea, the Lord's sanctuary, broke up the Jewish nation, "destroyed the city and the (Jews') sanctuary." Jesus told his disciples how to proceed when they saw this overspreading of abominations, the Roman power.

"When ye therefore shall see the abomination of desolation, spoken of by Daniel the prophet, stand in the holy place (Judea), (whoso readeth, let him understand): Then let them which be in Judea flee into the mountains." Matt. xxiv. 15, 16.

"And Jerusalem shall be trodden down of the Gentiles until the times of the Gentiles be fulfilled." Luke xxi. 24.

The war is not yet ended, the overspreading of abominations is not stayed, the treading down of the city and of the Lord's holy mountain and land is not finished, but it is soon to be closed up in "the consummation." The Roman kingdom has existed as the central power, imperial, kingly, or Papal, from that time onward until now. It was to "be broken without hand." Such will be the final fate of Rome as a ruling power.

The vision covers "2300 days (years); then shall the sanctuary be cleansed." The earth will be cleansed, of which Judea was a type. That the "year-day theory" is the true one the explanation of this vision, alone, would establish. The events symbolized, as stated by Gabriel, must extend through a space much longer than six years and four months, literal days; they have now occupied about 2300 years. And Gabriel said to Daniel:

"Behold, I will make thee know what shall be in the last end of the indignation: for at the time appointed the end shall be."

The 9th, 10th, 11th, and 12th chapters are occupied in more full explanations of the events of this interesting space of time, from the zenith of Medo-Persian power to the second personal advent of Christ, to raise the dead, judge the world, cleanse the earth, and "set up a kingdom which shall never be destroyed," "under the whole heaven."[1]

---

[1] For information on the chronology of the 2300 days, the 70 weeks, 1260 and 1335 days, see pp. 460 to 480 of this book. We should state to our readers that Eld. J. Litch, from whom we have quoted freely, has abandoned the year-day theory, and is teaching that these periods are all literal days, and the events connected with them are yet to come; that the little horn of Dan. 7th and also the one of the 8th chapter represent a future anti-Christ; also, that nearly all of Revelation, after the fifth chapter, is yet for future fulfillment, but to be immediately fulfilled and the Lord then come.

CHAPTER XXI.

THE PRE-EXISTENCE OF CHRIST—LIFE AND DEATH—DUTY OF WATCHFULNESS.

THE PRE–EXISTENCE OF CHRIST—BY ELD. J. H. WHITMORE.

"All men should honor the Son, even as they honor the Father. He that honoreth not the Son honoreth not the Father who hath sent him."—John v. 23.

The question to be considered in this article is, did Christ exist as a person before his incarnation?

This is eminently a theological question, and in answering it we shall appeal not to the speculations of philosophy, but to the plain declarations of the Scriptures. Accepting the Bible as the standard authority, we hope to bring to its study a teachable spririt and a grateful heart. The abstractions of philosophy, and the speculations of metaphysics, may answer for the sceptic and the rationalist, but with the devout believer in inspiration, nothing can take the place of the Holy Scriptures, which are able to make him "wise unto salvation through faith which is in Christ Jesus." Many vitally important truths are written in the fifth chapter of John's Gospel, one of which is embraced in the passage which stands at the head of this article: "He that honoreth not the Son honoreth not the Father." Our Lord was addressing the Jews who had sought to kill him for healing the impotent man on the Sabbath day, and for saying "that God was his Father, making himself equal with God." Our Saviour instead of attempting to allay their hostility by disclaiming Divine rank or power proceeded to say that the Father had committed all judgment unto the Son, *that all men should honor the Son even as they honor the Father.* That the hour had come when the dead should hear the voice of the Son of God, and they that heard should live; that as the Father had life in himself, so had he given the Son to have life in himself; that they were not to wonder at this, for the hour was coming in the which all that were in the graves should hear his voice and should come forth, they that had done good, unto the resurrection of life, and they that had done evil, unto the resurrection of damnation. In these tremendous utterances our Lord certainly claimed for himself divine prerogatives; therefore all men should honor him, even as they honor the Father who sent him. If *we* would thus honor the Son we must *believe* the record which God hath given of him, and accept as *true* the testimony of the faithful witness, who is emphatically styled the Way, the Truth, and the Life.

The first question properly to be considered in Christology, is that of Christ's pre-existence. The Apostle John begins his gospel with the announcement that "*In the beginning was the Word*, and the Word was with God, and the Word was God. The same was *in the beginning* with God." "All things were made by him; and without him was not anything made that was made." In this important passage three things are distinctly stated: (1) In the beginning the Word was with God; (2) the Word was God; and (3) the Word created all things. If there were nothing else to the purpose in the whole of the New Testament, these first three verses of the fourth Gospel in connection with the fourteenth verse would suffice to persuade a believer in Holy Scripture of the truth of Christ's pre-existence and Divinity. Without preface or words of introduction, disdaining the verbiage and formulas of scholastic philosophy, the apostle John, instead of beginning his narrative at the human birth of our Lord, or at the commencement of his ministry, opens his treatise as it were with a peal of thunder in the sublime announcement, IN THE BEGINNING WAS THE WORD. Thus, before time began, or at a point to which man cannot apply his finite conception of time, there existed the *Logos* or Word. When as yet the heavens and the earth were not, he *was*. He existed before the creation, for he was the Creator of all things. The personality of the *Logos* is carefully protected by the language used. The evangelist speaks of *him*, not of it; of a *person*, not of an attribute. John talks not like one speaking of an ideal existence, or of a divine energy. He worshiped the Word as the Creator, and adored him as his Saviour. To him the life of Jesus was as the light of heaven. He never seeks to idealize the Master. To his conception, Jesus is above and beyond all idealization. The Word of whom he writes is also the Son, the only begotton Son of God. "He that hath the Son hath life, and he that hath not the Son of God hath not life." "God sent his only begotton Son into the world that we might live through him."

We have also in the opening chapter of John's Gospel the testimony of John the Baptist, whom our Lord declares to be a true witness. (John v. 32.) "John bore witness of him, and cried, saying, This was he of whom I spoke, he that cometh after me is preferred before me: *for he was before me.*" The followers of Socinus, who denied the pre-existence of Christ will not allow the obvious teaching of the passage, but paraphrase it thus: "The Christ who is to begin his ministry after me has, by the divine appointment, been preferred before me, because he is my chief or superior." Thus they explain the clause "for he was before me" in the sense of superior rank or dignity, instead of *time.* John, however, uses the same word —*protos*—several times in his Gospel to denote priority of time. Examples: "The world hated me *before* it hated you." (John xv. 18.) "He *first* findeth his own brother Simon." (i. 41.) "The other disciples did outrun Peter and came *first* to the sepulchre." (xx. 4.) The verb in the last clause, "He *was* before me," is sufficient to fix the meaning of *protos* as indicating priority of time. Had the Baptist referred to the rank or dignity of Christ as separable from the idea of time, he would not have said "He *was*," but "He *is* before me."

OUR LORD'S DIRECT TESTIMONY.

Our Lord's discourses, in which he claims to have had a pre-existence in heaven, must carry with them the absolute conviction to every Christian heart of the truthfulness of the great doctrine therein enunciated. To the Jewish Ruler he said: "No man hath ascended up to heaven, but he that came down from heaven, even the Son of man which is in heaven." (John iii. 13.) When preaching in the great synagogue of Capernaum he used the following significant language: "I came down from heaven, not to do mine own will, but the will of him that sent me." (ch. vi. 38.) "I am the living Bread which came down from heaven." (ch. vi. 51.) "The Jews then murmured at him because he said, I am the Bread which came down from heaven. And they said, is not this Jesus, the son of Joseph, whose father and mother we know? How is it then that he saith, I came down from heaven." (ch. vi. 41, 42.) The Jews objected that they knew his father and mother, and could not, therefore, understand his claim to a pre-existent life. Instead of attempting to remove the impression which his words had made upon his auditors, our Lord proceeded to re-assert his pre-existence in the same terms as before. (vs. 44–58.) He carried the doctrine into its mysterious consequences. Since he was the Bread of Life which came down from heaven, his flesh was meat indeed, and his blood was drink indeed. They only would have eternal life who should eat this flesh and drink this blood. When many of the disciples murmured at this doctrine as "a hard saying," our Lord met their objections by predicting his return to heaven as an event that would justify his allusions to his pre-existence. "What and if ye shall see *the Son of man ascend up* WHERE HE WAS BEFORE." (John vi. 62.) In what manner are declarations so plain and unequivocal to be avoided? It is said that Socinus and his early disciples, in order to account for these phrases, supposed that Christ, between the time of his birth and entrance upon his ministry, was translated into heaven, and there remained some time, that he might see and hear those things which he was to publish to the world.[1] For such a supposition, however, no warrant of Scripture can be found, and the position is therefore clearly an untenable one. Another hypothesis, and the one generally adopted by modern Socinians, is that our Lord's words do not necessarily imply a literal ascent and descent, but merely that "he alone was admitted to an intimate knowledge of the divine will, and was commissioned to reveal it to men."[2] But to this it is obvious to reply that if the first of these two opposite phrases of "ascending into heaven," and "coming down from heaven," be explained figuratively to mean becoming acquainted with God's will, the second phrase must signify to become *un*acquainted with the divine will. Whatever "*ascending* to heaven" may be supposed to mean, in any figure, *descending* from heaven must mean the opposite. If, therefore, to ascend be to *learn*, to descend must be to *unlearn.*[3]

Again, if to come down from heaven signifies to bring a divine commission to teach, is it not passing strange that the expression

---

[1] Watson's Inst., Part II., p. 241. [2] Beltham's Inquiry. [3] Magee on the Atonement.

should never have been used in reference to Moses or David, to John or Paul, or to any other of the inspired writers? So decisive is the passage in John vi. 62 that even Strauss concedes that the language of Jesus is "in its intrinsic meaning, as well as in that which is reflected on it from other passages, unequivocally significative of actual, not merely of ideal, pre-existence."[1]

On another occasion, our Lord, in addressing the Jews in the temple, said: "If a man keep *my* saying, he shall never see death." (John viii. 54.) The Jews, thinking that by such an announcement he assumed to be greater than Abraham and the prophets, indignantly asked, "Whom makest thou thyself?" Jesus replied, "Your father Abraham rejoiced to see my day, and he saw it and was glad." Abraham had seen the day of Christ by the light of prophecy, and accordingly this statement was a claim on the part of Jesus to be the true Messiah.

The Jews evidently thought that Jesus meant by his "day" something more than the years of his human life. At least, they determined by asking him a question, to know whether he claimed to have lived in the days of Abraham. "Then said the Jews unto him, Thou art not yet fifty years old, and hast thou seen Abraham?" Thus, by perverting the Master's language, they directly raised the question of pre-existence. Now, if our Lord had only claimed to be a human Messiah, he undoubtedly would have most earnestly disclaimed any such inference from his words. He had not said that he had seen Abraham, but that Abraham had seen his day. By the light of prophecy and with the eye of faith Abraham had seen the day of Christ and rejoiced thereat. Abraham had looked forward to Christ as the promised seed in whom all the nations should be blessed. (Gen. xxii. 18, Gal. iii. 16.) Our Lord's design appears to have been to show that Abraham believed that in due time the Messiah would come, and that to him would the gathering of the nations be, and that, as a consequence, he, as the true Messiah, was greater than Abraham. He might, indeed, have replied to the impertinent question of the Jews by assuring them that he meant only that Abraham saw him by the light of prophecy, and that this did not necessarily imply that he was Abraham's contemporary. But in his actual answer he mounted up far beyond Abraham, both in rank and

---

[1] Leben Jesu, ch. 4, § 65.

time, and more than justified the suspicions of his jealous examiners concerning his real meaning. "Jesus said unto them, Verily, verily, I say unto you, *Before Abraham was, I am*."[1] Greek—*Prin Abraam genesthai*, "before Abraham was born, that is, before he had an existence, *ego simi, I am*." Observe, our Lord does not say "Before Abraham was, I was," but "I am." He claims pre-existence indeed, but he claims more than this. He is the I AM. The speaker was "Jesus Christ, the same yesterday, and to-day, and forever." (Heb. xiii. 8.) The phrase "I am" denotes existence merely, with no note of beginning or end. "Applied to God it denotes *continued* existence without respect to time, so far as he is concerned. . . . The manner in which Jesus used it would strikingly suggest the application of the same language to God. The question here was about the pre-existence of Jesus. The objection of the Jews was that he was not fifty years old and could not, therefore, have seen Abraham. Jesus replied to that that he *existed before Abraham*.[2] The passage corresponds with John's affirmation, already noticed, that '*in the beginning was the Word*,' and proves most conclusively the personal pre-existence of Christ. . . . It may be interesting to notice the Socinian hypothesis by which the plain teaching of this passage is sought to be evaded. The first exposition is, 'That Christ existed before the patriarch Abraham had become, according to the import of his name, the father of many nations, that is, before the Gentiles were called.' The second is, 'Before Abraham was' born, I am he, *i. e.*, the Christ, in the destination and appointment of God."[3]

A little attention will serve to show the exceeding absurdity of these expositions. Neither of them claims anything peculiar for Christ, nothing indeed more than his auditors, without arrogance, might have claimed for themselves. The first would make our Lord talk thus irrelevantly: "I solemnly assure you [verily, verily, I say unto you], before Abraham shall have become what his name signifies, the father of many nations, I am. Be not indignant at this answer, nor think I magnify myself, for what I assert of myself is equally true of each of you; for *before Abram be made Abraham*,

[1] Meyer in loc.: "Ehe Abraham ward, bin Ich, alter als Abraham's werden ist meine existenz." Erasmus in loc.: "Antequam Abraham nasceretur ego sum."

[2] Barnes' Notes on John viii. 58.

[3] Watson's Inst., Part II., p. 243.

ye are." The second would make him say to the Jews: "Do not look thus angrily upon me and contemptuously ask, hast thou seen Abraham? It is true that Abraham has been dead eighteen centuries, and also true that I am not yet forty years old; but notwithstanding this I repeat it, *before Abraham was born, I was.* But do not mistake my meaning, I claim only to have existed in the foreknowledge and decree of God. Nor do I elevate myself above humanity by this claim, for each of you likewise thus existed before Abraham was born."[1] It is difficult to understand how such expositions could ever have been received by any Christian, and utterly impossible to account thereby for the exasperation of the Jews. *They* evidently understood him as claiming all the attributes and majesty of the Messiah, and the highest honors of God. The action of the Jews showed in what light they regarded his words. Filled with rage at the blasphemy, as they thought it, of his claiming divinity for himself, "they took up stones to cast at him, but Jesus hid himself, and went out of the temple, going through the midst of them, and so passed by." There is nothing in the text or context of this famous passage that serves to support the Socinian scheme. Observe the force of the expression, "*Before Abraham was, I am*," or, as Dr. Murdock's translation of the Syriac reads, "*Before Abraham existed, I was.*" Just so surely as he spoke of Abraham as a person, just so surely did he speak of himself as a person; and just as certainly as Abraham had a real existence, just so certainly had Christ a real existence before Abraham was born.

The attention of the reader is next called to the solemn and significant language in which our Lord addressed his disciples on the eve of his betrayal. "The Father himself loveth you *because ye have loved me, and have believed that I came out from God. I came forth from the Father, and am come into the world: again I leave the world, and go to the Father.*" (John xvi. 28.) This language is very explict and to the point. Just as certainly as the second clause of the last verse quoted, is to be understood literally, just so certainly must the first clause of the same verse be taken in its literal sense; or, as certainly as Jesus now exists personally with the Father, just so certainly did he exist with the Father before he came into the world.

---

[1] **Pearson on the Creed.**

That our Lord's language was neither ambiguous nor obscure is clearly seen from the disciples' reply. They said unto him, "*Lo, now speakest thou plainly*, and speakest no proverb. *Now* are we sure that thou knowest all things, and needest not that any man should ask thee: *by this we believe that thou camest forth from God.*" Well would it be if all would have the disciples' implicit faith in the words of the Master, and not seek, as do many, to obscure or destroy his meaning by resolving his words into some figure of speech that will inevitably destroy the sense intended. The language of John xvi. 28, literally understood, would forever settle the question of Christ's pre-existence. Few and feeble have been the efforts of Socinian writers to meet the direct and conclusive testimony of this remarkable passage. The disciples acknowledged as clear what had before been obscure, and confessed their belief that he had come from God. In plain language when one speaks of his existence, he is never understood as speaking of an ideal existence, but always and invariably of a real or personal existence. In John xvi. 28, our Saviour uses what the disciples acknowledge to be plain language, and therefore, the conclusion is inevitable, that the existence which he said he had with the Father was a personal and not merely an ideal existence; or in other words, that Christ pre-existed as a person, and not as an attribute merely.

In connection with this, and as fixing the sense of the passage beyond successful controversy, the reader is referred to Paul's language in the fourth chapter of his letter to the Ephesians. Speaking of Christ's glorious ascension after his resurrection—as most expositors allow—the apostle by way of parenthesis exclaims—"Now that he ascended, what is it but that he also descended first into to the lower parts of the earth? He that descended is the same also that ascended up far above all heavens that he might fulfill all things." It is here unequivocally declared that the same person—meaning Christ—who ascended above all heavens, was the same Being who first descended into the lower parts of the earth. On no other supposition than that of his pre-existence as the Son of God, does the assertion that he ascended imply that he first descended. As he was exalted, so was he first abased; as he rose victorious over death, so was he first placed under its dominion; as he returned *to* his Father, so he first came *from* his Father.

Again, how full of solemn significance is that passage in our Lord's intercessory prayer, in which he asks—"O Father, glorify thou me with thine own self, with the glory which I had with thee before the world was!" (John xvii. 5.) There could hardly be a more distinct declaration of the pre-existence of Christ than this. So far as this great doctrine is concerned, this text ought at once to remove every doubt, silence every cavil, and answer every objection. The Socinians, who deny, not only our Lord's Divinity, but his existence before he appeared in the world, make a very weak attempt to evade the obvious teaching of this important passage. Their exposition may be seen in the following paraphrase: "O Father, glorify thou me, with the glory which I had with thee *in thy immutable decree*, before the world was." But it is obvious that our Lord did not ask to be glorified with *predetermined glory*, but with the glory which he had with the Father, before the world was. He had once possessed glory with the Father, but he divested himself of this glory when he took upon himself the nature of man. He desired to be re-invested with heavenly honor and dignity. It seems very unlikely that Jesus in his last solemn prayer with his disciples, should speak of *having enjoyed* blessings with the Father which were only to be given to him *in the future.* It is also clear that since our Lord had glory with the Father before the world was, that he then existed as a person, and not merely as an attribute. His pre-existence was personal, not ideal. It would not only be absurd, but irreverent, to represent the Son of God as asking his heavenly Father to re-invest him with the glory which he had with him as a divine attribute, purpose, or idea.

In fact, so decisive is this passage, so impregnable does it stand against all Socinian assaults, that, as Dr. Harwood very justly observes, "were there no intimation in the whole New Testament of the pre-existence of Christ, this single text would irrefragibly demonstrate and establish it. Our Saviour, here in a solemn act of devotion, declares to the Almighty that he had glory with him before the world was, and fervently supplicates that he would be graciously pleased to reinstate him in his former felicity. The language is plain and clear. Every word has great emphasis: "*Glorify thou me with thine own self, with the glory which I had with thee before the world was.* Upon this single text I lay my finger. And if plain words be designedly employed to convey any determinate meaning, if the modes of human speech have any precision, I am convinced that this plain declaration of our Lord, in an act of devotion, exhibits a great and important truth, which can never be subverted or invalidated by any accurate and satisfactory criticism." [1]

PAUL'S CHRISTOLOGY.

There are many passages in the writings of Paul in which the doctrine of the pre-existence of Christ is very clearly taught. Two of these we will notice. In the second chapter of his letter to the Philippians, the apostle, in exhorting his readers to practice humility, presents for their imitation the example of Christ, "*who being in the form of God, thought it not robbery to be equal with God; but made himself of no reputation, and took upon him the form of a servant, and was made in the likeness of men.*"

The antithesis in this passage is between the expressions "form of God" and "form of servant." In his pre-existent state Christ was in the form of God; but, when born into the world he appeared in the form of a servant. Leaving the glory which he enjoyed in the presence of God, "he made himself of no reputation,"—Greek, *eautone eknose*, literally, *he emptied himself;* divested himself of the form of God, and took upon himself the form of man.

In another place the apostle Paul, speaking of Christ, says: "By him were all things created, that are in heaven, and that are in earth, visible and invisible, whether they be thrones, or dominions, or principalities, or powers; *all things were created by him and for him.* And *he is before all things*, and by him all things consist." [2] In this passage, which is paralleled only by the prologue to John's Gospel, Christ is said to have existed before the universe, and to have created it. The language, though grand in expression, and sublime in meaning, is utterly misleading unless it teaches the personal pre-existence of Christ. If Jesus had no pre-existence, how did he, though rich, for our sakes become poor? (2 Cor. viii. 9.) Of what riches did he divest himself? If he had no conscious existence before his incarnation, how could he say, "I proceeded forth and came from God, neither came I of myself, but he sent me."

---

[1] **Harwood's Socinian Scheme.**

[2] **Benson in loc.**

(John viii. 42.) Observe that the *I*, the *person* speaking, is ever the same, whether in the form of God, or in the form of a servant; whether as the Son of God, or as the Son of man; whether as the divine Logos, or as Jesus of Nazareth, the personal identity is ever preserved,—"Jesus Christ *the same yesterday*, *to-day*, *and forever*."

In the days of Noah he preached by the Spirit to the wicked antediluvians; but this could not have been the case if he was not formerly existent at that time. From the Theophanies and Messianic prophecies of the Old Testament, very plausible, if not wholly conclusive, arguments may be found to show that he who was called the Angel of the Lord (Ex. iii. 2), the Angel of God's presence (Is. lxiii. 9), and the Messenger of the Covenant (Mal. iii. 1), was none other than the pre-existent Jesus. Micah evidently alludes to Christ where he speaks of him who is "to be Ruler in Israel, whose goings forth have been from of old, from everlasting." (Micah v. 2.) Isaiah calls him Emanuel (Is. vii. 14), and Jeremiah says his name shall be called the Lord our Righteousness. (Jer. xxiii. 6.) Zachariah terms him the Fellow of the Lord of Hosts (Zach. xiii. 7), and Malachi points to him as the Angel of the Covenant, who would suddenly come to his temple. (Mal. iii. 1.)

The time is fast hastening, and cannot be far distant, when the blessed Jesus shall come "to be glorified in his saints, and to be admired in all them that believe in that day."[1]

"Soon *all* shall hail our Jesus' name,
Angels shall prostrate fall;
For him the brightest glory claim,
And crown him Lord of all."

LIFE AND DEATH—BY JAMES H. WHITMORE.

"The wages of sin is death; but the gift of God is eternal life through Jesus Christ our Lord." (Rom. 6:23.)

Of all words none have for the human race so transcendent an interest as those little monosyllables life and death. They are the terms which are used in Scripture to express the respective future destinies of the righteous and the wicked. To correctly understand their meaning, therefore, is a matter of very great importance. This ought not to be a difficult task. Nor would it be were it not

[1] Advent Christian Quarterly, Vol. ii. 134.

for the interposition of what are called "theological definitions." There is no difference of opinion among men anywhere concerning the *literal* meaning of the words life and death.

Without attempting a scientific definition of these terms, it will suffice for the present to say that LIFE means *vital existence*, and that its opposite DEATH means the *extinction of life* or the *cessation of vital existence.*[1] These definitions will be generally accepted as the true meaning of the words life and death when applied to the lower animals, although they are not commonly allowed when spoken of man. But in popular theology man is regarded as an immortal being, and the terms life and death, when applied to him in a future state, are necessarily understood in a figurative sense. Says a distinguished English writer:

"A being who believes he has life already by original creation, in the sense of an unending or immortal existence, is necessiated to understand the promise of life as synonymous with the promise of happiness, and when death is predicated of such a being, it also must be understood in the metaphorical sense of misery, since it is presumed that this native immortality will never be alienated.

"Does not this conversion of the most commonplace terms from their familiar and natural use to a use both unfamiliar and unnatural appear, to say the least, a very singular circumstance? If the lan-

---

[1] The words LIFE and DEATH, with their derivatives, appear to be employed in Scripture to denote the following ideas: LIFE stands for the idea of—

1. *Vital existence*, as distinct from the death or dissolution of vegetable or animal structures; and as opposed to the insensibility of material things. Also, it signifies ETERNAL LIFE.
2. *Activity of movement or agency;* as "living waters;" "the word of God is *quick* [living] and powerful;" "*quicken* thou me in thy way."
3. *Happy existence;* not *happiness* alone, but *happy life.* "In thy favor is life;" "wisdom is a tree of life;" "now I live, if ye stand fast in the Lord."
4. "*To be alive in the Spirit*" is to be living a spiritual life, in opposition to that carnal one of which Paul says, "If ye *live* after the flesh, ye shall die" (Rom. vi. 11), and the "life of God," or godly life.(Eph. iv. 18.)

But LIFE *never* seems to stand for *holiness* alone, or a state of union with God, as is commonly supposed. This appears to be a *purely gratuitous assertion;* on which rests the whole fabric of the opinions which we are venturing to reject. At the same time, it is readily granted that the term *life* is properly *associated* in the case of the righteous with the idea of *holiness*, as it is also with the idea of *happiness: but that it ever loses its proper radical meaning of existence has yet to be proved, and of course the burden of proof lies with the opposite party.*

DEATH, on the other hand, stands for—

1. *The loss or destruction of vegetable or animal life.* "A dead tree;" "a dead lion;" "a dead body."
2. The state of *condemnation to such literal death.* "Thou art but a dead man." (Gen. xx. 7.)
3. *Danger of death.* "Thanks be to God who hath delivered us from so great death." So also "destruction of the flesh," in 1 Cor. v. 5, is used for a *mortal disease.*
4. To be "*dead to*" anything, signifies *to cease to be or to live in certain relationships to it.* "Dead to the world"—"to sin"—"to the law." But the phrase "dead to God" *never occurs.*
5. To *mortify*, or put to death, signifies to destroy the life of anything, either literally, or in the sense of its *activity and power;* as when it is said "Nabal's heart became *dead* within him."
6. It has never been shown that *death* stands for a state of *misery*, or of *sinfulness, apart from the idea of that literal destruction, or death*, which is the wages of sin.
7. The expression, *spiritual death*, and the distinction between *temporal and eternal death*, are alike unknown to the Holy Scriptures. They are, we venture to think, the necessary creations of an erroneous theory.—*Life in Christ*, by the Rev. Edward White.

guage in which the original Scriptures were written could not furnish terms to express the ideas of happiness and misery, then there might be some plausibility for the appropriation of these terms in this arbitrary sense: but the rudest language has its signs for these ideas; and, therefore, there could have been no need, and we should think, too, no reason to set aside the appropriate words, and to employ others in a sense so different from their peculiar signification. Thus employed, the words life and death part with their proper and distinctive signification; and one term especially—the term death—is employed in a sense the very opposite of its original and conventional meaning: *death*, according to the popular theory, is made to signify a *life in misery!*

"Now, there are grave objections to this figurative use of the words life and death. In the first place, we have seen they have a very arbitrary and unnatural meaning forced upon them. And in the second place, the conversion of these words from their proper to a very violent and arbitrary meaning has no authority from nor is it demanded by the written word.

"The Bible professing to be the teacher of mankind in religion, the most interesting and important subjects, would, of course, not construct a terminology of its own; but make use of the language which the people understood, and employ the terms of such language in their current and conventional meaning; and whenever it was necessary to employ a word different from its customary usage, either the context would make this apparent or there would be some cautionary observation to prevent the possibility of mistake.

"All language is, more or less, figurative; and of all imaginations, the Oriental is the most imaginative; and, therefore, it was to be expected that words would not invariably be used in their strict primary signification: but whenever it should be necessary to employ a word in an unusual sense, there would be ample evidence of its new appropriation. Should there be any danger of misunderstanding the sense in which a word is used, especially if upon that word depended important doctrine, then we might expect such a cautionary notice of its new meaning, as is furnished, for example, in the book of Revelation (chapter xi. 8), where the great city is called Sodom and Egypt, and we are carefully informed that it is so called 'spiritually.' [See another example in John vii. 38, 39; also, Gal. iii. 23–25.]

"But the words in question have no such admonitory notice, which is the more surprising since such a usage of them, as the Scriptures are alleged to furnish, is contrary to all custom; and being employed to teach very vital doctrines, such an admonition is the more necessary, and to be expected. The fact that the Bible has no inspired glossary or explanation of terms, renders it the more imperative that all its words should be employed according to established usage; and is in itself a tacit proof that such *is* the sense in which every word is used. I conclude, therefore, that the words life and death, as used in the Bible, are to be understood in the same sense they obtain in ordinary language—that is, except when obvious reasons demand a figurative meaning for them—in their plain, literal, conventional signification—not respectively happiness and misery, but existence and non-existence."[1]

It is plain to all that *life* does not necessarily include the idea of *happiness;* since one may possess life and not happiness. The converse of this, however, is not true. If we possess happiness we must necessarily possess life. Life is the necessary foundation of all positive good. To borrow the language of Abp. Whately:

"It is certain that the words life, eternal life, immortality, etc., are always applied to the condition of those, and of those only, who shall at the last day be approved as 'good and faithful servants, who are to enter into the joy of their Lord.' 'Life,' as applied to their condition, is usually understood to mean 'happy' life. And that theirs will be a happy life we are indeed plainly taught; but I do not think we are anywhere taught that the word 'life' does of itself necessarily imply happiness. If so indeed, it would be a mere tautology to speak of a 'happy life;' and a contradiction to speak of a 'miserable life,' which we know is not the case, according to the usage of any language. In all ages and countries, 'life,' and the words answering to it in other languages, have always been applied in ordinary discourse to a wretched life no less properly than to a happy one. Life, therefore, in the received sense of the word, would apply equally to the condition of the blest, and of the condemned, supposing these last to be destined to continue forever living in a state of misery. And yet, to *their* condition the words 'life' and 'immortality' never are applied in Scripture. If therefore we sup-

---

[1] *Life and Death,* by J. Panton Ham, ch. 2.

pose the hearers of Jesus and his apostles to have understood, as nearly as possible, in the ordinary sense, the words employed, they must naturally have conceived them to mean (if they were taught nothing to the contrary) that the condemned were really and literally to be 'destroyed,' and cease to exist; not that they were to exist forever in a state of wretchedness. For they are never spoken of as being kept alive, but as *forfeiting* life: as for instance: 'Ye will not come unto me that ye may *have life*.' 'He that hath the Son hath life; and he that hath not the Son of God hath *not* life.' And again, 'perdition,' 'death,' 'destruction,' are employed in numerous passages to express the doom of the condemned. All which expressions would, as I have said, be naturally taken in their usual and obvious sense, if nothing were taught to the contrary."[1]

Hiram Mattison, in a recently published work, says:

"Future *happiness alone* is conditioned upon faith in Christ, and *not our future being*. Consequently, the future non-existence of the wicked cannot follow for lack of a vital connection with Christ, by faith in him. He is 'our life' in that he restores the soul to spiritual life by his Spirit, raises our bodies from the dead, and finally crowns the righteous with glory in heaven. But *our immortal existence is not made dependent on the reception or rejection of salvation through his name*. We shall exist forever, whether in happiness through faith in Christ and a holy life, or in misery through a life of sin and the rejection of offered mercy through him, the only Saviour."[2]

In accordance with this statement of Orthodoxy, is the assertion of a writer in the *Eclectic Review* for August, 1845:

"The term life, when used descriptively of the future state of the righteous, does not denote existence, but happiness exclusively."[3]

Let us proceed at once to try these confident assertions of Orthodoxy, by an appeal to the supreme authority of the Scriptures. Fortunately we have an inspired definition of the term "life," which furnishes the highest and most satisfactory proof, that the Holy Spirit dictated the word in its literal sense:

"He asked *life* of thee, and thou gavest *it* him, *even* LENGTH OF DAYS FOREVER AND EVER." (Ps. 21: 4.)

---

[1] *Scripture Revelations of a Future State*, p. 228.

[2] *Bible Doctrine of Immortality*, p. 63.

[3] See Dobney, *Future Punishment*, p. 192.

Here we have one of the most explicit phrases for "immortal existence," used to define 'life' [eternal life], and applied to one who asked it of God. Again we read: "His seed shall endure forever." (Ps. 89: 36.) "With long life will I satisfy him." (Ps 91: 16.) It may he said that these passages refer to Christ, and that they cannot, therefore, be used as evidence to show the meaning of the word "life" when applied to the future condition of righteous *men*. This anticipated objection, however, would not prove that these passages are impertinent to the question discussed; for Jesus said to his disciples, "Because I live, ye shall live also." (John 14: 19.) And the author of the epistle to the Hebrews says: "Wherefore he is able also to save them to the uttermost that come unto God by him, seeing that he ever liveth to make intercession for them." (ch. 7: 25.) And again Jesus says, "I give unto my sheep *eternal life*, and they shall never perish." (John 10: 28.) Will the reader be so kind as to carefully notice the absolute conclusiveness of the above passages? The eternal life promised to the faithful follower of Christ is 'LENGTH OF DAYS FOREVER AND EVER.' How brightly the truth shines when contrasted with error!

Notice the significant contrasts in the following passages:

"The thief cometh not, but for to steal and to *kill* and to *destroy;* I am come that they might have *life*, and that they might have it more abundantly." (John 10: 10.)

"Whosoever believeth in him should not *perish*, but have *everlasting life.*" (John 3: 16.)

In these passages, if a metaphorical meaning be placed upon the word 'life,' then the contrasted terms 'destroy' and 'perish' must also be metaphorically explained. But where, it may be asked, is the similitude or resemblance between *destruction* and a *life* of endless misery? Life *may* include happiness; but destruction *cannot* include the idea of endless misery.

If on the other hand we examine the literal meaning of the words 'destroy' and 'perish' we shall find that they are directly opposed to the idea of the continuance in being of the object to which they are applied. (The only exceptions to this rule are found in "theological definitions.") To destroy means to demolish; to ruin; to bring to naught; to annihilate; to kill; to extirpate; to put an end to. Perish (literally to depart wholly); to die; to lose life in any manner; to be destroyed; to come to nothing. The apostle Peter speaking of the final doom of wicked men, says "they shall *utterly perish* in their own corruption." (2 Pet. 2: 12.) The language here used is so forcible that even President Dwight says: "It cannot be denied that the destruction spoken of in this passage is declared to be absolute, and must be either annihilation or eternal woe."[1]

The apostle Paul in speaking of the wicked at the second coming of Christ, says: "Who shall be punished with everlasting destruction from the presence of the Lord, and from the glory of his power." (2 Thes. 1 : 9.) Orthodoxy interprets this passage to mean that the wicked shall be punished with everlasting misery! And when the same apostle says "the wages of sin is *death*," this "tremendous Orthodxy" says, Not so; for the wages of sin is not literal destruction, but eternal life in torment! This shocking perversion of Scripture is directly traceable to the metaphorical sense invariably given by popular theology to the words "life" and "death" when applied to the future state of the righteous and wicked of the human race.

Mr. Mattison has a chapter entitled, "Immortal existence not a result of faith in Christ."[2] This sentiment is indorsed by the leading Protestant Church of America; and not only this Church, but all Orthodox Churches must admit the conclusion, as they accept the premises upon which it is legitimately based. The reader's special attention is invited to the issue thus fairly joined between Orthodoxy and the Bible. What then is the testimony? What saith the faithful Witness?

> "If we receive the witness of men, the witness of God is greater: for this is the witness of God, which he hath testified of his Son. He that believeth on the Son of God hath the witness in himself; he that believeth not God hath made him a liar; because he believeth not the record that God gave of his Son. And this is the record, that God hath given to us eternal life, and *this life is in his Son. He that hath the Son* HATH LIFE; and *he that hath not the Son of God hath not life.*" (John v. 9–12.)

The phrase "immortal existence" when applied to man means the same as "eternal life." The full sense of the passage would be preserved if it were read thus: "And this is the record, that God hath given to us an immortal existence, and this existence is in his Son!

---

[1] *Theology*, vol. 4, p. 460.

[2] Bible Doctrine of Immortality, ch. 6.

He that hath the Son hath an immortal existence; and he that hath not the Son of God hath not an immortal existence."

It is written, "The just shall live by his faith." (Hab. ii. 4.) This text is quoted by the apostle Paul in Rom. i. 17, and Gal. iii. 11. It is also said, "Without faith it is impossible to please him." (Heb. xi. 6.) "For ye are all the children of God by faith in Jesus Christ." (Gal. iii. 25.) "These are written that ye might believe that Jesus is the Christ, the Son of God; and that believing, ye might have *life* through his name." (John xx. 31.) "The gift of God is eternal life through Jesus Christ our Lord." (Rom. vi. 23.) "He that believeth not the Son shall not see life." (John iii. 36.) These passages conclusively prove that "eternal life" or immortal existence is a result of faith in Christ.

The same conclusion is reached from considering the distinctive titles given to Christ by the writers of the New Testament. He is called "the Prince of life" (or Author of life, margin) in Acts iii. 15; "Christ, our Life" in Col. iii. 4; and in the Syriac Version, he is frequently called the "Vivifier" and the "Life-giver."[1] There are many passages of Scripture which support his right to those titles. Jesus himself said: "My sheep hear my voice, and I know them, and they follow me; and I give unto them eternal life." (John x. 27, 28.) "That he should give eternal life to as many as thou hast given him.' (John xvii. 2.) "Whosoever drinketh of the water that I shall give him shall never thirst: but the water that I shall give him shall be in him a well of water springing up to everlasting life." (John iv. 14; see also Ps. xxxvi. 9.) "To him that overcometh will I give to eat of the tree of life, which is in the midst of the Paradise of God." (Rev. ii. 7.) Every one of these passages is directly opposed to the notion

---

[1] In the Syraic version of the New Testament the subject of *life* is made more prominent than in the "authorized English version." This will be noticed in the following passages from Prof. Murdock's translation:

Acts iv. 12: "There is not another name under heaven, which is given to men, *whereby to live*."

Acts v. 31: "Him hath God established as a Head and *Life-giver*."

Rom. i. 16: "I am not ashamed of the Gospel, for it is the power of God *unto life*, to all who believe."

John xii. 47: "I did not come to judge the world, but to *vivify* the world."

Acts xvi. 31: "Believe on the name of our Lord Jesus Messiah, *thou wilt have* LIFE."

Phil. iii. 20: "Our concern is from heaven; and from thence we expect our VIVIFIER, our Lord Jesus Messiah."

Heb. vii. 25: "And he is able to *vivify* forever them who come to God by him."

2 Tim. i. 10: "The appearing of our *Life-giver*, Jesus the Messiah, who hath abolished death, and hath made manifest life and immortality by the Gospel."

2 Tim. iii. 15: "From thy childhood thou was taught the holy books, which can make thee wise unto *life*, by faith in Jesus the Messiah."

2 Tim. iv. 18: "My Lord will rescue me from every evil work; and will give me *life* in his heavenly kingdom."

of man's natural immortality. For it is evident that eternal life is not promised to all men, but to the faithful alone. If all men have an immortal existence guaranteed to them by the deathlessness of their nature, in what sense is Christ called the Life-giver?

The tree of life in Eden was to Adam a pledge of immortality so long as he preserved his innocence.

It was not the emblem of "happiness exclusively," but of life in its literal sense of continued existence. So, too, the tree of life in the Paradise of God is the symbol of eternal life or immortal existence. But this magnificent inheritance is only promised "to him that overcometh." The result to Adam of being driven out from the tree of life in Eden, was not merely unhappiness, but literal death. In carrying out the analogy, therefore, we cannot suppose that those who are to be excluded from the tree of life in Paradise will be immortal.

That Christ is the bestower of life in the literal sense of that term, is further evident from his language in John v. 21: "As the Father raiseth up the dead, and quickeneth them; even so the Son quickeneth whom he will." To this agrees the language of the apostle Paul: "The last Adam was made a quickening (that is a life-giving) Spirit" (1 Cor. xv. 45.) We cannot in this place substitute the metaphorical sense of the word life, by saying that Christ bestows life on whom he will, in the sense of bestowing happiness only; for the subject of both paragraphs is the resurrection or re-enlivening of dead men, and not the conferring of happiness upon those who were already in possession of eternal life.

Let me now pause to ask, In which of the recorded discourses of our Lord or of his apostles shall we find the unconditional immortality of all men affirmed?

And if for the very best of reasons this question cannot be answered, let me ask, Where have we any Scriptural authority for saying that Christ is the bestower of *happiness*, but not of *life?*

No interpretation will take us through the New Testament without manifest absurdities or obvious contradictions, except that which attaches to the phrase eternal life the meaning of *immortal existence.* In support of this assertion, and as further evidence in favor of the literal sense of the word life, some additional passages from the Gospel of John may be adduced, which appear to be fatal to the popular theory. The most prominent feature in the recorded discourses of our Lord is the promise of EVERLASTING LIFE. The assertion of the apostle in the opening of the chapter is most significant. "IN HIM WAS LIFE; and THE LIFE was the light of man." (ch. i. 4.) This passage evidently denotes that he who is expressly desiginated as "THE LIFE," had the power to impart life to others. The same meaning is seen in the parallel passage. (John v. 26:) "For as the Father hath life in himself; so hath he given to the Son to have life in himself." Here life cannot be taken to mean happiness merely, without destroying the congruous signification of the whole passage. The context would not justify the use of the word "life" as a meta-aphor. For in the preceding verses our Lord ascribed to himself the power to raise up and give life to the dead; and in ch. vi. 53, 54, he says: "Except ye eat the flesh of the Son of man, and drink his blood, ye have no life in you. Whosoever eateth my flesh and drinketh my blood, hath eternal life, and I will raise him up at the last day." How plainly do these passages teach that immortality is conditional, and that the expression "eternal life" is to be taken in its strictly literal sense of immortal existence!

This conclusion is supported by the language of our Lord in ch. vi. 57. "As the living Father hath sent me, and I live by the Father; so he that eateth me, even he shall live by me." And in ch. v. 28, 29, he says, "Marvel not at this, for the hour is coming, in the which all that are in the graves shall hear his voice and shall come forth; they that have done good unto the resurrection of life; and they that have done evil unto the resurrection of damnation." Here it is impossible to spiritualize the word "life" without destroying the sense of the whole passage. The wicked as well as the righteous are to be raised from the graves; but only those who have "done good" shall obtain the "resurrection of life." The frequent reference in the fifth and sixth chapters to the physical ideas of the resurrection from "the graves," and to the privilege of living instead of dying, as the fathers in the wilderness died, shows very decisively that the future "life" promised is intended in a literal and not in a metaphorical sense.

Our Lord said to the Jews: "Your fathers did eat manna in the wilderness, and are dead. This is the bread which cometh down from heaven, that a man may eat thereof and not die. I am the living bread which came down from heaven; if any man eat this bread he shall live forever; and the bread that I will give is my flesh, which I will give for the life of the world." (John vi. 49, 51.) "I will raise him up at the last day." (ch. vi. 40, 44, 54.) Why is reference made to the resurrection of the dead, if the life spoken of as the result of it means only the happiness of beings already immortal? Were there not words enough in the Greek language to properly express such a meaning, had it been intended? If so, how are we justified in uniformly giving a figurative term to words which everywhere else are taken in their literal sense?

Will it be said that the life spoken of includes the resurrection of the body, *and* the happiness of the soul already immortal? What then mean these words: "Except ye eat the flesh of the Son of man, and drink his blood, *ye have no life in you?*" (John vi. 53.) Will our Orthodox opponents say that the WICKED will not be raised to have an eternal existence in the body? An affirmative answer would end the controversy.

When our Lord represents himself as "the bread of life," he plainly intimates thereby that the one great object of his mission was to *give life.* A self-reliant and spiritualistic Orthodoxy confidently asserts that the Lord Jesus is not the source of future life to believers; that all men are to have an immortal existence, let their conduct be what it may; that it is not as the bestower of immortality, but of everlasting happiness, that he styles himself the "BREAD OF LIFE." Such a doctrine finds not the slightest support in Scripture, unless it be in Gen. iii. 4, where the Serpent said to our common mother, "ye shall not surely die."

The immediate object of the use of bread is to sustain life, not to confer happiness. There are thousands at this very hour who have an abundance of bread, and yet lead a most wretched life. It is not then as the bestower of "happiness exclusively" that Christ is called the Bread of Life, but because the Father has constituted him as the Giver of immortality to all who obey him.

Another very plain instance of the use of the word "life" in its literal sense occurs in the statement of our Lord to Martha, in John xi. 25, 26: "I am the resurrection and the *life;* he that believeth in me though he were dead, yet shall he live; and whosoever liveth and believeth in me shall never die." Now the word "resurrection" in this passage must of necessity be taken in its literal sense. It would therefore, be a violation of all just principles of interpretation to say that the word "life" in this sentence must be taken figuratively. For it is obvious that in the same sense that Christ is the "resurrection" he is "the life." "I am the resurrection *and the life.*" To take one of these words literally, and to convert the other into a metaphor, would be a perversion of Scripture to serve a theory. Besides, the context exhibits the sense in which the words were used. Our Lord teaches that he would raise to life those who had believed in him, but were already dead; while of living believers he asserts they "shall never die," that is, according to the literal rendering of the Greek, "they shall not die forever." They shall not die in the absolute sense in which the term "second death" is used, but their death will be a falling asleep in Jesus.[1]

It will not do to spiritualize the words "life" and he "shall live," "dead," and "shall not die forever;" for there is no question raised either in the text or context about spiritual death and life, nor about happiness and misery.

Once more: in ch. xii. 25, our Lord, in addressing the Greeks, who came up to worship at the feast, uses this remarkable language: "He that loveth his life shall lose it; and he that hateth his life in this world shall keep it unto life eternal."

No ingenuity of reasoning can make this passage teach the popular doctrine. It is utterly opposed to the idea that men have eternal life in themselves. For it is plain that a man cannot lose his life and have it at the same time; yet our Lord declares "he that loveth his life *shall* lose it." What is it which a man is here represented as loving? And what is it he will keep unto eternal life if he hate it in this world? The obvious answer to these questions must carry with it the conviction to every unbiased mind, that Christ is truly the *Life-giver*, in the sense that he gives the priceless boon of IMMORTALITY to all who love and obey him.

The great theme upon which Christ and his apostles delighted to dwell was life, *eternal life.* Well did Peter say unto his Lord, "Thou hast the words of eternal life." (John vi. 68.) An inspired apostle has declared that "Christ hath abolished death, and brought life and immortality to light through the Gospel." (2 Tim. i. 10.)

---

[1] Another exposition makes this promise refer to the living saints at the second coming of Christ. See 1 Thess. iv. 15, . 1 Cor. xv. 21.

This revelation was brought about by the personal resurrection of Christ, who afterwards appearing to John in Patmos, says (Rev. i. 18): "I am he that *liveth* and was dead; and behold, I am alive forevermore." When we read this sublime utterance, our hearts are cheered with the hope of life, for we remember that precious promise of the *Life-giver*, "Because I live, ye shall live also." (John xiv. 19.) He might just as easily have said, "Because I am happy, ye shall be happy also;" but this would not have been the full or radical idea intended. He and his apostles uniformly use the more comprehensive term "life," without which no other good is possible. But it may be asked, Will not the future life of the redeemed be a happy one? Most assuredly it will; but we do not get this idea from the word life itself, but from those passages of Scripture in which the felicity of those who receive the gift of life is specially mentioned.

The question at issue is not whether Christ bestows mere existence only, but whether he bestows existence at all. The Orthodox position is, that he is the bestower of happiness *only;* that men are not dependent upon him for future *life*, as they are naturally immortal, and consequently deathless.

The utter absence of any necessity for substituting the word "happiness" for "life," when the latter term is applied to describe the future state of the righteous, is seen from the following language of Scripture:

"Eye hath not seen, nor ear heard, neither hath entered into the heart of man, the things which God hath prepared for them that love him." (1 Cor. ii. 9.) "In thy presence is FULLNESS OF JOY; at thy right hand are PLEASURES FOR EVERMORE." (Ps. xvi. 11.)

"In my Father's house are many mansions; if it were not so I would have told you. I go to prepare a place for you, and if I go and prepare a place for you *I will come again, and receive you unto myself, that where I am there ye may be also.*" (John xiv. 2, 3.) "We shall ever be with the Lord." (1 Thes. iv. 17.) "Then shall the king say unto them on his right hand, COME YE BLESSED OF MY FATHER, inherit the kingdom prepared for you from the foundation of the world." (Matt. xxv. 34.)

"*Blessed* and holy is he that hath part in the first resurrection; on such the second death hath no power." (Rev. xx. 6.)

"And I heard a great voice out of heaven saying, Behold, the tabernacle of God is with men, and he will dwell with them, and they shall be his people, *and God himself shall be with them, and be their God. And God shall wipe away all tears from their eyes; and there shall be* NO MORE DEATH, *neither sorrow nor crying, neither shall there be any more pain,* for the former things are passed away." (Rev. xxi. 3, 4.)

What a magnificent destiny awaits the faithful follower of Christ! To be forever with the Lord; to share in the pure pleasures of the angels; to be forever free from all pain and sorrow; to be assured that perfect peace will never be disturbed by the corroding cares of mortal life—all this will be inexpressibly glorious!

If a righteous man has even in this world, while fully trusting in God, a "peace which passeth all understanding," what pencil can paint, or pen portray, the beatific vision which shall unfold to his enraptured gaze when, admitted to the new heavens and new earth, he beholds the glory of his Redeemer, and is permitted to share in the perpetual pleasures of the Paradise of God? In that bright world, sickness and sorrow, disease and death, will be unknown. There will be no mourners there to weep over the sad ravages of the king of terrors, "for God shall wipe away all tears from their eyes, and there shall be *no more death*."

This glorious promise, made by him whose word is truth, leads to the remark that the Scriptures not only represent Christ as the giver of "life," but also as the destroyer of death. Coeval with the entrance of sin into the world was the promise that the Seed of the woman should bruise the serpent's head.[1] And the apostle John says:

"For this purpose the Son of God was manifested, that he might destroy the works of the devil." (1 John iii. 8.)

The language of the author of the epistle to the Hebrews is still more explicit:

"Forasmuch then as the children are partakers of flesh and blood, he also himself likewise took part of the same, that through death he *might destroy him that had the power of death, that is, the devil.*" (ch. ii. 14.)

"He will swallow up *death* in victory." (Is. xxv. 8.)

"*The last enemy that shall be destroyed is death.*" (1 Cor. xv. 26.)

"And death and *hades* were cast into the lake of fire. This is the second death." (Rev. xx. 14.)

Only one question remains—What is meant by the expression "death shall be destroyed?" The "second death" is, in the Orthodox vocabulary, called "eternal death," and is defined to be "the

---

[1] Literally, "*crush* the serpent's head."

death that never dies." Hence the expression is spiritualized to read, "the last enemy that shall be endlessly preserved is death." But how contrary would such an interpretation be to reason as well as to revelation! Who does not know that death will never be destroyed so long as he has *living victims* to prey upon? We can never understand what is meant by death being the last enemy that shall be destroyed so long as we define eternal *death* to mean eternal life in misery. When death "is swallowed up in victory," and "*mortality* is swallowed up of LIFE," *then will death be destroyed.* Then "the Most High shall appear upon the seat of judgment, and misery shall pass away, and the longsuffering shall have an end." (2 Esd. vii. 33.)

The Orthodox interpretation of the words "life" and "death" is an outrage upon human reason, and a reflection upon the character of God. It deprives our glorious Redeemer of the honor of dispensing immortality to his faithful subjects, and disguises under the sentence of death a life of interminable woe.

So long as men feel that they are already immortal, so long will they be unable to realize the great central fact of the Gospel, that Christ is the *Life-giver*, and that he is coming the second time to confer immortality upon all who truly love and obey him.

Why is it that the doctrine of Christ's second advent is so unpopular among modern Christians? Is it not because they fail to realize the great object of his coming? Orthodoxy confidently proclaims that "death is the Prince of peace," and the usher of the happy soul to the realms of glory. It is plain that if Christians believe that they shall go to Christ in heaven when they die, they will not expect him to come to earth again, unless it be in a spiritual manner. Christ said, "I am come that ye might have *life.*" And again, "Ye will not come to ME that ye might have LIFE." But Orthodoxy only seems to hear that other voice, "Ye shall not surely die;" and turns away with the virtual response: "We already have *life*, IMMORTAL LIFE. We will accept *happiness* at thy hands, but we have all the *life* that we need."

The language of Scripture is, "*When* Christ who is our life shall appear, *then* shall *ye also appear* with him in glory." Our Lord taught his disciples that he would come to *them*, *not* that they should go to him.

The hour is surely coming, nor can it be far distant, when he who is the Resurrection and the Life will come to bestow the priceless pearl of immortality upon all who have sought for it by patient continuance in well doing. (Rom. ii. 6, 7.) Then "the ransomed of the Lord shall return, and come to Zion with songs and everlasting joy upon their heads; they shall obtain joy and gladness, and sorrow and sighing shall flee away." (Is. xxxv. 10.)

"It is not," says Prof. Hudson, the author of *Christ our Life*, "the integrity of Scripture language only that is affected by our decision on the subject of immortality; but it may be truly said, that on the right apprehension of this one doctrine of revelation depends our having perfectly just and Scriptural views of all its other doctrines—of the corruption of human nature, the person and divinity of Jesus Christ, the atonement, the office of the Spirit and regeneration, the union with Christ, the resurrection from the dead, the final judgment, together with the ultimate end or consummation of redemption." (pp. 4, 5.)

There are two words in the Greek translated in our English Bible "immortality," viz.: *aphanasia* and *aptharsia*. Both are found in 1 Cor. xv. 53, 54, the former being rendered "*immortality*," the latter "*incorruption*." The only other place in which *aphanasia* occurs is in 1 Tim. vi. 16, "Who only hath *immortality*." The other instances in which *aptharsia* occurs are Rom. ii. 7, 1 Cor. xv. 42–50, 2 Tim. i. 10, excepting Eph. vi. 24, and Titus ii. 7, where it is used in a moral sense for futurity and rendered "*sincerity*."

The adjective, *apthartos*, occurs seven times in the New Testament: Rom. i. 23, 1 Cor. ix. 25, xv. 52, 1 Tim. i. 17, 1 Peter i. 4, 23, iii. 4. In all which passages it will be observed, and the fact is surely of great significance, the application of these words is, *exclusively*, either to God, or that which is of God—his people, their inheritance, resurrection, and reward.

Even Mr. James Grant, when he has not a theory to maintain, can write: "The brutes, we are elsewhere told, are destined to perish; *that is, that when they die there is nothing more of them*, and we hear nothing more of them!" (p. 262.) Can Mr. Grant give us any good and sufficient reason why "perish," as applied to an animal, should mean one thing, but when applied to a man the very opposite? We trow not.

RETROSPECTIVE THOUGHTS.

In carefully considering the historical facts we have presented concerning the awakening and action of a large number of the Lord's watchmen and laymen, upon the subject of our Lord's immediate coming and the events connected therewith, together with the Scriptural arguments which have induced this movement, with constant developments in the present events which fulfill prophetic Scriptures, increasing the interest and the number of believers, we are assured that the end of probationary time is near.

The kingdoms designated have occupied their places, accomplished their work, and filled the mould of prophecy to its last point. The prophetic time for the work of the visions has run to the last extremity, and is nearly exhausted. The day of the Lord must soon open upon an unprepared and astonished world; but with great joy shall an expectant, watching Church hail her coming Lord and Redeemer.

We cannot better state the fevered and excited condition of society than in the following language of Dr. H. Bonar:

The restlessness of *Christian mind* and *Christian thought* amongst us is alarming. Some new thing in doctrine is demanded, we might say, week by week, to feed the excitement which everywhere prevails. The eager way in which many, of whom greater steadfastness might have been expected, snatch at each new speculation that is broached, shows how many "unstable souls" we have; how many "itching ears;" how many "stony-ground" hearers; how many "seducing spirits;" how many vendors of "profane and old wives' fables;" how many "men of corrupt minds, and destitute of the truth;" how many who do not "shun profane and vain babblings;" how many "creepers into houses, leading captive silly women;" how many who "will not endure sound doctrine;" how many "carried about with divers and strange doctrines." They run from man to man, from doctrine to doctrine, from creed to creed, from church to church, in quest of novelty, perverting Scripture in support of their opinions, and parading some one text or set of texts as proof, in one-sided neglect of other passages which are needful for the adjustment of the truth. The church, no less than the world, is in a state of fermentation, and nothing now satisfies save a constant relay of new teachers and new speculations. *Theological sensation-*

alism, yes, and *prophetical sensationalism* are in demand at the present day. Sober-minded and wholesome literature is at a discount; but a sensational pamphlet, fixing some date, or depicting some personage, or foretelling some portentous change, circulates by thousands. "Evil men and seducers wax worse and worse, deceiving and being deceived."

Ritualism is doing its best to buy up for itself all goodly Babylonish garments, and to flaunt the ancient harlotry before church and nation. Broad Churchism undermines the Scriptures, hews down the cross, and sneers at the great white throne. . . . The foundations are being rapidly undermined, and a few years will witness the shaking of the whole fabric. The things that can be shaken are being shaken, that those things that cannot be shaken may remain.

The great truth of Christ's personal and pre-millennial advent has been established in the full strength of Scriptural demonstration. No doctrine seems to us more clearly proved than this, that the heavens are to retain Christ only until the times of the restitution of all things, and that then he comes in glory to deliver creation, to destroy Anti-christ, to re-gather Israel, to bind Satan, and to glorify his church. For that coming we watch as men who know not when their Lord doth come. We see no ground, indeed, for what is called the "secret rapture of the saints;" but we are not of those who see anything interposed between us and the Advent. There *may be* an interval still, but we are not prepared to affirm that there *must be*. There *may be* events still intervening, but we are not prepared to say that there *must be*. We *watch*, and we do so because we know neither the day nor the hour when the Son of man cometh; nay, because we know that in such an hour as we think not he will come; and the signs given, both by himself and his apostles, are largely unfolding themselves, and that with a distinctness such as they have never done in any former ages. When we see these things come to pass we know that he is near, even at the doors. Post-millennarians have interposed a thousand years between us and his coming; let us beware of, in a similar way, interposing other periods, which would enable any one to say, if that be the case, he *cannot* come for centuries, and we need not *watch* for his coming as a thief in the night.

Then, the extreme minuteness of *detail* into which some literalists have gone as to future events, and especially as to their relative allocation, has, by the puzzles and perplexities thus introduced, repelled not a few. The way in which the present dispensation has been treated as a mere parenthesis, in which minute events in Israel's future have been (in a most peremptory way) assorted so as to fit it with foregone conclusions and preconceived theories, has made many who wished to study the subject shrink back in despair. The *unproved* assertions (and they are legion) made by dogmatical writers and speakers, under the boasted presidency of the Holy Ghost, has made many ask, in wonder and despair, if anything can be proved at all. *Unproved assertions* may not seem very offensive or injurious things, yet they are so. "*Prove* all things" is the apostolic statute, which some in our day seem to understand as meaning "assert all things."

But let us not turn away from the prophetic word, though thus disfigured. It is a light shining in a dark place, until the day dawn and the day-star arise. Let us walk in the light, and all the more because the ruler of the darkness of this world seeks to quench or hide it from our view. Let Christ's ministers be faithful in proclaiming his advent boldly.

The truth is that the Master may be nearer than we think. It will be well for us, when he comes, to be found, not only waiting for his appearing, but searching his Word.[1]

"Behold the measure of the promise filled;
See Salem built the labor of a God!
Bright as a sun the sacred city shines.
All kingdoms, and all princes of the earth
Flock to that light; the glory of all lands
Flows into her; unbounded is her joy,
And endless her increase——
Praise is in all her gates. Upon her walls,
And in her streets, and in her spacious courts,
Is heard salvation. . . .
. . . . Her report has traveled forth
Into all lands. From every clime they come
To see thy beauty, and to share thy joy,
Oh Zion! An assembly such as earth
Saw never, such as heaven stoops down to see!"

---

[1] London Quarterly Journal of Prophecy, Oct., 1873.

SHALL WE BELIEVE THE BIBLE OR MEN?

To them that seek for immortality God will render eternal life.—Rom. 2: 6, 7.
The immortality of the soul is like that of God.—AUGUSTINE.
The body is our clog.—PLATO.
Our organized bodies are no part of ourselves.—BISHOP BUTLER. Analogy.
The soul of the wicked is immortal.—CLEMENTINE HOMILIES.
Every soul is immortal.—TERTULLIAN.
The doctrine of the endless pains of the wicked follows as an easy consequence when the immortality of the soul is once granted.—HOOKER. Eccl. Polity.
Immortal souls were guilty of the trespass, and must therefore immortally suffer the pains.—RICHARD BAXTER. 'Saint's Rest.
The soul that sinneth it shall die.—Ezek. 18: 4. *If ye live after the flesh ye shall die.*—Rom. 8: 13.
The never-dying soul.—CLEMENTINE HOMILIES.
The wicked have not even the hope of dying.—Rev. C. H. SPURGEON.
The wicked shall never die.—JAMES GRANT. Religious Tendencies.
The wages of sin is Death.—Rom. 6: 23. *He which converteth a sinner shall save a soul from Death.*—James 5: 20.
How will they call and cry, O Death, whither art thou now gone!—RICHARD BAXTER.
Their souls shall not be put to death.—BARTLETT. Life and Death Eternal.
Does Death come? No. Death flies away from them.—Rev. J. FURNISS.
If any man eat of this bread he shall live forever.—John 6: 51.
Lest he eat, and live forever.—Genesis 3: 22.
In hell they must live.—Rev. J. FURNISS.
The wicked will live on forever.—Rev. Dr. ANGUS. Future Punishment.
The sinner shall live on through eternity.—JAMES GRANT.
The righteous shall go into life eternal.—Matthew 25: 46.
Eternal life will be the lot of the damned.—TERTULLIAN.
God is able to destroy both body and soul in hell.—Matthew 10: 28. *All the wicked will God destroy.*—Psalm 145: 20.
The wicked are rebuilt in union indestructible.—POLLOK. Course of time.
God will not destroy one single soul or body which he has created.—JAMES GRANT.
They will be pained, but undestroyed.—Rev. C. H. SPURGEON.
The wicked shall consume; into smoke shall they consume away.—Psalm 37: 20,
The fire of hell does not consume.—JOHN BUNYAN.
The wicked shall never be consumed.—EDWARDS, WESLEY, BAXTER.
A destruction not consuming.—ROBERT BAXTER. God's Purpose in Judgment.
Them that perish.—2 Cor. 2: 15. *The wicked shall utterly perish.*—2 Pet. 2: 12.
He that soweth to the flesh, shall of the flesh reap corruption.—Galatians 6: 8.
The bodies of the wicked shall be rendered incorruptible.—THOMAS SCOTT.
The bodies of the wicked shall be changed to fit them for eternal torments without corruption.—JONATHAN EDWARDS.
Are not my ways equal?—Ezek. 18: 29. *I, the Lord, am a just God.*—Isaiah 45: 21.
Vindictive justice here displays its power in sustaining dying lives under those great and excruciating pains which scarce an angel's strength could undergo.—JOHN BUNYAN.
We can hardly tell how to reconcile it (eternal pain) with the justice and goodness of God.—ARCHBISHOP TILLOTSON.
The dark side is appalling. We stumble at the thought.—R. B. GIRDLESTONE.
I see not one ray to disclose to me the reason why man must suffer to all eternity.—ALBERT BARNES. Practical Sermons.
God must keep the wicked alive to show his power to restrain them.—Mr. LORD.
Whatsoever a man soweth, that shall he also reap.—Gal. 6: 7.
The punishments of hell are but the perpetual vengeance that accompanies the sins of hell.—Rev. W. A. BUTLER.
Punishment will be just as sin will continue in hell.—JONATHAN EDWARDS.
The Lord is very pitiful.—James 5: 11. *Be pitiful.*—1 Pet. 3: 8.
The woes of sinners will not be a cause of grief to the saints in heaven, but of rejoicing.—JONATHAN EDWARDS.
God will rejoice in their misery, and will do so forever.—JOHN BUNYAN.
It is the highest degree of faith to believe that God is merciful.—LUTHER.
As long as general indifference to human suffering continued, so long was little pain felt at the thought that others are doomed to eternal misery.—Dr. SALMON.
It may seem to our weak mind to clash with the statement that God is love.—Rev. EDWARD NANGLE. Achil Herald.
"A hundred difficulties meet the mind, when we think on this great subject; and they meet us when we endeavour to urge our fellow sinners to be reconciled to God, and to put confidence in Him. I confess for one I feel these, and feel them more sensibly and powerfully the more I look at them, and the longer I live. I do not know that I have a ray of light on this subject, which I had not when the subject first flashed across my soul. I have read to some extent what wise and good men have written. I have looked at their theories and explanations. I have endeavored to weigh their arguments, for my whole soul pants for light and relief on these subjects; but I get neither; and in the distress and anguish of my own spirit, I confess that I see no light whatever."—ALBERT BARNES, D. D.

IMMORTALITY.

God created man in his own image.—Gen. 1: 27. *God said, in the day that thou eatest thereof thou shalt die.*—Gen. 2: 17.

God intrusted Adam with a spark of immortality; he foolishly blew it out by sin.—MATTHEW HENRY. Commentary on Gen. 3: 19.

Adam forfeited the blessing of immortality.—THOMAS SCOTT.

Man abideth not: he is like the beasts that perish.—Ps. 49: 12.

The immortality of the soul is neither argued nor affirmed in the Old Testament.—Professor PEROWNE. Hulsean Lectures.

The doctrine of the immortality of the soul, and the name, are alike unknown to the entire Bible.—Dr. OLSHAUSEN.

In fact no such doctrine is revealed to us.—Archbishop WHATELY.

The Bible is silent on the point of an absolute and unconditional immortality for all men.—Rev. H. H. DOBNEY. Letter Abp. Cantuar.

Search the Bible from beginning to end, and you will nowhere find sinners addressed as immortal beings.—Rev. THOMAS DAVIS.

Eternal fixity and duration belongs only to those who are in accordance with God. DEAN ALFORD on 1 John 2: 17.

My sheep hear my voice: and I give unto them eternal life; and they shall never perish.—John 10: 27-8. *To them who seek for immortality God will render eternal life.*—Rom. 2: 6, 7.

If there be one blessing more than another, which the Scriptures agree in ascribing to Christ as its author, and for which the believer is taught that he is wholly indebted to redemption, it is Immortality.—Rev. Dr. DE BURGH. Christ our life.

We are candidates for Immortality.—Professor PEROWNE.

Christianity treats man not as immortal, but as a candidate for Immortality.—Rev. Dr. PARKER.

As God is eternal, so is all that is in communion with him.—DEAN ALFORD.

Sinful man is not by nature immortal but mortal. If Immortality is to be his, it must be as a gift and not inherited. It must become his by virtue of some new provision of grace. This was the Gospel of Christ.—Rev. H. CONSTABLE. Restitution of all things.

It was just when the coming of Christ was begun to be lost sight of that the doctrine of the Immortality of the soul came to replace that of the Resurrection.—JOHN NELSON DARBY.

The earliest Christian Writings considered Immortality as the peculiar portion of believers in Christ.—J. M. DENNISTON, A. M. Perishing Soul.

From beginning to end of the Apostolical Fathers there is not one word said of the Immortality of the soul. Immortality is asserted by them to be peculiar to the redeemed.—Rev. H. CONSTABLE. Duration and Nature of Future Punishment.

The soul that sinneth it shall die.—Ezekiel 18: 4. *All the wicked will God destroy.*—Ps. 145: 20. *They shall utterly perish.*—2 Pet. 2: 12.

The literal sense of the words descriptive of future punishment overturns the systems of Augustine and Origen.—Rev. H. CONSTABLE. Restitution, &c.

It seems a strange way of understanding a law which requires the plainest words, that by death should be meant eternal life in misery.—JOHN LOCKE.

My mind fails to conceive a grosser misinterpretation of language than when five or six of the strongest words which the Greek tongue possesses, signifying "Destroy" or "Destruction," are explained to mean maintaining an everlasting but wretched existence. To translate black as white is nothing to this.—R. F. WEYMOUTH.

A New Bible would be required to convey that doctrine at all.—Rev. S. MINTON.

The doom of the wicked is everywhere spoken of in Holy Scripture in terms which imply the obliteration of their entire being and existence.—Rev. W. KER.

The final destiny of man as a sinner is that he shall be in the end as though he had never been.—Rev. E. W. TAUNTON. Life in Christ. See Obadiah 16.

These shall go away into everlasting punishment.—Mat. 25: 46. *They shall be punished with everlasting destruction.*—2 Thes. 1: 9.

May it not be reckoned an infinite punishment, should God doom man to total annihilation?—HERMAN WITSIUS.

Endless annihilation is an endless or an infinite punishment. Final annihilation is an infinite evil, as it is inflicted in disapprobation of sin.—President EDWARDS. Review of Chauncey.

Everlasting destruction is an everlasting punishment.—Rev. H. CONSTABLE.

Shall not the Judge of all the earth do right?—Gen. 18: 25. *O House of Israel, are not my ways equal?*—Ezek. 18: 29. *Why even of yourselves judge ye not what is right?*—Luke 12: 57.

I believe that the popular doctrine is the direct occasion of much positive infidelity. Rev. S. MINTON, M. A. The Way Everlasting.

The dogma of eternal suffering involves nothing less than the moral character of God. W. MAUDE. The Rainbow.

We fail in presenting thoroughly God's truth to the heathen nations, because we have encumbered Christianity with a doctrine of hell, so unjust, so indiscriminate, so hardening in its frightful proportions, that men's consciences refuse to receive it.—Rev. E. WHITE.

It is a fearful thing to fall into the hands of the living God.—Heb. 10: 31.

I cannot see what great comfort sinners can take in the thought of a tedious time of terrible torment, ending at last in annihilation, and the utter extinction of their being.—Archbishop TILLOTSON.

It seems all but inconceivable that when God is all in all there should be some dark spot where, amid endlessly self-inflicted suffering, or in the enhancement of ever-enduring hate, rebel hands should be forever raised against the Eternal Father and the God of everlasting love.—Bishop ELLICOTT. The Church and The Age.

Scripture vs. Popular Misconceptions.

A FEW PLAIN FACTS FOR THOUGHTFUL CHRISTIANS.

BY PROF. C. L. IVES, YALE COLLEGE.

1. **Scripture declares,** that the "everlasting punishment" (Matt. xxv. 46) of the wicked will consist of "everlasting destruction" (2 Thess. i. 9). The popular theory teaches, that it will consist of everlasting pain.

2. **Scripture declares,** that God will "destroy both body and soul in hell." Matt. x. 28. The popular theory teaches, that He will destroy neither one nor the other; but will preserve both of them alive forever in unmitigated agony.

3. **Scripture declares,** that "our God is a consuming fire." Heb. xii. 20. The popular theory teaches, that he is only a scorching fire.

4. **Scripture declares,** that the "fiery indignation" will "devour the adversaries." Heb. x. 27. The popular theory teaches, that it will do no such thing, but only torture them.

5. **Scripture declares,** that the wicked will "perish like natural brute beasts." 2 Peter ii. 12. The popular theory teaches, that there will be no analogy whatever between the two cases.

6. **Scripture declares,** that whosoever "will save his life" by unfaithfulness to Christ, shall ultimately "lose it" (Matt. xvi. 25) in a far more terrible manner. The popular theory teaches, that no man can lose his life, and that the second death is no death at all, but eternal life in sin and misery.

7. **Scripture declares,** that "whosoever doeth the will of God abideth forever." 1 John ii. 17. The popular theory teaches, that every man will abide forever, whether he does the will of God or not.

8. **Scripture declares,** that if we desire "immortality," we must seek it "by patient continuance in well-doing." Rom. ii. 7. The popular theory teaches, that every man possesses inherent, indefeasible immortality, and what we have to seek for is, that it may prove a blessing and not a curse to us.

9. **Scripture declares,** that "the wages of sin is death." Rom. vi. 23. The popular theory teaches, that it is eternal life in misery; in other words, that God will inflict upon impenitent sinners a punishment *infinitely greater* than what he has pronounced to be their due.

10. **Scripture declares,** that "the gift of God is eternal life through Jesus Christ our Lord." Rom. vi. 23. The popular theory teaches, that eternal life is the common possession of all men, and that the gift of God through Jesus Christ is the privilege of spending it in holiness and happiness.

11. **Scripture declares,** that "the Son of God was manifested that he might destroy the works of the devil." 1 John iii. 8. The popular theory teaches, that they will never be destroyed at all, but that a portion of the universe will be specially set apart for the eternal exhibition of them in their fullest maturity.

12. **Scripture declares,** that Christ is to "reconcile all things to God. Col. i. 20. The popular theory teaches, that all things will *never* be reconciled to God; that discord and disorder will never *cease*, but only be confined to one particular locality.

13. **Scripture declares,** that in Christ "all things consist." Col. 1. 17. The popular theory teaches, that a whole kingdom will "consist" forever, although *not* "in Him."

14. **Scripture declares,** "He that hath the Son hath life, but he that hath not the Son of God hath not life" (1 John v. 12); that "if we live after the flesh we shall die, but if through the Spirit we mortify the deeds of the body we shall live." Rom. viii. 13. The advocates of the popular theory say, that the life of believers and unbelievers must be of equal duration.

QUESTIONS FOR THE CLERGY.

1. Is the soul a part of God or a part of man?
2. If it is a part of God, can it sin?
3. If it is a part of man, is it not mortal and subject to death?
4. Is there an intimation in the Bible that God put a soul (mortal or immortal) into Adam at his creation? but as he was made of dust, is it not said that this man of dust became a living soul?
5. If men can exist without bodies, why were Enoch and Elijah taken out of the world bodily?
6. If the body is a prison-house for the soul, are not these good prophets (Enoch and Elijah) still in prison?
7. If the body is a prison-house, why was Adam's soul put into it before it sinned?
8. When the soul—the prisoner—becomes guilty, why is the prison—the body—destroyed to let it out?
9. Did not Christ suffer the penalty due to Adam's transgression in making the atonement?
10. Then if that penalty was moral or spiritual death, did not Christ suffer it?
11. If in Adam all die a spiritual death, and if as the clergy say—this same all that died in Adam will be made alive—then will not all be made spiritually alive in Christ?
12. If the soul is an immortal or spiritual thing, must it not, if it dies, die a spiritual death?
13. As nothing can die except what is mortal, if the soul dies a spiritual death, must it not be spiritually mortal?
14. If the soul is a spiritual thing and immortal, how, then, can it die a spiritual death?
15. If literal death destroys a literal thing, must not spiritual death destroy a spiritual thing?

Name Index

Editor's Note: The book History of the Second Advent Message and Mission, Doctrine and People, *as originally authored by Isaac C. Wellcome, contained no index. This name index was compiled by Michael Coe and Gabriel Johnson when they were staff members at the Ellen G. White Estate. Minor editorial changes in this index were later made in preparation for publication in this volume.*

General Index

Editor's Note: The book History of the Second Advent Message and Mission, Doctrine and People, *as originally authored by Isaac C. Wellcome, contained no index. This general index developed by Andrews University Press is not intended to be a complete and exhaustive resource. Derived primarily from the terms appearing in the extensive table of contents in Wellcome's volume, the index also includes some additional entries and corrections. Despite these acknowledged limitations, this index should be useful as a guide for the reader to the most prominent subjects and persons.*

Gary Land, professor of history at Andrews University and chair of the department, earned a Ph.D. in history from the University of California at Santa Barbara. The *Historical Dictionary of the Seventh-day Adventists* is one of his published books, and he has edited such works as *Adventism in America* and *The World of Ellen G. White*.

George R. Knight, emeritus professor of church history at Andrews University, is an authority on Adventist history. The lengthy list of his published works includes *Millenial Fever and the End of the World: A Study of Millerite Adventism*; *A Brief History of Seventh-day Adventists*; and *A Search for Identity: The Development of Seventh-day Adventist Beliefs*.